CHILDHOOD STRESS

CHILDHOOD STRESS

Edited by
L. EUGENE ARNOLD
The Ohio State University

A Wiley-Interscience Publication
JOHN WILEY & SONS, INC.
New York   Chichester   Brisbane   Toronto   Singapore

Copyright © 1990 by John Wiley & Sons, Inc.

This publication is designed to provide accurate and authoritative information in regard to the subject matter covered. It is sold with the understanding that the publisher is not engaged in rendering legal, accounting, or other professional service. If legal advice or other expert assistance is required, the services of a competent professional person should be sought. *From a Declaration of Principles jointly adopted by a Committee of the American Bar Association and a Committee of Publishers.*

Library of Congress Cataloging-in-Publication Data:
Childhood stress / edited by L. Eugene Arnold.
p.   cm. — (Wiley series in child mental health)
Includes bibliographical references.
ISBN 0-471-50868-3
1. Stress in children.   2. Stress in teenagers.   3. Stress in children—Prevention.   4. Stress in teenagers—Prevention.
I. Arnold, L. Eugene, 1936-   . II. Series.
BF723.S75C47   1990
155.4′18—dc20   90-30610

Printed in the United States of America

10 9 8 7 6 5 4 3 2 1

Dedicated to Rev. Mary M. Janata, M.Div. (1926–1987), the first full-time program director of the Commission on Interprofessional Education and Practice at Ohio State University, and to all those who labor under stress for the benefit of children:

To teachers, principals, and other educators who help children learn the knowledge and skills needed in the modern world.

To ministers, priests, and rabbis who try to guide children along the paths of reason and social responsibility.

To social workers who try to relieve socioeconomic stress and improve the home and community environment.

To psychologists, psychiatrists, and other mental health professionals who help children cope with stress.

To pediatricians, family practitioners, and other physicians who promote children's health.

To nurses who work for a healthful environment in hospital, home, and community.

To allied medical professionals, dentists, and other health care professionals who round out the team fighting for children's physical and mental health.

To attorneys, judges, and others who assist children through the labyrinths of justice.

To business people, politicians, and others who try to help arrange adequate day care.

Most of all, to parents who try to preserve islands of security for children in a mad world.

Contributors

L. Eugene Arnold, M.Ed., M.D., Professor of Psychiatry, Pediatrics, and Neuroscience, The Ohio State University, Columbus, Ohio

Marianne L. Barton, Ph.D., Clinical Assistant Professor of Psychiatry and Human Behavior, Brown University Program in Medicine, Providence, Rhode Island

William Beardslee, M.D., Clinical Director, Department of Psychiatry, Children's Hospital of Boston, Boston, Massachusetts

Robert T. Brown, M.D., Associate Professor of Pediatrics, The Ohio State University, Columbus, Ohio

Elizabeth M. Burns, R.S.M., R.N., Ph.D., Professor of Nursing, Psychiatry and Neuroscience, The Ohio State University, Columbus, Ohio

John A. Carnahan, J.D., Attorney, Columbus, Ohio

Daniel J. Christie, Ph.D., Associate Professor of Psychology, The Ohio State University, Marion, Ohio

Debra S. Cohn, Ph.D., Social Work Consultant, Child Abuse Program, Children's Hospital, Columbus, Ohio

Rebecca del Carmen, Ph.D., Laboratory of Comparative Ethology, National Institute of Child Health and Human Development, Bethesda, Maryland

Spencer Eth, M.D., Assistant Professor of Psychiatry, UCLA School of Medicine, Los Angeles, California

Norman Garmezy, Ph.D., Professor of Psychology, University of Minnesota, Minneapolis, Minnesota

Edward Greenblatt, Ph.D., Cornell University Medical Center, Westchester Division, White Plains, New York

Robert L. Hendren, D.O., Associate Professor of Psychiatry and Pediatrics, University of New Mexico, Albuquerque, New Mexico

Lynne C. Huffman, M.D., Laboratory of Comparative Ethology, National Institute of Child Health and Human Development, Bethesda, Maryland

Charles F. Johnson, M.D., Professor of Pediatrics, The Ohio State University College of Medicine, Columbus, Ohio

Judith Kimchi, R.N., M.S., Graduate Trainee, Research Foundation, College of Nursing, The Ohio State University, Columbus, Ohio

Elliot M. Kranzler, M.D., Assistant Professor of Clinical Psychiatry, Columbia University, New York, New York

Marie L. Lobo, Ph.D., Assistant Professor, Department of Family and Community, College of Nursing, The Ohio State University, Columbus, Ohio

Ann Masten, Ph.D., Department of Psychology, University of Minnesota, Minneapolis, Minnesota

Joanne Milburn, Ph.D., Hannah Neil Center for Children, Columbus, Ohio

Joseph D. Noshpitz, M.D., Private Practice, Washington, D.C.

Margaret O'Dougherty, Ph.D, Assistant Professor of Pediatrics and Psychology, The Ohio State University, Columbus, Ohio

Nancy M. Ryan-Wenger, R.N., Ph.D., Assistant Professor, Life Span Process, College of Nursing, The Ohio State University, Columbus, Ohio

Barbara Schaffner, R.N., M.S.N., College of Nursing, The Ohio State University, Columbus, Ohio

Susah Jones Sears, Ph.D., Associate Professor of Education, The Ohio State University, Columbus, Ohio

Beverly G. Toomey, Ph.D., Associate Professor, College of Social Work, The Ohio State University, Columbus, Ohio

Paul V. Trad, M.D., Director, Child and Adolescent Outpatient Department, Cornell University Medical Center, Westchester Division, White Plains, New York

Susan Beckwitt Turkel, M.D., Associate Professor of Psychiatry, Pediatrics and Pathology, USC Medical Center, Los Angeles, California

Charles H. Zeanah, M.D., Associate Professor of Psychiatry and Human Behavior, Brown University Program in Medicine, Providence, Rhode Island

Series Preface

This series is intended to serve a number of functions. It includes works on child development; it presents material on child advocacy; it publishes contributions to child psychiatry; and it gives expression to cogent views on child rearing and child management. The mental health of parents and their interaction with their children is a major theme of the series, and emphasis is placed on the child as individual, as family member, and as a part of the larger social surround.

Child development is regarded as the basic science of child mental health, and within that framework research works are included in this series. The many ethical and legal dimensions of the way society relates to its children are the central theme of the child advocacy publications, as well as a primarily demographic approach that highlights the role and status of children within society. The child psychiatry publications span studies that concern the diagnosis, description, therapeutics, rehabilitation, and prevention of the emotional disorders of childhood. And the views of thoughtful and creative contributors to the handling of children under many different circumstances (retardation, acute and chronic illness, hospitalization, handicap, disturbed social conditions, etc.) find expression within the framework of child rearing and child management.

Family studies with a central child mental health perspective are included in the series, and explorations into the nature of parenthood and the parenting process are emphasized. This includes books about divorce, the single parent, the absent parent, parents with physical and emotional illnesses, and other conditions that significantly affect the parent-child relationship.

Finally, the series examines the impact of larger social forces, such as war, famine, migration, and economic failure, on the adaptation of children and families. In the largest sense, the series is devoted to books that illuminate the special needs, status, and history of children and their families, within all perspectives that bear on their collective mental health.

JOSEPH D. NOSHPITZ

Washington, D.C.

Acknowledgments

This book was inspired and encouraged by the Commission on Interprofessional Education and Practice at the Ohio State University and by the Alfred L. Willson Fund of the Columbus Foundation. The influence of these two organizations can be found in the emphasis on interprofessional prevention, with contributions from education, law, nursing, pediatrics/phoebeatrics, psychiatry, psychology, social work, and theology. Some of the early work was made possible by staff and programs funded by the Kellogg Foundation.

A particular debt is owed to the late Rev. Mary M. Janata, who for 11 years as Program Director of the Commission on Interprofessional Education and Practice fostered a fertile interprofessional intellectual atmosphere conducive to such undertakings, and to her successor, R. Michael Casto, Ph.D., Associate Director of the Commission. Background support was offered by Luverne L. Cunningham, Ph.D., Director of the Commission.

Manuscript preparation depended heavily on the invaluable assistance of Mrs. Elaine Proper and was expedited by the help of Ms. Mary Ann Rausch, Ms. Beth Deley, Ms. Tracy Mazik, and Ms. Anita Pryor.

Contents

PART I: THE TWO FACES OF STRESS: PSYCHOLOGICAL AND BIOLOGICAL

PART II: STRESS AT DIFFERENT DEVELOPMENTAL STAGES

**PART III: SOURCES OF STRESS IN CHILDHOOD
(INCLUDING PUBLIC HEALTH ASPECTS)**

Stress in Children and Adolescents: Introduction and Summary

L. Eugene Arnold

The word stress has evolved several meanings, including emphasis, intensity, and effort. As used in physics, it referred to a constraining, deforming, or distorting force or pressure. The distortion in the stressed object was called the strain. Then the terminology "stress and strain" was applied to the psychosocial as well as physical realm. Eventually, "stress" came to refer to the strain as well as (or even rather than) the stress. An illustration of this semantic evolution can be found in the *Diagnostic and Statistical Manual of Mental Disorders* (DSM-III-R), where a patient's response to a catastrophic situation is called "post-traumatic stress disorder," and the relatively new word "stressor" is used to refer to the causal stress. To encompass both meanings (stressor and strain), child stress might be defined as any intrusion into children's normal physical or psychosocial life experiences that acutely or chronically unbalances physiological or psychological equilibrium, threatens security or safety, or distorts physical or psychological growth/development, and the psychophysiological consequences of such intrusion or distortion.

Caplan (1981) defined stress as "a marked discrepancy between the demands made . . . and the organism's capability to respond, the consequences of which will be detrimental. . . ." (p. 414). Such definitions imply that stress is always destructive or harmful. However, many authors adduce evidence that the dose-response curve for stress is nonlinear: mild stressors often seem benign and sometimes even seem growth-promoting. Such complications have induced most of the chapter contributors in this book to offer their own definitional refinements and clarifications.

For example, Norman Garmezy and Ann Masten (Chapter 17) define stress by four features: (1) stress is a manifest stimulus event; (2) this event is capable of modifying physiological and/or psychological equilibrium; (3) this disequilibrium is reflected in a state of arousal with neurophysiological, cognitive, and emotional consequences; and (4) these changes can disrupt the adaptation of the person. The effort at resolution that follows the stress is called coping.

Stress has physical, chemical, biological, psychological, and socioeconomic/cultural sources. Examples of these are listed in Table 0.1. For convenience in discussion, the first three sources can be lumped as biological and the last two as psychological. Such lumping is easily justified because it is difficult to find a given type of stressor in pure form. Stresses tend to cluster and interact.

Stressors can act additively and synergistically. For example, deprivation or malnutrition can compound fetal alcohol effects. Iron deficiency or zinc deficiency can aggravate lead poisoning. Discrimination can aggravate poverty, and both can aggravate the effects of illness. Even the same cause can stress the child through two or more different mechanisms, or in different ways. For example, maternal alcoholism can stress

TABLE 0.1.   *Sampling of the Range of Child and Adolescent Stressors*

Category of Stress	Examples (with Chapter in Which Discussed)
Physical	Accidents (12, 21)
	Battering (10)
	Biological clock disruption by electric lights, variable schedules (3)
	Iatrogenic stress: shots, rectal exam, sutures (6, 12)
	Premature contact sports
	Some types of sexual abuse (10)
Chemical	Adulteration of food
	Fetal alcohol effects (3)
	Insecticides, solvents (3)
	Lead, other heavy metals
	Nicotine exposure (fetus or nursling)
	Other drugs
Biological	Disability, handicap (12)
	Genetic vulnerability as narrowing of life options (12)
	Infection (12)
	Other illness (12)
	Malnutrition (3)
	Puberty (9)
Psychological	Absence of parent: illness, depression (13)
	Catastrophe (1, 2, 16)
	Deprivation (6)
	Excessive television, media violence (Introduction)
	Iatrogenic stress: interviews about abuse, psychotherapy, hospitalization (7, 10, 12)
	Legal majority (9)
	Loss of parent: death (15), divorce (14)
	Sexual and emotional abuse (10)
	Threats, fears of violence (11)
Socioeconomic/ Cultural	Competition (16)
	Discrimination (16)
	Future shock (Introduction)
	Poverty, unemployment (16)
	Social role contradictions (8, 9)
	Threats in school and neighborhood (11)
	Traditions of domestic violence (10)
	"Working" parents (Introduction, 7)

the fetal brain chemically/physically, and then psychologically stress the newborn infant through maternal unavailability, neglect, or abuse. Poverty can stress the child through malnutrition, poor environmental stimulation, and poor parenting due to worry, preoccupation, discouragement, or resentment of another mouth to feed.

ORGANIZATION OF THE BOOK

To consider this complex subject in a comprehensive and systematic manner applicable to children and adolescents, the book is organized into four major parts. Part I focuses in detail on the psychological and biological aspects of stress. These are treated in the same section because they are inseparable in actual experience, but in separate chapters for ease of conceptualization and study. Part II considers the interactions of developmental age with stress, including stresses created by development itself and stresses peculiar to each age/stage. Part III studies various types of stressors and their ramifications, including public health aspects. Part IV concentrates in a special way on assessment, treatment, and prevention, including risk, preventive factors, and intervention techniques.

Because these topics cannot be neatly pigeonholed, chapters in one section often touch on issues relevant to another section or chapter. Where this occurs, cross-references guide the reader to the appropriate supplemental chapter. The rest of this introduction will summarize highlights from each topic area, relate the chapters to one another, and supplement these with additional material and overarching discussion.

THE TWO FACES OF STRESS: PSYCHOLOGICAL AND BIOLOGICAL

The term "faces" was deliberately chosen to emphasize that these are two aspects of the same complex phenomenon, not two different entities. This fact is underscored by the need for the chapters on psychological aspects to mention some biological effects, and for the chapters on biological aspects to mention some psychological factors. One might argue that even at the theoretical level the two cannot be divorced, that psychology could be subsumed under biology. After all, only living organisms can feel, perceive, and behave in the usual sense.

The artificial dichotomy of biological (including physical and chemical) and psychological (including social) applies both to the source of stress (stressor) and to the response of child or adolescent (including strain, coping, adjustment, and adaptation). Thus we could construct a 2 × 2 matrix as shown in Table 0.2.

In Chapter 1, Paul V. Trad discusses psychological aspects and portrays the broad spectrum of possible child stress responses, including coping. In Chapter 3, Elizabeth M. Burns and L. Eugene Arnold discuss biological aspects, including a chemical stress example and neurohormonal, psychoimmunological, and nutritional considerations. Each of these two general chapters is followed by a chapter on the respective pathological responses. Although practically any psychiatric disorder can be aggravated or even elicited by stress, two examples of psychopathology are

TABLE 0.2.   *Possible Combinations of Stress Source and Response in Regard to the Psychological–Biological Dichotomy.* Numbers refer to the chapters that discuss each issue. Underlined numbers are the primary chapters for the topic.

| | | Response or Effect | |
		Psychological	Biological
Source	Psychological (including Social)	Chap. 1, 2, 7–11, 13–16	(Psychosomatic) Chap. 1, 3, 4, 6
	Biological (including Chemical and Physical)	(Somatopsychic) Chap. 3, 6, 9, 10, 12	Chap. 3, 6

definitionally recognized to be stress-caused: adjustment disorder and post-traumatic stress disorder. These are discussed by Susan Beckwitt Turkel and Spencer Eth in Chapter 2.

Another category of pathology popularly (and correctly) associated with stress is the psychosomatic. Nancy A. Ryan-Wenger discusses this in Chapter 4 and elaborates on the three biological responses to stress: autonomic (immediate), neuroendocrine (intermediate), and endocrine (delayed).

Coping

Stress responses may be visualized or plotted on two intersecting axes: the psychological–physiological spectrum and the pathological versus adaptive coping spectrum. No stress response is purely psychological, purely physiological, or completely pathological, and whether a completely adaptive response ever occurs may be questionable. The simultaneous psychological and physiological arousal induced by stress is largely dependent on perception of the event as stressful. A child in "blissful ignorance" is not stressed—in danger perhaps, but not stressed. Sometimes numbing, withdrawal, or denial is the most adaptive response that conditions allow, as, for example, when nothing can be done about the stressor and nothing can be done to save oneself. Other situations favor a different coping style: for example, if the stressor can be mastered or fled. These different coping styles may be associated with different relative levels of the various adrenal hormones that are elicited by stress (Trad, Chapter 1).

Each individual has a favored coping style or combination of coping styles. Although this may be modified somewhat by different stressors, there is still a tendency to resort to one's favorite coping style under stress. If this does not work because of a different or more intense than usual stress, one may escalate the inadequate coping behavior in an attempt to find the same relief this coping mechanism brought on previous occasions. A vicious cycle can be initiated by stress, in which the discomfort elicits habitual coping behavior, which is inadequate to bring relief, and this inadequacy itself becomes a new stressor, which brings further discomfort, which elicits more of the same inadequate coping. When this cycle escalates sufficiently, it can spin off suicide, other violence, substance abuse, psychosis, running away, or dropping out as a centrifugal behavior. Similarly, a virtuous cycle can operate through stress mastery: the memory of previous success under stress imparts a relaxed self-confidence conducive to flexible perseverance.

Caplan (1981) distinguished four types of successful coping: (1) mitigating the stressor or fleeing from it; (2) enhancing one's stress management capability, as by enlisting a support network; (3) defending against arousal dysphoria (anxiety, depression, fear) by utilizing appropriate mental defense mechanisms; and (4) internal readjustment to the event and its sequelae ("worry work" and "grief work"). Trad (Chapter 1) identified the following as important in coping: adaptable temperament (however, in Chapter 6 Lobo gives an interesting example of a special circumstance where a "difficult" temperament led to better coping), attachment, family support, older age, internal locus of control, social support, and correct appraisal of whether the stressor can best be mastered, fled, or accepted as inevitable.

Signal-to-Noise Ratio Effect on Coping.   Noshpitz and Coddington (1989) propose that the efficiency and adaptiveness of stress response is influenced by the ratio of signal to noise in the demands of the stress stimuli and in their perception. A clear signal about what kind of coping is needed, coupled with little noise (conflicting or distracting demands) facilitates healthy coping/adaptation. High noise or low signal disrupts or impedes coping. For example, losing one's home by fire might be more easily adapted to than the less tragic losing of it by parental job promotion requiring a move. In the case of fire, clear goals and action are indicated, such as rebuilding and observing fire precautions in the future, with little ambivalence or conflict. But in the move due to promotion, it is not so clear what should be done about the loss, and there may be much ambivalence, perhaps even a prohibition against recognizing it as a loss or expressing negative affect about it.

Biological Aspects of Stress

Although the popular press often implies that stress is mainly psychosocial, stress was originally a physical concept that seemed applicable to people as functioning biobehavioral units. The brain is the basis of cognition, emotion, and behavior; it can be affected by the health of the rest of the body and can affect the physiology and even growth of the rest of the body. The brain and the rest of the body are tied together through the endocrine and autonomic nervous systems, as well as by the voluntary motor and sensory peripheral nerves. This allows for both psychosomatic and somatopsychic interactions in health and disease. Apprehension of stress can trigger messages from the brain throughout the body, resulting in somatic changes. Physical-chemical-biological stresses can find their way to the brain to affect it directly (as with toxins); but the brain can also be affected indirectly, by apprehension of a peripheral physical disability or illness. In Chapter 9 Robert L. Hendren gives an interesting example of a *somatosocial* stress chain. An adolescent's blossoming sexual maturity is perceived by the parent, who reacts to it (perhaps out of stress) with changed behavior and attitudes that may stress the adolescent.

In Chapter 3, Elizabeth M. Burns and L. Eugene Arnold discuss some direct and indirect chemical effects on the developing brain, using alcohol as an example. The developing brain is particularly vulnerable during organogenesis (gestational weeks 3–9), rapid neuronal proliferation (gestational weeks 12–20), and the brain growth spurt, which spans the last ten weeks of gestation and the first 18 to 24 postnatal months. The brain growth spurt is characterized by dendritic arborization, axonal growth, synaptogenesis, myelination, and maturation of synaptic structures. Alcohol, as a solvent, can distort the neuronal membranes, which contain the molecular "signatures" that guide the axonal growth cones to the appropriate synaptic connection. Fortunately, the time of greatest vulnerability is also the time of greatest plasticity and hope for repair of damage. Thus, an infant suffering fetal alcohol effects may be salvaged by appropriate stimulation during the first 2 years of life. That's the good news. The bad news is that recent research is suggesting that even one or two drinks a day during pregnancy may have a deleterious effect on the fetal brain. In addition, some pediatric medications have an amount of alcohol that could be deleterious.

Even psychosocial stress, when perceived, can elicit signals from the brain to arouse the autonomic nervous system and the limbic–hypothalamic pituitary-adrenal axis; and then prolonged high levels of adrenal hormones can affect brain development. There are receptors for various hormones in the brain. In some cases these act by affecting protein synthesis, so that brain structure and behavior are affected long after the peak hormone level.

In Chapter 12, Margaret O'Dougherty and Robert T. Brown describe indirect effects of somatic disorder on mind/brain function, resulting from the perception of disability or chronic illness. Surprisingly, the severity of physical disability has not consistently correlated with poor adjustment. This suggests that the stress is not inherent in the illness itself, but in the child's perception of and response to the illness. The illness may be seen as a challenge, an enemy, a punishment, a failing or weakness, a manipulative opportunity to avoid demands or to secure affection or attention, a loss, or an opportunity for moral growth.

These considerations apply not only to primary physical illness, but also to secondary, or psychosomatic, illness. In Chapter 4, Nancy M. Ryan-Wenger describes how the autonomic and endocrine arousal from stress can cause such peripheral physical changes as bronchoconstriction, increased or decreased secretions, increased ventilatory demands from increased oxygen consumption, hyperglycemia, increased joint inflammation, increased blood pressure, muscle spasm or tension, increased or decreased gastrointestinal function, and vascular engorgement or pallor of various organs or regions. Such changes, when symptomatic, can lead to diagnosable chronic psychosomatic illness. Once established, such an illness constitutes a source of stress like any other chronic illness. Thus the stress cycle comes full circle: a psychosomatic illness is both effect and cause of stress. Some individuals seem constitutionally (genetically?) more predisposed than others in one or another target organ and have poor coping skills, setting the stage for precipitation of illness by a stressful event in the setting of a nonsupportive family.

STRESS AT DIFFERENT DEVELOPMENTAL AGES

The main justification for a book on childhood stress is the developmental variable, including special vulnerabilities and strengths with which children and adolescents confront stress. These vulnerabilities and strengths vary with developmental stage, but not in a strictly linear fashion with age. There is a hierarchical logical dependency in which coping ability depends on emotional maturity, which depends on cognitive and psychomotor abilities, which depend on neurophysiological maturation. There are developmental feedback loops in which the effects of stress can affect any of these developmental parameters, either beneficially or pathologically, and modify later ability to tolerate or master stress. There can be critical stages at which certain stressors have a profound impact. Garmezy and Rutter (1983) point out that coping takes different forms at different ages. In memory, young children have a tendency to confuse plan with action retrospectively, and this tendency appears to increase if the plan was formulated and inhibited under stress (Pynoos & Nader, 1989). Such considerations certainly warrant a special section on the typical stresses encountered at each stage of development and the typical coping and other responses of the child/adolescent at each developmental stage.

In Chapter 5, Lynne C. Huffman and Rebecca del Carmen start this section with discussion of prenatal stress. They thoroughly and critically review the animal and human literature that suggests stressing of a pregnant mother can affect fetal development, and come up with some interesting conclusions. One is that in addition to harmful effects, stress may sometimes have beneficial effects. Further considerations include preconceptional stress (the preceding parental stresses that predispose attitudes toward the pregnancy and offspring) and the "psychological layette"—cultural, familial, and parental values and expectations—that can later impact child and adolescent.

In Chapter 6, Marie L. Lobo describes some stresses of infancy and their effects. These include neonatal intensive care, deprivation, and blood draw and circumcision pain. Despite methodological difficulties in measuring infant stress, Lobo is able to cite convincing documentation that infants do respond to stress. One stress effect at this age is the disruption of cue-giving and perceiving in the caretaking dyad.

In Chapter 7, Marianne L. Barton and Charles H. Zeanah review typical preschool stressors, vulnerability, and coping options. Preschoolers are especially prone to regress and disorganize under stress. Their cognitive limitations lead them to misunderstand or feel responsible for stressful events. Their relative dependence, aggravated by regression, leads to attention seeking (often misbehavior) to secure more contact with attachment figures, usually parents. They benefit even more than older children from explanation and parental support.

In Chapter 8, Susan Jones Sears and Joanne F. Milburn summarize the typical stresses of school-age children. Because the main developmental task of this stage concerns schooling, many of the stresses are school-related. Accordingly, Sears and Milburn focus in detail on three school-related problems: test-taking, fear of failure or success, and school fears, including school phobia. In these, as in so many other children's stresses, the quality of parental support is crucial.

In Chapter 9, Robert L. Hendren describes some typical stresses of adolescence, including peer pressure and the need to adjust to physical changes, along with some typical mental defense mechanisms that adolescents often use in coping. With adolescents, the psychological–biological stress spectrum comes full circle. It started with a heavy loading of biological stress in the prenatal stage, with increasing emphasis on psychological stresses through the prepubertal school age, and then comes back toward the biological with the effects of pubertal sex hormones. By late adolescence the pendulum has settled near the center, with a more adult-type balance of psychological and biological stresses. This will swing more toward the biological again in senescence, with increasing physical disability, but that is beyond the scope of this book.

The attention to age/stage considerations pervades the whole book. For example, in Chapter 2 Turkel and Eth describe the age-specific typical post-traumatic stress symptoms of preschoolers (e.g., regression), school-age children (e.g., somatization), and adolescents. In Chapter 12, Margaret O'Dougherty and Robert T. Brown review the different responses to illness elicited at different stages of development. During infancy, separation anxiety and stranger fear may be intensified. A toddler is likely to regress. Preschoolers are likely to perceive painful treatments as punishment for Oedipal or other guilt. Elementary-school-aged children may mistakenly ascribe physical illness to family conflict and may associate pain with persecution and punishment. They may have a fear of being under someone's control. They may explain illness as contamination or as internalization. Being separated from peers by long hospitalization or homebound illness is an important additional stress of chronic illness. Although adolescents can appreciate the full impact of death fears, they may fear a loss of physical integrity (e.g., loss of hair from cancer chemotherapy) perhaps even more than death. Because of their concern with separating successfully from parents, they may fear chronic dependence. Closely related to this is the fear of loss of control. An equally prevalent fear for peer-conforming adolescents is that of being different from peers.

Age appears to be both a risk factor and a protective factor. The positive correlation of cut-off norms with age on the Coddington Life Events Scales for Children and Adolescents (Coddington, 1981) implies that children suffer more annual life event stress each year as they age. At the same time they obviously develop better abilities to cope with the increasing stress (at least if development goes well).

SOME SPECIFIC STRESSES

Abuse

One of the most stressful experiences for children is to be abused by their caretakers. Witnessing violence perpetrated against one parent by another or against a grandparent by a parent is also stressful: it threatens the security and stability of the child's home, distorts the child's sense of right and wrong, and complicates the child's identification with the same-sex parent (whether perpetrator or victim). In Chapter 10, Charles F. Johnson and Debra S. Cohn describe the grim statistics of domestic violence, discuss some causes and effects, and propose some logical preventive steps. Prevention of abuse is complicated by unclarity of definition, difficulty of determining exact prevalence, oversimplified causal explanations, and associated problems of poverty, social stress, isolation, and low self-concept. It is further hampered by division of responsibility among professions and agencies, the tension between compassion and control, the competition for scarce resources, and the emotionality and reactiveness surrounding abuse. Possible interventions include eliminating the norms and means that legitimize and glorify violence, reducing violence-provoking stress, integrating families into a community network, eliminating sexism, and breaking family cycles of violence.

Threat

The threat of violence can be almost as stressful as actually suffering or witnessing violence. As described by Daniel J. Christie and Beverly G. Toomey in Chapter 11, this generation grew up under the shadow of the nuclear threat. By early adolescence, a third of one sample listed nuclear war as one of their three top fears. Children think about the possibility of nuclear war, have nightmares about it, and have their lives colored by vulnerability and tenuousness. Over 40% of American children and 12% of Soviet children consider nuclear war inevitable in their lifetime. Further, less than 25% of American and less than 3% of Soviet children believe they would survive a nuclear war. Could it be that the conviction of nuclear inevitability has contributed to the tripling of teenage suicide in the past two or three decades? Possible antidotes are actions aimed at reducing the threat, rethinking the good-guy/bad-guy mentality, learning more about the enemy, and humanizing the enemy.

However, children and adolescents do not need to look toward global war to find threats of violence. These can be found in their own community and even in their own school, with extortion, mugging, and even rape and occasional murder occurring on school grounds. The trip to and from school is fraught with danger for many children. While only a minority of children actually suffer violence in school or en route, most children and adolescents are affected by the threat of knowing they could be the next victim. Of a national sample studied, 38% said they avoid certain locations in school to avoid being hurt or bothered, 20% were afraid at least sometimes in school, and 4% had stayed home to avoid being hurt or bothered. Possibly 100,000 students per year drop out because of fear. A useful intervention is to teach children their rights, problem-solving skills, and appreciation of cultural diversity.

Competition

Threat of violence is not the only stressor found in our schools. In Chapter 8, Sears and Milburn describe the threats posed by academic competition, failure, and even success. The latter may be a particular problem for girls, who often are still socially programmed to be non-competitive and not too smart, but who at the same time are expected to succeed academically. This poses a role conflict that can be very stressful. For most children, failure is more of a threat than is success, and the effect of failure is mediated by a student's personal explanatory beliefs. Those who believe in luck and fate drift into hopelessness, whereas those who believe in personal responsibility tend to try harder. Even the latter outcome, however, is not an unmixed blessing. The stress of highly motivated, intense striving can take its own toll. Perhaps the high truancy and dropout rates are the way some youngsters cope with the stressful school environment.

Socioeconomic Inequities. In Chapter 16, Toomey and Christie describe the stress of poverty and discrimination, which can stunt or warp development. Despite the great efforts and gains of the last three decades, stressful levels of residual racial/ethnic/class discrimination remain to confront minority children at unexpected turns. Some of this is imbedded in culture and language, not necessarily intentional by the majority. Minority children and adolescents, especially if poor, have a special need for independent self-appraisal rather than accepting the definition of their worth implied by the larger society.

The Stress of Parent Loss or Absence

A special stress for children is loss or absence of caretaker or fear of such. The absence can be physical, as through divorce or death, or can be mental/emotional, by preoccupation or unavailability of the parent, as in depression, psychosis, or other chronic illness.

Parent Illness. With over 5% of adults experiencing severe depression at some point in their lives, a large number of children are exposed to severe depression of a parent during their formative years. In Chapter 13, William Beardslee discusses the stresses this poses for children of such parents and describes some of his preventive work. These children and adolescents have a dual burden: they must cope not only with the illness of a parent, but also with the fact that they themselves carry a high genetic vulnerability to development of depression. Such children are often confused by the emotional unresponsiveness of their depressed parent, who appears superficially normal, but who does not give them the affective attention they need. In attempting to adapt to this, the child may erroneously conclude that the problem is the child's rather than the parent's. Beardslee has developed a structured short-term educational/cognitive/behavioral family therapy. He explains the problem to the children and their parents and helps them find alternate ways of coping to prevent child frustration or erroneous conclusions. He also educates them about their own risk so that they can seek early treatment at the first sign of depression.

Divorce. In Chapter 14, L. Eugene Arnold and John A. Carnahan discuss the ramifications of the most common cause for parent absence—divorce. Children and adolescents are stressed by divorce in several ways. The most obvious is that they must be separated from one of their parents. In addition, they may be trapped in a feud between the divorcing parents, sometimes used as pawns, but more commonly merely torn in their loyalties, with each parent lobbying for the children's affection. The legal system may impose additional stresses even in its efforts to be helpful and fair. For example, the right of the child to state a preference of custodian or to elect a custodian at a statutory age may be an unwelcome privilege for the child who does not wish to take sides. Furthermore, the possibility of such election may induce parents to more intense lobbying and manipulation of the child's affections. Even in "civilized" divorces, with cooperation by both parents for the welfare of the children, the children's lives are disrupted. The disruption reaches catastrophic proportions if one of the parents finds it necessary to move to another state, making frequent visits inconvenient. Cooperation among parents, attorneys, mental health professionals, and the court is necessary to prevent the child's stress being any greater than necessary.

Parent Death. The ultimate parent loss, of course, is death. In Chapter 15, Elliot M. Kranzler describes the effects on a child of losing a parent through death. The grieving process can both affect and be affected by development. For example, children below age 8 have difficulty comprehending the finality of death; preschoolers may appear scandalously unconcerned or cheerful at their parent's funeral because of inability to understand the situation. If a parent dies at a critical transitional stage of the child's development, passage to the next stage may be delayed, stymied, or incomplete.

Iatrogenic Stress of Children

Although the term "iatrogenic" strictly refers to physician-caused stress, the concept can be more broadly applied to stress inadvertently caused by any helping professional. Obvious examples are physical or dental examinations, shots, hospitalizations, and interviews or testimony of abused children for the purpose of prosecuting the perpetrator. Less obvious are such stressors as psychotherapy or being offered the right to elect the custodial parent. In Chapter 10, Johnson and Cohn discuss how the helping professions may re-abuse children in an effort to protect or treat them. In Chapter 19, L. Eugene Arnold offers some poignant examples of how all adults—both professionals and parents—frequently stress children with good intentions.

While the routine "practice" of experienced professionals considerably stresses children, the learning "practice" of students in the helping professions may pose even more stress. For example, in Chapter 6 Marie Lobo describes evidence that an inexperienced circumcisor stressed infants more than the same resident physician did after gaining experience. Such findings constitute an argument for child specialists in each profession, who would have the necessary trained experience. But they also constitute an ethical dilemma for the academic institutions that sponsor such training. One solution might be tighter supervision, but the cost might not be justified by the amount of child stress reduction compared to spending the same money some other way for children's benefit. It is not clear what would constitute appropriate informed consent. Although beyond the scope of this book, resolution of such ethical issues is one of the goals of the Ohio State University Commission on Interprofessional Education and Practice, which sponsored development of the book.

Technological Stress and Future Shock

In many ways the accelerating pace of technological/cultural change, sometimes called future shock or the communication revolution or postindustrial revolution, is not as stressful for children and adolescents as it is for adults. Children do not have the dual burden of unlearning the familiar while adjusting to the new. To a young child, the whole world is a new, unfamiliar place. Everything is something new to be assimilated, whether kerosene lamp or laser, horse-drawn carriage or space shuttle, printed page or electronic mail. The most likely source of child stress from technological change is the change in availability of parents resulting from parent stress. One technological parent stress is unemployment resulting from obsolescence of job skills. This is discussed by Toomey and Christie in Chapter 16. Another socioeconomic aspect of the industrial and postindustrial revolutions is the increasing need for parents to work outside of the home, away from ready access to their children. This occurred first with fathers in the first industrial revolution. Prior to that time, both parents in most families worked at home, on the family farm or in a small family business, with which the children assisted, resulting in many hours of parent-child contact. The effects of losing this contact were not at first notable because in most instances the child still had the mother at home, and half a loaf is infinitely better than none. The problem began to receive more scrutiny when mothers also were pulled away from home to work in factories, offices, and other commerce. It then became known as the problem of "the working mother," even though it more properly should have been recognized earlier as the problem of the working parent. Since 1980, the year when the number of married women who were employed outside the home exceeded 50%, the working mother has become the norm. In Chapter 7, Barton and Zeanah discuss some evidence that maternal role dissatisfaction may be more important than employment per se. This issue and other aspects of the parent-child relationship in a changing society are more extensively discussed in a previous book, *Parents, Children, and Change* (Arnold, 1985).

In some instances, technology may impact children and adolescents directly more than it does adults. One example of this is the effect of electric lights on growth and age of puberty, discussed by Burns and Arnold in Chapter 3. The earlier onset of puberty, possibly before the adolescent is cognitively and emotionally ready, can be a special stress; Hendren describes the effects in Chapter 9.

Television Stress. Another mundane example of technological im-pact on children and adolescents is the effect of commercial television. Numerous studies have demonstrated that frequent and prolonged tele-vision watching, especially of crime stories and violent cartoons, causes increased aggressiveness (e.g., Singer, 1985; Zuckerman & Zuckerman, 1985). Even some programs that appear benign, such as exciting game shows, may be overarousing to toddlers and preschoolers. There is also a suspicion that regardless of content, many hours in front of the "boob tube" have a stultifying effect on children's cognitive, emotional, social, and academic development, although this is not as well established as the aggression link. Nonaggressive emotional symptoms can also result from media experiences. It is not surprising that children would have night-mares and fears after watching a horror movie or episode, but even presentations apparently designed for children can be stressful. One 5-year-old boy (at the expected age for castration anxiety) had nightmares for a week after intently watching "The Land of Oz," in which a boy discovered at the end that he actually was a princess.

It is noteworthy that electric lights, movies, and television were all initiated as improvements or conveniences not suspected to be stressful to children and adolescents. The effects on children were discovered only after they had become a common part of modern life. Who knows what current innovations will be discovered in the future to have a now-unsuspected stressful effect on children? Do we need a child-development impact statement similar to the environmental impact statement required before introducing new technology? The implica-tions are mind boggling, but these are issues that will need to be faced if the human species is to avoid changing the environment too rapidly and stressfully for its own evolution to keep pace.

INTERPROFESSIONAL PREVENTION, ASSESSMENT, AND TREATMENT

Prevention of stress symptoms is certainly not a new idea. For example, in 1920 Alfred L. Willson established a foundation for "scientific prevention in early youth" of mental/emotional disorders, which he conceptualized as stress-related. In 1968 Skipper and Leonard reported that anticipatory guidance of parents in supporting 3- to 9-year-old children through tonsillectomy significantly decreased their fever, vomiting, and emotional disturbance, compared to a control group. They also found a lasting benefit: fewer fears, less crying, and less sleep disturbance a week later at home. Today's children have benefited from application of such findings, but at the same time, new stresses have arisen, calling for additional preventive efforts.

A recurring theme throughout this book is the opportunity and need for interprofessional preventive planning and action. Because the stresses impacting children cover the spectrum from physical and chemical through biological and psychological to socioeconomic and cultural, no one profession can address them all. Effective prevention or amelioration requires communication and collaboration among all the helping professions.

For example, physicians, nurses, and allied medical professionals have the opportunity and expertise to monitor prenatal maternal health, nutrition, and substance abuse, and educate prospective parents about the optimum intrauterine and postnatal environment for their infant. However, they cannot do much alone about poverty or other social or cultural situations that might stress children or prevent the parents from acting constructively. Here social work, public health nursing, law, and theology have more to offer. The impact of lifestyle on children's development can be addressed by social work, theology, psychology, law, and education. Educators have a special opportunity to help enlighten the attitudes and developing habits of children and adolescents (the future parents), who are not nearly as accessible to the other professions.

The legal profession shapes the structure of society through laws, the interpretation thereof, and such issues as vigor of liability pursuit. In fact, attorneys have a great impact on what the other professions can do, are allowed to do, and are willing to risk doing. They also have a profound impact on family life through the manner in which divorces are handled and the outcome of regulations on such matters as television or other media content that comes into the home.

Psychologists and psychiatrists have a special opportunity to ameliorate the stress on children of parental depression, psychosis, or other absences through mental illness, but they alone cannot do this without the support of social work and other health professionals within a framework allowed by law. They will not even have the opportunity to help many children with chronic illness or disability unless these are referred by other helping professions, who themselves need to find ways to support such children psychologically in their day-to-day contact. Mental health professionals can call on education for expertise in techniques of enlightening children about their genetic risks. And when they reach the limits of what they can do, they need to call on theology's capacity to find the meaning in apparently meaningless and hopeless situations. With their knowledge of human behavior and motivation, they can assist educators, social workers, and others who are attempting to educate and influence customs, policies, and individual habits. Only by such sharing of expertise and legally sanctioned roles can the helping professions ameliorate the stresses of childhood. In Chapter 19, Arnold illustrates with a case example the assessment of stress and interprofessional prevention opportunities.

Risk and Protective Factors

The authors of each chapter discuss relevant factors that modify the response to the particular stress they are examining. These modifying factors can be roughly categorized as risk factors—variables that predispose to a pathological or maladaptive reaction—and protective factors. Some protective factors are merely the converse of respective risk factors (e.g., female vs. male for aggressive misbehavior as a stress reaction). Others may be qualitatively different concepts. Of particular interest is resilience, a summary concept of protective factor efficacy.

Since not all children and adolescents seem vulnerable even under catastrophic stress, Norman Garmezy and Ann Masten pose questions in Chapter 17 about why some children are so resilient, so able to cope. Through the process of appraisal, stressed people decide whether their abilities can meet the demands of the event, in which case it becomes a growth experience, or whether their abilities are unequal to the demands, in which case the event is disruptive. Garmezy and Masten discuss risk factors ranging from genetic/biological to sociocultural, and note that considerably less than 100% of those at risk develop a disorder or otherwise show the ravages of stress. For example, less than half the children exposed to the worst combination of delinquency risk factors actually become delinquent, and the half who do not become delinquent cannot be distinguished in the degree of known risk from those who do. Prematurity is a good example of combining biological and socioeconomic risks: although premature birth carries greater risk at any socioeconomic level, in poor mothers it combines maternal undernourishment and inadequate prenatal care and perhaps infant malnutrition with impaired mothering due to economic stress on the mother. Garmezy and Masten cite four possible protective factors emerging from study of the children of the Holocaust: the power of religious belief; the reconstructive or healing power of a strong, loving caregiver; a sense of social responsibility and awareness of family and community bonds; and identification with the memory of competent dead parents.

In Chapter 7, Barton and Zeanah discuss protective factors relevant to preschool children. In Chapter 1, Trad discusses resilience as one of the modifiers of psychological stress response. In Chapter 18, Judith Kimchi and Barbara Schaffner provide a more comprehensive review of protective factors, including the concept of constitutional hardiness. They provide a table summarizing the available literature and discuss the ramifications.

Prevention and Treatment Interventions

Chapter 20 by Paul V. Trad and Chapter 21 by Joseph D. Noshpitz together provide an overview of prevention and treatment possibilities and practice. Chapter 20 focuses on the preschool age and on psychodynamic psychotherapy, while Chapter 21 focuses on older children and adolescents and covers other treatment/prevention. Other chapters, notably 4, 8, and 13, also discuss treatment.

Many of the same strategies and techniques useful for treatment can also be implemented preventively. These include education about stress in general and about particular stressors, self-relaxation/hypnosis, enhancement of feelings of mastery, cognitive-behavioral modification of coping skills, self-help groups, family therapy, and parent guidance. Notable exceptions are psychopharmacotherapy and Amytal catharsis, which would generally be used only after stress symptoms appear. In addition to techniques, Noshpitz provides in Chapter 21 a theoretical background and literature review for prevention.

One issue that arises is whether stress *should* be prevented, or more accurately, whether all of it should be prevented. In Chapter 17, Garmezy and Masten point out that in some cases mastery of stress can be a growth experience bringing out the best in an individual. On the other hand, overwhelming stress can be destructive. An analogy might be conditioning of an athlete to a hot climate: some moderate workouts in the heat can help adjust the athlete's metabolism and homeostatic mechanisms to cope with heat in the athletic contest, but extreme workouts to the point of heat exhaustion could lead to brain damage or even death. Since it is unlikely that we would ever be able to completely eliminate stress anyhow, and since the ordinary challenges of growing up would seem to supply enough stress for the average child, it seems reasonable for helping professionals to collaborate in reducing the stresses that currently assault children. When we have done this, then perhaps we can say that we stress (emphasize) the needs of children and adolescents rather than stressing and straining their psychobiological development.

REFERENCES

Arnold, L. E. (1985). *Parents, children, and change.* Lexington, MA: D.C. Heath & Co.

Caplan, G. (1981). Mastery of stress: Psychosocial aspects. *American Journal of Psychiatry, 138*(4), 413–420.

Coddington, R. D. (1981). *Life event scales for children and adolescents.* Author, 100 W. Main St., St. Clairsville, OH, 43950.

Garmezy, N., & Rutter, M. (1983). *Stress, coping, and development in children.* New York: McGraw Hill.

Noshpitz, J. D., & Coddington, R. D. (1989). Adjustment disorders. In B. Karasu, (Ed.), *Treatments of psychiatric disorders: A task force report of the American Psychiatric Association* (p. 2502). Washington, DC: APA Press.

Pynoos, R. S., & Nader, K. (1989). Children's memory and proximity to violence. *Journal of the American Academy of Child and Adolescent Psychiatry, 28*(2), 236–241.

Singer, D. G. (1985). Does violent television produce aggressive children? *Pediatric Annals, 14*(12), 804–810.

Skipper, J. K., & Leonard, R. C. (1968). Children, stress, and hospitalization: A field experiment. *Journal of Health and Social Behavior, 9,* 275–287.

Zuckerman, D. M., & Zuckerman, B. S. (1985). Television's impact on children. *Pediatrics, 75*(2), 233–240.

Part I

The Two Faces of Stress: Psychological and Biological

Psychological Aspects of Child Stress: Development and the Spectrum of Coping Responses

Paul V. Trad
Edward Greenblatt

Our world is no longer a simple place for children; they are as much affected by the diverse pressures of their environment as are adults. There is considerable evidence linking stressful life events to psychiatric disorders in adults (Andrews & Tennant, 1978; Brown & Harris, 1978; Lloyd, 1980; Paykel, 1978). But where stressful events in adults have been demonstrated to have physiologic or psychological sequelae, in children there is another dimension to consider: development. To what degree do stressful events affect a child's development and, conversely, to what degree does children's development protect or put them at risk for problems arising from such events?

SOME COMPLEXITIES OF STRESS AND COPING CONCEPTS

One difficulty researchers have encountered in answering these questions arises from the term "stress" itself. As Rutter (1983) noted, the term used popularly is too nebulous to have much scientific meaning. A civil engineer refers to stress on a load-bearing column or wall; a linguist speaks of stress as a spoken emphasis. And yet the word "stress," in one of its several definitions, has considerable application to the study of behavior. Stress is a physical, emotional, or chemical factor that exerts significant pressure on an individual's ability to function adaptively. An individual may make a satisfactory or unsatisfactory adaptation to a stressor; it is the range of responses of the human being to stressors, and the factors which create those responses, that concern us. Each event has a meaning of its own to the individual it affects, and that meaning, as much as the players and incidents of the event itself, constitutes an important facet of the stress (Rutter, 1983). Garmezy and Masten (1986) and Garmezy and Rutter (1983), attempting to further refine the concept of stress, have noted that stress usually pertains to a particular event or situation and evokes an emotional reaction that may serve as the basis for behavioral disorder, often brief and usually reversible. Knapp (1980) characterized stress as short-termed homeostatic perturbation, the result of the body preparing itself for an emergency response to a threatening situation. It is important, Knapp noted, to distinguish between external stress—stimuli that impinge on the individual from the environment—and internal stress which may derive from the individual's innate biological mechanisms. While it would be useful in examining the link between stress, behavior, and the physical health of the individual to consider innate biological stress, this chapter will deal with external stressors.

Garmezy and Rutter (1983) introduced five categories of stressors: loss; chronically disturbed relationships; events that change the family status quo, such as the birth of a sibling; events that require social adaptation;

and acute negative events such as physical trauma. These researchers targeted the last group in their discussion of acute reactions to stress. Their categories are well defined, but they focused narrowly on one short range of the spectrum of stress events. Therefore, we have decided to discuss the effects of stress on children in terms of the acute or unforeseeable and the chronic or foreseeable. A third category, neutral stress, overlaps with these; it may be acute, chronic, or repeated, but it is mundane and expectable as part of life.

By acute, unforeseeable stressors I mean negative events such as assault or disaster, as well as less spectacular but no less stressful events such as divorce. Such events are generally sudden, may be unforeseen and unplanned for, and by their nature may encompass other stressors, such as loss of, or separation from, parents, disturbance of normal relationships, and a sense of helplessness. Bereavement or divorce, as a single event, is in this schema an acute stressor, but its effects on children are generally long term. Chronic, or foreseeable, stressors are those which essentially form a persistently adverse theme in the child's life. Thus, chronic stressors may include the ongoing disturbance emanating from divorce or separation, socioeconomic disadvantage, handicapping condition, or chronic illness. This category of stressors also includes many events that disrupt the child's accustomed routine, such as the birth of a sibling or a move to a new neighborhood. Neutral stressors refer to those less calamitous, more mundane events that create a feeling of pressure but usually do not cause maladaptive responses, for example, an imminent school examination.

The Spectrum of Stress Responses

A stress event may call up an array of responses, based on a child's perception of the event, developmental level, and innate ability to cope with the strain the event creates. The significance of a loss event (such as bereavement or separation) in the etiology of behavioral and psychiatric disorder is, of course, well documented. Certain other kinds of stress events, such as hospitalization or chronic abuse, have also been much examined for links to later psychological disorders. Stress may be less a cause of later profound behavioral disorders than the root of physical or emotional symptoms that can affect children's development and hence their lifelong ability to cope and achieve. But even in experiences of the most severe stress (such as war, kidnapping, or natural disaster), some children exhibit an ability to cope adaptively with the most intense terror and disorientation (Garmezy, Masten & Tellegen, 1984; Rutter, 1979a). Where do these coping resources come from?

Historically, psychiatrists and developmental psychologists have pursued an understanding of negative results in the lives and behavior of children, but in the 1980s there was an increasing awareness of the need for an approach that embraces the study of stress resistance in children (Garmezy, Masten, & Tellegen, 1984; Hetherington, 1989; Masten & Tellegen, 1984; Rutter, 1979). Because "stress-resistant" children manifest the ability to deal effectively, even gracefully, with events that traumatize their peers, study of their coping styles may help us teach "stress competence" to all children (Garmezy & Rutter, 1983). The idea of somehow "immunizing" a child against the worst effects of physical or emotional trauma has been examined by a number of researchers who have attempted to teach coping skills to children (Ayalon, 1983; Dweck & Elliott, 1983; Janis, 1971; Keister & Updegraff, 1937; Kendall & Kriss, 1983; Meichenbaum, 1975; Meichenbaum & Novaco, 1978).

It may be most useful to view childhood stress responses not as a series of isolated potential reactions, but as part of a continuum. Almost any response to stress can fall within the realm of adaptive or maladaptive, depending upon its context and sequelae. Garmezy (1985) cited Bleuler's study of the children of schizophrenics, and in particular one child, Vreni, the daughter of a substance-abusive mother and a father who was both alcoholic and schizophrenic. Because of her parents' incapacities, at 14 years Vreni was surrogate parent to four younger siblings, not only performing routine household tasks, cooking and washing, but also nurturing her siblings, even making sure that their schoolwork was completed and that they attended school regularly. Vreni was also a "nurturer" to her parents, at the expense of her own education and plans for the future. Yet despite her grim and demanding adolescence, Vreni grew up to be a loving, adaptive parent and a happy wife. Clearly, for this child pseudomaturity and hyperresponsibility in response to a stressful home environment were adaptive, and they did not prevent her from forming successful attachments or creating a successful life for herself as an adult. Rather, her adjustment permitted her to feel "heroic" and pivotal to her family's successful functioning. Another child who responded with the same hyperresponsibility (which would appear to be an appropriate short-term response) might later use responsibility to her family as an excuse to avoid the future or the stress of new attachments or further challenges, carrying the adaptation too far, into the realm of the maladaptive.

If reaction to stress is a defense—or attempted defense—against anxiety, then maladaptive stress reaction may only be a more extreme version of an initial reaction that failed to alleviate stress. One child may be able to deflect the confusion and fear of loss created by his parents' divorce by increased self-reliance, taking strength from a perception of mastery or competence, while another child may find that mere mastery of individual tasks is not sufficient to allay anxieties and may become rigidly controlling or may ritualize life in order to minimize the chance of further anxiety.

Perhaps an ideal stress reaction is one which responds not only to the anxiety a stress event elicits, but to the stressor itself. Stress events often require that the target individual cope with some problem immediately. Therefore, children who react to the stress of an important examination with redoubled effort may not only achieve a soothing sense that some-thing positive is being done (mastery through activity), but also improve their chances of doing well on the examination. Conversely, children who respond to an examination with paralysis or regression are likely only to confirm their fears of failure and heighten anxiety.

Even in very young children, response to stress has its own internal logic: the 5-year-old who regresses to enuresis after the birth of a sibling may be seeking to compete as a baby with the new infant; a child who is accosted by a schoolyard bully and becomes abusive in turn may be trying to "court" his persecutor's favor; and a child whose mother is hospitalized and suddenly not available may become insatiable for reas-surance and attention. Depending on the duration and severity of the stress involved, these stress reactions are generally short lived and adap-tive. The examples given above are deliberately culled from the everyday, and in each example these reactions are normal, even predictable. Where the stresses are extraordinary, even normal reactions are likely to be more intense. In this chapter we will briefly examine some acute, chronic, and neutral stress events, the normal spectrum of child coping and adaptation, and the factors that appear to influence coping and vulnerability.

SPECIFIC STRESSORS AND THEIR PSYCHOLOGICAL CONSEQUENCES

Chronic Stressors and Their Consequences

Chronic stressors tend to create an aura or background of stress against which an individual lives, or strives to live, a normal life. Of the chronic stressors discussed here, only one, chronic illness or handicap, generally derives from sources outside human control. The others—abuse, ongo-ing family disturbance, socioeconomic deprivation, and the effects of a substance-abusing or emotionally disordered parent–emanate from the actions of human beings. According to the *Diagnostic and Statistical Man-ual of Mental Disorders* (DSM-III-R; APA, 1987), post-traumatic stress disor-der is generally more powerful when the event has a human origin. Applying this notion to chronic stressors, can it be that "man-made" chronic stressors such as parental discord are more disruptive to a child than "natural" stressors such as illness or handicap? At present, no data exist to strongly support this notion. Chronic stressful conditions not only cause pain and anxiety in a child in isolated instances, but also form a backdrop of adversity that may distort the child's growth and development.

Children who grow up to an accompaniment of parental bickering, or who are bystanders in an acrimonious divorce, suffer from ongoing stress that can exert a debilitating effect through family functioning (Rice, 1987). Such children show a higher incidence of physiological responses such as hyperactivity, sleep disturbances, and tension than do children from intact families (Brady, Bray, & Zeeb, 1986). Some of the stresses created by divorce or parental strife appear to derive from the fact that marital dysfunction, divorce, and the exigencies of life after a divorce may absorb the time, attention, and energy of the parents to the extent that their needed support is not available to the child. As Rutter (1979b) noted, there is frequently a tendency to regard divorce as the final, positive solution to the negative experience of marital dysfunction. However, a divorce is no guarantee that parental hostility will cease. Indeed, it may escalate over matters such as child support or custody, and the child may become the target of rejection or hostility. In this case, the child faces bereavement of a sort as well as the considerable strain of parental hostility. It is possible that the true bereavement of a total loss might be less detrimental to the child's development than the stress evoked by the isolation that can be imposed by a hostile divorce (Rutter, 1979b). (See Chapter 14 for more about divorce stress.)

There has been considerable investigation into the experience of children of schizophrenic, depressed, or addicted parents. Studies by Fergusson, Horwood, and Shannon (1984) and by Livingston, Nugent, Rader, and Smith (1985) linked maternal depression with child-rearing problems, and with childhood depression or severe anxiety. (See Chapter 13 for more about parental depression.) Pfeffer (1986) found a strong association between childhood suicidal behavior and parental alcoholism and between such behavior and divorce or separation. The ongoing stress a child experiences in dealing with the discordant communications of an impaired parent may be expressed in low self-esteem, depression, or anxiety disorders, as well as in accident-proneness or a decline in physical health. Conversely, such stress may compel the child to a new level of competence or mastery which becomes the foundation for future stress-competence. Because the disordered function of one parent will often force the other parent to carry a double financial and emotional load, the child's normal relationship with the healthy parent may be jeopardized (Trad, 1988).

With stressors such as emotional, physical, or sexual abuse, each blow or cruel word or distressing touch is an event in itself, but each also adds to an aura of stress with which such a child's life is cloaked (Trad, 1987, 1988). Thus, repeated abuse becomes a chronic stressor in a child's life. As with children of impaired parents, abused children experience a high degree of noncontingency, impaired dyadic interaction, and lowered self-esteem; they are strongly at risk for depression (Trad, 1986, 1988). (See Chapter 10 for more about abuse.)

A chronic illness or handicap may create an ongoing stress, for it establishes rules and limitations that clearly mark the child as different from peers. Chronic illness or handicap can call the child's competence into question, especially when the illness impairs the exercise of newly developed skills (Emde, Gaensbauer, & Harmon, 1981). The fact that an illness such as juvenile diabetes or a congenital heart murmur is chronic—that it will be with the child always, without regard to any solution he or she tries—may also put the child at risk for learned helplessness depression (Trad, 1988). Because chronic illness or handicap often affects the entire family, putting strain on the emotional and financial resources of parents and other siblings, the handicapped child may respond with pseudomaturity, aggressive self-reliance, or almost unnaturally good behavior, designed to offset the trouble the child feels he or she has caused. (See Chapter 12 for more about chronic illness.)

Acute Stressors and Their Consequences

Acute stressors, in the sense intended here, are not limited to traumatic events such as those outlined by Garmezy and Rutter (1985) in discussing acute reactions to stress. Stressors producing post-traumatic stress disorder (see Chapter 2) are generally those outside the common order of experience, whereas some of the events we have classified as acute are relatively common, but profound enough and of short enough duration to warrant the term *acute*. These include accident or sudden physical injury and the immediate events surrounding a bereavement or divorce.

The effect on a child of an event such as the 1976 Chowchilla bus kidnapping may be very similar in symptoms to that of a Jamaican child who survived 1988's Hurricane Gilbert, or of a child evacuated from the area surrounding the Three Mile Island nuclear plant. Manifestations of unsuccessful coping may include nightmares and "flashbacks," detachment, sleeplessness, guilt, depression, hypervigilance, anxiety, and irritability (Garmezy & Rutter, 1985).

Like other traumatic stress events, war and terrorism may comprise a number of stressors, including separation, deprivation, fear, physical danger, anxiety associated with the loss of a parent, and lack of control (Freud & Burlingham, 1943). The child is knocked out of his accustomed routine, in some cases deliberately separated from his home or family, and may be caught up by the contagious fear that his parents and other adults around him communicate. In fact, a child's reaction to the stressful event of war may be heavily influenced by the reactions of his parents (Garmezy, 1985). Children who are not swayed by the fears of adults may view an experience of war as an adventure in which they can be heroes. Rutter (1985) suggested that if the child does not experience a significant personal loss, the experience of war, while frightening, may not create lasting sequelae; perhaps it is possible that such children will find new mastery skills and self-confidence in coping with the chaos of war experience. However, where the experience has a strong personal connotation—the child has a direct contact with the war or with a terrorist act or has sustained a significant loss—the likelihood of psychiatric disorder is much greater. Terrorism, like violent crime, often touches its victims more directly than a distant battle. Terrorist attack or violent crime can give rise to anxiety, physiological disorders, emotional lability, forgetfulness, and disturbed orientation, which linger for some time after the incident, but there is generally no lasting psychosis (Trad, 1988). (See Chapter 11 for more about threats of violence.)

A number of studies have investigated the effect on children of what Garmezy and Rutter (1985) termed "the prototypic situation for eliciting post-traumatic stress reactions in adults and children": disaster (Kinston & Rosser, 1974). Disasters are by their nature sudden and unexpected; they vary in form, duration, extent, and the degree to which a stricken community is prepared beforehand (Barton, 1969). A child who survives a disaster, whether natural or man made, is likely to experience guilt, psychic numbing, and an indelible image of the event and its destruction. Apathy, hostility, emotional outbursts, somatic complaints, and behavioral disorganization may follow (Lifton, 1967, 1980). In reviewing studies that have focused on the effect of disaster on children, particularly the Buffalo Creek Flood in Appalachia and the Three Mile Island nuclear accident, Garmezy and Rutter (1985) concluded that "behavioral disturbances appear to be less intense than might have been anticipated; a majority of children show a moderate amount of fear and anxiety, but this subsides; regressive behaviour . . . mild sleep disturbance . . . a later less severe stressor such as a storm may lead to a temporary increase in emotional distress, although this is variable; enuresis occurs in some cases, while hypersensitivity to loud noises may be evident in others" (p. 162). (See Chapter 16 for more about disasters.)

In stress situations arising from disaster, combat, or other violent trauma, the child's perception of his or her own role ("I was a hero!" or "I was a victim!") appears to be an important factor in the severity of the stress experience. It is not surprising that so much of children's literature is comprised of stories in which a child faces a great challenge—a stressor—and triumphs, thereby gaining new skills and self-esteem. A further discussion of stress perception appears below.

Accidental injury, by its nature, is a sudden, unplanned occurrence, and one that can be shrouded in feelings of guilt or fear; a child who is badly hurt contends with more than the pain of the injury alone. The kind of injury a child sustains may have some bearing on how stressful the injury event is. For instance, research on burn victims consistently shows an increase in emotional disturbance following the accident (Garmezy & Rutter, 1985). This may be due to a number of factors, including the necessity for prolonged hospitalization, separation from parents, fear for other people who might have been burned in the same accident, repeated painful dressing changes, and fear of disfigurement or crippling. In addition, burn victims often face multiple hospital admissions and rehabilitation programs that keep the image of the hospital and trauma unsettlingly fresh. Hospitalization itself can constitute a very stressful event for a child, who may be separated from his or her parents and surrounded by adult strangers, strangers who appear to understand the workings of the child's body far better than the child does. The whole experience may evoke feelings of helplessness and anxiety, although the daily presence of a parent or family member will considerably lessen that anxiety (Robertson & Robertson, 1971). As with other stressful events, the attitudes broadcast by the child's parents can have a significant impact on whether the child copes successfully with the experience of hospitalization. It has been observed also that while one episode of hospitalization does not appear to produce long-term psychiatric distress, two or more episodes create a substantially higher risk of disorder (Douglas, 1975; Quinton & Rutter, 1976; Rutter, 1983). (See Chapter 12 for more about illness effects.)

Finally, in discussing acute stressors, we must again mention divorce. In a seminal study of children of divorced parents, Wallerstein (1983) noted that divorce represents a uniquely stressful experience for a child who has been reared in a two-parent household. The formerly close bonds of the family community are severed, and the child faces a kind of bereavement. The child's response, which may be intense but more short-lived than that of the parents, may involve anger, profound misery, a sense of vulnerability, anxiety about the parents' safety, conflicting loyalties, and an overall sense of neediness.

Neutral Stressors and Their Consequences

Neutral stressors are stressors that most children face: the birth of a sibling, starting school, changing schools, or moving. They generally have some effect on children's accustomed environment, introducing a change in their life (a sibling, a visitor). The stresses are essentially without value connotation; that is, it is the child's own perception of the event that determines whether it is stressful and whether the response to that stress will be predominantly negative or positive. The birth of a sibling may well be felt as a negative event by an older child: Dunn and Kendrick (1980b) found that after the birth of a second child, mothers tend to play with their firstborn children less and to issue more prohibitions and orders. With neutral stressors what is important is apparently less the degree of change the event causes than the perceived degree of unpleasantness the child experiences (Holmes & Rahe, 1967). Moreover, even "positive" stressful events can be overwhelming. A child who experiences success or is praised for work accomplished with intense effort may interpret that praise as a message that his normal work, outside the range of that intense effort, is not sufficient. Praise or success may thus come to be viewed by such a child as pressure. Generally, neutral stress events lead to "adaptation reactions" in which no obvious emotional pathology need be apparent. Such reactions are often transient and reversible, and even ostensibly emotional reactions are unlikely to lead to major behavioral problems (Trad, 1988).

Stress, whether chronic, acute, or neutral, exacts a physiological (see Chapters 3 and 4) as well as a psychological response from a child. Often a child is required to cope with an event whose potential for stress would seem crushing even to an adult, and yet such children often find ways to cope, to adjust, and even to emerge stronger for the expression (Bleuler, 1978). The resources upon which they draw and the forces that nurture this ability to cope are explored in the next sections.

INTERACTIONS OF STRESS AND DEVELOPMENT

There is evidence linking specific stressful experiences to psychiatric disorder in children. The psychopathology attendant on maternal separation has been documented by Bowlby (1969) and Ainsworth (1972). Children who encounter the disturbed relationships inherent in maternal depression, parental substance abuse, or abusive behavior may be at risk for depression or suicidal behavior (Jacobs, Prusoff, & Paykel, 1974; Trad, 1987, 1988). On the other hand, while researchers such as Terr (1979, 1981a, 1981b, 1983), Handford et al. (1986), Malmquist (1984), Tuckman (1973), and Gleser et al. (1981) have provided compelling evidence that acute stressors such as disaster or assault can leave a child with an aftermath of disorientation and behavioral dysfunction, it appears that in most cases such dysfunction is transient and does not lead to a full-fledged psychiatric disorder.

But what of the effects of such stress on the development of a child? Does stress deflect or enhance developmental achievements? Can it have a serious impact on the progression of development? What are the factors that promote resiliency in the child? Answers to these questions depend on a large number of factors, including the child's age, temperament, the relationship with the attachment figure, cognitive skills, locus of control, and skills at seeking social support. It can also be argued that chronic stressors are more likely to create a long-term developmental burden than are acute stressors, although there appears to be little or no difference between the neuroendocrine reactions to acute and chronic stressors (Trad, 1988).

Age is a particularly crucial factor in determining the developmental effects of a stressful event: stress seems to have a graver developmental effect on a young child than on an older one, according to Rutter (1983). He suggested that the important product of stress is an altered form of response to future stress, rather than any specific disorder. An early experience of stress may elicit a coping style that persists for reasons unrelated to the original event. A child whose intense emotional neediness during an early stress event was satisfied might later develop neediness as a style, perceiving that it was successful in allaying stress once and thus will always be a successful strategy. An early stressful event may cause physical changes that influence the child's most developed coping abilities. The stressful experience may sensitize the child to future events; that is, an early experience of stress may serve to change the child's coping style in such a way as to increase vulnerability to, or give limited immunity to, later stresses (Rutter, 1983). Finally, family functioning may be so disrupted by the stress situation as to constitute a stressful condition in itself.

The age at which a stressful event occurs will determine, to a certain extent, the repertoire of developmental skills the child brings to it. A securely attached 1-year-old infant is more likely to be severely disrupted by hospitalization than is a 4-month-old, whose attachment bond is still tenuous. Similarly, 5-year-olds are likely to weather hospitalization better than 3-year-olds because they are better able to understand that the separation from home and parents does not mean abandonment, and because parents may more readily prepare them for the experience they face (Trad, 1987). Obviously, developed coping skills are less likely to be altered or hampered than nascent or newly acquired skills.

Perhaps the most crucial area of development in terms of stress is competence or mastery. Children whose locus-of-control orientation is internal, and who have a body of mastery experience to reinforce their belief in their own powers, are more likely to cope successfully with stress. Conversely, children with little or no mastery experience or a strongly external locus of control may be at risk for learned helplessness depression. Although an internal locus of control is likely to affect how well a child copes with stress, locus-of-control orientation is not likely to be affected by the event itself (Trad, 1986, 1988). Nevertheless, the effect of stress on mastery or competence may be to reinforce or even enhance the child's current level of development in that area. Thus, the effect of stressful events on development depends on how successfully the child is able to manage the stress at the time it occurs. Overcoming the potentially debilitating effects of a stress experience can reinforce the child's sense of mastery, insulating the child from the effects of learned helplessness and perhaps immunizing him or her against future stress. An unsuccessfully managed stress experience carries with it both the onus of nonmastery and the full brunt of the stress event itself (Rutter, 1983). Acute or chronic stress experience may have considerable effect on development, but developmental factors, in turn, have great impact on the child's ability to cope, to resist the destructive power of stress.

FACTORS IN COPING AND STRESS RESISTANCE

In discussing the factors that influence the impact of stress events in the lives of children, two categories can be observed: those factors that are intrinsic to the child (such as temperament, age, sex, and competence) and those that are environmental, such as the family milieu and available social support.

Temperament

Temperament may be one of the leading factors determining vulnerability and ability to cope with stress. The tripartite classification of easy, difficult, and slow-to-warm-up temperaments made by Thomas, Chess, and Birch (1970) and Thomas and Chess (1984) encompasses such dimensions as emotional flexibility, regularity, threshold of stimulus response, attention span or persistence level, prevailing mood, and intensity of reaction. These dimensions tend to cluster in patterns that identify the three temperament types. These clusters give significant clues as to the role temperament will play in a child's reaction to stress. A child of easy temperament, for example, tends to be adaptable and positive in outlook, curious and persistent in explorations. A child of difficult temperament is generally inflexible and easily alarmed by new stimuli, negative in outlook, irregular, and intense in reaction. The slow-to-warm-up child, as the name suggests, displays slow adaptability, a certain reluctance to explore or confront new stimuli, and a low intensity of reaction. With these characteristics in mind, it is not difficult to see that children of difficult or slow-to-warm-up temperament may be particularly affected by stressful experience. Given their low level of adaptability, such children may be particularly prone to physiologic disorders (reduced ability to regulate biological reactivity). Emotional flexibility and positive emotional outlook may be the most important temperamental factors governing a child's response to stress, giving the child the affective resources to express his or her experience (Trad, 1986, 1988). Persistence, as a temperamental factor, may also enhance the child's ability to seek solutions or ameliorate the stress that is faced.

Another approach to the question of temperament and stress has been posited by Block and Block (1980), who advanced the construct of ego resiliency. Ego-resilient children are resourceful and creative in dealing with challenges and barriers, can maintain behavior and performance under stress, are able to process competing stimuli, and essentially adapt to meet the requirements of the situation they face. Nonresilient children, by contrast, are rigid and only narrowly adaptive; paralyzed, repetitive, or diffuse when under stress; brittle; and generally unable to meet conflicting demands. In many ways there is overlap between the adaptive characteristics of the ego-resilient individual and the individual of easy temperament, and overlap between the brittle, unyielding character of the ego-unresilient individual and the individual of difficult temperament. The response of the easy/resilient individual or the difficult/unresilient individual to stressful events is, of course, implied by the characteristics of each mode.

Relatively little research exists that clearly defines the specific role of temperament in stress responses. However, Dunn et al. found that temperament could predict behavioral changes following a sibling's birth (Dunn, Kendrick, & MacNamee, 1981), as well as changes in the pattern of mother–child interaction that followed the birth (Dunn & Kendrick, 1980a). It has also been observed that children of different temperamental typologies are protected from or vulnerable to stress, in part because of the effects of their temperaments on the parent–child relationship. Rutter (1978) has observed that children with unfavorable temperamental predisposition were twice as liable to parental criticism as other children. Does this imply some favorable or protective aura for the child of easy temperament? [Not always, according to Lobo in Chapter 6—*Ed.*]

Hinkle (1974) makes a point that persons with a pattern of high stress resistance or stress competence may often have a "sociopathic" quality to their personalities. Tenuous attachment, which can be shifted if the object is too demanding, seems to offer some kind of protective quality to these people, but at a cost.

Attachment and Family Support

The status of a child's attachment to parents and the milieu of origin are crucial factors in stress resistance and vulnerability. Werner and Smith (1982) found that a child with a secure, supportive attachment to parents and a home environment that is supportive and fosters respect for all family members is likely to recuperate quickly from illnesses and is generally responsible and given to a "positive social orientation." Girls from such a background have fewer teen pregnancies, teen marriages, and accidents. Other researchers such as Garmezy (1985) and Block (1971) have pointed to (1) secure attachment; (2) parents who are confident and open, with a genuine concern for the goals of the child; and (3) a home marked by limit-setting, closeness, and shared values. Interestingly, Garmezy found that family intactness was not a factor in identifying resilient, stress-competent children. In supportive single-parent families the parent was as actively involved in promoting her child's aspirations and interests as were parents in more traditionally structured families.

The warmth and sense of control that a child derives from a secure attachment and supportive family environment creates a powerful protective aura around the child, in sharp contrast to an unsupportive or actively hostile family milieu. Garmezy (1985) has noted six family variables associated with high incidence of psychiatric disorders in children: marital turmoil, low socioeconomic status of the family, overcrowding or a large family, paternal criminality, maternal psychiatric disorder, and a child's admission into the custody of local authorities. A number of these variables can also be considered chronic stressors in the scheme proposed earlier in this chapter. After hospitalization, children with a tenuous parent–child attachment and those from poor or deprived families are more likely to experience persistent disturbance, even after a return home (Quinton & Rutter, 1976; Stacey, Dearden, Pill, & Robinson, 1970). Characteristics of families that "nurture" unresilient or stress-incompetent children include enmeshment, overprotectiveness, rigidity, and lack of conflict resolution mechanisms (Trad, 1988).

Age

We have already touched on the relationship between age and the effect of hospitalization on children. Because age and stage of development are linked, it is difficult not to consider the two factors together. However, there are certain aspects to the question of age and stress that are not specifically linked to development. In discussing the birth of a sibling, both Dunn et al. (1981) and Moore (1975) found that younger children were more likely to display clinging or other forms of disturbed behavior. As Rutter (1983) suggests, this may be because an older child is less likely to try to compete with the new infant or because an older child may be "brought in" on the process of tending the baby, thus enhancing the older child's sense of mastery and self-esteem. A wider gap in age between infant and older sibling may also mean that maternal patterns of interaction with the older child are set and are less likely to be disrupted by the arrival of the infant.

Bowlby (1980) and Rutter (1966) both noted that, in bereavement, younger children tend to have shorter, milder grief reactions than those of adolescents or adults. On the other hand, bereavement tends to have delayed consequences for young children, which can be significantly more profound (Rutter, 1966). The younger child's ability or inability to understand the nature of death and to express feelings of loss may be the determining factor. Certainly young children are not capable of predicting the range of changes a bereavement will make in their lives, and these changes, as much as the loss, may be responsible for the delayed response. (See Chapter 15 for more about bereavement. See also the discussion of sense of coherence (SOC) under "Resilience" below.)

Neuroendocrine Correlates of Coping

An examination of neuroendocrine reactivity to stress interfaces with the study of temperament, which is also a hierarchically interlocked system (Derryberry & Rothbart, 1984). The correlation of neuroendocrinological differences with observed differences in temperament at an early age would be a valuable tool for studying the development of stress-coping mechanisms.

A major step in this direction was taken by Tennes, Downey, and Vernadakis (1977), who monitored urinary cortisol rates every 8 hours over 3 days in 20 infants age 11 to 13 months. After baseline cortisol levels had been obtained on the first day, the infants were separated from their mothers for 1 hour on the second day. When tested after the separation, infants who reacted with fear or anxiety when their mothers left were found to have higher levels of cortisol. Further testing revealed that those infants had chronically higher levels of cortisol even before separation than infants who did not react fearfully. Among members of the fear/anxiety group, there were two distinct subgroups. Response to separation by one group was marked by distinct affective reactions (crying or clinging to the mother). However, members of the other group became immobilized and passive, in what might have been a physiological regression to a drowsy state, allowing them to withdraw from interaction with the environment. Psychological regression to an earlier state of helplessness may have been involved as well. Members of the latter group had lower levels of cortisol both chronically and in association with the stress event than did those who exhibited more overt anxious reactions. It thus appears that hyperactivity and hypoactivity may be used to predict two different types of bio-behavioral reactivity to stress. When the infants were re-categorized according to their response to toys during a play session (happy, indifferent, or fearful), it was observed that the "happy" or "indifferent" infants had cortisol levels similar to those of securely separating infants, whereas infants who reacted fearfully to the toys showed cortisol levels on a par with those seen in infants who experienced anxiety on being separated from their mothers.

The fact that psychoendocrine correlates in 1-year-old infants who were separated from their mothers for 1 hour are similar to findings in highly emotional versus more reserved adults is an indication of the rapidity with which neuroendocrine systems mature. Disturbance of the attachment bond may provide a useful paradigm of stress-coping states in infancy, especially in light of the intensity of despair response and the physiological changes known to occur upon traumatic separation: for example, changes in sleep patterns, monoamine systems, immune function, body temperature, and endocrine function (Gunnar, Mangelsdorf, Larson, & Hertsgaard, 1989; Kalin & Carnes, 1984; Trad, 1986, 1987).

Gunnar (1987) has suggested that the secretion of cortisol, rather than being purely reactive, may be part of a coping mechanism triggered by new and/or unexpected stimuli, so that, while it may be activated simultaneously with emotion and emotional reaction, it has no one-to-one relationship with them. However, Henry (1980) has suggested that perhaps cortisol secretion is an adaptive response to situations which require submission and the learning of new roles or behaviors. In Henry's view, attempts to manage or cope with a stressor should be marked by elevations in norepinephrine; attempts to avoid or flee the stressor should be marked by elevated epinephrine; and a lack of action or depression should be marked by elevated cortisol. Each of these reactions are designed to elicit a very different coping mechanism from the individual under stress. (See Chapters 3 and 4 for more about neuro-hormonal responses to stress.)

Sex

There is some evidence that boys are, on the whole, more vulnerable to stress than girls. This does not appear to depend on specific stress events: whether faced with hospitalization, the birth of a sibling, or divorce, boys are the more likely to evidence withdrawal or aggression (Dunn et al., 1981; Rutter, 1981, 1983; Wallerstein & Kelly, 1980). The reasons for this gender vulnerability are not clearly drawn. There may be a sociological impulse at work here: parents may be less likely to support boys during stressful times than girls, or may be impatient with a boy's expression of distress (Hetherington, 1980). There may be sex-linked temperamentally or biologically increased vulnerability to stressful events or physical hazard (Eme, 1979; Rutter, 1970). Or in some way the significance of a stress event may be heightened for boys (Block, Block, & Morrison, 1981).

Control

One of the recurrent themes that appears in connection with any discussion of stress and coping is the perception of control. Paykel (1974) noted that the link between stress and psychiatric disorder is much stronger when the stressful event is seen as uncontrollable. Children's ability to control their environment, and their faith in that ability, is one of the strongest protective factors for stress. Children with a strong internal locus of control are apt to face the world with a sense that they can control it; those with an external locus of control tend to feel controlled, at the mercy of forces and powers outside themselves. The issue of control, both of the self and of external events, is central to the discussion of stress resistance, for closely linked to control is competence, children's mastery of skills and situations, by which they control themselves and the world around them (Trad, 1988).

Block and Block (1980), in discussing the roles of control and stress, referred to overcontrollers and undercontrollers. Here the term *over-controller* refers to a child who tries to control his environment and himself, endeavoring to reduce the risks that more spontaneous, flexible behavior might create. An *undercontroller* refers to a child who has the confidence to function in a flexible, even adventurous way, without seeking to control his environment. Block and Block found that un-dercontrol is displayed in the child's confident, active engagement with tasks, in curiosity and willingness to explore, in expressiveness and im-pulsiveness, but also in a lack of compliance and relaxation. For an undercontrolling child, the quality of ego resilience (discussed above) moderates impulse without dampening spontaneity, curiosity, or enthu-siasm. Without ego resilience, an undercontrolled child is likely to be restless, impulsive, manipulative, and brittle. For overcontrolling chil-dren, too, ego resilience is a moderating factor. Resilient overcontrollers tend to be relaxed and empathic, highly socialized, compliant, and ac-cepting of themselves and the people around them. In marked contrast, unresilient overcontrollers are inhibited, anxious, reserved, threatened by ambiguous or challenging situations, and often appear victimized or overwhelmed. Resiliency appears to play an important role in mediating the effects of ego control, particularly under stress.

The degree to which the child is able to take command of himself during and after a stressful experience appears to mitigate not only the experience itself, but its aftereffects. However, a strongly internal locus of control orientation may be a mixed blessing in a situation of extreme stress if it causes the child to assign guilt for the stressful event to himself.

Event Perception

The way in which the child under stress views the experience is an important factor in stress competence. An event is stressful if it awakens a perception of threat accompanied by physiological reactions. But per-ception of stress may vary from person to person, depending on the individual's perception of himself and his own competence to deal with the threat; in fact, the way an individual copes with a stressful event may be of more lasting importance than the event itself (Garmezy & Rutter, 1985; Lazarus & Launier, 1978). Children with an internal locus of control may be exhilarated by the challenge to their powers, as in Garmezy, Masten, and Tellegen's Challenge Model of Competence (1984). Rutter (1979a) suggests that some individuals may have a heightened awareness of stressful events, which increases their vulnerability to them, while some others are able to suppress awareness of a threatening stimulus, enabling them to cope with the stressful event without succumbing to it.

A discussion of perception also allows us to question what a stress is. Obviously, violent assault, hospitalization, or natural disaster will not be perceived as pleasant experiences, but in the gray areas of human experience, stress may be literally what the individual makes of it. As Rutter commented, "many of the minor hassles and pleasures of the day are brought about, at least in part, by persons themselves as a consequence of the way they are feeling" (1983, p. 16). While children and adolescents, questioned about the most stressful events in their lives, catalogue expected stressors such as the birth of a sibling, parental divorce, and chronic family turmoil, they often contradict the expectations of psychiatric professionals about the relative stress of an event. Yamamoto (1979) discovered that children felt parental quarreling was more stressful than the birth of a sibling. Adolescents generally rank the chronic family turmoil created by parental alcoholism, unemployment, or illness higher than adult professionals would rank them (Garmezy & Rutter, 1985).

Social Support

Among the factors listed as stress-protective, temperament, attachment, and social support are probably the most often cited. Cobb (1976) defined social support as information leading to a sense that one is loved and valued. There is evidence that in conditions as varied as low birth weight, arthritis, and depression, social support may facilitate compliance with medical regimens and thus recovery (Trad, 1988). Support may come from extended family members or extrafamilial sources; from peers, trusted adults, teachers, and school personnel, and from groups— from membership in a scout troop or church organization, for instance. Henderson (1981) noted that, in adults, social support is of little help in protecting against or mitigating the effect of stress unless the individual uses that support.

How—or whether—a child perceives the support available was studied by Zill (1977) in a comparison of adult and child assessment of lifestyle (which encompassed numerous factors, including friendship and support groups). When parents were interviewed, 60% reported that their children had good to excellent lifestyles; but less than 30% of the children so reported. A child may not realize that support is available, or may have compelling reasons (such as family loyalty or feelings of guilt) not to seek out support. Finally, aloneness—as opposed to isolation—apparently is a source of support to many children, who cite the opportunity to be alone as a desirable and nourishing factor in dealing with stressful situations (Wolfe, 1978).

Resiliency

Garmezy, Masten, and Tellegen (1984), in outlining the assumptions behind their Project Competence study, hypothesized that a child's competence level might serve as a protective factor under stress. These researchers posited three models of competency: the Compensatory Model, in which stress factors are compensated for by the child's own attributes; the Challenge Model, in which the child rises to meet the challenge a stress event poses; and the Immunity/Vulnerability Model, in which the child's attributes modify or exacerbate the severity of the event. The question of vulnerability, both physiological and psychological, has been approached by a number of authorities. Block and Block (1980) suggested that precursors of resilience likely are rooted in both genetic and temperamental factors, and are most easily demonstrated by temperamental values such as the infant's response to change, ease of comforting, and self-quieting.

Studying a group of adolescents in Israeli settlements during the 1982 evacuation of the Sinai peninsula, Antonovsky and Sagy (1986) found confirmation of the notion of Sense of Coherence (SOC) as a factor in stress resiliency. Antonovsky (1979) defined sense of coherence as an individual's pervasive, enduring confidence in the predictability and manageability of his environment, and his belief that events will tend to work out as well as possible. According to Antonovsky, SOC develops throughout childhood, is formed but labile during adolescence, and probably reaches its final, concrete form by about the age of 30; thus age at the time of a stress event is an important factor in how protective SOC will be. Attachment and good communication with parents were also posited as important factors in SOC, but in fact neither of these was proved important in the Sinai evacuation study. The Sinai study did show that a stable community is a precursor for SOC. It appears that the more children's lives are marked by consistency, involvement in the decisions that shape their lives, and a balance of stimuli, the greater their SOC will be. Finally, it appears that boys have an overall higher SOC than girls do—perhaps, Antonovsky and Sagy suggested, because of the differing attributes of and expectations for girls and boys.

While boys' superiority on sense of coherence appears to contradict findings reported above about boys being more vulnerable to stress, it is possible that while boys tend to have a higher SOC, girls are generally more flexible and immediately adaptive. The two qualities are neither mutually exclusive nor congruent.

Individuals with a high sense of coherence do not appear to perceive stressful situations as threatening or uncontrollable. Since confidence in the predictability and manageability of the environment is one of the qualities of SOC, it is not unreasonable that Antonovsky and Sagy (1986) found a correlation between high SOC and a lower level of anxiety in stressful situations. However, it appears that an acutely stressful event may "override" the protective influence of SOC, when situational characteristics are more influential than personality characteristics on the individual's ability to cope (Gal & Israelshvily, 1978).

Molina (1983) saw the individual's vulnerability to stress as in constant flux. The biological and psychosocial systems are interactive and are vulnerable to disruption by the alteration of another system. This vulnerability begins on the genetic level: genetic predispositions for metabolic, endocrine, cardiovascular, or psychiatric disorders have been demonstrated by research. Pre- and perinatal influences and experiences are part of this "vulnerability profile." Psychological vulnerability evolves from the action of the individual's personal experiences on the unique blend of history, temperament, and biology (Hetherington, 1989; Trad, 1988, 1989). Molina cited poor frustration tolerance, learned helplessness, low self-esteem, fear of intimacy, limited trust in others, and lack of a secure attachment as factors in the individual who is vulnerable or at risk for stress. Additionally, it is possible that early stress experiences may create a kind of hypersensitivity in an individual, creating an increased vulnerability to a particular kind of stress event or to environmental stress generally. (See Chapter 3 for neurochemical research evidence for this possible "priming" effect.)

Factors such as learned helplessness may play a role in vulnerability to stress beyond that already cited here. Such an orientation may actually corrupt the hormonal and immunologic mechanisms, damaging the ability of these systems to emit adaptive neuroendocrine regulation and thus jeopardizing health during a stressful period (Trad, 1988). Knapp (1980) noted that immunological triggers, which play an important role in the origins of organic illness, co-depend on psychological catalyzers, in an intricate protective–adaptive mechanism which is easily disrupted if the individual is subjected to stress.

Challenge

Bleuler (1978), writing his longitudinal study of 208 schizophrenic probands, hypothesized that suffering has a toughening effect on the personalities of some children, enabling them to master their lives despite obstacles. This notion of toughening or steeling dovetails with the Challenge Model of Competence advanced by Garmezy, Masten, and Tellegen (1984). These researchers noted a phenomenon in which the adverse conditions in which children develop actually allow them to increase their sense of mastery and accomplishment—a phenomenon which is essentially the converse of Seligman's (1975) Learned Helplessness paradigm. By applying their own talents and deriving pleasure from their ability to cope with a stressful environment, children demonstrate what Rachman (1978) termed "required helpfulness."

This kind of coping strategy lessens children's vulnerability to stress because it adds an element of controllability and of predictability to their lives, if the task required is one they can accomplish (Garmezy, 1985). Other researchers (Radke-Yarrow & Zahn-Waxler, 1984; Radke-Yarrow, Zahn-Waxler, & Chapman, 1984) have also observed this prosocial familial helpfulness among children with impaired parents.

CONCLUSION

It is perhaps a natural tendency to view childhood stress—and stress responses—in terms of negative, positive, and neutral values. Perhaps it is more effective to think in terms of a scale on which the same stresses may have different values, depending upon the myriad factors of temperament, age, sex, environment, and available support which each child brings to bear in dealing with them. A child whose difficult temperament makes challenges and mild changes equally daunting may be deeply affected by the relatively mild stress of a family move to another house in the same town. One whose tenuous family attachments establish a pattern that makes it difficult for him to reach out for support may experience school pressures or the casual bullying of the schoolyard as events of harrowing significance. On the other hand, a child whose locus of control is rooted firmly in his own powers and potential is likely to confront even major stresses with confidence and creativity.

It is interesting to consider that the literature of and about childhood is filled with stories of children who confront terrific stressors and not only survive but become stronger. Tom Sawyer, Jane Eyre, Oliver Twist, and Jim Hawkins are literary examples of children who face cruelty and violence, survive, and are made stronger. Children thrive on such stories of childhood heroism and survival. It can be argued that most children expect to survive; that stress competence is something even young children view as desirable, if not heroic.

It can also be argued that the heroic children of literature accurately reflect the successful coping of many real children. Even without financial advantage or copious social support, a child such as Vreni is able to deal with an incapacitated parent, take over much of the nurturing role in her family, and emerge from her childhood strong and competent. While stress may cause short-term responses such as those discussed here, it may also give children an opportunity to rise to the occasion, to contribute to the welfare of the people around them, and to strengthen the skills and confidence with which they face the world and all future challenges.

REFERENCES

Ainsworth, M. D. S. (1972). Attachment and dependency: A comparison. In J. Gerwitz (Ed.), *Attachment and dependency* (pp. 97–137). New York: Harcourt Brace Jovanovich.

American Psychiatric Association. (1987). *Diagnostic and Statistical Manual of Mental Disorders* (3rd ed., rev.). Washington, DC: American Psychiatric Press.

Andrews, G., & Tennant, C. (1978). Life event stress and psychiatric illness. *Psychological Medicine, 8,* 545–549.

Antonovsky, A. (1979). *Health, stress and coping.* San Francisco: Jossey-Bass.

Antonovsky, H., & Sagy, S. (1986). The development of a sense of coherence and its impact on responses to stress situations. *Journal of Social Psychology, 126*(2), 213–225.

Ayalon, O. (1983). Coping with terrorism: The Israeli case. In D. Meichenbaum & M. E. Jaremko (Eds.), *Stress reduction and prevention* (pp. 293–339). New York: Plenum.

Barton, A. H. (1969). *Communists in disaster: A sociological analysis of collective stress situations.* New York: Doubleday.

Bleuler, M. (1978). *The schizophrenic disorders: Long-term patient and family studies.* New Haven: Yale University Press.

Block, J. (1971). *Lives through time.* Berkeley, CA: Bancroft Books.

Block, J. H., & Block, J. (1980). The role of ego-control and ego-resiliency in the organization of behavior. In W. A. Collins (Ed.), *Development of cognition, affect, and social relations. The Minnesota symposia on child psychology* (Vol. 13). Hilldale, NJ: Erlbaum.

Block, J. H., Block, J., & Morrison, A. (1981). Parental agreement-disagreement on childbearing orientations and gender-related personality correlates in children. *Child Development, 52,* 965–974.

Bowlby, J. (1969). *Attachment and loss: Vol. 1. Attachment.* London: Hogarth Press.

Bowlby, J. (1980). *Attachment and loss: Vol. III. Loss, sadness and depression.* New York: Basic Books.

Brady, C. P., Bray, J. H., & Zeeb, L. (1986). Behavior problems of clinic children: Relation to parental marital status, age and sex of child. *American Journal of Orthopsychiatry, 56*(3), 399–412.

Brown, G. W., & Harris, T. (1978). *Social origins of depression: A study of psychiatric disorder in women.* London: Tavistock Publications.

Cobb, S. (1976). Social support as a moderator of life stress: Presidential address. *Psychosomatic Medicine, 38*(5), 300–314.

Derryberry, D., & Rothbart, M. K. (1984). Emotion, attention and temperament. In C. E. Izard, J. Kagan, & R. B. Zajonic (Eds.), *Emotions, cognition and behavior* (pp. 132–166). Cambridge, England: Cambridge University Press.

Douglas, J. W. B. (1975). Early hospital admissions and later disturbances of behavior and learning. *Developmental Medicine and Child Neurology, 17,* 456–480.

Dunn, J., & Kendrick, C. (1980a). Studying temperament and parent–child interaction: Comparison of interview and direct observation. *Developmental Medicine and Child Neurology, 4,* 484–496.

Dunn, J., & Kendrick, C. (1980b). The arrival of a sibling: Changes in patterns of interaction between mother and first born child. *Journal of Child Psychology and Psychiatry, 21,* 119–132.

Dunn, J., Kendrick, C., & MacNamee, R. (1981). The reaction of first-born children to the birth of a sibling: Mother's reports. *Journal of Child Psychology and Psychiatry, 22,* 1–18.

Dweck, C. S., & Elliott, E. S. (1983). Achievement motivation. In E. M. Hetherington (Ed.), *Socialization, personality and social development. Handbook of child psychology, Vol. 4,* (4th ed., pp. 643–691). New York: Wiley.

Emde, R. N., Gaensbauer, T., & Harmon, R. J. (1981). Using our emotions: Some principles for appraising emotional development and intervention. In M. Lewis & L. T. Taft (Eds.), *Developmental disabilities, theories, assessment, and intervention.* New York: SP Medical & Scientific Books.

Eme, R. F. (1979). Sex differences in childhood psychopathology: A review. *Psychological Bulletin, 86,* 574–595.

Fergusson, D. M., Horwood, L. J., & Shannon, F. T. (1984). Relationship of family life events, maternal depression, and child-rearing problems. *Pediatrics, 73*(6), 773–776.

Freud, A., & Burlingham, D. T. (1943). *War and children.* London: Medical War Books.

Gal, R., & Israelshvily, M. (1978). *Personality traits vs. situational factors as determinants of an individual's coping with stress: A theoretical model.* Paper presented at the Second International Conference on Psychological Stress and Adjustment in Time of War and Peace, Tel Aviv.

Garmezy, N. (1985). Stress-resistant children: The search for protective factors. In J. E. Stevenson (Ed.), *Recent research in developmental psychopathology. Journal of Child Psychology & Psychiatry* (Book Suppl.). Oxford: Pergamon.

Garmezy, N., & Masten, A. S. (1986). Stress, competence, and resilience: Common frontiers for therapist and psychopathologist. *Behavior Therapy, 17,* 500–521.

Garmezy, N., Masten, A. S., & Tellegen, A. (1984). The study of stress and competence in children: A building block for developmental psychopathology. *Child Development, 55*(1), 97–111.

Garmezy, N., & Rutter, M. (1983). *Stress, coping, and development in children.* New York: McGraw-Hill.

Garmezy, N., & Rutter, M. (1985). Acute reactions to stress. In M. Rutter & L.

Hersov (Eds.), *Child and adolescent psychiatry: Modern approaches* (2nd ed., pp. 152–176). Oxford: Blackwell Scientific.

Gleser, G. C., Green, B. L., & Winget, C. (1981). *Prolonged psychosocial effects of disaster: A study of Buffalo Creek.* New York: Academic Press.

Gunnar, M. R. (1987). Psychobiological studies of stress and coping: An introduction. *Child Development, 58*(6), 1403–1407.

Gunnar, M. R., Mangelsdorf, S., Larson, M., & Hertsgaard, L. (1989). Attachment, temperament, and the adrenocortical activity in infancy: A study of psychoendocrine regulation. *Development Psychology, 25,* 355–363.

Handford, H. A., Mayes, S. D., Mattison, R. E., Humphrey, F. J. II, Bagnato, S., Bixler, E. O., & Kales, J. D. (1986). Three Mile Island nuclear accident: A disaster study of child and parent reaction. *Journal of the American Academy of Child Psychiatry, 25,* 346–356.

Henderson, S. (1981). Social relationships, adversity and neurosis: An analysis of prospective observations. *British Journal of Psychiatry, 138,* 3 398.

Henry, J. P. (1980). Present concept of stress theory. In E. Ursdin, R. Kvetnansky & I. J. Kopin (Eds.), *Catecholamines and stress* (pp. 557–571). New York: Elsevier.

Hetherington, E. M. (1989). Coping with family transitions: Winners, losers, and survivors. *Child Development, 60,* 1–14.

Hetherington, E. M. (1980). Children and divorce. In R. Henderson (Ed.), *Parent–child interaction: Theory, research and prospect.* New York: Academic Press.

Hinkle, L. E. (1974). The effect of exposure to culture change, social change, and changes in interpersonal relationships on health. In B. S. Dohrenwend & B. P. Dohrenwend (Eds.), *Stressful life events: Their nature and effects.* New York: Wiley.

Holmes, T. H., & Rahe, R. H. (1967). The social readjustment rating scale. *Journal of Psychosomatic Research, 11,* 213–218.

Jacobs, S. C., Prusoff, B. A., & Paykel, E. S. (1974). Recent life events in schizophrenia and depression. *Psychological Medicine, 4,* 444–453.

Janis, I. L. (1971). *Stress and frustration.* New York: Harcourt Brace Jovanovich.

Kalin, N. H., & Carnes, M. (1984). Biological correlates of attachment bond disruption in human and nonhuman primates. *Progress in Neuropsychopharmacology and Biological Psychiatry, 8,* 459–469.

Keister, M. E., & Updegraff, R. (1937). A study of children's reactions to failure and an experimental attempt to modify them. *Child Development, 8,* 241–248.

Kendall, P. C., & Kriss, M. R. (1983). Cognitive-behavioral interaction. In C. E. Walker (Ed.), *The handbook of clinical psychology: Theory, research, and practice* (pp. 770–819). Illinois: Dorsey.

Kinston W., & Rosser, R. (1974). Disaster: Effects on mental and physical state. *Journal of Psychosomatic Research, 18*(6), 437–456.

Knapp, P. H. (1980). Free association as a biopsychosocial probe. *Psychosomatic Medicine, 42* (1 Suppl.), 197–219.

Lazarus, R. S., & Launier, R. (1978). Stress-related transactions between person and environment. In L. A. Pervin & M. Lewis (Eds.), *Perspectives in interactional psychology.* New York: Plenum Press.

Lifton, R. J. (1967). *Death in life: Survivors of Hiroshima.* New York: Simon and Schuster.

Lifton, R. J. (1980). The concept of the survivor. In J. E. Dimsdale (Ed.), *Survivors, victims, and perpetrators. Essays on the Nazi Holocaust* (pp. 113–126). Washington DC: Hemisphere Publishing Corp.

Livingston, R., Nugent, H., Rader, L., & Smith, G. R. (1985). Family histories of depressed and severely anxious children. *American Journal of Psychiatry, 142*(12), 1497–1499.

Lloyd, C. (1980). Life events and depressive disorder reviewed: II. Events as precipitating factors. *Archives of General Psychiatry, 37,* 541–548.

Malmquist, C. P. (1984). Children who witness parental murder: Post-traumatic and legal issues. *Journal of the American Academy of Child Psychiatry.*

Meichenbaum, D. (1975). Self-instructional methods. In F. Kanfer & A. Goldstein (Eds.), *Helping people change* (pp. 357–391). New York: Pergammon Press.

Meichenbaum, D., & Novaco, R. (1978). Stress inoculation: A preventive approach. In C. D. Spielberger & I. G. Sarason (Eds.), *Stress and anxiety,* (Vol. 5, pp. 317–330). New York: Wiley.

Molina, J. A. (1983). *International Journal of Psychiatry in Medicine, 13*(1), 29–36.

Moore, T. (1975). Stress in normal childhood. In L. Levi (Ed.), *Society, stress and disease: Childhood and adolescence* (Vol. 2). London: Oxford University Press.

Paykel, E. S. (1974). Life stress and psychiatric disorder: Applications of the clinical approach. In B. S. Dohrenwend & B. P. Dohrenwend (Eds.), *Stressful life events: Their nature and effects.* New York: Wiley.

Paykel, E. S. (1978). Contribution of life events to causation of psychiatric illness. *Psychological Medicine, 8,* 245–254.

Pfeffer, C. R. (1986). *The suicidal child.* New York: Guilford Press.

Quinton, D., & Rutter, M. (1976). Early hospital admissions and later disturbances of behaviour: An attempted replication of Douglas' findings. *Developmental Medicine and Child Neurology, 18,* 447–459.

Rachman, S. J. (1978). *Fear and courage.* San Francisco: Freeman.

Radke-Yarrow, M., & Zahn-Waxler, C. (1984). Roots, motives and patterns in children's prosocial behavior. In J. Reykowski, D. Karylowski, & E. Staub (Eds.), *The development and maintenance of prosocial behaviors: International perspectives.* New York: Plenum.

Radke-Yarrow, M., Zahn-Waxler, C., & Chapman, M. (1984). Children's prosocial dispositions and behavior. In P. H. Mussen (Ed.), *Carmichael's Manual of Child Psychology, 4* (4th ed., pp. 469–545). New York: Wiley.

Rice, P. L. (1987). *Stress and health: Principles and practice for coping and wellness.* Monterey, CA: Brooks/Cole Publishing.

Robertson, J., & Robertson, J. (1971). Young children in brief separation: A fresh look. *Psychoanalytic Study of the Child, 26,* 264–315.

Rutter, M. (1966). *Children of sick parents: An environmental and psychiatric study.* Institute of Psychiatry Maudsley Monographs No. 16. London: Oxford University Press.

Rutter, M. (1970). Sex differences in children's responses to family stress. In E. J. Anthony & C. Koupernik (Eds.), *The child and his family.* New York: Wiley.

Rutter, M. (1978). Early sources of security and competence. In J. S. Bruner & A. Garton (Eds.), *Human growth and development.* London: Oxford University Press.

Rutter, M. (1979a). Protective factors in children's responses to stress and disadvantage. In M. W. Kent & J. E. Rolf (Eds.), *Primary prevention of psychopathology, Vol. 3: Social competence in children.* Hanover, NH: University Press of New England.

Rutter, M. (1979b). Maternal deprivation, 1972–1978: New findings, new concepts, new approaches. *Child Development, 50*(2), 283–305.

Rutter, M. (1981). Stress, coping, and development: Some issues and some questions. *Journal of Child Psychology and Psychiatry, 22,* 323–356.

Rutter, M. (1983). Stress, coping, and development: Some issues and some questions. In N. Garmezy & M. Rutter (Eds.), *Stress, coping, and development in children.* New York: McGraw-Hill.

Rutter, M. (1985). *Child psychiatry: The interface between clinical and developmental research.* Inaugural lecture at the opening of the MRC Child Psychiatry Unit, Institute of Psychiatry, London.

Seligman, M. E. P. (1975). *Helplessness: On depression, development and death.* San Francisco: Freeman.

Stacey, M., Dearden, R., Pill, R., & Robinson, D. (1970). *Hospitals, children and their families: The report of a pilot study.* London: Routledge and Keagan Paul.

Tennes, K., Downey, K., & Vernadakis, A. (1977). Urinary cortisol excretion rates and anxiety in normal 1-year-old infants. *Psychosomatic Medicine, 39,* 178–187.

Terr, L. C. (1979). Children of Chowchilla: A study of psychic trauma. *Psychoanalytic Study of Children, 34,* 552–623.

Terr, L. C. (1981a). Psychic trauma in children: Observations following the Chowchilla school-bus kidnapping. *American Journal of Psychiatry, 138,* 14–19.

Terr, L. C. (1981b). Forbidden games: Post-traumatic child's play. *Journal of the American Academy of Child Psychiatry, 20,* 741–760.

Terr, L. C. (1983). Chowchilla revisited: The effects of psychic trauma four years after a school-bus kidnapping. *American Journal of Psychiatry, 140,* 1543–1550.

Thomas, A., & Chess, S. (1984). Genesis and evolution of behavior disorders: From infancy to early adult life. *American Journal of Psychiatry, 141,* 1–9.

Thomas, A., Chess, S., & Birch, H. G. (1970). The origin of personality. *Scientific American, 223*(2), 102–109.

Trad, P. (1986). *Infant depression: Paradigms and paradoxes.* New York: Springer-Verlag.

Trad, P. (1987). *Infant and childhood depression: Developmental factors.* New York: Wiley.

Trad, P. (1988). *Psychosocial scenarios for pediatrics.* New York: Springer-Verlag.

Trad, P. (1989). *The preschool child.* New York: Wiley.

Tuckman, A. J. (1973). Disaster and mental health intervention. *Community Mental Health Journal, 9,* 151–157.

Wallerstein, J. S. (1983). Children of divorce: The psychological tasks of the child. *American Journal of Orthopsychiatry, 53*(2), 230–243.

Wallerstein, J. S., & Kelly, J. B. (1980). *Surviving the break up: How children and parents cope with divorce.* New York: Basic Books; London: Grant McIntyre.

Werner, E. E., & Smith, R. S. (1982). *Vulnerable, but invisible: A Study of Resilient Children.* New York: McGraw-Hill.

Wolfe, M. (1978). Childhood and privacy. In I. Altman & J. F. Wohlwill (Eds.), *Children and the environment.* New York: Plenum.

Yamamoto, K. (1979). Children's ratings of the stressfulness of experiences. *Developmental Psychology, 15,* 581–582.

Zill, N. (1977). *National survey of children: Summary of preliminary results.* Unpublished manuscript, Foundation for Child Development, New York.

CHAPTER TWO

Psychopathological Responses to Stress: Adjustment Disorder and Post-Traumatic Stress Disorder in Children and Adolescents

Susan Beckwitt Turkel
Spencer Eth

Children are constantly being subjected to stress and conflict in their external environment: from family, school, work, and nature; and in their internal environment: from feelings of anger, anxiety, sadness, and loneliness. Ordinarily, they adapt to these difficulties with varying degrees of success and resolution; only rarely do they become symptomatic. But sometimes even such common problems as divorce, crime, illness, and accidents will result in more intense reactions and maladaptive responses. Although many psychiatric disorders may be related to stress and most are exacerbated by stress, two specific diagnostic entities are especially acknowledged to be stress induced. Adjustment Disorder and Post-Traumatic Stress Disorder (PTSD) refer to the milder and more severe psychopathologic responses seen following stress.

The American Psychiatric Association's 1987 *Diagnostic and Statistical Manual of Mental Disorders,* Third Edition, Revised (DSM-III-R) defines the criteria for the diagnoses of Adjustment Disorder and Post-Traumatic Stress Disorder (PTSD) on Axis I. Adjustment Disorder refers to maladaptive and symptomatic responses to stress with observed changes in mood, conduct, or functioning. Table 2.1 lists the nine subtypes of Adjustment Disorder based on the predominant symptoms (APA, 1987; Barker, 1988). Post-Traumatic Stress Disorder is classified as a form of Anxiety Disorder (APA, 1987). Axis IV of the multiaxial system specifically designates the degree of stress in the individual's life and is related to these two major stress-induced diagnoses (APA, 1987). See Chapter 19 for more about Axis IV.

ADJUSTMENT DISORDER

There is no typical clinical picture of Adjustment Disorder in children, and the reaction to stress depends on many variables (Masten et al., 1988). In adults the typical clinical pattern is less heterogeneous and its self-limited nature is part of the diagnosis. Most adults eventually recover (Looney & Gunderson, 1978). In adolescents the outcome is not as predictable: about half will recover, while the other half will progress to more pervasive and persistent problems (Andreasen & Hoenk, 1982). But in children it is difficult to define clearly the limits of the maladaptive and symptomatic responses that constitute Adjustment Disorder, and any psychologic injury may potentially have a very wide impact on the child's development and subsequent course.

Children are especially vulnerable to the vicissitudes of life, and they are greatly influenced by the adults in their environment. When adults are supportive and calm, their children usually can weather adversity and develop resilience and coping skills in the process. But if the adults themselves are overwhelmed, or if the relationship between adult and

TABLE 2.1. *Comparison of Clinical Features of Adjustment Disorder and Post-Traumatic Stress Disorder (PTSD)*

	Adjustment Disorder	Post-Traumatic Stress Disorder
Clinical Pattern	Variable and individual, with disturbance of mood, conduct, and/or functioning.	Predictable after catastrophic event: re-experiencing in nightmares and flashbacks; avoidance; psychic numbing; increased arousal.
Onset	Within 3 months of stress.	Immediate or delayed 6 months or more.
Duration	Persists no longer than 6 months after stress.	At least 1 month; may be prolonged indefinitely.
Type of Stress	Mild to major identifiable stressor or multiple stressors in the range of expected experience.	Catastrophic: outside range of expected experience.
Classification in DSM-III-R	Own separate category on Axis I.	Under Anxiety Disorder on Axis I.
Subtypes	With: Anxious Mood Depressed Mood Disturbance of Conduct Mixed Disturbance of Emotions and Conduct Mixed Emotional Features Physical Complaints Withdrawal Work/Academic Inhibition Not Otherwise Specified	PTSD, acute; PTSD, delayed onset.

child is fraught with conflict, the young are then more likely to demonstrate maladaptive behavior and disturbances of mood.

Different personalities react differently to the same stress. If affect can be modulated until after the crisis has passed, this may allow for better cognitive efforts and more satisfactory resolutions. "Denial of affect" helps the child and family to function more normally in the time of crisis, allowing the affect to be confronted after the immediate crisis situation has passed (Chess & Hassibi, 1986). But denial of affect should not be mistaken for denial of fact, for when a child or family fails to acknowledge a real threat, they cannot respond to the crisis and symptoms will ensue (Chess & Hassibi, 1986).

Intervention is important, for psychologic stress may increase vulnerability to other mental and physical illnesses. Prevention and intervention strategies involving support and education may prepare the child and facilitate mastery of the stressful situation. Social support and cognitive guidance, which increase problem-solving capacity and mastery of affect, are particularly recommended (Caplan, 1981).

Not all children are adversely affected by identical stresses in the same way; some appear to be more resilient while others are more vulnerable. The most vulnerable cope poorly even with the minor problems of daily life. It is the responsibility of adults to protect these children and to intervene when needed. Unfortunately, when parents are themselves stressed, their availability to their children is compromised (Eisen, 1979). Parental problems that result in disorganization, violence, family disruption, and mental illness have a decidedly negative impact on the child (Woolston, 1986). Problems in the family may then be passed on to subsequent generations (Sigal, DiNocola, & Bounvino, 1988).

Negative life events, or "stressors," can be correlated with symptoms in both adolescents and children. In a clinic population, family or marital stress, accidents, and illness correlated with conduct problems, while permanent separations correlated with somatic and mood disturbances (Goodyer, Kolvin, & Gatzanis, 1985). Stressful events can cause at least short-term disturbances in children, as after a bush fire in Australia, in which the child's and parent's responses were highly correlated (McFarlane, 1988). When the mother lacks social supports and has poor confiding relationships in her own life, she is at greater risk for distress following stressful events. In turn, her child is at risk for emotional disorder (Goodyer, Wright, & Altham, 1988). When the mother is well supported, she is able to buffer stressful experiences and mitigate their negative influence on her child. Without support herself, she is usually unsuccessful in shielding her child.

Studies of the incidence and etiology of Adjustment Disorder have been difficult because of the protean nature of the syndrome. In a study of the 1-year prevalence of psychiatric disorders in primary care pediatrics, the diagnoses of Adjustment Disorder or Post-Traumatic Stress Disorder were not made in any of the 789 children surveyed (Costello et al., 1988). However, when a community survey was undertaken in Puerto Rico, with rates of adult psychopathology similar to those in the United States Epidemiologic Catchment Area survey, the DSM-III-R diagnosis of Adjustment Disorder was found in approximately 4% of children aged 4 to 16 years (Bird et al., 1988).

Adjustment Disorder in Adolescence

Adolescence may be a time of special vulnerability for symptoms follow-ing stress. Adolescents rely on their peer group perhaps as much as family, but disturbance in their peers may erode this base of support (van der Kolk, 1985). Adjustment Disorder has been found to be the second most common cause for psychiatric hospitalization of adolescents (Faulstich et al., 1986). The more common stressors precipitating Adjust-ment Disorder in adolescents include school problems, feelings of paren-tal rejection, sexual problems, and drug or alcohol abuse (Andreasen & Wasek, 1980). Those with parental conflict have the best prognosis in long-term follow-up (Fard, Hudgens, & Welner, 1978). Those adolescents who present with primarily depressive symptoms also seem to have a better prognosis than those with behavioral and conduct disturbance, but no other factors have been clearly identified as predictors of out-come (Andreasen & Wasek, 1980). Regardless of what the stresses might have been, their pathogenic potential can be seen as a three- to sixfold risk for conduct or emotional symptoms in the year following the event. With additional stress, the effect is additive over the 12-month period (Goodyer, Kolvin, & Gatzanis, 1987).

"Normal adolescent turmoil" is probably a myth, and the DSM-II diag-nosis "Adjustment Reaction of Adolescence" does not appear in the DSM-III-R (APA, 1980; APA, 1987; Oldham, 1978). Normal adolescents may have brief, single episodes of mild behavioral or affective disturb-ance, as adults may, but this can be distinguished from the more severe and prolonged symptoms of the adolescent suffering from a Personality Disorder, Adjustment Disorder, PTSD, or early Schizophrenia or Mood Disorders (Masterson & Washburne, 1966). The more severe symptoms in adolescents are often indicative of the beginning of a lifetime of psychiatric illness (Masterson, 1967). Adolescents do not "grow out of" their problems as was once thought, and severe disturbances of behavior or affect require prompt intervention (Masterson, 1968). If the symptoms are mild, the prognosis is favorable, but again treatment may be indi-cated to achieve a good outcome (Thomas & Chess, 1976).

An important issue affecting outcome is the perception of stress termed "locus of control." With an internal locus of control—the sense that one's own actions influence events—there is a greater sense of self-esteem and ego strength, which correlates in most instances with greater coping skills (Sadowski et al., 1983). Locus of control is an intel-lectual function, and it develops at different rates in children relative to their cognitive performance in other spheres (Skinner, Chapman, & Baltes, 1988). An adolescent's cognitive view of personal influence on events is intimately related to individual response to stress, and cognitive distortions are a better predictor for depression after stressful events than the nature of the event itself (Deal & Williams, 1988). A prospective study of stress and well-being in adolescents demonstrated that an internal sense or "stable global attribution" that negative events were due to uncontrollable causes correlated with an increased rate of depression. Conversely, when events were considered to be due to controlled and controllable causes, depression was rare (Brown & Siegel, 1988).

Variables Influencing Development of Adjustment Disorder

Adjustment Disorder is an individual's reaction to an identifiable stressor and represents that person's effort to cope, albeit in maladaptive and symptomatic ways. Various factors have been identified as important variables in a child's responses (Rutter, 1981; Woolston, 1986; Woolston, 1988).

Sex. Girls seem to be more successful in adapting to stress in the short term; their early outcome may be more favorable than boys, who are more apt to demonstrate behavioral or conduct problems when emotionally upset. But girls usually show their disturbance in less conspicuous ways, with more depressive and anxious symptoms, that are less likely to draw the attention of others unless severe (Breslau, Klein, & Allen, 1988; Woolston, 1988).

Age. Younger children have fewer coping strategies in their repertoire and suffer more serious and pervasive long-term sequelae. Older children may have the benefit of greater experience and a wider array of responses, which can mitigate a possible negative outcome (Woolston, 1988).

Temperament. Some children have been extremely sensitive to change since infancy, and they are constitutionally more vulnerable to stress. Others are even-tempered and tolerant, and seem more resilient (Werner, 1989). These overall patterns of reactivity are quite stable in individuals over time (Thomas & Chess, 1984; Woolston, 1988). How an individual will respond to stress also reflects personal style of "ego defenses." Children who rely on higher level, mature defenses fare better than those whose ego is prone to regression and disintegration (Woolston, 1988).

Previous Experience. A history of previous traumatic experiences usually will weaken an individual and increase susceptibility to psychologic injury and distress. But if the previous stressors were minor or if they were successfully overcome, these experiences may enhance coping skills and resilience and allow the child to negotiate subsequent challenges more easily (Woolston, 1988).

Stress Itself. The nature, duration, and intensity of the stress are critical. Severe enough catastrophes will cause symptoms in virtually everyone, and the diagnosis of Post-Traumatic Stress Disorder may then be appropriate. A brief, self-limited stressor is more likely to be successfully surmounted than a chronic, diffuse, or recurrent one, which drains the resources and continuously strains the person's ability to cope and elicit support (Woolston, 1988).

With a favorable temperament, a nurturing family milieu, and other external supports, a good outcome following adversity is likely. But with a hypersensitive nature, conflict in family relationships, and minimal external support, adjustment is likely to be maladaptive and symptomatic (Woolston, 1988). A child's general adjustment and behavior before a stress may be more important in predicting the outcome and the type and severity of a child's symptoms, if any, than the specific insult itself. The child's idiosyncratic experience of the stress is perhaps the most important factor of all, for it is this subjective response which is most variable and individual, and which may become the focus of therapeutic intervention.

Patterns of Response to Specific Stresses

The following discussions of stressors include preventive possibilities for each.

Divorce. Perhaps the most common and potentially most disruptive crisis that many children and adolescents face is the divorce of their parents. The effects of divorce have been studied, most notably by Wallerstein and Kelly, who prospectively followed a group of 131 children aged 2 to 18 years in 60 families (Kelly & Wallerstein, 1976; Wallerstein & Kelly, 1974, 1975, 1976).

The youngest preschoolers, aged 2½ to 3½, after divorce were irritable and anxious initially, with behavioral regression and tantrums. Aside from a generally increased neediness for adults, these youngest children usually did well after 1 year. The slightly older children, aged 3¾ to 4¾, seemed to suffer more disruption, with confusion and fear of losing both parents. Children ages 5 to 6 were, in general, anxious and aggressive following their father's departure, and in some their problems persisted, especially if the relationship between their parents remained chaotic and unresolved (Wallerstein & Kelly, 1975).

By school age, the 7- to 10-year-old group differed greatly in their responses. Initial sadness, fear, and feelings of deprivation were common, and their father's visits were often of little comfort. Individual capacities and personalities in the children were more apparent in this age group, and some seemed unaffected by their parents' divorce, maintaining their self-esteem, self-reliance, and involvements outside the home (Kelly & Wallerstein, 1976).

The older school children, ages 9 to 10 years, employed more varied coping responses and efforts at mastery to contain their psychic pain. By this age the children could well understand the meaning and consequences of divorce, and felt intensely angry and isolated. By 1 year afterward, half the children resumed normal function following the initial disturbance, while the other half showed more profound distress and disruption (Wallerstein & Kelly, 1976).

Adolescents often responded to their parents' divorce with a rapid acceleration and telescoping of the normal conflicts and responses of the individuation process. If there were longstanding problems and conflicts before the divorce, then a more symptomatic response occurred. In most, however, the emotional distance the adolescent had already achieved from the parental problems was proportional to his or her mastery of the stress. Those adolescents who did best afterwards were the ones who were able to separate themselves and employ denial of affect during the crisis (Wallerstein & Kelly, 1974).

When custody arrangements are made by an adversarial process, they may embody the conflicts and respond to the problems of the adults while inadequately meeting the children's needs. With arbitration and mediated custody decrees, increased cooperation between the parents can sometimes be effected, and the children can then benefit from the resolution of parental tension (Frankel, 1985). Unfortunately, this rarely happens (Benedek & Schetky, 1985; Wallerstein, 1985). (See Chapter 14 for further discussion about the effects of divorce.)

Illness. Chronic physical illness is an example of a potentially disruptive process in a child's life, perhaps involving recurrent separations, pain, and other frightening events. It can be upsetting to both parents and child, and can produce a chronically stressful situation resulting in maladaptive behavior and emotional symptoms. The problems of chronic illness are pervasive and can produce a financial and emotional burden, with severe guilt and anxiety (Cytryn, Moore, & Robinson, 1973; de Traubenberg, 1973). Fortunately, this rarely occurs; most children, adolescents, and their families can cope successfully with the stresses of chronic physical illness.

In a study of chronically ill adolescents with a variety of disorders, who were compared to matched controls, there were no differences in levels of anxiety or self-esteem. Both the ill and healthy youth held a similarly positive outlook on life (Kellerman et al., 1980; Zeltzer et al., 1980). This finding may be related to their ability to deny the worst aspects and consequences of their illness in order to function adaptatively, or may be related to their experience coping with multiple minor stresses resulting in greater resilience and more successful coping strategies their healthy peers had no impetus to develop. Adolescent juvenile diabetics who are considered well controlled medically tend also to be well adjusted at home and with peers, are appropriately independent, and have good self-esteem and a sense of internal control (Swift, Seidman, & Stein, 1967). There appears to be a direct relationship between the diabetic adolescent's emotional and physical well-being (Johnson, 1988).

Children with chronic illness are not a homogeneous group; rather, they have had very different life experiences, irrespective of their medical condition (Bedell et al., 1977). The presence of a chronic physical illness by itself is insufficient to produce psychologic illness, but it may make the child more vulnerable to other stress, including conflict and confusion in the family (Bedell et al., 1977). When illness is experienced as an insurmountable obstacle or the cause of rejection by loved ones, the child may react with extreme emotional distress, and suicidal ideation and behavior may occur (Weinberg, 1970).

In studies of children and adolescents with juvenile rheumatoid arthritis, those with less severe physical disabilities were often more affected psychologically, and it was found that the child's adjustment was primarily determined by the family's attitude. If the parents were pessimistic and guilt-ridden, their children had more emotional and social problems (McAnarney et al., 1974).

Hemophilia is an example of a chronic and potentially lethal inherited disorder. Most boys and their families adapt well, and they maintain age-appropriate function at home and at school, despite their illness (Mattson & Gross, 1966). The minority who show a poor adjustment tend to have overprotective, overanxious, or guilt-ridden mothers, to whom they respond with either social withdrawal and fear or inappropriate recklessness (Mattson & Gross, 1966). (See Chapter 12 for further discussion about the effects of illness.)

Hospitalization. The psychologic effects of medical hospitalization depend on the child's age, family, and previous experience. Infants older than 7 months protest initially, appear uncooperative and subdued in the hospital, and then require a readjustment period on returning home. Infants younger than 7 months rarely protest the separation from their mothers and seem to accept more easily substitute caretakers in the hospital, but then may appear briefly but dramatically upset on returning home (Schaffer & Callender, 1959). The long-term effects of this early separation have not been studied.

Preschool-age children seem to be more upset by hospitalization than older children or younger infants, but they also are the most likely to show benefit and respond positively if their environment is supportive (Vernon & Schulman, 1964). Early studies of the effects of hospitalization revealed detrimental effects, and this led to changes in pediatric hospital policy. When preparation is given the child beforehand and parental visits are encouraged while the child is hospitalized, permitting the parents to participate in the child's care, the emotionally traumatic effects of hospitalization need not occur (Freud, 1952; Prugh et al., 1953).

Illness in older children involves not only separation from their families, but increasing awareness of the personal significance and implication of the illness itself. Adaptation increases with cognitive function, and parents who have coped successfully with their child's illness are able to enhance their child's understanding of the illness, facilitate self-care and independence in their child, and isolate their own fear and anxiety (denial of affect) during crises (Mattson, 1972).

Surgery. Surgical procedures provide a finite stress and allow study of a child's response. Some predominantly psychoanalytic studies of the effect of tonsillectomy concluded that this operation was an important and stressful experience for every child (Jessner, Blom, & Waldfogel, 1952), but others found that the majority of children were scarcely affected by the experience (Jackson et al., 1953). Children with a history of previous trauma reacted less well to tonsillectomy, and although younger children had several mild adverse behavioral changes, more than 90% underwent the procedure without negative consequences (Jackson et al., 1953). Some procedures may be more disturbing than others, and when comparisons were made, children were found to have more emotional problems after genitourinary surgery than after tonsillectomy (Blotcky & Grossman, 1978).

Following cardiac catheterization, younger children are upset by the pain and the separation from their parents, while older children and adolescents are more aware of their physical status and the long-term implications of their condition (Aisenberg et al., 1973). Problems in adjustment occur following both cardiac (Freeman et al., 1988) and renal transplantation, reflecting the patient's previous level of emotional adjustment rather than a specific response to the procedure (Tisza, Dorsett, & Morse, 1976). Accommodating to complete heart block and the implantation of a cardiac pacemaker would also seem likely to produce emotional distress, but intellectualization, identification with medical personnel, and denial of affect during crises allow children and adolescents to undergo the procedure without psychiatric symptoms (Galdston & Gamble, 1969).

Summary of Adjustment Disorder

In children and adolescents, although the diagnosis of Adjustment Disorder is often made, it may not indicate a homogeneous, distinct entity.

Whether a stressor will be followed by an emotional or behavioral disturbance is not entirely predictable and depends to a great extent on individual differences in personality, temperament, and experience, and on environmental differences in family conflict, support, and coping strategies.

POST-TRAUMATIC STRESS DISORDER

In contrast to Adjustment Disorder, where the natural history of the syndrome is unclear and the nature of the adjustment problems are as individual as the people who suffer them, Post-Traumatic Stress Disorder (PTSD) is a more clinically discrete diagnostic entity resulting from exposure to catastrophic events. Nevertheless, the specific expression of PTSD is influenced by the individual's prior life experiences, personality, temperament, and available supports.

The term Post-Traumatic Stress Disorder was introduced into the psychiatric nomenclature with the publication of DSM-III in 1980 (APA, 1980). When first delineated, examples of symptoms in children and adolescents were not included, but in the revised edition, DSM-III-R (APA, 1987), there are references to younger sufferers of catastrophic trauma.

There is no direct information on the prevalence, sex ratio, or familial patterns of PTSD, but the psychologic impact of a variety of natural and man-made disasters has been studied and this provides data on the susceptibility and modifying factors following trauma (Bloch, Silber, & Perry, 1956; Burke et al., 1982; Burke et al., 1986; Glover, 1942; Lacey, 1972; Milgram & Milgram, 1976; Newman, 1976). Studies include investigations of the impact of bush fire (McFarlane, 1987; McFarlane, Policansky, & Irwin, 1978), kidnapping (Terr, 1981), sniper attack (Pynoos et al., 1987), terrorism (Eth, 1987), warfare (Arroyo & Eth, 1985) and violent crime (Eth, 1988; Pynoos et al., 1987). PTSD seems to be more severe and persistent when the trauma is life threatening and of human design (APA, 1987). The cumulative effect of exposure to repeated trauma may be significant (Terr, 1983), and ongoing reactions of the child's mother or primary caregiver to the traumatic event are critical. Post-traumatic symptoms in the parents, overprotective parenting, maternal separation, and changed family function are powerful determinants of emotional and behavioral symptoms in the children (McFarlane, 1987). As observed during World War II, "children measure the danger that threatens them chiefly by the reactions of those about them, especially of their trusted parents and teachers" (Papanek, 1942).

There appears to be a dose-response relationship between degree of exposure to a traumatic experience and the risk of developing PTSD.

Following a sniper attack on an elementary school, 80% of the children under fire showed PTSD symptoms immediately, and those who were not in direct danger rarely developed acute PTSD unless other situational risk factors were also present (Pynoos et al., 1987). That the incidence of PTSD is very high following particularly intense stressors has also been demonstrated in studies of kidnapping (Terr, 1981), sexual molestation (Kiser et al., 1988; McLeer et al., 1988) and witnessing of parental rape (Pynoos & Nader, 1988) or homicide (Eth, in press).

Clinical Features of PTSD

By definition, PTSD refers to the cluster of symptoms that arises after an extremely disturbing event which is outside the range of usual human experience and which would be markedly distressing to almost anyone. Traumatic events usually involve a serious life threat, often in the form of a natural or human-induced disaster, accident, or violent crime. The person experiencing the psychic trauma may be the direct victim or an eyewitness to the tragic occurrence. The clear psychosocial stressor precipitates an initial response of intense fear, terror, and helplessness, which leads in turn to the core symptoms of PTSD: re-experiencing the trauma, psychic numbing, and increased arousal (APA, 1987).

The traumatic event may be re-experienced in a variety of ways. There may be recurrent, intrusive, markedly dysphoric memories and dreams of the trauma, and, in younger children, repetitive, stereotyped, joyless reenactments of the trauma in their play (Terr, 1979). Flashbacks and hallucinations are rare in children. Dissociative symptoms, not uncommon after repeated trauma such as repeated sexual abuse, may signal a risk for the development of multiple personality disorder (Kluft, 1985).

Psychic numbing refers to a range of reactions from the inability to remember the traumatic event to a blocking of all affect and enjoyment in life. Very young children may regress significantly, stop talking, become enuretic, and show disturbance of sleep or appetite. The child may try to suppress all thoughts and feelings of the traumatic event and to avoid any activity or situation even vaguely reminiscent of the event in an attempt to impose some feeling of control over intolerable circumstances (Terr, 1988).

Irritability, hypervigilance, exaggerated startle response, sleep disturbance, and poor concentration are all indicative of an abnormally heightened state of psychophysiologic arousal, which is another characteristic feature of PTSD. The state of arousal can be measured in the laboratory, providing an objective method of validating the diagnosis (Keane, Wolfe, & Taylor, 1987). Further, there appear to be some lasting neurophysiologic correlates of PTSD, including a loss of the normal inhibitory modulation of the startle response (Ornitz & Pynoos, 1989), and possible chronic alterations of neurohormones related to memory (Pitman, 1989).

Progression of Symptoms

The natural history of disaster-related PTSD has been studied, and a typical sequence of psychologic responses has been described. Denial of the impending danger is common in the initial "threat" phase (Kinston & Rosser, 1974). This is followed by the "impact" phase, in which there is the realization of danger and an intense affective response when the person may seem stunned, dazed, terrified, unresponsive, or even elated. Children in this traumatic state of regression and helplessness may have severely disorganized thoughts and behavior, appearing numb or frenzied or exhibiting autonomic dysfunction (Solnit & Kris, 1967). During the "recoil" phase there is a return to awareness and an ability to recall the event. As the child struggles to cope in the "aftermath" phase, symptoms of dependency, hyperactivity, and irrationality may persist, but gradually abate in most children as they begin to regain personal stability and social function (Kinston & Ross, 1974). Unfortunately, coping strategies and available supports are usually inadequate to meet this challenge completely, and fears, anxiety, sadness, and regressions persist, evolving and crystallizing into the recognizable clinical pattern of PTSD.

Patterns of Response in Children of Different Ages

Children generally respond to severe psychic trauma with changes in cognition, affect, interpersonal relations, impulse control, behavior, and vegetative function, and these responses differ with age (Eth & Pynoos, 1985). Infants respond to psychic trauma in nonspecific ways, and it is only after the capacity to encode and retrieve verbal memory develops, usually between 30 and 36 months, that children react with a distinct symptom pattern and an associated memory following a traumatic event (Terr, 1988).

Preschoolers. Preschoolers are particularly helpless when confronted by great danger, and they have the most limited repertoire of coping strategies. They may require the most assistance to recover after a catastrophe and are most influenced by the adults in their environment. Preschool children often appear withdrawn, subdued, or even mute. These young children are especially prone to regression in the wake of a traumatic experience, with anxious attachment behavior, intensified separation and stranger anxiety, dependence on transitional objects and caregivers, lapses in toilet training, crying, whining, and throwing tantrums (Elizur & Kaffman, 1982). Preschool children typically engage in reenactments and play around traumatic themes, tending to disregard peripheral details and focusing on the central action of the trauma in their play (Bergen, 1958; Maclean, 1977).

School-age Children.   School-age children exhibit a wider range of cognitive, behavioral, and emotional responses to psychic trauma, and their repertoire of coping skills may be greater. Cognitive constriction and impairment is common in this age and is manifested in poor concentration and declining performance in school. Some children seem preoccupied with the fine details of their traumatic experience, while simultaneously denying the affect associated with the event. To some degree, this denial of affect may be an adaptive defense, but journalistic accountings and a failure to acknowledge the personal impact of the event preclude mastery (Pynoos & Eth, 1986). Some children remain in a perpetual state of arousal and hypervigilence, as if continuously prepared for imminent danger but unable to overcome the one that has occurred (Eth, 1987).

School-age children may appear different and inconsistent after experiencing a severe psychic trauma, occasionally becoming irritable, rude, provocative, or infantile and clinging. Children may be aware of the changes in themselves, and may react with a loss of self-esteem and self-confidence. Their friends may also notice a change, and peer relationships will suffer as the child becomes unpredictable or inappropriately inhibited or aggressive. They may try to involve their friends in redramatizations and trauma-related games with mixed responses from their peers (Arroyo & Eth, 1985). School-age children are particularly susceptible to developing psychosomatic symptoms, such as stomach pains, headaches, and other complaints (Krystal, 1978).

Adolescents.   Adolescents suffering PTSD often resemble adults with this disorder. In fact, a not-uncommon response to trauma in adolescence is the precipitation of precocious entrance into adulthood. The traumatized adolescent frequently becomes disenchanted and rebellious. The combination of poor impulse control, bad judgment, and reenactment behavior can be life-threatening. Suicidal behavior and drug abuse are common, as are truancy, sexual indiscretion, and delinquency. Adolescents are very sensitive to the implications and stigmatization of experiencing severe trauma, and chronic problems in interpersonal relationships are frequent (Eth, in press).

In a study of PTSD incidence, 1% was found in the total population, 3.5% in civilians exposed to physical attack or in Viet Nam veterans who were not wounded, and 20% in veterans wounded in Viet Nam (Helzer, Robins, & McEvoy, 1987). Viet Nam veterans with PTSD are more likely to have been adolescents while in combat. These adolescent soldiers were more likely to develop PTSD than older GIs, especially if they experienced loss of group support at the time of injury (van der Kolk, 1985). On return home, this group has been especially prone to drug abuse, rage, and despair, suffering profound disillusionment and moral stagnation, as if languishing in a state of perpetual, pathological adolescence (Jackson, 1982).

CONCLUSION

Many event-related factors influence the child or adolescent's response to emotional stress or trauma, including the origin, nature, intensity, speed of onset, social preparedness, duration, scope of impact, degree of life threat and suffering, and the potential for recurrence of the event. How a particular child will respond depends on his or her life history, personality, emotional development, state of mind, autonomic regulation, coping skills, social and familial supports, and ability to detach and deny intense affect.

When the child is exposed to an overwhelming event causing helplessness in the face of fear, anxiety, and arousal, PTSD may result. When the child confronts instead a less severe stress, but the coping and support mechanisms are insufficient to counteract the stress completely, the maladaptive behaviors and emotional symptoms of Adjustment Disorder may result. When the stress is less severe or the child's available coping skills and support mechanisms are adequate, the child may have minimal if any symptoms, and learn from the experience.

Stress and trauma are endemic in our society, and children must also face these threats. Although many contend successfully with life events, others fall prey to the psychopathological conditions discussed in this chapter.

REFERENCES

Aisenberg, R. B., Wolff, P. H., Rosenfeld, A., & Nadas, A. S. (1973). Psychologic impact of cardiac catheterization. *Pediatrics, 51,* 1051–1059.

American Psychiatric Association (APA). (1980). *Diagnostic and statistical manual of mental disorders* (3d ed.). Washington, DC: American Psychiatric Press.

American Psychiatric Association (APA). (1987). *Diagnostic and statistical manual of mental disorders* (3d ed., rev.). Washington, DC: American Psychiatric Press.

Andreasen N. C., & Hoenk, P. R. (1982). The predictive value of adjustment disorders: A follow-up study. *American Journal of Psychiatry, 139,* 584–590.

Andreasen, N. C., & Wasek, P. (1980). Adjustment disorders in adolescents and adults. *Archives of General Psychiatry, 37,* 1166–1170.

Arroyo, W., & Eth, S. (1985). Children traumatized by Central American warfare. In S. Eth & R. S. Pynoos (Eds.), *Post-Traumatic Stress Disorder in children* (pp. 101–120). Washington, DC: American Psychiatric Press.

Barker, P. (1988). *Basic child psychiatry* (5th ed., pp. 196–199). Oxford: Blackwell Scientific Publications.

Bedell, J. R., Giordani, B., Amour, J. L., Tavormina, J., & Boll, T. (1977). Life stress and the psychological and medical adjustment of chronically ill children. *Journal of Psychosomatic Research, 21,* 237–242.

Benedek, E. P., & Schetky, D. H. (1985). Custody and visitation: Problems and perspectives. *Psychiatric Clinics of North America, 8,* 857–873.

Bergen, M. (1958). Effect of severe trauma on a 4-year-old child. *Psychoanalytic Study of the Child, 13,* 407–429.

Bird, H. R., Canino, G., Rubio-Stipec, M., Gould, M. S., Ribera, J., Sesman, M., Woodbury, M., Huertas-Goldman, S., Pagan, A., Sanchez-Lacay, A., & Moscoso, M. (1988). Estimates of the prevalence of childhood maladjustment in a community survey in Puerto Rico. *Archives of General Psychiatry, 45,* 1120–1126.

Block, D. A., Silber, E., & Perry, S. E. (1956). Some factors in the emotional reaction of children to disaster. *American Journal of Psychiatry, 113,* 416–422.

Blotcky, M. J., & Grossman, I. (1978). Psychologic implications of childhood genitourinary surgery: An empirical study. *Journal of the American Academy of Child Psychiatry, 17,* 488–497.

Breslau, N., Klein, N., & Allen, L. (1988). Very low birthweight: Behavioral sequelae at nine years of age. *Journal of the American Academy of Child and Adolescent Psychiatry, 27,* 605–612.

Brown, J. D., & Siegel, J. M. (1988). Attributions for negative life events and depression: The role of perceived control. *Journal of Personality and Social Psychology, 54,* 316–322.

Burke, J. D., Borus, J. F., Burns, B. J., Millstein, K. H., & Beasley, M. C. (1982). Changes in children's behavior after a natural disaster. *American Journal of Psychiatry, 139,* 107–113.

Burke, J. D., Moccia, P., Borus, J. F., & Burns, B. J. (1986). Emotional distress in fifth grade children ten months after natural disaster. *Journal of the American Academy of Child and Adolescent Psychiatry, 25,* 536–541.

Caplan, G. (1981). Mastery of stress: Psychological aspects. *American Journal of Psychiatry, 138,* 413–420.

Chess, S., & Hassibi, M. (1986). *Principles and practice of child psychiatry* (2nd ed., pp. 215–220). New York: Plenum Press.

Costello, E. J., Costello, A. J., Edelbrock, C., Burns, B. J., Dulcan, M. K., Brent, D., & Janiszewski, S. (1988). Psychiatric disorders in pediatric primary care: Prevalence and risk factors. *Archives of General Psychiatry, 45,* 1107–1116.

Cytryn, L., Moore, P. V. P., & Robinson, M. E. (1973). Psychologic adjustment of children with cystic fibrosis. In E. J. Anthony & C. Koupernik (Eds.), *The child in his family* (Vol. II, pp. 37–47). New York: John Wiley and Sons.

de Traubenberg, N. R. (1973). Psychologic aspects of congenital heart disease in children. In E. J. Anthony & C. Koupernik (Eds.), *The child in his family* (Vol. II, pp. 75–83). New York: John Wiley and Sons.

Deal, S. L., & Williams, J. E. (1988). Cognitive distortions as mediators between life stress and depression in adolescents. *Adolescence, 23,* 477–490.

Eisen, P. (1979). Children under stress. *Australian and New Zealand Journal of Psychiatry, 13,* 193–207.

Elizur, E., & Kaffman, M. (1982). Children's bereavement reactions following death of the father, II. *Journal of the American Academy of Child Psychiatry, 21,* 474–480.

Eth, S., & Pynoos, R. S. (1985). Developmental perspective on psychic trauma in childhood. In C. Figley (Ed.), *Trauma and its wake* (pp. 36–52). New York: Brunner-Mazel.

Eth, S. (1987). Long-term effects of terrorism on children. *Western Journal of Medicine, 147,* 73–74.

Eth, S. (1988). The child victim as witness in sexual abuse proceedings. *Psychiatry, 51,* 221–232.

Eth, S. (in press). The adolescent witness to homicide. In E. P. Benedek & D. G. Cornell, (Eds.), *Juvenile homicide.* Washington, DC: American Psychiatric Press.

Fard, K., Hudgens, R. W., & Welner, A. (1978). Undiagnosed psychiatric illness in adolescents: A prospective study and seven-year follow-up. *Archives of General Psychiatry, 35,* 279–282.

Faulstich, M. E., Moore, J. R., Carey, M. P., Ruggiero, L., & Gresham, F. (1986). Prevalence of DSM-III conduct and adjustment disorders for adolescent psychiatric inpatients. *Adolescence, 21,* 333–337.

Frankel, S. A. (1985). Joint custody awards and children: A theoretical framework and some practical considerations. *Psychiatry, 48,* 318–328.

Freeman, A. M., Sokol, R. S., Folks, D. G., McVay, R. F., McGriffin, A. F., & Fahs, J. J. (1988). Psychiatric characteristics of patients undergoing cardiac transplantation. *Psychiatric Medicine, 6,* 8–23.

Freud, A. (1952). The role of bodily illness in the mental life of children. *Psychoanalytic Study of the Child, 7,* 69–81.

Galdston, R., & Gamble, W. J. (1969). On borrowed time: Observations on children with implanted cardiac pacemakers and their families. *American Journal of Psychiatry, 126,* 104–108.

Glover, E. (1942). Notes on the psychological effects of war conditions on the civilian population. *International Journal of Psychoanalysis, 23,* 17–37.

Goodyer, I., Kolvin, I., & Gatzanis, S. (1985). Recent undesirable life events and psychiatric disorder in childhood and adolescence. *British Journal of Psychiatry, 147,* 517–523.

Goodyer, I. M., Kolvin, I., & Gatzanis, S. (1987). The impact of recent undesirable life events on psychiatric disorders in childhood and adolescence. *British Journal of Psychiatry, 151,* 179–184.

Goodyer, I. M., Wright, C., & Altham, P. M. E. (1988). Maternal adversity and recent stressful life events in anxious and depressed children. *Journal of Child Psychology and Psychiatry, 29,* 651–667.

Helzer, J. E., Robins, L. N., & McEvoy, L. (1987). Post-traumatic stress disorder in the general population: Findings of the epidemiologic catchment area survey. *New England Journal of Medicine, 317,* 1630–1634.

Jackson, H. C. (1982). Moral nihilism: Developmental arrest as a sequela to combat stress. *Adolescent Psychiatry, 10,* 228–242.

Jackson, K., Winkley, R., Faust, O. A., Cermak, E. G., & Burtt, M. M. (1953). Behavioral changes indicating emotional trauma in tonsillectomized children: Final report. *Pediatrics, 12,* 23–28.

Jessner, L., Blom, G. E., & Waldfogel, S. (1952). Emotional implications of tonsillectomy and adenoidectomy on children. *Psychoanalytic Study of the Child, 7,* 126–169.

Johnson, S. B. (1988). Psychologic aspects of childhood diabetes. *Journal of Child Psychology and Psychiatry, 29,* 729–738.

Keane, T. M., Wolfe, J., & Taylor, K. J. (1987). Post-traumatic stress disorder: Evidence for diagnostic validity and methods of psychologic assessment. *Journal of Clinical Psychology, 43,* 32–43.

Kellerman, J., Zeltzer, L., Ellenberg, L., Dash, J., & Rigler, D. (1980). Psychological effects of illness in adolescents: I. Anxiety, self-esteem, and perception of control. *Journal of Pediatrics, 97,* 126–131.

Kelly, J. B., & Wallerstein, J. S. (1976). The effects of parental divorce: Experiences of the child in early latency. *American Journal of Orthopsychiatry, 46,* 20–32.

Kinston, W., & Rosser, R. (1974). Disaster: Effects on mental and physical state. *Journal of Psychosomatic Research, 18,* 437–456.

Kiser, L. J., Ackerman, B. J., Brown, E., Edwards, N. B., McCalgan, E., Pugh, R., & Pruitt, D. B. (1988). Post-traumatic stress disorder in young children: A reaction to purported sexual abuse. *Journal of the American Academy of Child and Adolescent Psychiatry, 27,* 645–649.

Kluft, R. P. (1985). *Childhood antecedents of multiple personality.* Washington, DC: American Psychiatric Press.

Krystal, H. (1978). Trauma and affects. *Psychoanalytic Study of the Child, 22,* 81–116.

Lacey, G. (1972). Observations on Aberfan. *Journal of Psychosomatic Research, 16,* 257–260.

Looney, J. C., & Gunderson, E. K. E. (1978). Transient situational disturbances: Course and outcome. *American Journal of Psychiatry, 135,* 660–663.

Maclean, G. (1977). Psychic trauma and traumatic neurosis. *Canadian Psychiatric Association Journal, 22,* 71–76.

Masten, A. S., Garmezy, N., Tellegen, A., Pellegrini, D. S., Larkin, K., & Larsen, A. (1988). Competence and stress in school children: The moderating effects of individual and family qualities. *Journal of Child Psychology and Psychiatry, 29,* 745–764.

Masterson, J. F. (1967). The symptomatic adolescent five years later: He didn't grow out of it. *American Journal of Psychiatry, 123,* 1338–1345.

Masterson, J. F. (1968). The psychiatric significance of adolescent turmoil. *American Journal of Psychiatry, 124,* 1549–1554.

Masterson, J. F., & Washburne, A. (1966). The symptomatic adolescent: Psychiatric illness or adolescent turmoil? *American Journal of Psychiatry, 122,* 1240–1247.

Mattson, A. (1972). Long-term physical illness in childhood: A challenge to psychosocial adaptation. *Pediatrics, 50,* 801–811.

Mattson, A., & Gross, S. (1966). Adaptation and defensive behavior in young hemophiliacs and their parents. *American Journal of Psychiatry, 122,* 1349–1356.

McAnarney, E. R., Plese, I. B., Satterwhite, B., & Friedman, S. B. (1974). Psychological problems of children with chronic juvenile arthritis. *Pediatrics, 53,* 523–528.

McFarlane, A. C. (1987). Post-traumatic phenomena in a longitudinal study of children following a natural disaster. *Journal of the American Academy of Child and Adolescent Psychiatry, 26,* 746–760.

McFarlane, A. C. (1988). Recent life events and psychiatric disorder in children: The interaction with preceding extreme adversity. *Journal of Child Psychology and Psychiatry, 29,* 677–690.

McFarlane, A. C., Policansky, S. K., & Irwin, C. (1978). A longitudinal study of psychological morbidity in children due to natural disaster. *Psychologic Medicine, 17,* 727–738.

McLeer, S. V., Deblinger, E., Atkins, M. S., Foa, E. B., & Ralphe, D. L. (1988). Post-traumatic stress disorder in sexually abused children. *Journal of the American Academy of Child and Adolescent Psychiatry, 27,* 650–654.

Milgram, R. M., & Milgram, N. A. (1976). The effects of the Yom Kippur war on anxiety level in Israeli children. *Journal of Psychology, 94,* 107–113.

Newman, C. J. (1976). Children of disaster: Clinical observations at Buffalo Creek. *American Journal of Psychiatry, 133,* 306–312.

Oldham, D. G. (1978). Adolescent turmoil: A myth revisited. *Adolescent Psychiatry, 6,* 267–280.

Ornitz, E. M., & Pynoos, R. S. (1989). Startle modulation in children with post-traumatic stress disorder. *American Journal of Psychiatry 146,* 866–870.

Papanek, E. (1942). My experiences with fugitive children in Europe. *Nervous Child, 2,* 301–307.

Pitman, R. K. (1989). Post-traumatic stress disorder, hormones and memory. *Biologic Psychiatry, 26,* 221–223.

Prugh, D. G., Staub, E. M., Sands, H. H., Kirschbaum, R. M., & Lenihan, E. A. (1953). A study of the emotional reactions of children and families to hospitalization and illness. *American Journal of Orthopsychiatry, 23,* 70–106.

Pynoos, R. S., & Eth, S. (1986). Witness to violence: The child interview. *Journal of the American Academy of Child and Adolescent Psychiatry, 25,* 306–319.

Pynoos, R. S., Frederick, C., Nader, K., Arroyo, W., Steinberg, A., Eth, S., Nunez, F., & Fairbanks, L. (1987). Life threat and post-traumatic stress in school-age children. *Archives of General Psychiatry, 44,* 1057–1063.

Pynoos, R. S., & Nader, K. (1988). Children who witness the sexual assaults of their mothers. *Journal of the American Academy of Child and Adolescent Psychiatry, 27,* 567–572.

Rutter, M. (1981). Stress, coping and development: Some issues and some questions. *Journal of Child Psychology and Psychiatry, 22,* 323–356.

Sadowski, C. J., Woodward, H. R., Davis, S. F., & Elsbury, D. L. (1983). Sex differences in correlates of locus of control dimensions. *Journal of Personality Assessment, 47,* 627–631.

Schaffer, H. R., & Callender, W. M. (1959). Psychologic effects of hospitalization in infancy. *Pediatrics, 24,* 528–539.

Sigal, J. J., DiNocola, V. F., & Bounvino, M. (1988). Grandchildren of survivors: Can negative effects of prolonged exposure to excessive stress be observed two generations later? *Canadian Journal of Psychiatry, 33,* 207–212.

Skinner, E. A., Chapman, M., & Baltes, P. B. (1988). Control, means-ends, and agency beliefs: A new conceptualization and its measurement in childhood. *Journal of Personality and Social Psychology, 54,* 117–133.

Solnit, A. J., & Kris, M. (1967). Trauma and infantile experience. In S. S. Furst (Ed.), *Psychic trauma* (pp. 179–220). New York: Basic Books.

Swift, C. R., Seidman, F., & Stein, H. (1967). Adjustment problems in juvenile diabetes. *Psychosomatic Medicine, 29,* 555–571.

Terr, L. (1979). Children of Chowchilla: A study of psychic trauma. *Psychoanalytic Study of the Child, 34,* 547–623.

Terr, L. (1981). Psychic trauma in children: Observations following the Chowchilla school-bus kidnapping. *American Journal of Psychiatry, 138,* 14–19.

Terr, L. (1983). Life attitudes, dreams, and psychic trauma in a group of "normal" children. *Journal of the American Academy of Child Psychiatry, 22,* 221–230.

Terr, L. (1988). What happens to early memories of trauma? A study of twenty children under age 5 at the time of documented traumatic events. *Journal of the American Academy of Child and Adolescent Psychiatry, 27,* 96–104.

Thomas, A., & Chess, S. (1976). Evolution of behavior disorders into adolescence. *American Journal of Psychiatry, 133,* 539–542.

Thomas, A., & Chess, S. (1984). Genesis and evolution of behavioral disorders from infancy to early adult life. *American Journal of Psychiatry, 141,* 1–9.

Tisza, V. B., Dorsett, P., & Morse, J. (1976). Psychologic implications of renal transplantation. *Journal of the American Academy of Child Psychiatry, 15,* 709–720.

van der Kolk, B. A. (1985). Adolescent vulnerability to post-traumatic stress disorder. *Psychiatry, 48,* 365–370.

Vernon, D. T. A., & Schulman, J. L. (1964). Hospitalization as a source of psychologic benefit to children. *Pediatrics, 23,* 694–696.

Wallerstein, J. S. (1985). Children of divorce: Emerging trends. *Psychiatric Clinics of North America, 8,* 837–853.

.Wallerstein, J. S., & Kelly, J. B. (1974). The effects of parental divorce: The adolescent experience. In E. J. Anthony & C. Koupernik (Eds.), The child in his family (Vol. III, pp. 479–505). New York: John Wiley and Sons.

Wallerstein, J. S., & Kelly, J. B. (1975). The effects of parental divorce: Experiences of the preschool child. *Journal of the American Academy of Child Psychiatry, 15,* 600–616.

Wallerstein, J. S., & Kelly, J. B. (1976). The effects of parental divorce: Experiences of the child in later latency. *American Journal of Orthopsychiatry, 46,* 256–269.

Weinberg, S. (1970). Suicidal intent in adolescence: A hypothesis about the role of physical illness. *Journal of Pediatrics, 77,* 579–586.

Werner, E. E. (1989). High-risk children in young adulthood: A longitudinal study from birth to 32 years. *American Journal of Orthopsychiatry, 59,* 72–81.

Woolston, J. L. (1988). Theoretical considerations of the adjustment disorders. *Journal of the American Academy of Child and Adolescent Psychiatry, 27,* 280–287.

Woolston, J. L. (1986). A child's reaction to his parents' problems. *Pediatrics in Review, 8,* 169–176.

Zeltzer, L., Kellerman, J., Ellenberg, L., Dash, J., & Rigler, D. (1980). Psychological effects of illness in adolescents: II. Impact of illness in adolescents—crucial issues and coping styles. *Journal of Pediatrics, 97,* 132–138.

CHAPTER THREE

Biological Aspects of Stress: Effects on the Developing Brain

Elizabeth M. Burns
L. Eugene Arnold

This chapter focuses on the physical (biological) aspects of stress: physical stressors and physical responses to stress, with special attention to the developing child's brain. Nevertheless, since "all stress reactions involve integrated physiologic and psychologic" responses (Corson & Corson, 1980), it will be impossible to exclude consideration of psychological stressors and responses.

The young developing brain reacts to stressors—whether physical, chemical, infectious, psychological, social, or nutritional—differently from an adult brain. The brain consumes nearly half an infant's resting caloric requirement, compared to one-fourth or less for an adult. The infant's brain requires such a large proportion of nutritional intake because of its active growth and development. It triples in size from birth to age 2. More remarkable yet is its development: a "building boom" of seething construction, tearing down, transportation (migration of cells), remodeling, reshaping, pruning, elaboration, refinement, specialization, and interconnection of cells, membranes, dendrites, axons, spines, synapses, and supporting structures. This complex process continually integrates genetic programming with environmental input to produce a dynamic electrochemical-neuroanatomical harmony of checks and balances. That the process succeeds at all in the best of circumstances seems a minor miracle. We should not be surprised that many stressors can disrupt the delicate developmental process, sometimes irreversibly.

In the first part of this chapter we describe the effects of a biological-chemical stress, using alcohol as an example. Other examples of chemical stressors, such as lead, nicotine, pesticides/herbicides, or maternal use of street drugs, could have been used. Eskanazi (1984), Weston et al. (1989), and others have documented effects from such chemicals, including behavior and learning disorders and reduction in expected intelligence (IQ). Alcohol makes an especially apt example because it is one of the better (albeit incompletely) studied chemical stressors and because it illustrates how we can stress our children without realizing it: moderate social drinking by pregnant and nursing mothers traditionally has been assumed to be innocuous. In the second part of the chapter we describe some ways in which psychosocial stresses can affect the developing brain via adrenal and other hormonal mechanisms, and touch on psychoimmunology and nutritional aspects of stress.

CHEMICAL STRESS

Any force capable of deforming or distorting brain cell membranes is a brain stressor. Alcohol and other solvents increase the fluidity of the lipid-rich neuronal membrane, expand membrane surfaces, disorganize membrane constituents (alter lipid composition, distort the stearic arrangement of proteins, and alter the carbohydrate composition of membrane bound glycoconjugates), affect the activity of membrane-bound enzymes, and disturb membrane transport mechanisms (Hunt, 1985). According to Tabakoff, Noble, and Warren (1979), the effects of alcohol on the adult rat brain include: a decrease in the synthesis of brain nuclear and mitochondrial RNA; adverse effects on the proper association of ribosomal subunits (which in turn affect protein synthesis); inhibition of the increase of glucose utilization that occurs in activated neurons; inhibition of $Na+/K+$ ATPase at high blood alcohol concentrations (which in turn interferes with brain carbohydrate metabolism associated with increased brain glucose levels); and, adverse effects on brain cell membranes. Alcohol is known to be a human teratogen (Clarren & Smith, 1978). The impact of alcohol stress during brain development is serious and, in the case of the fetal alcohol syndrome, is catastrophic.

The Fetal Alcohol Syndrome and Fetal Alcohol Effects

Maternal alcohol intake during pregnancy is reported to be detrimental to the human fetus (Alpert et al., 1981; Clarren et al., 1978; Jones & Smith, 1973; Jones et al., 1974; Landesman-Dwyer & Ragozin, 1981; Warren, 1977). The offspring of alcoholic mothers (whose daily alcohol intake is at least six drinks per day) are at risk for the fetal alcohol syndrome, a constellation of developmental anomalies first given worldwide attention in 1973 by Jones and Smith. The incidence of this syndrome is approximately 3% in infants born of alcoholic mothers (Hanson, Streissguth, & Smith, 1978). Characteristics of the syndrome include: prenatal and postnatal growth deficiency, microcephaly, extensive neuropathology (neuroglial heterotopias, dysplasias, ectopic disorganized neuronal arrangements, and disruption of cell laminae and neuronal projections in cerebral cortex, cerebellum, and hippocampus), craniofacial dysmorphology, limb and organ anomalies, mental retardation, and behavioral disorders. The full-blown syndrome has been observed only in offspring of chronically alcoholic women.

The severity of alcohol-induced brain deficits ranges from the full-blown fetal alcohol syndrome to the more subtle though serious abnormalities described as fetal alcohol effects. The former is attributed to the high blood alcohol concentrations characteristic of chronic alcoholism, and the latter to lower blood alcohol concentrations associated with light or moderate social drinking. Fetal alcohol effects include attention deficit disorder (Shaywitz, Griffieth, & Warshaw, 1979), hyperactivity (Clarren & Smith, 1978), and other less clearly understood brain deficits thought to be related to altered synaptic structure and/or function.

Vulnerable Periods of Brain Development

An important teratological principle is: the more rapid the growth rate of a tissue, the greater its vulnerability. Based on this principle, three phases of human neuro-ontogeny have been identified as critically vulnerable periods:

- Organogenesis (gestation weeks 3–9)
- Rapid neuronal proliferation (gestation weeks 12–20)
- The brain growth spurt (gestation weeks 30–40 and the first 18–24 months after birth).

In general, CNS development (in contrast to development of the rest of the organism) proceeds in a sequential caudocranial manner (Timiras, Vernadakis, & Sherwood, 1968), with maturation of the spinal cord preceding that of myelencephalon, mesencephalon, diencephalon, and telencephalon, respectively (Vernadakis & Woodbury, 1969). For example, a major portion of cerebellar development occurs postnatally (Altman, 1969; Altman, 1972a; Altman, 1972b; Altman, 1972c; Ito, 1984). Thus, during any specific time frame, exposure to a teratogen may selectively and significantly affect specific brain regions, systems, or parts of systems that are the most vulnerable at the time of exposure.

Organogenesis (gestation weeks 3–9) is a time of critical vulnerability for the entire organism. Neuro-ontogenetic events characteristic of this developmental phase include establishment of the basic embryonic plan of the brain and induction of the future central and peripheral nervous systems. These events are mediated by cell proliferation, migration, differentiation, and cellular death. The effects of teratogenic agents during organogenesis are likely to be devastating and may give rise to major deformities or embryonal death (Moore, 1977). In this light, a 17% perinatal mortality rate in offspring of alcoholic women as compared with 2% for non-alcoholic women (Jones et al., 1974) is not surprising. Further, Clarren et al. (1978) observed gross neuropathology (neuroglial heterotopias, dysplasias, and ectopic disorganized neuronal arrangements) in the brains of infants who died perinatally and whose mothers were chronic alcoholics. These neuropathological changes probably resulted from injury during organogenesis (Lemire et al., 1975). Dow and Riopelle (1985) have suggested that alcohol alters neuronal growth cone formation (Figure 3.1) and the production of neurotrophic factors, thus interfering with essential mechanisms mediating embryonal central nervous system development.

A second vulnerable period in human brain ontogeny (Dobbing, 1974) occurs during gestation weeks 12–20. The final critically vulnerable period for the developing human brain begins during the last trimester of

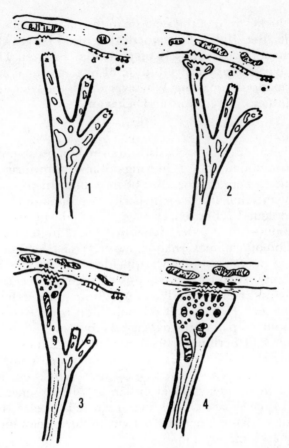

Figure 3.1. A schema representing selected events (recognition and adhesion) that occur during synaptogenesis. 1. Axonal growth cones (a, b and c) approach targets (a′, d′ and e′). 2. The 'signature' on growth cone (a) recognizes its target 'signature' (a′) on the postsynaptic membrane. 3. Adhesion occurs between axonal growth cone (a) and its postsynaptic target (a′). Growth cones b and c, in the absence of appropriate target 'signatures', regress. 4. The structural machinery of the synapse is elaborated after synaptic connectivity is established.

pregnancy and continues throughout the first 18 to 24 months after birth. This time frame encompasses the most rapid phase of brain growth and is known as the *brain growth spurt*. It is characterized by dendritic arborization, axonal growth, peak synaptogenesis, gliogenesis, myelination, and maturation of structures and mechanisms involved in synaptic neurotransmission (Dobbing 1971; Dobbing, & Sands, 1979; Dobbing & Smart, 1973).

Because of the key role of the synapse in the maintenance of nervous system integrity, the effects of alcohol during the brain growth spurt on synaptic biochemical ontogeny is of particular interest. The synapse provides the dynamic physical substrate of interneuronal communication and information processing. Whatever affects the synapse will affect neurological function, cognition, and behavior.

Synaptogenesis. Synaptogenesis is the single most important event during brain development for achieving optimal, appropriate interneuronal connections. Some of the most obvious and frustrating effects of damage during this time frame are hyperkinesis, impaired learning, and behavioral problems in children. Damage during the brain growth spurt is likely to be permanent unless rehabilitation is undertaken immediately. The period of maximal synaptic plasticity (i.e., the time of greatest potential for optimal development) coincides with that of maximal synaptic vulnerability. Therefore, if synaptic damage has occurred prior to birth, aggressive intervention early postnatally may repair the damage, at least to some extent. However, if rehabilitation is delayed beyond the brain growth spurt, repair of the damage is minimal.

Burry, Kniss, and Scribner (1984) recently hypothesized that synaptogenesis proceeds by a series of events in which completion of a preceding event is required before the subsequent event is initiated. Completion of the sequence of events in an orderly manner enables development of the synaptic machinery required for effective synaptic function. Feedback from functional activity of the developing synapse is essential to synaptic maturation.

During ontogeny, terminals of axons must find and attach to their appropriate targets. This involves guided outgrowth of the leading edge of the growth cone (Figure 3.1), recognition of appropriate target sites, and attachment and adhesion of presynaptic and postsynaptic elements.

Four factors influence the recognition-adhesion process (humoral substances, intercellular matrix, cell surfaces, and feedback). The single most important of these factors is the cell surface, i.e., synaptic plasma membrane microarchitectonics, or "signatures" on the leading edge of the growth cone and on the future postsynaptic target site. Numerous studies have shown that alteration of these "signatures," i.e., alteration of the biochemical molecular structure of the involved membranes, leads to changes in cellular behavior (Edelman, 1976).

During synaptogenesis, alcohol-induced alterations in membrane fluidity (also known to occur in the adult neuronal membrane) would be expected to distort "signatures" of developing synaptic elements. If so, disorder would be introduced into the sequential series of synaptic events, thus interfering with normal synaptogenesis. Further, alcohol depresses synaptic function, decreasing feedback to the synapse, thus further disturbing normal synaptogenesis.

Because the human brain growth spurt is perinatal, extending through the first 18–24 months postnatally, it is important to note that human milk alcohol concentrations reach measurable levels within 30 minutes and persist for several hours after a drink (Kerfoot, Kruckeberg, & Burns, 1985; Kesaniemi, 1974). Alcohol 0.6 g/kg (15% solution in water) consumed in 5 minutes yielded a peak milk alcohol concentration in 30 minutes of 78 mg/dl (Kesaniemi, 1974) and alcohol 1 g/kg (10% solution) consumed slowly in three hours yielded a peak milk alcohol concentration in 215 minutes of 90 mg/dl (Kerfoot, Kruckeberg, & Burns, 1985). Breast-fed infants of social-drinking mothers may be exposed to significant amounts of alcohol.

Some Effects of Alcohol During Synaptogenesis in an Animal Model

It is well known that in adult animals acute alcohol increases the fluidity of synaptic membranes (Crews, Majchrowicz, & Meeks, 1983; Michaelis, Michaelis, & Tehan, 1983) and that chronic alcohol increases the resistance to its fluidizing effects (Chin, Parsons, & Goldstein, 1978). Alterations in membrane fluidity in immature brain might interfere with axonal or dendritic growth cone formation, recognition and adhesion processes during synaptogenesis, or in brain capillary and/or blood-brain barrier tight junction development. Immature synapses and brain capillaries, including blood-brain barrier characteristics, may be prime targets for the effects of alcohol. Disruption of the blood-brain barrier can subject the brain to other circulating toxins that it otherwise might have been spared.

To test the hypothesis that chronic exposure to low alcohol concentrations, as in moderate social drinking, during the brain growth spurt may alter synaptic biochemistry, we (E.M.B. and colleagues) studied the effects of alcohol 4 g/kg body weight per day during the brain growth spurt (postnatal days 6–16) in the rat. This dose is approximately one-third of that used in this animal model to mimic maternal alcoholism. Because the metabolism of alcohol is three times as fast in the rat as in the human, this dose is equivalent to about 1.3 g/kg in a human, or approximately three drinks consumed by a woman. Postnatal days 6–16 in the rat correspond to late third trimester and early infancy in the human because the rat's brain growth spurt peaks later.

The results revealed significantly reduced synaptosomal sialic acid content (equally distributed between glycoprotein- and glycolipid-bound sialic acid); significantly diminished activity of ecto-sialyltransferase; no change in neuraminidase activity; and no change in either total protein or lipid (Stibler et al., 1983). No effect of alcohol on body temperature was found in these preweanling rats (Kruckeberg et al., 1984). Thus, the altered synaptic biochemistry was not due to alcoholinduced hypothermia. Sialic acid is thought to be a constituent of the "signatures" on growth cones and their target sites. Decreased synaptosomal sialic acid content could, therefore, interfere with normal synaptogenesis, and this neuropathology might then be reflected in problems associated with fetal alcohol effects. Later we found in this animal model altered synaptosomal galactose content (Stibler et al., 1985), but no difference in synaptosomal Na + /K + -ATPase activity.

Micromorphological studies in these animals revealed nonsignificant structural changes in the cerebellum, lobule IX, at the light and electron microscopic levels (Burns et al., 1984). The numbers of cerebellar Purkinje cells and synaptic profiles per unit volume were less in alcohol-treated than in control animals, but these differences were not statistically significant. A decreased number of cerebellar cells (based on DNA content) was observed in alcohol-treated animals. Thus, the subtle damage that was significant at the biochemical level was not statistically significant at the micromorphological level. However, the trends were consistent across all parameters. Obviously, further studies are indicated.

We compared the effects of alcohol 6 g/kg given on one day only (day 6 postnatally), corresponding to episodic or binge drinking, with the effects of alcohol 4 g/kg throughout the brain growth spurt. Six g/kg in a rat would be approximately equivalent to five or six drinks by a woman on one occasion. Alcohol-treated animals performed less well than controls on all tests of balancing ability, but not significantly so (Burns et al., 1986).

Body, whole brain, and cerebellar weights were significantly lower in both groups of alcohol-treated rats as compared with controls on postnatal day 17. By 70 days of age, no body weight differences from controls in either males or females were observed; however, between-group whole brain and cerebellar weight differences remained. At both 17 and 70 days after birth, in the two alcohol-treated groups, the cerebellum was disproportionately decreased in weight with respect to the brain as a whole. The number of cerebellar cells (based on DNA content) also was significantly decreased in both sexes in both alcohol-treated groups, as compared with controls.

Discussion of Findings from Animal Studies

These results underline the importance of timing, intensity, and duration of alcohol exposure during ontogeny and how lasting effects can be produced during this critically vulnerable phase.

A proposed criterion of nutritional adequacy in animals treated with alcohol during ontogeny (Wiener et al., 1981) is normalcy of body and brain weights. Dobbing and colleagues (Dobbing, 1971; Dobbing & Smart, 1973; Sands & Dobbing, 1981) found that brain weight was less affected than body weight by malnutrition. This gave rise to the misleading concept of "brain sparing." Although brain weight is less affected than body weight by malnutrition during the brain growth spurt, a small decrement localized to a critical area can be extremely important. For example, a critical decrease in numbers of neurons or synaptic connections within a small circumscribed brain region (e.g., brain stem centers regulating respiration or circulation) might seriously affect autonomic function without significantly altering brain weight.

According to Dobbing and Sands (1971), an irreversible true microcephaly results in rats from severe malnutrition during the brain growth spurt, the "once-only" opportunity for building the brain. Dobbing and Smart (1973) showed that retardation of body growth by malnutrition during the brain growth spurt results in a permanent body weight deficit which resists rehabilitative efforts.

Microcephaly is among the most important morphological characteristics of the full-blown fetal alcohol syndrome. The significantly decreased brain weights in our "social-drinking" alcohol-treated rats as compared with controls shows a trend towards microcephaly. It is generally accepted that the fetal alcohol syndrome is not produced by severe nutritional deprivation in the absence of alcoholism per se. Therefore, the microcephaly associated with the fetal alcohol syndrome seems to be a direct pharmacological effect of alcohol on the brain, with subsequent accommodation of the infant's head size to brain size. If microcephaly in the fetal alcohol syndrome is indeed a pharmacological effect of alcohol, then the trend towards microcephaly in our alcohol treated rats, in spite of no permanent effects on body weight in these animals, suggests that in rats alcohol levels that mimic moderate social drinking in the human do indeed produce "a touch of microcephaly."

Body weights in our alcohol-treated animals were reduced by only about one-third as much as in malnutrition during the same time period (Culley & Lineberger, 1968). Brain weight reduction in our animals was closely comparable to that observed by Culley and Lineberger in their malnourished animals. By 70 days of age, body weight in both of our alcohol-treated groups had caught up completely with that of controls. However, brain weight was just as significantly decreased at 70 days as it had been at 17 days of age. In malnourished animals, neither body nor brain weight caught up by 110 days of age (Culley & Lineberger, 1968).

Therefore the complete catch-up in body weight by 70 days of age in our animals suggests that the brain deficits are due to the pharmacological effects of alcohol rather than to alcohol-induced malnutrition. Thus, alcohol exposure during the critically vulnerable brain growth spurt is reflected in altered whole brain and regional brain weights, regardless of how precisely nutritional status is controlled in alcohol-treated animals.

Although animal findings are not conclusive for the human, it is wise to consider the potential danger of alcohol exposure of the human brain during the brain growth spurt. Insofar as extrapolation is permissible, moderate social drinking and binge drinking by pregnant women during the third trimester and lactation may interfere with normal dendritic arborization, axonal growth, synaptogenesis, myelination, and maturation of neurotransmitter systems and neurotransmission.

Recently, Mills and colleagues (1984) reported a prospective study of 31,604 pregnancies from 1974 to 1977. They found that the percentage of newborns below the tenth percentile of weight for gestational age increased sharply with increasing maternal alcohol intake. Also, they found that "consumption of one to two drinks daily was associated with a substantially increased risk of producing a growth-retarded infant" (p. 1877). Because no safe level of alcohol intake has been established, they advised that pregnant women limit alcoholic beverage intake to an "occasional" drink or at least not more than one drink per day. In view of their findings that one to two drinks a day was associated with significant risk, allowing one drink a day seems to be cutting it rather fine. Their data did not permit assessment of binge drinking nor of drinking beyond the first trimester of pregnancy. Unfortunately, this suggests that they saw no need to evaluate the effects of alcohol exposure during the brain growth spurt. The animal data described above suggest a need to consider late effects.

Again insofar as extrapolation is permitted, the disproportionate severity of the observed cerebellar effects in rats suggests implications for both the neuromotor and mental health of affected children. Berntson and Torello (1982) pointed out that ascending paleocerebellar limbic projections modulate mechanisms involved in motivation, emotional behaviors, and behavioral integration. Cerebellar damage, therefore, may be reflected not only in altered motor, sensory, and autonomic functions, but also in disturbances of emotion, motivation, and behavior.

Caution to Obstetrical and Pediatric Care Providers

Landesman-Dwyer (1981) reviewed the use of alcohol for inhibition of premature labor. Beta-2 agonists have also been used to inhibit premature labor (Weiner, 1980); however, they have their own problems and have not completely replaced alcohol. Recently alcohol was still listed among the inhibitors of premature labor (Andersson, 1982; Caritis et al., 1982; Fuchs & Fuchs, 1981; Souney, Kaul, & Osathanondh, 1983). Sisenwein et al. (1983) reported that a subgroup of children born during or within 15 hours of alcohol infusion showed significant pathology upon developmental testing and personality inventory at ages 4 to 7 years. Behavioral assessment of such children has been extremely limited (Landesman-Dwyer, 1981). Alcohol has also been used in hyperalimentation in small-for-date infants. Infantile intoxication during hyperalimentation was reported by Peden, Sammon, & Downey (1973), who found blood alcohol concentrations as high as 163–183 mg/dl in several lethargic, small-for-date infants. Cook, Shott, & Andrews (1975) also stressed the dangers associated with alcohol hyperalimentation of small-for-date infants. These recent clinical uses of alcohol in obstetrics and pediatrics suggest a lack of awareness of the potential dangers of alcohol exposure during the brain growth spurt. It is important for clinicians to be aware that alcohol or its metabolites may act directly or may interact with other drugs or with neurotransmitter or hormone molecules to affect the developing brain adversely. The American Academy of Pediatrics (AAP) Committee on Drugs (1984) reported finding more than 700 liquid pharmaceutical preparations for children containing alcohol in concentrations from 0.35% to 68%. The AAP report emphasized the potential toxicity of this alcoholic content.

A Lethal Complication of Brain Maldevelopment. Synaptic alterations in brainstem respiratory centers may result from low blood alcohol concentrations during the brain growth spurt. Could these increase the risk of the sudden infant death syndrome (SIDS)? Although SIDS is the leading cause of death during the first postnatal year (Merritt & Valdes-Dapena, 1984), its etiology and neuropathological basis remain unknown.

Subtle brainstem pathology, in the absence of infectious or chemical stress, might cause no apparent problem. If the stress of an acute upper respiratory infection is superimposed on already compromised regulatory systems, an infant's capacity to cope may be exceeded. Further, depressant effects of alcohol contained in medications used to treat upper respiratory or other minor illnesses might suffice to tip the balance, allowing SIDS to occur.

Possible Interaction of Ethanol and Thyroxine. Animal experiments suggest that exposure of the brain during the brain growth spurt to low thyroxine levels, alone or in combination with alcohol or any central nervous system depressant, may increase the risk of SIDS.

Brain changes that occur in experimental animals from low thyroxine levels during the brain growth spurt include: a decrease in mean cell size, with an increase in cellular numerical density; a hypoplastic axonal network; a reduction in dendritic branching; an abnormal distribution of dendritic spines; decreased synaptic connectivity; and altered vascularity (Eayrs, 1954; 1971; Eayrs & Goodhead, 1959). These changes may be related to any of a diverse multiplicity of thyroxine effects on RNA and protein synthesis (Legrand, Clos, & Legrand, 1982). According to Hamburgh (1969), low thyroxine during brain development results in decreased brain vascularization. If brainstem vascularity or synaptic and/or blood-brain barrier development are affected, then the risk of SIDS may be increased. Walsh (1986) showed that ethanol 0.6 g/kg (used in the diluent for isopropylnorepinephrine) caused apnea frequently in hypothyroid rats but infrequently in control animals. Ethanol 0.6 g/kg in a rat is approximately equivalent to 0.2 g/kg in a human, and is closely comparable to the amount of ethanol in an infant's dose of an elixir containing 18% alcohol.

Effects of Ethanol During the Human Brain Growth Spurt. Several studies on the effects of low alcohol levels on fetal breathing were done in women (light social drinkers) at 37–40 weeks gestation, using real-time ultrasonic scanning, prior to and after ingestion of either 31 ml (one ounce) of Vodka in diet ginger ale (Fox et al., 1978) or 0.25 g alcohol per kg body weight (1.5 ounces of Vodka for a 125-lb woman) (Lewis & Boylan, 1979; McLeod et al., 1983; 1984). In all subjects, within 30 minutes after the ingestion of alcohol, fetal respiratory movements were virtually abolished and remained so throughout the three hours of monitoring. These findings illustrate the extreme sensitivity of the brainstem respiratory center to the neurotoxicity of alcohol during the brain growth spurt. Depriving the brainstem of the feedback normally provided by fetal respiratory movements would be likely to interfere with normal synaptic maturation.

Summary of Alcohol Effects

There are potential dangers of relatively low-intensity and/or short-duration alcohol exposures during critically vulnerable phases of brain ontogeny. The seriousness of alcohol exposure during the brain growth spurt (late gestation to 2 years) is underlined by the heightened susceptibility of rapidly developing synaptic structures during this developmental period. Subtle though serious synaptic biochemical alterations may result from low-intensity, short-duration alcohol exposures during the brain growth spurt. Such exposures could result from the common frequency of light and moderate social drinking. Birth weight is signficantly less in offspring of women who consume one to two drinks per day, and low birth weight is widely recognized to be associated with many subtle behavioral and educational handicaps. Synaptic integrity is essential for information processing and interneuronal communication in the central nervous system. Alcohol-induced synaptic distortion may be reflected in altered biological organization, which can result in altered behavior and learning.

Implications for Maternal and Infant Health: Interprofessional Prevention

An interprofessional approach to prevention is needed. Every helping professional is responsible for prevention in a special way:

- Educators at all levels—kindergarten through the Ph.D., M.D., L.L.D., etc.—are responsible for providing factual information relative to alcohol. This involves a two-directional interchange of learning and teaching. Educators need to learn the latest information from the other professions and then in turn teach it to the future professionals as they grow up (as well as to the rest of the public).
- Nurses, physicians, pharmacists, nutritionists, and other allied health professionals share responsibilities for the delivery of health care that includes prevention and treatment of mental and physical health problems related to the use of alcohol.
- Obstetricians, pediatricians, family physicians, nurses, and allied medical professionals need to educate parents and to beware of the use of alcohol in labor and in pediatric medications.
- Psychologists in addition to designing and executing infant rehabilitation can collaboratively design strategies and techniques for reshaping social behaviors in such a way as to discourage drinking by pregnant and nursing mothers.
- Social workers have a special responsibility for educating the poor, who may not be reached by the other professions, and for collaborating with the other professions to counteract the social pressures that induce pregnant and nursing mothers to drink.
- The legal profession, through legislation and jurisprudence, has responsibility for the laws governing alcohol availability and use and for interpreting the liability of those who disregard the information above.
- Theologians and pastoral counselors interpret the moral responsibilities of pregnant and nursing mothers in regard to protecting their fetuses and infants. They also carry the message of forgiveness to those who fail to heed the warning in time and interpret the innocence of those who did not know in time.

Prevention includes dissemination of information to raise consciousness about the potential dangers of alcohol use for the developing brain. Professionals need to know something about:

- Human prenatal growth and development, including periods of maximal vulnerability as well as maximal plasticity (wherein rehabilitation is most effective).

- Teratological principles related to timing, intensity, and duration of potential insults to brain growth and development.
- Nutritional requirements and other means for promoting whole-ness/wellness.
- Knowledge of the effects of alcohol (and/or other central nervous system depressants) on neuropsychological function as a backdrop for decision-making relative to the nature and extent of clients' problems.

Assessment requires:

- Knowledge of the blood alcohol concentration capable of causing damage and how to calculate absolute alcohol content in order to determine the nature and extent of clients' problems.
- Skillful history-taking to obtain essential information from clients and their families relative to the use of alcohol and other central nervous system depressants.
- Skillful mental and physical assessment of clients.

Treatment and prevention are based on knowledge of how to:

- Maintain an atmosphere of acceptance, care, and concern for the client as a person—neither condoning nor condemning.
- Work with client and family or significant other.
- Build self-esteem in the client; be reassuring, supportive.
- Provide information needed by the client and his or her family that will enable informed decision making.
- Teach clients and families decision-making skills, including how to say no to alcoholic beverages (and other substances of abuse).
- Avoid causing feelings of guilt without minimizing the importance of principles relevant to potential dangers.
- Arrange prompt rehabilitation of infants born to drinking mothers because, paradoxically, during the brain growth spurt the brain is not only most susceptible to damage but also most plastic. Hence, this stage encompasses the time of greatest potential for deriving benefit from rehabilitative measures.

A Dilemma about New Knowledge.   During preparation of this chap-ter, a colleague objected to disseminating the information above because it might cause guilt in social-drinking mothers of brain-damaged chil-dren. He thought that a general warning should await more definitive scientific evidence, and felt that in the meantime pregnant women would continue to drink anyhow and should not be made to feel guilty or be otherwise stressed about it. Since there are many causes of developmental brain damage, many mothers of handicapped children would blame the damage on their own social drinking erroneously. Thus, an attempt to prevent chemical stress might produce psychological stress.

Though these considerations are weighty, our position is that the opportunity for a prevention decision should not be withheld from responsible future mothers merely to protect those who already have a handicapped child or those who will not heed the warning. Our colleague's concerns can be dealt with by assuring those who did not know in time that they are innocent, not responsible for something they did not know. Various counselling professionals can help them realize this. For those who know but ignore the warning, some guilt is appropriate, but theological professionals can help them find forgiveness. Since no one has claimed that maternal drinking benefits the fetus, we resolve the dilemma by advocating abstention for pregnant and nursing mothers until safe levels can be determined.

NEUROHORMONAL MEDIATION OF STRESS EFFECTS: PSYCHOSOCIAL IMPACT ON THE BRAIN

Table 3.1 summarizes some of the neuro-hormonal effects of stress. It has been known for some time that psychological and social stress can elicit the same "fight or flight" physiological reaction (Cannon, 1939) as physical danger. This includes activation of the autonomic (sympathetic-adrenergic and parasympathetic-cholinergic) nervous system and an increase of adrenal and possibly other hormones. At first the adrenal glands pour the catecholamines epinephrine (adrenalin), norepinephrine (noradrenalin), and to some extent dopamine, into the circulation. Soon, especially with repeated or chronic activation (chronic stress), the adrenals also release high levels of steroid adrenocortical hormones (corticosteroids), leading to the "general adaptation syndrome" (Selye, 1936; 1956). Stress-induced activation of brain muscarinic (cholinergic) mechanisms may also contribute to activation of the limbic-hypothalamic-pituitary-adrenal axis, either directly or through intermediary adrenergic activation (Dilsaver, 1985). For example, cholinergic stimulation activates the locus coeruleus, which noradrenergically activates other brain structures, including many in the limbic system. When first increased, the corticosteroids promote repair and moderate the danger of epinephrine flooding; but with chronic elevation they alter sleep and attentional states and eventually lead to neuronal death.

In chronic stress, a neuroendocrine vicious cycle can develop from the following factors: adrenergic (sympathetic) activation stimulates the limbic-

TABLE 3.1. Some Neuro-hormonal Effects of Stress

Effects	Results
Immediate, acute:	
Autonomic activation	Adrenal medulla → catecholamines (epinephrine, norepinephrine, dopamine)
	BP and other circulatory changes, ↑ heart rate, sweating, pallor, ↑ muscle tone (→ tension)
	Suppression of insulin response to glucose
	Effects on immune function
Brain adrenergic activation	↑ Vigilance, ↑ alertness, ↓ reaction time
	Activation of hypothalamic-pituitary-adrenal axis
Brain muscarinic (cholinergic) activation	Adrenergic activation
	Activation of limbic-hypothalamic-pituitary-adrenocortical axis
Delayed or chronic:	
↑ Circulating ACTH	
↑ Circulating corticosteroids (e.g., cortisol) from adrenal cortex, possibly gonads (from chronic activation of limbic-hypothalamus-pituitary adrenal axis)	Variable effects on neuromuscular development
	At first, corticosteroids promote neuronal repair, but chronically:
	Disturbed sleep and concentration, possible depression
	Neuronal death
	↓ Neuron mitosis, growth, + branching
	Influences on synthesis of messenger RNA and other neuronal proteins

↑ Adrenergic autonomic + serotonergic CNS development;
↑ Hippocampal vasoactive intestinal peptide;
↓ Hippocampal GABA transport;
↓ Immune response

↓ Growth hormone (rare: only in deprivation or abuse)

Psychosocial dwarfism

↑ Beta-endorphin

Possible aggravation of fetal hypoxic damage

Possible changes in sex hormones and other hormones

Changes in sexual differentiation of developing brain. Testosterone defeminizes brain of fetus Estrogens: ↑ Axon growth; ↑ progesterone receptors; ↓ hypothalamic MAO + tyrosine hydroxylase; ↑ preoptic choline acetyltransferase.

Suppression of immune response
↓ Natural killer cell activity
↓ Mitogen response
↑ EBV & herpes titer
↓ % helper T lymphocytes
↓ Interferon
↓ Repair of DNA radiation damage

↑ Susceptibility to infection and cancer

Sources: Beumont (1979), Dilsaver (1988), Gorman & Locke (1989), Kennedy, Kiecolt-Glaser, & Glaser (1988), Kiecolt-Glaser & Glaser (1986, 1988), Locke & Gorman (1988), McEweSn (1986), Sandman et al. (1990). See also Fig 4.1, Chapter 4.

hypothalamic-pituitary-adrenal (LHPA) axis. In this axis, the brain's chemical messenger to the pituitary to release ACTH (corticotrophin) is corticotrophin-releasing hormone (CRH or CRF), which is thus increased with activation of the LHPA axis. However, CRH itself stimulates central sympathetic outflow. One way it does this is by increasing the firing rate of the norepinephrine-rich locus coeruleus, generally believed to be involved in anxiety disorders. Incidentally, the locus coeruleus of juvenile lab animals does not respond as vigorously to noxious (or innocuous) stimuli as does that of young adult animals (Charney et al., 1989). Thus, infants and children may be biologically protected from stress effects in this one way (immaturity of locus coeruleus function), even though they are more vulnerable in other ways.

Because of the intimate feedback mechanisms between the LHPA axis and the gonads (and because the adrenal cortex also produces some sex hormones), stress can also affect levels of steroid sex hormones. For example, Mason, Giller, & Ostroff (1984) and Rose (1984) report testosterone fluctuations with stress. Further, stress during pregnancy in rats can interfere with normal androgen effects in the brain of a male fetus (Fleming et al., 1986). Growth hormone, produced by the pituitary, can also be affected. In fact, no hormone can safely be presumed unaffected by stress. (See Figure 4.1, Chapter 4, for some of the hormonal pathways.)

Hormone Effects on Developing Brain

All these hormones have neurophysiological effects in the brain, and these effects vary according to stage of development. In some cases the effects result in neuroanatomical changes in neuronal or brain tissue structure. The subtle, sometimes permanent, effects of the hormones on the developing brain are just now being elucidated. The review below is summarized mainly from McEwen's (1985) superb review, based largely on animal studies.

Steroid hormones can affect brain development in three ways: through promoting or inhibiting the normal process of cell loss ("pruning"); through promoting or slowing growth of individual neurons; and through influencing the process of differentiation of neurons into different neurotransmitter types (e.g., serotonergic vs. dopaminergic vs. cholinergic). Receptors for the steroid hormones (adrenal cortical hormones such as cortisol, cortisone, and corticosterone; sex hormones such as estrogen, progestins, and androgens) are located in critical parts of the brain as well as in the pituitary gland and peripheral target organs. These are specialized high-molecular-weight cell membrane sites, which are adapted to react in contact with a steroid hormone in such a way as to excite or inhibit various neural or metabolic pathways. Although each receptor is specific for a given hormone, the receptors for each hormone are similar regardless of organ location. The exact effects of stimulating a receptor depend on the location (e.g., hippocampus vs. hypothalamus) and the age or stage of development of the organism. For example, in early development, estrogen receptors promote sexual differentiation of the brain. Paradoxically, estrogen acts by de-feminizing the brains of males. The estradiol (estrogen) available to the brain estrogen receptors comes from brain aromatization of testosterone to estradiol, which has a de-feminizing effect only at the stage of development when testosterone can enter the brain from the blood, but estrogen is bound by circulating alpha-fetoprotein. Estrogen receptors are more numerous in the left cortex of male rat fetuses and in the right cortex of females. Estrogen decreases cortical thickness, and sex differences in relative cortical thickness of the two hemispheres correlate with estrogen receptors (Diamond, 1989). Testosterone apparently continues to influence differentiation of brain anatomy into adulthood (Brown & Grober, 1983), but in a different manner from the fetal mechanism.

Evidence from animal experiments suggests that steroid hormones in some instances act by influencing production of messenger RNA and other proteins, which presumably could be incorporated into neuronal growth. Because the effect is mediated via protein synthesis, the effects of hormones in these cases are not immediately apparent, but show up in later behavior, which tends to persist beyond the exposure to the hormone (McEwen, 1985).

The glucocorticoids (such as cortisol, hydrocortisone) cause a wide range of brain development effects, from extremely deleterious to enhancing of specific pathways or systems, depending on levels, age of development, and brain region. They can block neuronal mitosis and growth, including branching. On the other hand, they facilitate adrenergic autonomic development and development of central serotonin systems. They influence the process of myelination, which is so important in brain maturation and function from birth on. They have many effects in the hippocampus, a brain area essential for memory and cognitive learning. These include: inhibiting transport of gamma-amino-butyric acid (GABA); raising hippocampal vasoactive intestinal peptide (VIP) and synapsin levels; and altering histamine and norepinephrine (noradrenalin) responses. In high doses in old rodents, adrenal glucocorticoids seem to cause hippocampal cell destruction, possibly linked to memory deterioration of old age (McEwen, 1985).

Sex steroid hormones appear to differentiate brain development of the two sexes by specific effects on the neuroanatomy of discrete areas of the brain, such as the visual cortex. They also have more general effects. Estrogens have largely trophic effects, including axon growth (only during development) and enhanced preoptic choline acetyltransferase, an enzyme necessary for production of acetylcholine, an essential neurotransmitter. Estrogens elicit development of progestin receptors and inhibit monoamine oxidase and tyrosine hydroxylase in the neurohormonally important hypothalamus. They also "influence the levels of serotonergic and muscarinic receptors in various brain regions." (McEwen, 1985, p. 24). One result of brain sexual differentiation is a sex difference in the serotonin behavioral syndrome resulting from high doses of serotonin agonists (Fischette, Biegon, & McEwen, 1984). Serotonin aberrations have been implicated in such disorders as autism and hyperactivity, which have a dramatic sex difference in prevalence. Fleming et al. (1986) found that third-trimester stress of a pregnant rat eliminated the right-cortical dominance of the male pups. At maturity these males mimicked female sexual behavior. (In Chapter 9, Hendren reviews the relationship of pubertal pituitary and gonadal hormones to adolescent adjustment and cognitive abilities.)

Neurohormonal Mediation of Psychosocial Stress Effects

Any stress, including psychosocial, that affects the level or proportion of steroid hormones in the developing brain could conceivably have an enduring effect on brain microanatomy and neurochemical function. Breier et al. (1988) found in a sample of adults who had lost a parent (mostly through death) between ages 2 and 17 that those with a subsequent poor home life and personal adaptation later had significantly more adult psychiatric disorders. Importantly, they also had significantly elevated plasma cortisol and beta-endorphin (produced from the same molecule as adrenocorticotrophic hormone, ACTH) even when not psychiatrically ill. Furthermore, adult plasma levels of cortisol and ACTH correlated significantly with scores on the retrospective scale of home life and personal adjustment immediately following loss of parent. This scale considered such things as relationship with surviving parent, stability of home life, and relationship with caretakers.

Such retrospective findings are supported by findings from a prospective study of childhood bereavement at Ohio State University by Weller, Weller, Fristad, and Bowes (1989). Studying young children without psychiatric history who lost a parent by death, they found 39% to have a positive (nonsuppressed) dexamethasone suppression test (DST), generally accepted as a neurohormonal marker of depression. The postdexamethasone cortisol levels ranged from 1.0 to 18.2, with levels above 5 considered significant; these illustrate the wide range of individual response to a similar stressor. The cortisol levels correlated with suicidal ideation at 0.67 ($p < .001$). Children with a positive DST averaged almost twice as many depression symptoms elicited in a structured interview as those with a normal DST. Such data suggest strong links among psychosocial stress, neurohormonal response, and psychopathological stress effects.

The importance of psychological stress in eliciting the adrenal response (undoubtedly mediated initially through the brain) is underscored by Corson and Corson (1985) in their critique of the debate between Selye and Mason that is described in Chapter 4 by Ryan. It appears that the *perception* of stress is as important as the stressor itself in raising adrenal cortical hormone levels, even in the case of such physical stressors as fasting and heat extremes. Many stressors, such as crowding or noise, combine in their essence physical and psychological substresses. Diamond (1989) found differences in thickness and structure of cortex between rats raised in solitary, boring, small cages and those raised in a large "enriched" cage with "toys" and other rats, space and variety closer to the natural wild setting. However, she apparently did not check for evidence that such differences might be mediated by adrenal hormones. Interestingly, male rats showed more impact of environmental impoverishment on visual (occipital) cortex while female rats showed a more generalized cortical change, including somatosensory cortex.

Another hormone, growth hormone, shows stress effects in the rare but highly informative syndrome of psychosocial dwarfism (Brown, 1976). Children from deprived, neglectful, chaotic, or sometimes abusive homes have been found whose height is about half that of the age-peer mean, with retardation of bone age but not teeth. They show low levels of not only corticosteroids and ACTH, but more importantly, growth hormone. Upon being removed from the stressful environment, they secrete more growth hormone and resume growing. Although malnutrition may be involved, it is important to note that dwarfism from simple malnutrition shows high growth hormone levels, in contrast to the low levels in psychosocial dwarfism (Beumont, 1979). Imura, Yoshima, & Ikekubo (1971) and others reported evidence that adrenergic activation may be involved in stress-induced suppression of growth hormone. Although prolactin is also necessary for growth and prolactin release is inhibited by dopamine, one of the stress-induced catecholamines, no evidence was found on cursory review that this may be a supplementary mechanism.

"Priming" Effect of Stress. Kalivas & Duffy (1989) report animal evidence that repeated stress alters the neurochemical response to subsequent stress. Prestressed rats showed a significant increase in dopamine response of prefrontal cortex and nucleus accumbus with subsequent similar stress, but a decrease in dopamine in the A10 region. They propose that repeated stress alters the mesocorticolimbic dopamine neurons by increasing axonal neurotransmission in the terminal fields and decreasing somatodendritic transmission. This alters the neurochemical brain response to subsequent stress, undoubtedly relevant to the sensitizing and immunizing psychological effects of stress discussed elsewhere in this book. Pitman (1989) even suggests that the memory of a particularly traumatic stress may act as a repeat stressor in a hormonally mediated

vicious cycle build-up of intrusive recollections. Ornitz and Pynoos (1989) report that 1 ½ years after a major stress, six children age 8 to 13 suffered significant impairment of the normal prestimulation inhibition of startle response, which usually matures by age 8. These children regressed to a 5-year-old level of startle inhibition. The authors concluded that the stressor may have induced a lasting change in brainstem function, which altered subsequent responses to such neutral stimuli as white noise bursts. Alternately, perhaps rather than inducing a brainstem change, the stressor may have "undone" a normal developmental change.

Stress and Memory. The "stress-responsive neuromodulators" (Gold, 1988) include epinephrine, norepinephrine, ACTH, ACTH fragments, and vasopressin. These affect memory mechanisms, probably in an inverted U-shaped curve such that moderate amounts enhance memory—"emblazon on the memory"—but extremes may interfere with memory. This may explain the apparently contradictory post-stress phenomena of flashbacks/intrusive recollections and amnesia (Pitman, 1989). Other stress-induced neurohormones (endorphins and oxytocin) tend mainly to interfere with memory. The implications for stress effects on learning of schoolchildren require much further study: perhaps a titration of stress in the classroom will be needed.

Biological Clocks, Light, and Technological Stress

Humans evolved as diurnal creatures in a 24-hour cycle. Neuro-hormonal activity, including body temperature and secretion of such hormones as the corticoids, catecholamines, and growth hormone, naturally ebbs and flows in synchrony with the cycle of day and night, of light and darkness. The neurophysiological cycle is maintained even when individuals are deprived of light-dark cues, leading to the inference of a biological clock embedded in the central nervous system. However, the biological cycle, if chronically deprived of day-night cues, tends to drift "out of synch."

Though the light-dark cycle is not the only "Zeitgeber" (time giver) synchronizing the biological clock, it is the most powerful (Aschoff, 1980). The modulating effect of light probably operates through the eyes and involves the pineal gland as well as the better-known neuroendocrine centers. The acrophase (daily time of peak secretion) for some hormones varies by age. For example, peak daily cortisol secretion occurs earlier with older age (Halbreich, 1987). Memory efficiency, most important for school children, varies with the arousal cycle. For learning experiences in the early morning, at low arousal, immediate recall is better but long-term memory is poorer than for material learned in the afternoon or evening, at high arousal (Monk, 1987). In fact, the response to almost any stimulus, including chemical and infectious agents, varies with the arousal phase of the daily cycle (Aschoff, 1980).

Numerous experiments have demonstrated that the biological daily cycle can be manipulated by contrived artificial lighting. "Jet lag" is believed to be the readjustment period for the biological clock to resynchronize with the environmental day-night cycle (Aschoff, 1980). At a more widespread level, in the past century electric lighting has brought the opportunity for people to inadvertently stress their own biological rhythms. It is not clear whether young children are more or less vulnerable than adults in this regard. However, it seems intuitively credible that the developmental encoding of the timing of biological rhythms could be influenced by growing up in an environment where the effective onset of darkness is delayed, with a lengthening of the light segment of the daily cycle. This would seem an interesting area for further research.

Much is already known about the effect of artificial light on growth and the age of puberty. Human observations have suggested that availability of electricity is associated with earlier onset of menarche. Of course, the more rapid maturity is undoubtedly explained in part by better nutrition in electrified, industrialized cultures. Nevertheless, controlled experiments with farm animals have confirmed that supplementing daylight with artificial nocturnal light (increasing the total hours of light) promotes more rapid growth (Peters & Tucker, 1981), earlier onset of fertility, and even increased reproductive vigor (Amir et al., 1987). The light-induced growth acceleration is associated with increased food intake, possibly more efficient food utilization, higher levels of prolactin (Peters et al., 1981), and probably melatonin changes. (Prolactin is one of the essential human growth factors.) Continuous light does not induce as much growth as a 16:8 ratio of light to dark (Peters & Tucker, 1981). Interestingly, exposure of pregnant ewes to light supplementation increased the growth rate of the subsequent offspring even though the lambs themselves were not directly exposed to supplemental light (Amir, Thimonier, & Gacitua, 1987). Although rapid growth is generally considered a sign of vigor and robust good health, it is possible that such rapid change somehow stresses the body. Certainly, early puberty can be a cause of psychosocial stress, as a youngster finds himself or herself being related to or reacted to sexually before developing the emotional maturity to cope with it. (In Chapter 9, Hendren describes the special emotional risk for girls of early puberty.)

Psychoneuroimmunology

The 1980s saw an explosion of interest in psychogenic stress-induced suppression of immune function. Reviews by Kiecolt-Glaser and Glaser (1986, 1988), Kennedy, Kiecolt-Glaser, and Glaser (1988), and Gorman and Locke (1989) collected the following aggregate significant stress effects from various studies, all in the direction of impaired immune response or increased morbidity:

1. Decreased blastogenesis of lymphocytes in response to known mitogens.
2. Lower percent of helper T lymphocytes (necessary to stimulate production of immunoglobulins by lymphocytes).
3. Decreased natural killer cell activity.
4. Decreased interferon.
5. Decreased repair of DNA damage from radiation.
6. Increased titers of herpes simplex and Epstein-Barr virus (reflecting decreased cellular immunity).
7. Increased death rates.
8. Increased rates of cancer and several infectious diseases.

There are two limitations to most of the research: First, most of the studies linked only two of the three factors essential to establishing the full hypothesis: stressor (life event), immune suppression, and morbidity/mortality. Many studies seem to have firmly established associations between two of these in each combination, but few studies examined all three simultaneously (Glaser et al., 1987). The second limitation for our purposes is that little of the research was focused on children. One study that did show associations among all three (stressful event, immune impairment, and increased morbidity) was a year-long longitudinal study of medical students by Glaser et al. (1987). Around examination time they showed an increase of infectious illness as well as impairments on four measures of immune function. During summer vacation immune function recovered to normal except in those with high scores on a loneliness scale.

Animal studies suggest that early experiences (prenatal or postnatal) can increase or suppress various immune functions, but the results are ambiguous. For example, brief separation of infant primates from their mothers induce suppression of mitogen-induced T cell function, reversible on reunion but appearing again in adulthood, while those chronically isolated after birth show increased mitogen responses as adults. Prematurely weaned rat pups develop more infections and cancer, with decreased mitogen response, but obviously the physical deprivation of something in the mother's milk may be of greater importance than the stress (Gorman & Locke, 1989).

The immunological effects of stress are undoubtedly related in some way to the endocrine effects and/or autonomic arousal (Locke & Gorman, 1988). Autonomic fibers innervate such immunological organs as thymus, spleen, lymph nodes, and bone marrow. Immunological tissues and cells have receptors for such neurotransmitters as acetylcholine, histamine, and the catecholamines, and for such hormones as adrenocorticotrophic hormone (ACTH), growth hormone, somatostatin, testosterone, insulin, triiodothyronine, glucagon, and corticosteroids. Corticosteroids are known inhibitors of immune function and are elevated in the late stages of stress response as well as in major psychiatric depression. Kiecolt-Glaser et al. (1984) found in psychiatric inpatients significant associations between loneliness scores, distress levels on the Minnesota Multiphasic Personality Inventory, urinary cortisol levels, and two measures of immune suppression (natural killer cell activity and T-lymphocyte response to phytohemagglutinin). Su, London, & Jaffe (1988) reported evidence that progesterone and other steroid hormones bind to sigma receptors in brain and lymphoid tissue. They suggested that the same receptor, when activated, might affect immune function, cause psychosis, and alter mood, depending on location.

Another hypothesis concerns endogenous opioids, such as β-endorphin, which metabolically originate from the same long polypeptide as ACTH and some other hormones. Since opiate addicts are known to have suppressed immune function, since opiates injected into the periaqueductal gray area (PAG) of the rat mesencephalon suppress natural killer cell activity, and since electric stimulation of rat PAG promotes cancer, it is possible that endogenous opioids, released under stress as natural painkillers, may as a side effect suppress immune function (Fackelmann, 1989). Sandman et al. (1990) have also proposed that β-endorphin elicited by maternal stress may aggravate hypoxic fetal brain damage.

Interactions with Brain Development. Geschwind and his associates (e.g., Behan & Geschwind, 1985; Geschwind & Galaburda, 1985) suggest an important possible prenatal influence of immunity and hormones on brain development. They reviewed numerous data linking left-handedness, male sex, maternal rho antibodies, and such disorders as dyslexia, autism, and language disorders, and examined post-mortem brains of dyslexics. In the latter they found perisylvian ectopia (islands of cortical cells out of proper place, presumably because of disrupted fetal migration), dysplasia (pockets of abnormal small cells disrupting the cortical layers), and micropolygyria (numerous abnormally small folds of cortex), all more marked on the left, near language areas. The "Geschwind hypothesis" is that the later-developing left cerebral hemisphere may have its cortical cell migration disrupted by excess testosterone or maternal auto-antibodies, with effects on the wiring of both hemispheres. Fride and Weinstock (1987) found in rats that random maternal stress (noise and light) throughout gestation reversed the pups' normal cerebral and behavioral lateralization, significantly increased the interhemispheric coupling of dopamine (one of the adrenergic catechol-amines), and reduced the pups' later ability to cope with anxiety as adults.

Relationship to Biological Clock.   Animal experiments have demon-strated that resistance to infection varies with the phase of the daily neurophysiological cycle, being greatest in the middle of the activity phase, at a time of high arousal and temperature (Aschoff, 1980). This poses a seeming paradox because of the similarities between stress re-sponse and the arousal phase of the daily cycle. In many ways, the neuroendocrine stress response seems an exaggeration of the daily arousal phase, yet the former seems to impair immune function and the latter seems to promote it. The explanation may be a curvilinear relation-ship (inverted U) between arousal and immune competence, with too little or too much arousal lowering immune response. If so, this may be another argument for a little stress sometimes being good—at least enough stress to keep a person awake and alert at appropriate times!

Nutrition, Stress, and Brain Development

In addition to making an individual more vulnerable to other stresses, malnutrition itself is a potentially important stressor for many children, especially in the third world. Severe protein/caloric deficiency (kwashiorkor) has been known since the 1960s to be associated with apathy and depressed mental performance persisting on follow-up stud-ies (Susser, 1987). In laboratory animals, both general undernutrition (Juorio, 1987) and thiamine (B1) deficiency (Butterworth, 1987) signifi-cantly reduce brain levels of serotonin, an essential neurotransmitter manufactured in the brain from dietary tryptophan, an essential amino acid. More recent human studies have not been able to demonstrate unequivocally a direct effect of malnutrition itself on "mental compe-tence" (IQ and related measures) separate from the socioeconomic/cultural deprivation that usually accompanies it (Susser, 1987). Review of relevant human studies by Stein and Susser (1987) resulted in these conclusions:

1. Specific dietary deficiencies seem to underlie many forms of men-tal impairment, but seem most related to the preconceptional and embryonic phases.
2. Otherwise, malnutrition (acute or chronic) before late infancy has not been proven to be an enduring cause of mental impairment.
3. However, combining chronic malnutrition with social deprivation

does result in depressed cognitive performance. How much the effects persist into adulthood is not known.

Rosso (1987), also reviewing the literature, arrived at a more pessimistic conclusion for gestational malnutrition. He cited evidence that maternal undernutrition during the last half of gestation decreases the full-term birth weight and coupled this with numerous studies linking lower full-term birth weight with such sequelae as lower intelligence, learning problems, and impairment of coordination and fine motor ability. However, it is not unequivocally clear that lower birth weight solely from undernutrition, independent of other insults and socioeconomic status, causes the same problem. For "significant" deficits in later life, it appears that growth retardation must begin before gestational week 26 (Harvey, Prince, Bunton, Parkinson, & Campbell, 1982).

For milder deleterious effects, the causal link with malnutrition seems better established. For example, Galler and Ramsey (1989), controlling for socioeconomic and home environment factors, found a significant association between attention deficit at age 9–15 and a history of moderate to severe protein-energy malnutrition in the first year of life.

The popular conception that better or altered nutrition is required under stress receives a bit of scientific support, especially for biological stressors. For example, people with marginal thiamine (B1) deficiency may function adequately for long periods but then acutely develop clinical signs and symptoms of beriberi during the course of certain infectious diseases, notably gastroenteritis (Butterworth, 1987). It is common clinical knowledge that massive wound healing requires extra ascorbate (vitamin C) and protein and that certain metabolically stressful drugs require additional amounts of specific B vitamins to prevent or ameliorate side effects. Lehnert et al. (1984) reported that supplemental tyrosine (an amino acid dietary precursor of the adrenergic catecholamines utilized under stress) could prevent stress-induced behavioral depression and brain biochemical change. Ordinarily, rats subjected to acute, uncontrollable stress suffer depletion of brain norepinephrine (one of the catecholamines) in the locus coeruleus, hypothalamus, and hippocampus, and show decreased open-field spontaneous activity, exploratory hole-poking, and rearing up on hind legs (compared to controls). Rats eating diets supplemented with additional tyrosine (a normal constituent of dietary protein) resembled unstressed controls behaviorally and did not show norepinephrine depletion. Further research is needed to determine how (and if) such findings should be applied to children's diets. Meanwhile, these suggestive studies add one more reason for ensuring that all children receive a calorically sufficient diet with generous proportions of protein and the recommended daily allowances of vitamins and minerals.

CONCLUSION

Lauretta Bender, a child psychiatrist who developed the widely used Bender gestalt test for visual-motor function, once remarked in a lecture that "we are all a little bit brain damaged." By this she meant that the developing brain is so vulnerable to insult and so precariously programmed that few survive the developmental years unscathed by some biological or psychosocial stress. Fortunately, the potential of most brains is such that 90% attainment of our true potential is sufficient to let some of us muddle through professional or other schools and write chapters like this. Civilization was built mainly by brains that had not realized their full potential. Think what could be accomplished if we could increase the average realization of brain potential by 5%! Such a possibility is coming more within our reach with what we are now learning about stress effects on the developing brain.

REFERENCES

Alpert, J. J., Day, N., Dooling, E., Hingson, R., Oppenheimer, E., Rosett, H. L., Weiner, L., & Zukerman, B. (1981). Maternal alcohol consumption and newborn assessment: Methodology of the Boston City Hospital prospective study. *Neurobehavioral Toxicology and Teratology, 3*, 187–194.

Altman, J. (1969). Autoradiographic and histological studies of postnatal neurogenesis: III. Dating the time of production and onset of differentiation of cerebellar microneurons in rats. *Journal of Comparative Neurology, 136*, 269–294.

Altman, J. (1972a). Postnatal development of the cerebellar cortex in the rat: I. The external germinal layer and the transitional molecular layer. *Journal of Comparative Neurology, 145*, 353–398.

Altman, J. (1972b). Postnatal development of the cerebellar cortex in the rat: II. Phases in the maturation of purkinje cells and of the molecular layer. *Journal of Comparative Neurology, 145*, 399–464.

Altman, J. (1972c). Postnatal development of the cerebellar cortex in the rat: III. Maturation of the components of the granular layer. *Journal of Comparative Neurology, 145*, 465–514.

American Academy of Pediatrics. (1984). Ethanol in liquid preparations intended for children. *Pediatrics, 73*(3), 405–407.

Amir, D., Thimonier, J., & Gacitua, H. (1987). The effect of a light pulse and melatonin, alone or in combination, on the reproductive performance of Finn-cross ewes in spring in Israel. *Journal of Agricultural Science, 109*, 273–279.

Andersson, K. (1982). Pharmacological inhibition of uterine activity. *Acta Obstetrica Gynecologica Scandinavica (Suppl.), 108*, 17–23.

Aschoff, J. (1980). The circadian system in man. In D. T. Krieger & J. C. Hughes (Eds.), *Neuroendocrinology*. New York: H. P. Publishing Co.

Behan, P. O., & Geschwind, N. (1985). Hemispheric laterality and immunity. In R. Guilleman et al. (Eds.), *Mental modulation of immunity.* New York: Raven Press.

Berntson, G. G., & Torello, M. W. (1982). Paleocerebellum in the integration of behavioral function. *Physiological Psychology, 10,* 2–12.

Beumont, P. J. V. (1979). The endocrinology of psychiatry. In K. Granville-Grossman (Ed.), *Recent advances in clinical psychiatry* (3rd ed., pp. 185–224). New York: Churchill-Livingston.

Breier, A., Kelsoe, J. R., Kirwin, P. D., et al. (1988, November). Early parental loss and development of adult psychopathology. *Archives of General Psychiatry, 45,* 987–993.

Brown, G. M. (1976). Endocrine aspects of psychosocial dwarfism. In E. J. Sachar (Ed.), *Hormones, behavior, and psychopathology.* New York: Raven Press.

Brown, J. W., & Grober, E. (1983). Age, sex and aphasia type: Evidence for a regional cerebral growth process underlying lateralization. *Journal of Nervous and Mental Disorders, 171,* 431–434.

Burns, E. M., Kruckeberg, T. W., Kanak, M. F., & Stibler, H. (1986). Ethanol exposure during brain ontogeny: Some long-term effects. *Neurobehavioral Toxicology and Teratology, 8,* 383–389.

Burns, E. M., Kruckeberg, T. W., Stibler, H., Cerven, E., & Borg, S. (1984). Ethanol exposure during brain growth spurt. *Teratology, 9,* 251–258.

Burry, R. W., Kniss, D. A., & Scribner, L. R. (1984). Mechanisms of synapse formation and maturation. In D. R. Jones (Ed.), *Current topics in research on synapses* (Vol. 1, pp. 1–51). New York: Alan R. Liss.

Butterworth, R. F. (1987). Thiamine malnutrition and brain development. In D. K. Rassin, B. Haber, & B. Drujan (Eds.), *Current topics in nutrition and disease* (Vol. 16). New York: Alan R. Liss.

Cannon, W. B. (1939). *The wisdom of the body* (2nd ed.). New York: W. W. Norton.

Caritis, S. N., Carson, D., Greebon, D., McCormick, M., Edelstone, D. I., & Mueller-Heuback, E. (1982). A comparison of terbutaline and ethanol in treatment of preterm labor. *American Journal of Obstetrics and Gynecology, 142,* 183–190.

Charney, D. S., Woods, S. W., Krystal, J. H., & Heninger, G. R. (1989, May). Panic disorder strongly linked to neuronal dysfunction. *The Psychiatric Times, VI*(5), 1–43.

Chin, J. H., Parsons, L. M., & Goldstein, D. B. (1978). Increased cholesterol content of erythrocyte and brain membranes in ethanol-tolerant mice. *Biochemica Biophysica Acta, 513,* 358–363.

Clarren, S. K., Alvord, E. C., Sumi, S. M., Streissguth, A. P., & Smith, D. W. (1978). Brain malformations related to prenatal exposure to ethanol. *Journal of Pediatrics, 92,* 64–67.

Clarren, S. K., & Smith, D. W. (1978). The fetal alcohol syndrome. *The New England Journal of Medicine, 298*(19), 1063–1067.

Cook, L. N., Shott, R. J., & Andrews, B. F. (1975). Acute transplacental ethanol intoxication. *American Journal of Disease of Children, 129,* 1075–1076.

Corson, S. A., & Corson, E. O. (1980). Biopsychogenic stress. In H. Selye (Ed.), *Selye's guide to stress research*, Vol 2. New York: Van Nostrand Reinhold.

Crews, F. T., Majchrowicz, E., & Meeks, R. (1983). Changes in cortical synaptosomal plasma membrane fluidity and composition in ethanol-dependent rats. *Psychopharmacology, 81,* 208–213.

Culley, W. J., & Lineberger, R. O. (1968). Effect of undernutrition on the size and composition of the rat brain. *Journal of Nutrition, 96,* 375–381.

Diamond, M. C. (1989). Sex and the cerebral cortex. *Biological Psychiatry, 25,* 823–825.

Dilsaver, S. C. (1988). Effects of stress on muscarinic mechanisms. *Neuroscience & Biobehavioral Reviews, 12*(1), 23–28.

Dobbing, J. (1971). Undernutrition and the developing brain. In R. Paoletti & A. N. Davison (Eds.), *Chemistry and brain development: Advances in experimental medicine and biology* (Vol. 13, pp. 399–412). New York: Plenum.

Dobbing, J. (1974). The later growth of the brain and its vulnerability. *Pediatrics, 53,* 2–6.

Dobbing, J., & Sands, J. (1971). Vulnerability of developing brain. *Biology of the Neonate, 19,* 363–378.

Dobbing, J., & Sands, J. (1979). Comparative aspects of the brain growth spurt. *Early Human Development, 3,* 79–83.

Dobbing, J., & Smart, J. L. (1973). Early undernutrition, brain development and behavior. In S. A. Barnett (Ed.), *Ethology and development. Clinics in developmental medicine* (No. 47, pp. 16–36). Philadelphia: Lippincott.

Dow, K. E., & Riopelle, R. J. (1985). Ethanol neurotoxicity: Effects on neurite formation and neurotrophic factor production in vitro. *Science, 28,* 591–593.

Eayrs, J. T. (1954). The vascularity of the cerebral cortex in normal and cretinous rats. *Journal of Anatomy, 88,* 164–173.

Eayrs, J. T. (1971). Thyroid and the developing brain: Anatomical and behavioral effects. In M. Hamburgh & E. J. W. Barrington (Eds.), *Hormones in development* (pp. 345–355). New York: Appleton-Century-Crofts Educational Division, Meredith Co.

Eayrs, J. T., & Goodhead, B. (1959). Postnatal development of the cerebral cortex in the rat. *Anatomy, 93,* 385–402.

Edelman, G. M. (1976). Surface modulation in cell recognition and cell growth. Some new hypotheses on phenotypic alteration and transmembranous control of cell surface receptors. *Science, 192,* 218–226.

Eskanazi, B. (1984). Neural behavioral teratology. In M.B. Bracken (Ed.), *Perinatal epidemiology.* New York: Oxford Press.

Fackelmann, K. A. (1989). Brain and immunity: Mapping the link. *Science News, 136*(3), 36.

Fischette, C. T., Biegon, A., & McEwen, B. S. (1984). Sex steroid modulation of the serotonin behavioral syndrome. *Life Sciences, 35,* 1197–1206.

Fleming, D. E., Anderson, R. H., Rhees, R. W., Kinghorn, E., & Bakaitis, J. (1986).

Effects of prenatal stress on sexually dimorphic asymmetries in the cerebral cortex of the male rat. *Brain Research Bulletin, 16,* 395–398.

Fox, H. E., Steinbrecher, M., Pressel, D., Inglis, J., Medvid, L., & Angel, E. (1978). Maternal ethanol ingestion and the occurrence of human fetal breathing movements. *American Journal of Obstetrics and Gynecology, 132,* 354–358.

Fride, E., & Weinstock, M. (1987). Increased interhemispheric coupling of the dopamine systems induced by prenatal stress. *Brain Research Bulletin, 18*(3), 457–461.

Fuchs, A.-R., & Fuchs, F. (1981). Ethanol for prevention of preterm birth. *Seminars in Perinatology, 5,* 236–251.

Galler, J. R., & Ramsey, F. (1989). A follow-up study of the influence of early malnutrition on development: Behavior at home and at school. *Journal of American Academy of Child and Adolescent Psychiatry, 28*(2), 254–261.

Geschwind, N., & Galaburda, A. M. (1985). Cerebral lateralization: Biological mechanisms, associations, and pathology: A hypothesis and a program for research. *Archives of Neurology, 42,* 428–459.

Glaser, R., Rice, J., Sheridan, J., et al. (1987). Stress related immune suppression: Health implications. *Brain, Behavior & Immunity, 1,* 7–20.

Gold, P. W. (1988). Stress-responsive neuromodulators. *Biological Psychiatry, 24,* 371–374.

Gorman, J. R., & Locke, S. E. (1989). Neural, endocrine and immune interactions. In H. I. Kaplan & B. J. Sadock (Eds.), *Comprehensive textbook of psychiatry* (Vol. 5). Baltimore: William & Wilkins.

Halbreich, U. (1987). The circadian rhythm of cortisol and MHPG in depressives and normals. In A. Halaris (Ed.), *Chronobiology and psychiatric disorders.* New York: Elsevier.

Hamburgh, M. (1969). The role of thyroid and growth hormones in neurogenesis. *Current Topics in Developmental Biology, 4,* 109–148.

Hanson, J. W., Streissguth, A. P., & Smith, D. W. (1978). The effects of moderate alcohol consumption during pregnancy on fetal growth and morphogenesis. *Journal of Pediatrics, 92,* 457.

Harvey, D., Prince, J., Bunton, J., Parkinson, C., & Campbell, S. (1982). Abilities of children who were small-for-gestational-age babies. *Pediatrics, 69*(3), 296–300.

Hunt, W. A. (1985). *Alcohol and biological membranes.* New York: The Guilford Press.

Imura, H., Yoshima, T., & Ikekubo, K. (1971). Growth hormone secretion in a patient with deprivation dwarfism. *Endocrinologica Japanica, 18,* 301–304.

Ito, M. (1984). Purkinje cells: Morphology and development. In *The cerebellum and neural control* (pp. 21–39). New York: Raven Press.

Jones, K. L., & Smith, D. W. (1973). Recognition of the fetal alcohol syndrome in early infancy. *Lancet, 2,* 999–1001.

Jones, K. L., Smith, D. W., Streissguth, A. P., & Myrianthopoulos, N. C. (1974). Outcome in offspring of chronic alcoholic women. *Lancet, 1,* 2076–2078.

Juorio, A. V. (1987). Interactions Between Nutritional States and Some Brain

Biogenic Amines. In D. K. Rassin, B. Haber, & B. Drujan (Eds.), *Current topics in nutrition and disease* (Vol. 16). New York: Alan R. Liss.

Kalivas, P. W., & Duffy, P. (1989). Similar effects of daily cocaine and stress on mesocorticolimbic dopamine neurotransmission in the rat. *Biological Psychiatry, 25,* 913–928.

Kennedy, S., Kiecolt-Glaser, J. K., & Glaser, R. (1988). Immunological consequences of acute and chronic stressors: Mediating role of interpersonal relationships. *British Journal of Medical Psychology, 61,* 77–85.

Kerfoot, K. M., Kruckeberg, T. W., & Burns, E. M. (1985). Maternal ethanol consumption and levels of ethanol in breast milk. *Abstracts of Papers presented at the 34th International Congress on Alcoholism and Drug Dependence,* Calgary, Alberta, Canada, August 4–10, 1985 (p. 124).

Kesaniemi, Y. A. (1974). Ethanol and acetaldehyde in the milk and peripheral blood of lactating women after ethanol consumption. *Journal of Obstetrics and Gynecology, 81,* 84–86.

Kiecolt-Glaser, J., & Glaser, R. (1986). Psychological influences on immunity. *Psychosomatics, 27*(9), 621–624.

Kiecolt-Glaser, J., & Glaser, R. (1988). Major life changes, chronic stress and immunity. In T. P. Bridge et al. (Eds.), *Psychological, neuropsychiatric, and substance abuse aspects of AIDS.* New York: Raven Press.

Kiecolt-Glaser, J. K., Ricker, D., George, J., Messick, G., Speicher, C. E., Garner, W., & Glaser, R. (1984). Urinary cortisol levels, cellular immunocompetency, and loneliness in psychiatric inpatients. *Psychosomatic Medicine, 46*(1), 15–23.

Kruckeberg, T. W., Gaetano, P. K., Burns, E. M., Cerven, E., & Borg, S. (1984). Ethanol in preweanling rats with dams: Body temperature unaffected. *Neurobehavioral Toxicology and Teratology, 6,* 307–312.

Landesman-Dwyer, S. (1981). The relationship of children's behavior to maternal alcohol consumption. In A. L. Abel (Ed.), *Fetal alcohol syndrome* (Vol. II, pp. 127–148). Boca Raton, FL: CRC Press.

Landesman-Dwyer, S., & Ragozin, A. S. (1981). Behavioral correlates of prenatal alcohol exposure: A four-year follow-up study. *Neurobehavioral Toxicology and Teratology, 3,* 187–194.

Legrand, C., Clos, J., & Legrand, J. (1982). Influence of altered thyroid and nutritional states on early histogenesis of the rat cerebellar cortex with special reference to synaptogenesis. *Reproduction, Nutrition, Development, 22,* 201–208.

Lehnert, H., Reinstein, D. K., Strowbridge, B. W., et al. (1984). Neurochemical and behavioral consequences of acute, uncontrollable stress: Effects of dietary tyrosine. *Brain Research, 303,* 215–223.

Lemire, R. J., Loeser, J. D., Leech, R. W., & Alvord, E. C., Jr. (1975). *Normal and abnormal development of the human nervous system.* Hagerstown, MD: Harper & Row.

Lewis, P. J., & Boylan, P. (1979). Alcohol and fetal breathing. *Lancet, 1,* 388.

Mason, J. W., Giller, E. L., & Ostroff, R. B. (1984). Relationships between psychological mechanisms and the pituitary-gonadal system. *Current Clinical Practice Series, 26,* 215–228.

McEwen, B. S. (1985). Steroids and brain function. *TIPS, 6,* 22–25.

McLeod, W., Brien, J., Carmichael, L., Probert, C., Steenaart, N., & Patrick, J. (1984). Maternal glucose injections do not alter the suppression of fetal breathing following maternal ethanol ingestion. *American Journal of Obstetrics and Gynecology, 148,* 634–639.

McLeod, W., Brien, J., Loomis, C., Carmichael, L., Probert, C., & Patrick, J. (1983). Effect of maternal ethanol ingestion on fetal breathing movements, gross body movements, and heart rate at 37–40 weeks gestation. *American Journal of Obstetrics and Gynecology, 145,* 251–257.

Merritt, T. A., & Valdes-Dapena, M. (1984). Sudden infant death research update. *Pediatric Annals, 13*(3), 193–207.

Michaelis, M. L., Michaelis, E. K., & Tehan, T. (1983). Alcohol effects on synaptic membrane calcium ion fluxes. *Pharmacology, Biochemistry, and Behavior, 18* (Suppl. 1), 19–23.

Mills, J. L., Graubard, B. I., Harley, E. E., Rhoads, G. G., & Berendes, H. W. (1984). Maternal alcohol consumption and birth weight: How much drinking during pregnancy is safe? *Journal of the American Medical Association, 252,* 1875–1879.

Monk, T. H. (1987). Circadian rhythms in human performance and subjective activation. In A. Halaris (Ed.), *Chronobiology and psychiatric disorders.* New York: Elsevier.

Moore, K. L. (1977). *The developing human: Clinically oriented embryology.* (2nd ed., pp. 33–95; 319–358). Philadelphia: W.A. Saunders Company.

Ornitz, E. M., & Pynoos, R. S. (1989). Startle modulation in children with post-traumatic stress disorder. *American Journal of Psychiatry, 146,* 866–870.

Peden, V. H., Sammon, T. J., & Downey, D. A. (1973). Intravenously induced infantile intoxication with ethanol. *Fetal and Neonatal Medicine, 83*(3), 490–493.

Peters, R. R., Chapin, L. T., Emery, R. S., & Tucker, H. A. (1981). Milk yield, feed intake, prolactin, growth hormone, and glucocorticoid response of cows to supplemental light. *Journal of Dairy Science, 64,* 1671–1678.

Peters, R. R., & Tucker, H. A. (1981). Light your way to better production. *Dairy Herd Management, 18,* 56–70.

Pitman, R. K. (1989). Post-traumatic stress disorder, hormones, and memory. *Biological Psychiatry, 26,* 221–223.

Rose, R. M. (1984). Overview of endocrinology of stress. In G. Brown (Ed.), *Neuroendocrinology and psychiatric disorder* (pp. 95–122). New York: Raven Press.

Rosso, P. (1987). Maternal nutrition and fetal growth: Implications for subsequent mental competence. In D. K. Rassin, B. Haber, B. Drujan (Eds.), *Current topics in nutrition and disease* (Vol. 16). New York: Alan R. Liss.

Sandman, C. A., Barron, J. L., Demet, E. M., Chicz-Demet, A., Rothenberg, S. J., & Zea, F. J. (1990). Opioid peptides and perinatal development: Is beta-endorphin a natural teratogen? In G. F. Koob, C. A. Sandman, & F. L. Strand (Eds.), A decade of neuropeptides: Past, present, and future. *Annals of the New York Academy of Sciences, 579,* 91–108.

Sands, J., & Dobbing, J. (1981). Nutritional growth restriction and catch-up failure. In M. Monset-Couchard & A. Minkowski (Eds.), *Physiological and biochemical basis for perinatal medicine* (pp. 245–259). New York: S. Karger.

Selye, H. (1936). A syndrome produced by diverse nocuous agents. *Nature, 138,* 132.

Selye, H. (1956). *The stress of life.* New York: McGraw-Hill.

Shaywitz, B. A., Griffieth, G. G., & Warshaw, J. B. (1979). Hyperactivity and cognitive deficits in developing rat pups born to alcoholic mothers: An experimental model of EFAS. *Neurobehavioral Toxicology and Teratology, 1*(2), 113–122.

Sisenwein, F. E., Tejani, N. A., Boxer, H. S., & Digiuseppo, R. (1983). Effects of maternal ethanol infusion during pregnancy on the growth and development of children of four to seven years of age. *American Journal of Obstetrics and Gynecology, 147,* 52.

Souney, P. F., Kaul, A. F., & Osathanondh, R. (1983). Pharmacology of preterm labor. *Clinical Pharmacology, 2,* 29–44.

Stein, Z., & Susser, M. (1987). Early nutrition, fetal growth, and mental function: Observations in our species. In D. K. Rassin, B. Haber, & B. Drujan (Eds.), *Current topics in nutrition and disease* (Vol. 16). New York: Alan R. Liss.

Stibler, H., Burns, E. M., Kruckeberg, T. W., Cerven, E., & Borg, S. (1985). Changes of synaptosomal surface carbohydrates after ethanol exposure during synaptogenesis. In H. Parvez, E. Burns, Y. Burov, & S. Parvez (Eds.), *Progress in alcohol research* (pp. 37–49). Utrecht, Holland: VNU Science Press.

Stibler, H., Burns, E., Kruckeberg, T. W., Gaetano, P., Cerven, E., Borg, S., & Tabakoff, B. (1983). Effect of ethanol on synaptosomal sialic acid metabolism in the developing rat brain. *Journal of the Neurological Sciences, 59,* 21–35.

Su, T. P., London, E. D., & Jaffe, J. H. (1988, April 8). Steroid binding at σ receptors suggests link between endocrine, nervous, and immune systems. *Science, 240,* 219–221.

Susser, M. (1987). Perspective: The development of studies of nutrition, the brain, and mental performance. In D. K. Rassin, B. Haber, & B. Drujan (Eds.), *Current topics in nutrition and disease* (Vol. 16). New York: Alan R. Liss.

Tabakoff, B., Noble, E. P., & Warren, K. R. (1979). Alcohol, nutrition, and the brain. In R. J. Wurtman & J. J. Wurtman (Eds.), *Nutrition and the brain* (Vol. 4, pp. 159–213). New York: Raven Press.

Timiras, P. S., Vernadakis, A., & Sherwood, N. M. (1968). Development and plasticity of the nervous system. In. N. S. Assali (Ed.), *Biology of gestation* (pp. 261–319). New York: Academic Press.

Vernadakis, A., & Woodbury, D. M. (1969). The developing animal as a model. *Epilepsia, 10,* 163–178.

Walsh, R. R. (1986). [Functional sites of cardiac acceleration in hypothyroid neonatal rats]. Unpublished raw data.

Warren, K. R. (1977). *Critical review of the fetal alcohol syndrome.* National Institute of Alcohol Abuse and Alcoholism. Available through the National Clearinghouse for Alcohol Information. P.O. Box 2345, Rockville, MD, 20852.

Weiner, N. (1980). Norepinephrine, epinephrine, and the sympathomimetic amines. In A. G. Gilman, L. S. Goodman, & A. Gilman (Eds.), *The Pharmacological basis of therapeutics* (6th ed, pp. 138–175). New York: Macmillan.

Weller, E. B., Weller, R. A., Fristad, M. A., & Bowes, J. M. (1989). Personal communication.

Weston, R., Ivins, B., Zuckerman, B., Jones, C., & Lopez, R. (1989, June). Drug exposed babies: Research and clinical issues. *Bulletin of National Center for Clinical Infant Programs, 9*(5), 1–7.

Wiener, S. G., Shoemaker, W. J., Koda, L. Y., & Bloom, F. E. (1981). Interaction of ethanol and nutrition during gestation: Influence on maternal and offspring development in the rat. *Journal of Pharmacological and Experimental Therapeutics, 216,* 572–579.

CHAPTER FOUR

Children's Psychosomatic Responses to Stress

Nancy M. Ryan-Wenger

The ways that children respond to stress may either promote growth and a sense of efficacy (Mechanic, 1983) or cause behavioral, social, academic, or psychosomatic problems (Garmezy & Rutter, 1983). This chapter focuses on children's primary and secondary psychosomatic responses to stress (Minuchin, Rosman, & Baker, 1978). Primary psychosomatic symptoms occur when symptoms of a pre-existing physiologic disorder such as diabetes or asthma are aggravated during a stress response. Secondary psychosomatic symptoms are the result of somatization of emotional responses to stress with no obvious predisposing condition, as in recurrent abdominal pain or headaches. Treatment and prevention of secondary psychosomatic symptoms are of special concern because exaggerated and prolonged somatic responses to stress may eventually cause structural changes and tissue damage (Eaton, Peterson, & Davis, 1981; Henker, 1984; Wolf & Goodell, 1979).

Most of what is known about stress, coping, and morbidity is based on empirical studies and theories developed by and for adults. The validity of applying this knowledge to the explanation, treatment, and prevention of symptoms in children has been assumed, but not formally tested (Ryan, 1988). This chapter will examine the theoretical and empirical evidence regarding the scope of psychosomatic symptoms in children, proposed biophysiological mechanisms for the development of symptoms, risk factors and causes of psychosomatic symptoms, and prevention or treatment of symptoms.

PREVALENCE OF PSYCHOSOMATIC SYMPTOMS IN CHILDREN

Actual prevalence rates of primary psychosomatic symptoms in children are unknown, and the role of stress in the etiology of chronic illness is controversial. However, most experts agree that the potential for stress-related aggravation of symptoms exists for all children with such chronic conditions as diabetes mellitus (Jacobson & Leibovich, 1984); juvenile rheumatoid arthritis (Singsen, Johnson, & Bernstein, 1979); migraine (Barlow, 1984); asthma (Fritz, 1983; Jones, 1976); and dermatitis (Teshima et al., 1982).

Based on several studies and clinical observations, an estimated 10% of children in the general population experience secondary psychosomatic symptoms. This percentage is most likely underestimated, since children normally must depend upon their parents to seek medical treatment, with the result that many children with symptoms are not identified (Schor, 1986).

A longitudinal examination of services used by 47,145 children in a prepaid health maintenance organization (HMO) showed that psychosomatic symptoms accounted for 17.3% of the diagnoses for all children up to age 11 (Starfield et al., 1980). This sample was primarily white middle class and therefore not representative of all children, but there is no reason to suspect fewer psychosomatic diagnoses among other social classes. In a cross-sectional study of an HMO population of 1521 children, Schor (1986) found that of all diagnoses, the number of psychosomatic diagnoses peaked at age 7 (7.2%) for boys and at ages 6 (6.2%) and 16 (6.2%) for girls. These studies indicate the frequency of diagnoses, not the percentage of children. There is some evidence that morbidity occurs in clusters. In a study of a school-based clinic in which self-initiated care was encouraged, a small number of the same children repeatedly seeking treatment for a variety of symptoms accounted for most of the visits (Lewis et al., 1977). In a secondary analysis of data from the Starfield et al. (1980) longitudinal study, about 20% of the children had at least eight different complaints during the six-year period (Starfield et al., 1984).

The most widely studied secondary psychosomatic symptom among children is recurrent abdominal pain (RAP). RAP accounted for 5.8% of all diagnoses in the Starfield et al. (1980) study. Studies of specific populations in England and the United States revealed that 3% of preschool children (Zuckerman, Stevenson, & Bailey, 1987) and 10–15% of school-age children experienced RAP (Apley & Hale, 1975; Parcel, Nader, & Meyer, 1977; Pringle, Butler, & Davie, 1966; Sharrer & Ryan-Wenger, in review), while 23.2% of an adolescent clinic population complained of RAP and/or chest pain (Greene et al., 1985).

Psychogenic headaches are believed to be uncommon among children (Barlow, 1984). Of all diagnoses in the Starfield et al. (1980) study, 7.1% were headache. A community sample of 308 preschool children indicated that 3% had recurrent headaches (Zuckerman, Stevenson, & Bailey, 1987), but a school-based study of 250 8- to 12-year-olds revealed that 17.2% complained of frequent headaches (Sharrer & Ryan-Wenger, in review). Longitudinal studies of children from all socioeconomic groups are needed. However, even a conservative estimate of 10% prevalence legitimizes the need for further study and prevention. The latter requires an understanding of the complex physiologic changes that occur during a normal stress response.

NORMAL PHYSIOLOGIC STRESS RESPONSE

A stressful psychosocial event is perceived by the sensory system. The stressor is interpreted cognitively by the brain's cortex and integrated affectively via the limbic system (Everly & Rosenfeld, 1981). If stressors are perceived as a threat or challenge, the body responds via a variety of physiological axes, some of which exhibit an immediate effect, while others are slower to develop, but longer in duration. These axes will be described in increasing order of the time required for a response (Figure 4.1).

Stressors that are perceived as threatening cause a stimulation of the posterior hypothalamus and an immediate response of the autonomic nervous system via neural pathways. Although immediate, the effects have a relatively short duration (Asterita, 1985). Stimulation of thoraco-lumbar regions of the spinal cord elicits direct autonomic effects on sympathetically innervated end-organs. Sympathetic effects on the various body systems prepare the body for action (Table 4.1). Similarly, end-organs innervated by the parasympathetic nervous system are affected by stimulation of the craniosacral regions of the spinal cord. Parasympathetic effects are often paradoxical to sympathetic effects, and tend to relax and restore body functions (Table 4.1).

An intermediate response to stress via neuroendocrine axes was first described by Cannon (1914, 1953) as the "fight or flight" response. This response involves both direct autonomic effects via neural pathways on sympathetically innervated end-organs and a neuroendocrine effect via the circulatory system. Stimulation of the adrenal medulla (Figure 4.1) releases catecholamines: 80% epinephrine and 20% norepinephrine. Catecholamine effects on end-organs (Table 4.1) are similar to direct sympathetic stimulation except that there is a 20–30 second delay of onset and the effect lasts approximately ten times longer (Usdin, Kretnansky, & Kopin, 1976).

Delayed Stress Response

Three endocrine axes (adrenocortical, somatotropic, thyroid) must rely on the circulatory system for hormonal transfer and are therefore the slowest to respond. Compared to autonomic and neuroendocrine axes, a greater intensity of stimulation is required to activate the endocrine responses, but the effects last longer. The adrenocortical hormones are mineralocorticoids, glucocorticoids, and sex hormones. The main mineralocorticoid is aldosterone, which has an antidiuretic effect. The antidiuretic effect of stress is probably potentiated by a release of vaso-pressin (ADH) from the posterior pituitary (Everly & Rosenfeld, 1981). The glucocorticoids secreted are 95% cortisol and 5% corticosterone and cortisone. Sex hormones do not appear to play a role in the stress response. Somatotropin is also called growth hormone. Thyroid hormones are thyroxine (T4) and tri-iodothyrinine (T3). The effects of the three endocrine axes on various body systems (Mason, 1968; Selye, 1976) can be seen in Table 4.2.

Selye (1956) offered the General Adaptation Syndrome (GAS), a generalized, non-specific response to stressors, as a theoretical framework to describe the role of the three endocrine axes during chronic stress. The

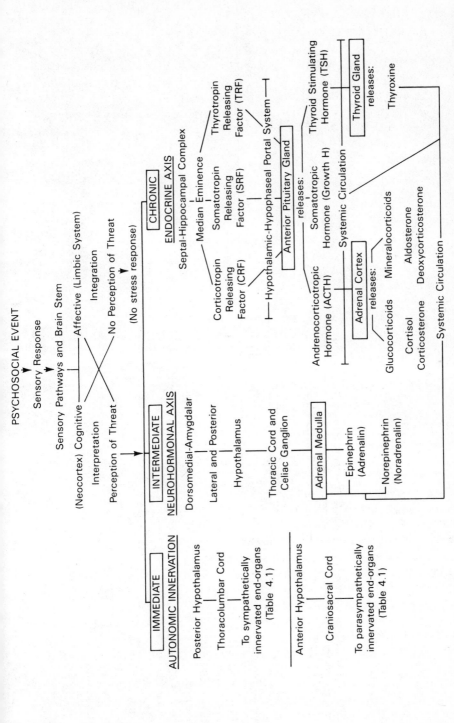

Figure 4.1. A model of potential pathways for stress reactivity to psychosocial stimuli. [Adapted from: Everly G.S., & Rosenfeld, R. (Eds.). (1981). *The nature and treatment of the stress response* (p. 31). New York: Plenum Press, Reprinted by permission.]

TABLE 4.1. *Immediate and Intermediate Effects of Stress on Body Organ Systems*

	Immediate Effects		Intermediate Effects	
	Autonomic Innervation		Neuroendocrine	
Organ System	Sympathetic	Parasympathetic	Epinephrine	Norepinephrine
Central Nervous System	Increase mental activity		Increase anxiety	
Bronchi/bronchioles	Dilate	Constrict	Dilate	Dilate (less potent)
Respiration	Increase rate	Decrease rate	Increase rate & depth	Increase (less potent)
Gastrointestinal smooth muscle	Decrease tone	Increase tone	Decrease tone	Decrease tone
Peristalsis	Decrease	Increase	Decrease	Decrease
Abdominal and stomach muscles	Relax		Relax	Relax
Pyloric sphincter	Contract	Relax	Contract	Contract
Blood cells			Decrease eosinophils and coagulation time; increase red blood cells	

Heart rate	Increase	Decrease	Increase	Increase (less potent)
Force of contraction	Increase	Decrease (atrial)	Increase	Increase (less potent)
Peripheral muscle circulation	Constrict		Constrict	Constrict
Skeletal muscle circulation	Varies with alpha or beta receptors		Dilate	Constrict (more potent)
Blood pressure (BP)			Increase systolic BP	Increase mean arterial pressure
Basal Metabolic Rate	Increase		Increase	
Liver	Increase glucose release	Slight glycogen synthesis	Increase glycogenolysis	
Pancreas			Decrease insulin secretion	Decrease insulin
Skeletal muscle	Increase glycogenolysis, Increase strength		Increase glycogenolysis	
Pupils	Dilate	Constrict	Dilate	Dilate
Sweat glands	Increase sweating		Increase sweating	Increase sweating

TABLE 4.2. *Delayed Endocrine Effects of Chronic Stress on Body Organ Systems*

| Organ System | Adrenocortical | | Somatotropic | Thyroid |
	Mineralocorticoids	Glucocorticoids	Growth Hormone	Thyroxine and Tri-iodothyrinine
Central Nervous System				Increase nervousness and anxiety
Respiration				Increase rate and depth
Stomach		Increase secretion of HCl and pepsin; decrease secretion of gastric mucus		Increase gastric juices; increase motility
Blood		Decrease eosinophils, white blood cells, lymphocytes, antibodies and fibroblast activity; increase red blood cells; increase glucose concentration; decrease inflammatory response		
Heart				Increase heart rate and force of contraction

Metabolism	Decrease protein synthesis; increase protein catabolism	Increase amino acid uptake; increase mobilization of energy resources	Increase gluconeogenesis; increase basal metabolic rate; increase protein metabolism; increase metabolism in most cells; increase intracellular enzymes
Liver	Increase gluconeogenesis; increase glycogen stores		
Pancreas	Increase secretion of trypsinogen		Decrease insulin production
Skeletal muscle	Release of amino acids from muscle; decrease glucose uptake in fat, skin and muscle; weakening effect		Energy depletion
Kidney	Increase reabsorption of sodium and excretion of potassium		
Adipose tissue	Increase fat catabolism		Increase fat metabolism; decrease cholesterol, phospholipids and triglycerides
Endocrine glands			Increase hormone secretion

alarm phase results in stimulation of the three endocrine axes, but the adrenocortical response is the most critical. The *stage of resistance* represents the body's attempt to maintain homeostasis. Here, the somatotropic axis takes priority, while adrenocortical responses decrease. If the stressor persists, energy to maintain homeostasis is depleted. All three axes are highly activated during the *stage of exhaustion*, and if they continue, may result in permanent damage to circulatory, digestive, immune, and cardiovascular systems. Psychosomatic symptom development represents the body's response to prolonged or frequent attempts to maintain homeostasis. Selye's non-specificity theory of the GAS has been disputed by Mason's studies (1971, 1975a, 1975b) which show that stimulation of the pituitary-adrenocortical system is not "non-specific," but responds differently to different stimuli.

Experts in the field of psychoneuroimmunology have further explicated the body's neurological and hormonal responses to stressors (Axelrod & Reisine, 1984; Amkraut & Solomon, 1975; Kiecolt-Glaser et al., 1985; Solomon & Amkraut, 1981). Stress related to marital disruption results in poorer immune response in both men and women who are separated/divorced compared to their married peers. The women showed increased lymphocyte production in response to two mitogen assays, lower helper T lymphocytes, and higher Epstein-Barr virus titers (Keicolt-Glaser & Glaser, 1986), while men had no significant T cell differences, but higher antibody titers to two herpes viruses (Keicolt-Glaser et al., 1988). Commonplace stressors like examinations and loneliness also caused impairment of immune function in medical students (Glaser et al., 1985; Keicolt-Glaser et al., 1984). The cathartic effect of writing about traumatic experiences as a form of psychotherapy was hypothesized to have a positive influence on immune function (Pennebaker, Keicolt-Glaser, & Glaser, 1988). In fact, compared to a control group, undergraduate students who wrote about traumatic experiences experienced fewer health center visits and better immune function. A relationship between stress-related immune suppression and AIDS is hypothesized by Glaser and his colleagues (1986, 1988). Stress is known to depress interferon production by leukocytes, as well as natural killer cell activity (Glaser et al., 1986). Studies of immune function and stress have not yet been conducted on children, but the implications can probably be extrapolated to children.

PROPOSED MECHANISMS FOR DEVELOPMENT OF SPECIFIC PSYCHOSOMATIC SYMPTOMS

It is important to distinguish causes of symptoms from mechanisms. Causes vary according to the *sources* of stress and can be psychological, social, or physical in nature. Causes activate *mechanisms,* both organic and functional, which can be explained in physiologic terms (Wolf & Goodell, 1979). One school of thought regarding development of psychosomatic symptoms is that neurohormonal responses to stress disrupt normal tissue function (Holroyd & Lazarus, 1982). For example, epinephrine causes a constriction of peripheral muscle tissue circulation, which may result in ischemic pain. Another school of thought is that adaptive efforts are faulty in kind and duration (Holmes & Masuda, 1974). A normal physiologic stress response may stimulate an irritating body process (Zegans, 1982). As an example, cortisol's effect of increasing gastric HCl secretion but decreasing gastric mucus production can aggravate an existing ulcerous condition. Many theories about the physiologic mechanisms of psychosomatic symptom development are based on the notion of homeostatic failure; that is, the symptoms are the result of normal bodily processes "gone wrong" (Wolf & Goodell, 1979).

For example, *bronchial spasms* that occur in asthmatic children as a result of emotional responses to stress can be explained by the effects of parasympathetic and sympathetic stimulation (Behrman & Vaughan, 1987; Stein, 1982). Parasympathetic stimulation causes bronchoconstriction and release of "mediators" from mast cells in the lungs. Humoral mediators such as histamine, slow-reacting substance of anaphylaxis, and prostaglandins cause bronchoconstriction, vascular permeability, and increased mucus secretion. Sympathetic stimulation causes the adrenal medulla to release epinephrine and norepinephrine, which in turn, relax bronchial muscles and inhibit mediator release. However, these sympathetic effects are not as strong as the paradoxical parasympathetic effects. Autonomic-induced metabolic activity in the liver, muscle, and bone marrow increases oxygen consumption by 20–40%, increasing ventilatory demands. The energy required for all these changes decreases cAMP levels inside the cells, which leads to contraction of the bronchial smooth muscles. Another theory is that during stress, prostaglandins are synthesized in the lungs, causing further inhibition of cAMP levels, inhibition of norepinephrine secretion, and subsequent constriction of smooth muscle in the lungs.

Hyperglycemic episodes in children with diabetes can occur during a stress response (Behrman & Vaughan, 1987; Jacobson & Leibovich, 1984). Blood glucose levels are increased when sympathetic stimulation causes production of epinephrine by the adrenal medulla. Epinephrine stimulates glycogenolysis in the liver and inhibits insulin release by already depleted beta cells in the pancreas. Glucocorticoids produced by the adrenal cortex stimulate glucose secretion and gluconeogenesis in the liver, and inhibition of glucose uptake by the peripheral tissues.

The *inflammation of joints* that occurs in juvenile rheumatoid arthritis can be aggravated by the stress response (Amkraut & Solomon, 1975). If release of epinephrine and norepinephrine is continuous or frequent, tissue cells that are already injured or sensitive will release histamine;

plasmin is produced, which leads to breakdown of serum globulin and release of bradykinin. Bradykinin causes vasodilation, which attracts white blood cells, increases capillary permeability, and stimulates pain fibers, resulting in the redness, swelling, warmth, and pain of inflammation. Further, the inflammatory response ". . . becomes self-perpetuating in the connective tissue diseases instead of limited, as in wound healing . . ." (Cassidy, 1982, p. 68).

The *nonorganic failure to thrive* syndrome observed in emotionally deprived infants whose families experience numerous psychosocial stressors is a result of malnutrition (Pollett & Leibel, 1980) and, in part, inhibition of growth hormone (GH) production (Drotar, 1985; Yoos, 1984). Prolonged emotional stress causes stimulation of the hypothalamus by the limbic system; increased production of somatostatin (GH release inhibiting factor) decreases the circulating levels of growth hormone. Also, stress stimulates the anterior pituitary to produce adrenocorticotropic hormone (ACTH), which causes increased levels of cortisol. Cortisol inhibits protein synthesis and increases amino acid release from skeletal muscle and other tissues (Bithoney & Dubowitz, 1985). Normal protein catabolism continues, leading to wasting of soft tissues, osteoporosis, and decreased production of growth hormone.

Although *abdominal pain* and *headache* are the most common secondary psychosomatic symptoms in children, little is known about the mechanisms that cause the pain. Pain may be due to prolonged tension-induced muscle contraction, which decreases circulation to the tissues, causing an increase in metabolites and pain (Everly & Rosenfeld, 1981). Once tension is released, pain tends to disappear. There is some argument that explanation of headache pain as muscle contraction is too simplistic (Martin, 1983). Abdominal pain may be due to spasm of involuntary muscle (Apley, 1975). Apley noted that autonomic reactivity that occurs during stress causes vasomotor changes as evidenced by skin pallor, and hypothesized that the blood converges in the gut, causing pain. None of the above hypotheses have been tested empirically on children.

Any psychosomatic symptom that develops as a result of stress can itself be stress-producing, and thus may perpetuate itself. An example of such a vicious cycle is shown in Figure 4.2.

RISK FACTORS THAT INFLUENCE DEVELOPMENT OF PSYCHOSOMATIC SYMPTOMS IN CHILDREN

It is generally agreed that an individual's emotional reactions to stressors must be intense, chronic, or both for psychosomatic symptoms to develop. Because not all individuals develop such symptoms, other factors

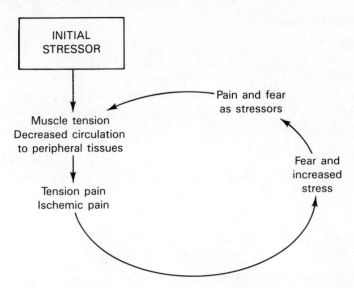

Figure 4.2. Vicious cycle of psychosomatic symptom development and perpetuation.

must place certain individuals at risk. These mediating, or risk factors, as outlined by Lachman (1972, pp. 68–70) and supported theoretically and empirically by others, are described below.

Specific Structures Involved in Physiologic Reactivity

Individuals have characteristic psychophysiologic reactivity levels which then predispose certain organs or structures to damage (Sternbach, 1966). Believed to be most at risk are body parts innervated by the sympathetic and parasympathetic nervous system (Eaton, Peterson, & Davis, 1981; Henker, 1984). An individual typically copes with specific stressors with a fight-flight response, which primarily activates catecholamines, or with a conservation-withdrawal response, which primarily activates corticoids, causing a helpless, depressed appearance (Henry, 1980; Henry & Stephens, 1977). This theory is supported by evidence that autonomic-altering and anti-anxiety drugs are effective for some patients with psychosomatic symptoms (Henker, 1984). Zegans (1982) identified particularly vulnerable regions as the hypothalamic-pituitary-endocrine axis, autonomic nervous system-adrenal medulla, immune system, reticular activating system, involuntary and striated muscle systems, and cognitive-affective integrating centers in the brain. Stress response stereotypy (Sternbach, 1966) places a strain on those organs most frequently affected during stress.

Biological Condition of the Structure

If an organ is already diseased or damaged by predisposing conditions, the normal acute stress response may cause further damage; even an occasional insult to the system may lead to permanent tissue damage (Eaton, Peterson, & Davis, 1981; Zegans, 1982). This "weak-link" theory (Sternbach, 1966) suggests that physiologic vulnerability is a key factor in the development and maintenance of psychosomatic symptoms (Minuchin et al., 1975). Children with predisposing physical conditions already have vulnerable organs, and may benefit most from interventions which serve to moderate the level of their stress responses.

Reactivity of the Structure: Threshold, Intensity, Frequency, and Duration of the Stress Response

It has been hypothesized that some structures have lower reactivity thresholds than others, making them the most likely to be affected by the stress response (Lachman, 1972). It is likely that frequent activation of the stress response with slow return to baseline causes a strain on the system and eventual structural damage (Sternbach, 1966). A further strain on the system may result when a minor stressor causes an inappropriately severe physiological response (Zegans, 1982). The combination of undischarged emotions, maintenance of a tension state, and the physiological stress response could eventually lead to structural damage (Eaton, Peterson, & Davis, 1981). Even if a severe stressor has been eliminated, an acute physiological response can become chronic if it becomes conditioned to a benign but frequently occurring stimulus similar to the original stressor (Zegans, 1982).

Studies of autonomic nervous system reactivity related to pupillary response, intestinal motility, and rectal tone were conducted about twenty years ago. Healthy children and children with RAP showed no significant differences in pupillary reactivity at rest or under the stress of a cold pressor test (Apley, Haslam, & Tulloh, 1971; Rubin, Barbero, & Sibinga, 1967). However, pupillary recovery time after stress was significantly slower among children with RAP in one study (Rubin, Barbero, & Sibinga, 1967). After injection of prostigmine, children with RAP had a heightened response and greater rectosigmoid motility than healthy children (Kopel, Kim, & Barbero, 1967). Measurement of rectal tone revealed significant abnormalities among children with RAP compared to children with other organic diseases (Kline et al., 1979). Another laboratory study compared RAP children with hospitalized and healthy children regarding autonomic, somatic, subjective, and behavioral arousal to a cold pressor test. No significant differential responses were noted across the three groups, and no recovery deficit was observed (Fuerstein et al., 1982). Inconsistent results and lack of recent research along these lines suggests that the heightened reactivity theory has been abandoned.

Corson et al.'s animal model research suggests that different patterns of renal responses to stress occur in dogs with different constitutional make-ups. When placed in an aversive environment, dogs of certain excitable breeds such as terriers and cocker spaniels exhibited signs of poor adaptation. Four components of the typical "fight or flight" response to stress were evident in these breeds: antidiuresis, hyperpnea, salivation, and tachycardia. The responses were intense, persistent, and highly fluctuating. Less excitable dogs, such as beagles and hounds, consistently showed rapid habituation and no antidiuresis (Corson & Corson, 1979). Anxiolytic drugs (meprobamate, phenobarbital, diazepam) eliminated or markedly decreased all four components of the stress response (Corson & Corson, 1968, 1973). The similarity between Type A versus Type B personalities and low versus high adaptability dog breeds was examined with respect to susceptibility to psychosomatic cardiorespiratory disorders (Corson, Corson, & Andrysco, 1982; Corson & Corson, 1987). It was found that the "dynamics of the development and extinction of cardiac and respiratory orienting responses could be used as predictors of high or low adaptability to psychologically aversive environments" (Corson, Corson, & Andrysco, 1982, p. 8). The similarity between hyperkinesis in children and the hyperexcitability in some breeds of dogs suggests that differential responses to stress of hyperkinetic versus adaptable children could be postulated.

Genetic Factors that Predispose the Structure to Harm from Psychophysiological Arousal

The prevalence of psychosomatic symptoms among members of the same family suggests either that a genetic predisposition exists, or, alternatively, that such illness behavior is learned (Apley, 1975). When fingerprints of 155 patients with psychosomatic gastrointestinal complaints were examined for congenital markers, digital arches were found in 64% of patients who had constipation and abdominal pain before age 10, compared to 10% of patients without such complaints ($p < .001$) (Gottlieb & Schuster, 1986). Solomon & Moos (1965) hypothesize that even in the presence of genetic predisposition to an autoimmune disease, the disease will develop only in individuals with significant emotional distress and failed psychological defense mechanisms. This hypothesis has been supported by recent psychoneuroimmunology studies (Solomon & Amkraut, 1981).

Developmental Level

Although developmental level was not mentioned by Lachman (1972) as a mediating factor in the development of psychosomatic symptoms, this category should be added. Because of the many physiological, cognitive, psychological, and social changes that occur from infancy through adolescence, it is possible that stress response mechanisms also change over time. Certainly sources of stress, perceptions of stress, and methods of coping change as a child develops (Maccoby, 1983; see also Chapters 5–9 of this book). There is evidence that the prevalence of specific psychosomatic symptoms differs according to the developmental level of the child. For example, infants manifest the failure to thrive syndrome, preschoolers often experience enuresis, school-agers complain of frequent abdominal pain, and anorexia nervosa occurs most often in adolescents. Garmezy (1983) suggests that children may be more vulnerable to stress during periods of destabilization, such as maturational changes, because otherwise normal stress responses may negatively affect systems that are experiencing change. The mechanisms by which developmental level influences psychosomatic symptom development are not well understood.

CAUSES OF PSYCHOSOMATIC SYMPTOM DEVELOPMENT IN CHILDREN

Psychosomatic medicine is based on the belief that electrochemical neural circuits in the brain that interpret life experiences influence all types of visceral mechanisms (Wolf & Goodell, 1979). Most of the literature on causes of psychosomatic symptoms in children is theoretical and speculative, based primarily on clinical observations. Three categories of causes will be examined: non-supportive family and social environments, stressful life events, and ineffective coping strategies. Most of the research has been done on children with recurrent abdominal pain (RAP).

Non-Supportive Family and Social Environments

Non-supportive and disruptive family and social environments have been implicated as a primary cause of psychosomatic symptom development in children. There is evidence that individuals who do not get positive feedback about their behaviors from persons in their social environment have an increased susceptibility to disease (Cassell, 1976). Through a review of research, Haggerty (1986) provides convincing evidence that stressful family environments are related to illness episodes in children. Solomon & Amkraut (1981) review evidence that emotional factors and failure of psychological defenses lead to decreased immunologic resistance to disease. An alternative hypothesis is that some psychological and social environments lead an individual to minimize the significance of certain symptoms (Holroyd & Lazarus, 1982). Lack of attention to stressors and untreated symptoms may lead to permanent damage to body tissues.

In a classic article, Solnit and Green (1964) identified the "vulnerable child syndrome" in which children who had been expected by their parents to die at an early age, but survived, tend to demonstrate behavioral, academic, and somatic problems. The parents overprotect, underdiscipline, and infantilize the vulnerable child. The children experience difficulty with separation and have numerous bodily concerns.

In addition to the physiological vulnerability of some children, Minuchin and others (1975) propose that the development and maintenance of psychosomatic symptoms in children requires that the child be involved in parental conflict within a family organization characterized by enmeshment, overprotection, rigidity, and lack of conflict resolution. Symptoms are maintained because they become embedded in the family organization. A type of operant conditioning occurs, with attention reinforcing the symptom. Family history often reveals similarities in symptoms among generations of family members (Apley, 1975; Minuchin et al., 1975). Mechanic (1983) proposed that adolescents, who are experiencing normal maturational changes and increased self-awareness, cope better with painful self-perceptions in a stable family, school, and peer environment. Adolescents who experience discontinuities with their environment are at risk for excessive self-awareness. Such increased attention to inner feelings and bodily changes increases awareness and potency of distress and the prevalence of reported symptoms.

Only a few empirical studies have tested the relationship between quality of family and social environment and development of psychosomatic symptoms. Studies of this type are all limited by the lack of reliable and valid instruments to measure the quality of a child's environment. A longitudinal study in Helsinki of 90 children from age 11 through 19 showed significant negative correlations between scores on the Habitual Somatic Discomfort Questionnaire and "satisfaction with home" scores at ages 13, 15, and 18 for boys ($r = -.31$ to $-.42$), but only at age 15 for girls ($r = -.45$) (Rauste-von Wright & von Wright, 1981). Of 152 children seen for psychiatric consultation (Hughes, 1984), 47 had RAP as the major presenting complaint. Interviews with 23 of them revealed preoccupation with family problems. Family histories included many illnesses, deaths, and other threatened losses. The mothers' intense concerns about the children's symptoms were disproportionate to the children's apparent good health. When compared to mothers of healthy children, mothers of children with RAP were significantly more likely to be emotionally depressed, have marital problems, and perceive their own health to be poor (Zuckerman, Stevenson, & Bailey, 1987). On the other hand, a comparative study of RAP and healthy children and their parents showed no significant differences between groups with respect to measures of depression, marital dissatisfaction, or other personality variables usually equated with psychogenicity (McGrath et al., 1983). A study of 100 families of children with cystic fibrosis revealed that the children's pulmonary functioning decreased as family life changes increased ($r = -.26, p < .01$) (Patterson & McCubbin, 1983).

Stressful Life Events

Life events research was originally based on the assumption that the amount of life change or social readjustment produced by stressful life events, not the events themselves, cause an individual to be at risk for health problems (Holmes & Masuda, 1974). A desire to demonstrate a relationship between stress and morbidity in adults led Holmes and Rahe (1967) to develop the familiar Social Readjustment Rating Scale and its resultant Life Change Unit (LCU) scores. Coddington (1972a, 1972b, 1984) developed similar instruments for four different age groups of children. The relative stressfulness of each event was determined by child health professionals and teachers.

A competing stress-coping theory by Lazarus and Folkman (1984) suggests that the individual's cognitive appraisal of stressors and coping resources determines how well an individual will cope with stressors. This theory and dissatisfaction with the fact that the individual's perceptions of stressors are not accounted for by LCU scores led to development of other instruments, which include the individual's perception of the frequency and severity of life events. The Feel Bad Scale (FBS) is a life events instrument developed from the children's perspective (Lewis, Siegel, & Lewis, 1984). The FBS measures children's perceptions of the frequency and severity of the stressors, not adults' inferences about the stressfulness of the events. In contrast to the preponderance of one-time catastrophic events on the Coddington scales, the FBS items include typical "daily hassles" that children themselves perceive to be stressful (Lewis, Siegel, & Lewis, 1984). In adults, there is some evidence that persistent or daily hassles that irritate or distress people "may be even more important in adaptation and health" than major, dramatic life changes (Lazarus & Folkman, 1984, p. 13). This may also be true of children.

Results of studies that correlate stress and morbidity in children are inconsistent. The variety of life events scales used makes comparison difficult. Scores of 136 seventh- and eighth-grade children on interval-level measures of stressful life events, social support, and symptom patterns were reduced to dichotomous categories of "high" and "low," resulting in a loss of sensitivity of the original data. Gamma correlations between perceived stress and symptoms were still significant ($r = .40$, $p < .02$), as were correlations between social support and symptoms ($r = -.33$, $p < .05$) (Yarcheski & Mahon, 1986). It is not known what the correlations of interval level data would have been. However, in a study of 44 children with atopic dermatitis, correlations of major life events scores and everyday problem scores with symptom scores were not significant (Gil et al., 1987).

Studies that compare life event scores of children with and without psychosomatic symptoms also show inconsistent results. In two studies, children with RAP had significantly more stressful life events and higher mean stress scores than healthy children (Hodges et al., 1984; Scharrer & Ryan, in review). Children who were seen in a clinic for either RAP or chest pain had similar *positive* life change scores, but significantly higher *negative* life change scores than children who were seen for routine checkups (Greene et al., 1985). On the other hand, two studies showed no significant differences between RAP and healthy children on the number of stressful life events experienced (Raymer, Weininger, & Hamilton, 1984), or between children with migraines and their best friends on LCU scores (Cooper et al., 1987).

Ineffective Coping Strategies

Lazarus and Launier (1978) suggest that the ways people cope with stress may be ". . . even more important to overall morale, social functioning and health/illness than the frequency and severity of stress episodes themselves" (p. 308). "Coping affects health outcomes by influencing the frequency, intensity, and patterning of neuroendocrine stress responses" (Holroyd & Lazarus, 1982, p. 26). Children's coping styles have been described by Chess and colleagues (Chess, 1967; Thomas et al., 1963) and Murphy (Murphy, 1962, 1973; Murphy & Moriarty, 1976) in separate longitudinal studies of children. Coping *styles,* however, are more descriptive of personality traits that persist over time than of specific behaviors or *strategies* used to cope. In order to accurately test the relationship between coping and development of psychosomatic symptoms in children, coping strategies used by children need to be explicated and incorporated into instruments to measure coping.

Inappropriate instruments and faulty assumptions about the developmental capabilities of children resulted in a study with significant but questionable results. Seventh- and eighth-grade students were given a symptom pattern instrument and a modification of the Jalowiec Coping Scale, an instrument designed to measure coping in adults (Yarcheski & Mahon, 1986). The scale was modified to include only the emotion-

focused coping strategies. Based on the false assumption that early adolescents are not capable of problem solving, the authors eliminated all
the problem-solving strategies. The authors assumed that emotion-
focused strategies were ineffective strategies, because they do not address
the actual stressor, and hypothesized that emotion-focused strategies are
likely to be associated with symptoms. When coping scores were dichoto-
mized into high and low, gamma correlations between coping and symptom patterns were significant (gamma $= -.43$, $p < .007$), but it is not
known if problem solving or other types of coping strategies would also
be related to symptoms.

In an attempt to develop an instrument to measure children's coping
from the children's perspective, 103 eight- to twelve-year-old, lower class
to upper middle class white children were asked what they do when they
feel stressed, that is, "bad, nervous or worried" (Ryan, 1989). The 518
coping strategies obtained were inductively sorted into 13 categories of
coping behaviors. Among these coping strategies were cognitive behaviors, like "think what to do," "do something about it," and read, write, or
draw. Seeking support from family and friends was a common strategy,
as were isolating behaviors and distracting behaviors. Representative
strategies from each category were included in a self-report instrument
called the Schoolagers' Coping Strategies Inventory (SCSI), which measures frequency of use and perceived effectiveness of coping strategies
(Ryan-Wenger, in press). Low scores reflect less coping ability than do
high scores. When compared to a group of asymptomatic children, lower
mean coping scores were reported by children with one or more stress-
related symptoms (Ryan-Wenger, in press).

Low correlations and proportions found in stressor and morbidity
studies are often blamed on the instruments, sample size, sampling
method or statistical analysis. Figure 4.3 illustrates the more likely reason
why research results do not support the hypothesis that cases (Group A)
have high stress and controls (Group D) have low stress. Subjects who fall
in Groups B and C weaken expected statistical results. Researchers
should focus their attention on Group B children who, despite high stress
scores, do *not* become ill. These are the resilient or invulnerable children,
from whom much can be learned about inherent and learned characteristics that help them to cope with stressors (Anthony & Cohler, 1987;
Garmezy, 1983). Perhaps stress-coping strategies used by resilient children could be taught to the vulnerable children in Group C, who, despite
relatively low stress levels, still become ill.

The distribution of subjects in Groups A, B, C, and D is evidence of the
complexity of the stress-coping process. Many factors other than stressors
and coping contribute to or protect an individual from the development
of morbidity. Drotar (1981) has suggested that, rather than focusing on
the differences between chronically ill and physically healthy children,

	Illness	No Illness
High Stress	CASES A	RESILIENT B
Low Stress	VULNERABLE C	CONTROLS D

Figure 4.3. Potential distribution of subjects in a case/control study by levels of stress and presence of illness.

or on factors that lead to unsuccessful coping, researchers should examine factors that lead to *successful* coping in family, school, and social relationships. Prospective studies from a developmental perspective will help to determine the vulnerability factors that jeopardize the vulnerable children and the protective factors that guard the resilient children. (See Chapters 13, 17, and 18 for more about these.)

PREVENTION AND TREATMENT OF PSYCHOSOMATIC SYMPTOMS IN CHILDREN

Most intervention programs for children are derived from adult-level theory or practical successes, with no evaluation of efficacy in children nor much research to support what should be included. Interventions have focused on the individual child, groups of children, or the families of symptomatic children. Four basic types are reviewed below: medical interventions, ameliorating the stressors, changing the individual's interpretation of stressors, and improving the stress-coping strategies.

Medical Interventions

There is some concern about the role of medical treatments, such as medication and surgical intervention, in the care of children with psychosomatic symptoms. Apley (1975) believes that although the short-term success in relief of symptoms may help a child to focus on causes rather than symptoms, medical interventions are not an appropriate long-term solution. Symptomatic children would benefit more from a type of informal psychotherapy: ". . . reassurance based on sympathetic listening, explanations and discussions" (Apley, 1975; Apley, MacKeith, & Meadow, 1978).

Changing the Stressors

Brenner (1984) suggests that health professionals help children by assisting them to remove at least one stressor. This requires that children be helped to identify their own stressors and evaluate the extent to which the stressors can be changed. Interviews, diaries, and self-report instruments can be used to identify sources of stress. If parental cooperation can be obtained, family therapy and counseling may help identify the role of family dynamics in symptom maintenance, sources of stress in the family environment, and ways to change dysfunctional patterns (Minuchin, Rosman, & Baker, 1978). Unfortunately, many of the family and school-related stressors that children experience are outside the control of children and of health professionals as well. In such cases, children could still be helped to change their perceptions of the stressors, or change the ways that they deal with stressors (Ryan, 1988).

Changing Perceptions of Stressors

The ways that the brain organizes and interprets information about stressors predisposes to either adaptive or maladaptive responses. Therefore, interventions may focus on changing interpretations of stressors (Wolf & Goodell, 1979). Changing children's appraisal of stressors requires individual counseling of a supportive type. While investigative or psychodynamic psychotherapy appears to be successful for adults (Eaton, Peterson, & Davis, 1981), Mechanic (1983) warns that introspective counseling with children may ". . . exacerbate difficulties by reinforcing an already dysfunctional overconcern with the self" (p. 12). Children need reassurance that their feelings and symptoms are not as unique or deviant as they seem (Mechanic, 1983). Although it is generally agreed that children should be assisted to reframe their perceptions of stressors from negative to positive, from hopeless to hopeful, or from destructive to growth-producing, specific methods for accomplishing this have not been identified.

Changing Coping Strategies

Because coping strategies are learned and can be acquired, changed, or eliminated (Moos, 1976), cognitive-behavioral interventions may be successful in preventing and treating psychosomatic symptoms (Holroyd & Lazarus, 1982). A child's repertoire of coping strategies should first be assessed by interview, observation, and self-report, then the child's perceived effectiveness of the strategies should be evaluated. Adults' perceptions of effectiveness or adequacy of coping strategies may be quite different from children's perceptions (Ryan, 1988). Although some adults may believe that only strategies that focus on changing the stressor are adaptive (Yarcheski & Mahon, 1986), others assert that coping strategies that serve to distract from or ignore the stressor are sometimes appropriate when stressors cannot be changed (Lazarus & Folkman, 1984). Coping strategies used in anticipation of stressors are often different from those used during or after a stressful event (Lazarus & Folkman, 1984). Children can be taught to anticipate stressors and use anticipatory coping strategies, which might be more flexible or wider-spectrum. A study of 103 children eight to twelve years old revealed that the children most frequently used social support, isolating and avoidant strategies *before* a stressor, social support *during* a stressor, and avoidant and distracting strategies *after* a stressor (Ryan, 1989).

Little is known about the validity of teaching children new coping strategies, such as relaxation or imagery (Beckemeyer & Bahn, 1980; LaMontagne, Mason, & Hepworth, 1985; Petosa & Oldfield, 1985; Stanton, 1985). It may be best to encourage greater use of strategies in their own repertoire that children have found to be successful, and discourage use of strategies that they report are ineffective, but which they use anyway. Zegans (1982) warns that if certain coping behaviors are successful in mastering the stressor, but the physiologic aspect of "blocked action" continues to be expressed, a "reverberating circuit" may be established because no appropriate cut-off signal is received. The applicability of this theory to children has not been tested empirically, but may explain a continuation of symptoms despite removal of maladaptive coping strategies.

Creative coping-skills programs are taught in small groups or classroom settings, although the efficacy of this method has not been validated. The contents of such programs typically consist of social competence skills, self-awareness, and stress-reduction techniques such as imagery, meditation, progressive relaxation, and the quieting reflex (Brenner, 1984; Humphrey, 1984; Humphrey & Humphrey, 1985; Medeiros, Porter, & Welch, 1983). More typical coping strategies that children themselves find useful should also be included in these programs, such as physical exercise, distracting behaviors, and cognitive strategies like thinking about the problem, reading, writing, and drawing (Ryan, 1989).

The complexity of psychosomatic symptom development in children has led some health professionals to employ a combination of the above treatment techniques with both the child and the family, since there is often dysfunction on more than one level (Schaefer, Millman, & Levine, 1979).

CONCLUSION

Current knowledge about mechanisms, causes, treatment, and prevention of psychosomatic symptoms in children is highly speculative. The absence of a theory to describe, explain, and predict psychosomatic symptom development in children has resulted in diverse branches of biopsychosocial research, but has hindered systematic knowledge development. Multidisciplinary professional groups, journals and conferences specific to the phenomenon of stress in children are needed to consolidate existing knowledge, develop theory, and stimulate collaborative research programs.

REFERENCES

Amkraut, A., & Solomon, G. F. (1975). From symbolic stimulus to the pathophysiologic response: Immune mechanisms. *International Journal of Psychiatry Medicine, 5,* 541–562.

Anthony, E. J., & Cohler, B. J. (1987). *The invulnerable child.* New York: Guilford Press.

Apley, J. (1975). *The child with abdominal pains.* London: Blackwell Scientific Publications.

Apley, J., & Hale, B. (1975). Children with recurrent abdominal pain: How do they grow up? *British Medical Journal, 3,* 7–9.

Apley, J., Haslam, D. R., & Tulloh, G. (1971). Pupillary reaction in children with recurrent pain. *Archives of Disease in Childhood, 46,* 337–340.

Apley, J., MacKeith, R. C., & Meadow, R. (1978). *The child and his symptoms.* Oxford: Blackwell Scientific Publications.

Asterita, M. F. (1985). *The physiology of stress.* New York: Human Sciences Press.

Axelrod, J., & Reisine, T. D. (1984). Stress hormones: Their interaction and regulation. *Science, 4*(224), 452–459.

Barlow, C. F. (1984). *Headaches and migraine in childhood.* Philadelphia: Lippincott.

Beckemeyer, P., & Bahn, J. E. (1980). Helping toddlers and preschoolers cope while suturing their minor lacerations. *American Journal of Maternal Child Nursing, 5,* 326–330.

Behrman, R. E., & Vaughan, V. C. (1987). *Nelson textbook of pediatrics* (13th ed.). Philadelphia: Saunders.

Bithoney, W. G., & Dubowitz, H. (1985). Organic concomitants of nonorganic failure to thrive: Implications for research. In D. Drotar (Ed.), *New directions in failure to thrive* (pp. 47–68). New York: Plenum Press.

Brenner, A. (1984). *Helping children cope with stress.* Lexington, MA: Lexington Books.

Cannon, W. B. (1914). The emergency function of the adrenal medulla in pain and in the major emotions. *American Journal of Physiology, 33,* 356–372.

Cannon, W. B. (1953). *Bodily changes in pain, hunger, fear and rage.* Boston: C. T. Branford.

Cassel, J. (1976). The contribution of the social environment to host resistance. *American Journal of Epidemiology, 104,* 107–123.

Cassidy, J. T. (1982). Basic concepts in the pathogenesis of autoimmune diseases. In J. T. Cassidy (Ed.), *Textbook of pediatric rheumatology* (pp. 47–98). New York: Wiley.

Chess, S. (1967). *Exceptional infant* (Vol. I). New York: Basic Books.

Coddington, R. D. (1972a). The significance of life events as etiologic factors in the diseases of children. II. A study of a normal population. *Journal of Psychosomatic Research, 16,* 205–213.

Coddington, R. D. (1972b). The significance of life events as etiologic factors in the diseases of children. I. A survey of professional workers. *Journal of Psychosomatic Research, 16,* 7–18.

Coddington, R. D. (1984). Measuring the stressfulness of a child's environment. In J. H. Humphrey (Ed.), *Stress in childhood* (pp. 97–126). New York: AMS Press.

Cooper, P. J., Bawden, H. N., Camfield, P. R., & Camfield, C. S. (1987). Anxiety and life events in childhood migraine. *Pediatrics, 79*(6), 999–1004.

Corson, S. A., & Corson, E. O. (1968). The effects of psychotropic drugs on conditioning of water and electrolyte excretion: Experimental research and clinical implications. *Excerpta Medica International Congress Series,* No. 182, 147–164.

Corson, S. A., & Corson, E. O. (1973). Animal models of psychosocial stress reactions. *Psychopharmacology Bulletin, 9* (4), 42–44.

Corson, S. A., & Corson, E. O. (1979). Interaction of genetic and psychosocial factors in stress-reaction patterns: A systems approach to the investigation of stress-coping mechanisms. *Psychotherapy and Psychosomatics, 31,* 161–171.

Corson, S. A., & Corson, E. O. (1987). Type A behavior pattern and heart disease: A critical review of contradictory data. *Pavlovian Journal of Biological Sciences, 22,* 31–37.

Corson, S. A., Corson, E. O., & Andrysco, R. M. (1982). Cardiac and respiratory orienting reflexes as indices of susceptibility to psychosomatic cardio-respiratory disorders. In M. Horvath & E. Frantik (Eds.), *Psychophysiological risk factors of cardiovascular diseases: Psychosocial stress, personality and occupational specificity* (pp. 351–372). Praha: Avicenum, Czechoslovak Medical Press.

Drotar, D. (1981). Psychological perspectives in chronic childhood illness. *Journal of Pediatric Psychology, 6,* 211–228.

Drotar, D. (1985). *New directions in failure to thrive.* New York: Plenum Press.

Eaton, M. T., Peterson, M. H., & Davis, J. A. (1981). Psychological factors affecting physical conditions. In M. T. Eaton, M. H. Peterson, & J. A. Davis (Eds.), *Psychiatry* (pp. 181–191). Garden City, NY: Medical Examination Publishing Company.

Everly, G. S., & Rosenfeld, R. (1981). *The nature and treatment of the stress response: A practical guide for clinicians.* New York: Plenum Press.

Feuerstein, M., Barr, R. G., Francoeur, T. E., Houle, M., & Rafman, S. (1982).

Potential biobehavioral mechanisms of recurrent abdominal pain in children. *Pain, 13,* 287–298.

Fritz, G. K. (1983). Childhood asthma. *Psychosomatics, 24*(11), 959–967.

Garmezy, N. (1983). Stressors of childhood. In N. Garmezy & M. Rutter (Eds.), *Stress, coping and development in children* (pp. 43–84). New York: McGraw-Hill.

Garmezy, N., & Rutter, M. (1983). *Stress, coping and development in children.* New York: McGraw-Hill.

Gil, K. M., Keefe, F. J., Sampson, H. A., McCaskill, C. C., et al. (1987). The relation of stress and family environment to atopic dermatitis symptoms in children. *Journal of Psychosomatic Research, 31,* 673–684.

Glaser, R., & Kiecolt-Glaser, J. K. (1988). Stress-associated immune suppression and AIDS. *Advances in Biochemistry and Psychopharmacology, 44,* 217–224.

Glaser, R., Kiecolt-Glaser, J. K., Speicher, C. E., & Holliday, J. E. (1985). Stress, loneliness and changes in herpesvirus latency. *Journal of Behavioral Medicine, 8,* 249–260.

Glaser, R., Rice, J., Speicher, C. E., Stout, J. C., & Kiecolt-Glaser, J. K. (1986). Stress depresses interferon production concomitant with a decrease in natural killer cell activity. *Behavioral Neuroscience, 100,* 675–678.

Gottlieb, S. H., & Schuster, M. M. (1986). Dermatoglyphic (fingerprint) evidence for a congenital syndrome of early onset constipation and abdominal pain. *Gastroenterology, 91,* 428–432.

Greene, J. W., Walker, L. S., Hickson, G., & Thompson, J. (1985). Stressful life events and somatic complaints in adolescents. *Pediatrics, 75*(1), 19–22.

Haggerty, R. J. (1986). Stress and illness in children. *Bulletin of the New York Academy of Medicine, 62*(7), 707–718.

Henker, F. O. (1984). Psychosomatic illness: Biochemical and physiologic foundations. *Psychosomatics, 25*(1), 19–24.

Henry, J. P. (1980). Present concept of stress theory. In E. Usdin, R. Kvetnansky, & I. J. Kopin (Eds.), *Catecholamines & stress: Recent advances* (pp. 557–571). New York: Elsevier Press.

Henry, J. P., & Stephens, P. (1977). *Stress, health and the social environment.* New York: Springer.

Hodges, K., Kline, J. J., Barbero, G., & Flanery, R. (1984). Life events occurring in families of children with recurrent abdominal pain. *Journal of Psychosomatic Research, 28*(3), 185–188.

Holmes, T. H., & Masuda, M. (1974). Life change and illness susceptibility. In B. S. Dohrenwend & B. P. Dohrenwend (Eds.), *Stressful life events: Their nature and effects* (pp. 45–72). New York: Wiley.

Holmes, T. H., & Rahe, R. R. (1967). The social readjustment rating scale. *Journal of Psychosomatic Research, 11,* 216.

Holroyd, K. A., & Lazarus, R. S. (1982). Stress, coping and somatic adaptation. In L. Goldberger & S. Breznitz (Eds.), *Handbook of stress* (pp. 21–35). New York: Free Press.

Hughes, M. C. (1984). Recurrent abdominal pain and childhood depression:

Clinical observations of 23 children and their families. *American Journal of Orthopsychiatry, 54*(1), 146–155.

Humphrey, J. H. (1984). *Stress in childhood.* New York: AMS Press.

Humphrey, J. H., & Humphrey, J. N. (1985). *Controlling stress in children.* Springfield, IL: C. C. Thomas.

Jacobson, A. M., & Leibovich, J. B. (1984). Psychological issues in diabetes mellitus. *Psychosomatics, 25*(1), 7–15.

Jones, R. S. (1976). *Asthma in children.* Acton, MA: Publishing Sciences.

Kiecolt-Glaser, J. K., Garner, W., Speicher, C. E., et al. (1984). Psychosocial modifiers of immunocompetence in medical students. *Psychosomatic Medicine, 46,* 7–14.

Kiecolt-Glaser, J. K., & Glaser, R. (1986). Psychological influences on immunity. *Psychosomatics, 27,* 621–624.

Kiecolt-Glaser, J. K., Kennedy, S., Malkoff, S., Fisher, L., Speicher, C. E., & Glaser, R. (1988). Marital discord and immunity in males. *Psychosomatic Medicine, 50,* 213–229.

Kiecolt-Glaser, J. K., Stephens, R. E., Lipetz, P. D., Speicher, C. E., & Glaser, R. (1985). Distress and DNA repair in human lymphocytes. *Journal of Behavioral Medicine, 8*(4), 311–320.

Kline, J. J., Hodges, V. K., Cameron, A., & Barbero, G. J. (1979). Rectal tonometry in recurrent abdominal pain of childhood (RAP). *American Journal of Gastroenterology, 72*(3), 337.

Kopel, F. B., Kim, I. C., & Barbero, G. J. (1967). Comparison of rectosigmoid motility in normal children, children with recurrent abdominal pain and children with ulcerative colitis. *Pediatrics, 39*(4), 539–545.

Lachman, S. (1972). *Psychosomatic disorders: A behavioristic interpretation.* New York: Wiley.

LaMontagne, L. L., Mason, D. R., & Hepworth, J. T. (1985). Effects of relaxation on anxiety in children: Implications for coping with stress. *Nursing Research, 34,* 289–292.

Lazarus, R. S., & Folkman, S. (1984). *Stress, appraisal and coping.* New York: Springer.

Lazarus, R. S., & Launier, R. (1978). Stress-related transactions between person and environment. In L. A. Pervin & M. Lewis (Eds.), *Perspectives in interactional psychology* (pp. 287–327). New York: Plenum Press.

Lewis, C. E., Lewis, M. S., Lorimer, A. A., & Palmer, B. B. (1977). Child-initiated care: The use of school nursing services in an adult-free system. *Pediatrics, 60,* 499–507.

Lewis, C. E., Siegel, J. M., & Lewis, M. A. (1984). Feeling bad: exploring sources of distress among pre-adolescent children. *American Journal of Public Health, 74*(2), 117–122.

Maccoby, E. E. (1983). Social-emotional development and response to stressors. In N. Garmezy & M. Rutter (Eds.), *Stress, coping and development in children* (pp. 217–234). New York: McGraw Hill.

Martin, M. J. (1983). Muscle contraction (tension) headache. *Psychosomatics, 24*(4), 319–323.

Mason, J. (1968). Organization of psychoendocrine mechanisms. *Psychosomatic Medicine, 30,* (Entire Part II).

Mason, J. (1971). A re-evaluation of the concept of non-specificity in stress theory. *Journal of Psychological Research, 8,* 323–333.

Mason, J. (1975a). A historical view of the stress field. *Journal of Human Stress, 1,* 6–12, 22–37.

Mason, J. (1975b). Endocrine parameters and emotion. In L. Levi (Ed.), *Emotions—Their parameters and measurement.* New York: Raven Press.

McGrath, P. J., Goodman, J. T., Firestone, P., Shipman, R., & Peters, S. (1983). Recurrent abdominal pain: A psychogenic disorder? *Archives of Disease in Childhood, 58,* 888–890.

Mechanic, D. (1983). Adolescent health and illness behavior: Review of the literature and a new hypothesis for the study of stress. *Journal of Human Stress, 9*(2), 4–13.

Medeiros, D. C., Porter, B. J., & Welch, I. D. (1983). *Children under stress.* Englewood Cliffs, NJ: Prentice Hall.

Minuchin, S., Baker, L., Rosman, B. L., Liebman, R., Milman, L., & Todd, T. C. (1975). A conceptual model of psychosomatic illness in children. *Archives of General Psychiatry, 32,* 1031–1038.

Minuchin, S., Rosman, B. S., & Baker, L. (1978). *Psychosomatic families: Anorexia nervosa in context.* Cambridge, MA: Harvard University Press.

Moos, R. (1976). *Human adaptation: Coping with life crises.* Lexington, MA: D. C. Heath & Co.

Murphy, L. B. (1962). *The widening world of childhood.* New York: Basic Books.

Murphy, L. B. (1973). Prediction and consistency: Basic determinants of coping style. In L. J. Stone, J. T. Smith, & L. B. Murphy (Eds.), *The competent infant* (pp. 76–77). New York: Basic Books.

Murphy, L. B., & Moriarty, A. E. (1976). *Vulnerability, coping and growth.* New Haven: Yale University Press.

Parcel, G. S., Nader, P. R., & Meyer, M. P. (1977). Adolescent health concerns, problems and patterns of utilization in a true ethnic urban population. *Pediatrics, 60,* 157–163.

Patterson, J. M., & McCubbin, H. I. (1983). The impact of family life events and changes on the health of a chronically ill child. *Family Relations, 32,* 255–264.

Pennebaker, J. W., Keicolt-Glaser, J. K., & Glaser, R. (1988). Disclosure of traumas and immune function: Health implications for psychotherapy. *Journal of Consulting and Clinical Psychology, 56,* 239–245.

Petosa, R., & Oldfield, D. (1985). A pilot study of the impact of stress management techniques on the classroom behavior of elementary school students. *Journal of School Health, 55*(2), 69–70.

Pollett, E., & Leibel, R. (1980). Biological and social correlates of failure to thrive. In L. S. Greene & F. E. Johnston (Eds.), *Social and biological predictors of nutritional status, physical growth, and neurological development* (pp. 173–200). New York: Academic Press.

Pringle, M. D. D., Butler, N. R., & Davie, R. (1966). *11,000 seven-year-olds.* London: Longman Group Ltd.

Rauste-von Wright, M., & von Wright, J. (1981). A longitudinal study of psychosomatic symptoms in healthy 11–18 year old girls and boys. *Journal of Psychosomatic Research, 25*(6), 525–534.

Raymer, D., Weininger, O., & Hamilton, J. R. (1984, Feb. 5). Psychological problems in children with abdominal pain. *Lancet,* 439–440.

Rubin, L. S., Barbero, G. J., & Sibinga, M. S. (1967). Pupillary reactivity in children with recurrent abdominal pain. *Psychosomatic Medicine, 29*(2), 111–120.

Ryan, N. M. (1988). The stress-coping process in school-age children: Gaps in the knowledge needed for health promotion. *Advances in Nursing Science, 11*(1), 1–12.

Ryan, N. M. (1989). Identification of children's coping strategies from the school-agers' perspective. *Research in Nursing and Health, 12,* 111–122.

Ryan-Wenger, N. M. (in press). Development and psychometrics of the school-agers' coping strategies inventory. *Nursing Research.*

Schaefer, C. E., Millman, H. L., & Levine, G. F. (1979). *Therapies for psychosomatic disorders in children.* San Francisco: Jossey Bass.

Schor, E. L. (1986). Use of health care services by children and diagnoses received during presumably stressful life transitions. *Pediatrics, 77*(6), 834–841.

Selye, H. (1976). *Stress in health and disease.* Reading, MA: Butterworth's.

Selye, H. (1956). *The stress of life.* New York: McGraw Hill.

Sharrer, V., & Ryan, N. M. (in review). Measures of stress and coping of children with and without recurrent abdominal pain.

Singsen, B. H., Johnson, M. A., & Bernstein, B. A. (1979). Psychodynamics of juvenile rheumatoid arthritis. In J. N. Miller (Ed.), *Juvenile rheumatoid arthritis* (pp. 249–265). Littleton, MA: PSG Publishing Company.

Solnit, A. J., & Green, M. (1964, July). Reactions to the threatened loss of a child: A vulnerable child syndrome: Pediatric management of the dying child, Part III. *Pediatrics, 34,* 58–66.

Solomon, G. F., & Amkraut, G. F. (1981). Psychoneuroendocrinological effects on the immune response. *Annual Review of Microbiology, 35,* 155–184.

Solomon, G. F., & Moos, R. H. (1965). The relationship of personality to the presence of rheumatoid factor in asymptomatic relatives of patients with rheumatoid arthritis. *Psychosomatic Medicine, 27*(4), 350–360.

Stanton, H. E. (1985). The reduction of children's school-related stress. *Australian Psychologist, 20*(2), 171–193.

Starfield, B., Gross, E., Wood, M., Pantell, R., Allen, C., et al. (1980). Psychosocial and psychosomatic diagnoses in primary care of children. *Pediatrics, 66*(2), 159–167.

Starfield, B., Katz, H., Gabriel, A., Livingston, G., Benson, B. A., et al. (1984).

Morbidity in childhood: A longitudinal view. *New England Journal of Medicine, 310*(13), 824–829.

Stein, M. (1982). Biopsychosocial factors in asthma. In L. J. West & M. Stein (Eds.), *Critical issues in behavioral medicine* (pp. 159–182). Philadelphia: Lippincott.

Sternbach, R. (1966). *Principles of psychophysiology.* New York: Academic Press.

Teshima, H., Kubo, C., Kihara, H., Imada, Y., Nagata, S., Ago, Y., & Ikemi, Y. (1982). Psychosomatic aspects of skin diseases from the standpoint of immunology. *Psychotherapy and Psychosomatics, 37,* 165–175.

Thomas, A., Birch, H. G., Chess, S., Hertzig, M. E., & Korn, S. (1963). *Behavioral individuality in early childhood.* New York: New York University Press.

Usdin, E., Kretnansky, R., & Kopin, I. (1976). *Catecholamines and stress.* Oxford: Pergamon Press.

Wolf, S., & Goodell, H. (1979, March). Causes and mechanisms in psychosomatic phenomena. *Journal of Human Stress,* 9–18.

Yarcheski, A., & Mahon, N. E. (1986). Perceived stress and symptom patterns in early adolescents: The role of mediating variables. *Research in Nursing and Health, 9,* 289–297.

Yoos, L. (1984). Taking another look at failure to thrive. *MCN: American Journal of Maternal Child Nursing, 9*(1), 32–36.

Zegans, L. S. (1982). Stress and the development of somatic disorders. In L. Goldberger & S. Breznitz (Eds.), *Handbook of stress* (pp. 134–152). New York: Free Press.

Zuckerman, B., Stevenson, J., & Bailey, V. (1987). Stomachaches and headaches in a community sample of preschool children. *Pediatrics, 79*(5), 677–682.

Part II

Stress at Different Developmental Stages

CHAPTER FIVE

Prenatal Stress

Lynne C. Huffman
Rebecca del Carmen

Stress affects the developing organism at any stage of the life cycle. As originally defined by Selye (1950), a stressor was an agent that produced assorted physiological changes. He further described a General Adaptation Syndrome of three stages: an alarm reaction, with an initial shock phase and subsequent countershock phase; a stage of resistance; and a stage of exhaustion. More recently, stress has been defined as "any real or imagined trauma, physical or psychological, that leads to the release of stress hormones associated with the adrenal glands" (Herrenkohl, 1986, p. 120). With increasing precision of the definition of stress, there is a growing body of work identifying measures of prenatal stress. These measures have included both markers of the autonomic nervous system (e.g., Bryan et al., 1989; Lacey, 1967; Sontag, 1944), endocrinologic system, and immunologic system (Solomon, Amkraut, & Rubin, 1985), and also other physiological signs of stress response, such as pilo-erection and excessive urination and defecation in rats (Thompson, 1957). In addition, subjective self-report measures traditionally have been employed.

Early reports concluded that prenatal psychological stress in human subjects may influence the behavior of the offspring. This prompted a large number of studies in experimental animals attempting to provide more precise information about the nature of the changes induced by such stress and their underlying mechanisms. Many studies, however, were methodologically flawed and difficult to interpret. The purpose of this chapter is to review the human and animal research on the role of prenatal stress in determining development and behavior of the offspring.

First, the various types of prenatal stressors are reviewed (see Table 5.1), including both external physical events (e.g., environmental changes, exercise) and psychosocial influences (e.g., life stress, anxiety). In this review, we assess factors that are potentially capable of influencing the developing fetus by their effects on the mother and the presumed transplacental transfer of active substances to the fetus. In general, we do not examine biological stressors which have, among other possible mechanisms, direct effects on the fetus (e.g., radiation, hormones, drugs, infectious agents). These stressors are better classified as behavioral teratogens, and have been thoroughly reviewed recently by Riley and Vorhees (1986). (See also Chapter 2 for an example.) This discussion is followed by a summary of confounding and modifying factors and methodological problems in the overall design of many studies. Next, we integrate the research findings on specific mechanisms of prenatal stress. Finally, in the last section, we provide suggestions for future research strategies.

TABLE 5.1. ***Prenatal Stressors.*** All of the following have been suggested by the literature to stress the fetus in measurable degree, either in animal or human studies. However, the quality of documentation (research design, sample selection, etc.) is highly variable. (Well-doc. = Well-documented; A = Animal studies; H = Human studies)

Prenatal Stressors	Likely Results	Documentation Quality (Animal or Human)
	Biological (Physical/Chemical)	
Drugs		
Alcohol	Anatomic dysmorphology (1st trimester exposure)	Well-doc. (A + H)
	Lower birthweight (3rd trimester exposure)	Probable (A + H)
	Disordered behavior	Probable (A + H)
	Delayed physical development	Questionable (A)
	Disordered learning	Probable (A)
CNS stimulants	Disordered behavior	Questionable (A)
Antianxiety agents	Disordered behavior	Questionable (A)
Anticonvulsants	Anatomic dysmorphology	Probable (A + H)
	Disordered behavior	Questionable (A + H)
Environmental Agents		
Lead	Delayed behavior development	Well-doc. (A)
	Disordered learning	Well-doc. (A + H)
	Disordered social behavior	Questionable (H)
Insecticides	Growth retardation	Questionable (A)
Solvents	Growth retardation	Questionable (A)
	Disordered learning/memory	Probable (A)
	Disordered sensation	Questionable (A)
Special Agents		
Malnutrition	Lower birthweight	Well-doc. (A + H)
	Delayed neurological development	Probable (A + H)
Excessive exercise	Lower birthweight	Well-doc. (A + H)
Ionizing irradiation	Growth retardation (3rd trimester exposure)	Well-doc. (A)
	Delayed physical development	Questionable (A)
Gonadal/Adrenal steroids	Disordered behavior	Well-doc. (A)

(continued)

TABLE 5.1. **(Continued)**

Prenatal Stressors	Likely Results	Documentation Quality (Animal or Human)
Environmental Extremes		
Noise	Delayed motor development	Probable (A)
	Anatomic dysmorphology	Questionable (A + H)
	Lower birthweight	Questionable (A + H)
Heat	Lower birthweight (3rd trimester exposure)	Probable (A)
	Altered sex differentiation	Well-doc. (A)
Crowding*	Altered sex differentiation	Probable (A)
	Disordered behavior	Probable (A)

	Psychosocial	
Acute Life Stress		
Critical life events	Obstetric complications	Questionable (H)
	Physical illness	Questionable (H)
	Disordered behavior	Questionable (H)
Nonspecific psychosocial stress	Disordered behavior	Questionable (H)
Trauma	Disordered fetal behavior	Questionable (H)
Maternal anxiety	Disordered neonatal activity	Questionable (H)
	Obstetric complications	Questionable (H)

*Crowding can also be considered a psychosocial stressor and is a good example of the difficulty of dichotomizing stress into biological/physical and psychosocial.

PHYSICAL STRESSORS

The study of physical stressors, in part, represents an attempt to identify stimuli that are as simple as possible, in the hope that they elicit relatively selective or specific disturbances. Once this is done, then it may be more feasible to attempt interpretation of obstetric, fetal, and infant outcome under more complex conditions, such as psychosocial stress.

Heat, Light, and Restraint

With some variation, this stress cluster typically is measured by restraining an animal in a small Plexiglas holder onto which 200 foot-candles of light are directed with a concurrent increase in heat of approximately 2 degrees Centigrade. The treatment is administered several times daily (Ward & Reed, 1985). At the anatomic level, this type of stress on Sprague-Dawley rats during late pregnancy (days 14–20) significantly reduced the area of the sexually dimorphic nucleus in the preoptic area of the hypothalamus in male offspring (Anderson, 1985). This area is presumed to be of significance in the masculinization of the rat brain. Barlow, Knight, and Sullivan (1978) noted earlier parturition in a group of Porton-Wistar albino rats stressed by heat, light, and restraint during late pregnancy. It is unclear whether this accounts entirely for the consistent finding of several investigators who have noted that stressed Sprague-Dawley rats have offspring with decreased birthweight (Herrenkohl & Whitney, 1976; Rhees & Fleming, 1981). In a study using a different rat strain, this effect was more marked in male compared to female offspring (Barlow et al., 1978). The latter report also noted a delay in ear-opening for the stressed group.

In the arena of neurobehavioral development, Morra (1965) used various levels of heat stress in a preconceptional avoidance training paradigm, where female Wistar albino rats were pretrained to avoid intense radiant heat (unconditioned stimulus) at the sound of a buzzer (conditioned stimulus). He reported less open-field activity, faster swimming time, and greater T maze accuracy (presumed to be measures of emotionality) in the offspring of rats subjected to greater levels of conditioned stress. In addition, decreased viability by age 25 days was associated with the higher-stressed groups. This study is confounded by the absence of cross-fostering, though it was noted that each group was handled equally. In their report, Barlow et al. (1978) also found that the offspring of stressed mother rats were retarded in the development of the auditory startle reflex and cliff-avoidance.

It is known that exposure of rats to prenatal heat and restraint leads to disruptions in the normal course of sexual differentiation and subsequent alterations in reproductive behavior (Rhees & Fleming, 1981). Specifically, Ward and colleagues found impaired ejaculatory behavior and increased female lordotic behavior in male offspring of stressed mother Sprague-Dawley rats (Ward, 1972; Ward & Reed, 1985). While no litter effects were noted, the absence of a cross-fostering design does not eliminate the possibility that the effects could have been caused by prepartal-stress-induced disturbances in maternal behavior. Dahlöf, Hard, and Larsson (1978) also noted that the restraint of pregnant Wistar rats between days 14–21 of gestation caused, in male newborn offspring, a significant reduction in testes and adrenal weight as well as decreased anogenital distance (where anogenital distance is a measure of the virilization of the somatotype). In Rockland-Swiss albino mice, prenatal heat and restraint stress in late pregnancy decreased aggressive behavior in male offspring (Kinsley & Svare, 1986a). In female offspring, a consensus is yet to be reached: one report of Rockland-Swiss albino mice noted a decreased intensity of aggression during pregnancy but elevated aggression during lactation (Kinsley & Svare, 1988), while another study of albino CD-1 mice noted a reduction in exhibited attacks postpartum (Politch & Herrenkohl, 1979).

Studies of the effect of heat and restraint on neonatal outcome may be confounded by lack of cross-fostering designs (Joffe, 1965), uncontrolled litter effects—i.e., innate similarity of litter mates (Chapman & Stern, 1979), different species and strains of animals (Archer & Blackman, 1971)—or by alterations in maternal food/water intake and body weight gain (Kinsley & Svare, 1986b).

Intermittent Noise and Light

Bättig, Zeier, Müller, and Buzzi (1980) found that aircraft noise in the field, irregular and unforseeable in nature, provided a continuous subjective irritation to humans and was accompanied by physiological reactions of stress (increased heart rate, respiratory rate, and skin conductance). Laboratory studies have made use of an electric bell (sound intensity 90–95 dBA), sometimes paired with a light (20 foot-candles), controlled to give noise bursts and light flashes for a period of time each day (Fride & Weinstock, 1984).

In a study addressing changes in offspring brain morphology resulting from prenatal noise stress, Fride et al. (1985) demonstrated that the number of hippocampal benzodiazepine (BZ) binding sites were significantly reduced in prenatally stressed Sabra albino rats. The authors concluded that this may express a decreased ability to cope with anxiety-provoking situations. The septo-hippocampal system is thought to be important in the regulation of anxiety response (Smotherman et al., 1981) and contains specific BZ binding sites, which are reduced in the hippocampi of strains of highly emotional rats (Gentsch, Lichtsteiner, & Feer, 1981). While the report of Fride et al. (1985) documented no differences in litter size, sex ratio, gross anatomical malformations, or weight of rat pups born to noise-stressed and control mothers, limited work in human populations did suggest gross effects. In land tracts within the outdoor-noise 90dBA contour around the Los Angeles airport landing pattern, aircraft noise appeared related to an increase in the incidence of congenital malformations (combined rates of spina bifida and anencephaly) in human infants (Jones & Tauscher, 1978). A similar study, using a slightly lower noise criterion (65–75 dBA) and studying singleton hospital births in Amsterdam, suggested that aircraft noise can decrease birthweight. (Knipschild, Meier, & Salle, 1981). While the confounds of socioeconomic status, maternal age, and twinship are controlled for in this human work, other variables, such as jet aircraft pollutants, cannot be discounted.

At a neurobehavioral level, DeFries and Weir (1964) found that the effects of prenatal stress in C57BL/6J mice offspring (i.e., decreased open-field activity level) are manifested at 120 days of age only if the offspring have undergone previous test experience in the open field. This suggests that postnatal experiences interact in the expression of prenatally induced effects. In Sabra albino rats, Fride and Weinstock (1984) compared the effects of stress applied daily throughout pregnancy, randomly throughout pregnancy, or daily from day 14–21. They noted that offspring of mother rats in the random group showed delayed appearance of motor activities, whereas offspring of the late daily stress group developed more quickly than did control animals. They concluded that the same type of maternal stress can either increase or delay the rate of maturation of early motor skills according to the timing of its application. A later study by Fride and colleagues (Fride et al., 1985) using the same rat strain found that prenatally stressed female offspring later showed disruption of their own maternal behavior during conflict (i.e., pup retrieval through an airstream). However, they were raised by their biological mothers and postnatal maternal behavior cannot be excluded as an important mediating influence. In humans, Sontag (1970) has reported "hyperkinetic" fetal behavior in response to noise and a statistical relationship between increased fetal activity and behavioral abnormalities such as social apprehension and fear of novelty.

In all of these studies, a direct effect of noise on the developing fetus cannot be ruled out.

Crowding and Handling

Rodents exposed to crowded environments have increased adrenocortical activity, increased adrenal weight, and other signs of stress (Christian, 1975). In the laboratory, crowding procedures have included placing large numbers of animals in one cage (Bush & Leathwood, 1975) or placing the pregnant female in a cage with a number of aggressive males (Dahlöf, Hård, & Larsson, 1977). In contrast to other stressors, such as noise and restraint, Dahlöf et al. (1978) demonstrated that rat offspring of mothers stressed by crowding had higher birthweights than did control offspring.

Behaviorally, Bush and Leathwood (1975) showed that Swiss white mice raised in large litters (20 pups/litter) showed marked effects, including delayed development of reflex behavior and poor adult shuttle-box avoidance performance; these effects were felt to arise from a combination of social and nutritional factors. In a study placing many pregnant albino mice together in a cage (Keeley, 1962), litters from crowded mothers were less active and slower to respond to unfamiliar stimuli than controls born to uncrowded mothers. These differences existed regardless of postnatal rearing, age, or starvation status. Ader and Conklin (1963) found that, when cross-fostered and tested at 45 and 100 days of age, the offspring of gestationally handled mother Sprague-Dawley rats were found to be generally less emotional, showing decreased defecation under stress compared to controls. Similarly, Lieberman (1963) found increased activity and decreased defecation in the offspring of crowded C57B16 mice when compared to controls at 35 days of age. However, the study was limited by its small sample size and lack of cross-fostering design.

Prenatal crowding with aggressive males also has been shown to increase the probability of later adult lordosis (a female sexual behavior) in the male offspring (Dahlöf et al., 1977) and to decrease anogenital distances in newborn male rats of two different strains (Wistar rats: Dahlöf et al., 1978; Long-Evans rats: Moore & Power, 1986). Moore and Power (1986) concluded that crowding increases corticosteroid secretion by the stressed mother and subsequently suppresses fetal gonadal secretions, thereby interfering with the perinatal androgen condition and masculine development.

Exercise

Offspring effects of exercise training before pregnancy and continued through pregnancy have been addressed utilizing treadmills (Treadway et al., 1986; Wilson & Gisolfi, 1980) and cycles (Hall & Kaufmann, 1987).

Wilson and Gisolfi (1980) demonstrated greater offspring mortality during the first 28 days of life in Sprague-Dawley rats when preconceptional high-intensity exercise levels were maintained during pregnancy. However, this finding is confounded by the fact that exercise was maintained using a shock-avoidance contingency. In the pregnant ewe without preconceptional exercise training, sustained low-level maternal exercise produced significant changes in fetal parameters (e.g., decreased fetal arterial pO_2) only if exercise was continued to the point of maternal exhaustion. No evidence of fetal compromise, such as acidosis in fetal tissues, was demonstrated (Clapp, 1980).

Animal studies demonstrate that preconceptional exercise training, with or without exercise during gestation, produced smaller offspring (ICR-JCL mice: Terada, 1974; Wistar rats: Treadway et al., 1986). While delayed ossification in mouse fetuses was noted in one study (Terada, 1974), no physical malformations have been found (Terada, 1974; Swiss-Webster mice: Boehnke, Chernoff, & Finnell, 1987).

In humans, investigators have demonstrated that heavy physical work in a group of undernourished women (Tafari, Naeye, & Gobezie, 1980) and the maintenance of preconceptional exercise levels (Clapp & Dickstein, 1984) during pregnancy decrease infant birthweight. In contrast, Hall and Kaufmann (1987) found that infant birthweights and infant Apgar scores were significantly higher in a group of women who participated in a physical conditioning exercise program (i.e., cycling) during pregnancy than in a control group. The prospective study by Erkkola (1976) also showed that women with a high physical work capacity tend to have bigger infants.

Malnutrition

Both human and animal data have suggested that the earlier the malnutrition, the more severe and more permanent are the effects (Winick, 1969). During the prenatal period in particular, all fetal organs are in the hyperplastic phase of development and therefore should be maximally sensitive to nutritional influence (Winick & Nobel, 1966, 1967).

Numerous studies have reported low-birthweight rodent offspring following full-term prenatal malnutrition (Berg, 1965; Bush & Leathwood, 1975; Morgane et al., 1978; Rhees & Fleming, 1981; Stephan & Chow, 1968). Offspring also show retarded development of physical features such as ear opening, fur eruption, and eye opening (Bush & Leathwood, 1975). The issue of low birthweight is particularly relevant to human infant outcome. In the recent past, between 30% and 50% of surviving term infants who had low birthweights eventually demonstrated impaired neurologic and intellectual development (Drillien, 1970; Lubchenco, 1970). Chase and colleagues (1972) demonstrated that human infants with low birthweights for gestational age had low cerebrum-brain stem and cerebellum weights. They also found brain biochemical alterations (decreased total DNA and cholesterol), particularly of the cerebellum and of the myelin lipids cerebroside and sulfatide. Similarly, Bush and Leathwood (1975) showed that prenatal nutritional deprivation in mice resulted in decreased forebrain weight and DNA content.

In contrast, Jones and Crnic (1988) have demonstrated that, when food restriction in rats is limited to the first two trimesters of pregnancy, male offspring develop obesity as adults. These results parallel data reported by Ravelli, Stein, and Susser (1976) in a historical cohort study of 19-year-old male offspring of women exposed to the Dutch famine of 1944–1945. This study suggested that qualitative differences in outcome can be induced by simple variations in the timing of gestational undernutrition.

In regard to neurobehavioral development, Bush and Leathwood (1975) demonstrated that mouse pups born of protein-restricted mothers had delayed development of reflex behavior (e.g., grasping, righting, crawling, and auditory startle) and poor adult shuttle-box avoidance performance, even if reared from birth by well-nourished mothers.

Animal studies of malnutrition are important because controlled studies in humans would be impossible. Although malnutrition is a major health problem in many parts of the world and is particularly devastating to the young, it seldom occurs alone (Scrimshaw & Behar, 1965). There are only limited opportunities to study the effect of deprivations of any kind on human brain development (Chase et al., 1972; Rosso, Hormazabel, & Winick, 1970), and these few chances are confounded by postnatal effects. However, the results of animal studies must be applied cautiously to human situations. As Morgane et al. (1978) noted, the impact of prenatal undernutrition on brain growth in the rat does not directly correlate with the human situation because neuronal multiplication occurs toward the end of gestation in the rat and occurs earlier (the second trimester) in humans.

Clearly, the fetus is no longer regarded as extracting its nutrients from the mother regardless of her nutritional status (Frazer & Huggett, 1970). Although maternal stores can be drawn upon to palliate acute or mild malnutrition, fetal development *can* be affected when a pregnant mother suffers nutritional insufficiencies.

PSYCHOSOCIAL STRESSORS

While psychosocial stress has been linked successfully to a variety of physical disorders (e.g., Diamond, 1982; Eliot & Eisdorfer, 1982; Sklar & Anisman, 1981), its role in the outcome of pregnancy remains more elusive.

Direct assessment of stress-related physiological changes in humans generally is invasive and can threaten the viability of the fetus (Istvan, 1986). Therefore, researchers have relied upon animal research or upon non-experimental studies. Consequently, it is difficult to make interpretations and statements regarding causal relations of stress and pregnancy outcome in humans. Further, many human studies have been methodologically flawed by heavy reliance upon retrospective data and self-report measures, inadequate sample descriptions, small sample sizes or inadequate controls, and a lack of specificity with respect to predictor and criterion variables (Istvan, 1986; McDonald, 1968; Omer & Everly, 1988).

Nevertheless, prenatal psychosocial stress effects on human birth outcomes continues to be a source of theoretical intrigue. In part, this interest lies in its potential for interventions aimed at modifying or enhancing the psychosocial factors leading to optimal pregnancy and neonatal outcome. In fact, several studies recently reported success in reducing pregnancy anxiety and improving reproductive functioning or neonatal status by using ultrasound feedback (Field et al., 1985; Sparling, Seeds, & Farran, 1988) or hypnotic relaxation (Omer et al., 1986). Nonetheless, given the variety and complexity of interacting psychosocial factors involved in pregnancy and labor, as well as the difficulty in isolating one variable from another in human studies (Wolkind, 1981a), researchers have become increasingly cautious in their assertions regarding the link between psychosocial stress and pregnancy outcome. For example, in a recent review article on stress, anxiety, and birth outcomes, Istvan (1986) emphasized that the supporting evidence for the relationships between these variables is very weak. Omer and Everly (1988) suggested that the effects of prenatal stress and anxiety are stronger when specific predictor and criterion variables (e.g., preterm delivery, neonatal status) are clearly differentiated from one another rather than grouped together (e.g., "abnormal pregnancy").

As in other areas of stress research, the study of stress influences during pregnancy includes investigation into the effects of acute life stress and more pervasive psychological distress (Holmes & Rahe, 1967; Spielberger & Jacobs, 1978). What follows is a review of the literature on both acute life stress and psychological distress during pregnancy as they relate to birth outcome.

Acute Life Stress

Acute life stress often involves critical events which require considerable life readjustment (Holmes & Rahe, 1967). Examples include death of a spouse, divorce, and loss of a job. Research suggests that individuals experiencing a significant amount of life change may be more at risk for the occurrence of physical illnesses than those individuals whose environments are more stable (Holmes & Masuda, 1974; Holmes & Rahe, 1967; Rahe, 1974). This body of research led investigators to study the impact of acute life stress on pregnancy outcome. Specifically, variables examined in relation to childbirth and offspring status include critical life events, nonspecific psychosocial stress, and trauma.

Critical Life Events. In a series of studies designed to assess the effects of acute prenatal stress on behavior of offspring, Huttenen (1988) concluded that stress operating through the mother on the fetus can have permanent deleterious effects on offspring. After observing in one preliminary study that the effects of stress in the last trimester of rat pregnancy resulted in a significant increase in offspring turnover of intracerebrally injected radioactive norepinephrine, he decided to examine the impact of prenatal life stress on human psychological disorders (Huttenen & Niskanen, 1978). He used epidemiological data to assess the effects of prenatal loss of the father on the later incidence of psychiatric disturbance in the offspring. Compared to a control group whose mothers experienced mate loss after the birth of the child, there was an increased incidence of adult psychopathology, particularly schizophrenia, among a group of individuals whose fathers died during their gestation. Although these results suggested that prenatal stress may be a risk factor in offspring psychopathology, they are not conclusive given that the outcome variable consisted of adult psychopathology, and environmental factors throughout the individual's life cannot be excluded. To control for confounding postnatal environmental factors influencing the offspring, outcome variables often are restricted to assessment of obstetric complications, neonatal status, or infant characteristics rather than older children and adults.

In a subsequent study, Huttenen (1988) assessed the influence of prenatal stress on infant temperament at 6–8 months of age. The study consisted of prospective data (prenatal and postnatal assessments) on 240 mother-infant dyads. There was a significant relationship between maternal stress during the first trimester of the pregnancy and temperamental features (e.g., slow adaptability, negative mood, easy distractibility, high intensity). Although the study employed maternal self-report measures to assess both maternal and infant status, mothers' reports of stress during the second and third trimesters were unrelated to infant temperament. Also, the extent and distribution of stress was of the same magnitude during all phases of the pregnancy.

Gorsuch and Key (1974) found that life stress predicted obstetric complications and infant status. Life change was scored for two years preceding delivery. Obstetric complications were recorded from medical records and included marginal placenta, preeclampsia, threatened abortion, precipitate labor, infant respiratory distress, low Apgar scores (6 or less), and low birthweight. Results indicated that stressful life events in the second and third trimesters predicted obstetric complications and neonatal status.

The fact that Huttenen (1988) found that stress in the first trimester predicted infant status while Gorsuch and Key (1974) found no relation with first trimester stress highlights the importance of timing and type of measures used to assess life stress and infant status. Although both studies utilized prenatal assessments, Gorsuch and Key (1974) combined prenatal with postnatal (retrospective) assessments of life events, which may have confounded their data with biased postnatal accounts of prenatal stress. Also, the outcome measures varied in each study with Huttenen (1988) assessing infant status via maternal report at 6–8 months and Gorsuch and Key (1974) evaluating medical records for birth complications.

In contrast, Stott (1973) found that interpersonal difficulty, but not life events (including death or severe illness of a family member), predicted offspring status. Prenatal stress was assessed retrospectively in 153 mothers one month after delivery. Offspring characteristics were assessed every six months in the first two years and subsequently every year until the children were 4 years of age. Prenatal interpersonal conflict (marital conflict, interpersonal problems with family and friends) correlated with the incidence of children's physical and psychological problems including physical illness, neurological dysfunction, physical defects, developmental delays, and behavioral disturbances.

Surprisingly, Jones (1978) found, in 178 white women of low socioeconomic status, that lower life change scores predicted a greater probability of obstetric complications (precipitate labor, premature rupture of membranes, prolonged labor, Apgar scores of less than 7, stillbirth, or neonatal death). One possible interpretation provided by the author was that individuals who had experienced higher prepregnancy conflict were more capable of coping with stress and were less affected physiologically at the time of the delivery compared to patients with lower levels of previous life change.

Nonspecific Psychosocial Stress. Rather than measuring critical life events, Newton et al. (1979) assessed perceived nonspecific psychosocial stress (amount of general tension and worry over particular events) in relation to preterm delivery. They found that nonspecific worry and life stress in the week preceding the onset of labor (assessed retrospectively 3–4 days after delivery) was much higher in mothers who gave birth prematurely. Similarly, Blau and his colleagues (1963) conducted a study on the relations of maternal personality and attitudes to preterm delivery. Sixty mothers were assessed retrospectively and assigned to either a preterm or a control group. Each mother was rated on a variety of personality traits, including attitudes towards the pregnancy, level of maturity, and interpersonal relations. Mothers with preterm deliveries showed more negative attitudes, greater emotional immaturity, and less adequate resolution of family problems. Although these results suggested that prenatal worries and negative attitudes predict preterm delivery, the retrospective design inherently confounds prenatal stress with birth outcome. In a prospective study, however, Ferreira (1960) examined prenatal attitudes towards the pregnancy and the baby as they relate to infant status and also found a significant relationship. Specifically, "deviant behavior" in the first five days of life (amount of crying, amount of sleep, degree of irritability, bowel movements, and feeding) was associated with negative prenatal attitudes ("fear of harming the baby" and "rejection of the pregnancy").

Trauma. In an early study, Sontag (1941) found that distress during pregnancy produced a marked increase in fetal activity. Similarly,

Ianniruberto and Tajani (1981) examined 28 panic-stricken pregnant women (18–36 weeks gestational age) during an earthquake in Italy. None of the mothers suffered physical trauma. All of the fetuses showed intense hyperkinesia, which lasted from 2 to 8 hours. In 20 cases this was followed by a period of reduced motility lasting 24–72 hours; the remaining 8 fetuses recovered immediately. Rofe and Goldberg (1983) examined the prenatal effects of living in an area which had been the target of terrorist activity in the Middle East. In particular, blood pressure of over 5,000 pregnant women was assessed. Subjects were classified as living in a high-, middle-, or low-stressed areas based on the varying intensity of terrorist activity. Results indicated that the women in the high-stress environment displayed significantly higher systolic and diastolic blood pressure, which can severely threaten both mother and fetus (Wolkind, 1981b). Results also indicated that the younger women displayed greater increase in systolic blood pressure than older women.

This body of research on the effects of life stress on obstetric, neonatal, and infant status highlights the need to provide more systematic and objective measures of both predictor and outcome variables. When relations between prenatal stress and birth outcome are found, studies often use retrospective accounts or self-report data to assess both prenatal maternal stress and infant status. Careful attention must be given to both the timing of the prenatal assessments and the occurrence of the life event (e.g., two years prior to delivery vs. two years prior to conception), with more theory-driven hypotheses rather than arbitrarily selecting temporal points during the pregnancy and infancy periods.

Psychological Distress: Prenatal Anxiety

Many studies indicate that pregnancy is typically associated with increased distress and anxiety. For example, Shereshefsky and Yarrow (1973) interviewed 60 middle-class primiparous women during their pregnancy and found that three quarters reported anxiety, which decreased slightly in the second trimester but increased as labor approached. Similarly, Pedersen et al. (1989) assessed a variety of psychological constructs and found that prenatal anxiety and self-efficacy emerged as the most salient predictor variables in the psychological functioning of normal, primiparous subjects. Currently, researchers are struggling to differentiate "normal" anxieties, which may be constructive, from those associated with negative birth outcomes (Zajicek, 1981). Moderate levels of depression and anxiety during the pregnancy are not necessarily signs of maladjustment. In fact, a psychologically healthy woman may be more perceptive and sensitive to the normal disequilibrations of pregnancy. Breen (1975) noted that women who were well-adjusted in the preconceptional and postnatal periods reported more distress during the pregnancy than those who were maladjusted before and after the pregnancy.

More extreme levels of anxiety both before and during the pregnancy may have more negative implications for maternal and infant well-being. Zajicek (1981) examined the relationship between prenatal conflicts and pre-pregnancy psychiatric history and found that women who had psychiatric problems before pregnancy continued to experience them while they were pregnant. Similarly, Grimm (1961) found that extreme levels of psychological tension during the pregnancy predicted obstetric outcome, including spontaneous abortion and preterm delivery. More moderate levels of prenatal tension were unrelated to obstetric complications.

A large body of research in the 1950s and 1960s found associations between prenatal anxiety and a variety of obstetric problems including miscarriages, prolonged or painful labor, and preterm delivery (Cramond, 1954; Davids, DeVault, & Talmadge, 1961; Grimm, 1961; Gunter, 1963; Joffe, 1969; Spielberger & Jacobs, 1978). McDonald (1968) reviewed much of this early literature and concluded that higher levels of prenatal anxiety were significantly related to obstetric complications.

One of the most consistent findings reported is that prenatal anxiety and distress predicts preterm delivery (Berkowitz & Kasl, 1983; Gunter, 1963; Newton et al., 1979; Schwartz, 1977). However, most of these studies utilized retrospective designs. The findings from such an approach are inconclusive, since women with preterm deliveries may recall experiencing more prenatal anxiety. Prospective studies are more desirable, but they often are difficult to conduct, since only a small proportion of mothers experience a particular obstetric problem of interest (McDonald, 1968; Omer & Everly, 1988; Spielberger & Jacobs, 1978).

Davids et al. (1961) assessed anxiety during the seventh month of pregnancy and again at 6 weeks following delivery. They noted that "women who were later to experience complications in delivery or were to give birth to children with abnormalities tended to report relatively high amounts of disturbing anxiety while they were pregnant" (p. 76). Similarly, Gorsuch and Key (1974) assessed anxiety (and life stress) in mothers of low socioeconomic status and reported that anxiety in the first trimester predicted "abnormalities of pregnancy" (p. 360). Findings must be interpreted with caution without more precisely defined variables. When more extensive assessments are made, results frequently vary as a function of specific outcome measure. Beck et al. (1980) found that maternal preparation, anxiety, and attitudes did influence some aspects of delivery, but the predictive power depended on the criterion measure selected. Subjects were randomly assigned to a standard prenatal preparatory class or a standard class plus desensitization to a hierarchy of labor and delivery related scores. A control group consisted of women who did not request a preparatory class. Fears of pregnancy and levels of anxiety were assessed in the last trimester and upon admission to the labor room. Criterion variables included obstetric complications (e.g., length of labor, use of analgesia or anesthesia, type of delivery, Apgar scores, etc.); rating scales of pain and mangeability completed by obstetrical staff; and self-rated pain levels within 24 hours of delivery. Results indicated that participation in the prenatal classes was significantly related to lower pain ratings, but not to other obstetric variables. Prenatal anxiety in the third trimester did not predict obstetric complications.

Researchers have successfully linked prenatal anxiety to neonatal activity. Standley, Soule, and Copans (1979) assessed the effect of specific dimensions of prenatal anxiety on perinatal outcome, including birthweight, infant alertness, and motor maturity. Anxieties about pregnancy, childbirth, and parenting were related to motor maturity of the neonate. Also, women who were young and not well-educated were more anxious during pregnancy. Similarly, Ottinger and Simmons (1964) were interested in the effects of prenatal maternal anxiety on neonatal body activity and crying activity assessed on the second, third, and fourth days of life. They found that prenatal anxiety was significantly related to neonatal crying. However, they noted that the design of their study did not reveal the mechanisms responsible for this effect.

CONFOUNDING AND MODIFYING FACTORS

In many studies, it is possible that the effects on offspring behavior were the result of some variable other than the stress during gestation alone. Confounding factors in the animal work comprise both prenatal and postnatal variables. Prenatal variables include timing and configuration of stress applications, maternal species, strain and genotype (which determine the intrauterine environment and the inheritance of conceptus). Postnatal variables include the number and composition of litter mates. In species that give birth to multiple offspring, there is often a correlation between litter mates on several traits. If data analyses make use of each subject, the effect of treatment tends to be overestimated. Maternal effects postnatally may also be potential confounds; in an attempt to eliminate this confound, a cross-fostering design can be employed. In this experimental design, a factorial combination is conducted so that pups from each of the prenatal treatment conditions are raised by mothers from each of the treatment groups. Additionally, nutritional status and the age of the offspring at testing may affect results.

Furthermore, there are limitations in the application of animal work to humans. Frequently, investigations deal with species-specific behavior with questionable predictive validity for humans. The human work is even more problematic in that it is usually retrospective and non-experimental, in some cases taking advantage of actuarial surveys.

The mixture of physical elements in "physical stress" situations can make it difficult to interpret findings. As Kinsley and Svare (1986b) noted, studies of prenatal heat/light/restraint stress may also involve varying degrees of dehydration and malnutrition. Also, it is difficult to identify, much less eliminate or minimize, psychological factors in laboratory animals. For example, monkeys have shown emotional reactions when forced to exercise on a treadmill; the largest adrenal cortical stress responses occurred when the monkey refused to do the hard labor rather than when a substantial amount of muscular work was performed (Mason, 1968).

Results from empirical studies provide equivocal support for the effects of prenatal stress and anxiety on obstetric and birth outcome. Findings are often inconsistent and inconclusive due largely to methodological shortcomings including a heavy reliance on retrospective data and a lack of specificity with respect to the outcome variables.

The retrospective design that characterizes much of the work in this area clearly is problematic since it confounds prenatal stress with perinatal or postnatal factors. Of the research on prenatal stress and anxiety in humans reviewed in the present chapter, approximately one-half employed prospective designs (e.g. Beck et al., 1980; Burstein, Kinch, & Stern, 1974; Crandon, 1979; Davids et al., 1961; Ferreira, 1960; Grimm & Venet, 1966; Huttenen, 1988; Ottinger & Simmons, 1964; Standley et al., 1979). Even conclusions based on prospective work, however, are equivocal. Some prospective studies show that stress and anxiety during pregnancy predict obstetric complications (Davids et al., 1961), infant temperament (Huttenen, 1988), neonatal motor maturity (Standley et al., 1979), noenatal crying (Ottinger & Simmons, 1964), and abnormal neonatal behavioral patterns (e.g., sleep disruption, irritability, changes in bowel movements, and feeding problems [Ferreira, 1960]). Other prospective studies, however, suggest no relation of prenatal stress or anxiety to obstetric or neonatal outcome (Beck et al., 1980; Grimm, 1961; Grimm & Venet, 1966; Jones, 1978; McDonald & Christakos, 1963).

When specific outcome variables are considered, additional inconsistencies become apparent. For example, anxiety has repeatedly been associated both with preterm delivery (Gunter, 1963; Newton et al., 1979; Schwartz, 1977) and with less effective uterine contractions and prolonged labor (e.g., Lederman et al., 1978).

Social Support

In addition to issues of methodology and specificity of outcome variables, inconsistencies may result from failure to account for individual differences that mediate the effects of stress and anxiety on pregnancy and infant outcome. Individual differences in social support have been found to be related to postnatal functioning (Dimitrovsky, Perez-Hirshberg, & Itskowitz, 1987; Nuckolls, Cassel, & Kaplan, 1972; Sosa et al., 1980). Dimitrovsky et al. (1987) assessed depression and quality of family relations during the last trimester of pregnancy and eight weeks postpartum. Their results indicated that a poor marital relationship predicted both prenatal and postnatal depression. They conclude that a good marital relationship may protect some women from prenatal distress. Nuckolls, Cassell, and Kaplan (1972) report that "psychosocial assets" including family and social support assessed prenatally lowered the rate of birth complications when high levels of stress were present. Similarly, Sosa et al. (1980) assessed the effect of a supportive female companion on length of labor and mother-infant interaction following delivery. The companion, assigned upon admission, provided social and emotional support including friendly verbalization and physical contact (holding hands, rubbing the mother's back). Compared to a control group, labor was shortened and some aspects of maternal behaviors in the first hour after delivery (stroking, vocalization) were enhanced. Also, certain problems requiring intervention (stillbirth, Caesarean section, oxytocin augmentation, forceps) were decreased for mothers who had a supportive companion. The authors noted that their particular setting in Guatemala (crowded hospital conditions, absence of prenatal preparatory classes) may have increased maternal anxiety and exaggerated the effect of a supportive environment. They also speculate that their effects were correlated with catecholamine levels and changes in plasma epinephrine, although they did not study these biochemical factors directly.

Benefits of Stress

An interesting set of findings are those which, as a group, represent beneficial effects of stress. Moderate exercise stress in humans has been shown to increase infant birthweight and Apgar scores (Erkkola, 1976; Hall & Kaufmann, 1987). Fride and Weinstock (1984) noted that offspring of mother rats in a group which received daily noise stress late in pregnancy developed early motor skills more quickly than did control animals. The offspring of rat mothers stressed by crowding had higher birthweights as well as less emotionality, measured by increased activity and decreased defecation, than did control offspring (Dahlöf et al., 1978; Lieberman, 1963). Ader and Conklin (1963) also found that the offspring of handled mother rats were found to be generally less emotional, showing decreased defecation compared to controls. To the extent that lower birthweight, delayed motor skills, and high emotionality may be considered maladaptive, such results contradict any expectation that only negative effects can result from prenatal stress.

MECHANISMS OF PRENATAL STRESS

In general, the stress response in humans is a result of cognitive interpretation of a stimulus with or without emotional arousal of the organism (Asterita, 1985). As noted in Chapters 3 and 4, two main physiological axes are activated. The neural axis is most rapid and allows, through the anterior and posterior hypothalamus, for respective activation of the sympathetic and parasympathetic nervous systems. The sympathetic nervous system dictates adrenal medullary release of catecholamines (e.g., epinephrine and norepinephrine). The neuroendocrine axis response is more prolonged. Hypothalamic releasing factors from the median eminence cause the anterior pituitary to release trophic hormones, including adrenocorticotrophic hormone (ACTH). ACTH then acts upon the adrenal cortex to secrete steroid hormones: sex hormones (e.g. androgens), glucocorticoids (e.g. cortisol), and mineralocorticoids (e.g. aldosterone).

With regard to prenatal stressors and the specific impact of those stressors on the offspring, external events are potentially capable of influencing the developing fetus by direct effects, by mechanical effects, or by the transplacental transfer of active substances, such as neurochemicals, hormones, and immune factors to the fetus. Because this chapter has been limited to those stressors which do not have primarily direct effects, only mechanisms for the second and third effects will be discussed, with the most substantive data supporting the third.

Mechanical Effects

The major hemodynamic response to exercise is the selective redistribution of blood flow to the working muscles, with a reduction in blood flow to the splanchnic organs and potentially to the pregnant uterus as well as to the fetus (Morris et al., 1956; Rosenfeld & West, 1977). Such changes have recently been confirmed by Clapp (1980) in the pregnant sheep model.

There are several ways in which nutrient flow to the fetus could be diminished during maternal malnutrition. It is possible that maternal nutrient concentrations could be diminished and these deficits could be passed on to the fetus; however, the best documented mechanism in rats is that the malnourished dam fails to adequately increase her blood volume, thereby limiting the normal expansion of uterine blood flow. It is also possible that placental transport capacity could be reduced, either because of reduced growth of the placenta, histological abnormalities, or decreased fuel necessary for active transport of some nutrients (reviewed by Jones & Crnic, 1988).

Mednick (1970) hypothesized that the higher incidence of "pregnancy and birth complications" in a group of individuals at high risk for schizophrenia might be caused by the sensitivity of fetal neural tissue to anoxia secondary to vascular obstruction. Kelly (1962) has shown that fear increases uterine activity. Myers (1975) later postulated that if background uterine tone were sufficiently increased, it might provoke tetanic contractions and fetal asphyxia. However, the episodes of psychosocial stress in his study of rhesus monkeys failed to produce such changes in uterine activity; thus, the enhanced asphyxia of the fetuses could not be attributed to a mechanical cause.

Transfer of Active Substances to Fetus

Neurochemical Effects. In pregnant rats, Moyer, Herrenkohl, and Jacobowitz (1977) showed that prenatal stress reduced maternal brain levels of norepinephrine in the ventral ascending bundle (i.e., medial preoptic nucleus, anterior hypothalamus, medial forebrain bundle). Similar changes occurred in male offspring of stressed mothers. At the level of discrete brain regions, Moyer and colleagues (1978) found that, compared to normal adult male rats, prenatally stressed males had significantly less norepinephrine in the medial preoptic nucleus and median eminence. These are areas involved with neuroendocrine control mechanisms, including sexual behavior (Lisk, 1967) and are target regions for gonadal steroids (Grant & Stumpf, 1975). These reductions in norepinephrine concentrations to within normal female range may relate to the feminized adult sexual behavior of prenatally stressed male offspring (Ward, 1972). Lieberman (1963) also noted that prenatal injections of epinephrine and norepinephrine altered offspring behavior; epinephrine, in particular, mimicked the behavioral results of the crowding stressor.

Very few studies directly assess stress-related neurochemical factors in human pregnancy. Omer (Omer & Everly, 1988; Omer et al., 1986) suggested the possible involvement of catecholamines in preterm labor, with norepinephrine increasing uterine contractions (Danforth, 1982; Lederman et al., 1978) and epinephrine decreasing these contractions in the short run but increasing them in the long run (Ishikawah & Fuchs, 1978; Tothill, Rothbine, & Willman, 1971). Lederman et al. (1978) presented one of the few studies directly assessing relations of maternal anxiety, selected neurohormones, and progress in labor. Measures of plasma epinephrine, norepinephrine, and cortisol were obtained in third-trimester pregnancy, during labor, and after delivery. Plasma epinephrine levels drawn at 3 cm of cervical dilation were significantly related to self-rated anxiety and lower uterine contractility.

Pregnant women respond to induced exercise with significant increases in epinephrine and norepinephrine (Artal et al., 1981; Rauramo, Andersson, & Laatikainen, 1982). Artal and colleagues (1981) noted, in exercise-stressed pregnant women, a predominant rise in norepinephrine in comparison to epinephrine, suggesting that exercise activates the sympathetic nerves to a greater extent than the adrenal medulla. There were no changes in cortisol concentration with mild exercise.

Sandman and colleagues (1990) have posited an endorphinergic mechanism for the effects of stress on the fetus and on infant outcome. To support this model, they cite earlier work (Chernick & Craig, 1982) which suggested that endogenous opiates are the primary cause of neurological complications related to hypoxia. Pregnant rabbits were pretreated with naloxone (an opiate antagonist) or placebo, then asphyxiated and delivered of offspring by Cesarean section. Although pups born to placebo-pretreated mothers were not viable, pups born to naloxone-pretreated mothers were. Proposing a biopsychological model of stress in pregnant women, Sandman concluded that beta-endorphin, an endogenous opiate that increases in amniotic fluid and cord blood with perinatal stress, may be a final common pathway for the fetal effects of stress-related complications of pregnancy.

Hormonal Effects. It has been suggested that maternal pituitary-adrenal hormones reaching the fetal hippocampus at a critical time during development can cause permanent alterations in the reactivity of the hypothalamic-pituitary-adrenal (HPA) axis (Sapolsky, Krey, & McEwen, 1984), which in turn might result in changes in behavior, particularly under stressful conditions. To date, studies testing this hypothesis are inconsistent. Ader and Plaut (1968) found decreased plasma corticosterone levels in response to stress in prenatally stressed offspring, while Peters (1982) found that handling combined with saline injection of rat dams produced an increased corticosterone response in the offspring after stress, compared to controls.

Anogenital distances of restraint/light/heat prenatally stressed females were shorter than those of control females, suggesting that alterations in fetal testosterone exposure may be responsible for disruptions in behavior and reproduction (Kinsley & Svare, 1988). In a fostering study, Power and Moore (1986) and Moore and Power (1986) showed that rat dams respond differently to pups whose mothers were stressed by crowding with aggressive males during the last week of pregnancy: stressed male pups received lower levels of maternal licking from the same foster mothers than did unstressed males. The investigators determined that this difference originated from a change in the urinary chemosignals produced by prenatally stressed males. They concluded that the crowding procedure interfered with the production of male-typical odors by interfering with male-typical levels of prenatal testosterone secretion.

Restraint stress has been found to feminize male sexual behavior in adult rats (Ward, 1972, 1984). Diminished exposure of fetal males to gonadal androgens is presumed to be the result of increased exposure to stress steroids (Ward, 1972). Similar abnormalities can be produced by maternal treatment with opiates (Ward, Orth, & Weisz, 1983); this finding suggests the abnormalities in male sexual development may be mediated by excess fetal opioidergic activity induced by stress. In support of this suggestion is the work of Ward, Monaghan, and Ward (1986), who found that maternal treatment with an opioid receptor antagonist could prevent the adverse effects of prenatal stress on male sexual development and behavior.

There are very few human studies that have explored the relation between maternal hormonal correlates of stress and infant status. Vaughn et al. (1987) presented data assessing the hypothesis that maternal anxiety influences infant temperament via intrauterine environment. They obtained assessments of maternal psychological adjustment (including anxiety level) and blood samples for cortisol, ACTH, and beta-endorphin (1) during the third trimester of the pregnancy; (2) during the early labor; (3) after cervical dilation; and (4) one day postpartum. They also obtained a sample of placental blood at the time of delivery. They concluded that the neuroendocrine data have no interpretable relation to infant temperament. In contrast, maternal anxiety was significantly related to infant temperament (as was first-trimester stress in Huttenen's 1988 report). However, their results remain largely inconclusive, since both maternal anxiety and infant temperament were assessed via maternal report.

With regard to other hormones, Pugh, Newton, and Piercy (1979) speculated in an anecdotal report that maternal gastrin crossing the placenta mediated the fatal acute gastric ulcerative hemorrhage in a 21-hour-old infant boy.

Immune Factor Effects. While the nature and mechanisms of stress effects on the immune system are being unraveled and have recently been the subject of excellent reviews (Plotnikoff et al., 1986; Solomon et al., 1985), there has been no specific implication of these effects in the area of prenatal stress. However, see the description of the Geschwind hypothesis in Chapter 3.

DIRECTIONS FOR FUTURE RESEARCH

Despite four decades of research, well-developed theory about the relation between prenatal psychosocial stress and birth or neonatal status in humans does not exist. The type of research that has characterized much of the literature on humans is often inconclusive and has limited the development of theoretical and conceptual models. Many limitations of previous studies stem from a failure to capture in the research designs a multidimensional perspective of prenatal psychosocial stress as it relates to obstetric and neonatal outcome. New directions and strategies for future research should include:

1. Control or assess individual differences that may relate to heterogeneity of outcome, including social support, coping mechanisms, and biochemical reactivity.
2. Provide objective, independent measures of maternal and infant status whenever possible, particularly when assessing infant temperament.
3. Utilize prospective rather than retrospective research designs whenever possible to avoid "retrospectoscopic" confounding of perinatal or postnatal factors with prenatal influences.
4. Provide multiple prenatal assessments as well as preconception baseline data.
5. Delineate prenatal predictor and obstetric or neonatal criterion variables with increased specificity.
6. Exercise care in generalizing between species and between stressors of varying severity.
7. Allow for emergence of a "dose-response curve" for stress effects (which may well be curvilinear).
8. Allow for finding specific beneficial effects of stress (in specific situations and at specific stress levels) as well as specific harmful effects.

These recommendations may help us advance toward research designs that are clearly more complex but which yield more reliable and concise findings on the actual effects of prenatal stress.

REFERENCES

Ader, R., & Conklin, P. M. (1963). Handling of pregnant rats: Effects on emotionality of their offspring. *Science, 142*, 411–412.

Ader, R., & Plaut, S. M. (1968). Effects of prenatal maternal handling and differential housing on offspring emotionality, plasma corticosterone levels, and susceptibility to gastric erosions. *Psychosomatic Medicine, 30*, 277–286.

Anderson, D. K. (1985). Effects of prenatal stress on the differentiation of the sexually dimorphic nucleus of the preoptic area (SDN-POA) of the rat brain. *Brain Research, 332*, 113–118.

Archer, J. E., & Blackman, D. E. (1971). Prenatal psychological stress and off-spring behavior in rats and mice. *Developmental Psychobiology, 4,* 193–248.

Artal, R., Platt, L. D., Sperling, M., Kammula, R. K., Jilek, J., & Nakamura, R. (1981). Exercise in pregnancy. I. Maternal cardiovascular and metabolic responses in normal pregnancy. *American Journal of Obstetrics and Gynecology, 140,* 123–127.

Asterita, M. F. (1985). *The physiology of stress.* New York: Human Sciences Press.

Barlow, S. M., Knight, A., & Sullivan, F. M. (1978). *Teratology, 18,* 211–218.

Bättig, K., Zeier, H., Muller, R., & Buzzi, R. (1980). A field study on vegetative effects of aircraft noise. *Archives of Environmental Health, 35,* 228–235.

Beck, N. C., Siegel, L. J., Davidson, N. P., Kormeier, S., Breitenstein, A., & Hall, D. G. (1980). The prediction of pregnancy outcome: Maternal preparation, anxiety, and sets. *Journal of Psychosomatic Research, 24,* 341–343.

Berg, B. N. (1965). Dietary restriction and reproduction in the rat. *Journal of Nutrition, 87,* 344–350.

Berkowitz, G. S., & Kasl, S. V. (1983). The role of psychosocial factors in spontaneous preterm delivery. *Journal of Psychosomatic Research, 27,* 283–290.

Blau, A., Slaffe, B., Easton, K., Welkowitz, J., Springarn, J., & Cohen, J. (1963). The psychogenic etiology of premature births: A preliminary report. *Psychosomatic Medicine, 25*(3), 201–211.

Boehnke, W. H., Chernoff, G. F., & Finnell, R. H. (1987). Investigation of the teratogenic effects of exercise on pregnancy outcome in mice. *Teratogenesis, Carcinogenesis, and Mutagenesis, 7,* 391–397.

Breen, D. (1975). *The birth of a first child.* London: Tavistock Publications.

Bryan, Y. E., Huffman, L. C., Pedersen, F. A., & Porges, S. W. (1989). *The ontogeny of maternal responsiveness: Prenatal influences.* Manuscript in preparation.

Burstein, I., Kinch, R. A. H., & Stern, L. (1974). Anxiety, pregnancy, labor, and the neonate. *American Journal of Obstetrics and Gynecology, 118*(2), 195–199.

Bush, M., & Leathwood, P. D. (1975). Effects of differing regimens of early malnutrition on behavioral development and adult avoidance learning in Swiss white mice. *British Journal of Nutrition, 33,* 373–385.

Chapman, R. H., & Stern, J. M. (1979). Failure of severe maternal stress or ACTH during pregnancy to affect emotionality of male rat offspring. Implications of litter effects for prenatal studies. *Developmental Psychobiology, 12,* 255–267.

Chase, H. P., Welch, N. N., Dabiere, C. S., Vasan, N. S. & Butterfield, L. J. (1972). Alterations in human brain chemistry following intrauterine growth retardation. *Pediatrics, 50,* 403–411.

Chernick, V., & Craig, R. J. (1982). Naloxone reverses neonatal depression caused by fetal asphyxia. *Science, 216,* 1252–1253.

Christian, J. J. (1975). Hormonal control of population growth. In B. E. Eleftheriou & R. L. Sprott (Eds.), *Hormonal correlates of behavior,* Vol. 1. (pp. 205–274). New York: Plenum.

Clapp, J. F. (1980). Acute exercise stress in the pregnant ewe. *American Journal of Obstetrics and Gynecology, 136,* 489.

Clapp, J. F., & Dickstein, S. (1984). Endurance exercise and pregnancy outcome. *Medical Science and Sports Exercise, 16,* 556–562.

Cramond, W. (1954). Psychological aspects of uterine dysfunction. *Lancet, 2,* 1241–1245.

Crandon, A. J. (1979). Maternal anxiety and neonatal well-being. *Journal of Psychosomatic Research, 23,* 113–115.

Dahlöf, L., Hård, E., & Larsson, K. (1977). Influence of maternal stress on offspring sexual behavior. *Animal Behavior, 25,* 958–963.

Dahlöf, L., Hård, E., & Larsson, K. (1978). Influence of maternal stress on the development of the genital system. *Physiology and Behavior, 20,* 193–195.

Danforth, D. N. (Ed.) (1982). *Obstetrics and Gynecology.* Philadelphia: J.B. Lippincott.

Davids, A., DeVault, S., & Talmadge, M. (1961). Anxiety, pregnancy, and childbirth abnormalities. *Journal of Consulting Psychology, 25*(1), 74–77.

DeFries, J. C., & Weir, M. W. (1964). Open field behavior of C57BL/6J mice as a function of age, experience, and prenatal maternal stress. *Psychonomic Science, 1,* 389–390.

Diamond, E. (1982). The role of anger and hostility in essential hypertension and coronary heart disease. *Psychological Bulletin, 92,* 410–433.

Dimitrovsky, L., Perez-Hirshberg, M., & Itskowitz, R. (1987). Depression during and following pregnancy: Quality of family relationships. *The Journal of Psychology, 121*(3), 213–218.

Drillien, C. M. (1970). Intellectual sequelae of "fetal malnutrition." In H. A. Waisman & G. Kerr (Eds.), *Fetal growth and development* (p. 271). New York: McGraw-Hill.

Eliot, G., & Eisdorfer, D. (Eds.) (1982). *Stress and human health: Analysis and implications of research.* New York: Springer.

Erkkola, R. (1976). The physical work capacity of the expectant mother and its effect on pregnancy, labour and the newborn. *International Journal of Gynaecology and Obstetrics, 14,* 153–159.

Ferreira, A. J. (1960). The pregnant mother's emotional attitude and its reflection upon the newborn. *American Journal of Orthopsychiatry, 30,* 553–561.

Field, T., Sandberg, D., Quetel, T. A., Garcia, R., & Rosario, M. (1985). Effects of ultrasound feedback on pregnancy anxiety, fetal activity, and neonatal outcome. *Obstetrics and Gynecology, 66*(4), 525–528.

Frazer, J. F. D., & Huggett, A. (1970). The partition of nutrients between mother and conceptus in the pregnant rat. *Journal of Physiology, 207,* 783–788.

Fride, E., Dan, Y., Gavish, M., & Weinstock, M. (1985). Prenatal stress impairs maternal behavior in a conflict situation and reduces hippocampal benzodiazepine receptors. *Life Sciences, 36,* 2103–2109.

Fride, E., & Weinstock, M. (1984). The effects of prenatal exposure to predictable or unpredictable stress on early development in the rat. *Developmental Psychobiology, 17,* 651–660.

Gentsch, C., Lichtsteiner, M., & Feer, H. (1981). 3H-Diazepam binding sites in Roman high- and low-avoidance rats. *Experientia, 37,* 183–186.

Gorsuch, R. L., & Key, M. K. (1974). Abnormalities of pregnancy as a function of anxiety and life stress. *Psychosomatic Medicine, 36,* 352–361.

Grant, L. D., & Stumpf, W. E. (1975). Hormone uptake sites in relation to CNS biogenic amine systems. In W. E. Stumpf & L. D. Grant (Eds.), *Anatomical neuroendocrinology* (pp. 445–463). New York: Karger.

Grimm, E. R. (1961). Psychological tension in pregnancy. *Psychosomatic Medicine, 23*(6), 1961.

Grimm, E. R., & Venet, W. R. (1966). The relationship of emotional adjustment and attitudes to the course and outcome of pregnancy. *Psychosomatic Medicine, 28,* 34–49.

Gunter, L. M. (1963). Psychopathology and stress in the life experience of mothers of premature infants. *American Journal of Obstetrics and Gynecology, 86,* 333–340.

Hall, D. C., & Kaufmann, D. A. (1987). Effects of aerobic and strength conditioning on pregnancy outcomes. *American Journal of Obstetrics and Gynecology, 157,* 1199–1203.

Herrenkohl, L. R. (1986). Prenatal stress disrupts reproductive behavior and physiology in offspring. *Annals of the New York Academy of Sciences, 474,* 120–128.

Herrenkohl, L. R., & Whitney, J. B. (1976). Effects of prepartal stress on postnatal nursing behavior, litter development and adult sexual behavior. *Physiology and Behavior, 17,* 1019–1021.

Holmes, T. H., & Masuda, M. (1974). Life change and illness susceptibility. In B. S. Dohrenwend & B. P. Dohrenwend (Eds.), *Stressful life events: Their nature and occurrence.* New York: Wiley.

Holmes, T. H., & Rahe, R. H. (1967). The social readjustment rating scale. *Journal of Psychosomatic Research, 11,* 213–218.

Huttenen, M. O. (1988). Maternal stress during pregnancy and the behavior of the offspring. In S. Doxiadis (Ed.), *Early influences shaping the individual.* New York: Plenum Press.

Huttunen, M. O., & Niskanen, P. (1978). Prenatal loss of father and psychiatric disorders. *Archives of General Psychiatry, 35,* 429.

Ianniruberto, A., & Tajani, E. (1981). Ultrasonographic study of fetal movements. *Seminars in Perinatology, 5*(2), 175–181.

Ishikawa, M., & Fuchs, A. (1978). Effects of epinephrine and oxytocin on the release of prostaglandin F from the rat uterus. *Nature, 223,* 89–101.

Istvan, J. (1986). Stress, anxiety, and birth outcomes: A critical review of the evidence. *Psychological Bulletin, 100*(3), 331–348.

Joffe, J. M. (1965). Effect of foster-mothers strain and prenatal experience on adult behavior in rats. *Nature, 208,* 815–816.

Joffe, J. M. (1969). *Prenatal determinants of behavior.* Oxford: Pergamon.

Jones, A. C. (1978). Life change and psychological distress as predictors of pregnancy outcome. *Psychosomatic Medicine, 40*(5), 402–411.

Jones, A. P., & Crnic, L. S. (1988). Maternal mediation of the effects of malnutrition. In E. P. Riley & C. V. Vorhees (Eds.), *Handbook of behavioral teratology* (pp. 409–426). New York: Plenum.

Jones, F. N., & Tauscher, J. (1978). Residence under an airport landing pattern as a factor in teratism. *Archives of Environmental Health, 33,* 10–12.

Keeley, K. (1962). Prenatal influence on behavior of offspring of crowded mice. *Science, 135,* 44–45.

Kelly, J. V. (1962). Effect of fear on uterine motility. *American Journal of Obstetrics and Gynecology, 83,* 576–581.

Kinsley, C., & Svare, B. (1986a). Prenatal stress reduces intermale aggression in mice. *Physiology and Behavior, 36,* 783–786.

Kinsley, C., & Svare, B. (1986b). Prenatal stress effects: Are they mediated by reductions in maternal food and water intake and body weight gain? *Physiology and Behavior, 37,* 191–193.

Kinsley, C., & Svare, B. (1988). Prenatal stress alters maternal aggression in mice. *Physiology and Behavior, 42,* 7–13.

Knipschild, P., Meier, H., & Salle, H. (1981). Aircraft noise and birth weight. *International Archives of Occupational and Environmental Health, 48,* 131–136.

Lacey, J. I. (1967). Somatic response patterning and stress: Some revisions of activation theory. In M. H. Appley & R. Trumbull (Eds.), *Psychological stress: Issues in research.* New York: Appleton.

Lederman, R. P., Lederman, E., Work, B. A., & McCann, D. S. (1978). The relationship of maternal anxiety, plasma catecholamines, and plasma cortisol to progress in labor. *American Journal of Obstetrics and Gynecology, 2*(10), 495–500.

Lieberman, M. W. (1963). Early developmental stress and later behavior. *Science, 141,* 824–825.

Lisk, R. D. (1967). Sexual behavior: Hormonal control. In L. Martini & W. F. Ganong (Eds.), *Neuroendocrinology* (Vol. 2, pp. 197–239). New York: Academic Press.

Lubchenco, L. O. (1970). Assessment of gestational age and development at birth. *Pediatric Clinics of North America, 17,* 125–135.

Mason, J. W. (1968). "Overall" hormonal balance as a key to endocrine organization. *Psychosomatic Medicine, 30,* 791–808.

McDonald, R. L. (1968). The role of emotional factors in obstetric complications: A review. *Psychosomatic Medicine, 30*(2), 222–237.

McDonald, R. L., & Christakos, A. C. (1963). Relationship of emotional adjustment during pregnancy to obstetric complications. *American Journal of Obstetrics and Gynecology, 86,* 341–348.

Mednick, S. A. (1970). Breakdown in individuals at high risk for schizophrenia: Possible predispositional perinatal factors. *Mental Hygiene, 54,* 50–63.

Moore, C. L., & Power, K. L. (1986). Prenatal stress affects mother-infant interaction in Norway rats. *Developmental Psychobiology, 19,* 235–245.

Morgane, P. J., Miller, M., Kemper, T., Stern, W., Forbes, W., Hall, R., Bronzino, J., Kissane, J., Hawrylewicz, E., & Resnick, O. (1978). The effects of protein malnutrition on the developing central nervous system in the rat. *Neuroscience and Biobehavioral Reviews, 2,* 137–230.

Morra, M. (1965). Level of maternal stress during two pregnancy periods on rat offspring behavior. *Psychonomic Science, 3,* 7–8.

Morris, N., Osorn, S., Wright, H., & Hart, A. (1956). Effective uterine blood-flow during exercise in normal and pre-eclamptic pregnancies. *Lancet, 2,* 481.

Moyer, J. A., Herrenkohl, L. R., & Jacobowitz, D. M. (1977). Effects of stress during pregnancy on catecholamines in discrete brain regions. *Brain Research, 121,* 385–393.

Moyer, J. A., Herrenkohl, L. R., & Jacobowitz, D. M. (1978). Stress during pregnancy: Effect on catecholamines in discrete brain regions of offspring as adults. *Brain Research, 144,* 173–178.

Myers, R. E. (1975). Maternal psychological stress and fetal asphyxia: A study in the monkey. *American Journal of Obstetrics and Gynecology, 122,* 47–59.

Newton, R. W., Webster, P. A., Binu, P. S., Maskrey, N., & Phillips, A. B. (1979). Psychosocial stress in pregnancy and its relation to the onset of premature labour. *British Medical Journal, ii,* 411–413.

Nuckolls, K. B., Cassel, J., & Kaplan, B. H. (1972). Psychosocial assets, life crisis, and the prognosis of pregnancy. *American Journal of Epidemiology, 95,* 431–441.

Omer, H., & Everly, G. S. (1988). Psychological factors in preterm labor: Critical review and theoretical synthesis. *American Journal of Psychiatry, 145*(12), 1507–1513.

Omer, H., Friedlander, D., Palti, Z., & Shekel, I. (1986). Life stresses and premature labor: Real connection or artifactual findings? *Psychosomatic Medicine, 48*(5), 362–369.

Ottinger, D. R., & Simmons, J. E. (1964). Behavior of human neonates and prenatal maternal anxiety. *Psychological Reports, 14,* 391–394.

Pedersen, F. A., Bryan, Y., Huffman, L., & Del Carmen, R. (1989). *Construction of self and offspring in the pregnancy and early infancy periods.* Paper presented at the Biennial Meeting of the Society for Research in Child Development, Kansas City, Missouri.

Peters, D. A. V. (1982). Prenatal stress: Effects on brain biogenic amine and plasma corticosterone levels. *Pharmacology and Biochemistry of Behavior, 17,* 721–725.

Plotnikoff, N. P., Faith, R. E., Murgo, A. J., & Good, R. A. (Eds.) (1986). *Enkephalins and endorphins: Stress and the immune system.* New York: Plenum.

Politch, J. A., & Herrenkohl, L. R. (1979). Prenatal stress reduces maternal aggression by mice offspring. *Physiology and Behavior, 23,* 415–418.

Power, K. L., & Moore, C. L. (1986). Prenatal stress eliminates differential maternal attention to male offspring in Norway rats. *Physiology and Behavior, 38,* 667–671.

Pugh, R. J., Newton, R. W., & Piercy, D. M. (1979). Fatal bleeding from gastric ulceration during the first day of life: Possible association with social stress. *Archives of Diseases in Childhood, 54,* 146–148.

Rahe, R. H. (1974). Life change and subsequent illness reports. In E. K. Gunderson & R. H. Rahe (Eds.), *Life stress and illness*. Springfield, IL: Charles C. Thomas.

Rauramo, I., Andersson, B., & Laatikainen, T. (1982). Stress hormones and placental steroids in physical exercise during pregnancy. *British Journal of Obstetrics and Gynaecology, 89,* 921–925.

Ravelli, G.-P., Stein, Z., & Susser, M. (1976). Obesity in young men after famine exposure *in utero* and early infancy. *New England Journal of Medicine, 295,* 349–353.

Rhees, R. W., & Fleming, D. E. (1981). Effects of malnutrition, maternal stress or ACTH injections during pregnancy on sexual behavior of male offspring. *Physiology and Behavior, 27,* 879–882.

Riley, E. P., & Vorhees, C. V. (Eds.) (1986). *Handbook of behavioral teratology*. New York: Plenum.

Rofe, Y., & Goldberg, J. (1983). Prolonged exposure to a war environment and its effects on the blood pressure of pregnant women. *British Journal of Medical Psychology, 56,* 305–311.

Rosenfeld, C. R., & West, J. (1977). Circulatory response to systemic infusion of norepinephrine in the pregnant ewe. *American Journal of Obstetrics and Gynecology, 127,* 376–383.

Rosso, P., Hormazabel, J., & Winick, M. (1970). Changes in brain weight, cholesterol, phospholipid and DNA of marasmic children. *American Journal of Clinical Nutrition, 23,* 1275–1279.

Sandman, C. A., Barron, J. L., Demet, E. M., Chicz-Demet, A., Rothenberg, S. J., & Zea, F. J. (1990). Opioid peptides and perinatal development: Is beta-endorphin a natural teratogen? In G. F. Koob, C. A. Sandman, & F. L. Strand (Eds.), A decade of neuropeptides: Past, present, and future. *Annals of the New York Academy of Sciences, 579,* 91–108.

Sapolsky, R. M., Krey, L. C., & McEwen, B. S. (1984). Stress down-regulates corticosterone receptors in a site-specific manner in the brain. *Endocrinology, 114,* 287–292.

Schwartz, J. L. (1977). A study of the relationship between maternal life-change events and preterm delivery. In J. L. Schwartz & L. M. Schwartz (Eds.), *Vulnerable infants: A psychosocial dilemma*. New York: McGraw-Hill.

Scrimshaw, N. S., & Behar, M. (1965). Malnutrition in underdeveloped countries. *New England Journal of Medicine, 272,* 137–144.

Selye, H. (1950). *The physiology and pathology of exposure to stress*. Montreal: Medical Publishers.

Shereshefsky, P. M., & Yarrow, L. J. (1973). Psychological aspects of a first pregnancy and early postnatal adaptation. New York: Raven Press.

Sklar, L. S., & Anisman, H. (1981). Stress and cancer. *Psychological Bulletin, 89,* 369–406.

Smotherman, W. P., Burt, G., Kimble, D., Strickrod, G., & Bremiller, R. (1981). Behavioral and corticosterone effects in conditioned taste aversion following hippocampal lesions. *Physiology and Behavior, 627,* 569–574.

Solomon, G. F., Amkraut, A. A., & Rubin, R. T. (1985). Stress, hormones, neuroregulation and immunity. In S. R. Burchfield (Ed.), *Stress: Psychological and physiological interactions.* Washington, DC: Hemisphere.

Sontag, L. W. (1941). The significance of fetal environmental differences. *American Journal of Obstetrics and Gynecology, 42,* 996–1003.

Sontag, L. W. (1944). Differences in modifiability of fetal behavior and physiology. *Psychosomatic Medicine, 6,* 151–154.

Sontag, L. W. (1970). Effect of noise during pregnancy upon foetal and subsequent adult behavior. In B. L. Welch & A. S. Welch (Eds.), *Physiological effects of noise* (pp. 131–141). New York: Plenum Press.

Sosa, R., Kennell, J., Klaus, M., Robertson, S., & Urrutia, J. (1980). The effect of a supportive companion on perinatal problems, length of labor, and mother-infant interaction. *The New England Journal of Medicine, 303*(11), 597–600.

Sparling, J. W., Seeds, J. W., & Farran, D. C. (1988). The relationship of obstetric ultrasound to parent and infant behavior. *Obstetrics and Gynecology, 72*(6), 902–907.

Spielberger, C. D., & Jacobs, G. A. (1978). Stress and anxiety during pregnancy and labor. In L. Carenza, P. Pancheri, & L. Zichella (Eds.), *Clinical psychoneuroendocrinology in reproduction.* New York: Academic Press.

Standley, K., Soule, B., & Copans, S. A. (1979). Dimensions of prenatal anxiety and their influence on pregnancy outcome. *American Journal of Obstetrics and Gynecology, 135*(1), 23–26.

Stephan, J. K., & Chow, B. F. (1968). Growth of progeny from rats underfed during gestation only. *Federation Proceedings, 27,* 728.

Stott, D. H. (1973). Follow-up study from birth of the effects of prenatal stresses. *Developmental Medicine and Child Neurology, 15,* 770–787.

Tafari, N., Naeye, R., & Gobezie, A. (1980). Effects of maternal undernutrition and heavy physical work during pregnancy on birth weight. *British Journal of Obstetrics and Gynecology, 87,* 222–226.

Terada, M. (1974). Effect of physical activity before pregnancy on fetuses of mice exercised forcibly during pregnancy. *Teratology, 10,* 141–144.

Thompson, W. R. (1957). Influence of maternal anxiety on emotionality in young rats. *Science, 125,* 698–699.

Tothill, A., Rothbine, L., & Willman, F. (1971). Relation between prostaglandin E2 and adrenaline reversal in the rat uterus. *Nature, 223,* 56–57.

Treadway, J., Dover, E. V., Morse, W., Newcomer, L., & Craig, B. W. (1986). Influence of exercise training on maternal and fetal morphological characteristics in the rat. *Journal of Applied Physiology, 60,* 1700–1703.

Vaughn, B. E., Bradley, C. F., Joffe, L. S., Seifer, R., & Barglow, P. (1987). Maternal characteristics measured prenatally are predictive of ratings of temperamental "difficulty" on the Carey Infant Temperament Questionnaire. *Developmental Psychology, 23*(1), 152–161.

Ward, I. L. (1972). Prenatal stress feminizes and demasculinizes the behavior of males. *Science, 175,* 82–84.

Ward, I. L. (1984). The prenatal stress syndrome: Current status. *Psychoneuroendocrinology, 9,* 3–11.

Ward, I. L., & Reed, J. (1985). Prenatal stress and prepuberal social rearing conditions interact to determine sexual behavior in male rats. *Behavioral Neurosciences, 99,* 301–309.

Ward, O. B., Monaghan, E. P., & Ward, I. L. (1986). Naltrexone blocks the effects of prenatal stress on sexual behavior differentiation in male rats. *Pharmacology, Biochemistry and Behavior, 25,* 573–576.

Ward, O.B., Orth, J. M., & Weisz, J. (1983). A possible role of opiates in modifying sexual differentiation. In M. Schlumpf & W. Lichtensteiger (Eds.), *Monographs in Neural Sciences. 9. Drugs and Hormones in Brain Development* (pp. 194–200). New York: Karger.

Wilson, N., & Gisolfi, C. (1980). Effects of exercising rats during pregnancy. *Journal of Applied Physiology, 48,* 34–40.

Winick, M. (1969). Malnutrition and brain development. *Journal of Pediatrics, 74,* 667–679.

Winick, M., & Noble, A. (1966). Cellular response with increased feeding in neonatal rats. *Journal of Nutrition, 89,* 300.

Winick, M., & Nobel, A. (1967). Cellular response during malnutrition at various ages. *Journal of Nutrition, 91,* 179–182.

Wolkind, S. (1981a). Prenatal emotional stress-effects on the foetus. In S. Wolkind & E. Zajicek (Eds.), *Pregnancy: A psychological and social study.* New York: Academic Press.

Wolkind, S. (1981b). Hypertension of pregnancy. In S. Wolkind & E. Zajicek (Eds.), *Pregnancy: A psychological and social study.* New York: Academic Press.

Zajicek, E. (1981). Psychiatric problems during pregnancy. In S. Wolkind & E. Zajicek (Eds.), *Pregnancy: A psychological and social study.* New York: Academic Press.

CHAPTER SIX

Stress in Infancy

Marie L. Lobo

Much of the literature does not specifically use the term "stress" in the discussions of infants and their environments. Analyzing the literature on infant stress is particularly difficult, given the measurement issues. In school-aged children and adults, self-reports frequently are used to identify stressful situations. Obviously, infants cannot complete self-reports. Physiological indicators of stress, such as increased serum cortisol levels, are also difficult to interpret because of the difficulties inherent in obtaining the serum from the infant. Identification of a true baseline is confounded by the trauma caused by obtaining the necessary blood sample. Because of the extrapolation needed to conclude infant stress, this chapter includes several exemplars to describe stressful situations in infancy and their consequences.

GENERAL CONSIDERATIONS ABOUT INFANT STRESS

According to Lyon and Werner (1987), stress can be defined as a stimulus, a response, or a transaction. This definition provides much latitude in determining what is stress and whether "stress" is the event affecting the infant ("stressor") or the infant's response to an event ("strain"). Levine (1983) proposed that stress was a coping response: "the individual is presumed to be coping if his behavior consists of responses that permit him to master the situation" (p. 110). Selye (1976) defined stress as "the state manifested by a specific syndrome which consists of all the nonspecifically induced changes within a biological system" (p. 64). This is the definition most often cited in the literature.

In his treatise on adaptation, Dubos (1965) traces the origin of the term stress from the word "distress." The use of the term meant to "impose strain on, to coerce or compel" (p. 27), and the definition continues to be meaningful. Dubos contends the "most fundamental discrepancies between the nature of environmental stimuli and their biological effects come from the fact that the conditions under which man lives now are very different from those which shaped his biological constitution during evolutionary development" (pp. 27–28). Infancy is the stage when the modern, changing environment first impacts fully on the developing human.

Difficulties in Measuring the Infant's
Physiological Response to Stress

Physiological indicators of stress usually are measured in the bodily secretions of blood, urine, or saliva. The collection of body fluids from an infant is stressful to the infant due, at the least, to restraint and pain. Blood is obtained either from a heel stick or venipuncture. Most infants are swaddled in a blanket or clothed in such a manner that neither a vein nor a foot is readily accessible without disturbing the infant. In a heel stick, often viewed as least stressful, the infant's heel is squeezed or pressure is applied so that a lancet can be used to puncture the infant's heel to obtain the blood in a small tube. By the time the blood is obtained, the infant is crying and flailing and would be described as most distressed. It is difficult to know how the serum cortisol level is affected by the trauma of this data collection procedure. Since much of the research done to date has been on infants who have been circumcised, there is not a good understanding of the cumulative effect of the restraint, the circumcision, and the blood collection on response to stress, nor are there data available on female infants.

It may appear less stressful to collect a urine specimen from an infant. However, placing an adhesive-backed plastic bag over the infant's genitals can also be an uncomfortable and stressful experience. The adhesive, while necessary, makes the bags difficult to position, particularly on females, and removal often results in infant behaviors of crying, kicking, and other gross motor body movements. There can also be problems with leakage of urine from the bag or contamination by feces if the collection device is not properly applied.

The collection of saliva is least intrusive. However, the infants are often in a prefeeding state, cueing the caregiver that they are hungry. It is unknown how stressful it is to the infant to have feeding delayed and a syringe-type instrument instead of the nipple inserted into the mouth. Infants are reported to have nonsignificantly higher cortisol levels during the prefeeding state, with a mean prefeed serum cortisol of 97.2 ng/ml with a range of 17–342 ng/ml, while postfeed cortisols were 89.2 ng/ml with a range of 22–252 ng/ml (Blank, 1986, p. 350). No reports of the difference in pre- and postfeeding salivary cortisol have been found. See Chapter 2 for some interesting cortisol correlates of differential infant reactions to separation from mothers.

INFANT EXPOSURE TO STRESSORS

Developing infants have the potential for exposure to many stressors in their everyday life. How infants interpret these experiences is not understood. Most research on children's response to stress has been with school-aged or adolescent children. However, it is known that infants have both physiological and psychosocial reactions to the environmental stressors to which they are exposed.

A literature search failed to reveal any data-based reports related to an infant having positive responses to stress. Most of the literature supports the need for a positive, low-stress or nonstressful environment to ensure optimum health of the infant. However, some developmental theorists have stated that some stress in the environment may promote growth in infancy. The stressors described were such things as a toy being out of reach, forcing the infant to crawl to the toy.

An infant's exposure to stress may be mediated by some other factor in the environment. Scientists continue their search to define mediating factors and develop strategies to enhance the mediating factors in the infant's environment. Rutter (1985) states: "The infancy years are not determinative; cognitive processes play a major role in emotional and behavioural responses; temperamental features are influential, but oper-ate through interactions as much as individual reactivity; much behavior is context-related; many of the links in development are social rather than individual; continuities over time are usually indirect rather than direct; and fluidity in functioning continues right into adult life" (p. 606). Because of the multiple factors that influence the infant and growing child over time, it is often difficult to predict what the long-term conse-quences of early stressors will be.

Stress may also be a necessary component of the environment, encour-aging the infant to perform new behaviors. Mothers who have more complex verbal and nonverbal interactions with their infant may stimu-late development in the infant. For instance, the parent who throws a ball to the infant will stimulate better eye/hand coordination, and the parent who describes food with color and texture will stimulate cognitive and language development. The infant may need to be stressed to do new tasks.

Environment—The Small World

There are various characteristics of the infant's environment that can support or fail to support physical, mental, and social growth and devel-opment. Bronfenbrenner (1979) views the environment as an ecological system that can serve as a predisposer to stressful responses in the infant, or can be a mediator of stressful experiences for the infant.

Characteristics of the environment which must be considered are the "animate" or live part of the environment, including people and pets, and the "inanimate" or structural part of the environment, including toys, furniture, and buildings. The "people" part of the animate environ-ment includes mothers, fathers, siblings, grandparents, aunts, uncles, and other individuals with whom the infant has regular contact. To mediate stressful events, the animate environment must be responsive to the infant's cues (Douglas & Snyder, 1974; Lendzion, 1974; Yarrow, 1968).

Infants control and/or modify their environment by the cues they present to their caregivers. Infant cues are those behaviors presented by the infant that signal to the caregiver the infant's needs. Distress cues are cues that allow the infant to disengage from his environment, and include crying, back arching, gaze aversion, head shaking, and tray pounding (Barnard, 1978). The infant may need a diaper change or be hungry, in pain, satiated, or overstimulated when presenting these cues. It is the responsibility of the caregiver to correctly interpret and respond to these cues. Positive responses, such as feeding the infant when a hunger cry is presented, would be supportive to the infant's growth and development. Thus, a supportive animate environment could be considered both growth fostering and less stressful. If the animate responses are negative, such as yelling in response to the infant's hunger cry or hitting the infant rather than feeding, the environment is considered nonsupportive or stressful. Infants also cue satisfaction with their environment by smiling, cooing, and seeking eye contact or physical proximity with the individuals in their environment. These behaviors provide the infant with the ability to adapt to as well as influence the environment.

Attachment is usually referred to as "any form of behavior that results in a person attaining or retaining proximity to some other differentiated and preferred individual" (Bowlby, 1980, p. 39). Ainsworth et al. (1978) defined attachment as "the affectional bond or tie that an infant forms between himself and his mother figure—a bond that tends to be enduring and independent of specific situations" (p. 302). Bowlby postulates that attachment behavior is instinctive and can be described using animal models (1969, 1973, 1980, 1988). The primary method of describing attachment behaviors in both animals and humans has been the description of reunification behaviors when the infant has been separated from mother or mother figure (Ainsworth et al., 1978; Bowlby, 1969, 1973, 1980, 1988). Separation from the primary caretaker is stressful to the infant, with prolonged separation having long-term negative outcomes for the infant.

Bradley's and Caldwell's (1984) work supports not only the importance of the infant's primary caretaker, but also the exposure to a varied, yet stable, animate environment. Infants obtain a great deal of positive stimulation from such activities as trips to the grocery store and regular contacts with adults other than their parent. The key characteristic to this aspect of the supportive animate environment is the ongoing contact with the *same* relative or other adult who is not the primary caretaker.

There are also supportive and nonsupportive inanimate environments. An infant needs access to the stimulation of toys, different colors, and textures to assist in the development of his fine and gross motor skills and sense of touch and smell. Bradley's and Caldwell's (1984) research on the long-term consequences of the early environment of the infant have clearly demonstrated the need for a varied inanimate environment. Toys that interest the infant and are developmentally appropriate are important aspects of the inanimate environment, as are toys that challenge the infant to reach towards the next phase of development. Visual and auditory stimulation are also important for the infant's growth and development. A nonsupportive inanimate environment may be one void of toys and without visual and auditory stimulation.

The classic description of a nonsupportive animate and inanimate environment was published by Spitz in his 1945 description of "hospitalism." He found the infant units "bleak and deserted" with caregivers present only during feeding. Thus, these infants lacked a supportive animate environment. There were no activities to attract the babies' attention. Part of their standard care was to hang white bed sheets over the foot and the side railing of each crib, screening the child from the environment except for the ceiling. Spitz goes on to describe that when the study began, the infants in the Foundling Home had no toys in their cribs. This created a lack of a supportive inanimate environment. With the current understanding of the importance of the environment on infant growth and development, this is a chilling description of a nonsupportive environment. That the morbidity and mortality of these infants were high is not surprising, for they had so few growth-fostering experiences.

Relationship Between Family Stress and Illness.   There are no known studies demonstrating a relationship between stressful family life and infant infection, but in older children Roghman and Haggarty (1972) demonstrated a relationship between family stresses and the incidence of streptococcal throat infections. A relationship between severe family dysfunction and infants' failure to thrive has been demonstrated (Altemeir et al., 1985; Crittendon, 1987; Drotar & Strum, 1987; Fosson & Wilson, 1987).

SPECIFIC STRESSES AND INFANT REACTIONS

The most stressful event an infant experiences is its own birth. The infant must suddenly begin obtaining its own supply of oxygen rather than depending on the maternal blood supply, and must achieve the ability of thermoregulation to cope with the temperature changes in the environment. In addition, the infant must be able to respond to the increased sensory stimuli from lights and sound no longer filtered by amniotic fluid. These stimuli lack the temporal pattern provided by the mother's heartbeat and other familiar bodily sounds heard by the fetus in the intrauterine environment. A major physiological adaptation is the shift from fetal to infant circulation, with the closure of the ductus venosus, the ductus arteriosus, the foramen ovale, and the umbilical arteries and vein. Thus, the newborn infant must demonstrate extraordinary ability to adapt to the physiological stress of birth.

An infant's response to stress can be difficult to evaluate and categorize because of the interpretation needed relative to the infant's inability to articulate. Nevertheless, several stressful areas of infant life have been studied extensively. First, the preterm infant's response to the high-stress environment of the neonatal intensive care unit provided evidence that even the least developed infant can and does respond to stressful environments. Second, failure to thrive (FTT) from environmental deprivation has provided a perspective of the infant's maladaptive response to a nonsupportive animate environment. Third, studies of protein-calorie malnutrition (PCM) provide some interesting insights into nature-nurture and biosocial interactions under stress. Fourth, data on infants' responses to painful situations have provided some information on the physiological responses the infant has to aversive stimuli. While a degree of stress can be viewed as positive for the adult, and even for the older child, it is not known whether the presence of any stress can be positive for the infant.

Neonatal Intensive Care Units: A High-Stress Environment

One of the most stressful environments in which an infant can be placed without ethical conflict is the neonatal intensive care unit (NICU). These units tend to be high-technology, low-touch environments with an enormous amount of aversive auditory, visual, and tactile stimulation, as well as a lack of consistent caregivers. The most frequent type of physical contact is for medical or nursing care, with little contact for rocking or other type of comfort (Gottfried, 1985). Stimulation to the infant is not contingent on the infant's cues and, in fact, may disrupt the infant's state. Historically, it was thought the infant in a NICU was deprived of stimulation; however, current understanding of the physiological and social needs of the preterm infant indicates the average NICU may in fact be overstimulating. The overstimulation is stressful to the at-risk infant in the NICU.

Continuous exposure to fluorescent lights affects the infant's diurnal rhythm. Phototherapy used for the treatment of hyperbilirubinemia may damage the retina. Noise appears to be related to a higher incidence of sensory hearing loss among low-birthweight infants. Loud noises, such as slamming the incubator door shut, cause the infant to startle and cry, leading to a decreased transcutaneous pO_2 (oxygen level measured through the skin), followed by an increase in intracranial pressure (increased pressure in the brain). In the very early gestational age premature infants (24 to 26 weeks gestation), there is an increased incidence of intraventricular hemorrhage (IVH or bleeding into the brain), which leads to cognitive and psychomotor dysfunctions in the infants who survive. The relationship between increased intracranial pressure and IVH is not understood, but appears to deserve study (Gottfried, 1985; Peabody & Lewis, 1985).

The temperature of the environment can also affect the infant. For example, hypothermia may contribute to an increase in apneic episodes. Incubators may over- or underheat, causing the infant to become hyper- or hypothermic. The uterus is considered a "neutral thermal environment," and the first thermal stress may come in the delivery room, where the infant may lose as much as 3 degrees centigrade of temperature within the first five minutes of life through evaporation and convective heat loss (Peabody & Lewis, 1985). When an infant is placed in an NICU, the caregiver must remember, "every characteristic of these highly technical nurseries has the potential to harm as well as help" (Peabody & Lewis, 1985, p. 219).

Interventions are being developed to counteract the stressful NICU environment. One intervention currently being tested is "kangarooing" (Anderson, 1989; Anderson, Marks, & Wahlberg, 1986). This is a process where the mother "wears" the baby between her breasts, allowing the infant to breast-feed at will and absorb the mother's warmth through skin-to-skin contact. This process allows the infant to have contact with the maternal heartbeat, voice, and touch while maintaining warmth. Infants monitored during this treatment remain physiologically stable, maintaining temperature and transcutaneous pO_2 levels, and with decreased apnea and bradycardia. One mother, an NICU nurse, "kangarooed" her 32-week gestation preterm infant from birth. He went home at 3 weeks of age, having an average weight gain of 21.4 grams per day from birth, compared to other infants in the same stepdown nursery who gained from 6.9 to 11.1 grams per day (Anderson, 1989). The latter group included infants whose mothers visited them and "kangarooed" them, although not continuously. It is not clear how to interpret the relative weight gain in view of Klaus and Fanaroff's (1986) report of 30.7 grams per day weight gain as optimum for preterm infants between 32 and 36 weeks gestation (p. 117). Nevertheless, this high-touch rather than high-technology approach to the preterm infant holds much promise for mediating the iatrogenic effects of Western society's stressful NICU environments.

Infant Response to a Nonsupportive Environment: Deprivation

In addition to the necessity of an optimum animate environment, a nonsupportive or deprived inanimate environment has also been shown to cause a decrease in cognitive and social development (Gottfried, 1984). Nonorganic failure to thrive (NOFTT) can be used as an examplar to demonstrate the combined effect of the inadequate or nonsupportive inanimate (physical) and animate (social) environment. The infant reared in a nonsupportive environment will not develop optimum physical, mental, or social health. At the extreme, such problems as NOFTT (Accardo, 1982) and psychosocial dwarfism may result (Annecillo, 1986; see also Chapters 3 and 4).

Historically, failure to thrive (FTT) was attributed to maternal deprivation, with the focus on the study and treatment of the inadequacies in the mother. Potential contributions of the father, the infant, or the inanimate environment were not acknowledged. Accardo (1982) states that FTT is not a diagnosis but a presenting symptom. The symptom is a result of any number of stresses on the infant. The stressor may be internal (such as a congenital defect), external animate (such as a mother who uses drugs or a nonsupportive animate environment), or external inanimate (such as pesticides or sensory deprivation). Any of these can interfere with normal growth and development of the infant.

As with other disorders with unclear or mixed etiologies, FTT is defined in many different ways. One definition is "the term commonly used to describe the condition of an infant or young child who is not growing adequately or may actually lose weight without obvious reason" (Garfunkle, 1977, p. 123). A more operational definition of FTT is: a descriptive term for a syndrome occurring in infancy and early childhood in which the height and weight are below the third percentile for age. The diagnosis of FTT should be made only after other biological impairments have been ruled out. See Table 6.1 for possible causes of FTT. Classic FTT is associated with maternal deprivation or some form of impaired interaction between the caregiver and the infant. Protein-calorie malnutrition, from a nutritional/poverty perspective, is also mentioned as a cause (Green, 1977). "Organic FTT" and protein-calorie malnutrition, while defined anatomically as FTT, have been considered as very different problems from NOFTT associated with impaired interaction between the caregiver and the infant.

There are few formal research studies testing interventions to enhance the environment of the infant experiencing NOFTT. Many papers are reports of specific case studies, with little or no analysis of which intervention presented to the family was most effective in improving the status of the infant (Clark, 1975; Durand, 1975; Joslen, 1975; Shapiro, Fraiberg, & Adelson, 1976). Intervention research with this population is ethically difficult because the infant with NOFTT at or below the third percentile is in a precarious position for survival.

Etiology of FTT. In a study of growth failures in a clinic population Larken et al. (1976) found no single etiological factor that manifested in each case. In a retrospective study of 140 children labeled as abused or

TABLE 6.1. Possible Causes of Failure to Thrive (FTT; height and weight are below the third percentile for age).

1. "Organic" FTT as a result of anatomical/physiological impairment.
    (a) Cardiac defects
    (b) Gastrointestinal dysfunction
    (c) Renal dysfunction
    (d) Neurologic dysfunction
    (e) Infectious process
    (f) Intrauterine growth retardation
    (g) Fetal alcohol syndrome
2. Protein-calorie malnutrition—failure to grow as a result of inadequate intake of protein and other nutrients.
    (a) Famine
    (b) Cult diets, vegetarian diets with decreased protein
    (c) Lack of understanding of infant dietary needs
    (d) Extreme pica (substituting non-nutritive materials for nutritive)
3. Parent-infant interaction problems—impaired relationships between the infant and the caregiver, creating environmental deprivation and "nonorganic" FTT.
    (a) Environmental deprivation (inanimate)
    (b) Maternal or parental deprivation (animate environment)
    (c) Impaired parent-child interaction
    (d) Abuse

neglected, Goldson et al. (1976) found that 18 children, or 11.5%, were described as having FTT. In a comparison of an NOFTT population and a control sample, Pollitt (1975, 1976; Pollitt, Eickler, & Chen, 1975) found that control children had more frequent and more positive contacts with their mothers than did children with NOFTT. Parents and infants with NOFTT may develop mutual patterns that interfere with the establishment of a synchronous relationship. Pollitt's findings are supported by the recent family-focused studies cited earlier (Altemeir et al., 1985; Crittendon, 1987; Drotar & Strum, 1987; Fosson & Wilson, 1987). There continues to be a need for further definition of the critical variables in the animate environments of infants with NOFTT and their families. Meanwhile, intervention programs need to focus on the family system, not just on the mother or the infant.

Mixed Organic-Nonorganic Failure to Thrive

When an infant is evaluated for FTT, organic causes must be ruled out. There may be infants who present an organic problem as well as behaviors often associated with nonorganic FTT (Homer & Ludwig, 1981; Lobo & Barnard, in press). In a retrospective chart analysis of 82 hospital-

TABLE 6.2.   *Nursing Child Assessment Feeding Scale (NCAFS).*

Guidelines designed to assess the contributions and characteristics, unique to the feeding interaction, of both parent and child during the first year of life.

Sensitivity to Cues: Parents' ability to "read" the infant's behavior and appropriately modify their own behavior.

Response to Distress: Parents' ability to read infant signals that assistance is needed from the parents; parents should appropriately assist the infant in a timely manner.

Cognitive Growth Fostering: Providing stimulation just above the child's current level of understanding.

Social-Emotional Growth Fostering: Playing, affectionately engaging in social interaction with the child during eating or teaching; appropriate social reinforcement of desired behavior.

Clarity of Cues: Skill and understandability with which infant signals caregiver so the parent can "read" and modify own behavior, facilitating a flow of synchronous interaction. Ambiguous or confusing signals can interrupt or mislead the caregiver's adaptive activities.

Responsiveness to Parent: Infant's "reading" of caregiver's behavior so infant can modify own behavior.

(Adapted from Barnard, 1978, by permission of the author.)

ized children with a diagnosis of FTT, 40 cases were found to have organic causes of FTT. Of the 40 cases, 19 presented with both organic and nonorganic FTT. Their families were often characterized as being dysfunctional. Parents were often dysfunctional due to psychosis or drug abuse, or the child was difficult to feed, with decreased feedback to the caregiver (Homer & Ludwig, 1981).

Two studies utilizing the Nursing Child Assessment Feeding Scale (NCAFS) (Barnard, 1978; see Table 6.2) show significant findings on observation of the feeding dyad. In a study of 12 infants under one year of age admitted to a major children's medical center with a diagnosis of FTT, infants with organic causes were found to present less clear cues and to be less responsive to parents than healthy infants. Their responsiveness to the parent was more like infants with nonorganic FTT (Lobo & Barnard, in press). Details are shown in Table 6.3. It is important to note that 12 of the 24 FTT families recruited into the study did not complete data collection, a further indication of the difficulty in studying these families.

Infants with congenital heart disease (CHD) were found to provide significantly less clear cues to their mothers and to be less responsive to their mothers than were age-matched controls (Lobo, in press). Details are shown in Table 6.4). The mothers of infants with CHD provided

**TABLE 6.3.   Scores for Age-Matched Normal Controls and FTT Infants
on the Nursing Child Assessment Feeding Scale.** (See Table 6.2 for definition
and description of subscales. FTT = Failure to Thrive, PCM = Protein-Calorie
Malnutrition, PII = Parent-Infant Interaction FTT, ORG = Organic cause
for FTT.)

Subscales/ (Possible Points)	Control $N = 17$	FTT $N = 12$	PCM** $N = 2$	PII $N = 5$	ORG $N = 5$
Sensitivity to Cues (16)	13.4	12.3	15.0	10.6	13.0
Response to Distress (11)	10.3	10.0	11.0	9.8	9.6
Social-emotional (14)	11.9	11.5	12.5	10.4	12.2
Cognitive (9)	6.5	6.1	7.5	4.8	6.8
Mother subtotal (50)	42.2	39.9	46.5	35.6	41.6
Clarity of Cues (15)	11.7	11.5	13.0	10.6	11.8
Responsiveness to Parent (11)	7.1	6.3	9.0	5.6	6.0
Child subtotal (26)	18.6	17.8	22.0	16.2	17.8
Total NCAFS Score (76)	60.8*	57.8	68.5	51.8*	59.4

*Mann-Whitney test, $Z = 1.9625, p = .0497$
**PCM subjects were omitted from tests for significance

significantly less social-emotional growth-fostering behaviors to their infants. The nature of the development of the interaction is not known.
However, infants with CHD presented significantly less clear cues to
their mothers and the mothers did not interact with their infants during
feeding in the same manner that mothers of healthy infants do. Figure
6.1 illustrates the cycle of each individual's contribution to the relationship. If the infant gives unclear cues, the caregiver (mother) becomes

**TABLE 6.4.   Paired T-Tests for Age-Matched Normal Controls and Infants
with Cardiac Defects on the Nursing Child Assessment Feeding Scale.** (See Table 6.2
for definition and description of subscales.)

Subscales	Control $(n = 10)$	Cardiac $(n = 10)$	t	p
Sensitivity to Cues	14.5	13.0	1.25	.245
Response to Distress	10.5	10.3	0.90	.394
Social Emotional	13.2	11.6	2.28	.049
Cognitive	8.4	7.3	1.86	.096
Mother subtotal	46.6	42.5	2.03	.072
Clarity of Cues	12.6	10.7	2.30	.047
Responsiveness to Parent	10.0	7.7	2.41	.039
Infant subtotal	21.6	18.4	2.63	.027
Total NCAFS Score	68.2	60.9	2.78	.022

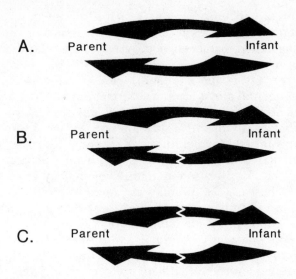

Figure 6.1. Disrupted interaction model (adapted from Barnard, 1985). A. A normal, healthy infant gives the mother cues to which she responds, eliciting more normal behavior in a cycle indicating reciprocity between mother and infant. B. An infant with congenital heart disease or other problem gives unclear and confusing cues, disrupting the infant's contribution to the parent-infant interaction experience. C. Eventually the mother becomes confused by the infant's unclear cues and also begins to give less clear cues to her infant and is less responsive to the infant's cues.

confused as to how to respond, which in turn may cause her to give less growth-fostering behaviors to the infant, thus setting up an FTT confounded with both organic and inorganic characteristics.

Infants with the physiological stress of a congenital defect or other pathophysiology must be carefully examined for their responses to additional stress from both the animate and inanimate environments. The caregiver provides cues to the infant and in turn must read the infant's cues. If this process is unclear for either participant in the interaction, an increased risk for mixed organic-nonorganic FTT will be present. A chaotic inanimate environment may also be a factor in mixed organic-nonorganic FTT by overstimulating the infant, preventing the infant from presenting clearly readable cues (Lobo & Robinson, 1988).

Protein-Calorie Malnutrition: Interaction with Temperament

There is some evidence that infants' individual characteristics may influence how they respond to stressful environments. Some infants may present different behaviors or cues, which allows them to be more successful in adapting to a stressful environment. The importance of individual characteristics has been demonstrated in infants with FTT or marasmus from protein calorie malnutrition (PCM).

Infants of the Masai tribe, a nomadic tribe in East Africa, experienced harsh environmental stress when a severe drought accompanied by social upheaval occurred in the 1970s. A study was implemented to test the hypothesis that an infant with a difficult temperament would stress the already compromised Masai mother and extended family, placing the infant at particular risk for behavioral and health problems (deVries, 1984). Using the classification system developed by Carey (1973) and Thomas and Chess (1977), infants were rated as either "difficult" (less adaptable, more irregular, more intense, and showing greater negative reactions) or "easy" (more adaptable, more regular, less intense, quieter, and more easily managed). Originally, 48 infants were evaluated using the Infant Temperament Questionnaire. Of these, 13 of the 20 families with the easiest or most difficult infants were contacted two to three months after the initial evaluation. Of the 7 infants rated as having easy temperament, 5 had died, while only 1 of the 6 infants rated as difficult had died. It was hypothesized that the more difficult infant with more irritable behaviors received more attention and food from the mother. Observations of mother-infant interaction confirmed that the infant who cried more frequently was put to breast more frequently in this setting, where demand feeding was the norm. The difficult infants spent more time suckling than did the easy infants. Thus, the difficult temperament, assumed a priori to be maladaptive, turned out to have surprising survival value under this particular stress.

The influence of nutrition on an infant's ability to respond to a stressful environment has also been demonstrated by Chavez, Martinez, and Yaschine (1975). Infants whose mothers were placed on a supplemental nutrition program prenatally and who received supplemental nutrition from 12 to 16 weeks of age were more physically active, played more, and received more verbal interactions from both the father and the mother. Additionally, fathers were found to have more physical contact with their infants as they carried them around the village to "show them off" to their friends, bragging about how much weight the infants had gained and how beautiful they were, thus enhancing the social environment of the infant. While the influence of the infant's nutritional status on environmental interaction was very evident, there was no attempt to address the impact of study participation on the parents. In the families of the infants who received supplemental nutrition, there were more frequent contacts with the study staff. This contact could have influenced parental self-esteem as well as increased the value of the infant because of the special attention the infant received (Chavez et al., 1975).

Long-Term Consequences of Deprivation

A number of investigators have attempted to examine the long-term impact of early deprivation. The areas most frequently examined are physical and cognitive growth and development. A few investigators have focused on social and behavioral consequences. A major problem with the studies is the multiple factors present in the lives of the children, which could be influencing their long-term cognitive, social, and physical development. Ernst (1988) found that later childhood experiences of children suffering early maternal deprivation included parental discord, divorce, psychosocial disorders in parents, and other factors that could have influenced the outcome. Ernst's conclusions have been supported by Bradley, Caldwell, and Rock (1988) and Kolvin, Miller, Fleeting, and Kolvin (1988).

Some investigators have found both lower intelligence scores and subnormal growth and development in school-aged children who experienced early NOFTT (Cabak & Najdanvic, 1965; Elmer, Gregg, & Ellison, 1969; Oates, Peacock, & Forrest, 1985; Stoch & Smythe, 1976). Other studies indicated behavioral problems, with young children developing "inhibitory coping strategies" or a compliant behavior pattern, which reduced the chances that the parent would become abusive to the child (Crittenden & DiLalla, 1988). One study found that parents of school-aged children with a history of NOFTT had less knowledge about their children's education and the children had a higher incidence of school problems than a control group matched for age, sex, social class, and ethnic group (Oates et al., 1985). Graham (1967) focused only on physical growth and concluded that "when near starvation occurs during a significant part of the first year, failure to grow in length and head size is so striking that even under the best circumstances significant permanent deficits occur" (p. 142).

The long-term consequences of early deprivation can have a profound impact on the physical, social, and emotional growth and development of a child. The home environment must be monitored and assistance given to parents if the child is to be salvaged. The deprivation experience interacts in a complex manner with subsequent supportive or non-supportive environments to produce diverse outcomes.

Response to a Common Stressor: Pain

Integrating a series of studies that they completed on the neonate's response to circumcision, restraint, and blood sampling, Gunnar, Malone, & Fisch, (1985) demonstrated the healthy newborn's "inherent resilience" in a stressful situation. In their research, prior to data collection, restrictions were placed on other procedures that might be stressful to the infant, such as bathing, weighing, blood sampling, or any other stimulation that was potentially arousing. While acknowledging that data-collection methods can be stressful in and of themselves, Gunnar et al. demonstrated that neonates had differing levels of plasma cortisol related to the stress they experienced. The infant adrenocortical system was "shown to respond to aversive, stressful stimulation, and behavioral distress (e.g., crying) was associated with elevated cortisol levels, while sleep was associated with low levels of circulating adrenocortical hormones or their urinary metabolites" (p. 179). In fact, plasma cortisol levels were negatively correlated with quiet sleep and positively correlated with all of the awake states.

The results of the four studies reported by Gunnar and colleagues (1985) indicated that the neonatal adrenocortical system not only responded to stress, but even discriminated finely among different degrees of stress. Three increasingly complex conditions were studied: blood sampling, blood sampling with restraint, and combined blood sampling, restraint, and circumcision. As the conditions became more stressful— that is, more complex—the plasma cortisol levels 30 minutes following the onset of the stress increased.

A disturbing aspect of Gunnar et al.'s work was the effect of both the animate and inanimate environment on the infant. In a private hospital with fewer interns and residents, the plasma cortisol levels were lower than in a teaching hospital. They also found changes over time in the plasma cortisol levels of the infants circumcised by the same physician. The first infant tested was also the first infant the physician had ever circumcised, and the infant's plasma cortisol level was high. The cortisol levels on infants the physician subsequently circumcised gradually decreased throughout the study as she became more adept at the procedure (Gunnar et al., 1985). This suggests that infants may be placed in very stressful situations to facilitate the learning of a health professional; the long-term consequences to the infant are not understood. This finding poses a complicated ethical dilemma which needs further study.

SUMMARY

Human responses to stress begin prenatally and develop more fully as infants interact with their environment. Infants are exposed to many stressors from both their animate and inanimate environments. The infant's response to stressors can be placed on a continuum ranging from very adaptive to very maladaptive. This review focused on the maladaptive responses which endanger the infant's well-being. The Masai infants of difficult temperament showed response to their stress by demanding, and receiving, more from their animate environment. The infants with nonorganic FTT responded to their nonsupportive environment in a maladaptive manner, failing to grow physically, socially, and emotionally. Infants with combined organic problems and characteristics of nonorganic FTT may be demonstrating responses to stress, such as disengagement of eye contact, to which the caregiver does not know how to respond, creating discord in the relationship.

Providers of infant care must be aware of the impact of stress on the infant's developing physical, social, and emotional well-being. Stress in the situation of nonsupportive animate and inanimate environments, aversive stimulation, and lack of response to infant cues may lead to maladaptation on the part of the infant. Although not proven by research evidence, appropriate challenges or stressors may assist the infant to reach the next stage of physical, social, and emotional well-being in an adaptive manner. The stress in an infant's environment needs to be structured and modulated to allow growth. Under severe stress conditions, the figures in the animate environment need to intervene to decrease the impact of the stress on the infant.

REFERENCES

Accardo, P. J. (1982). Growth and development: An interactional context for failure to thrive. In P. J. Accardo (Ed.), *Failure to thrive in infancy and early childhood: A multidisciplinary team approach* (pp. 5–18). Baltimore: University Park Press.

Ainsworth, M. D. S., Blehar, M. C., Waters, E., & Wall, S. (1978). *Patterns of attachment: A psychological study of the strange situation.* Hillsdale, NJ: Lawrence Erlbaum.

Altemeier, W. A., O'Connor, S. M., Sherrod, K. B., & Vietze, P. M. (1985). Prospective study of antecedents for nonorganic failure to thrive. *The Journal of Pediatrics, 106,* 360–365.

Anderson, G. C. (1989). Skin to skin: Kangaroo care in Western Europe. *American Journal of Nursing, 89,* 662–666.

Anderson, G. C., Marks, E., & Wahlberg, V. (1986). Kangaroo care for premature infants. *American Journal of Nursing, 86,* 807–809.

Annecillo, C. (1986). Environment and intelligence: Reversible impairment of intellectual growth in the syndrome of abuse dwarfism. In B. Stabler & L. E. Underwood (Eds.), *Slow grows the child: Psychosocial aspects of growth delay* (pp. 168–177). Hillsdale, NJ: Lawrence Erlbaum.

Barnard, K. (1978). *Nursing Child Assessment Feeding Scale.* Seattle: University of Washington School of Nursing.

Barnard, K. (1985). *Nursing child assessment satellite training: Instructor's learning resources manual* (rev. ed.). Seattle: University of Washington School of Nursing.

Blank, D. M. (1986). Relating mother's anxiety and perception to infant satiety, anxiety, and feeding behavior. *Nursing Research, 35,* 347–351.

Bowlby, J. (1969). *Attachment.* New York: Basic Books.

Bowlby, J. (1973). *Separation: Anxiety and anger.* New York: Basic Books.

Bowlby, J. (1980). *Loss: Sadness and depression.* New York: Basic Books.

Bowlby, J. (1988). Developmental psychiatry comes of age. *The American Journal of Psychiatry, 145,* 1–10.

Bradley, R. H., & Caldwell, B. M. (1984). One hundred seventy-five children: A study of the relationship between home environment and cognitive development during the first 5 years. In A. W. Gottfried (Ed.), *Home environment and early cognitive development: Longitudinal research* (pp. 5–56). New York: Academic Press.

Bradley, R. H., Caldwell, B. M., & Rock, S. L. (1988). Home environment and school performances: A ten-year follow-up and examination of three models of environmental action. *Child Development, 59,* 852–867.

Bronfenbrenner, U. (1979). *The ecology of human development: Experiments by nature.* Cambridge, MA: Harvard University Press.

Cabak, V., & Najdanvic, R. (1965). Effects of undernutrition in early life on physical and mental development. *Archives of Disease in Childhood, 40,* 532–534.

Carey, W. B. (1973). Measurement of infant temperament in pediatric practice. In J. C. Westman (Ed.), *Individual differences in children.* New York: John Wiley.

Chavez, A., Martinez, C., & Yashine, T. (1975). Nutrition, behavioral development, and mother child interaction in young rural children. *Federation Proceedings, 34,* 1574–1582.

Clark, D. (1975). Rumination in a failure to thrive infant. *The American Journal of Maternal Child Nursing, 4*(1), 9–22.

Crittenden, P. M. (1987). Non-organic failure-to-thrive: Deprivation or distortion? *Infant Mental Health Journal, 8,* 51–64.

Crittenden, P. M., & DiLalla, D. L. (1988). Compulsive compliance: The development of an inhibitory coping strategy in infancy. *Journal of Abnormal Child Psychology, 16,* 585–599.

deVries, M. W. (1984). Temperament and infant mortality among the Masai of East Africa. *American Journal of Psychiatry, 141,* 1189–1194.

Douglas, H. B., & Snyder, C. (1979). The inanimate environment. In K. E. Barnard & H. B. Douglas (Eds.), *Child health assessment part I: A literature review* (pp. 103–114). (DHEW Publication No. HRA 75-30). Bethesda, MD: U.S. Department of Health, Education, and Welfare.

Drotar, D., & Sturm, L. (1987). Paternal influences in non-organic failure to thrive: Implications for psychosocial management. *Infant Mental Health Journal, 8,* 37–50.

Dubos, R. (1965). *Man adapting.* New Haven: Yale University Press.

Durand, B. (1975). A clinical nursing study: Failure to thrive in a child with Down's Syndrome. *Nursing Research, 24*(4), 272–286.

Elmer, E., Gregg, G. S., & Ellison, P. (1969). Late results of the "failure to thrive" syndrome. *Clinical Pediatrics, 8,* 584–589.

Ernst, C. (1988). Are early childhood experiences overrated? A reassessment of maternal deprivation. *European Archives of Psychiatry and Neurological Sciences, 237,* 80–90.

Fosson, A., & Wilson, J. (1987). Family interactions surrounding feedings of infants with nonorganic failure to thrive. *Clinical Pediatrics, 26,* 518–523.

Garfunkle, J. M. (1977). Failure to thrive in infants and young children. *The Journal of Family Practice, 5,* 123–126.

Goldson, E., Cadol, R. V., Fitch, M., & Umlauf, L. (1976). Non-accidental trauma and failure to thrive. *American Journal of Diseases of Children, 130,* 490–492.

Gottfried, A. W. (1984). Home environment and early cognitive development: Integration, meta-analysis, and conclusions. In A. W. Gottfried (Ed.), *Home environment and early cognitive development: Longitudinal research* (pp. 329–342). New York: Academic Press.

Gottfried, A. W. (1985). Environment of newborn infants in special care units. In A. W. Gottfried & J. L. Gaiter (Eds.), *Infant stress under intensive care* (pp. 23–54). Baltimore: University Park Press.

Graham, G. G. (1967). Effect of infantile malnutrition on growth. *Federation Proceedings, 26,* 139–143.

Green, L. S. (Ed.). (1977). *Malnutrition, behavior and social organization.* New York: Academic Press.

Gunnar, M. R., Malone, S., & Fisch, R. O. (1985). The psychobiology of stress and coping in the human neonate: Studies of adrenocortical activity in response to aversive stimulation. In T. M. Field, P. M. McCabe, & N. Schneiderman (Eds.), *Stress and coping* (pp. 179–196). Hillsdale, NJ: Lawrence Erlbaum.

Homer, C., & Ludwig, S. (1981). Categorization of etiology of failure to thrive. *American Journal of Diseases of Children, 135,* 848–851.

Joslen, F. (1975). The treatment of an abused family. *The American Journal of Maternal Child Nursing, 4*(1), 23–34.

Klaus, M., & Fanaroff, A. (1986). *Care of the high risk neonate.* Philadelphia: Saunders.

Kolvin, I., Miller, F. J. W., Fleeting, M., & Kolvin, P. A. (1988). Social and parenting factors affecting criminal-offence rates: Findings from the Newcastle Thousand Family Study (1947–1980). *British Journal of Psychiatry, 152,* 80–90.

Larken, F., Perri, K. P., Bursich, J. H., & Polson, J. R. K. (1976). Etiology of growth failure in a clinic population. *Journal of the American Dietetic Association, 69*(5), 506–510.

Lendzion, A. (1974). The animate environment. In K. E. Barnard & H. B. Douglas (Eds.), *Child health assessment part I: A literature review* (pp. 87–101). (DHEW Publication No. HRA 75-30). Bethesda, MD: U.S. Department of Health, Education, and Welfare.

Levine, S. (1983). A psychobiological approach to the ontogeny of coping. In N. Garmezy & M. Rutter (Eds.), *Stress, coping, and development in children* (pp. 107–131). New York: McGraw-Hill.

Lobo, M. L. (In press). *Parent-infant interaction during feeding of infants with congenital heart disease. Journal of Pediatric Nursing.*

Lobo, M. L., & Barnard, K. E. (In press). Failure to thrive: A parent-child interaction perspective. *Journal of Pediatric Nursing.*

Lobo, M. L., & Robinson, J. L., (1988). [Unpublished raw data].

Lyon, B. L., & Werner, J. S. (1987). Stress. In J. J. Fitzpatrick & R. L. Taunton (Eds.), *Annual review of nursing research* (Vol. 5, pp. 1–22). New York: Springer.

Oates, R. K., Peacock, A., & Forrest, D. (1985). Long-term effects of nonorganic failure to thrive. *Pediatrics, 75,* 36–40.

Peabody, J. L., & Lewis, K. (1985). Consequences of newborn intensive care. In A. W. Gottfried & J. L. Gaiter (Eds.), *Infant stress under intensive care* (pp. 199–226). Baltimore: University Park Press.

Pollitt, E. (1975). Socioeconomic, dietary intake and mother-child interaction data. *Federation Proceedings, 34*(7), 1593–1597.

Pollitt, E. (1976). Behavioral disturbances among failure to thrive children. *American Journal of Diseases of Children, 30,* 24–26.

Pollitt, E., Eickler, A. W., & Chen, C. K. (1975). Psychological development and behavior of mothers of failure to thrive children. *American Journal of Orthopsychiatry, 45*(4), 525–537.

Roghmann, K. J., & Haggarty, R. J. (1972). Family stress and the use of health services. *International Journal of Epidemiology, 1*(3), 279–286.

Rutter, M. (1985). Resilience in the face of adversity: Protective factors and resistance to psychiatric disorder. *British Journal of Psychiatry, 147,* 598–611.

Selye, H. (1976). *The stress of life* (rev. ed.). New York: McGraw-Hill.

Shapiro, V., Fraiberg, S., & Adelson, E. (1976). Infant parent psychotherapy on behalf of a child in a critical nutritional state. *The Psychoanalytic Study of the Child, 31,* 23–34.

Spitz, R. A. (1945). Hospitalism: An inquiry into the genesis of psychiatric conditions in early childhood. *The Psychoanalytic Study of the Child, 1,* 53–74.

Stoch, M.B., & Smythe, P. M. (1976). Fifteen-year developmental study on effects of severe undernutrition during infancy on subsequent physical growth and intellectual functioning. *Archives of Disease in Childhood, 51,* 327–336.

Thomas, A., & Chess, S. (1977). *Temperament and development.* New York: Brunner/Mazel.

Yarrow, L. (1968). Conceptualizing the early environment. In L. Dittman (Ed.), *Early child care* (pp. 15–27). New York: Atherton.

CHAPTER SEVEN

Stress in the Preschool Years

Marianne L. Barton
Charles H. Zeanah

Acknowledgments: Dr. Zeanah is supported in part by a Research Scientist Development Award from NIMH (MH 00691).

For the purpose of this chapter, stress is defined as an environmental event that requires adaptation or change and arouses an individual's subjective experience of discomfort. In this definition, stress is presumed to refer to an event or a stimulus (stressor) and not to an individual's response (strain or coping) or to some interaction between individual and stimulus. Forms of response reviewed in the following pages include behavioral changes, psychiatric disorder, and the positive responses typically referred to as coping.

This definition of stress focuses on events, not chronic environmental situations that are presumed to exert a negative influence, such as high levels of noise or crowding. Such conditions presumably do not require adaptation or change upon occurrence, but instead require sustained alterations in response, which become habitual over time. There are few data available on the effects of such chronic environmental stress on young children. What data are available concern maternal deprivation, a condition that clearly exerts significant negative influences beyond those experienced as subjectively stressful.

Unfortunately, this definition blurs the distinction between kinds of disruptive events that have been shown to influence individual functioning in unique ways. Rutter (1983) cautions repeatedly about the importance of differentiating the kinds of negative events experienced in order to isolate their potential effects. We concur and delineate below broad classes of stressful events and their sequelae.

In this chapter we selectively review data to answer the following questions regarding the experience of stress in preschool children: What are the specific developmental characteristics of preschoolers mediating their experience of and response to stressful events? What kinds of events elicit discomfort and require adaptation in preschool children? What are the typical responses, both positive and negative, of preschool children to stress? Are there protective factors that modulate the negative effects of stressful events in preschoolers? If so, how do such factors exert their influence?

DEVELOPMENTAL FACTORS AND PRESCHOOL RESPONSE TO STRESS

Kagan (1983) argues that the effects of any potentially stressful event must be measured against the organism's capacity to respond to it. He says, "the consequences of an event are dependent upon the structural readiness of the organism." Thus, the developmental status of the child is critical to understanding a particular event and the child's capacity to respond to it.

Several characteristics of the preschool child's functioning have a significant impact on stress response. These include the cognitive achievements and limitations of the preschool period, the salience of emotional concerns with competence and mastery, the preschooler's increasing awareness of the self in relation to others, and the fact that the child's primary attachment relationships may be in a process of formation early in the preschool period.

Preschool Cognitive Function

According to Piaget (1952, 1960), the cognitive functioning of 2- to 4-year-old children is characterized by preconceptual thought. They do not make abstract generalizations, nor do they categorize information actively. Instead, their thinking is closely tied to the physical properties of objects or events, with few mechanisms for understanding causality. Preconceptual thinking is characterized by two features: *animism,* or the attribution of human qualities to inanimate objects, and *egocentrism,* or the proclivity to view any event solely from the perspective of its meaning to the self.

As children approach school age, they begin to make more causal and conceptual links, but their reasoning is intuitive, subject to frequent errors and idiosyncracies. For example, preschool children tend to understand illness as having magical causes; they may believe that illness is a punishment for transgression (Perrin & Gerrity, 1981; Potter & Roberts, 1984). The belief that the child is responsible for negative events such as family dissolution or divorce is likewise common among preschoolers and is related to the egocentric as well as the magical quality of their thinking.

Preschoolers' cognitive limitations predispose them to experience unexpected events as particularly frightening, in part because of their inability to comprehend causal processes. Consequently, as young children are provided increased realistic information regarding a traumatic event (such as hospitalization), their level of fear decreases and with it evidence of distress reactions (Rutter, 1981b). Indeed, hospitalization becomes a less powerful stressor past the age of 4 in part because children's increased cognitive skills render preparation more feasible and more useful to them.

Control Issues

Numerous writers (e.g., Erikson, 1959) have described the child's struggle to achieve psychological autonomy and eventually mastery and competence in the preschool period. Control over one's immediate environment, while critical at many developmental stages, is particularly important to preschoolers, who have struggled only recently to gain control over their own behavior and who continue to struggle toward a wider range of competencies.

The threat posed by many events experienced as stressful by the pre-school child centers around a loss of control, including the inability of trusted adults to control environmental events. The effort to regain control, to achieve some measure of mastery over the uncontrollable, is seen dramatically in the preschooler's play. The child uses pretend to enact stressful events with the self in the role of powerful adult or agent of control. In Chapter 20, Trad and his colleagues present a fuller description of the importance of turning passivity into action in the play of preschoolers, emphasizing again the salience of this dimension in young children's experience of themselves in their world. It is clearly linked both to the cognitive capacities described above and to the interpersonal context reviewed below.

Awareness of Self and Others

With toddlerhood come dramatic changes in children's sense of themselves in relationship to others. First, they achieve the ability to recognize themselves as separate and as agents who can affect others (Kagan, 1983). As the preschool years progress, this is complimented by an emerging ability to detect and empathize with the emotional states of others. As a result, preschoolers become aware of receiving differential amounts of attention, or of being more or less successful in bids for attention. In essence, they become aware of being treated differently from others. While preschoolers may be unlikely to experience this as an affront to self-esteem, they nonetheless experience it as a negative affective state. At the same time, they are sufficiently able to identify with preferred states of others to feel disappointed by comparison.

These emerging skills mark impressive gains in the growth of social cognition. Unfortunately, they also render young children especially vulnerable to certain kinds of stress. For example, Koch (1965, cited in Rutter, 1983) noted that the birth of new siblings was most stressful to children in the 2- to 4-year-old range. Presumably, children's increased sensitivity to social relationships in general and threats of displacement in particular combine with their ongoing dependency on the family to make them especially vulnerable to anxiety and distress. Similarly, as children's social relationships outside the family increase in the later preschool years, threats to newly formed friendships become intensely disruptive and anxiety provoking.

Attachment

Finally, preschool children's struggle with the continuing development of attachment relationships renders them particularly vulnerable to events that threaten to disrupt those relationships. Bowlby (1969) viewed the first three years of life as heavily involved in the development of attachment relationships which are internalized as part of the child's sense of self in relation to others. Disruptions in the attachment process, most often occasioned by unexpected separation from attachment figures, are likely to be particularly painful during the toddler and early preschool years. Separation from attachment figures in the first half of the first year of life is relatively less disruptive, in large measure because specific attachments are still forming (Kagan, Kearsley, & Zelazo, 1978). Separation after the age of 4 is likewise less disruptive because children have acquired the cognitive skills to maintain an internalized image of their absent attachment figures, and so can comfort and reassure themselves.

During the period between 1 and 4 years, stressors that threaten the primary attachment relationship are likely to be experienced as particularly difficult. As children approach school age, their repertoire of self-soothing skills as well as their networks of extra-familial relationships expand, and with those, their ability to find comfort from persons other than primary attachment figures in times of stress.

TYPICAL PRESCHOOL RESPONSES TO STRESS

The most common stress-induced behaviors of preschoolers can be grouped into four general categories: regression to immature forms of behavior, increased attention seeking, withdrawal from social contact, and changes in play. Beyond these rather general patterns of response to stressful events, more specific responses have also been noted, especially a variety of anxiety symptoms. In most cases these are relatively short-term responses. Data on children's long-term responses are relatively rarer and permit fewer systematic generalizations.

Regression

Perhaps the most commonly reported response to stress in preschool children is a regression to immature, often disorganized behavior. Maccoby (1983) hypothesizes that when a stressful, arousing event leads to strong negative affect, the younger the child, the greater the likelihood of extensive behavioral disorganization. Behavioral organization in young children frequently represents a recently achieved progression from more primitive organizational capacities. As a result, according to Maccoby, young children have fewer strategies available in their efforts to simplify organizational demands before their capacity for maintaining organized behavior breaks down entirely.

The loss of organizational capacity in response to stress is evidenced perhaps most clearly in the response to fatigue. Tired children frequently exhibit crying and irritability typical of earlier ages and a markedly decreased capacity to maintain organization. A common sequel to the birth of a new sibling is a regression to earlier patterns of behavior on the part of older siblings (Dunn & Kendrik, 1982). Wallerstein and Kelly (1982) noted regressive behavior, including increased frequency of sleep disturbances, separation protest, tearfulness, irritability, and aggressiveness, in young children whose parents divorced. Others report increased clinging and attention-seeking behavior following periods of separation from parents (e.g., Field & Reite, 1984; Robertson & Robertson, 1971). Some researchers have also reported an interruption in developmental progression in response to stress. For example, Heinicke and Westheimer (1966) note that 2-year-olds who were separated from their parents ceased to make gains in language acquisition and resumed their progress only after a period of reunion with their parents. It seems clear that potent stressors can overtax young children's coping resources, resulting in the abandonment of developmental goals and the loss of previously achieved organizational skills. Typically, such regressions are short-lived and are supplanted over a brief period of time by a return to more typical modes of functioning.

Attention Seeking

A second category of preschool response to stressful events is an increase in behavior designed to elicit adult attention. In girls, this may take the form of increased shyness, clinging, and inhibition; in boys, it is more likely to take the form of increased aggressiveness and noncompliance. Like temporary regressions, these are likely to be short-lived. They may be viewed in many cases as a relatively adaptive response designed to elicit increased adult support and involvement. Indeed, much of what is labelled regressive as well as attention-seeking behavior serves the general function of increasing contact with attachment figures during times of stress. Review of the literature reveals that when attention-seeking behavior is ineffective in eliciting increased support from adults, then such behaviors persist as more chronic consequences of stressful events.

Social Withdrawal

Among the preschool child's most troubling responses to stress is withdrawal from social contact, with associated symptoms of apathy and depression. This reaction was first described by René Spitz (1946) in his studies of infants reared in institutions; it continues to be associated with children who experience relatively severe or prolonged stress. More recently it has been described in the clinical literature about children who have experienced maltreatment (abuse/neglect) (Mueller & Silverman, 1989), as well as those who have experienced severely traumatic events like violent crimes or natural disasters (Eth & Pynoos, 1985; Newman, 1976). Prolonged social withdrawal is one symptom of post-traumatic stress disorder, a more general and enduring pattern of maladaptation.

Changes in Play

Wallerstein (1977) noted that following divorce, preschool children were likely to show an inhibition of play. Attachment studies of younger children likewise reveal that children who are highly stressed by a brief separation show periods of immobility, diminished duration of play episodes, and regression to less complex forms of toy usage (Maccoby & Feldman, 1972). Other studies suggest that children under stress show increased use of play, possibly as one strategy to master the stressful experience (Field & Reite, 1984).

Play seems to serve two critical functions for the young child during periods of stress. It offers an opportunity to retreat from difficult reality experience into a less troubled and potentially restorative sphere of activity. Second, play offers the child the chance to re-enact stressful events in an effort to master them and to achieve some measure of cognitive affective accommodation. Like adults who recount traumatic events over and over or watch repeated news footage of the tragedy, children at play seek to replay a stressful event until they can develop some cognitive assimilation of it as well as some affective reconciliation. Terr (1981) described post-traumatic play as a particular form in which young children attempt to master major, traumatic events. Because the trauma is not a product of their imagination but a real event, they become stuck in the play, unable to assimilate the event or to reconcile themselves to it.

PRESCHOOL STRESSORS IN NORMAL DEVELOPMENT

To look more incisively at the effects of stress on preschool children, we review a variety of potentially stressful events. These include stressors typically experienced as part of normal development, and those viewed as less common and potentially more disruptive.

Maternal Employment

Dramatic changes in families during the past three decades have led researchers to assess the effects of maternal employment on child development. At present, roughly half the mothers of preschool children are employed outside the home (Waldman, 1983) and a number of studies have examined child intellectual, language, and socioemotional out-comes in these children compared to children whose mothers remain at home. Reviews of these studies indicate that maternal employment per se is not an especially important influence on children's development (Hoffman, 1979; Lerner & Galambos, 1986; Siegel, 1984). Apparently this is true even in nontraditional families, such as those in communal living or social contract marriages (Zimmerman & Bernstein, 1983).

Recent research has attempted to assess the importance of mediating variables. For instance, maternal role satisfaction has been proposed as a more direct link to child outcomes than employment status. Having a paying job outside of the home often exerts a positive influence on the mother's sense of well-being, and this is associated with more positive child outcomes (Hoffman, 1979; Rutter, 1981a). Maternal role dissatisfaction has been associated with more negative behavior of both parents with their preschool children (Stuckey, McGhee, & Bell, 1982). Farel (1980) found that poorly adjusted children were more likely to have mothers who were unemployed and wanted a job. (See Chapter 16 for more about effects of parental unemployment.) Children of mothers who were dissatisfied with their employment status were less socially competent. Although no effects of maternal employment status on pre-school child outcomes were apparent in the New York Longitudinal Sample, the investigators found, using a path analytic model, that mater-nal role dissatisfaction was related to problematic mother-child interac-tion, which was in turn related to difficult child behavior (Lerner & Galambos, 1986).

Child Care

Related to the question of the effects of maternal employment is the question of the effects of child care away from home. The most compre-hensive reviews of the effects of daycare on children's development have concluded that there are no systematically harmful effects in preschool-ers, although quality of the care provided appears to be a crucial variable (Belsky & Steinberg, 1978; Rutter, 1981a). The consensus seems clear enough that currently the concern is about possible harmful effects of daycare in the first year of life (Belsky, 1988; Clarke-Stewart, 1988) rather than in the preschool years.

Group daycare does not appear to increase or decrease psychological symptoms or disorders in preschool children, although it may lead both to increased assertiveness and peer interaction (Rutter, 1981a). In-home daycare differs from group daycare somewhat in terms of amount of time caregivers spend with children, but if there are adequate numbers of caregivers for children, no differences in effects on children's develop-ment are apparent (Stallings & Porter, 1980, cited in Rutter, 1981a).

Despite important policy implications, research to date on daycare leaves many questions unanswered. As with other stressors in normal development, daycare may be helpful or harmful to the development of preschool children, depending on a host of other variables (Belsky & Steinberg, 1978; Rutter, 1981a). What we know is that good-quality daycare with stable caregiving arrangements is not harmful to preschoolers, that it does not adversely affect attachments to parents, and that it is associated with different, though not necessarily better or worse, social outcomes for children (Rutter, 1981a).

Birth of a Sibling

One of the most common stressors for young children is the birth of a sibling. Despite its near ubiquity and potential long-term importance, the effects of sibling birth on children have only recently been well-studied.

From these investigations we know that some changes in the behavior of the oldest child may become apparent during the mother's second pregnancy. Nadelman and Begun (1982) found that some of the children in their sample had increased negative behavior during the pregnancy, which actually decreased after the birth of the second child. These children seemed to have reacted to changes in the family environment created by the pregnancy and the anticipated new baby.

Field and Reite (1984) demonstrated behavioral and physiological changes in young children separated from their mothers during sibling birth. They videotaped parent-child play sessions before, during, and after the mother's hospitalization for delivery of the new baby, monitored activity level and heart rate during these sessions, and used time-lapse videotapes of three nights of sleep. They found increased activity level, heart rate, night wakings, crying, and negative affect during the separation. All of these diminished following the mother's return. In addition to separation, these children were also coping with their parents' preoccupation with the new sibling and their loss of the parents' availability. Fantasy play themes following the new sibling's arrival were primarily hostile: blocks falling on the new baby, having the baby dive off a bridge, running over the new baby with a car.

According to one of the most thorough longitudinal investigations in this area, changes in the parent-child relationship are not temporary. Dunn and Kendrick (1982) studied the impact of the birth of a second child in 40 working class families in Cambridge, England. From home observations they found that the time that mother and older sibling spent together playing and focusing on a subject of common interest decreased markedly after the birth of the second child. The number of conversations between these two that were initiated by the mother also decreased markedly. Further, there was a significant decrease in the mothers' responses to bids for attention by the older child after the birth of the sibling. These findings were still true 14 months after the birth of the second child. The birth of the sibling led to renegotiation of the parent-child relationship. Conflict between the mother and older child increased. In fact, 93% of the first children were defiant, demanding, and negative when their mothers paid attention to the new baby. As a result, confrontations between the two increased markedly. Conversations between the mothers and the older children concerning control of the older children's behavior increased significantly. Seventy percent of mothers reported regressed behaviors in their older children, including thumbsucking, loss of toilet training, and increased night waking. Fears, worries, and miserable moods increased over the period from pregnancy to the 14-month interviews, although demandingness and sleep problems declined significantly.

Another long-term effect of sibling birth was demonstrated by McCall (1984). Using data from the Fels Longitudinal Study, he found that IQ of the oldest children measured at ages 3 to 7 years dropped ten points relative to singleton children and six points relative to last-born children. Group differences were no longer significant by age 17 years in this sample.

The initial adjustment does not constitute the entire or even the major stressor associated with a new sibling. Afterwards the relationship between the preschool child and the new sibling plays an ongoing role in the older child's adaptation. Stillwell and Dunn (1985) found that early patterns of sibling relationships tend to persist over time. Nevertheless, there are few data available on the long-term effects of these relationships. Despite claims to the contrary, there is no clear evidence that spacing of children or sex of siblings is related to sibling closeness (Gallinsky & David, 1988). Family relationships outside the sibling dyad do appear to be important modifiers, however (Dunn, 1988).

PRESCHOOL STRESSORS BEYOND NORMAL DEVELOPMENT

Divorce

Two major longitudinal investigations have included sufficient numbers of preschool children to examine the impact of divorce. These have confirmed that divorce entails a number of immediate and long-term effects on preschool children's adaptation.

Wallerstein and Kelly (1982) studied 131 children in 60 divorcing middle-class families. Thirty-four of the children were aged 2 to 5 years at the time of the divorce. They appeared frightened and sad. They demonstrated emotional neediness and, at times, intense self-blame. Their play revealed mixtures of confusion about the separation and restorative fantasies. The investigators noted an increase in aggression, or less commonly an inhibition of aggression, immediately after the divorce. In a clinical-descriptive follow-up of these preschool children ten years after the divorce, Wallerstein (1984) reports that they fared better than their older siblings and that they looked forward optimistically to future marriage and family life. Thus, the same children who seemed most affected in their initial adaptation appeared to suffer the least long-term ill effects from the divorce (compared to older children).

Hetherington, Cox, & Cox (1982) studied 144 middle-class, white 4-year-olds, half from mother-custody divorced families and half from intact families. Within the first two years after divorce, children experienced psychological distress and health and behavior problems. Boys from divorced families had more behavior problems, noncompliance at home and school, difficulties in school achievement, and peer relationship problems.

Long-term problems in this sample depended upon initial coping as well as what occurred in the next four years. The occurrence of multiple stressors without available protective relationships and supports had the most deleterious effects on children's long-term adjustment. Authoritative parenting, as expected, was associated with high social and cognitive competence in the children. Mother-son relationships in divorced, non-remarried families were significantly more intense, ambivalent, and conflicted, typically with ineffectual control attempts by mothers. In contrast, mother-daughter relationships in divorced, non-remarried families were indistinguishable from mother-daughter relationships in non-divorced families (Hetherington, 1989). These results agree with Zaslow's (1989) extensive review of other published studies indicating that boys experience more problems with mothers who do not remarry but girls experience more problems in postdivorce families involving father custody or a stepfather.

Cluster analysis of Hetherington's sample six years after the divorce yielded three clusters of children: (1) aggressive, insecure (2) opportunistic-competent, and (3) caring-competent. The first group were lonely, angry, anxious, and insecure. Boys in this group had been rated temperamentally difficult earlier in life. Their homes were characterized by negative affect, conflict, and unsatisfactory conflict-resolution styles in parents, involving verbal or physical attacks, power assertion, or withdrawal rather than compromise. Children in the other two clusters were adapting well, with high self-esteem, academic achievement, and peer acceptance. Members of the opportunistic-competent group were distinguished by an interpersonal manipulativeness, ingratiating themselves to people in power and enjoying numerous but short-lived friendships. Those in the caring-competent group were less oriented to status and were significantly higher in helping and sharing than children in the other groups. Interestingly, 18 of the 23 children in this last cluster were girls, despite equal numbers of boys and girls in the total sample. They were characterized by having early experiences in caring for younger siblings or a less-than-adequately functioning mother. Thus, early care-giving experiences seemed to have been advantageous for girls but not for boys (Hetherington, 1988, 1989). (Further discussion of divorce stress can be found in Chapter 14.)

Hospitalization

Concern about the effects of hospitalization results from carefully con-trolled studies examining both single and repeated admissions of pre-school children. The evidence is clear that although a single hospital admission of one week or less often leads to acute distress, possibly persisting for some months after the return home, it does not lead to increased risk for long-term emotional or behavioral problems (Rutter, 1972). On the other hand, preschool children seem to be especially susceptible to harmful long-term effects after repeated admissions.

Two large studies have demonstrated increased psychiatric disorders following prolonged or repeated hospital admissions in preschool chil-dren (Douglas, 1975; Quinton & Rutter, 1976). These studies assessed outcome by different methods, including parental report, teacher ques-tionnaires, and direct assessments. Nevertheless, it was not possible to establish a causal link because children from more disadvantaged homes were more likely to experience repeated hospitalization (Quinton & Rutter, 1976). Since other stressors related to psychiatric disorders are also strongly associated with psychosocial disadvantage, it is not clear whether the outcomes were due to repeated hospital admissions or to the family characteristics of these children. Quinton and Rutter (1976) sug-gest that there is likely to be an interactive effect between social disadvan-tage and repeated admissions, since it is known that deprived children are most susceptible to harmful effects of stressful separations.

Maltreatment (Abuse or Neglect)

One of the most devastating stressors for preschool children is maltreat-ment by their parents (Galdston, 1965; Kempe & Kempe, 1978). The term "maltreatment" is a more convenient term referring to the abuse/sexual abuse/neglect spectrum discussed more fully for all ages by Johnson and Cohn in Chapter 10. More recent longitudinal studies that have exam-ined the effects on development have confirmed and extended the con-cerns raised by the earlier clinical reports.

In the Harvard Maltreatment Project, comprised of preschool and early school-age children, Aber and Allen (1987) and Aber et al. (1989) derived two summary outcome variables from factor-analysis of ten dependent variables assessing the children's relationships with novel adults, effectance motivation, and cognitive maturity. A "Secure Readiness to Learn" factor comprised high effectance motivation, high cognitive maturity, and low dependency. An "Outer Directedness" factor included verbal attention seeking, smiles, lack of wariness, and imitation. On each of these factors, derived from developmentally appropriate measures of adaptive functioning, maltreated children were significantly impaired compared to control children. On the other hand, there were no differences in behavioral symptoms between poor maltreated and poor nonmaltreated children, although both of these groups were significantly higher than a nonclinical sample. In another investigation that also controlled for social class, abused children had significantly more behavioral problems than nonabused children five years after the abuse was identified (Oates, Peacock, & Forrest, 1984). Aber and Allen (1987) concluded that maltreatment disrupts a dynamic balance in young children between the motivation to establish safe, secure relationships with adults and the motivation to venture out to explore the world in a competency-promoting manner.

Another arena in which effects of child maltreatment have been examined is peer relations. The development of satisfying peer relationships is a central component of social competence in the preschool-age period (Howes, 1987). In their extensive review, Mueller and Silverman (1989) concluded that preschoolers with a history of maltreatment demonstrate two major effects: heightened aggression and social withdrawal or avoidance. Interestingly, the aggression toward peers demonstrated by maltreated children often occurs in the unusual context of another child's distress. Mueller and Silverman (1989) proposed that this reaction represents an identification with the aggressor and a defensive disavowal of distress, a disavowal necessary to maintain their own self-integrity, which has been threatened by previous experiences of distress. The withdrawal and avoidance of interaction that characterizes maltreated children apparently goes beyond passive avoidance and includes actually resisting friendly bids from other children.

Children who are maltreated in infancy appear to be more vulnerable to psychosocial disruptions of development in the preschool years (Gaensbauer, Mrazek, & Harmon, 1980; Gaensbauer & Sands, 1979; George & Main, 1979). Particularly when stage-salient developmental outcomes are examined, previously maltreated preschool children appear significantly more vulnerable than their non-maltreated peers (Aber & Cicchetti, 1984).

The prospective, longitudinal Minnesota Mother-Child Project (Erickson, Egeland, & Pianta, 1989) has examined the effects of different types of maltreatment on specific developmental tasks. Physically abused pre-school children demonstrated more aggressive, noncompliant, and acting-out behavior than comparison children in the same high-risk sample. They had poor adaptive behavior in kindergarten and were unable to solve problems without over-reliance on teachers. Children whose mothers were psychologically unavailable to them (maternally deprived) were less involved in structured tasks and functioned less adequately in social and academic situations in kindergarten. Children who were neglected demonstrated the most severe impairments, functioning less well socially, academically, emotionally, and behaviorally compared to the control group and to the other groups. Sexually abused preschool children demonstrated impulsivity, dependence, socially deviant behavior, and poor peer relations.

On the other hand, similarities in effects across maltreatment groups were also apparent. Children who had experienced each type of maltreatment demonstrated intense anxiety, anger, poor peer relations and unpopularity, and dependence significant enough that it interfered with adaptation in kindergarten. These results suggest that maltreatment in all of its forms has devastating effects on salient developmental tasks for preschool children, including developing a secure attachment, development of an autonomous self, symbolic representation, peer relations, and communicative behavior (Cicchetti, 1989).

Witnessing Violence

Even if children are not physically abused themselves, witnessing acts of domestic violence has immediate and long-term effects on them. For instance, one study (Hughes, 1988) compared anxiety and behavior problems in three groups of children: physically abused children who witnessed family violence, nonabused children who witnessed family violence, and a control group. Abused children exhibited significantly more distress and behavior problems than the others, with nonabused witness children generally falling in between them and the controls. Preschool children in a battered women's shelter were rated by their mothers as having more severe behavior problems than older children (Hughes & Barad, 1983).

Case reports of young children who have witnessed their mothers being raped have suggested that a variety of post-traumatic symptoms occur in the children (reviewed in Pynoos & Eth, 1988). No systematic investigations of preschool children's responses are yet available. Witnessing serious but unsuccessful suicide attempts apparently also leads to post-traumatic symptoms in young children (Pynoos, Gilmore, & Shapiro, 1981).

Concern about long-term effects of maltreatment and witnessing of violence also comes from studies of perpetrators of marital and child abuse. In studies of battered women, investigators have found that one-half to three-quarters of the perpetrators and one-quarter to one-third of the victims had had violent childhoods (Gayford, 1975; Roy, 1977). Steinmetz (1986) pointed out that witnessing violence may be especially harmful for boys. She cites findings by Rosenbaum and O'Leary (1981) that abusive husbands were significantly more likely to have witnessed family violence in their childhoods than nonabusive husbands. Similarly, Strauss, Gelles, and Steinmetz (1980) reported that men who grew up in violent homes had a rate of abusing their wives 1000% greater than men who grew up in nonviolent homes. These retrospective results point to the need for longitudinal, prospective investigations to examine factors related to repetition of or escape from the transgenerational cycle of family violence.

Loss of a Parent

Descriptive studies of bereavement in young children have demonstrated that their acute reactions are quite similar to the reactions of bereaved adults (Becker & Margolin, 1967; Furman, 1974). Garmezy (1983), on the other hand, suggests that younger children may experience milder and relatively briefer grief reactions than do adolescents or adults, largely because they have a less clear understanding of death and its finality. Links between childhood loss of a parent and later development of adult depression have been reported repeatedly, although the links apparently are not direct (Harris, Brown, & Bifulco, 1986). Bowlby's (1980, 1988) careful reviews of these investigations and other available clinical data suggest a number of factors important to healthy resolution of mourning in young children. These include: a reasonably good parent-child relationship prior to the loss, prompt access to accurate information about the death, opportunities for inquiring about the death, participation in funeral rites, and the comforting presence of the surviving parent or other trusted adult figure. Prospective studies are needed to assess the relative importance of these clinically meaningful variables.

Violent Loss of a Parent.   When loss of the parent occurs from homicide or suicide, the effects on children may be even more profound. This problem is apparently far more common than is generally recognized. Pynoos and Eth (1984) reported that in Los Angeles County in 1981, at least 200 young children witnessed a parent-parent homicide. Clinical reports of such cases have revealed a variety of post-traumatic symptoms in these children, including new fears, generalized anxiety, post-traumatic play, affective or behavioral constriction, and sleep disturbances

(Bergen, 1958; Malmquist, 1982; Pruett, 1979; Pynoos & Eth, 1984; Zeanah & Burk, 1984). The largest sample studied to date are 50 children in Los Angeles whom Pynoos and Eth (1988) report exhibited numerous symptoms and were especially preoccupied by intrusive recollections of the traumatic event.

Long-term effects of violent loss also may occur in these children. A sample of 21 clinic-referred children who lost a parent through violence (15 were less than 5 years old), received diagnoses of overanxious, dysthymic, or conduct disorders (Payton & Krocker-Tuskan, 1988). As the authors acknowledged, it was impossible to weigh the contribution of other variables that antedated and followed the losses and also might have contributed to the development of psychiatric disorders in these children. Nevertheless, from a practical standpoint, violent loss of a parent clearly identifies a group of preschool children who have experienced a uniquely traumatic experience and who are at high risk for subsequent psychiatric disorder.

MODIFYING VARIABLES

The impact of stress on preschool children is modified by individual differences, protective factors, and coping skills.

Individual Differences that Modify Stress Response

Many individual differences can also be considered risk factors (e.g., male sex, younger age) or protective factors (e.g., female sex, older age).

Sex of Child. An increasing body of data suggests that in response to stress, preschool boys evidence greater behavioral disruption than girls, at least in the short run. Boys are more likely than girls to show an increase in withdrawal subsequent to the birth of a sibling (Dunn et al., 1981) and exhibit greater behavioral disinhibition at entry into daycare (Rutter, 1981a). A recent investigation of post-traumatic stress disorder in young children reveals that boys may suffer more severe and more slowly resolved reactions at the time of the event, although girls are more likely to experience a recurrence of symptoms later in development (Kiser et al., 1988). Boys also are more likely to evidence increases in their aggression level with increases in parental discord and disharmony (Rutter, 1981b).

Both Hetherington, Cox, & Cox, (1977) and Wallerstein and Kelly (1982) reported that behavioral difficulties, including aggression and noncompliance, were much more severe and of longer duration in boys than in girls in the year immediately following divorce. Subsequent data (Hetherington et al., 1982) reveal marked deterioration in divorced mothers' interaction with their sons in the first year after divorce, including decreased positive behavior, affection, and affiliation, and increased threats and commands with little enforcement. These data suggest an interaction between preschool boys' relatively greater need for consistent limit setting and structure, and their mothers' diminished availability for those functions following disruptive family events; these combine to produce apparent gender-specific effects.

Age of Child. Preschool-aged children seem particularly vulnerable to certain kinds of stressful events, primarily because of the cognitive and emotional tasks of the preschool period. Events likely to be particularly stressful to preschoolers include hospitalization and the birth of a new sibling. However, except for the special separation vulnerability at ages 1–4 compared to ages 4–6 (discussed earlier), there are few data bearing on the question of differing vulnerabilities at different ages within the preschool period. The reactions of children to stressful events vary by age and developmental level, but there is little to suggest that such variation is consistently related to differential long-term outcomes.

Intelligence. Although intuitively we would expect intelligence to be a moderating variable in children's response to stress, this has not been studied in preschoolers. However, we might extrapolate from a study of 168 middle-class school-aged children which revealed that when previously high-achieving youngsters experienced moderate to high levels of family stress, their academic performance improved. The opposite pattern was observed in less scholastically competent children whose families experienced similar levels of stress (Barton, 1985). These data suggest that for some children, scholastic ability may serve as a buffer to familial stress, permitting increased focus, at least in the short term, on areas of positive functioning.

Temperament. The notion of temperament, or biologically determined variations in behavioral style and reactivity, is frequently advanced as one explanation for children's differential response to stress. Nonetheless, there is little direct evidence available. It is quite clear that temperamentally difficult children exhibit, among other characteristics, avoidance or distress in new situations and slow adaptation to unfamiliar events. They tend to be highly reactive and extreme in their reactions (Chess, Thomas, & Birch, 1968; Grahem, Rutter, & George, 1973) and present a higher incidence of behavior problems (Carey, 1981). Temperamentally difficult children are more likely to elicit negative reactions from adults (Keogh & Pullis, 1980 cited in Rutter, 1981a; Rutter, 1978) and are more likely to experience difficulties forming secure attachments under conditions of high environmental stress or low maternal support (Goldberg, 1981). Thus, it seems likely that temperamentally difficult children may experience greater difficulty adjusting to stressful events and may be more likely to experience negative interactions and reduced interpersonal support. Taken together, these qualities may indeed render temperamentally difficult children more vulnerable to stress.

A recent study by Wertlieb et al. (1988) of 158 school-age children reveals that both difficult temperament and increased stress were related to a higher incidence of behavior problems. These factors interacted only modestly, however, to produce slightly increased vulnerability when they occurred simultaneously.

Two empirical investigations involving preschool children bear directly on this point. First, Dunn et al. (1981) used interview measures of temperament to predict changes in children's behavior after the birth of a sibling. In a subsequent investigation, Dunn and Kendrick (1982) reported that children with adverse temperaments were most likely to demonstrate problem behaviors eight months after birth of a sibling.

Rutter (1981b) has argued that temperamental differences in response to stress may be mediated by differential patterns of parent-child interaction, with more difficult children and their parents sharing more negative interactive patterns. Hetherington (1989) offers evidence in support of this view from her six-year follow-up of the children of divorced parents. She noted that for difficult children, increased stress was associated with diminished adaptability. Furthermore, when mothers' aversive responses to children increased with deterioration in mothers' own level of functioning, the increases were most notable with difficult children.

Thus, it appears that temperament may exert significant influence on children's reaction to stress, but it is highly colored by the larger environmental context. Extremes of environment may even "reverse the polarity" and make a difficult temperament a survival asset, as mentioned by Lobo in Chapter 6. In general, though, difficult temperament may be most usefully viewed as a risk factor whose presence may predispose children to negative interaction patterns, which in turn undermine their capacity to cope with stress.

Preschool Protective Factors

Protective factors are characteristics or circumstances that protect children from the effects of stressful events or mitigate those effects when they occur.

Structure and Stability.   Given the preschooler's inability to maintain organization in the face of stress, the provision of environmental structure would seem critical to mediating the immediate effects of stress. A familiar environment that provides structure and restores routine facilitates the young child's ability to maintain behavioral organization. Indeed, studies of divorce suggest that significant alterations in environmental structure (e.g., moves, parents' return to work, economic instability) are important contributors to the behavioral instability reported after divorce.

The importance of stability extends to the parent's emotional state. Children of divorcing parents clearly did much better during and after the initial adjustment period when their custodial parents evidenced relatively more stable functioning or sought supportive counseling.

Availability of Attachment Figures. Obviously, one component of the child's environment directly related to the experience of stress is the availability of primary attachment figures. As Maccoby (1983) notes, the young child has an immediate and all-purpose response to stress, namely the seeking of contact with attachment figures (parents or parent substitutes).

In describing the reaction of British children to the air raids of the second World War, Freud and Burlingham (1944) noted that when young children remained with their mothers or mother substitutes, they showed no untoward reaction to the bombings. Similar findings have been reported by more recent investigations of children in violent, strife-ridden contexts (Ziv & Isreali, 1973). In addition, numerous studies have revealed that parents' presence during a child's hospitalization greatly reduces the distress experienced by the child, as does frequent contact with a consistently present nurse (Rutter, 1983). Children of divorcing parents adjusted much better when the children were able to maintain close relationships with the non-custodial parent (Hetherington et al., 1977). Thus, it seems clear that the availability of a parent or parent substitute greatly reduces the experience of stress in young children.

Quality of Parent-Child Relationship. Equally important to mediating the effects of stress on the young child is the nature of the child's tie to the primary caregivers. Numerous studies have demonstrated that young children with secure attachment relationships are likely to exhibit improved social functioning, empathy, and self-esteem in the nursery school setting. In contrast, children with insecure attachment relationships are likely to evidence a variety of negative interactive patterns with peers and teachers (Sroufe, 1983). They are also more likely to experience difficulty in interacting with their mothers in a mildly stressful laboratory task (Matas, Arend, & Sroufe, 1978). In addition, children whose mothers are insecurely attached themselves tend to be over-represented in clinical samples (Benoit, Zeanah, & Barton, 1989; Crowell, Feldman, & Ginsberg, 1988). Since nearly half the mothers in control groups were insecurely attached in these samples, mothers' insecurity is not a significant risk factor for child problems. On the other hand, almost no mothers in the clinical samples were securely attached, suggesting that maternal security of attachment is an important protective factor with regard to psychiatric disorders in the children.

Similarly, in studies of the children of psychiatric patients, Rutter (1971) reports that in homes characterized by high levels of discord, children with a positive relationship with one parent were much less likely to develop conduct disorders than children who lacked such relationships. In families without such discord, the presence of a supportive relationship with one parent did not distinguish outcome.

The quality of other relationships within the family has also been related to the responses of children exposed to chronic stress. Elder (1977, cited in Rutter, 1981b) reported that among children reared amidst severe economic depression, a supportive relationship between parents reduced the likelihood of a depressive response in children.

Obviously, the quality of parent-child relationships is influenced by a variety of factors. These include the relationship history and its meaning to the participants, as well as more specific characteristics of the child and the parents. Child characteristics include such factors as sex and temperament, discussed earlier. Parent characteristics include their ability to respond to stress in adaptive ways. An example of parent characteristics is found in Dunn's 1985 study of children's adaptation to the birth of a sibling. The most important variable in preschoolers' reactions is how well their parents negotiate the increased demands and role changes following the birth of a second child. The children who developed the most positive relationships with new siblings had mothers who did not become too fatigued or depressed after the baby's birth. These mothers were also able to continue to enjoy their older child. Since 95% of the older children in the study wanted to become involved in caring for the new baby, parents have an opportunity to improve preschoolers' adaptation. Children whose mothers talked to them about the infant as a person with needs, wants, and feelings were more likely to develop a positive relationship with the new sibling.

Resilience. Some research on the coping responses of children exposed to high levels of severe stress, such as war, has focused on delineating the characteristics of the invulnerable or resilient child. Garmezy (1983) reviews five investigations of such children and proposes that they share three central characteristics: (1) dispositional attributes in the child, such as social skills, emotional stability, internal locus of control, and independence; (2) family cohesion, warmth, or support; and (3) a support system outside of the family, which provides identification models or reinforcement for coping skills. None of these studies focused exclusively on preschool children, and it seems likely that given the increased dependence of the young child on the family context, the presence of support systems outside of the family may be less critical. What is central to the young child's adjustment, however, is the provision of extra-familial support services to their parents.

Numerous studies of adults have found increased coping skills in response to stress in the presence of social supports (Rutter, 1983). Recent research on young children suggests that the provision of such support may translate into social environments that support children's improved functioning. Hetherington (1989) described a complex interactive pattern involving parental functioning, social support, child temperament, and observable parent-child interaction, which predicted young children's response to divorce at a six-year follow-up. She found that under conditions of a stable maternal personality and low stress, there were no differences in mothers' negative responses to temperamentally easy or difficult children, although difficult children evidence more aversive behaviors. The co-occurrence of personality problems in mothers and high levels of stress significantly increased maternal aversive responses over the level found with either stress or personality problems alone, especially with difficult children and with sons. There were no differences in the adaptive behavior of easy and difficult children under conditions of low stress and high support. When support was not readily available, however, differences between easy and difficult children appeared. For difficult children, increased stress was associated with less adaptability. For easy children, a curvilinear relationship emerged: under supportive conditions these children actually increased adaptive skills when stress levels were moderate rather than high or low.

In summary, then, protective factors in young children include individual difference variables that may render some children less vulnerable to stress and a host of other factors that center upon continued environmental stability. The latter must include the availability of consistent, well functioning, and well supported attachment figures.

Augmenting the Coping Skills of Preschool Children

Given the data available on preschoolers' responses to stress, what strategies might be employed to augment the child's coping resources?

Information.   Several studies of young children's response to hospitalization have documented that providing specific information about the event prior to admission allays children's anxiety (Ferguson, 1979; Wolfer & Visentainer, 1979). In general, the provision of clear, simple explanations of events prior to their occurrence or as quickly as possible thereafter appears to be helpful in reducing anticipatory anxiety and correcting misattributions of blame or causality.

Ventilation. Providing the child the opportunity to express distress, ambivalence, and intense affective reactions both directly and in play frequently contributes to mastering the event and improving the perspective on the self. (The use of play therapy in helping preschoolers cope with stress is reviewed in Chapter 20.)

Rituals. Participation in rituals surrounding the event, or becoming actively involved in practices designed to make the child feel part of the event, are also of help.

Routine and Relationships. The maintenance of familiar routine and the maintenance of attachment relationships or frequent contact with substitute attachment figures is highly effective in reducing the young child's distress in response to environmental upheaval. To the extent that social supports provided to the family augment the coping skills of adults and permit their greater emotional availability to young children, such support is advantageous as well.

Cognition. Finally, researchers have recently focused on altering the young child's cognitive response to stress. Shure and Spivack (1980) and Spivack and Shure (1982) have provided evidence that the ability to generate alternative solutions to a problem is apparent by age 4 or 5, and is related to a reduced incidence of behavior problems. They argue that it may also be related to modifications in the impact of stress on young children. The relationship between efforts to teach problem-solving skills and improved adjustment is not supported by unequivocal data, but some writers suggest that such intervention efforts may be most effective for those children experiencing high levels of stress (Compas, 1988).

Applications

Gallinsky and David (1988) discuss examples of all of the above strategies in their review of parental interventions helpful in reducing the stress inherent in the birth of a sibling. These include preparing the child before birth, introducing the child to the new sibling, acknowledging the child's new role, accepting the child's ambivalence, minimizing changes in the child's life, maintaining attentiveness to the child, maintaining positive discipline techniques, and including the child in caregiving activities. Many of these strategies may be viewed as maintaining the quality and pattern of the parent-child relationship while acknowledging obvious changes and adaptations in familial routine.

CONCLUSION

All of the data reviewed here point to the complex interplay of factors affecting the preschool child's successful adaptation to stress. While recent studies on the effects of divorce, sibling birth, and maltreatment have enhanced our understanding of how best to ameliorate the preschooler's response to stress, much remains to be learned. Given the pace of our society and the increasing incidence of both familial instability and environmental upheaval, the experience of stress among preschoolers seems destined to increase. The future will likely continue to challenge both the state of our knowledge regarding the preschooler's response to stress and our ability to provide resources to support developmentally appropriate coping strategies in young children and their families.

REFERENCES

Aber, J. L., & Allen, J. P. (1987). Effects of maltreatment on young children's socioemotional development: An attachment theory perspective. *Developmental Psychology, 23,* 406–414.

Aber, J. L., Allen, J. P., Carlson, V., & Cicchetti, D. (1989). The effects of maltreatment on development during early childhood: Recent studies and their theoretical, clinical and policy implications. In D. Cicchetti & V. Carlson (Eds.), *Child maltreatment: Theory and research on the causes and consequences of child abuse and neglect.* Cambridge, MA: Cambridge University Press.

Aber, J. L., & Cicchetti, D. (1984). The socioemotional development of maltreated children: An empirical and theoretical analysis. In H. Fitzgerald, B. Lester, & M. Yogman (Eds.), *Theory and research in behavioral pediatrics* (Vol. 2). New York: Plenum Press.

Barton, M. (1985). *Behavioral stability in the elementary school years and the effects of environmental stress.* Paper presented at the meetings of the American Psychological Association, Los Angeles, CA.

Becker, D., & Margolin, F. (1967). How surviving parents handled their young children's adaptation to the crisis of loss. *American Journal of Orthopsychiatry, 37,* 753–757.

Belsky, J. (1988). The effects of infant day care reconsidered. *Early Childhood Research Quarterly, 3,* 235–272.

Belsky, J., & Steinberg, L. (1978). The effects of daycare: A critical review. *Child Development, 49,* 929–949.

Benoit, D., Zeanah, C. H., & Barton, M. (1989). Attachment disturbances in failure to thrive. *Infant Mental Health Journal, 10,* 185–202.

Bergen, M. E. (1958). The effect of severe trauma on a four-year-old child. *Psychoanalytic Study of the Child, 13,* 407–429.

Bowlby, J. (1969). *Attachment.* London: Hogarth Press.

Bowlby, J. (1980). *Loss.* New York: Basic Books.

Bowlby, J. (1988). Developmental psychiatry comes of age. *American Journal of Psychiatry, 145,* 1–10.

Carey, W. (1981). The importance of temperament-environment interaction for child health and development. In M. Lewis & L. Rosenblum (Eds.), *The uncommon child.* New York: Plenum Press.

Chess, S., Thomas, A., & Birch, H. G. (1968). Behavioral problems revisited. In S. Chess & H. Birch (Eds.), *Annual progress in child psychiatry and development.* New York: Bruner/Mazel.

Cicchetti, D. (1989). How research on child maltreatment has informed the study of child development: Perspectives on developmental psychopathology. In D. Cicchetti & V. Carlson (Eds.), *Child maltreatment: Theory and research on the causes and consequences of child abuse and neglect.* Cambridge, MA: Cambridge University Press.

Clarke-Stewart, A. K. (1988). "The 'effects' of infant day care reconsidered" reconsidered: Risks for parents, children, and researchers. *Early Childhood Research Quarterly, 3,* 293–318.

Compas, B. (1988). Coping with stress during childhood and adolescence. In S. Chess, A. Thomas, & M. Hertzig (Eds.), *Annual progress in child psychiatry and development.* New York: Bruner/Mazel.

Crowell, J. A., Feldman, S. S., & Ginsberg, N. (1988). Mothers' internal models of relationships and children's behavioral and developmental status: A study of mother-child interaction. *Child Development, 59,* 1273–1285.

Douglas, J. W. B. (1975). Early hospital admissions and later disturbances of behavior and learning. *Developmental Medicine and Child Neurology, 17,* 456–480.

Dunn, J. (1985). *Sisters and brothers.* Cambridge, MA: Harvard University Press.

Dunn, J. (1988). Normative life events as risk factors in childhood. In M. Rutter (Ed.), *Studies of psychosocial risk: The power of longitudinal data.* New York: Cambridge University Press.

Dunn, J., & Kendrick, C. (1982). *Siblings: Love, envy, and understanding.* Cambridge, MA: Harvard University Press.

Dunn, J., Kendrick, C., & MacNamee, R. (1981). The reaction of first born children to the birth of a sibling: Mothers' reports. *Journal of Child Psychiatry and Psychology, 22,* 1–18.

Erickson, M. F., Egeland, B., & Pianta, R. (1989). The effects of maltreatment on the development of young children. In D. Cicchetti & V. Carlson (Eds.), *Child maltreatment: Theory and research on the causes and consequences of child abuse and neglect.* Cambridge, MA: Cambridge University Press.

Erikson, E. (1959). Identity and the life cycle. *Psychological Issues, I,* 18–184.

Eth, S., & Pynoos R. (1985). Developmental perspective on psychic trauma in childhood. In C. R. Figley (Ed.), *Trauma and its wake*. New York: Bruner/Mazel.

Farel, A. N. (1980). Effects of preferred maternal roles, maternal employment, and sociographic status, on school adjustment and competence. *Child Development, 50,* 1179–1186.

Ferguson, B. F. (1979). Preparing young children for hospitalization: A comparison of two methods. *Pediatrics, 64,* 656–664.

Field, T., & Reite, M. (1984). Children's responses to separation from mother during the birth of another child. *Child Development, 55,* 1308–1316.

Freud, A., & Burlingham, D. (1944). *War and children*. London: Medical War Books.

Furman, E. (1974). *A child's parent dies*. New Haven: Yale University Press.

Gaensbauer, T. J., Mrazek, D., & Harmon, R. J. (1980). Affective behavior patterns in abused and/or neglected infants. In N. Frude (Ed.), *The understanding and prevention of child abuse: Psychological approaches*. London: Concord Press.

Gaensbauer, T. J., & Sands, S. K. (1979). Distorted affective communications in abused/neglected infants and their potential impact on caregivers. *Journal of the American Academy of Child Psychiatry, 18,* 236–250.

Galdston, R. (1965). Observations of children who have been physically abused and their parents. *American Journal of Psychiatry, 122,* 440–443.

Gallinsky, E., & David, J. (1988). *The preschool years*. New York: Times Books.

Garmezy, N. (1983). Stressors of childhood. In N. Garmezy & M. Rutter (Eds.), *Stress, coping and development in children*. New York: McGraw-Hill.

Gayford, J. J. (1975). Wife battering: A preliminary survey of 100 cases. *British Journal of Psychiatry, 25,* 194–197.

George, C., & Main, M. (1979). Social interactions of young abused children: Approach, avoidance and aggression. *Child Development, 50,* 306–318.

Goldberg, S. B. (1981). Infant irritability, mother responsiveness, and social support influences on the security of infant-mother attachment. *Child Development, 52,* 857–865.

Grahem, P., Rutter, M., & George, S. (1973). Temperamental characteristics as predictors of behavior disorders in children. *American Journal of Orthopsychiatry, 43,* 228–299.

Harris, T., Brown, G. W., & Bifulco, A. (1986). Loss of a parent in childhood and adult psychiatric disorder: The role of lack of parental care. *Psychological Medicine, 16,* 641–660.

Heinicke, C., & Westheimer, I. (1966). *Brief separation*. New York: International University Press.

Hetherington, E. M. (1988). Parents, children, and siblings six years after divorce. In R. A. Hinde & J. Stevenson-Hinde (Eds.), *Relationships within families*. Cambridge, MA: Cambridge University Press.

Hetherington, E. M. (1989). Coping with family transitions: Winners, losers, and survivors. *Child Development, 60,* 1–14.

Hetherington, E. M., Cox, M., & Cox, R. (1977). Beyond father absence: Conceptualization of the effects of divorce. In E. M. Hetherington & R. Parke (Eds.), *Contemporary readings in child psychology.* New York: McGraw-Hill.

Hetherington, E. M., Cox, M., & Cox, R. (1982). Effects of divorce on parents and children. In M. E. Lamb (Ed.), *Nontraditional families: Parenting and child development.* Hillsdale, NJ: Lawrence Erlbaum.

Hoffman, L. (1979). Maternal employment: 1979. *American Psychologist, 34,* 859–865.

Howes, C. (1987). The development of social competence with peers. *Developmental Review, 9,* 259–272.

Hughes, H. M. (1988). Psychological and behavioral correlates of family violence in child witnesses and victims. *American Journal of Orthopsychiatry, 58,* 77–90.

Hughes, H. M., & Barad, S. J. (1983). Psychological functioning of children in a battered women's shelter: A preliminary investigation. *American Journal of Orthopsychiatry, 53,* 525–531.

Kagan, J. (1983). Stress and coping in early development. In N. Garmezy & M. Rutter (Eds.), *Stress, coping and development in children.* New York: McGraw-Hill.

Kagan, J., Kearsley, R. B., & Zelazo, P. R. (1978). *Infancy: Its place in human development.* Cambridge, MA: Harvard University Press.

Kempe, R., & Kempe, C. H. (1978). *Child abuse.* Cambridge, MA: Harvard University Press.

Keogh, B. K., & Pullis, M. E. (1980). Temperamental influences on the development of exceptional children. *Advances in Special Education, 1,* 239–276.

Kiser, L., Ackerman, B., Brown, E., Edwards, N., McGolgan, E., Pugh, R., & Pruitt, D. (1988). Post traumatic stress disorders in young children: A reaction to purported sexual abuse. *Journal of the American Academy of Child Psychiatry, 29,* 645–676.

Lerner, J. V., & Galambos, N. L. (1986). Child development and family change: The influences of maternal employment in infants and toddlers. In L. P. Lipsitt & C. Rovee-Collier (Eds.), *Advances in infancy research* (Vol. 4, pp. 40–87). Norwood, NJ: Ablex.

Maccoby, E. (1983). Social emotional development and response to stressors. In N. Garmezy & M. Rutter (Eds.), *Stress, coping and development in children.* New York: McGraw-Hill.

Maccoby, E., & Feldman, S. S. (1972). Mother attachment and stranger reactions in the third year of life. *Monographs of the Society for Research in Child Development, 37,* No. 146.

Malmquist, C. (1982). *Children who witness parental murder: Posttraumatic and legal issues.* Paper presented to the Annual Meeting of the American Academy of Child and Adolescent Psychiatry, Washington, DC.

Matas, L., Arend, R. A., & Sroufe, L. A. (1978). Continuity of adaption in the second year: The relationship between quality of attachment and later competence. *Child Development, 49,* 547–556.

McCall, R. B. (1984). Developmental changes in mental performance: The effect of birth of a sibling. *Child Development, 55,* 1317–1321.

Mueller, E., & Silverman, N. (1989). Peer relations in maltreated children. In D.

Cicchetti & V. Carlson (Eds.), *Child maltreatment: Theory and research on the causes and consequences of child abuse and neglect.* Cambridge, MA: Cambridge University Press.

Nadelman, L., & Begun, A. (1982). The effect of the newborn on the older sibling. In M. E. Lamb & B. Sutton-Smith (Eds.), *Sibling relationships: Their nature and significance across the lifespan.* Hillsdale, NJ: Lawrence Erlbaum.

Newman, C. J. (1976). Children of disaster: Clinical observations at Buffalo Creek. *American Journal of Psychiatry, 133,* 206–312.

Oates, R. K., Peacock, A., & Forrest, D. (1984). The development of abused children. *Developmental Medicine and Child Neurology, 26,* 649–656.

Payton, J. B., & Krocker-Tuskan, M. (1988). Children's reactions to loss of a parent through violence. *Journal of the American Academy of Child and Adolescent Psychiatry, 27,* 563–566.

Perrin, E. C., & Gerrity, S. (1981). There's a demon in your belly: Children's understanding of illness. *Pediatrics, 67,* 841–849.

Piaget, J. (1952). *The origins of intelligence in children.* New York: International University Press.

Piaget, J. (1960). *The child's conception of the world.* London: Routledge.

Potter, P. C., & Roberts, M. C. (1984). Children's perceptions of chronic illness: The roles of disease symptoms, cognitive development, and information. *Journal of Pediatric Psychology, 9,* 13–27.

Pruett, K. B. (1979). Home treatment for two infants who witnessed their mother's murder. *Journal of the American Academy of Child Psychiatry, 18,* 647–657.

Pynoos, R., & Eth, S. (1984). The child as witness to homicide. *Journal of Social Issues, 40,* 269–290.

Pynoos, R., & Eth, S. (1988). Witnessing acts of personal violence. In S. Eth & R. Pynoos (Eds.), *Post-traumatic stress disorder in children.* Washington, DC: American Psychiatric Association Press.

Pynoos, R., Gilmore, K., & Shapiro, T. (1981). *Children's response to parental suicide behavior.* Paper presented to the Annual meeting of the American Academy of Child Psychiatry.

Quinton, D., & Rutter, M. (1976). Early hospital admissions and later disturbances of behavior. *Developmental Medicine and Child Neurology, 18,* 447–459.

Robertson, J., & Robertson, J. (1971). Young children in brief separation: A fresh look. *Psychoanalytic Study of the Child, 26,* 264–315.

Rosenbaum, A., & O'Leary, D. (1981). Children: The unintended victims of marital violence. *American Journal of Orthopsychiatry, 51,* 692–699.

Roy, M. (1977). A current survey of 150 cases. In M. Roy (Ed.), *Battered women: A psychosociological study of domestic violence.* New York: Van Nostrand Reinhold.

Rutter, M. (1971). Parent-child separation: Psychological effects on the child. *Journal of Child Psychology and Psychiatry, 12,* 233–260.

Rutter, M. (1972). *Maternal deprivation reassessed.* Harmondsworth: Penguin.

Rutter, M. (1978). Early sources of security and competence. In J. S. Bruner & A. Garten (Eds.), *Human growth and development.* London: Oxford University Press.

Rutter, M. (1981a). Social-emotional consequences of daycare for preschool children. *American Journal of Orthopsychiatry, 51,* 4–28.

Rutter, M. (1981b). Stress, coping and development: Some issues and some questions. *Journal of Child Psychology and Psychiatry, 22,* 323–356.

Rutter, M. (1983). Stress, coping and development: Some issues and some questions. In N. Garmezy & M. Rutter (Eds.), *Stress, coping and development in children.* New York: McGraw-Hill.

Shure, M. B., & Spivack, G. (1980). Interpersonal problem solving as a mediator of behavior adjustment in preschool and kindergarten children. *Journal of Applied Developmental Psychology, I,* 29–43.

Siegel, A. (1984). Working mothers and their children. *Journal of the American Academy of Child Psychiatry, 23,* 486–488.

Spitz, R. (1946). Anaclitic depression. *The Psychoanalytic Study of the Child, 2,* 313–342.

Spivack, G., & Shure, M. B. (1982). The cognition of social adjustment: Interpersonal, cognitive problem solving thinking. In B. B. Lahey & A. E. Kazdin (Eds.), *Advances in clinical child psychology* (Vol. 5). New York: Plenum Press.

Sroufe, L. A. (1983). Infant caregiver attachment and patterns of adaptation in preschool: The roots of maladaption and competence. In M. Perlmutter (Ed.), *Minnesota Symposium in Child Psychology,* No. 16. Hillsdale, NJ: Lawrence Erlbaum.

Stallings, J., & Porter, A. (1980). *National day care home study.* (Final report, Volume III, to the Department of Health and Human Services, Washington, DC, S.R.I. International.)

Steinmetz, S. K. (1986). The violent family. In M. Lystad (Ed.), *Violence in the home.* New York: Brunner/Mazel.

Stillwell, R., & Dunn, J. (1985). Continuities in sibling relationships: Patterns of aggression and friendliness. *Journal of Child Psychology, Psychiatry and Allied Disciplines, 26,* 627–637.

Strauss, M. A., Gelles, R. J., & Steinmetz, S. K. (1980). *Behind closed doors: Violence in American families.* New York: Doubleday.

Stuckey, M. F., McGhee, P. E., & Bell, N. J. (1982). Parent-child interaction: The influence of maternal employment. *Developmental Psychology, 18,* 635–644.

Terr, L. (1981). Forbidden games: post traumatic child's play. *Journal of the American Academy of Child Psychiatry, 20,* 742–759.

Waldman, E. (1983). Labor force statistics from the family perspective. *Monthly Labor Review, 106,* 16–19.

Wallerstein, J. (1977). Some observations regarding the effects of divorce on the psychological development of the preschool girl. In J. Oremland & E. Oremland (Eds.), *Sexual and gender development of young children.* Cambridge, MA: Ballinger Press.

Wallerstein, J. (1984). Children of divorce: Recent research. *Journal of the American Academy of Child Psychiatry, 23,* 515–517.

Wallerstein, J., & Kelly, J. (1982). *Surviving the breakup.* New York: Basic Books.

Wertlieb, O., Wiegal, C., Springer, T., & Feldstein, M. (1988). Temperament as a moderator of children's stressful experiences. In S. Chess, A. Thomas, & M. Hertzig (Eds.), *Annual progress in child psychiatry and development.* New York: Brunner/Mazel.

Wolfer, J. A., & Visentainer, M. A. (1979). Prehospital psychological preparation for tonsillectomy patients: Effects on children's and parents' adjustments. *Pediatrics, 64,* 646–655.

Zaslow, M. J. (1989). Sex differences in children's response to parental divorce: 2. Samples, variables, ages, and sources. *American Journal of Orthopsychiatry, 59,* 118–141.

Zeanah, C. H., & Burk, G. S. (1984). A young child who witnessed her mother's murder: Therapeutic and legal considerations. *American Journal of Psychotherapy, 38,* 132–145.

Zimmerman, I. L., & Bernstein, M. (1983). Parental work patterns in alternative families: Influence on child development. *American Journal of Orthopsychiatry, 53,* 418–425.

Ziv, A., & Isreali, R. (1973). Effects of bombardment on the manifest anxiety level of children living in kibbutzim. *Journal of Consulting and Clinical Psychology, 40,* 287–291.

CHAPTER EIGHT

School-Age Stress

Susan Jones Sears
Joanne Milburn

Elkind (1981) points out that today's parents are hurrying the growing-up process by treating children as adults and by burdening them with worry and anxiety, expecting them to aid adults in carrying life's load. This parent-induced stress compounds the natural stress of life events.

There is some evidence that stress may result in health and psychological adjustment problems in children similar to those in adults (Johnson & McCutcheon, 1980). For example, a relationship between life stress and respiratory-tract illness has been found (Boyce et al., 1977). Also, life stress was found to be related to frequency of accidents in children (Padilla, Rohsenow, & Bergman, 1976), and correlated with day-to-day changes in the health status of chronically ill children. Signals of stress overload in children (Elkind, 1981; Forbes, 1979) are listed in Table 8.1. These can also be considered symptoms or stress effects.

STRESS AND SCHOOL-AGE DEVELOPMENT

Table 8.2 lists some of the common stresses for school-age children. Note how many stresses are related to school. Only in recent years has research begun to explore childhood stress related to schooling. Elkind (1981) suggests that today's schools reflect the current bias toward having children grow up too fast. Schools have become so product-oriented that they hurry children by emphasizing achievement and test scores.

It is not surprising that so many child stresses relate to success and failure in school and that these concerns continue into adolescence and even into adulthood. "Industry vs. Inferiority" is Erikson's (1963) designation for the developmental stage when children enter school and begin to acquire the "fundamentals of technology" that will enable them to become productive citizens. According to Erikson, the danger for children in this stage is that they will develop a sense of inadequacy and inferiority if they fail to master the necessary tools and skills.

TABLE 8.1. Signals/Symptoms of Too Much Stress in School-Age Children

---

Regressing to infantile behavior: bed wetting, nail biting, thumb sucking
Uncharacteristic withdrawal: not talking to anyone, appearing depressed
Loss of motivation or inability to concentrate at school
Noticeable behavior changes
Poor appetite and sleeplessness
Unexplained irritability
Physical complaints: headache, stomach ache
Trouble getting along with peers

TABLE 8.2.   Some Common School-Age Stressors

Anxiety about going to school
Bullies
Changing schools
Conflict with the teacher
Competitive culture
Dental appointments
Difficulty with classmates
Embarassment about parental alcoholism, illness, or unemployment
Excessive television, especially violent programs
Fads and dares (pressure to buy or act)
Failing an exam
Failing marks at school
Failing to make an athletic team
Giving oral reports or speeches in front of the class
Lack of parental interest in achievements
Learning disorders
Not being able to complete homework assignments
Older siblings setting bad family reputation
Older siblings setting school expectations too high
Parental pressure to achieve
Peer teasing about glasses, dental braces, obesity, etc.
Pressure to take sides in parental conflicts/divorce
Special recognition for outstanding performance (e.g., honor roll)
Worry about taking tests
Younger siblings

Sources: Elkind, 1981; Sears & Navin, 1983. .

Developmental Issues and School-Age Coping

About the age of 6 or 7, children enter the stage of concrete operational thinking (called the "age of reason" by medieval philosophers). In contrast to their previous animistic, egocentric, magical thinking, they are now capable of rudimentary logic. Skills, concepts, and ideas begin to "click" (Lewis, 1982). Earlier gains are consolidated. Children apply this new ability to the task of "tooling up" for their later roles as productive adolescents and adults. They need to develop basic competence in many ways, not only in the "3 R's," but also in work habits, cooperative relationships (teamwork and team spirit), sense of confidence, athletic competence, ability to delay gratification in working towards a goal, etc.

This developmental task is aided by certain coping styles and mental defense mechanisms typical of school age: reality testing, a more obsessional organization, reaction formation, and shame/disgust/guilt about infantile urges. These reinforce the child's impulse control and drive towards more mature socialization. This frees more energy for learning and exploring, guided by a new respect for rules. The latter is fostered by the burgeoning conscience and other superego functions, with the capacity for guilt.

Responses to stress in the early school age often involve either regression or else fighting against the stress-induced urge to regress, perhaps by pseudomature behavior. There may be regression to phobic defenses characteristic of preschoolers. Acting-out misbehavior is a common way of "coping." This sometimes involves identification with the aggressor. Bravado may be a reaction to fears, especially among boys. Choosing sides and finding allies are common stress responses in action-oriented school-age children. Sublimation, of course, is one of the more desirable coping responses.

School-Related Stress

Entry into the school world means a host of new challenges that the child must meet. These include separation from parents, moving out into wider geographical space, acceptance of new authority figures, and encountering a new series of unfamiliar demands. These demands involve attending to and responding to unfamiliar stimuli, subordinating individual wishes to a group, and learning to socialize with large numbers of peers against whom the child must now be measured. The child's ability to meet all these new demands depends on such factors as cultural and familial expectations and norms, including the parents' attitudes toward learning and toward school as an authority; expectations related to gender; the amount of support available from various sources; the amount of self-confidence and sense of mastery the child has developed up to that point; and underlying genetic endowment.

Many school-related stress symptoms involve anxiety and fear. Theoreticians and researchers have attempted to distinguish among anxiety, fear, and phobia. Fears in young children are often considered to be a common, even normal and functional aspect of development, as temporary reactions to specific events the child interprets as threatening. Fear is thought to involve at least three response systems: (a) overt, motoric expressions, for example, moves toward avoidance, like running away; (b) unpleasant subjective feelings and thoughts about what is happening; and (c) physiological activities, such as increased heart rate, rapid breathing, and other stress-related bodily responses. Anxiety, although much like fear in its manifestation, is generally thought to be more diffuse and less specific in terms of the eliciting stimuli and may lead to a prolonged state of tension and apprehension. Phobias are irrational fears, more persistent, maladaptive, and extreme, leading to greater degrees of incapacity and based on underlying anxiety which becomes attached to a phobic target. Because fears are so common with children, a distinction has been made between the mildly fearful responses of many children and those fears that could be considered "clinical" (Graziano, DeGiovanni, & Garcia, 1979). The latter are defined as those lasting over two years and having an intensity that is debilitating to the child's everyday life.

Stress, fears, and anxieties specifically related to academic achievement form a continuum from mildly to severely disabling and can show a variety of manifestations:

> Mary may be afraid of success. She is in the sixth grade and until this year she has done well, always bringing home excellent marks. Now, all of a sudden, she is cutting classes, her grades are falling, and she has lost interest in school. Her mother is a fashion-conscious cosmetologist.
>
> John could be suffering from test anxiety. Before and during a test he experiences shortness of breath, headaches, and a tendency to perspire heavily. He finds it difficult to concentrate, and he keeps wanting to escape the test situation. His parents, both professionals, have criticized him for not getting straight A's like his brother.
>
> Susan may have school phobia. She has not attended school for several weeks. For several months before that she frequently experienced nausea and vomiting at school, dating from a bout of gastroenteritis that kept her out of school for three days, during which she fell behind in her work. Now that she is staying home, those symptoms have disappeared, but she is falling farther behind in her work.
>
> Tom may be afraid of failure. He studies incessantly, verbalizes fear of "flunking" despite a B+ average, and argues with the teacher several times a week over his quiz scores and homework grades. His father sports a "Born to lose" tatoo.

The bulk of this chapter discusses these three sources of school-related stress and anxiety: fear of success and fear of failure, test anxiety, and school phobia and school fears. Strategies to treat these are suggested and described.

FEAR OF SUCCESS AND FEAR OF FAILURE

Fear of Success

In 1968, Horner introduced the concept of "fear of success" as a partial explanation for the sex differences in need achievement. Horner's "motive to avoid success" was defined as "the arousal of expectancy, in competitive situations, that success will lead to negative consequences for women" (Horner, 1968, p. 16). Horner postulated that women were threatened by success because it was equated with loss of feminity and may result in social rejection.

Horner incorporates the concept of fear of success into Atkinson's theory of achievement motivation (Atkinson & Litwin, 1960). Atkinson viewed motives as latent and stable personality characteristics thought to be acquired during childhood. Motives are aroused whenever individuals expect that performances will be evaluated against some standard of excellence. Persons with high motives for success have large capacities for feeling proud at doing well, while persons with high motives to avoid failure are likely to have strong feelings of shame over failure. Tendencies to avoid failure or approach success in particular achievement situations are a result of the interaction of these motives with situational variables. Motives, then, determine behavior insofar as they lead to approach or avoidance tendencies.

Research on Horner's original hypothesis has resulted in mixed findings. Kimball and Leahy (1976) administered Horner's fear of success test to 303 children between the fourth and twelfth grades. There was an increase of fear of success imagery between the fourth and tenth grades and a decrease between tenth and twelfth grades. The finding of an increase between the fourth and tenth grades suggests that achievement during this age period had increasingly negative implications for the child. Speculations on what contributed to this increase can be offered. Since this age group is interested in the approval of peers, one factor contributing to fear of success in an academic setting may be that success often involves competition with peers and, consequently, conflicts with affiliative motives. A second interpretation could be that increases in the fear of success imagery are due to increasing verbal fluency in students. However, since a decrease between tenth and twelfth grades occurred, this explanation does not seem sufficient.

According to the Kimball and Leahy study, significant sex differences in fear of success did not appear until adolescence and were associated with the appropriateness of academic training to students' stereotyped sex roles. For example, the highest-ability girls pursuing the college preparatory program showed the highest fear of success, while the girls pursuing secretarial training showed the lowest fear of success. Both college preparatory boys and the secretarial course girls showed a decrease in fear of success in high school, suggesting that when a boy or girl is pursuing a "sex-appropriate" course of study, there is less ambivalence about the achievement of excellence.

David Tresemer (1976), however, reviewed over 100 studies assessing fear of success and concluded that while fear of success among females may exist, research has not proven its existence. In a reanalysis of

Horner's data, Tresemer suggested that the fear of success effect was strongly mediated by individuals' needs for achievement. In other words, negative thoughts can get in people's way if they are not motivated to try very hard in the first place. More effectively designed research is needed in this area.

Fear of Failure

The tendency to avoid the task in achievement situations is referred to as the "fear of failure." Feather (1969) has suggested that failure is especially distressing to males. Levine et al. (1976) found that males were more likely to attribute their successes to skill and their failures to luck, while females attributed both their successes and failures to skill. The authors suggested that males showed a self-defensive bias in their attributions and interpreted this self-defensive bias as indicating a greater fear of failure.

Examining fear of failure in children, researchers (Dweck, 1976; Dweck & Repucci, 1973) have hypothesized that children's reactions to failure are related to the way in which they interpret failure—whether they attribute it to factors within their control or beyond their control. Do children attribute the causes of their failures to internal factors, such as ability and effort, or to external factors, such as luck or difficulty of the task? Stated otherwise, do they attribute failure to factors within their control or beyond their control?

As a result of his studies, Heckhausen (1975) has suggested that in reaction to failure, fear-of-failure persons have a bias for "lack-of-ability" explanations, while "hope-for-success" persons have a bias for "lack-of-effort" explanations. The "lack-of-ability" causal attribution or explanation leads to more negative affect in self-reinforcement than "lack-of-effort" explanations.

The above reaction by fear-of-failure persons has implications for achievement behavior. If "lack of ability" is perceived as the main cause for failing at a new task, then with further failing the subjective probability of success diminishes rapidly, persistence is low, and emotional consequences are negative as compared with failure ascribed to momentary lack of effort. In giving up early, fear-of-failure persons restrict their opportunities to come up with success in the long run—a self-fulfilling fear. Figure 8.1 summarizes Heckhausen's conceptualization of the differences between fear-of-failure and hope-for-success persons.

Interventions for Fear of Failure or Success

Heckhausen (1975) viewed the fear-of-failure motive as a self-reinforcing motive system. Seen this way, a motive perpetuates a bias in outlook and action. It provides the individuals with the opportunity to condition

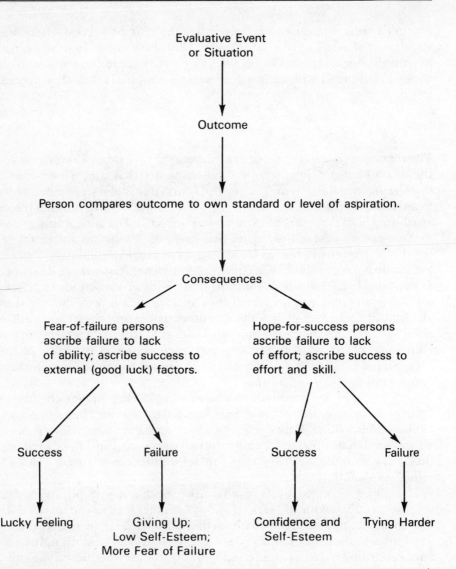

Figure 8.1. Differences in psychological impact of failure according to child's characteristic cognitive attributions.

their own self-reinforcements. The question arises: What can be done to alter this self-reinforcing system or intervene to reduce the fear-of-failure motive?

Cognitive approaches to treating fear of failure assume that fear and anxiety result from a person's interpretations of situations. Therefore, changing the individual's interpretation is critical. For example, replacing the one causal attribution explanation of "lack of ability" with one such as "you could do better with a little more effort" has been shown to have some degree of success in increasing the persistence of school-age children (Heckhausen, 1975). In each of twelve fourth-grade classrooms, three to eight underachieving, fear-of-failure students with typically biased causal attribution patterns were selected. Teachers in these classrooms were instructed in causal attribution theory and encouraged to try to increase their students' motivation by comments such as "you could do better if you would expend still more effort." A four-and-a-half-month treatment period revealed improved motivation compared with subjects in control classrooms. Failure was ascribed more to lack of effort than lack of ability. Level of aspiration was lowered less frequently in the face of failure. Anxiety also decreased.

Another cognitive approach, rational-emotive therapy, could be useful in the treatment of both fear of success and fear of failure. The main premise of this approach is that maladaptive behaviors result from irrational belief systems that influence what we say to ourselves. For example, the young girl who is an outstanding math student but tells herself that math is a masculine subject and she won't be accepted as feminine if she excels in that area is likely to exhibit maladaptive behavior by not trying to do as well as she can. The objective of rational emotive therapy is to help the individual identify and analyze irrational belief systems and substitute rational ones that are more likely to lead to adaptive behavior. The principles of rational-emotive therapy have been adapted by Knaus (1974) into an instructional program for children called Rational-Emotive Education (REE). Designed to be used by the classroom teacher, it involves five major learning areas:

1. *Feelings:* helping children become aware of feelings, their origins and various modes of expression.
2. *Challenging Irrational Beliefs:* helping children to recognize irrational belief systems and their effects and to develop cognitive styles that enable them to challenge these irrational thought patterns on their own.
3. *Challenging Feelings of Inferiority:* helping children recognize the complex nature of individuals, helping them understand that each person has positives as well as negatives, and that children should not view themselves or others in terms of a single attribute, whether good or bad.
4. *Learning, Mistake-making, and Imperfection:* helping children to understand the nature of the learning process, differences of opinion, and mistakes, in order to develop a more realistic approach toward learning and to avoid the pitfalls of perfectionism.

5. *Demanding, Catastrophizing, and Challenging:* teaching children to challenge irrational "must" and "should" systems which lead to "catastrophizing" and "awfulizing" and to replace them with more reasonable attitudes of "desire" and "prefer." Children will learn to think in terms of the things they would like to have happen rather than the things they demand should happen.

TEST ANXIETY

Test anxiety is a special case of general anxiety. Test anxiety refers to those phenomenological, physiological, and behavioral responses that accompany concern about failure. The stimuli, experiences, and responses of test anxiety seem to be as varied as those of general anxiety (Sieber, 1980).

Test anxiety is usually defined as a set of responses to a class of stimuli that have been associated with the individual's experience of evaluation or testing. Several researchers have attempted to describe the nature of and components of this process. In the 1950s, Mandler and Sarason (1952) suggested that the testing situation evokes both learned task drives and learned anxiety drives. Some of the anxiety drives are task-relevant, while others are task-irrelevant. The learned task drives and the task-relevant anxiety drives facilitate test performance, while the task-irrelevant anxiety drives decrease task performance.

Liebert and Morris (1967) hypothesized that test anxiety consisted of two conceptually different components: worry and emotionality. Worry refers to focusing of attention on concerns about performance, consequences of failure, negative self-evaluation, evaluation of one's ability relative to others, and the like. Emotionality, on the other hand, refers to the affective-physiological experience generated from increased autonomic arousal. Morris and Liebert (1970) reported evidence that worry was associated with performance decrements on cognitive and intellectual tasks, while emotionality was unrelated to task performance.

In a review of test anxiety literature, Wine (1971) hypothesized an attentional interpretation of the negative effects of test anxiety on performance. She contends that during tests or examinations, high test-anxious individuals divide their attention between task requirements and task-irrelevant cognitive activities such as worry. These worry cognitions distract individuals from task requirements and appear to interfere with effective use of their time, thereby contributing to performance decrements. Wine believes the highly test-anxious persons respond to evaluative testing conditions with worry and thus do not direct adequate attention to task-relevant variables.

After examining the various approaches, these commonalities regarding test anxiety emerge:

1. Test anxiety reflects individual differences in anxiety proneness in the exam situation.
2. Test-anxious people are more likely to perceive examination situations as more dangerous or threatening than do low-anxious persons.
3. Test-anxious persons experience worry cognitions and intense elevations in state anxiety in situations in which they are evaluated.

Further, Wine (1975) suggested that fear of negative evaluation appears to be a key ingredient of test anxiety, and test-anxious children are highly motivated to avoid disapproval. This fear of negative evaluation is accompanied by a general narrowing of the range of cue utilization in test-like situations; such students become more alert to evaluative cues, less alert to or aware of task cues, and more concerned about self-worth. In essence, the test-anxious person worries during tests.

Although the number of youngsters experiencing debilitating test anxiety is really not known (Johnson, 1979), Phillips et al. (1980) maintain that relatively large numbers, especially of minority children, are test-anxious. Hill (1972) suggests that children report increased levels of test anxiety across the elementary school years. Eysenck and Rachman (1965) believe that at least 20% of schoolchildren are negatively affected by test anxiety.

Etiology and Effects of Test Anxiety

Researchers generally agree that test anxiety results from children's reaction to evaluative experiences during preschool and early years. Sarason et al. (1960) view test anxiety as a personality characteristic that develops during the child's interactions with the parents during the preschool years and slowly stabilizes during the elementary years. High levels of evaluation anxiety result when children's performances and achievements do not live up to parents' expectations. Generally, the parents' expectations are unreasonably high. As a result, the parents' judgments of the children's performances are frequently negative. As the children internalize these negative parental feelings, hostile views of the rejecting parents develop. These hostile feelings create guilt in the children, and they begin to suppress the negative feelings toward their parents. Then the children fantasize about parental retaliation for the children's hostile feelings. This threat leads to the children engaging in behavior directed at satisfying their parents' wishes. The high test-anxious children may develop too much dependence upon adult direction and support in evaluative situations. Some children may attempt to avoid evaluative situations altogether unless adults are present.

Hermans, terLaak, and Maes (1972) have also examined parent-child relations pertaining to the development of test anxiety. In problem-solving situations, parents of high test-anxious children tend to be some-what negative toward their children. They ignore their children's bids for security, do not offer constructive help in problem solving, and may teach their children to engage in task-irrelevant and even taskinappropriate behaviors in problem solving or evaluative situations. Thus, the children come to rely on external supports from their parents or other adults to deal with evaluation and problem solving and to avoid criticism. Parents of low test-anxious children, on the other hand, offer effective problem-solving techniques and strategies without taking over the entire problem-solving situation. In short, they are teaching their children to rely on their own resources and to respond with task-oriented responses.

Test anxiety results in ineffective cognitive strategies and attentional deficits, causing poor task performance in evaluative situations. Low test-anxious children appear to become deeply involved in evaluative tasks, but high test-anxious children do not. High test-anxious children experience attentional blocks, extreme concern with emotional self-cues, and cognitive deficits such as misinterpretation of information. These attentional and cognitive deficits are likely to interfere with learning and responding in evaluative situations, and hence result in lowered per-formance.

The preceding comments suggest the importance of cognitive factors as mediating influences in the effects of test anxiety on both children's learning and their performance. Cognitive factors influence the percep-tion of a situation as evaluative or not. These cognitive factors are atten-tional in nature, e.g., the high test-anxious person's attention to self-stimuli rather than task stimuli. In fact, the test-anxious person di-vides attention between two kinds of self stimuli (worry and arousal) in addition to task stimuli. Morris and Liebert (1970) have examined this division of attention. Worry is seen as cognitive concern over per-formance in a task and emotionality is seen as an autonomic arousal. The adverse effects of test anxiety are presumably due to a division of atten-tion between concern over task performance on the one hand, and the physiological aspects of arousal on the other hand. The high test-anxious person attends more to the autonomic aspects of arousal and less to the task than does the low test-anxious person. This division of attention results in lowered performance by high test-anxious persons.

Assessment of Test Anxiety

Several questionnaires have been developed to measure test anxiety. This discussion describes only the Test Anxiety Scale for Children and two instruments used to measure the worry-emotionality components of test anxiety.

The Test Anxiety Scale for Children (TASC) is the most widely used scale to assess children's test anxiety. The TASC is a group-administered paper-and-pencil test consisting of 30 items to which the child responds "yes" or "no" by circling the appropriate response on an answer sheet as the questions are read by an examiner. Twelve of the items mention the word "test" specifically. Others ask about "worry" over classroom performance. The anxiety score is the number of "yes" responses (Spielberger et al., 1978).

Two separate self-report scales have been developed to measure the worry and emotionality aspects of test anxiety (Spielberger et al., 1978). One is the 10-item Worry-Emotionality Inventory. The other is the 16-item Inventory of Test Anxiety. Examining test items gives the reader a flavor of the tests:

Worry items include: (1) not feeling confident about performance; (2) worrying a great deal; (3) thinking how much brighter others are; (4) thinking about the consequences of failure; and (5) not feeling as prepared as possible.

Emotionality items include: (1) so nervous can't remember facts; (2) heart beating fast; (3) upset stomach; (4) uneasy, upset feeling; (5) feeling panicky. Examples: hands or arms shaking during exams and freezing up on exams.

Teachers and Test Anxiety

The role the teacher plays in influencing children's anxiety in the school setting in general, and in evaluative situations in particular, has been examined. Sarason et al. (1960) have hypothesized that test-anxious children's reactions to the test situation are at least partially a reflection of experiences at home. He further suggests that students may transfer unconscious feelings about evaluative situations from their parents to their teachers. Therefore, teacher-student relations may be an important factor in test anxiety. McKeachie et al. (1955) found that children's anxiety levels were a function of the way they perceived their teachers. If, for instance, the teacher was perceived as punitive and authoritarian, the student's performance deteriorated. On the other hand, if the teacher was perceived as nonpunitive, nonauthoritarian, and willing to help, the student's anxiety level was reduced. Sarason et al. (1960) maintained that teachers' instructional approaches or teaching techniques are an important variable in the performance of anxious children. He recommended that teachers use well-structured, clearly defined, and appropriately reinforced teaching techniques. Doyal and Forsyth (1973) examined teacher-student interaction in terms of teacher influence on students' test anxiety from a rather unique perspective. The researchers found that the teachers' own anxieties may influence their students' test anxiety as evidenced by a weak but positive correlation between teachers' Manifest Anxiety Scale scores and students' Test Anxiety Scale scores.

Interventions for Test Anxiety

Tryon (1980) reviewed the procedures used in the treatment of test anxiety. They are:

1. *Systematic Desensitization.* This is the most widely used behavioral technique for the treatment of anxiety. There is a general finding that systematic desensitization, and even relaxation alone, are effective in reducing self-reported test anxiety but are not as effective in improving grades. This would suggest that these treatments are helping the emotionality component of test anxiety rather than the worry component.

2. *Self-controlled Relaxation and Desensitization.* In this approach, individuals are taught to relax at the time when they would otherwise be anxious. In cue-controlled relaxation, students first relax and then pair a cue word such as "calm" with the exhalation of each breath. With repeated pairings, the cue word is predicted to elicit relaxation. Other self-control procedures are autogenic training and anxiety management training. All of these treatments have been found to be effective in the reduction of self-reported anxiety. Significant increases in grades have also been reported at post-treatment assessment.

3. *Cognitive Procedures.* Cognitive procedures are used to help the individual learn to focus on the task at hand rather than attend to interfering self-oriented responses. Wine (1971, 1980) has suggested using attention-focusing procedures to deal with the "worry" aspect of test anxiety. For example, using cognitive modification approaches, anxiety is explained to subjects as resulting from the thoughts and self-statements occurring before and during exams. Once aware of these statements, students are taught to focus their attention on replacing their self-defeating thoughts and self-statements with positive, task-oriented alternatives. Cognitive procedures result in significant reductions in self-reported test anxiety, accompanied by increased grades (Holroyd, 1976).

4. *Observational Learning.* Modeling and vicarious desensitization have been used to treat test anxiety. Observing others handling test situations in relaxed ways and observing others undergoing desensitization has resulted in reduction of self-reported test anxiety. In 75% of the studies reviewed, grades improved.

5. *Multicomponent Approach.* Meichenbaum and Butler (1980) suggested a variety of factors that influence task performance, including the larger meaning the individuals place on evaluation, their study skills, and their test-taking behaviors. Therefore, a multicomponent approach which influences the individuals' belief systems, self-talk, study-skills, and test-taking behavior would be more effective than any single approach.

SCHOOL PHOBIA AND OTHER SCHOOL FEARS

School phobia is an exaggerated fear associated with attending school. It may vary from mild anxiety to extreme panic, and is characterized by agitation, physical symptoms, and physical resistance to the school situation. It is usually clinically diagnosed as separation anxiety disorder (APA, 1987). Berg, Nichols, and Prichard (1969) have proposed the following operational description of school phobia:

1. severe difficulty in attending school, often amounting to prolonged absence;
2. severe emotional upset, shown by such symptoms as excessive fearfulness, undue tempers, misery, or complaints of feeling ill without obvious organic cause, when faced with the prospect of going to school;
3. staying home from school with the knowledge of the parents;
4. absence of significant antisocial disorders such as stealing, lying, wandering, destructiveness, and sexual misbehavior. (p. 123)

Not all of the fears and anxieties related to school can be labeled school phobia. School-related fears are common. For example, see Chapter 11 by Christie and Toomey for a discussion of fears of violence at school. Croake and Knox (1971) report that over 10% of the 212 ninth-graders in their study identified fears related to school. A relatively small percentage of these, however, would be likely to be considered school phobic. Miller, Barrett, and Hampe (1974), for example, estimated that 1% of the school-age population are school phobic. A frequently quoted figure is that of Kennedy (1965), who reports that 17 out of 1,000 children (one out of every 59) experience school phobia. Although findings in specific studies differ, in general, it appears that boys and girls are represented fairly equally among school-phobic children (Johnson, 1979). It is now thought that the previous statistics related to higher incidence in girls reflect a greater willingness on the part of girls to admit to their fears. School phobia is found both in young children and in adolescents, but

Johnson reports a peak around 11 years of age. It was thought at one time that these children were of above-average intelligence, but it appears now that school-phobic children are more likely to be of average intelligence but achieving to potential (Trueman, 1984). There is some agreement, however, that such children are frequently described as more immature, as more dependent, and as more depressed than their peers. Factoranalytic studies have identified a cluster of symptoms that describe the over-fearful child whose characteristic pattern of response is avoidance. These symptoms include anxiety, self-consciousness, social withdrawal, crying, worrying, hypersensitivity, and seclusiveness (Johnson & Melamed, 1983). It is not clear, however, whether this correlates with school phobia.

Etiology of School Phobia/Fears

Two principal viewpoints have contributed to etiological thinking in this area: the psychoanalytic or psychodynamic view and the behavioral position. Psychoanalytic theory considers school phobia to have specific precipitating events not directly related to school, such as death in the family or illness. Fear of leaving and losing the parent are considered to be displaced onto the school and persons in the school. Psychodynamic theory suggests that the parents have projected their own needs on the child and thus have imbued the child with unrealistic self-expectations. When the child is confronted at school with realistic limitations, the child is anxious and wants to avoid school.

Behavioral theory stresses aversive events related to school. These could include fear of another child at school, of a particular teacher, of failure when called on to recite, or of the school as a physical building. It could involve fear of getting on the bus or passing a specific corner on the way to school. Whatever the unpleasant event or stimulus, it creates anxiety and, therefore, avoidance of school. Remaining home provides reinforcement through the elimination of the anxiety. The longer the child stays home, however, the greater the anxiety associated with school and the more difficult the return. Thus, stresses and realistic fears proceed to phobia.

Most clinically oriented writers consider parental attitudes and behavior to be key factors in the origin of school-related fears. Fear of failure can be generated by too-high and perfectionistic parental expectations, by the fear of loss of parental approval, and in some cases by anticipation of punishment. Children may blame themselves for not meeting parental expectations and fear being exposed as worthless. This may lead them to avoid the learning situation and thus avoid evaluation (Schaefer & Millman, 1981). According to Gardner (1974), school-phobic children may have parents who are themselves phobic, suggesting a role of the parents as models for the child's behavior as well as a possible genetic vulnerability.

In addition to the parents' role in the origins of school-related fears, they may play a part in the maintenance of the child's avoidance behavior. For example, overprotective and overindulgent parents may reinforce the child's avoidance behavior by allowing the child to stay home. Gardner (1974) suggests that school-phobic children with separation anxiety may be complying with mother's unconscious desire that the child not go to school, reflecting the mother's resistance to the child's growing independence.

Assessment and Treatment of School Phobia and School Fears

Whether or not a child's fears/anxieties warrant some kind of therapeutic intervention depends, according to Morris and Kratochwill (1983), on whether the fear is found to (1) be excessive, (2) last over a relatively long period of time, and (3) create problems in living for the parent(s) and/or child. Since the predominant response of the child to fears related to school is avoidance of stimuli related to school, e.g., tests, assignments, etc., it is clear that problems of school avoidance can rapidly become compounded by the child's falling behind academically. Thus, school refusal can become a source of stress as well as a cause.

The most commonly used interventions are individual and family therapy; behavior modification programs in the home and school; systematic desensitization, usually combined with relaxation; and cognitive approaches. Regardless of orientation, most clinicians agree that the first step is returning the child to school, even though the child's return to school may be traumatic for the parents and child.

Gardner (1974) suggests a matter-of-fact approach, expecting the child to go to school, exhibiting surprise if he or she refuses. He suggests at least taking the child to the school building every day, even twice a day if necessary. The return to school needs to be accompanied by other interventions to eliminate the factors contributing to school avoidance and to support the child's remaining in school. There is also agreement that when academic deficiencies or poor study habits exist, these must be remediated as part of the treatment.

A variety of treatment approaches using behavior modification have been employed successfully in the treatment of school phobia (Trueman, 1984). The assumption in this approach is that school phobia is evoked by cues in the environment and is maintained by reinforcement from conditions or persons in the environment. Among the tools employed are token systems and contingency contracts administered by school personnel or parents, plus the elimination of reinforcers that may be contributing to making staying home more gratifying than going to school, for example, eliminating opportunities to be alone with the parent under reinforcing conditions. Similarly, the help of school personnel and possibly peers is necessary in order to increase the reward potential of the school environment and eliminate negative associations the child may have with school. In one case example, a principal coordinated a contingency program wherein a school-phobic boy could earn points to be traded for tickets to a football game.

Several studies have employed a behavioral "shaping" process to return the child to school by progressively longer periods of time in school and successive approximations of classroom attendance. In some cases, a child was first encouraged to go only as far as the playground, then the halls, or the office, ultimately moving back to the classroom. In other cases, a gradual separation of the child from the mother was shaped by bringing the mother into the school environment and then gradually phasing her out.

Systematic desensitization assumes that school phobia is a conditioned anxiety response occurring as a result of aversive events associated with the school situation. In one case, a 9-year-old boy was treated by first walking to school on a Sunday with a therapist whom he liked, then the following day walking from the house to the schoolyard talking about pleasant things, and on subsequent days going to an empty classroom, then entering the classroom with the therapist for a chat with the teacher, and after a week spending the morning in the classroom with the therapist waiting outside. School attendance was reinforced by praise and attention from school personnel, replacing the parent attention the child had received earlier for staying home (Lazarus, Davison, & Polefka, 1965).

Psychoanalytic or other psychodynamic principles assume that the child's school phobia is less related to the school environment than to conflicts within the family or to a neurotic relationship between the mother and the child. Treatment therefore is focused on family dynamics. Schaefer, Briesmeister, and Fitton (1984) summarize a number of case studies successfully using family therapy to treat school phobia. They recommend redirecting attention to family relationships and emotions (away from the child's symptoms), promoting communication, enhancing the marital relationship and familial mutual respect, and orchestrating the child's return to school. One variation in family therapy is a multi-family therapy approach in which families can provide mutual support to each other. Trueman (1984) reports there are no studies in the literature comparing behavioral and psychodynamic treatment of school phobia.

Regardless of approach used in the treatment of school phobia, both interprofessional cooperation and cooperation between professionals and the family are essential. Professionals can include physicians who may be evaluating the somatic complaints or providing psychiatric treat-ment, school psychologists, counselors, social workers, in some situations law enforcement agents, and a variety of school personnel. Children suffering from acute fears and anxieties may at times attempt to maintain their anxiety-reducing avoidance behaviors by engaging in manipulation of the adults involved. Agreement between professionals and parents on the strategies to be used and support for each other's efforts will help to ensure successful treatment.

PREVENTION AND MANAGEMENT OF SCHOOL STRESS: THE PARENTS' ROLE

Garmezy (1984), writing about the factors that protect children from destructive effects of various stressors, has identified three categories of protective variables:

1. personality dispositions of the child;
2. a supportive family milieu; and
3. an external support system that encourages and reinforces a child's coping efforts and strengthens them by inculcating positive values.

Some of these factors may be brought to bear in the prevention of school-related stress. Certainly one key lies in parenting, parent-child relationships, and the mental health of the family. Prevention has to begin with self-awareness on the part of the parents about what kinds of messages and cues they are giving the child about school and academic achievement. What kinds of expectations are they setting out, and how realistic are those expectations for their child? If expectations are too high, the child may give up. If they are too low, the child will respond accordingly. How interested are the parents in what the child accomplishes at school? Do they only reward spectacular success and take everything else for granted, or do they give approval for the child's efforts whatever the outcome? Is there too-frequent criticism, which may cause resentment and a desire to retaliate, possibly through lack of achievement?

Parents need also to be aware of the atmosphere that exists in the home. Frequent conflicts, tensions, and situations that threaten the child's security may precipitate a depressed child who cannot concen-trate and has little motivation. Parents need to assess their own fear level to make sure they are not creating an overprotective situation or model-ing fearfulness for the child. Parents should make sure they can be positive about the school, the teacher, and the learning requirements. If this is not possible, they need to try to work out an alternative school situation for the child that they can support. School for the child is a critical aspect of the "external support system" referred to by Garmezy as necessary for building resilience and coping skills.

Schaefer and Millman (1981) propose the following principles for parents:

1. Be accepting and encouraging.
2. Set realistic goals and expectations.
3. Teach and model active learning and problem solving.
4. Reward interest in learning and academic achievement.

Another approach to prevention focuses on the teaching of coping skills that will enable the child to handle anxiety in a constructive manner. A person can identify the indicators of anxiety and use these as cues to relax, at the same time eliminating self-statements that contribute to anxiety. There are reports of successful applications of coping skills training for the prevention of excessive fears in children undergoing medical or dental procedures (Kirschenbaum & Ordman, 1984). Although there is little research on such skills training for the prevention of school-related anxiety, the application of modeling and cognitive strategies seems promising as a means of helping children cope successfully with some of the stressful aspects of attending school.

SUMMARY

Most common school-age stresses relate in some way to school. Three relevant stress clusters are fear of success or failure, test anxiety, and fears associated with the school setting, which can include school phobia as the most extreme form. Fear of success—the expectation that, in competitive situations, success will lead to negative consequences for females—is an extensively researched hypothesis with mixed findings. While several studies suggest that fear of success appears during adolescence and is associated with the appropriateness of academic training to female/male stereotyped sex roles, other studies decry the lack of attention in the research to the mediating effects of individuals' needs for achievement. Fear of failure—the tendency to avoid the task in achievement situations—results in children restricting their opportunities for success. Since both fear of failure and fear of success appear to result from individuals' interpretations of academic situations, cognitive treatment approaches hold the most promise.

Test anxiety—a set of responses to stimuli that have been associated with one's experience of evaluation or testing—consists of two components: worry and emotionality. High levels of evaluation anxiety result when children's performances do not live up to parents' expectations. Systematic desensitization, relaxation, cognitive procedures, and observational learning have been used, with varying degrees of success, in the treatment of test anxiety. However, a multicomponent treatment which influences individuals' belief systems, self-talk, study skills, and test-taking behavior holds more promise than any single approach.

School phobia—an exaggerated fear related to attending school—can be severely incapacitating through prolonged absence from school and consequent academic losses. Attitudes and behavior of parents are important factors in the onset and maintenance of school-avoidance behavior. Treatment approaches stress returning the child to school as soon as possible, along with a variety of supportive interventions which may include family-oriented psychotherapy and/or behavioral approaches.

Because treatment of school-age stress may involve not only the family but a variety of professionals of different disciplines, interprofessional cooperation is essential for positive outcomes. Prevention of school-related stress and anxiety lies in the development of positive and realistic parental attitudes toward the child's abilities and achievement. Along with parental support and encouragement, a variety of coping strategies may be developed which can enable the child to master the challenges and demands of the school experience.

REFERENCES

American Psychiatric Association (APA). (1987). *Diagnostic and statistical manual of mental disorders (DSM III-R) Third Edition, Revised. Washington, DC: Author.*

Atkinson, J. W., & Litwin, G. H. (1960). Achievement motive and test anxiety conceived as motive to approach success and motive to avoid failure. *Journal of Counseling Psychology, 60,* 52–63.

Berg, I., Nichols, K., & Prichard, C. (1969). School phobia: Its classification and relationship to dependency. *Journal of Child Psychology and Psychiatry, 10,* 123–141.

Boyce, T. W., Jensen, E. W., Cassell, J. C., Collier, A. M., Smith, A. H., & Raimey, C. T. (1977). Influence of life events and family routines on childhood respiratory tract illness. *Pediatrics, 60,* 609–615.

Croake, J. W., & Knox, F. H. (1971). A second look at adolescent fears. *Adolescence, 6,* 279–284.

Dweck, C. S. (1976). Children's interpretation of evaluative feedback: The effect of social cues on learned helplessness. *Merrill-Palmer Quarterly, 22,* 105–109.

Dweck, C. S., & Repucci, N. D. (1973). Learned helplessness and reinforcement responsibility in children. *Journal of Personality and Social Psychology, 25*, 109–116.

Elkind, D. (1981). *The hurried child: Growing up too fast too soon.* Reading, MA: Addison-Wesley.

Erikson, E. H. (1963). *Childhood and society.* New York: W. W. Norton.

Eysenck, H. J., & Rachman, S. (1965). *The causes and cures of neurosis.* San Diego: Knapp.

Feather, N. T. (1969). Attribution of responsibility and valence of success and failure in relation to initial confidence and task performance. *Journal of Personality and Social Psychology, 13,* 129–144.

Forbes, R. (1979). *Life stress.* Garden City, NY: Doubleday.

Gardner, R. A. (1974). *Understanding children.* New York: Jason Aronson.

Garmezy, N. (1984). Stress-resistant children: The search for protective factors. In J. E. Stevenson (Ed.), Recent research in developmental psychopathology. *Journal of Child Psychology and Psychiatry Book Supplement No. 4.* Oxford: Pergamon Press.

Graziano, A. M., DeGiovanni, I. S., & Garcia, K. A. (1979). Behavioral treatment of children's fears: A review. *Psychological Bulletin, 86,* 804–830.

Heckhausen, H. (1975). Fear of failure as a self-reinforcing motive system. In I. G. Sarason & C. D. Speilberger (Eds.), *Stress and anxiety.* New York: Wiley.

Hermans, H., terLaak, J., & Maes, P. (1972). Achievement motivation and fear of failure in family and school. *Developmental Psychology, 6,* 520–528.

Hill, K. T. (1972). Anxiety in the evaluative context. In W. W. Hartup (Ed.), *The young child* (Vol. 2). Washington, DC: National Association for the Education of Young Children.

Holroyd, K. A. (1976). Cognition and desensitization in group treatment of test anxiety. *Journal of Consulting and Clinical Psychology, 44,* 991–1001.

Horner, M. (1968). *Sex differences in achievement motivation and performance in competitive and noncompetitive situations.* Unpublished doctoral dissertation, University of Michigan.

Johnson, J. H., & McCutcheon, S. (1980). Assessing life stress in older children and adolescents: Preliminary findings with the life events checklist. In I. G. Sarason & C. D. Spielberger (Eds.), *Stress and anxiety.* New York: Hemisphere.

Johnson, S. B. (1979). Children's fears in the classroom setting. *School Psychology Digest, 8,* 382–396.

Johnson, S. B., & Melamed, B. G. (1983). The assessment and treatment of children's fears. In B. B. Lahey & A. E. Kazdin (Eds.), *Advances in clinical child psychology.* New York: Plenum Press.

Kennedy, W. (1965). School phobia: Rapid treatment of fifty cases. *Journal of Abnormal Psychology, 70,* 285–289.

Kimball, B., & Leahy, R. L. (1976). Fear of success in males and females: Effects of developmental level and sex-linked course of study. *Sex Roles, 2,* 273–281.

Kirschenbaum, D. S., & Ordman, A. M. (1984). Preventive interventions for children: Cognitive behavior perspectives. In A. W. Meyers & W. E. Craighead (Eds.), *Cognitive behavior therapy with children.* New York: Plenum Press.

Knaus, W. J. (1974). *Rational emotive education.* New York: Institute for Rational Living.

Lazarus, A. A., Davison, G. C., & Polefka, D. A. (1965). Classical and operant factors in the treatment of a school phobia. *Journal of Abnormal Psychology, 70,* 225–229.

Levine, R., Reis, H. T., Sue, E., & Turner, E. S., & Turner, G. (1976). Fear of failure in males: A more salient factor than fear of success in females? *Sex Roles, 2,* 389–398.

Lewis, M. (1982). *Clinical aspects of child development.* Philadelphia: Lea & Febiger.

Liebert, R. M., & Morris, L. W. (1967). Cognitive and emotional components of test anxiety: A distinction and some initial data. *Psychological Reports, 20,* 975–978.

Mandler, G., & Sarason, S. B. (1952). A study of anxiety and learning. *Journal of Abnormal and Social Psychology, 47,* 166–173.

Meichenbaum, D., & Butler, L. (1980). Toward a conceptual model for the treatment of test anxiety: Implications for research and treatment. In I. G. Sarason (Ed.), *Test anxiety: Theory, research, and application.* Hillsdale, NJ: Erlbaum.

Miller, L. C., Barrett, C. L., & Hampe, E. (1974). Phobias of childhood in a prescientific era. In A. Davids (Ed.), *Child personality and psychopathology: Current topics.* New York: Wiley.

Morris, L. W., & Liebert, R. M. (1970). The relationship of cognitive and emotional components of test anxiety to physiological arousal and academic performance. *Journal of Consulting and Clinical Psychology, 35,* 332–337.

Morris, R. J., & Kratochwill, T. R. (1983). *Treating children's fears and phobias.* New York: Pergamon Press.

Padilla, E. R., Rohsenow, D. J., & Bergman, A. B. (1976). Predicting accident frequency in children. *Pediatrics, 58,* 223–226.

Phillips, B. N., Pitcher, G. D., Worsham, M. E., & Miller, S. C. (1980). Test anxiety and the school environment. In I. G. Sarason (Ed.), *Test anxiety: Theory, research, and applications.* Hillsdale, NJ: Erlbaum.

Sarason, S. B. (1966). The measurement of anxiety in children: Some questions and problems. In C. D. Spielberger (Ed.), *Anxiety and behavior.* New York: Academic Press.

Sarason, S. B., Davidson, K. S., Lightfall, F. F., Waite, R. R., & Ruebush, B. K. (1960). *Anxiety in elementary school children.* New York: Wiley.

Schaefer, C. E., Briesmeister, J. M., & Fitton, M. E. (1984). *Family therapy techniques for problem behaviors of children and teenagers.* San Francisco: Jossey-Bass.

Schaefer, C. E., & Millman, H. L. (1981). *How to help children with common problems.* New York: Van Nostrand Reinhold.

Sears, S. J., & Navin, S. L. (1983). Stressors in school counseling. *Education, 103,* 333–337.

Sieber, J. E. (1980). Defining test anxiety: Problems and approaches. In I. G.

Sarason (Ed.), *Test anxiety: Theory, research, and applications*. Hillsdale, NJ: Lawrence Erlbaum.

Spielberger, C. D., Gonzalez, H. P., Taylor, C. J., Algaze, B., & Anton, W. D. (1978). Examination stress and test anxiety. In C. D. Speilberger & I. G. Sarason (Eds.), *Stress and anxiety*. Washington, DC: Hemisphere.

Tresemer, D. (1976). The cumulative record of research on "fear of success." *Sex Roles, 2*, 217–235.

Trueman, D. (1984). The behavioral treatment of school phobia: A critical review. *Psychology in the Schools, 21*, 215–223.

Tryon, G. S. (1980). The measurement and treatment of test anxiety. *Review of Educational Research, 50*, 343–372.

Wine, J. D. (1971). Test anxiety and direction of attention. *Psychological Bulletin, 76*, 92–104.

Wine, J. D. (1975). Test anxiety and helping behaviour. *Canadian Journal of Behavioral Science, 3*, 216–222.

Wine, J. D. (1980). Cognitive attentional theory of test anxiety. In I. G. Sarason (Ed.), *Test anxiety: Theory, research, and application*. Hillsdale, NJ: Lawrence Erlbaum.

CHAPTER NINE

Stress in Adolescence

Robert L. Hendren

Adolescence is a time of special stress. A number of physical, psychological, and sociological influences are brought to bear on the individual at this stage of development (see Table 9.1). Pubertal growth produces profound anatomic and physiologic changes in the adolescent's body. Psychologically, the adolescent is faced with new challenges. Together with the difficult transition from the dependency of childhood to the independence and autonomy of adulthood, the adolescent is faced with the challenge of learning to use newly developed cognitive abilities. In this process, adolescents develop new relationships with their families and the culture that surrounds them.

Adolescents negotiate these stresses with varying degrees of mastery. Most do well. Others, who have not developed successful coping skills, may suffer stress related disorders. The expression of these disorders is often related to the societal pressures placed on the adolescent. Depression, eating disorders, and substance abuse are current expressions of stress in developed countries. This chapter describes the stresses of normal adolescent development and factors that are associated with both successful and maladaptive behavior elicited by those stresses.

BIOLOGICAL CHANGES IN ADOLESCENCE: HORMONE EFFECTS

Puberty is a process, not an event. It involves the change from an immature organism to a mature one with full reproductive potential (Grumbach, Grave, & Mayer, 1974). A growth spurt occurs in girls around 12 years of age, but may occur as early as 9 years of age. A similar growth spurt occurs in boys around 14 years of age, but may occur as early as $10^1/2$ years. The hormonal system needed to produce pubertal change actually develops prenatally, but is suppressed from birth until late childhood, when hormone levels begin to increase. This results in the gradual maturation of secondary sexual characteristics (Tanner, 1962).

That hormonal changes directly influence adolescent behavior is a commonly held belief. However, there are only a few scientific studies demonstrating this direct effect (Peterson, 1985). Nottelman et al. (1987) studied the relationship between adolescent psychosocial adjustment problems and markers of biologic development, including chronological age, pubertal status, and serum hormone levels, in 56 normal boys and 52 normal girls between ages 9 and 14. Adjustment problems such as poor self-image and behavior problems were associated in boys with a cluster of physical/biochemical findings characteristic of late maturers. These included lower sex steroid levels, lower pubertal stage, and relatively high adrenal androgen (androstenedione) levels, frequently in conjunction with higher chronological age. For girls, adjustment problems were

TABLE 9.1.   *Typical Adolescent Stressors*

Pubertal growth
Hormonal changes
Genetic vulnerability to illness
Heightened sexuality
Changed dependence/independence
Changed relationship to parents
Changed relationship of parents to adolescent
Newly developed cognitive abilities
Cultural and societal expectations
Gender role
Peer pressure
Parental psychopathology
School changes
Family moves
Parental marital discord and divorce
Encounters with legal authorities
Sexual mistreatment
Physical illness and hospitalization

associated with relatively high levels of gonadotropins, relatively low levels of dehydroepiandrosterone sulfate, and relatively high levels of androstenedione, by themselves or in conjunction with lower pubertal age. Androstenedione is a steroid particularly responsive to stress. Higher levels of this steroid were associated with adjustment problems in both boys and girls. The authors conclude that this relationship may reflect either endogenous hormone effects or the stresses of later maturation, such as adolescent self-comparisons with same-age peers.

A study of serum androgenic hormones in adolescent boys found that free testosterone was a strong predictor of sexual motivation and behavior, with no additional contribution from other hormones (Udry et al., 1985). Neither did measures of pubertal development and age demonstrate any additional effects, suggesting that free testosterone affects sexual motivation directly and does not work through the social interpretation of the accompanying pubertal development.

The direct relationship between hormone levels and cognitive function has been demonstrated in a series of studies performed by Gordon, Corbin, and Lee (1986). In male adolescents, follicle stimulating hormone (FSH) was significantly, but negatively correlated with three of four visuospatial skills. For adolescent females, this result was found with one visuospatial test. In addition, FSH was significantly and positively correlated with verbal fluency in females. In other words, FSH was negatively correlated with visuospatial performance abilities, in which men typically excel, and positively correlated with verbal fluency, an ability in which women excel. Additionally, injections of Luteinizing Hormone Releasing Hormone (LHRH) resulted in improved performance on fluency tests in males. No relationship between changes in testosterone and cognitive function were found.

While hormones may influence adolescent psychological adjustment directly, they also do so indirectly, through their effects on physical maturation and the subsequent reactions of the adolescent to these maturational changes as well as the responses from other people to these changes. Some important mediating factors include general social norms regarding deviance in timing, local social norms regarding preferred appearance, and gender (Petersen, 1985). In general, studies of the effects of the timing of maturation suggest that early maturation is more advantageous socially for boys, and middle or later maturation is advantageous socially for girls (Gross & Duke, 1980).

PSYCHOLOGICAL AND COGNITIVE DEVELOPMENT

Psychoanalytic theorists characterize adolescence as a period of internal intrapsychic struggle between the dependency needs of childhood and the drive for independence and autonomy (Blos, 1972; Freud, 1958). Freud (1958) describes adolescence as a period of increased anxiety due to drive development. This is accompanied by heightened conflict over impulse expression, intensified defenses against impulses, and emotional lability and regressions. However, more recent longitudinal studies have found that the majority of adolescents successfully negotiate adolescence without significant instability and upheaval (Offer, 1969).

Adolescence is also a time of developing and utilizing the new cognitive abilities young adolescents gain as they move into the stage of Formal Operational Thinking (Piaget, 1954). As this stage develops, the young person acquires a capacity for abstract reasoning, allowing for a greater understanding of the world and a greater preoccupation with vague or controversial issues such as religion, government, and relationships. The egocentrism of earlier stages becomes more balanced as the adolescent develops a broader and less immediate view of life. Superego or moral development also changes with these new cognitive abilities; the adolescent strives to develop an internal sense of morality (Kohlberg, 1971). While these new cognitive abilities help adolescents cope with their lives, anxiety is increased by these changes.

General characteristics of normal adolescent development are summarized in Table 9.2. Not all adolescents will develop evenly across all parameters, but variation from these guidelines suggests that the stress encountered by such adolescents is overwhelming their coping skills.

FAMILIAL AND CULTURAL DEVELOPMENTAL INFLUENCES: PARENTAL PUBERTY STRESS

As the adolescent moves developmentally to become more independent, the family of the young person also feels the stress of this process. Small, Cornelius, and Eastman (1983) report that potential stress is higher among mothers and fathers of early adolescents than among parents of preadolescent or middle adolescents. Parental conflict over the early adolescent's push for autonomy is suggested as the cause for this stress. Thus, the effects on the parents of the developmental changes occurring during adolescence produce another stress for the adolescent. Parents under stress are less able to be supportive of their adolescent. This can lead to an interaction between the parent and the adolescent which results in increasing stress for all involved (see Figure 9.1).

TABLE 9.2. Comparison of Developmental Characteristics at Three Stages of Adolescence

Early Adolescence (Puberty–14 Years)	Middle Adolescence (14–16 Years)	Late Adolescence (17–Adulthood)
Movement Towards Independence		
Struggle with sense of identity	Self-involvement, alternating unrealistically high expectations and poor self-concept	Firmer identity
Moodiness		Ability to delay gratification
Improved expression through speech	Complaints that parents interfere with independence	Ability to follow an idea to a conclusion
More likely to express feelings by action than words	Extremely concerned with appearance and body	Ability to express feelings in words
Close friendships gain importance	Feeling of strangeness about self and body	More developed sense of humor
Less affection shown to parents; occasional rudeness	Lowered opinion of parents; withdrawal of emotions from them	Stable interests
Realization that parents not perfect; identification of their faults	Effort to make new friends	Greater emotional stability
Search for new people to love besides parents	Emphasis on peer group; group identity of selectivity, superiority, competitiveness	Ability to make independent decision
Tendency to return to childish behavior, fought off by excessive activity	Sad periods as psychological loss of parents takes place	Ability to compromise
Peer group influences interests and clothing styles	Examination of inner experiences	Pride in one's work
		Self-reliance
		Greater concern for others

(continued)

TABLE 9.2.   (Continued)

Early Adolescence (Puberty–14 Years)	Middle Adolescence (14–16 Years)	Late Adolescence (17–Adulthood)
Sexuality		
Girls ahead of boys	Concerns about sexual attractiveness	Concerned with serious relationships
Same-sex friends and group activities	Frequently changing relationships	Clear sexual identity
Shyness, blushing, and modesty	Movement toward heterosexuality; fears of homosexuality	Capacities for tender and sensual love
Show-off qualities	Tenderness and fears shown towards opposite sex	
Greater interest in privacy	Feelings of love and passion	
Experimentation with body (masturbation)		
Worries about being normal		
Ethics and Self-Direction		
Rule and limit testing	Development of ideals; selection of role models	Capable of useful insight
Occasional experimentation with cigarettes, marijuana, and alcohol	More consistent evidence of conscience	Stress on personal dignity and self-esteem
Capacity for abstract thought	Greater capacity for setting goals	Ability to set goals and follow through
	Interest in moral reasoning	Acceptance of social institutions and cultural traditions
		Self-regulation of self-esteem

A survey of parents' reactions to the onset of adolescence found first-born children were perceived more negatively and generated more negative feelings in their parents (Cohen et al., 1986). In addition, older parents (aged 39 and above) perceived fewer negative changes and experienced fewer negative and anxious feelings toward their children than did younger parents (aged 38 and younger). This suggests older parents and later siblings benefit from increased parental experience, self-confidence, and knowledge in coping with the autonomy struggles of adolescence. Stress is likely to be higher if the parent feels that disagreement with the adolescent is a threat to parental control (Farrell & Rosenberg, 1981) or a general stressor within the context of family life (Pearlin & Lieberman, 1979).

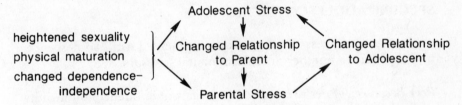

Figure 9.1. The parent-adolescent stress cycle initiated by puberty: a biopsychosocial family system. Although stressful, it ordinarily reaches a new level of healthy homeostasis if the preceding parent-child relationship was healthy and if no additional major stressor complicates it.

The stability and support available from the family is important in determining the adjustment of the adolescent. The perceived quality of attachment to parents is reported to be very significant in determining the well-being of the adolescent, even more so than the quality of attachment to peers (Greenberg, Siegel, & Leitch, 1983). The quality of this attachment is also shown to have a moderating effect on measures of self-esteem under conditions of high life stress.

Fathers and mothers are found to perceive the stress of having an adolescent somewhat differently. Mothers, but not fathers, appeared adversely affected by the intensity of the conflict they experienced with their sons or daughters (Silverberg & Steinberg, 1987). Parents' experiences of mid-life identity concerns were found to be positively related to the level of emotional autonomy of their same-sex child.

Social class is found to have a relationship to the amount of perceived conflict over adolescent autonomy struggles in families. Working-class fathers report stronger mid-life identity concerns around their sons' emotional autonomy than do white-collar and professional fathers (Silverberg & Steinberg, 1987). Blue-collar fathers also report less life satisfaction when their daughters are more emotionally autonomous. These differences may be due in part to working-class fathers placing greater value on conformity and obedience than on autonomy and independence for their adolescents (Kohn, 1977). Another factor among blue-collar fathers might be envy of their childrens' greater opportunities and potential accomplishments.

Interaction with social and cultural values is another important factor in determining the stress and coping ability of the maturing adolescent. Values given to physical size, body shape, gender stereotypes, and stereotypes about early and late maturers influence the adolescents' feelings about their bodies. Norms about expressions of sexuality, competition, and independence also vary in different societies, cultures, socioeconomic classes, and at various times. All of these must be considered in determining the nature and degree of stress faced by an adolescent.

SPECIFIC ADOLESCENT STRESSORS

In addition to the stress of normal development during adolescence, young people face a number of environmental stressors.

Peer Pressure. Peer pressure can have strong influences on healthy and unhealthy behavior. The stress of resisting unhealthy peer pressure can be buffered by good family relationships and a high self-esteem, and it is often those adolescents with neither who succumb to unhealthy pressure from their peers.

Parent Stress. Parental mental illness, parental unemployment, low socioeconomic status, and marital discord are a few of the important parent-related stresses faced by many adolescents (Stiffman, Jung, & Feldman, 1986). The parents' effect upon the adolescent is likely to be related to the young person's involvement in the parents' psychopathology and the modes of interaction that the parent has with the adolescent. (See Chapter 13 for more about parental depression.)

School Changes. During adolescence, most young people change schools (from elementary to junior high to high school) and change learning programs and expectations. School change is a stressful event for many adolescents and results in lowered self-esteem, especially for girls (Felner, Ginter, & Primavera, 1982; Simmons et al., 1979). This results in an increase in specific adjustment problems, especially when the school transition occurs at the same time as the peak of pubertal change (Simmons et al., 1979).

Moves. The stress of geographic mobility is also known to affect adolescent health. Adverse adjustment manifests itself in one of three ways: (1) the adolescent has increased physiological disorders, (2) the parent/child communication deteriorates, and (3) the adolescent develops psychological disorders most commonly associated with isolation and loneliness (Hendren, 1987). Adolescents who live within a harmonious family unit have been noted to adjust more readily to new environments. However, adolescents whose families do not function well or adolescents that have suffered pre-move disturbances are found to be much more vulnerable to the stresses of moving (Tooley, 1970).

Divorce. Parental divorce is yet another stress faced by a growing number of adolescents. More than 1.2 million children under 18 years of age live through the acute stages of parental divorce annually (Jellinek & Slovik, 1981). For adolescents, Wallerstein (1985) reports that one important factor is their real or perceived abandonment and rejection by the noncustodial parent. The stress of this perceived loss results in grief, depression, and possibly self-blame. The most important factor in predicting the post-divorce outcome is the adaptation of the post-divorce family. The success of the post-divorce family in adapting to its new circumstances is an important factor in how well the adolescent will withstand the stresses of the divorce. The greatest damage occurs when the divorce has both failed to solve any existing family problems and has created new ones, such as decreased finances, changes in residence, and loss of extended family members. Such continued stress can overwhelm the coping abilities of both the adolescent and the parents. (See Chapter 14 for more about divorce.)

Legal Stress. With increasing independence and decreased parental supervision, the adolescent has greater opportunity to encounter difficulty with legal authorities. Most young people obtain a driver's license and many have automobile accidents and/or traffic violations during adolescence. Other encounters with law enforcement officers and the legal system may occur as the adolescent experiments with different behaviors and moves beyond the limits of the family to test society's limits. When caught, the adolescent can experience a great deal of stress, increasing the likelihood of stress-related disorders such as depression and suicide.

Gender Role. Female adolescents are shown to experience greater stress in general than do males. Burke and Weir (1978) found female adolescents to be freer and more open with problem expression and also receive significantly more social support from peers. However, females report experiencing greater stress in their daily lives, particularly in such areas as acceptance by peers, relationships with the opposite sex, feelings of isolation and loneliness, and disagreements with parents. These young women also experienced more negative affect and had a greater number of psychosomatic symptoms. One possible explanation for this is the changing role of women in modern society, leaving adolescent females with a sense of confusion about and lack of control over their lives as they try to conform to ambiguous role definitions.

Sexual Mistreatment. The developing adolescent's struggles with autonomy, sexuality, and bodily changes are severely hampered when sexual abuse has occurred or is occurring in the family. The family is not a source of support, and the adolescent must struggle with all the normal stresses of adolescence plus those produced by sexual abuse with little or no support. (See Chapter 10 for more about abuse.)

Physical Illness and Hospitalization. Illness is another stress faced by many adolescents (Saylor et al., 1987). While healthy adolescents are struggling with their own attractiveness and ability to work and compete effectively, ill adolescents have even more reason to feel anxiety about their body and their ability to be independent. (See Chapter 12 for more about illness.)

COPING SKILLS, STRESS BUFFERS, AND MECHANISMS OF DEFENSE

The most significant factor in determining how adolescents respond to stress is the effectiveness of their coping skills. These include cognitive abilities, persistence, the ability to sustain friendships, problem-solving skills, ego strength, extroversion, and the manner in which one evaluates an event's stressfulness (Stiffman et al., 1986). Adolescents who function well in spite of great stress are typically characterized as having high levels of social competence (Werner & Smith, 1982). In a study of 306 children and adolescents whose parents have a mental illness, two environmental stressors (proportion of mentally ill family members and mother-child discord), two coping skills (activity competence and school competence) and an interaction (between proportion of mentally ill family members and activity competence) were found to explain 40% of the variance in behavior problems (Stiffman et al., 1986). Secure adolescents are characterized by peers as being more ego-resilient, less anxious, and less hostile, and they themselves report less distress and high levels of social support (Kobak & Sceery, 1988).

Psychological symptoms in adolescents are also found to be related to negative life events and psychosocial resources. Walker and Green (1987) found that perceived personal efficacy, peer support, and family cohesion directly affect symptom expression in both male and female adolescents. For males, peer support was a significant buffer against stress. However, high peer support did not buffer against stress in females. Low family cohesion was associated with high symptom levels for both males and females, even in the absence of negative life events.

Other factors associated with the successful coping with stress include having an internal locus of control (D'Arcy & Siddique, 1984), and a belief in one's personal efficacy (Wheaton, 1983). Both of these strengths reflect an ability to rely on oneself for direction and support rather than on one's parents or other external sources.

Adolescents attempt to cope with stress through the use of psychological defense mechanisms. Defense mechanisms are automatic and unconscious, and they alter the perception of both internal and external reality. Defenses commonly used by adolescents are listed in Table 9.3. They are

TABLE 9.3. *Psychological Defense Mechanisms from Immature to Mature*

Mechanism	Example
Denial is an unconscious mechanism that allows the adolescent to avoid awareness of thoughts, feelings, wishes, needs, or external reality factors that are consciously intolerable.	An adolescent denies any feeling of abandonment or rejection by the noncustodial parent after a divorce.
Projection is the unconscious mechanism whereby an unacceptable impulse, feeling, or idea is attributed to the external world.	An adolescent experiencing repeated trouble with the law claims all of the problems are due to law enforcement officers who have it in for him (projection of guilt).
Splitting occurs when the adolescent unconsciously views people or events as being at one extreme or the other.	A hospitalized patient views each of the medical staff as being all "good" or all "bad."
Acting out occurs when unconscious emotional conflicts or feelings are expressed in an arena different from the one in which they arose. Generally, acting out is a feeling expressed in actions rather than in words.	An adolescent girl who is angry at her family after being grounded runs away from home without verbally expressing her anger.
Regression is a partial or symbolic return to more infantile patterns of reacting or thinking.	An adolescent returns to childish and dependent behavior following a family move to a new city.
Counterphobia is seeking out experiences that are consciously or unconsciously feared.	An adolescent repeatedly engages in risk-taking behavior.
Identification occurs when a person unconsciously patterns himself after some other person. (Role modeling or imitation is similar to identification, but is a conscious process.)	An adolescent identifies with a rock star or an athletic coach whom he admires.
Reaction Formation unconsciously transforms unacceptable feelings, ideas, or impulses into their opposites.	An adolescent mother feels resentment toward the demands that caring for her child make on her. However, she repeatedly tells herself and others how wonderful motherhood is. At times she worries unnecessarily that some harm will come to her child.

(continued)

TABLE 9.3. **(Continued)**

Mechanism	Example
Repression (unconscious) and *Suppression* (conscious) occur when unacceptable thoughts, wishes, or impulses that would produce anxiety are pushed out of awareness.	An adolescent "forgets" to tell her parents of a failing grade in school.
Displacement occurs when emotions, ideas, or wishes are transferred from their original source or target to a more acceptable substitute.	An adolescent who is angry with a teacher berates a sibling for no apparent reason.
Isolation of affect is the separation of ideas or events from the feelings associated with them.	An adolescent, in a cool, unemotional manner, describes the circumstances of a serious automobile accident in which he received multiple injuries.
Rationalization uses reasoning and "rational" explanations, which may or may not be valid, to explain away unconscious conflicts and motivations.	An adolescent explains her drug abuse by saying that "everyone" does it.
Intellectualization controls affects and impulse by analyzing through excessive thought without experiencing the feeling.	When asked about the automobile accident in which his father was killed, an adolescent begins discussing the mechanics of trauma, velocity of impact, safety rules, and changing trends in life expectancy.
Sublimation unconsciously replaces an unacceptable feeling with a course of action that is personally and socially acceptable.	An adolescent whose father recently died from a myocardial infarction begins a vigorous exercise program.
Humor is used defensively to relieve anxiety caused by the discrepancies between what one wishes for himself and what actually happens.	An adolescent laughs about an embarrassing encounter with her school teacher.
Altruism is a seemingly unselfish interest in the welfare of others.	An adolescent whose parents are divorcing volunteers to work as a hospital aid.

listed in a progression from immature levels to mature levels of adaptive functioning. All defense mechanisms attempt to reduce stress, but immature defenses often have greater long-term consequences and are more likely to be associated with psychopathology.

STRESS-RELATED DISORDERS OF ADOLESCENCE

Variations in individual biological, psychological, and social characteristics interact with environmental stressors to create disorders in developing adolescents. Stress-related disorders prevalent in adolescents include depression, substance abuse, and eating disorders.

Adolescent Depression and Suicide

Genetic risk factors clearly influence the development of depression in adolescents (Wiener & Hendren, 1983). Evidence of abnormal amounts of neurotransmitters is found in young people with depression (Kashani & Cantwell, 1983). Children of depressed parents are at greater risk for developing depression, both from their increased genetic vulnerability and from the lack of availability and stability of their ill parent.

Reliable statistics regarding an apparent recent increase in adolescent depression are not available. However, statistics are available for suicide, often related to depression. The incidence of suicide in adolescence has nearly tripled since 1950. Suicide is, after accidents, the second leading cause of death in 15- to 24-year-olds (National Center for Health Statistics, 1987). In evaluating suicidal potential in an adolescent, it is important to assess both environmental stresses and the adolescent's coping ability. Part of the explanation for the recent rise in adolescent suicide is that stress upon adolescents has increased while environmental supports have decreased, leaving the adolescent more vulnerable. Recent studies also report a contagion effect that occurs when there is role modeling for suicide (Gould & Shaffer, 1986) or media publicity.

Developmental and Psychological Models. The life-stress model of Holmes and Rahe (1967) postulates that significant stresses, especially marital discord and family psychopathology, have a significant effect on adolescent depression. Kovacs and Beck (1977) developed a cognitive distortion model for depression resulting from unfavorable life experiences which lead to negative assumptions. They suggest that this explains the low self-esteem and poor body image observed in depressed children and adolescents. The learned helplessness model suggests that adolescents can learn a helpless and hopeless stance as a result of repeated failures (Dweck & Reppucci, 1973). Family systems are also found to be dysfunctional in depressed and suicidal children and adolescents (Pfeffer, 1981). Finally, the sociological model relates depression to a social structure that deprives certain individuals of desirable positions in society. (See Chapter 16.)

Adolescent Substance Abuse

Etiologic factors that characterize adolescent substance abusers include genetics and biological markers, parental values, culture, and individual characteristics, such as low self-esteem and the peer/social context. The stresses of adolescent development described earlier place young people at greater risk for misusing substances as an attempt to control these stresses. If environmental and personal supports are unable to help the adolescent cope with stresses, social pressures may lead the adolescent to drugs and alcohol (Pandina & Schuele, 1983). In the past 20 years, the dramatic increase in the number of adolescents who experiment with substances (National Institute of Drug Abuse, 1988) reflects the heightened stress of adolescence, the weakening environmental supports, and possibly the influence of the social context during this time period, when the social acceptability of substance use/abuse has increased.

Eating Disorders in Adolescence

No other illness illustrates the stress of development and its interaction with the biopsychosocial model as do eating disorders. The incidence of anorexia nervosa and bulimia has increased markedly in the past 30 years (Hendren et al., 1986), at a time when young women are facing new pressures from society to become more independent. Young women from upper-class families are at greatest risk for the development of these disorders. This is also the group which is under the greatest pressure to be attractive, a wife and mother, and a successful career woman. Eating disorders typically develop during a period of developmental crisis: when the child enters adolescence or when the adolescent leaves for college. The adolescent female who has trouble coping with these changes may feel inadequate and develop anorexia nervosa or bulimia in an attempt to appear successful by fulfilling the cultural standard for thinness.

Risk Factors and Pathogenesis. Eating-disordered women have a higher incidence of depression and substance abuse in their family history (Herzog & Copeland, 1985). Changes in neurotransmitters and hormone levels occur as the illness develops. These changes include alterations in stress-responsive hormones such as corticotropin-releasing factor (CRF), which decreases appetite, and in the neurotransmitters

norepinephrine, dopamine, and serotonin, which have all been implicated in the etiology and maintenance of both anorexia nervosa and
bulimia (Morley & Blundell, 1988). Psychological dysfunction is evident
in the eating-disordered adolescent's low self-esteem and in her difficulty
identifying and expressing feelings of ineffectiveness. In addition, the
social pressures in certain activities like ballet and athletics, which emphasize a sleek and slender body shape, place particular adolescents at
greater risk (Garfinkle & Garner, 1982). Thus, genetic and biological
vulnerability, difficulty in moving towards autonomy, and social expectations and pressures may combine in the development of an eating disorder as an ineffective attempt to cope with the stresses the adolescent is
facing.

CONCLUSION

The development of a young person through adolescence involves coping with stress and change in a number of areas. Bodily and cognitive
changes offer new challenges and opportunities, as does the movement
psychologically from dependence on the family to the autonomy of
healthy adulthood. The reactions of adolescents to these normal developmental changes depend on their sociocultural environment, family functioning, and basic endowment of healthy coping skills. Adolescents with
special environmental stresses, such as family dysfunction or frequent

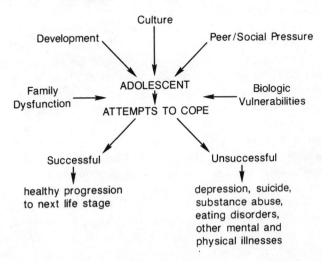

Figure 9.2. Some sources and outcomes of stress in adolescence. See text for
discussion.

moves, are at increased risk, as are those adolescents with deficient coping skills. Evaluation of these factors, along with the young person's stage of development and the current social values, can help explain prevalent stress related disorders, such as depression and suicide, substance abuse, and eating disorders (Figure 9.2). Recognition of these common stressors and coping reactions can be used to guide interventions, both for treatment of ill adolescents and for preventive efforts in the social environment.

REFERENCES

Blos, P. (1972). *On adolescence.* New York: Free Press.

Burke, R. J., & Weir, T. (1978). Sex differences in adolescent life stress, social support, and well-being. *Journal of Psychology, 98,* 277–288.

Cohen, M., Adler, N., Beck, A., & Irwin, C. E. (1986). Parental reactions to the onset of adolescence. *Journal of Adolescent Health Care, 7,* 101–106.

D'Arcy, C., & Siddique, C. M. (1984). Psychological distress among Canadian adolescents. *Psychological Medicine, 14,* 615–625.

Dweck, C. S., & Reppucci, N. D. (1973). Learned helplessness and reinforcement responsibility in children. *Journal of Personality and Social Psychology, 25,* 109–116.

Farrell, M. P., & Rosenberg, S. D. (1981). *Men at mid-life.* Dover, MA: Auburn House.

Felner, R. D., Ginter, M., & Primavera, J. (1982). Primary prevention during school transitions: Social support and environmental structure. *American Journal of Community Psychology, 10,* 277–290.

Freud, A. (1958). *Adolescence. Psychoanalytic study of the child* (Vol. 13). New York: International Universities Press.

Garfinkle, P. E., & Garner, D. M. (1982). *Anorexia nervosa: A multidimensional perspective* (pp. 112–119). New York: Brunner/Mazel.

Gordon, H. W., Corbin, E. D., & Lee, L. A. (1986). Changes in specialized cognitive function following changes in hormone levels. *Cortex, 22,* 399–415.

Gould, M. S., & Shaffer, D. (1986). The impact of suicides in television movies—Evidence of imitation. *New England Journal of Medicine, 315,* 690–694.

Greenberg, M. T., Siegel, J. M., & Leitch, C. J. (1983). The nature and importance of attachment relationships to parents and peers during adolescence. *Journal of Youth and Adolescence, 12*(5), 373–386.

Gross, R. T., & Duke, P. M. (1980). The effect of early versus late physical maturity on adolescent behavior. *Pediatric Clinics of North America, 27,* 71–77.

Grumbach, M. M., Grave, G. D., & Mayer, F. E. (Eds.) (1974). *The control of the onset of puberty.* New York: Wiley.

Hendren, R. L. (1987). Geographic mobility: Its unique stresses on children, adolescents, and their families. *Journal of Preventive Psychiatry, 3*(4), 303–308.

Hendren, R. L., Barber, J. K., & Sigafoos, A. (1986). Eating disordered symptoms in a non-clinical population: A study of female adolescents in two private schools. *Journal of the American Academy of Child Psychiatry, 25*(6), 836–840.

Herzog, D. B., & Copeland, P. M. (1985). Eating disorders. *New England Journal of Medicine, 313*(5), 295–303.

Holmes, C. H., & Rahe, R. H. (1967). The social readjustment rating scale. *Journal of Psychosomatic Research, 11,* 213–218.

Jellinek, M. S., & Slovik, L. S. (1981). Current concepts in psychiatry. Divorce: Impact on children. *New England Journal of Medicine, 305,* 557–560.

Kashani, J. H., & Cantwell, D. P. (1983). Etiology and treatment of childhood depression: A biopsychosocial perspective. *Comprehensive Psychiatry, 24,* 476–486.

Kobak, R. R., & Sceery, A. (1988). Attachment in late adolescence: Working models, affect regulation, and representations of self and others. *Child Development, 59,* 135–146.

Kohlberg, L. (1971). Moral stages and moralization: The cognitive developmental approach. In T. Labona (Ed.), *Moral development and epistemology.* New York: Academic Press.

Kohn, M. L. (1977). *Class and conformity* (2nd ed.). Chicago: University of Chicago Press.

Kovacs, M., & Beck, A. T. (1977). An empirical-clinical approach toward a definition of childhood depression. In J. G. Schultergrandt & A. Raskin, (Eds.), *Depression in childhood: Diagnosis, treatment and conceptual models.* New York: Raven Press.

Morley, J. E., & Blundell, J. E. (1988). The neurobiologic basis of eating disorders: Some formulations. *Biological Psychiatry, 23,* 53–78.

National Center for Health Statistics. (1987, August). *Death and death rates for the 10 leading causes of death in specific age groups: United States supplement.* Hyattsville, MD: National Center for Health Statistics.

National Institute of Drug Abuse. (1988). *High school senior drug use 1975–1987.* Rockville, MD: National Institute of Drug Abuse.

Nottelmann, E. D., Susman, E. J., Inoff-Germain, G., Cutler, G. B., Loriaux, D. L., & Chrousos, G. P. (1987). Developmental processes in early adolescence: Relationships between adolescent adjustment problems and chronological age, pubertal stage, and puberty-related serum hormone levels. *Journal of Pediatrics, 110*(3), 473–480.

Offer, D. (1969). *The psychological world of the teenager.* New York: Basic Books.

Pandina, R. J., & Schuele, J. A. (1983). Psychosocial correlates of alcohol and drug use of adolescent students and adolescents in treatment. *Journal of Studies on Alcohol, 44*(6), 950–973.

Pearlin, L. I., & Lieberman, M. A. (1979). Social sources of emotional stress. In R. G. Simmons (Ed.), *Research in community and mental health* (Vol. 1). Greenwich, CT: JAI Press.

Petersen, A. C. (1985). Pubertal development as a cause of disturbance: Myths, realities, and unanswered questions. *Genetic, Social and General Psychology Monographs, 111*(12), 205–232.

Pfeffer, C. R. (1981). The family system of suicidal children. *American Journal of Psychotherapy, 25,* 330–341.

Piaget, J. (1954). *The construction of reality in the child.* New York: Basic Books.

Saylor, C. F., Pallmeyer, T. P., Finch, A. J., Eason, L., Trieber, F., & Folger, C. (1987). Predictors of psychological distress in hospitalized pediatric patients. *Journal of the American Academy of Child and Adolescent Psychiatry, 26*(2), 232–236.

Silverberg, S. B., & Steinberg, L. (1987). Adolescent autonomy, parent-adolescent conflict, and parental well-being. *Journal of Youth and Adolescence, 16*(3), 293–312.

Simmons, R. G., Blyth, D. A., VanCleave, E. F., & Bush, D. M. (1979). Entry into early adolescence: The impact of school structure, puberty, and early dating on self-esteem. *American Sociological Review, 44,* 948–967.

Small, S. A., Cornelius, S., & Eastman, G. (1983). *Parenting adolescent children: A period of storm and stress?* Paper presented at the Ninety-first Annual Convention of the American Psychological Association, Anaheim, CA.

Stiffman, A. R., Jung, K. G., & Feldman, R. A. (1986). A multivariate risk model for childhood behavior problems. *American Journal of Orthopsychiatry, 56*(2), 204–211.

Tanner, F. M. (1962). *Growth at adolescence.* Oxford: Blackwell Scientific Publications.

Tooley, K. (1970). The role of geographic mobility in some adjustment problems of children and families. *Journal of the American Academy of Child Psychiatry, 9,* 366.

Udry, J. R., Billy, J. O. G., Morris, N. M., Groff, T. R., & Madhwa, R. A. (1985). Serum androgenic hormones motivate sexual behavior in adolescent boys. *Fertility and Sterility, 43*(1), 90–94.

Walker, L. S., & Greene, J. W. (1987). Negative life events, psychosocial resources, and psychophysiological symptoms in adolescents. *Journal of Clinical Child Psychology, 16*(1), 29–36.

Wallerstein, J. S. (1985). Children of divorce: Preliminary report of a ten-year follow-up of older children and adolescents. *American Journal of Orthopsychiatry, 24,* 545–553.

Werner, E., & Smith, R. (1982). *Vulnerable but invincible: A longitudinal study of resilient children and youths.* New York: McGraw Hill.

Wheaton, B. (1983). Stress, personal coping resources, and psychiatric symptoms: An investigation of interactive models. *Journal of Health and Social Behavior, 24,* 208–229.

Wiener, J. M., & Hendren, R. L. (1983). Childhood depression. *Developmental and Behavioral Pediatrics, 4*(1), 43–49.

Part III

Sources of Stress in Childhood (Including Public Health Aspects)

CHAPTER TEN

The Stress of Child Abuse and Other Family Violence

Charles F. Johnson
Debra S. Cohn

CHILD ABUSE AND NEGLECT: DEFINITIONS, INCIDENCE, AND CONSEQUENCES

Adults have many possible reactions to stress, which range from passivity and acceptance to fight or flight. If the source of stress is animate and easily overpowered, the option of aggression may be considered the most feasible choice by the stressed individual. The family is a common source of stress (Straus, Gelles, & Steinmetz, 1980).

Aggressive physical reactions against adult family members are termed spouse abuse, husband/wife battering, or family violence; when the target is a child, it is child abuse. When the adult's response to stress is inadequate care of or concern for the child, it is child neglect. Neglect of a dependent child may be as dangerous as physical abuse. Physical and verbal traumas that have minor consequences for adults may permanently injure children.

Child abuse and other forms of family violence have been an unpleasant aspect of childhood throughout recorded history (deMause, 1974; Solomon, 1973); however, child abuse came to the attention of the medical community relatively recently. In 1946, Dr. John Caffey, a radiologist, reported the frequent association of unexplained chronic head injuries and multiple fractures of long bones in children (Caffey, 1946), but it was not until 1962, when Dr. C. Henry Kempe coined the term "battered child syndrome," that the problem came to the attention of professionals (Kempe et al., 1962).

Other than in times of war, family violence is the most likely type of violence to be encountered by either adults or children (Straus, 1980; Straus et al., 1980). The demands made by family members for love, food, shelter, clothing, and medical care, and the demands by society for parents to raise successful and law-abiding citizens, serve as stressors that can result in violence. Inability to escape the source of stress aggravates the tendency to violence. Although women have demonstrated a tendency to react to stress with depression (Brown & Harris, 1978), some also react with violence to family members, including their children. The violence demonstrated by society and propagated through its media, i.e., "socially scripted responses" (Straus, 1980; Straus et al., 1980), and through certain religious teachings, provide ready models for family members.

Attacking the source of stress may be regarded as "productive" by the perpetrator; however, if the target is the biological progeny, and death or disability results, "reproductive" loss ensues. In lower primates, attacks on the infants of other fathers provide opportunity for increased survival of the aggressor's progeny. In our species, where the attacks also may be on the biological offspring of the aggressor, the modeled behavior for a *survivor* may reappear as abuse of the original perpetrator's grandchildren. Thus, abuse or neglect may be familial (Gelles, 1987; Kalmuss, 1984).

Definitions

The definition of child abuse has changed over time, as has the attitude of societies toward children and children's relationships with their parents. Contemporary parents may disagree about children's rights and appropriate discipline. The definition of child abuse also varies from country to country (Mouzakitis & Varghese, 1985) and, to a lesser extent, from state to state, courtroom to courtroom, professional to professional, and physician to physician (Morris, Johnson, & Clasen, 1985). The Federal Child Abuse Prevention and Treatment Act of 1974 (Public Law 93-247) defined child abuse and neglect as:

> *The physical or mental injury, sexual abuse or exploitation, negligent treatment, or maltreatment of a child under the age of eighteen, or the age specified by the child protection law of the state in question, by a person who is responsible for the child's welfare under circumstances which indicate that the child's health or welfare is harmed or threatened thereby, as determined in accordance with regulations prescribed by the Secretary.*

Professionals may suspect or document child maltreatment; however, it is the court which adjudicates a child as abused or neglected. Abuse is an act of commission; neglect is an act of omission. Neglect and abuse may be physical, sexual, or emotional. A functional medical definition of suspected physical abuse is "an injury to a child which is not in keeping with the history of the injury or the child's development" (Johnson & Coury, 1988). There is less physician disagreement about definitions of sexual abuse (Ladson, Johnson, & Doty, 1987) than physical abuse.

Emotional abuse and neglect are more difficult to define (Brassard, Germain, & Hart, 1987) and instances of emotional abuse are less likely to be recognized, reported, (Newberger, 1983) and adjudicated. Class and race influence abuse reporting rates (Newberger, 1983). Emotional maltreatment may be defined as an injury to the intellectual or psychological capacity of a child, as evidenced by an observable and substantial impairment in the child's ability to function within the normal cultural range of performance and behavior (Landau et al., 1980).

Incidence

In 1987, a 313-bed children's hospital reported 313 cases of physical abuse, 464 cases of sexual abuse and assault, 52 cases of neglect and nonorganic failure to thrive, no cases of emotional abuse, and one case of emotional neglect. Emotional abusers also tend to abuse physically (Straus, 1974); it is the physical manifestations that bring the child into the system.

At the national level, there were 1.3 million cases of child abuse, defined as observable harm as a result of abuse or neglect, reported to authorities in 1986; this is a 66% increase over 1980 data (NCPCA, 1988). The projected 1,100 deaths of children from abuse represents an increase of 10% over 1980. The true incidence of abuse is unknown because only reported abuse can be tabulated. Of those cases that are reported, 53% are substantiated (NCPCA, 1988). A lack of substantiation is not due solely to misdiagnosis. It may be impossible to prove that abuse or neglect was the cause of physical or emotional injury, especially in younger children. Results of a survey of 1,146 parents, using the Conflict Tactics Scale to determine violent acts occurring in the past year to children between ages 3 and 17 years, revealed an incidence rate of 14%. This was extrapolated to be 6.5 million of the 46 million children of this age group in 1980 (Straus, 1980). When "being hit with an object" (which is considered an act of abuse at Columbus Children's Hospital) was excluded, the incidence of abuse decreased to 3–4%, or 1.7 million children. Because the study did not include violent acts directed toward children less than two years of age and required an adult admission of the act, the rate may be significantly higher. Changes in the incidence (Gelles & Straus, 1987) and severity (Fouras & Johnson, in press) are in dispute.

Consequences

Although the reported incidences of emotional abuse and neglect are lower than other forms of abuse and neglect, emotional consequences are the common final pathway of physical and sexual abuse and neglect. Most forms of physical maltreatment heal within days to months of the injury, although certain consequences, such as brain damage and pregnancy, have lifelong effects on the child. The emotional scars resulting from maltreatment experiences may never heal completely and may surface later in childhood and adulthood.

A variety of behavioral/emotional symptoms have been associated with the consequences of physical and/or sexual abuse. Table 10.1 compares reported effects of physical and sexual child abuse. As shown in Column 2, although physical abuse and sexual abuse are distinct types of victimization, the impact on children may be similar.

The insult does not need to be aimed directly to the child to be stressful. Passively witnessing home violence (verbal or physical) can also stress the child. For example, there is increasing evidence that children

Effects of Physical Abuse	Effects Common to Physical or Sexual Abuse	Effects of Sexual Abuse	
Antisocial behavior	Aggression	Anger	Mistrust
Apathy	Anxiety	Appetite loss	Mood swings
Central nervous system impairment	Criminal involvement as adult	Betrayal, feelings of	Multiple personality disorder
Cognitive impairment	Delinquency	Borderline personality disorder	Need to control
Destructiveness	Depression	Clinging	Neurosis
Developmental impairment	Fear	Compulsive masturbation	Nightmares
Disfigurement	Low self-esteem	Compulsivity	Perception of self as victim (scripting)
Failure to thrive	Nightmares*	Dependency	Phobias
Hopelessness	Paranoid reactions and mistrust	Disruptive behavior	Powerlessness
Impaired impulse control	Poor interpersonal relationships	Dissociation	Running away
Learning disabilities	Poor school performance	Distorted beliefs about self and others	Sadness
Limited attachment	Post-traumatic stress disorder symptoms	Eating disorders	Self-blame
Non-compliance	Predisposition to becoming abuser	Employment problems	Self-destructive behaviors
Passivity	Regressive behavior	Fatigue	Sense of differentness
Permanent physical handicaps	School problems	Grief	Sexual acting-out
Predisposition to emotional disturbance	Sleep disorders	Guilt	Sexual confusion or misinformation
Secondary retardation	Suicidal behavior	Hostility	Sexual dysfunction, avoidance, or inhibition
Social skills deficits	Use of primitive defense mechanisms	Hyperactivity	Shame
	Withdrawal	Hypersexuality, precocious sexual awareness	Somatic complaints
		Impaired ability to judge trustworthiness of others	Stigmatization
		Impaired emotional functioning as adult	Substance abuse
		Isolation	Vulnerability to repeated victimization of self or children

*Although nightmares are well documented only for sexual abuse, it seems reasonable to expect them also in some cases of physical abuse.
Sources: Cohen & Mannarino, 1988; Finkelhor, 1987a, 1987b; Green, 1988; Kolko, Moser, & Weldy, 1988; Walker, Bonner, & Kaufman, 1988.

are adversely affected by passively participating in divorce (Bolton & MacEachron, 1986; Touflexis, 1989; see also Chapter 14).

STRESS AS A SPECIFIC CONSEQUENCE OF ABUSE

Stress has been described as being perpetuated by threats to one's life; threats of injury, pain, and disability; threats to relatives; and threats to one's values or self-image (Ayalon & Van Tassel, 1987). Little is written about stress as a specific consequence of abuse. More is written about the physical manifestations of abuse (Johnson & Showers, 1985). A major medical reference book discusses stress, in one sentence, as a possible *trigger* of abuse (Ellerstein, 1981). Parental stress is considered to be the major cause of child abuse (Gelles,1987; Straus, 1980).

Certainly an act of violence by a trusted caretaker or parent that causes pain, potential disfigurement, and lack of confidence in the ability or motivation of that caretaker to provide protection is stressful to a dependent child. Younger children do not use the term stress, but physical, emotional, or sexual abuse of children does threaten their security and safety. Attacks by infectious and toxic agents are abstract to the younger child. In contrast, an attack by a caretaker is more comprehensible and realistic. Anxiety and stress from abuse are more likely to persist when the offending agent remains in the environment. The older child, although unable to escape the consequences of genetic and environmental disease, can run from abuse and abuser. The typical runaway is likely to have come from an abusive family (Farber et al., 1984), indicating that the stresses of the home environment may be more intense than the uncertainties and potential misfortunes of life on the street. The child who has been abused suffers the acute consequences of the event, which in physical abuse are manifest externally as bruises, burns, erythema, and lacerations, and internally as hemorrhages, ruptures, and fractures (Johnson & Showers, 1985). The variety of injuries and objects used to abuse children (Johnson & Showers, 1985) suggests that the child has little warning about any one attack and probably little time for anxiety and anticipatory stress. Chronic abuse leads to chronic stress from anticipation of future attacks (Green, 1983). Wolfe (1987) proposes that the immediate stress associated with child abuse (or any critical life events) "may play a lessor role in making the abuse into a significant developmental hazard than do changes in the child's social environment that are associated with the event." His theory predicts that moving into foster care or having a perpetrator parent jailed may be more stressful for the child than the abusive act itself!

Post-Traumatic Stress Disorder

Post-Traumatic Stress Disorder (PTSD) has been proposed as one model for the long-term manifestations of sexual abuse (Finkelhor, 1987b; McLeer et al., 1988). Children's initial reactions to abuse may not predict future effects (Finkelhor, 1987b). The child who may have handled the stress through denial may be unable to make an association if the abuse is discovered much later. Propranolol treatment of the heightened "automatic reactivity" associated with acute PTSD is being studied (Famularo, Kinscherff, & Fenton, 1988).

Munchausen's Syndrome by Proxy

The most recently recognized form of child abuse is Munchausen's Syndrome by Proxy (MSBP), which results when the parent intentionally causes a condition in a child to deceive the physician (Rosenberg, 1987). Typical physical abusers may try to blame the child's condition on an accident or natural process like "easy bruising," but most do not purposefully create a condition that simulates a disease to elicit unnecessary medical evaluations, hospitalizations, and treatments. Lasting harm may result from both the actions of the MSBP parent, invariably the mother, and the medical interventions aimed at diagnosis and treatment. The stress-inducing fear, anger, and guilt found in children who are hospitalized with actual disease (Christ & Flomenhaft, 1982) is likely to occur in children with MSBP. This situation makes the MSBP perpetrator guilty of emotional abuse as well as the MSBP physical abuse.

The consequences of MSBP include "psychologic development thwarted at the most basic level—basic parental trust" (McGuire & Feldman, 1989). Behavioral responses include feeding disorders, withdrawal, hyperactivity, oppositional behaviors, and tendency for the victim to perpetuate the pattern of seeking medical involvement (McGuire & Feldman, 1989). The MSBP children passively tolerate the medical procedures (Guandolo, 1985; Sneed & Bell, 1976; Waller, 1983) in a manner similar to that described in premature infants in the NICU. Psychiatric hospitalization of the child (Rogers et al., 1976) and fears of poisoning and death (Hvizdala & Gellady, 1978; Rogers et al., 1976) are further consequences. The fears are reality based: the mortality rate in one review of 117 victims was 9% (Rosenberg, 1987). The mothers who perpetrate MSBP may be concurrent victims of physical and sexual abuse themselves (McGuire & Feldman, 1989), linking this type of abuse to wife battering. Abuse of siblings may continue after the index child dies (Berger, 1979; Rosen et al., 1983); this may reflect a lack of success for social services and psychological interventions involving the perpetrator (Nicol & Eccles, 1985).

ABUSE FORMULA

A formula used to describe how abuse occurs should include four variables (Figure 10.1): (1) risk factors in the caretaker; (2) risk factors in the child; (3) stress; and (4) a precipitating event.

Parents at Risk for Abusing

Risk factors have been demonstrated in studies of non-human primates (Reite & Caine, 1983) and humans. The following may predispose parents or caretakers to react with abuse or neglect: parents abused as children, adolescent parenthood, unplanned pregnancy, delivery problems, emotional illness, low IQ, lack of empathy, lack of control, and economic, housing, domestic and health stress (Altemeier et al., 1982; Browne, 1986; Goldson et al., 1978; Johnson, 1983; Kinard & Klerman, 1980; Letourneau, 1981; Oates, Davis, & Ryan, 1980; Smith, Hanson, & Noble, 1973; Sze & Lamar, 1981). The relationship of the child to the caretaker may be a factor in the seriousness of the consequences. It is considered more stressful to children to be abused by someone they know and trust. As indicated in Table 10.2, the perpetrator of physical abuse is most likely to be the child's mother. In sexual abuse, the perpetrator is more likely to be the father or another male known to the child. If the child is abused by a stranger, the family is more likely to be supportive of the child and angry at the perpetrator. Also, the child is likely to receive therapy, which may prevent or salve acute and chronic stress.

When the perpetrator is a parent, the child receives a negative message about his or her value and the availability of the parent for positive support. The parent who confesses and desires to receive treatment is more likely to be prosecuted by the court and separated from the child. If adult confession and apology are not forthcoming, the child may feel responsible for the act(s). Parental behavior that denies culpability to avoid parental stress creates stress for the child. Adults may intentionally use bribes and threats, and may blame the child victim for any potential emotional and economic disruption of the family. This intrafamilial

I. Risk Factors in Caretaker		II. Risk Factors in Child		III. Stress		IV. Precipitating Event	
	+		+		+		⟶ ABUSE

Figure 10.1. Abuse formula.

TABLE 10.2. *Perpetrators of Abuse of 497 Children Reported from Columbus Children's Hospital in 1987*

Suspected Perpetrators	Sexual Abuse		Physical Abuse	
	Number	%	Number	%
Mother	3	1.2	81	32.8
Father	68	27.0	77	31.2
Sister	1	.4	0	0
Brother	13	5.2	0	0
Aunt	1	.4	3	1.2
Uncle	31	12.3	1	.4
Grandmother	0	0	6	2.4
Grandfather	13	5.2	0	0
Cousin Male	14	5.6	1	.4
Cousin Female	1	.4	0	0
Stepmother	0	0	3	1.2
Step Father	39	15.5	13	5.3
Stepsister	0	0	1	.4
Stepbrother	8	3.2	0	0
Stepgrandfather	5	2.0	0	0
Stepuncle	3	1.2	0	0
Mother's Boyfriend	24	9.5	27	11.0
Father's Girlfriend	0	0	3	1.2
Father's Girlfriend's Son	1	.4	0	0
Brother-in-Law	2	.8	0	0
Grandmother's Boyfriend	1	.4	0	0
Adoptive Mother	0	0	0	0
Foster Mother	0	0	3	1.2
Foster Father	0	0	1	.4
Female Babysitter	0	0	20	8.1
Male Babysitter	10	4.0	1	.4
Babysitter's Son	6	2.4	1	.4
Babysitter's Husband	8	3.2	0	0
Female Teacher	0	0	0	0
Male Teacher	0	0	1	.4
Institutional Male	0	0	4	1.6
TOTAL	252		247	

Source: Child Abuse Program, 1988.

conflict is a most perplexing situation for the child, who must choose between the loss of the perpetrating parent and the love of family members on the one hand, and, on the other hand, the possibility that the abuse will recur if the child remains silent. This is one explanation why abused children may recant their stories.

Children at Risk for Being Abused

The second factor in the abuse formula is the child. Risk factors include children who are different or seen as different by the parent (Mullins, 1986); e.g., retarded, premature, or hyperactive children (Johnson, 1983). The premature child is especially vulnerable (Goldson et al., 1978) because of early separation from the mother and lack of bonding opportunity. The congenital abnormalities, developmental delays, and economic stress associated with prematurity are contributing factors. The consequences of abuse may result in a child whose appearance (from a burn scar) or behavior (retarded or hyperactive from head injury) places the child in further jeopardy. In this instance, the original stress—the third factor in the abuse formula of Figure 10.1—may be replaced with the stress of dealing with a child whose needs overwhelm the parents' ability to cope.

Stress and Stress Management

The focus of the literature on abuse is on the relationship between caretaker stress and the precipitation of abuse (Browne, 1986; Passman & Mulhern, 1977). The most common stressors among 1,146 adults with at least one child aged 3 through 17 years was death of someone close (37%); and serious problems with health or behavior of a family member (25%) (Straus, 1980). Parental stressors specifically related to children were stress from pregnancy or birth of a child (12%), apprehension of a child in an illegal act (4.2%), and suspension of a child from school (2.5%). The higher the stress score of fathers, the higher their rate of child abuse, but mothers, even under low stress conditions, had a higher abuse rate. Child abuse rates were found to increase as the number of stresses increased.

Stress may not be preventable, but parents, preferably pre-parents, must learn to manage stress in nonviolent ways. Of concern, if child abuse is to be prevented, is the lack of knowledge that potential parents have about normal behavior and development (Johnson, Loxterkamp, & Albanese, 1982; Showers & Johnson, 1984; Showers & Johnson, 1985). Unsophisticated parents may see a normal child's behavior as abnormal, stressing the child to perform beyond capacity and punishing the child for what the parent concludes is intransigence. Programs directed at preventing re-abuse must teach both stress management and parenting skills.

It is possible that the behaviors modeled by abusing parents are adopted by child victims, who later become abusive parents (Green, 1983; Straus, 1980). These behaviors include poor models of stress management as well as physical approaches to discipline. Studies indicate that women are more likely to use avoidance in managing stress, and this results in greater impairment of functioning (Billings & Moos, 1981). The violence-prone parent may be a different type of abuser than the parent who is simply using physical approaches to discipline. With the former type, the child is unlikely to understand the cause of the parental outburst since it may not be related to the child's behavior. Violent acts that cannot be predicted because they result from frustration not related to the child may stress more severely than those that result from the child's behaviors.

The Stress of Witnessing Violence

Kalmuss (1984) reported that sons who witnessed parental violence were more likely to batter as adults and daughters were more likely to become victims. Observation of hitting between one's parents was found to be "more strongly related to severe marital aggression than is being hit as a teenager by one's parents" (Kalmuss, 1984). Others have suggested links between spouse abuse and child abuse. Straus et al. (1980) reported that when wife battering occurred in a family, the child abuse rate was 30% higher than in nonviolent homes. Further, witnessing parental abuse may be as harmful to the child's development as direct physical abuse (Walker, 1984; Widom, 1989; Wolfe et al., 1985). Children who see or hear their fathers abusing their mothers undergo stressful, frightening experiences (Wolfe, 1987). In one study, 33% of boys and 20% of girls who had been exposed to marital violence were clinically distressed (Wolfe et al., 1985).

DEVELOPMENTAL CONCERNS: ABUSE AT DIFFERENT AGES

Often a frustration, and always a challenge in the care and understanding of children, are the physical, behavioral, and emotional changes associated with development. The child's age and development level influence the types of physical (Johnson & Showers, 1985) and sexual (Child Abuse Program, 1988) insults suffered by the child. In physical abuse, variables include the relative size of the child, health of the child, size of the adult, and force, heat, or caustic strength of the offending agents. Shaking (Duhaime et al., 1987; Dykes, 1986) will have more adverse effects on an infant than on an older child. Formulas have been devised to study the severity of physical injury (Fouras & Johnson, in press); however, little is known about the relationships of the physical injury and developmental level to short- or long-term consequences.

Prenatal Abuse and Neglect of the Fetus and Potential Child

Though a discussion of prenatal abuse or neglect may seem academic, consequences to the future child are serious. Prevention efforts to avoid abuse and its attendant stresses must begin early with appropriate preparation for a healthy pregnancy of a desired and desirable infant (Oates et al., 1980).

The physical development of the child begins with fertilization. Although many congenital anomalies are coded in the genes, other preconception factors, such as a lack of or poor preparation for parenting, also may influence the potential child. Parents who have been abused are at higher risk for abusing their own children (Gelles, 1987). A teenager who risks unplanned pregnancy because of a lack of knowledge of or concern for birth control is placing the potential child at risk for abuse and neglect. High-school students have inadequate knowledge of child health and child development; this lack of knowledge is associated with selection of abusive approaches to child rearing (Johnson et al., 1982; Showers & Johnson, 1984; Showers & Johnson, 1985). Pre-pregnancy neglect includes inadequate parenting knowledge and skills. Students are not exposed to these topics by school system personnel, who are economically or philosophically unable or unwilling to offer them.

From a child's point of view, a lack of planning, genetic counseling, and preparation for pregnancy and parenthood may be considered a form of preconception neglect—these are known risk factors for child abuse. If "future children" could be knowledgeable about the situations which lead to their conception, pregnancy, and rearing, many would experience their most intense stresses from the anticipation of catastrophe! Luckily, infants are unable to process the events that occur prior to delivery and through early infancy that impart messages of a lack of planning or desire for their birth.

The effects on the fetus from infectious and toxic agents in the first trimester can be devastating. Even the well-planning mother may not be able to avoid these agents; however, mothers may deliberately place their unborn children at risk. A challenging conflict between the rights of the unborn child and those of the mother has arisen recently in situations where the mother is a known alcoholic or abuser of cocaine or other substances known to be of danger to the fetus. Instruction on nonchemical stress management before pregnancy could help avert transmission of the consequences of stress to the fetus.

Issues of prenatal abuse and neglect are occupying the pages of medical ethics journals (Caplan & Cohen, 1987; MacKenzie, Nagel, & Rothman, 1986). Cases have appeared in the popular press in which attempts have been made to keep mothers who abuse substances from continuing to do so during pregnancy. A lack of stress avoidance, inappropriate management of stress with drugs, and dietary indiscretions are forms of prenatal abuse and neglect. Stress induced by family violence is another. (See Chapters 3 and 5 for more about fetal stress effects.)

Issues of abortion and the rights of the fetus further complicate issues of prenatal abuse and neglect. Medical science is now able to keep alive some infants who have been aborted. If the unwanted child remains with the mother, future acts of abuse or neglect are risked.

Newborn Abuse and Neglect

Debate and legal machinations continue about the need to provide medical care to newborns with severe congenital anomalies. By law, the medical community must provide services to all newborns despite the wishes of the parents. Interventions that assist a defective and unwanted newborn to survive are likely to be stressful on the parent-child relationship. Survival with a handicap is stressful to the parents, siblings, and the handicapped child, especially when the system does not provide adequate support. This lack of resources is a form of societal abuse and neglect that may culminate in child abuse and neglect. A viable alternative for the unwanted child whose parents are resistant to support is early and professional foster or adoptive care.

The mental and physical condition of the mother immediately after delivery can adversely affect the newborn (Richards & McIntosh, 1972). Postpartum depression may be a factor in sudden infant death syndrome (SIDS) and infanticide (Ash, 1968; D'Orban, 1979). Many of the risk factors associated with teenage pregnancy are shared with SIDS (Johnson, 1983). Continued depression or other forms of mental illness may result in emotional and medical neglect (Hinton, 1978; Tylden, 1978; see Beardslee's discussion in Chapter 13 for further details.)

A crying infant increases the likelihood of parental aggression (Berkowitz, 1974), acting as an arousing and adversive stimulus to abusive parents (Frodi & Lamb, 1980). The crying of an infant of an abusive parent, which is intended as a message for help, may result in painful experiences.

Communication problems may originate with the mother who is unable or unwilling to respond to the needs and demands of the infant. Abusive mothers in one study engaged in significantly less positive behavior toward their children and praised appropriate behavior less than control mothers (Shindler & Arkowitz, 1986). The final result may be infant death or nonorganic failure to thrive (Barbero & Shaheen, 1984; Bithoney & Rathbun, 1983; Goldbloom, 1982); the latter is defined as failure to gain weight, failure to relate to the environment, or distorted physical and psychological growth and development (see Chapter 6 by Lobo). These infants exhibit signs of acute or chronic stress including inappropriate stranger anxiety, intense watchfulness, diminished vocalizations and unusual postures or vocalizations (Krieger & Sargent, 1967; Leonard, Rhymes, & Solnit, 1966), avoidance of social contact, intense interest in inanimate objects or self-stimulatory behavior (Rosenn, Loeb, & Jura, 1980). Other variables affecting the outcome of nonorganic-failure-to-thrive infants include prematurity, physical illness, micronutrient deficiency, severity of growth deficiency, age of onset, family demographics, and relationships that may influence psychological prognosis (Drotar, 1989). The consequences of this syndrome are life-threatening to the infant. Obtaining adequate nutrition is a primary concern of the infant; a failure to meet this need, especially if coupled with an emotionally unresponsive parent, is a source of severe stress.

Poor communication of needs may exist especially in the infant who is unusual looking, retarded, deaf, or blind and is unable to stimulate mothering or caretaking behavior in the parents. Disturbances in mother-infant communication may lead to nonorganic failure to thrive.

Comparison of Iatrogenic and Parent-Induced Stresses. A number of iatrogenic newborn stresses affect immediate behavior. Studies in the newborn nursery may serve as models to illustrate the consequences of parental abuse and neglect of newborns. Ill effects have been postulated as being due to separation from the mother, injections of vitamin K, blood drawing, eye drops, and personal handling. Manifestations of stress include muscle tension, crying (Rice, 1985), pallor, flushing, cyanosis, respiratory and cardiac rate irregularities, spitting, or gagging (Cole, 1985). The more fragile premature is more likely to suffer stress from more chronic painful stimuli, including lavage feedings, ventilation, and isolation from sensory stimuli (Newman, 1981; Rice, 1985). Preterm and full-term infants who require intensive care perform more poorly than controls on motor and interactive items on the Brazelton Assessment Scale (Holmes et al., 1982). As in child abuse, the long-term effects of stressful iatrogenic newborn experiences are unknown; however, intervention (Cole, 1985) has improved mental and motor performance in the first 9 months post-term (Heidelise et al., 1986).

Adults have claimed to have vivid memories of their newborn experiences, with consequences affecting later attitudes, behaviors, and interpersonal relationships (Grof, 1976). Complete alleviation of stress of infants is considered ill advised, as it may be "an important impetus to growth" (Lawhon & Melzar, 1988). The preterm infant in the Newborn Intensive Care Unit (NICU) may not be deprived of stimulation but rather may receive inappropriate stimulation patterns or extensive stimuli that are detrimental to intrasensory integration (Lawson, Dawn, & Turkewitz, 1977) and the establishment of normal diurnal cycles (Anderson, 1986).

The passivity of the premature upon painful manipulations (Cole,

1985) has been theorized as to be inhibition of action of an organism unable to respond to stress by either fighting or fleeing (Rice, 1985). Infants may learn that their usual signals of pain and distress, which should elicit comforting, are useless in the NICU. This learned behavior also may apply to the abused and neglected infant. Extensive restraining of infants has been shown to decrease tactile exploration during hospitalization (Lopez, 1983). The infant under the care of a chronically abusive parent may also "react" with passivity to pain. When neglectful mothers provide inadequate or inappropriate stimuli, i.e., emotionally abuse or neglect their children, the consequences may be similar to those experienced by NICU infants. However, the non-abused infant, once discharged from the NICU, should resume its growth in a healthy and supportive family, whereas the abused or neglected infant does not have a favorable environment unless diagnosed and placed in a healthier setting.

Abuse and Neglect of Older Children

As children mature and remain unable to communicate or have their needs fulfilled, they are more likely to demonstrate stress behaviors. Parents who are unable to obtain quality care for their children may unwittingly participate in a lack of stimulation and neglect. The single working parent may be more vulnerable to this situation, being handicapped by not having a second parent in relief. Of course, a child's needs can also be neglected in a two-parent family with both parents at home full time. Parenting is a time-consuming and demanding occupation; it requires resources, skills, and motivation. A lack of these may result in stress to the child (i.e., neglect) and stress to the parents as targets of the behaviors that the child generates to gain attention. These behaviors may result in abuse and further stress to the child. Older children may accept an explanation for a painful experience; however, depending upon the severity and chronicity of the pain, the explanation may not endear their caretaker or health provider to them. Frequent dressing changes of burned children could be compared to the chronic intentional pain caused by abusive parents. In accidental injury, both the parent and an understanding supportive health professional are usually available to minimize stress to the child when the physical pain cannot be decreased. In treatment of intentional burns, the trauma of medical care is often more chronically painful than the original abuse.

Abuse of Handicapped Children

Older children generally have less serious physical sequelae than younger ones do from the same insult; however, because of their increasing ability to comprehend the meaning of the attacks, and to associate them with their own vulnerability and/or a specific attacker, the emotional impact of abuse should increase with age. This comprehension, which increases the potential for inducing stress, may be delayed in children who are retarded or who suffer processing problems or other handicaps, especially those affecting the sensory systems (Rusch, Hall, & Griffin, 1986). On the other hand, handicapped children do cause family stress (Hobbs, Perrin, & Ireys, 1985; Kazak, 1986; Straus et al., 1980) and are more likely to be harshly disciplined (Beavers & Hampson, 1986) and abused (Diamond & Jaudes,1983). It is possible that developmental problems may make the emotional and physical consequences of the abuse more severe and chronic. There are no studies about differences in emotional consequences of abuse in normal and handicapped children, although the literature does indicate that specific handicaps, including prematurity (Diamond & Jaudes, 1983; Klein & Stern, 1971; Mori, 1983; Parks, 1977; Seifert et al., 1983) influence reactions to stress. In certain cases, questions have been raised about whether retardation is a cause or product of child abuse (Straus et al., 1980).

The known stresses of chronic illness may be intensified by a parent who is unable or unwilling to provide for the extra needs and demands of the chronically ill child. Although this may be defined as both medical and emotional neglect, professions not providing parents with support may be unwitting accomplices. Conversely, attention to the handicapped child may adversely affect the behavior of siblings (Lavigne & Ryan, 1979; McAndrew, 1976) through gross neglect of their needs (McKeever, 1983).

THE STRESS OF BEING IDENTIFIED AS ABUSED

Children enter the system of abuse identification through various channels. The preverbal child is unable to reveal abuse by telling. In addition, the younger child is generally in the care of the offender (Table 10.2). Rarely do perpetrators present themselves as abusers needing help. More likely, in physical abuse, the injury or another health need brings the child to the emergency room or physician's office where the diagnosis is suspected and, one hopes, reported. Physical injury by a stranger is assault and is not reportable as physical abuse; the parents are encouraged to report the assault to police. Sexual acts involving preverbal children by strangers are handled in a similar manner. When the parent or primary caretaker abuses the child and the child is able to communicate the information to a relative, this abuse may or may not be reported. The other parent may decide not to tell because the child is not believed or because the economic and emotional consequences to that parent and to other family members may be of more concern than obtaining help for the perpetrator and child, possibly involving the police. The family may believe that the abusive activity will stop as the result of family pressure and vigilance.

The school-age child may reveal an abuse history to school personnel. The prevention programs being offered by the schools teach children about what constitutes abuse and the need to tell. They offer the opportunity for children to reveal abuse. Because of guilt from accepting bribes or from passive participation, or because of fear of retaliation, the child may be reluctant to reveal abuse. Why children choose particular individuals and times to reveal abuse is unknown. They must trust the individuals to whom they reveal and overcome the anticipation of possibly being blamed, hurt by the abuser, or being stigmatized. The child must surmount the stress of the events, the possibility of further events, and the possibility that revealing will not stop the abuse. Children may choose to internalize the stress rather than report the incident if they feel there is little to gain, anticipate being rejected, or fear being responsible for the potential break-up of the family (Faller, 1984). The older child who has revealed abuse and is returned to the abusive situation or to an abusive alternative placement is less likely to reveal again, and has the added stress of realizing that there may be no safe placement.

The individual whom children tell must reassure them that their behavior is appropriate and that they are not to blame for the incidents. It is easy to imagine the quandary faced by children who wish to share an unpleasant experience but fear the consequences to themselves and possibly to the perpetrator, whom they may not wish to harm.

As indicated in Figure 10.2, stress does not end after the abusive incident. The abuse investigation itself may be stressful. The child being evaluated for abuse may be seen in an emergency room, a less than ideal environment for discussing a sensitive and emotionally laden subject. The interview may need to be repeated by the social worker from the local protective agency, the police, and the prosecutor.

If the case goes to court, the child may need to testify in an environment that is designed for adults and stressful and inappropriate for children. Judges and legislators often refuse to accept that children cannot be interviewed like adults. For example, the constitutional guarantee that the accused has the right to face the accuser is often inhumane for allegedly abused children, but the United States Supreme Court upheld this interpretation in a 6–2 decision on June 29, 1988.

Thus, the system which is designed to protect children may cause more stress to the child in the process of investigation and trial than the abuse episodes (Coulter et al., 1985; Tyler & Brassard, 1984). The child may be in double jeopardy from the investigation and its consequences, as a stressed parent may cause stress in the child (Browne, 1986) and be less available as a source of support. Stress is known to result from loss or imprisonment of a friend or mate (Browne, 1986). Testimony in juvenile court has been found to relieve anxiety and elevate the mood of children; however, the stress of protracted criminal proceedings may cause adverse mental health consequences (Runyan et al., 1988) to the child and family.

Recent efforts have been made to decrease the trauma of the investigatory process and courtroom experience. However, attempts to use videotape or closed-circuit television "confrontations" have been challenged and their legality has yet to be settled. In some courtrooms, more age-appropriate types of questions are being allowed. More progress has been made in providing "one-stop" interviews involving representatives

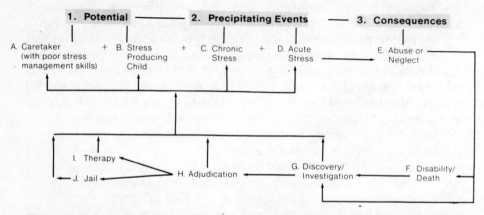

Figure 10.2. The abuse formula and stress. The combination of potential for abuse/neglect (1) and precipitating event(s) (2) result in consequences (3) for the child and family. The potential may exist in: a caretaker (A) with known risk factors, which may include poor stress management; and a child (B) whose potential existence (e.g., pregnancy) or behavior is stress producing. Chronic stress in the environment (C), which may include interpersonal or economic stresses, or acute stress (D) may lead to abuse or neglect (E). Thus, *any caretaker* is at risk for abusing a child. Although initial risk factors may be minimal, an increase in a caretaker's stress, as a result of a child's behavior or medical condition or adverse environmental changes, may precipitate abuse (acts of commission) or neglect (acts of omission). The consequences of the abuse, which may result in the child's disability or death (F), cause additional stress in parent(s) and the surviving child(ren). The abused child or surviving child(ren) may become more irritating to the parents. The parents may be overwhelmed by the recognition of their injurious behavior. Discovery (G), adjudication (H), and their consequences, which may include therapy (I) or jail (J), may cause further stress to the family. Relatives and other members of the parent's support system may feel guilty because they have protected the child inadequately and may withdraw their support from the parents. In order to prevent child abuse and its adverse consequences, treatment and change must be directed toward each segment of the formula.

from all the investigating agencies in lieu of multiple interviews; these changes are welcomed (American Academy of Child Psychiatry, 1986; MacFarlane & Krebs, 1986). This is expensive and requires coordination of agencies in systems that are not prepared to function together; continuing professional disagreement about optimal composition of inter-professional teams and procedures remain at issue (Boat & Everson, 1986; Mouzakitis, 1985).

Placement into another home, separation from siblings, and school changes are stressful and must be balanced against the need to protect the child (Pardeck, 1983). The child who remains in the home of a relative perpetrator may be pressured to recant. At the other extreme is the child who has been prompted to relate a story of abuse that is not true (Yates & Musty, 1988). This is often associated with custody battles and the child may be a willing or naive and unwilling participant. (See Chapter 14 for more details.) This places the child in a stressful situation of lying to please the parent. Older children may be teased by their peers if the events are made public. It has been recommended that the names of abused children be kept from the public to avoid this additional stress (Task Force, 1988).

THERAPY AS STRESSOR

Children who have been able to manage the stresses of abuse and reconstitute themselves in a manner that is comfortable with their personality and resources may not need therapy, especially if it forces them to re-experience the abusive episodes. Recalling a stressful event may lead to the re-release of stress hormones and may further enhance the strength of the painful memory (Pitman, 1989). There is disagreement about how much trauma remains after sexual abuse occurs (Elwell & Ephross, 1987). Schultz (1980) postulates that trauma to the child may be exaggerated due to naiveté about the role of sexuality in child development and an underestimate of the child's adaptive capacity. Adults may see fondling or exposure as more traumatic because they project their own values onto the child. The child who is "sexually abused" by a stranger by exhibitionism, fondling, or frottage may not be aware that he or she has been "violated" while the parents are incensed. The impact of stress, frustration, and pain differs in children based upon mitigating factors, defense mechanisms selected, and consequences of previous trauma (Murphy, 1974).

One cannot assume a negative outcome to child abuse—the impact depends upon the child's age, prior interactions with parents, and the child's interpretation of the abusive act (Kagan, 1983). Parents may be less upset by incest as they may protect the perpetrator-relative whom they do not or cannot believe would hurt the child. In the former in-stance, the child may be rushed to therapy; in the latter situation, the parents may resist. Interestingly, it is theorized that the child who has been abused by a stranger, and not physically harmed or threatened, is less affected than when physical trauma or a relative or known individual are involved. Thus, parents may resist therapy for the child who needs it most and seek it for the one who needs it least.

Difficulties Related to Treatment

Sadly, for those who can benefit from skilled therapy, limited resources result in the need for prioritization of cases. It is possible, since the child will rely on the family to provide transportation to therapy, that fewer children abused by caretakers will be able to cooperate with the case plan. Revealing the episodes may be tantamount, to the child, to betrayal of a friend, and the child may refuse to cooperate with therapy in order to serve the family's needs.

The motivation of the abuser may not be adequate, especially if the child is seen as responsible for the events, disliked and unvalued, or seen as the reason why the family must identify itself to the social and mental health systems. The latter may create further stress for the child as the family blames the child for the labeling and inconveniences. These ver-bal and nonverbal messages may cause the child to deny further abuse and guard behaviors that might indicate need for continued therapy.

Little is known about abused children's reaction to group therapy participation or to having friends and relatives know that they are at-tending therapy for events that they would prefer to forget or keep private. Group sessions in which the experiences of children having suffered more severe trauma than the index case are described may be stressful: the child may become concerned about the possibility of abuse being escalated.

Because the perpetrator may be jailed and unavailable to the therapist, it may appear again to the children that they are at fault for the episodes. Confession by the perpetrator to the child is not possible if the perpetra-tor is jailed. This circumstance must be balanced against society's need to punish illegal behaviors and protect itself from further transgressions. Poorly handled therapy, which forces confrontation with the abuser, may result in stress, as do pressures from the therapist or family for re-establishment of healthy parent-child relations before the child is ready.

PREVENTION OF ABUSE STRESS

Slow progress is being made in decreasing stress and other consequences of child abuse. Although not statistically significant, specific forms of physical and emotional neglect did decline between 1980 and 1986: delays in seeking health care; inadequate supervision; inadequate basic care; inadequate nurturance or affection; and spouse abuse and other forms of family violence observed by children (NCPCA, 1988). This suggests that prevention efforts directed toward new parents are having an effect.

Abuse prevention is tertiary when directed to abusers to prevent re-abuse, secondary when directed to at-risk populations, or primary when directed to the general population. When system resources are strained simply to identify abused children, only tertiary prevention may be possible. If the resources are inadequate, even the prevention of re-abuse may not be possible. Professionals may be reluctant to report abuse to agencies who seem to return children to abusive environments, have young and inexperienced workers, or workers with excessive caseloads.

Secondary abuse prevention relies on our ability to identify high-risk populations and risk factors. Programs are being directed to serve teen-age mothers and emphasize life skills, including stress management (Pearlin & Schooler, 1978; Schinke et al., 1986), in addition to parenting education. Eliciting parent participation, teaching stimulation techniques, and providing anticipatory guidance constitute part of the program recommended in the care of infants in the NICU (Lawhon & Melzar, 1988). These same techniques are appropriate for the parents of normal infants, to maximize development and minimize adverse effects from unavoidable adverse experiences. Babies whose behavior places them at high-risk for poor interaction with their parents (Thomas & Chess, 1984) can be identified by newborn nurses using standardized instruments (Maloni et al., 1986). Anticipatory guidance may prevent parental stress and attendant child abuse. Parents of handicapped children, who are at high risk for child abuse (Abbott & Meredith, 1986), should also receive intervention (Beavers & Hampson, 1986; Futcher, 1988).

Primary prevention requires a shift in the priorities of school systems toward teaching all students life skills, child development, child and adult health, and child-rearing alternatives. These programs must begin in preschool and kindergarten. Primary prevention also requires a reordering of the priorities of society (Johnson, 1986) toward concern for the invidious consequences of child abuse and family violence. This includes demands for the practice of nonviolent solutions to problems, and integration of families into kinship and community activities (Straus et al., 1980).

Most stressed parents do not abuse (Straus, 1980). We need to learn how managing the six components of stress (Farrington, 1980), which include subjective and objective factors and response capabilities in parents, stress stimuli from children, and environmental options, can mitigate the possibility of abuse. There is much to be learned about the origins and expressions of violence (Maiuro & Eberle, 1989), how to minimize stress to children in the face of violence (Milgram, 1982), and the dynamics of abuse (Newberger, Newberger, & Hampton, 1983) if we are to interrupt the cycle of abuse and its adverse effects on our society and its children.

REFERENCES

Abbott, D. A., & Meredith, W. H. (1986). Strength of parents with retarded children. *Family Relations, 35,* 371–375.

Altemeier, W. A., O'Connor, S., Vietze, P. M., Sandler, H. M., & Sherrod, K. B. (1982). Antecedents of child abuse. *Journal of Pediatrics, 100,* 823–829.

American Academy of Child Psychiatry (1986, February 9). Statement on protecting children undergoing abuse investigations and testimony. Adopted by Council.

Anderson, J. (1986). Sensory intervention with the pre-term infant in the neonatal intensive care unit. *American Journal of Occupational Therapy, 40,* 19–26.

Ash, S. (1968). Crib deaths: Their possible relationship to post-partum depression and infanticide. *Mount Sinai Journal of Medicine, 35,* 214.

Ayalon, O., & Van Tassel, E. (1977). Living in dangerous environments. In M. R. Brassard, R. Germain, & S. N. Stewart (Eds.), *Psychological maltreatment of children and youth* (pp. 171–182). New York: Pergamon Press.

Barbero, G. J., & Shaheen, E. (1984). Environmental failure to thrive: A clinical view. *Journal of Pediatrics, 71,* 639–644.

Beavers, J., & Hampson, R. B. (1986). Coping in families with a retarded child. *Family Process, 25,* 365–378.

Berger, D. (1979). Child abuse simulating apparent "near miss" sudden infant death syndrome. *Journal of Pediatrics, 95,* 554–556.

Berkowitz, L. (1974). Some determinants of impulsive aggression: Role of uneducated associations with reinforcement for aggression. *Psychological Review, 81,* 165–176.

Billings, A. G., & Moos, R. H. (1981). The role of coping responses and social resources in attenuating the stress of life events. *Journal of Behavioral Medicine, 4,* 139–157.

Bithoney, W. G., & Rathbun, J. M. (1983). Failure to thrive. In M. D. Levine, W. B. Carey, A. C. Crocker, & R. T. Gross (Eds.), *Developmental behavioral pediatrics,* (pp. 552–557). Philadelphia, PA: W. B. Saunders.

Boat, B. W., & Everson, M . D. (1986). *Using anatomical dolls: Guidelines for interviewing young children in sexual abuse investigations.* Chapel Hill, NC: University of North Carolina.

Bolton, F. G., & MacEachron, A. (1986). Assessing child maltreatment risk in the recently divorced parent-child relationship. *Journal of Family Violence, 1,* 259–275.

Brassard, M. R., Germain, R., & Hart, S. N. (1987). *Psychological maltreatment of children and youth.* New York: Pergamon Press.

Brown, G. W., & Harris, T. (1978). *Social origins of depression: A study of psychiatric disorder in women.* London: Tavistock Publications.

Browne, D. H. (1986). The role of stress in the commission of subsequent acts of child abuse and neglect. *Journal of Family Violence, 1,* 289–297.

Caffey, J. (1946). Multiple fractures in long bones of children suffering from chronic subdural hematoma. *American Journal of Roentgenology and Radium Therapy, 56,* 163–173.

Caplan, A., & Cohen, C. B. (1987). Imperiled newborns. *Hastings Center Report, 17,* 5–32.

Child Abuse Program (1988). *Annual Report 1986–1987.* Columbus, OH: Children's Hospital.

Christ, A. E., & Flomenhaft, K. (Eds.). (1982). *Psychosocial family interventions in chronic pediatric illness.* New York: Plenum Press.

Cohen, J. A., & Mannarino, A. P. (1988). Psychological symptoms in sexually abused girls. *Child Abuse and Neglect, 12,* 571–577.

Cole, J. (1985). Infant stimulation re-examined: An environmental and behavioral based approach. *Neonatal Network, 3,* 24–30.

Coulter, M. L., Runyan, D. K., Everson, M. D., Edelsohn, G. A., & King, N. M. P. (1985). Conflicting needs and interests of researchers and service providers in child sexual abuse cases. *Child Abuse and Neglect, 9,* 535–542.

deMause, L. (1974). The evolution of childhood. In L. deMause (Ed.), *The history of childhood* (pp. 1–74). New York: Psychohistory Press.

Diamond, L. J., & Jaudes, P. K. (1983). Child abuse in a cerebral palsied population. *Developmental Medicine in Child Neurology, 25,* 169–174.

d'Orban, P. (1979). Women who kill their children. *British Journal of Psychiatry, 134,* 560–571.

Drotar, D. (1989). Behavioral diagnosis in non-organic failure-to-thrive: A critique and suggested approach to psychological assessment. *Developmental and Behavioral Pediatrics, 10,* 48–55.

Duhaime, A. C., Gennarelli, T. A., Thibault, L. E., Derek, B. A., Margulies, S. S., & Wiser, R. (1987). The shaken baby syndrome. *Journal of Neurosurgery, 66,* 409–415.

Dykes, L. J. (1986). The whiplash shaken infant syndrome: What has been learned? *Child Abuse and Neglect, 10,* 211–221.

Ellerstein, N. S. (Ed.). (1981). *Child abuse and neglect.* New York: John Wiley.

Elwell, M. E., & Ephross, P. H. (1987). Initial reactions of sexually abused children. *Social Casework, 68,* 109–116.

Faller, K. C. (1984). Is the child victim of sexual abuse telling the truth? *Child Abuse and Neglect, 8,* 473–481.

Famularo, R., Kinscherff, R., & Fenton, T. (1988). Propranolol treatment for childhood post-traumatic stress disorder, acute type: A pilot study. *American Journal of Diseases of Children, 142,* 1244–1247.

Farber, E. D., Kinast, C., McCoard, W. D., & Falkner, D., (1984). Violence in families of adolescent runaways. *Child Abuse and Neglect, 18,* 295–299.

Farrington, K. (1980). Stress and family violence. In M. A. Straus & G. T. Hotaling (Eds.), *The social causes of husband-wife violence* (pp. 94–114). Minneapolis, MN: University of Minnesota Press.

Finkelhor, D. (1987a). The sexual abuse of children: Current research reviewed. *Psychiatric Annals, 17,* 233–241.

Finkelhor, D. (1987b). The trauma of child sexual abuse: Two models. *Journal of Interpersonal Violence, 2,* 348–366.

Fouras, G., & Johnson, C. F. (In press). Development of a formula to analyze severity of injury in child abuse. *Pediatric Emergency Care.*

Frodi, A. M., & Lamb, M. E. (1980). Child abuser's response to infant smiles and cries. *Child Development, 51,* 238–241.

Futcher, J. A. (1988). Chronic illness and family dynamics. *Pediatric Nursing, 14,* 381–385.

Gelles, R. (1987). The family and its role in the abuse of children. *Psychiatric Annals, 17,* 229–232.

Gelles, R. J., & Straus, M. A. (1987). Is violence toward children increasing? *Journal of Interpersonal Violence, 2,* 212–222.

Goldbloom, R. B. (1982). Failure to thrive. *The Pediatric Clinics of North America, 29,* 151–165.

Goldson, E., Fitch, M. J., Wendell, T. A., & Knapp, G. (1978). Child abuse: Its relationship to birth weight, Apgar score, and developmental testing. *American Journal of Diseases of Children, 132,* 790–793.

Green, A. H. (1983). Child abuse: Dimension of psychological trauma in abused children. *Journal of The American Academy of Child Psychiatry, 22,* 231–237.

Green, A. H. (1988). Child maltreatment and its victims: A comparison of physical and sexual abuse. *Psychiatric Clinics of North America, 11,* 591–610.

Grof, S. (1976). *Realm of the human unconscious.* New York: Dutton.

Guandolo, V. (1985). Munchausen syndrome by proxy: An outpatient challenge. *Pediatrics, 75,* 526–530..

Heidelise, A., Lawhon, G., Brown, E., Gibes, R., Duffy, F. H., McAnulty, G., & Blickman, J. G. (1986). Individualized behavioral and environmental care for the very low birth weight preterm infant at high risk for bronchopulmonary dysplasia: Neonatal intensive care unit and developmental outcome. *Pediatrics, 78,* 1123–1132.

Hinton, P. (1978). What kind of cot death? *British Medical Journal, 1,* 1345.

Hobbs, N., Perrin, J. M., & Ireys, H. T. (1985). *Chronically ill children and their families.* San Francisco: Jossey-Bass Publishers.

Holmes, D. L., Nagy, J. N., Slaymaker, F., Sosnowski, R. J., Prinz, S. M., & Pasternak, J. F. (1982). Early influences of prematurity, illness and prolonged hospitalization on infant behavior. *Developmental Psychology, 18,* 744–750.

Hvizdala, E. V., & Gellady, A. M. (1978). Intentional poisoning of two siblings by prescription drugs. *Clinical Pediatrics, 17,* 480–482.

Johnson, C. F. (1983). Sudden infant death syndrome vs. child abuse: The teenage connection. *Journal of Pedodontics, 7,* 196–208.

Johnson, C. F. (1986). Children's Hospital nuclear warhead bomb. *Pediatrics, 77,* 137.

Johnson, C. F., & Coury, D. L. (1988). Bruising and hemophilia: Accident or child abuse? *Child Abuse and Neglect, 12,* 409–415.

Johnson, C. F., Loxterkamp, D., & Albanese, M. (1982). Effects of high school students knowledge of child development and child health approaches to child discipline. *Pediatrics, 69,* 559–563.

Johnson, C. F., & Showers, J. (1985). Injury variables in child abuse. *Child Abuse and Neglect, 9,* 207–215.

Kagan, J. (1983). Stress and coping in early development. In N. Garmezy & M. Rutter (Eds.), *Stress, coping, and development in children* (pp. 191–216). New York: McGraw-Hill.

Kalmuss, D. (1984). The intergenerational transmission of marital aggression. *Journal of Marriage and the Family, 46,* 11–19.

Kazak, A. E. (1986). Families with physically handicapped children: Social ecology and family systems. *Family Process, 25,* 265–281.

Kempe, C. H., Silverman, F. H., Steele, B. F., Droegmueller, W., & Silver, H. K. (1962). The battered child syndrome. *Journal of American Medical Association, 181,* 17–24.

Kinard, E., & Klerman, L. (1980). Teenage parenting and child abuse: Are they related? *American Journal of Orthopsychiatry, 50,* 481–488.

Klein, M., & Stern, L. (1971). Low birth weight and the battered child syndrome. *American Journal of Diseases of Children, 122,* 15–18.

Kolko, D. J., Moser, J. T., & Weldy, S. R. (1988). Behavioral/emotional indicators of sexual abuse in child psychiatric inpatients: A controlled comparison with physical abuse. *Child Abuse and Neglect, 12,* 529–541.

Krieger, I., & Sargent, D. A. (1967). A postural sign in the sensory deprivation syndrome of infants. *Journal of Pediatrics, 70,* 332–335.

Ladson, S., Johnson, C. F., & Doty, R. E. (1987). Do physicians recognize sexual abuse? *American Journal of Diseases of Children, 141,* 411–415.

Landau, H. R., Salus, M. K., Stiffarm, T., & Kalb, N. L. (1980). *Child protection: The role of the courts.* Washington, DC: U.S. Government Printing Office.

Lavigne, J., & Ryan, M. (1979). Psychologic adjustment of siblings of children with chronic illness. *Pediatrics, 63,* 616–627.

Lawhon, G., & Melzar, A. (1988). Developmental care of the very low birth weight infant. *The Journal of Perinatal and Neonatal Nursing, 2,* 56–65.

Lawson, K., Dawn, C., & Turkewitz, G. (1977). Environmental characteristics of a neonatal intensive-care unit. *Child Development, 48,* 1633–1639.

Leonard, M. F., Rhymes, J. P., & Solnit, A. J. (1966). Failure to thrive in infants: A family problem. *American Journal of Diseases of Children, 111,* 600–612.

Letourneau, C. (1981). Empathy and stress: How they affect parental aggression. *Social Work, 26,* 383–389.

Lopez, C. J. (1983). Early experiences of premature infants and their providers: Psychodynamic and environmental factors in the neonatal intensive care. *Zero to Three, Bulletin of the National Center for Clinical Infant Programs, 2,* 7–11.

MacFarlane, K., & Krebs, S. (1986). Techniques for interviewing and gathering evidence. In K. MacFarlane, J. Waterman, S. Conerly, L. Damon, M. Durfee, & S. Long (Eds.), *Sexual abuse of young children: Evaluation and treatment* (pp. 67–100). New York: Guilford Press.

MacKenzie, T. B., Nagel, T. C., & Rothman, B. K. (1986). Case studies—When a pregnant woman endangers her fetus. *Hastings Center Report, 16,* 24–26.

Maiuro, R. D., & Eberle, J. A. (1989). New developments in research on aggression: An international report. *Violence and Victims, 4,* 3–15.

Maloni, J. A., Stegman, C. E., Taylor, P. M., & Brownell, C. A. (1986). Validation of infant behavior identified by neonatal nurses. *Nursing Research, 35,* 133–138.

McAndrew, I. (1976). Children with a handicap and their families: Child care. *Health and Development, 2,* 213–237.

McGuire, T. L., & Feldman, K. W. (1989). Psychologic morbidity of children subjected to Munchausen syndrome by proxy. *Pediatrics, 83,* 289–292.

McKeever, P. (1983). Siblings of chronically ill children: A literature review with implications for research and practice. *American Journal of Orthopsychiatry, 53,* 281–289.

McLeer, S. V., Deblinger, E., Atkins, M. S., Foa, E. B., & Ralphe, D. L. (1988). Post-traumatic stress disorder in sexually abused children. *Journal of the American Academy of Child and Adolescent Psychiatry, 27,* 650–654.

Milgram, N. A. (1982). War related stress in Israeli children and youth. In L. Goldberger and S. Breznitz (Eds.), *Handbook of stress: Theoretical and clinical aspects* (pp. 656–676). New York: The Free Press.

Mori, A. A. (1983). *Families of children with special needs: Early intervention techniques for the practitioner.* Rockville, MD: Aspen Systems.

Morris, J. L., Johnson, C. F., & Clasen, M. (1985). To report or not to report: Physician's attitudes toward discipline and child abuse. *American Journal of Diseases of Children, 139,* 194–197.

Mouzakitis, C. M. (1985). Interviewing in child protection. In C. M. Mouzakitis & R. Varghese (Eds.), *Social work treatment with abused and neglected children* (pp. 226–245). Springfield, IL: Charles C. Thomas.

Mouzakitis, C. M., & Varghese, R. (1985). Child abuse and neglect: An international perspective. In C. M. Mouzakitis and R. Varghese (Eds.), *Social work treatment with abused and neglected children* (pp. 17–34). Springfield, IL: Charles C. Thomas.

Mullins, J. B. (1986). The relationship between child abuse and handicapping conditions. *Journal of School Health, 56,* 134–136.

Murphy, L. B. (1974). Coping, vulnerability, and resilience in childhood. In G. V. Coelho, D. A. Hamburg, & J. E. Adams (Eds.), *Coping and adaptation* (pp. 69–100). New York: Basic Books.

National Committee for Prevention of Child Abuse (NCPCA). (1988, August).

NCPCA Memorandum: Study of the national incidence and prevalence of child abuse and neglect. Chicago, IL.

Newberger, E. H. (1983). The helping hand strikes again: Unintended consequences of child abuse report. *Journal of Clinical Psychology, 12,* 307–311.

Newberger, E. H., Newberger, C. M., & Hampton, R. L. (1983). Child abuse: The current theory base and future research needs. *Journal of the American Academy of Child and Adolescent Psychiatry, 22,* 262–268.

Newman, L. F. (1981). Social and sensory environment of low birth weight infants in a special care nursery: An anthropological investigation. *Journal of Nervous and Mental Disease, 169,* 448–455.

Nicol, A. R., & Eccles, M. (1985). Psychotherapy for Munchausen syndrome by proxy. *Archives of Diseases of Children, 60,* 344–348.

Oates, R. K., Davis, A. A., & Ryan, M. G. (1980). Predictive factors for child abuse. *Australian Paediatric Journal, 16,* 239–243.

Pardeck, J. T. (1983). An empirical analysis of behavioral and emotional problems of foster children as related to re-placement in care. *Child Abuse and Neglect, 7,* 75–78.

Parks, R. M. (1977). Parental reactions to the birth of a handicapped child. *Health and Social Work, 2,* 51–66.

Passman, R. H., & Mulhern, R. K. (1977). Maternal punitiveness as affected by situational stress: An experimental analogue of child abuse. *Journal of Abnormal Psychology, 86,* 565–569.

Pearlin, L. I., & Schooler, C. (1978). The structure of coping. *Journal of Health and Social Behavior, 19,* 2–21.

Pitman, R. K. (1989). Post-traumatic stress disorder, hormones, and memory. *Biological Psychiatry, 26,* 221–223.

Reite, M., & Caine, N. (1983). *Child abuse: The non-human primate data: Monographs in primatology* (Vol. 1). New York: Liss.

Rice, R. D. (1985). Infant stress and the relationship to violent behavior. *Neonatal Network, 3,* 39–43.

Richards, I., & McIntosh, H. (1972). Confidential injury to 226 consecutive infant deaths. *Archives of Diseases of Children, 47,* 697–706.

Rogers, D., Tripp, J., Bentovim, A., Robinson, A., Berry, D., & Goulding, R. (1976). Non-accidental poisoning: An extended syndrome of child abuse. *British Medical Journal, 1,* 793–796.

Rosen, C. L., Frost, J. D., Bricker, T., Tarnow, J. D., Gillette, P. C., & Dunlavy, S. (1983). Two siblings with recurrent cardiorespiratory arrest: Munchausen syndrome by proxy or child abuse? *Pediatrics, 71,* 715–720.

Rosenberg, D. A. (1987). Web of deceit: A literature review of Munchausen syndrome by proxy. *Child Abuse and Neglect, 11,* 547–563.

Rosenn, D. W., Loeb, L. S., & Jura, M. D. (1980). Differentiation of organic from non-organic failure to thrive syndrome in infancy. *Pediatrics, 66,* 698–704.

Runyan, D. K., Everson, M. D., Edelsohn, G. A., Hunter, W. M., & Coulter, M. L.

(1988). Impact of legal intervention on sexually abused children. *Journal of Pediatrics, 113,* 647–653.

Rusch, R. G., Hall, J. C., & Griffin, H. C. (1986). Abuse-provoking characteristics of institutionalized mentally retarded individuals. *American Journal of Mental Deficiency, 90,* 618–624.

Schinke, S. P., Schilling, R. F., Barth, R. P., Gilchrist, L. D., & Maxwell, J. S. (1986). Stress-management intervention to prevent family violence. *Journal of Family Violence, 1,* 13–26.

Schultz, L. G. (1980). Diagnosis and treatment: An introduction. In L. G. Schultz (Ed.), *The sexual victimology of youth* (pp. 39–42). Springfield, IL: Charles C. Thomas.

Seifert, K., Thompson, T., tenBensel, R. W., & Hunt, C. (1983). Perinatal stress: A study of factors linked to the risk of parenting problems. *Health and Social Work, 8,* 107–121.

Shindler, F., & Arkowitz, H. (1986). The assessment of mother-child interactions in physically abusive and non-abusive families. *Journal of Family Violence, 1,* 247–257.

Showers, J., & Johnson, C. F. (1984). Student's knowledge of child health and development: Effects on approaches to discipline. *Journal of School Health, 54,* 122–125.

Showers, J., & Johnson, C. F. (1985). Child development, child health and child rearing knowledge among urban adolescents: Are they adequately prepared for the challenges of parenthood? *Health Education, 16,* 37–41.

Smith, S., Hanson, R., & Noble, S. (1973). Parents of battered babies: A controlled study. *British Medical Journal, 4,* 388–391.

Sneed, R. C., & Bell, R. F. (1976). The dauphin of Munchausen: Factitious passage of renal stones in a child. *Pediatrics, 58,* 127–129.

Solomon, T. (1973). History and demography of child abuse. *Pediatrics, 51,* 773–776.

Straus, M. A. (1974). Leveling, civility, and violence in the family. *Journal of Marriage and the Family, 36,* 13–29.

Straus, M. A. (1980). Stress and physical child abuse. *Child Abuse and Neglect, 4,* 75–88.

Straus, M. A., Gelles, R. J., & Steinmetz, S. K. (1980). *Behind closed doors: Violence in the American family.* Garden City, NY: Anchor Press/Doubleday.

Sze, W., & Lamar, B. (1981). Causes of child abuse: A reexamination. *Health and Social Work, 6,* 19–25.

Task Force on Child Abuse and Neglect (1988). Public disclosure of private information about victims of abuse. *Pediatrics, 82,* 387.

Thomas, A., & Chess, S. (1984). Genesis and evolution of behavior disorders: From infancy to early adult life. *American Journal of Psychiatry, 141,* 1–9.

Touflexis, A. (1989, February 6). The lasting wounds of divorce. *Time, 133,* 61.

Tylden, E. (1978). What kind of cot death? *British Medical Journal, 1,* 1345.

Tyler, A. H., & Brassard, M. R. (1984). Abuse in the investigation and treatment of intrafamilial child sexual abuse. *Child Abuse and Neglect, 8,* 47–53.

Walker, C. E., Bonner, B. L., & Kaufman, K. L. (1988). *The physically and sexually abused child: Evaluation and treatment.* New York: Pergamon Press.

Walker, L. E. (1984). *The battered woman syndrome.* New York: Springer.

Waller, D. (1983). Obstacles to the treatment of Munchausen syndrome by proxy. *Journal of American Academy of Child Psychiatry, 22,* 80–85.

Widom, C. S. (1989). The cycle of violence. *Science, 244,* 160–166.

Wolfe, D. A. (1987). *Child abuse: Implications for child development and child psychopathology.* Newbury Park, CA: Sage Publications.

Wolfe, D. A., Jaffe, P. J., Wilson, S. K., & Zak, L. (1985). Children of battered women: The relation of child behavior to family violence and maternal stress. *Journal of Consulting and Clinical Psychology, 53,* 657–665.

Yates, A., & Musty, T. (1988). Preschool children's erroneous allegations of sexual molestation. *American Journal of Psychology, 145,* 989–992.

CHAPTER ELEVEN

The Stress of Violence: School, Community, and World

Daniel J. Christie
Beverly G. Toomey

Support for the research on the threat of nuclear war reported herein was provided by a grant by the Ohio Department of Mental Health, OSURF 721387.

Children growing up in the world today are frequently exposed to local, national, and world problems: violence, poverty, crime, hunger, drug abuse, and threats of war. The concerns of youth have changed from generation to generation. Annually since 1975, approximately 17,000 high school seniors have been administered questionnaires by the Survey Research Center of the University of Michigan. The questionnaires are designed to monitor young people's worries, concerns, and aspirations. Today's youth, when compared to samples from the mid-1970s, are less concerned with issues such as population growth, pollution, and energy shortages. They have remained quite highly concerned about crime, economic problems, and drug abuse. Worries about hunger, poverty, and race relations have not changed much over the years and remain a relatively low priority. What is most astounding is the dramatic increase in worry about the chance of nuclear war, a worry that hit its peak in 1982 and remained quite high at least until 1987 (Bachman, 1989), the year in which relations between the superpowers warmed significantly.

The everyday life experiences of children in some parts of the world include exposure to large-scale, life-threatening, institutionalized violence. Children in the United States today, unlike children in Northern Ireland or the West Bank, live in a country that is relatively stable and free from direct military confrontations. Yet, for many American children, the threat of nuclear war is salient among their concerns and represents a particular kind of stressor, threatening their sense of security.

This and the preceding chapter focus on violence and children. The term "violence" refers to the threat or actual use of force that may result in harm or injury to the child. Domestic violence is addressed in Chapter 10, and this chapter addresses "extramural" violence: in schools, communities, and the world. Violent acts represent a stressful intrusion into the child's life and may threaten the child's safety and security. The chapter is organized in a way that treats violent acts as stressors or independent variables that result in stress reactions. After reviewing school and community violence, childrens' reactions to the threat of world violence are examined.

SCHOOL AND COMMUNITY VIOLENCE

School and community violence are lumped together in one category deliberately because schools are embedded in communities. Figure 11.1 attempts to capture some hypothesized relationships between violence and children. The kinds of violence to which children might be exposed are many and varied—bullying, verbal harassment, name calling, etc. These violent acts may occur in either the school or in the surrounding

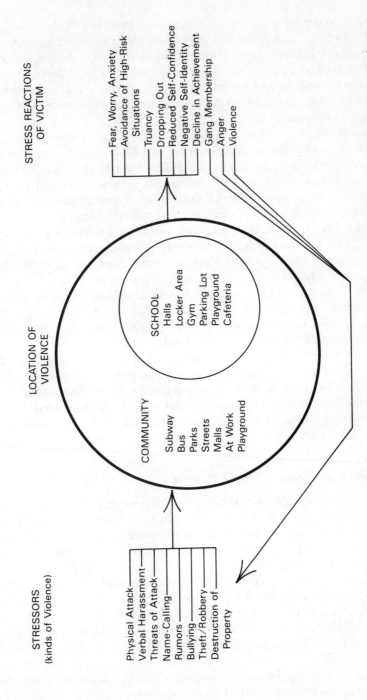

Figure 11.1. Various kinds of violence in school, community, or both produce stress reactions in children. At least three stress reactions—defensive gang membership, anger, and retaliatory violence—may lead to further violence.

community. In the figure, the school is represented as a circle embedded within the larger community; this is a geographic reality, and also makes the point that the kinds, perpetrators, and victims of violence are often the same in both settings. In the figure, a number of hypothesized stress reactions are presented, some of which (i.e., anger, gang membership, and violence) may produce vicious cycles as victims react in ways that perpetuate violent acts.

In general, while social and behavioral scientists have contributed a great deal to our understanding of ways in which certain forms of violence (e.g., television violence) affect children, little attention has been given to the impact of school and community violence on children. One unfortunate consequence is the difficulty of ascertaining trends in school and community violence over time, since meaningful baselines have not been established. Instead, the public receives through the popular press anecdotal and at times alarming reports of violence. Indeed, even a cursory review of the popular literature would lead one to expect that violence in the schools has reached crisis proportions.

With the exception of a few broad-based, carefully executed studies, the educational research literature offers little more than the popular literature. A short Department of Education (DOE) report, "Disorder in our Public Schools," was prepared in 1984. However, most of the report draws on data gathered in studies conducted in the 1970s. Among other points, the DOE report notes that more than 3 million crimes are committed in schools each month, with more than 282,000 students physically attacked (p. 5). The DOE report and others are examined here in more detail after a brief look at the way in which the popular press portrays school violence.

Popular Impressions of School Violence

Based on the popular press, it is estimated that on any given day 135,000 youngsters carry a gun to school in America ("These Perilous Halls," 1989). In 1987, in Boston, 55 young people were expelled and 300 were referred to a special program as a result of having a weapon in school ("Getting Tough," 1988).

In addition to violence committed by the schoolchildren themselves, outsiders also have used the school setting for irrational shooting sprees, killing children and teachers at random. In less than a year, beginning in the spring of 1988, three incidents—in Winnetka, Illinois; Stockton, California; and Greenwood, South Carolina—resulted in eight deaths and dozens wounded.

Nowadays, it is suggested, children go to school with greater awareness of violence in society, and acts of violence are increasingly spilling over into the "Halls of Ivy." It also is commonly believed that the increasing problem of drugs is linked to the use of weapons and the resultant violence in and around schools. From such a perspective, the school climate is merely reflecting the increasing levels of violence in society as a whole. Other viewpoints attribute school violence to the increases in student rights, which have eroded the authority of the teacher and thereby caused disorder in the school. Regardless of causal explanations, there seems to be a widespread perception in the popular press that problems of discipline and disorder in schools have become more serious, shifting in the last twenty years from minor incidents such as running in the halls to major crimes like assault and murder.

Scientific Research Literature

A review of the scholarly literature on violence and children presents a slightly different picture. While they recognize serious violence in some schools, educators and criminologists raise two questions to put this problem in perspective: (1) What is the prevalence of crime and violent behavior in the schools? and (2) Has the incidence of crime and violence increased in recent years?

The DOE's 1984 report, "Disorder in our Public Schools," could lead one to conclude that there is a significant amount of serious violence in the schools. However, some educators have criticized the alarmist tone of the report and have challenged the idea that crime is rampant in the schools. In an editorial in *The School Administrator,* Joseph Scherer and Jim Stimson (1984) wrote that the "crime" documented in the report includes relatively few serious crimes. For instance, in the crimes-against-people classification, robbery through force or threat is perhaps the most serious offense; "only" 120,000 of the 3 million crimes were in this category. Hence, in the 1984 report, lesser incidents of disruption have been classified with crime and violence. While student language and disrespectful behaviors are problematic in the schools, they should not be confused with crime or violence.

Challenging the notion that violence is a new phenomenon in public schools, Becker (1983) suggests that today's violence is consistent with a history of disorder in public schools. As long ago as 1843, Horace Mann noted that since there was no real curriculum, idleness and disorder were common, as was corporal punishment. In early times only the well-off sent their children to school. As education expanded, more children attended. Newman (1980) has noted that as public education reached a greater percentage of children, and as the number of years children stayed in school increased, the incidence of crime also increased. In the first quarter of this century, up to 75% of American children between the ages of 5 and 18 were in school. In this period, *The New York Times* (1917) reported riots in New York City schools in which "mobs of more than

5,000 students confronted the police in running battles" (p. 45). Westin (1970) also documented this pattern in education. Using major newspapers as his source, he identified a "continual stream of student protests and disruptions" between 1870 and 1950.

Rubel (1978) has cautioned that record keeping on disorder and crime in the schools is problematic. Definitions of offenses are unclear, so aggregating data across schools is methodologically unsound, and making comparisons between periods of time are tentative at best. Nevertheless, Rubel has identified two general areas of crime: those against property and those against persons. He reports that assaults against teachers almost tripled from 1957 to 1975, with a rate of 52 teachers per thousand assaulted. However, if petty theft and vandalism are excluded, serious violence such as teacher assaults (.5%) and student assaults (1.3%) occur in less than 2% of schools. Taken together, the foregoing research suggests several tentative conclusions: violence is not new to the public schools; it probably has increased over time; it often is exaggerated by the media; and it is largely understudied by educators and criminologists as well as social and behavioral scientists.

School Violence as a Stressor of Children

While it is possible to find some research on the causes and proposed remedies for the problem of violence, there is a paucity of research on the consequences of violence on children. Harlan and McDowell (1981) label the consequences of violence, such as fear in children, as "iceberg" issues: "One can sense that fear has an effect on the teaching-learning process, but there is [sic] very little data in the literature of crime in the schools that addresses this point" (p. 224).

There are two major surveys that have asked children about their concerns. The *Violent Schools—Safe Schools* study of the National Institute of Education (NIE) was conducted in junior and senior high schools in 1976–1977. Students were asked if they avoided places around school because they felt they would be hurt or bothered in those places. Thirty-eight percent of the youth acknowledged at least one such place in their school environment. Furthermore, 20% said they were afraid at least some of the time in school. Another 4% admitted that they had stayed home to avoid being hurt or bothered at school. Educators have noted that such fears can include not only fear of physical harm but also of insults, verbal abuse, and racial slurs (National Institute of Education, 1977).

A 1974 study of Philadelphia youngsters generally corroborates the findings of the NIE study with respect to the pervasiveness of fear associated with violence in and around schools. In the Philadelphia study, 54% of the boys felt the streets to and from school were dangerous; 44% felt

this was true of schoolyards, and 21% felt the schoolrooms were dangerous (Bayh, 1979).

At about the same time the NIE study was being conducted, a second
major study of violence and children was being undertaken by Hepburn
and Monti (1979). These investigators surveyed 1,799 junior and senior
high students in St. Louis and found that 40% felt afraid that they might
be hurt or bothered at school. Similarly, Carriere (1979) studied drop-
outs and found that 18% of males and 7% of females reported they
missed school because they were intimidated by would-be attackers. Of
the 750,000 youth that drop out of school each year, perhaps as many as
100,000 drop out because of fear.

Reviewing the St. Louis and NIE studies, McDermott (1980) suggests a
relationship between prior victimization and current fear. Not surprisingly, she also notes that the greater the amount of crime, the greater the
amount of apprehension even by non-victims. Fear of crime in school is
also related to fear of crime in general and to living in a high-crime area.
These findings are consistent with other findings indicating that schools
in high-crime, lower socioeconomic areas have more school violence
(Brodbelt, 1978).

In another paper, McDermott (1983) posits an interaction between
fear, victimization, and the perpetration of violence in the school and
community. As illustrated in Figure 11.2, McDermott proposes that there

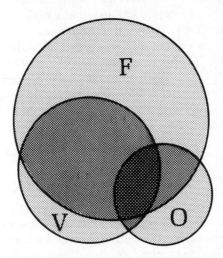

Figure 11.2. Overlap of subsets of a community's youth population: offenders
(O), victims (V), and fearful youth (F). [From McDermott, J. (1983). Crime in the
schools and in the community: Offenders, victims, and fearful youth. *Crime and
Delinquency, 29*(2), 270–282. Reprinted by permission of Sage Publications Inc.,
Copyright 1983.]

exist three groups with overlapping membership: fearful youths, offending youths, and victimized youths. She suggests that when youngsters are victimized and fearful, they may become perpetrators themselves out of anger about their own victimization. She also makes the point that victims may join youth gangs to build a sense of security and hedge against their fear. Thus, fear contributes to defensiveness and additional crime. Moreover, she insists these factors be viewed in the context of the problem of violence in the wider community.

Internal attributes of schools, like size and quality of the facility, are related to the incidence of violence. Larger schools and those with poor facilities seem to encourage more violent behavior (Brodbelt, 1978). And while inner-city youngsters appear most at risk, suburban schools are also beginning to encounter higher rates of violence (Bayh, 1979).

As a general rule, there is more crime and more fear of violence in secondary schools than in primary schools. High school girls are more fearful than boys, but in younger age groups, the levels of apprehension are similar between the groups. Data on differences in levels of fear by racial groups are inconclusive. The NIE study found minorities more fearful, but the St. Louis study concluded the opposite. In general, however, fear of crime is reported more by blacks than whites (McDermott, 1980). Studies by Angelino, Dolins, and Mech (1956) as well as the work by Jersild and Holmes (1935) indicate children from lower socioeconomic classes have more fears and tend to fear crime and violence more than middle-class youngsters. Fear may be a rational response because these youngsters usually live in neighborhoods where there is more crime to fear. Further analyses indicate that children who are more fearful may have less supportive parents and fewer connections through friendships. This is especially true for students new to a school. In short, children's fears of crime and violence in school appear clearly related to their direct experience with victimization and their secondary contact with others who have been victims (McDermott, 1983).

Developmental Perspective on Fear of School Violence

It seems likely that the fear of harm may inhibit the critical tasks of middle childhood: industry, achievement, and a sense of self-confidence. Adolescents attempting to consolidate a sense of identity and self-worth may be hampered in these important developments by failing to perceive fear as normal and acceptable. Instead, they may run the risk of accepting a negative self-identity. It also seems plausible that self-deprecation for lack of courage or lack of power may have a permanent effect at this time. This may be particularly true if parents are not aware of or responsive to the child's embarrassment. Negative consequences include lower indicated by research activity and publications tends to vary with public interest in the issue (Polyson, Hillmar, & Kriek, 1986).

Much of the research in the 1980s investigated the impact of the nuclear threat on children and adolescents. Studies have been completed in several countries, and taken together they suggest that children are aware of the threat of nuclear war and are concerned about the possibility of nuclear war (Beardslee & Mack, 1982; Chivian et al., 1985; Escalona, 1982; Goldberg et al., 1985; Goldenring & Doctor, 1983; Schwebel, 1982).

In a sense, the nuclear threat represents a stressor of a unique kind, one that is at once both an abstraction and a highly salient possibility to some individuals, particularly in view of the vast overkill potential that is stockpiled by the superpowers. Nuclear technology has transformed the nature of war. Children, youth, and adults all realize that life as we know it could be destroyed. The problem for children is a triple realization: the realization of the potentially devastating effects of nuclear war combined with the realizations that they are unable to protect themselves and that adults also are unable to protect them. The child's problem is embedded in the larger context of the family and the difficulty family members have coping with the threat of annihilation. Indeed, to adequately conceptualize the problem, one must examine the historical, technological, political, and psychological forces that have come together to spawn the nuclear threat. This is not to suggest that the nuclear problem is hopelessly intractable; rather, adults who want to deal with the issue in an honest way with children will have to be prepared for some tough questions about a complex and multidimensional problem.

Developmental Perspective on Fears and the Nuclear Threat

From a developmental perspective, it seems likely that childrens' thoughts, feelings, and coping strategies vary with age; however, in the available data only a rough outline of developmental changes can be discerned. The antecedents of child and adolescent fear may be found in early infancy, a time when most infants discriminate between familiar and unfamiliar persons and form an attachment to the primary caregiver. Although heightened fearfulness of strangers near the end of the infant's first year of life varies in intensity from infant to infant, the phenomenon seems nearly universal; for example, it has been found among Israeli, Guatemalan, and African infants (Kagan, 1976; Kagan, Kearsley, & Zelazo, 1978).

In early childhood, fears become associated with children's capacity to imagine and conceptualize, as contrasted with earlier developmental periods when fear responses were elicited by specific external stimuli (Jersild & Holmes, 1935). The fears of early childhood include those associated with ghosts and monsters. At about the same time, children

grades, absenteeism, truancy, and even dropping out of school (Carr
1979).

WORLD VIOLENCE: THREAT OF NUCLEAR WAR

Before discussing the implications and possibilities for prevention
amelioration of the stress of violence, we review data about the thre
nuclear war.

The Wax and Wane of Concerns about Nuclear War

The percentage of high school seniors who report that they w
"often" about the possibility of nuclear war quadrupled from 7% in
to 30% in 1982. During the same time period, the percentage of
school youth who indicated pessimism about the prospects of sui
varied between 20% and 30%; in particular, these youth "agreed
"mostly agree" with the proposition that nuclear or biological ann
tion probably will be the fate of all mankind, and within their life
(Bachman, 1983; Bachman, Johnson, & O'Malley, 1984).

These findings are not surprising when one considers that youth
were seniors in the early to mid 1980s essentially grew up during
some have dubbed "Cold War II"; indeed, relations between the s
powers became increasingly hostile since SALT I in 1972. Conside
example, one index of U.S.-Soviet relations—the doomsday clock o
cover of the *Bulletin of the Atomic Scientists.* The clock has come to sy
ize the nuclear threat hovering over humankind; the minute hand,
far from midnight, has advanced and retreated with the ebb and fl
relations between the nuclear superpowers. From 1981 to 1986, the
fluctuated within five minutes of doomsday, comparable to the
tions observed during the cold-war period of the early 1950s. It :
reasonable to assume that children and youth, not having directly
rienced historical freezes and thaws in U.S.-Soviet relations, quite
rally fear a nuclear war. In addition to not having a historical persp
on the wax and wane of the superpower relationship and the atte
threat of nuclear war, it seems likely that children have not develope
array of defenses that adults use to protect themselves against the ar
about annihilation (Lifton, 1979, 1982).

There is some evidence indicating that concern about nuclea
declined slightly in the latter part of the 1980s (Bachman, 1989)
worth noting that it is not only children and adolescents who se
respond to the political climate—so too do social and behavioral
tists, as well as mental health practitioners. Interest in nuclear iss

begin to develop the concept of nationalism and patriotism; they exhibit a strong attachment to their country, perceiving their country as benign, infallible, trustworthy, powerful, and superior to other countries. It has been suggested that children develop images of the enemy—the Soviet Union, for instance—that reinforce the notion of "us" versus "them." Distinguishing between us and them meets the child's need to develop a differentiated self rather than being fused with the environment as a drop of water is fused in a sea. The process of differentiation can be supported not only by distinguishing enemies from allies, but also by attaching to objects such as one's church, flag, and nation (Kohut, 1977; Volkan, 1985).

Since early childhood is dominated by egocentrism in that the child is unable to take another person's point of view (Flavell et al., 1981; Piaget, 1954), it seems likely that childrens' need for security is best met by reassuring them. Later, however, when children become better able to take various perspectives, it should be possible to discuss with them the notion of deterrence or countervailing forces—that one side would not attempt to harm the other for fear of retaliation.

While anecdotal and only suggestive, it is worth noting that one 10-year-old child seemed relieved to learn that a nuclear winter could engulf the earth after a nuclear war. He reasoned that the Russians wouldn't attack us because they would become victims of a nuclear winter, too. In a sense, this child was acquiring the notion of deterrence, albeit in an indirect way. While movement away from egocentrism would seem to be a necessary prerequisite for an understanding of deterrence, at present there is a paucity of research that examines the way in which perspective taking and other aspects of cognitive development affect childrens' perception of the threat of nuclear war.

At roughly middle childhood, if children verbalize their fears, adults will have to be prepared for very tough questions which challenge their capacity to protect children and to ensure their childrens' survival.

Some Interview and Survey Data

Precisely what can be said about the impact of the nuclear threat on children? A fair assessment, based primarily on interviews with children, is that children know about the threat, but scientists and practitioners have much to learn about how the threat affects them. Based on survey research, it is quite clear that American children are, by 12 years of age, well aware of the threat of nuclear war and that most of them are concerned about the possibility of nuclear war (Beardslee & Mack, 1982). Generally, their concern can be understood in terms of affective and cognitive responses characterized by fear, hopelessness, powerlessness, and denial (Christie, 1988).

In a number of studies, adolescents report that they *fear* the possibility of nuclear war (Escalona, 1982; Schwebel, 1982). Some have vivid images of nuclear warfare, images of their parents being dead, and dreams of world devastation.

Another theme that emerges from research on adolescents is their feelings of *hopelessness* about the future. They report their future seems uncertain or at risk because of the possibility of nuclear war (Beardslee & Mack, 1982; Goldberg et al., 1985). About half of the adolescents report that they expect nuclear war to occur within their lifetime (Chivian et al., 1985). On the basis of detailed interviews with 30 high school students, Goodman et al. (1983) suggest that nuclear death is a fate that adolescents have come to expect and that a pervasive sense of futurelessness impinges on their everyday lives.

In addition to fear and hopelessness, adolescents tend to feel *powerlessness* in the sense that they feel that they and others are unable to control or remove the threat of nuclear war (Escalona, 1982; Goldberg et al., 1985). And finally, a fourth theme that has been discovered with some consistency is the tendency for adolescents to suppress their thoughts of nuclear war; they report that they would feel miserable if they allowed themselves to think about it. Lifton (1982) has advanced the proposition that older children and adults defend against such fears by using *denial* or, more broadly, psychic numbing, which includes the unconscious mechanism of denial as well as a number of other ego defenses that block feelings.

Studies on the impact of the nuclear age on children and adolescents are not restricted to the United States. During the past few years, research has been conducted in Canada (Sommers et al., 1985), Finland (Solantaus, 1986), Malaysia (Christie & Zweigenhaft, 1989), the Soviet Union (Chivian et al., 1985), and Sweden (Holmborg & Bergstrom, 1985). As might be expected, differences across countries occur with respect to adolescents' opinions about the destructiveness of nuclear war and the possibility of preventing nuclear war. Usually, children and adolescents learn about nuclear war through the mass media. A robust set of relationships that is beginning to emerge across countries is that adolescents who worry frequently about the possibility of nuclear war tend to be optimistic about the prospect of preventing nuclear war (Goldenring & Doctor, 1983; Goldberg et al., 1985). Highly concerned adolescents also tend to be high achievers in school and tend to discuss their concerns with others (Goldberg et al., 1985; Solantaus, 1986).

Effects of the Threat of Nuclear War on Children

There is a great deal of variation in viewpoints with regard to how the nuclear threat affects children. It is possible to delimit two rather extreme positions. At one extreme is the opinion that the threat of nuclear war may actually alter childrens' personality development and distort normal processes of identity formation in adolescents. A stark conclusion of this position is that adolescents may internalize the notion that the way to survive is to trust no one and to destroy your opponents (Escalona, 1965). Escalona (1982) has argued that a social environment that tolerates or ignores the risk of total destruction promotes maladaptive patterns of personality functioning, such as powerlessness and cynical resignation.

Similarly, Newcomb (1986) has provided evidence suggesting that there are negative consequences due to living under the threat of nuclear war. He administered the Nuclear Attitudes Questionnaire to 722 young adults who had grown up in the nuclear age. High levels of nuclear anxiety as measured by the questionnaire were associated with "less purpose in life, less life satisfaction, more powerlessness, more depression, and more drug use" (p. 906). Alan Nelson (1985), a psychotherapist, concurs with the grim assessment of impact of the threat of nuclear war. Based on his experience in a clinical setting, he maintains that the threat of nuclear war leads to anger, anxiety, despair, bitterness, and, for young people, a hollow hedonism rooted in the expectation that the future is unlikely.

At the other extreme, Adelson and Finn (1985) have argued that the research on children and the threat of nuclear war is amateurish and politically motivated. Furthermore, they argue that if there are any effects, such effects are probably due to parents and teachers who have terrorized children by raising the nuclear issue. Coles (1985) offers a similar indictment and goes on to suggest that nuclear anxiety is likely to be most pronounced in—perhaps even limited to—upper-middle-class children who are not dealing with more pressing problems of financial difficulties or prejudice. Escalona (1965) also has suggested a relationship between social class and concern. Her overall impression based on questionnaires administered to 311 children is that lower-class children are more preoccupied than middle-class children with immediate concerns such as poverty, job scarcity, and hostile elements in the social environment (see Chapter 16), leaving less time and attention for more distant concerns.

It should be mentioned that there is no solid evidence supporting social class differences in adolescents' levels of concern (Diamond & Bachman, 1986); that is, when empirically examined with careful survey research, social class as indicated by various measures, including father's and mother's educational or income level, is not correlated with adolescents' level of concern.

Between the extreme positions—one which posits no effect and the other which argues that serious personality disorganization results from the threat—there is a more moderate position: that the threat of nuclear war may be a factor contributing to anxiety in children and youth (Schwebel, 1982). After all, only a small number of youngsters arrive at clinics with mental health problems directly attributable to the threat of nuclear war (Schwebel, 1965, 1982).

Coping with the Nuclear Threat: Stress Reactions

A wide variety of coping strategies, some adaptive and some more destructive to the child's efficient mastery of developmental tasks, may be used by children as they attempt to deal with the threat of nuclear war. It has been suggested that some children respond to the threat with *problems of impulse management,* by which is meant the inability to forego immediate gratification for longer term goals. Uncertain about the future, the child may adopt a "get it now" attitude. According to Beardslee and Mack (1982), their strongest finding was that children and youth experienced a "general unquiet or uneasiness about the future. . . ." (p. 89).

Others have encountered a related attitude, *anomie,* and its behavioral sequelae: Since I am going to die anyway, I might as well drop out, get high, and have indiscriminant sex (Goldenring & Doctor, 1983). Goldenring and Doctor (1983) suspect that 5–15% of their sample were very worried about the threat of nuclear war, so much so that they considered delaying plans for marriage and family life. Mack (1981) reports a similar trend with respect to doubts about planning a family. In short, some psychiatrists and psychologists suggest that the threat of nuclear war may make children and youth pessimistic about the future and less likely to develop a future orientation.

Some children express bitter *resentment* toward those in power who have brought the world to such a precarious balance of terror (Schwebel, 1982). Others experience a sense of *powerlessness* at a time when the development of a sense of mastery and achievement is critical. *Denial* is a common defense against anxiety for youth; they report that they would be miserable if they allowed themselves to think about the nuclear threat (Schwebel, 1982).

Repeated presentation of any stimulus leads to *habituation,* a psychophysiological process in which physiological responsivity to a specific stimulus gradually diminishes. It seems likely that over time a developing person would habituate to the threat of nuclear war. There are, of course, nuclear technology advances that occur periodically and effectively rekindle fear; however, habituation eventually runs its inevitable course (Milburn & Watman, 1982).

Another defense against fear is what Schwebel (1982) characterizes as a *macho* attitude: The fearful person maintains that "we'll win" or "we're smart enough to do them in before they get us" (p. 611).

In summary, some children and youth are fearful about nuclear war. Children may employ a variety of coping strategies and mental defense mechanisms, including denial, anomie, resentment of authority, and sometimes a macho attitude. They may experience uneasiness about the future, feel powerless, and may have little in the way of a future orientation.

The literature on children and the threat of nuclear war is replete with studies that allude to the umbrella term "nuclear anxiety" when describing the wide variety of reactions that youth may have in response to the threat. Diamond and Backman (1986) have made a convincing case for not treating "nuclear anxiety" as a unidimensional construct. At least two orthogonal components, and perhaps more, seem to underlie anxiety. In particular, they offer evidence for the importance of distinguishing between worry and despair. *Despair* characterizes those who believe that "nuclear or biological annihilation is likely and that the human race is not likely to come through these tough times" (p. 218). In contrast to despair, those who are *concerned* tend to worry about the risk of nuclear war; worry, in turn, is associated with interest in social issues. When correlating indices of concern and despair with mental health measures, only despair was found to yield significant effects. Despairing students were more likely to get into trouble, tended to dislike competition, and were absent from school more often than non-despairing students. Moreover, those students reporting despair had lower levels of self-esteem, tended to be dissatisfied with life, felt alienated from their countries, and tended to feel less able to control their life than non-despairing youth.

Another important factor influencing the ways in which children cope with the threat of nuclear war is the degree to which they feel that their actions make a difference, i.e., *self-efficacy.* Social and behavioral scientists have provided evidence for the proposition that perceived personal or collective efficacy differentiates those who are politically active from those who are not (Mohr, McLoughlin, & Silver, 1986; Smith, 1986; Tyler & McGraw, 1983). Notwithstanding the criticisms that have been leveled against studies which posit a relationship between personal efficacy and activism (Dyal & Morris, 1987), for practical purposes it is possible to hypothesize about some relationships between the constructs of personal efficacy, concern, and despair as they relate to the ways in which children cope with the threat of nuclear war.

Figure 11.3 suggests some tentative conceptual links between the child's perception of the threat of nuclear war, perception of self, and coping styles or stress reactions. The threat of nuclear war is represented as a stressor on the child. Salience of threat refers to the degree to which the child is concerned about nuclear war. Children who believe that their actions make a difference personally or politically would have higher levels of self-efficacy, while those who feel powerless would have a low

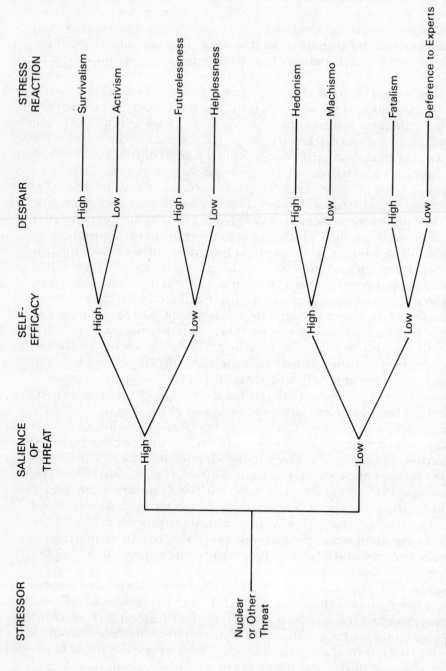

Figure 11.3. Some hypothesized relationships between the threat of nuclear war as a stressor and potential stress reactions of a child. Salience is partly cultural, partly the child's perception. Self-efficacy and despair are personality variables. See text for more explanation.

degree of self-efficacy. Finally, the degree to which the child believes that nuclear annihilation is likely is indicative of the degree of despair experienced by the child. The stress reactions depicted in the figure are inclusive of most of the kinds of reactions that have been reviewed in this chapter. Notice, for example, that the individual who holds an activist reaction or orientation would be characterized by a high degree of threat salience, high perceived self-efficacy, and a low level of despair.

Parents' Reactions to the Threat: Family Interactions

The reactions parents have to the threat also influence the developing child. There is some evidence, for example, of a significant relationship between parents expressing anxiety about nuclear war and their children expressing the same fear (Wrightsman, 1970). John Mack (1982) has made the point that adults also have feelings of powerlessness; they believe matters are out of their control. Since these feelings are not unlike the child's feelings, the adult may feel unable to help the child. Mack (1982) has argued that little can be done to help young people until the adults they depend on begin to address their own apathy and helplessness with respect to the arms race.

With respect to the family system, something akin to a "collective family secret" sometimes takes place in that everyone in the family knows about the threat of nuclear war but no one talks about it. Perhaps the silence is, in part, due to adults' use of denial as a mechanism that blocks feelings of fear and helplessness. It should be mentioned that adult denial is not based on ill intent, but rather is often a strategy that parents adopt to protect the child (Simon, 1984; Greenwald & Zeitlin, 1987). Moreover, the protective strategy of silence is mutual in the sense that some children learn to avoid challenging the helplessness of their parents. Such an analysis suggests that parents model the process of denial, and so it is not surprising to find the child adopting similar norms of behavior.

Figures 11.4 and 11.5 illustrate ways in which parents may try to protect their children regarding concerns about the threat of nuclear war. For example, if the child does not raise any concerns, parents may simply remain silent about the issue. This is shown in the vicious cycle of denial and feelings of powerlessness depicted in Figure 11.4. Figure 11.5 suggests that children who are able to discuss their concerns with adults gain an awareness of collective concern and, in turn, may develop an interest in political processes along with gaining a sense of self-efficacy.

An interesting relationship is beginning to emerge from data based on survey research (Chivian et al., 1985; Goldberg et al., 1985) and educational interventions (Christie & Nelson, 1988) with children and youth. In particular, these data indicate that frequent discussion or direct instruc-

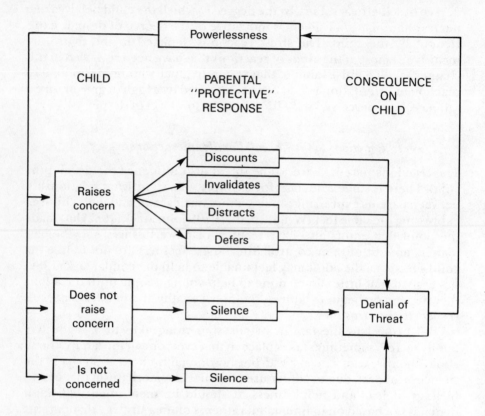

Figure 11.4. A hypothesized vicious cycle of parental "protective" responses and children's use of denial and sense of powerlessness.

tion about nuclear war is associated with more optimistic attitudes about the prospect of preventing nuclear war. Apparently, these children have a sense of efficacy—they believe that they and others can do something about the threat of nuclear war.

IMPLICATIONS FOR PROFESSIONAL INTERVENTION

School and Community Violence

In contrast to the threat of nuclear war, school and community violence are stressors that embody specific events that often directly impinge on the child and demand an adjustment on the part of the child. Accordingly, we would expect that training in social skills would be helpful. For

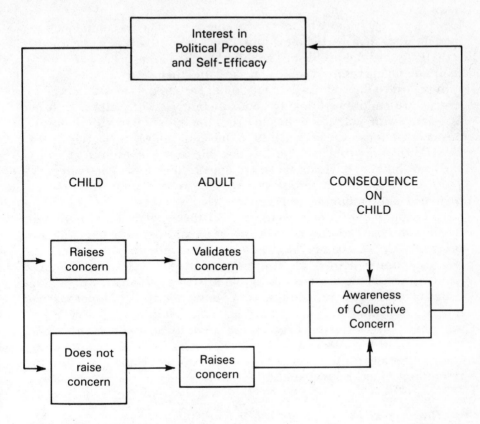

Figure 11.5. Hypothesized communication patterns between the child and adult that enhance the child's interest in political issues and sense of self-efficacy.

example, the fearful child might learn to avoid eye contact with certain individuals, not because he or she is foolish or cowardly, but because it is wise to do so. We have more to learn about the way in which some children prevent victimization while others present themselves as vulnerable to harassment.

It also might be worthwhile to encourage children to use resource persons, to tell someone about their particular problem. We should like to combat childrens' feelings of powerlessness by letting them actively deal with their concerns.

In addition to helping children learn behavioral strategies that effectively deal with violence, the child's emotional response to violence may require affirmation. Fear of the bully is a normal response. While parents may not know precisely what skills children need to cope with the problem, parents can share their *concern* about the children's welfare, thereby helping children bring their own coping strategies to bear on the problem. It is probably more beneficial for the child to have a compassionate model rather than one who exhibits a macho approach or a "be tough" attitude toward the problem. The difficulty for parents is in part due to their not having resolved some of these issues themselves.

In regard to the cognitive dimension of the child, it would be well to restructure children's thinking about themselves with respect to fears associated with violence. Being afraid of the bully is particularly insidious because it can cause the child to question self-worth. Certainly the child "owns the problem." Yet it is possible to teach children at a very early age that they have certain rights, one of which is personal integrity. They should know that no one has the right to harm them and to make them feel badly about themselves.

An encouraging development aimed at the reduction of school and community-based conflict and violence is the proliferation of mediation programs (cf. Cheatham, 1988). These programs are appearing in schools and communities across the country. Designed to teach ways of analyzing conflicts, managing those conflicts that arise, and resolving underlying issues that lead to conflict, these programs offer an additional mechanism to deal with the problem of violence. In addition to curricula that are primarily school-based (e.g., The Community Board Program, 1987), the American Bar Association has played a leading role in providing conferences and training related to both school and community dispute resolution (American Bar Association, 1988).

Dealing with the Threat of Nuclear War

It is probably clear that one bias running throughout this chapter is the importance placed on direct and honest communication as a means of breaking the silence that surrounds the nuclear issue. Adults might, for example, let children know that they too are afraid, that they care, and maybe even that they intend to do something about the problem. At a minimum, adults could let children know that childrens' fears are an understandable response to the threat of nuclear war. In these ways the child's fear is validated by an adult. It is O.K. to be afraid. Fear is the right emotion. Of course, hope also is needed.

Parents and professionals probably could do a better job of giving children hope for the future and confidence in their ability to shape their destinies. When asked if they "think nuclear war between the US and USSR can be prevented," 93.3% of the Soviet children say "yes," while only 65% of American children say "yes" (Chivian et al., 1985). Goldenring and Doctor (1983) indicate that one half of their sample of teens had never had the opportunity to talk with any adults about their fears. Goldenring and Doctor go on to suggest that a communication gap exists and currently is being filled by fear rather than hope. In various ways, such as active listening, children could be helped with their fears and, in the process, develop a sense of hope.

The importance of the children *actively* engaging in behaviors that are consistent with their convictions should be emphasized. For the nuclear issue, some children have written letters to the president. Others have joined the Children's Campaign for Nuclear Disarmament, an organization that encourages youngsters to have pen pals in the Soviet Union and to write directly to Soviet leaders. While such actions are unlikely to impact significantly on the arms race, the important point is that children perceive themselves as having done something about that which is bothering them. While the evidence at present is rather sparse, there is some research which underscores the value of perceived self-efficacy and the importance of engaging in issue-relevant behavior as means of enhancing mental health (Dyal & Morris, 1987).

Some of our characteristic *ways of thinking* remain maladaptive in the nuclear age. Jerome Frank (1982a, 1982b) has written about the importance of dispelling pro-nuclear thinking: more weapons mean more security; it's important to have superior nuclear forces. Actually, for deterrence to work, it is more rational to seek strategic parity. Further, children acquire an image of the enemy along with the implications that "we" are peace-loving and honorable while "they" are treacherous, cruel, and evil. A good-guy/bad-guy mentality of this kind probably plays a critical role in children's fear of nuclear war, for many countries have nuclear missiles and children are not afraid of all countries—certain ones, they are told, are friendly. We all share responsibility for what Morton Deutsch (1983) calls the malignant social process between the United States and the Soviet Union, a process that leaves both sides feeling more vulnerable and less secure despite defensive maneuvers.

Americans learn that the Soviets seek world domination, yet American scholars point out that such a position is largely an untestable assumption. There are curious mirror images between the attributions made by Americans and those made by ideologically equivalent persons in the Soviet Union. The ideological right in both countries argues that the other side is obstinate and imperialistic (Milburn, Stewart, & Herrmann, 1982). The media bear some of the responsibility for distorting images, since media coverage systematically highlights negative aspects of the other side. In the interest of intellectual honesty we should unilaterally counterbalance this with a representative sampling of Soviet life and behavior (cf. Cohen, 1984). This is not to suggest that Soviet motives are all or even typically benign, only that we all share the responsibility of dehumanizing enemy images that foster in-group/out-group distinctions and, at the same time, haunt many children.

The educational system could play a more active role in teaching children how to deal with fear. Children could begin to learn about nuclear issues so that they will be able to overcome at least one aspect of fear, that derived from ignorance. Peaceful coexistence can be taught at various levels of societal complexity. At the present time, peace curricula are being developed and used around the country. Typically, the curricula have multiple objectives, some of which include the reduction of ethnocentrism, the encouragement of a sense of political and self-efficacy, the honing of problem-solving skills that effectively deal with conflicts, awareness of nuclear issues, and the inculcation of world order values—peace, ecological balance, economic well-being, and human rights (cf. Riddle, 1988).

A Challenge to Professionals

Part of the problem when attempting to deal with the issue of violence is ideological polarization. Consider, for example, the tendency to construe solutions to the problem of violence in terms of either carrots or sticks. In the case of school violence, those on the ideological right argue for the reinstatement of discipline and a return to the image of teachers as authority figures. Often there is a call for more stringent punitive measures and, if necessary, the promotion of effective relations between police and public schools (cf. Blount, 1986). On the other hand, those associated with the ideological left may advocate the use of methods that promote cooperation and other forms of prosocial behaviors (cf. Staub, 1978, 1979) which engender concern about others along with feelings of responsibility for the welfare of others. The point is that these two viewpoints are not antithetical—there is no reason why one cannot shore up discipline practices and at the same time encourage the development of curricula or system-wide efforts that promote prosocial behavior patterns.

Similarly, when considering the threat of nuclear war, there are few political moderates who would argue against a credible nuclear deterrent if that means a survivable nuclear defense to be used for retaliatory (i.e., second strike) purposes. Even with a credible deterrent, the cooperative side of relations between nations can be pursued vigorously (cf. Milburn & Christie, 1989). To date, there is a paucity of research and practice that has attempted to enhance critical thinking in children by teaching them about the value of peace through strength and the "opposing" ideological position—peace through cooperation—as objectives that are not mutually exclusive (Kimmel, 1985).

In short, what is called for is a kind of cognitive flexibility among professionals that strips viewpoints from their ideological underpinnings. Both discipline and cooperation at the interpersonal level, as well as strength and cooperation at the international level, are compatible objectives.

A number of psychologists have addressed the problem of inaction on the part of adults with respect to important social issues (Fiske, 1987; Gilbert, 1988; Weick, 1984). Among other factors, professionals are likely to be inhibited by the maze of objectives or policy alternatives, with no clear indication as to which objectives are likely to be most efficacious. Moreover, the scale of the problem of violence in society may seem so large that any one individual is likely to feel helpless. The key challenge for professionals is to redefine the scale of the problem of violence (Weick, 1984) and make a modest contribution to its resolution. This may mean the active search for ways in which professionals can relate their practice to the problem of violence, thereby integrating ongoing professional activities with this important social issue.

In conclusion, the foregoing suggestions have been guided by a number of implicit values and convictions. Adults need to be aware of their own response to fear-provoking situations and images. They should practice rational ways of dealing with such responses. They should offer children the opportunity to discuss fears openly. It is not enough for the adult to exude confidence in the child's problem-solving ability; the child may also need guidance toward specific coping strategies. A key goal is to help children confront their fears with a sense of efficacy. Such a goal, we suggest, can be achieved by helping the child express feelings, gain knowledge, and act on convictions.

REFERENCES

Adelson, J., & Finn, C., Jr. (1985). Terrorizing children. *Commentary, 79*(4), 29.

American Bar Association (1988). *Dispute resolution.* Standing Committee on Dispute Resolution, 1800 M Street, N.W., Washington, DC 20036.

Angelino, H., Dolins, J., & Mech, E. (1956). Trends in the fears and worries of school children as related to socio-economic status and age. *Journal of Genetic Psychology, 89,* 263–276.

Bachman, J. G. (1983). American high school seniors view the military: 1976–1982. *Armed Forces and Society, 10*(1), 86–104.

Bachman, J. G. (1989). *Update on monitoring the future.* Personal communication, Survey Research Center, Institute for Social Research, The University of Michigan, Ann Arbor.

Bachman, J. G., Johnson, L. D., & O'Malley, P. M. (1984). Recent findings from Monitoring the Future: Continuing study of the lifestyles and values of youth. In F. Andrews (Ed.), *Research on the quality of life,* Ann Arbor, MI: Institute for Social Research.

Bayh, B. (1979). Battered schools: Violence and vandalism in public education. *Viewpoints in Teaching and Learning, 55,* 1–17.

Beardslee, W., & Mack, J. (1982). The impact on children and adolescents of nuclear developments. In Task Force Report 20, *Psychosocial aspects of nuclear developments* (pp. 64–93). Washington, DC: American Psychiatric Association.

Becker, D. C. (1983). Impact of crime and violence on schooling: Is there a solution? *Contemporary Education, 55*(1), 45–47.

Blount, E. C. (1986). *Model guidelines for effective police-public school relationships.* Springfield, IL: Charles C. Thomas.

Brodbelt, S. (1978). The epidemic of school violence. *The Clearing House, 51,* 383–388.

Carriere, R. (1979, January). Peer violence forces kids out of school. *The American School Board Journal,* 35–36.

Cheatham, A. (1988). *Directory of school mediation and conflict resolution programs.* Amherst, MA: National Association for Mediation in Education.

Chivian, E., Mack, J. E., Waletzky, J. P., Lazaroff, C., Doctor, R., & Goldenring, J. M. (1985, October). Soviet children and the threat of nuclear war: A preliminary study. *American Journal of Orthopsychiatry, 55*(4), 484–502.

Christie, D. J. (1988, August). Reducing fear and inducing complacency in students: A pseudodox in nuclear war education. In R. S. Moyer (Chair), *Effects of nuclear war education: Fear, indoctrination, or empowerment?* Symposium conducted at the 96th annual convention of the American Psychological Association, Atlanta, Georgia.

Christie, D. J., & Nelson, L. (1988). Students' reactions to nuclear education. *Bulletin of the Atomic Scientists, 44*(6), 22–23.

Christie, D. J., & Zweigenhaft, R. L. (1989, August). The third world and nuclear arms issues: A cross-cultural study of Malaysian and American students. In R. V. Wagner (Chair), *Nuclear threat anxiety and attitudes: Gender, cultural, and theoretical implications.* Symposium conducted at the 97th annual convention of the American Psychological Association, New Orleans, Louisiana.

Cohen, S. F. (1984, May). Societies. In *The nation,* reprinted by Promoting Enduring Peace, Woodmont, CT.

Coles, R. (1985, 8 December). Children and the bomb. *New York Times Magazine.*

The Community Board Program (1987). *Conflict resolution: A secondary school curriculum.* San Francisco, CA: The Community Board Program.

Deutsch, M. (1983). The prevention of World War III: A psychological perspective. *Political Psychology, 4*(1), 3–31.

Diamond, G., & Bachman, J. (1986). High-school seniors and the nuclear threat, 1975–1984: Political and mental health implications of concern and despair. *International Journal of Mental Health, 15,* 210–241.

Disorder in our public schools. (1984). Report of the Cabinet Council on Human Resources Working Group on School Violence/Discipline to the President. Washington, DC: U.S. Department of Education.

Dyal, J. A., & Morris, P. (1987, June). *Nuclear anxiety and issue-relevant behavior: Associations with mental health.* Paper presented at the 22nd annual conference of the Canadian Peace Research and Education Association, Hamilton, Ontario, Canada.

Escalona, S. K. (1965). Children and the threat of nuclear war. In M. Schwebel

(Ed.), *Behavioral science and human survival.* Palo Alto, CA: Behavioral Science Press.

Escalona, S. K. (1982). Growing up with the threat of nuclear war: Some indirect effects on personality development. *American Journal of Orthopsychiatry, 52*(4), 600–607.

Fiske, S. T. (1987). People's reactions to nuclear war: Implications for psychologists. *American Psychologist, 42*(3), 207–217.

Flavell, J. H., Everett, B. A., Croft, K., & Flavell, E. R. (1981). Young children's knowledge about visual perception: Further evidence for the Level 1-Level 2 distinction. *Developmental Psychology, 17,* 99–103.

Frank, J. (1982a). Prenuclear-age leaders and the nuclear arms race. *American Journal of Orthospsychiatry, 52*(4), 630–637.

Frank, J. D. (1982b). *Sanity and survival in the nuclear age: Psychological aspects of war and peace.* New York: Random House.

"Getting Tough." (1988). *Time,* 131, p. 52.

Gilbert, R. K. (1988). The dynamics of inaction: Psychological factors inhibiting arms control activism. *American Psychologist, 43*(10), 755–764.

Goldberg, S., LaCombe, S., Levinson, D., Parker, K. R., Ross, C., & Sommers, F. (1985, October). Thinking about the nuclear war: Relevance to mental health. *American Journal of Orthopsychiatry, 55*(4), 503–512.

Goldenring, J., & Doctor, R. (1983). *Adolescent concerns about the threat of nuclear war.* Testimony for the House of Representatives Select Committee on Children, Youth, and Families. Los Angeles, CA: Loyola Marymount University.

Goodman, L. A., Mack, J. B., Beardslee, W. R., & Snow, R. M. (1983). The threat of nuclear war and the nuclear arms race: Adolescent experiences and perceptions. *Political Psychology, 4*(3), 501–529.

Greenwald, D. S., & Zeitlin, S. J. (1987). *No reason to talk about it: Families confront the nuclear taboo.* New York: W. W. Norton.

Harlan, J. P., & McDowell, C. P. (1981). Crime and disorder in the public schools. *Education Studies, 12*(3), 221–229.

Hepburn, J. R., & Monti, D. J. (1979). Victimization, fear of crime, and adaptive responses among high school students. In W. H. Parsonage (Ed.), *Perspectives on victimology.* Beverly Hills, CA: Sage.

Holmborg, P. O., & Bergstrom, A. (1985). How Swedish teenagers think and feel concerning the nuclear threat. In T. Solantaus, E. Chivian, M. Vartanyan, & S. Chivian (Eds.), *Impact of nuclear war on children and adolescents: Proceedings of an international research symposium* (pp. 170–180). Boston, MA: International Physicians for the Prevention of Nuclear War.

Jersild, A., & Holmes, F. (1935). Children's fears. *Child Development Monographs, 20,* 358–408.

Kagan, J. (1976). Emergent themes in human development. *American Scientist, 64,* 186–196.

Kagan, J., Kearsley, R., & Zelazo, P. (1978). *Infancy: Its place in human development.* Cambridge, MA: Harvard University Press.

Kimmel, P. R. (1985). Learning about peace: Choices and the U.S. Institute of Peace as seen from two different perspectives. *American Psychologist, 40*(5), 536–541.

Kohut, H. (1977). *The restoration of self.* New York: International Universities Press.

Lifton, R. J. (1979). *The broken connection: On death and continuity of life.* New York: Simon & Schuster.

Lifton, R. J. (1982). Beyond psychic numbing: A call to awareness. *American Journal of Orthopsychiatry, 52*(4), 619–629.

Mack, J. E. (1981). Psychosocial effects of the arms race. *The Bulletin of the Atomic Scientists, 37*(4), 18–23.

Mack, J. E. (1982). The perception of U.S.–Soviet intentions and other psychological dimensions of the nuclear arms race. *American Journal of Orthopsychiatry, 52*(4), 590–599.

McDermott, J. (1980). High anxiety: Fear of crime in secondary schools. *Contemporary Education, 5*(1), 18–23.

McDermott, J. (1983). Crime in the schools and in the community: Offenders, victims, and fearful youth. *Crime and Delinquency, 29*(2), 270–282.

Milburn, T. W., & Christie, D. J. (1989). Rewarding in international politics. *Political Psychology, 10*(4), 625–645..

Milburn, T. W., Stewart, P. D., & Herrmann, R. K. (1982). Perceiving the other's intentions. In C. Kegley & P. McGowan (Eds.), *Foreign policy USA/USSR.* Beverly Hills, CA: Sage Publications

Milburn, T. W., & Watman, K. (1982, August). *Psychological paradoxes of strategic deterrence.* Paper presented at the meetings of the American Psychological Association, Washington, DC.

Mohr, D., McLoughlin, J., & Silver, R. L. (1986). Threat and collective control as moderators or peace activism: A comparison of peace activists and community residents. Unpublished paper, University of Waterloo.

National Institute of Education. (1977). *Violent schools—safe schools: The safe school study report to the Congress.* Washington, DC: U.S. Department of Health, Education, and Welfare.

Nelson, A. (1985). Psychological equivalence: Awareness and response-ability in our nuclear age. *American Psychologist, 40*(5), 549–556.

Newcomb, M. D. (1986). Nuclear attitudes and reactions: Associations with depression, drug use, and quality of life. *Journal of Personality and Social Psychology, 50*(5), 906–920.

Newman, J. (1980). From past to future: School violence in a broad view. *Contemporary Education, 52,* 7–12.

The New York Times (1917, October 17). Cited in Becker, D. C. (1983), Impact of crime and violence on schooling: Is there a solution? *Contemporary Education, 55*(1), 45–47.

Piaget, J. (1954). *The construction of reality in the child.* New York: Basic Books.

Polyson, J., Hillmar, J., & Kriek, D. (1986). Levels of public interest in nuclear war: 1945–1985. *Journal of Social Behavior and Personality, 1,* 397–401.

Riddle, R. (1988). *Bibliography of nuclear age educational resources.* Stanford, CA: International Security and Arms Control Project of the Stanford Program on International and Cross-Cultural Education.

Rubel, R. J. (1978). Analysis and critique of HEW's safe school study report to Congress. *Crime and Delinquency, 24*(3), 257–265.

Scherer, J. E., & Stimson, J. (1984). Is school violence a serious concern? *School Administrator, 41*(3), 19–20.

Schwebel, M. (1965). *Behavioral science and human survival.* Palo Alto, CA: Behavioral Science Press.

Schwebel, M. (1982). Effects of the nuclear war threat on children and teenagers: Implications for professionals. *American Journal of Orthopsychiatry, 52*(4), 608–618.

Simon, R. (1984). The nuclear family. *Family Therapy Networker, 8,* 30.

Smith, M. B. (1986). Kurt Lewin Memorial Address, 1986: War, peace, and psychology. *Journal of Social Issues, 42,* 23–38.

Solantaus, T. (1986). Adolescence and the nuclear threat in Finland: Anxiety and optimism. In B. Berger-Gould, S. Moon, & J. Van Hoorn (Eds.), *Growing up scared?* (pp. 210–223). Palo Alto, CA: Science and Behavior Books.

Sommers, F. G., Goldberg, S., Levinson, D., Ross, C., & LaCombe, S. (1985). Children's mental health and the threat of nuclear war. A Canadian pilot study. In T. Solantaus, E. Chivian, M. Vartanyan, & S. Chivian (Eds.), *Impact of the threat of nuclear war on children and adolescents: Proceedings of an international research symposium* (pp. 61–93). Boston, MA: International Physicians for the Prevention of Nuclear War.

Staub, E. (1978). *Positive social behavior and morality. Vol. I: Social and personal influences.* New York: Academic Press.

Staub, E. (1979). *Positive social behavior and morality. Vol. 2: Socialization and development.* New York: Academic Press.

"These Perilous Halls of Learning." (1989). *U.S. News and World Report, 106,* pp. 68–69.

Tyler, T. R., & McGraw, K. M. (1983). The threat of nuclear war: Risk interpretation and behavior response. *Journal of Social Issues, 39,* 25–40.

Volkan, V. D. (1985). The need to have enemies and allies: A developmental approach. *Political Psychology, 6*(2), 219–247.

Weick, K. E. (1984). Small wins: Redefining the scale of social problems. *American Psychologist, 39*(1), 40–49.

Westin, A. (1970). Facing the issues: Responding to rebels with a cause. In The Danforth Foundation and The Ford Foundation (Eds.), *The school and the democratic environment.* New York: Columbia University Press.

Wrightsman, L. S. (1970). Parental attitudes and behaviors as determinates of children's responses to the threat of nuclear war. In R. Sigel (Ed.), *Learning about politics.* New York: Random House.

CHAPTER TWELVE

The Stress
of Childhood Illness

Margaret O'Dougherty
Robert T. Brown

A child's illness, often accompanied by such stresses as hospitalizations, pain and malaise, extended diagnostic studies, surgery, medications, diet restrictions, activity limitations, school absences, and frequent medical crises, generates a number of fears, anxieties, and grief reactions. Chronic diseases are especially stressful. They constitute one of the major health problems of children; some consider them the nation's primary health problem (Pless & Satterwhite, 1975). About one child in ten experiences a chronic illness by the age of 15, and most of these children are cared for by their families at home (Pless, Roghmann, & Haggerty, 1972). Representative of the fears experienced by such children are fear of pain (juvenile rheumatoid arthritis), fear of major surgery (congenital heart defect), anxiety over disfigurement (colostomy for ulcerative colitis, amputation following malignancy), fear of death (leukemia, hemophilia), fear of the next acute episode (asthma and epilepsy), and depression about the gradual loss of health or functions in degenerative illness (muscular dystrophy, cystic fibrosis). Table 12.1 outlines specific stressors for several pediatric illnesses and highlights possible psychopathological effects if the stressful events extend, intensify, or cause ineffective coping strategies.

ILLNESS AND COPING

Examples of positive adaptation and maladaptation are evident within every illness and disability area. Although children who experience a chronic illness are at higher risk for experiencing psychosocial adjustment problems (Breslau, 1985; Cadman et al., 1987; Mattson, 1972; Mrazek, Anderson, & Strunk, 1985; O'Dougherty 1983; Pless & Roughmann, 1971; Rutter, Tizard, & Whitmore, 1970; Wallander et al., 1989), virtually all studies have documented significant variation in adjustment for each illness group and some studies have not found significant adjustment problems (Drotar et al., 1981; Tavormina et al., 1976). Some factors to consider in assessing the impact of the disease on the child include the child's age at onset; the severity, duration, symptomatology, and visibility of the illness; the type and extent of medical intervention; degree of family disruption and extent of financial burden; and individual child and parent characteristics that can moderate successful coping (e.g., SES, personality characteristics, IQ, social support) (O'Dougherty, 1983; Pless & Pinkerton, 1975).

One consistent finding has been that disorders involving documented brain damage are associated with poorer overall adaptation (Breslau, 1985; Rutter et al., 1970; Seidel, Chadwick, & Rutter, 1975). This finding likely relates to the powerful contribution of intelligence for successful coping.

TABLE 12.1. *Specific Illness Stressors and Possible Psychological Effects*

Illness	Stressful Medical Interventions	Possible Effects
Epilepsy: A condition in which there is a continuing proclivity to have seizures	Adverse anticonvulsant medication drug effects Regular blood tests Hospitalization for status epilepticus Brain surgery	Anxiety and fear of unconsciousness Sense of control and autonomy severely affected Social stigmatization, rejection, and discrimination Parental overprotection or rejection Heightened dependency on parents
Asthma: A respiratory disorder characterized by intermittent and reversible attacks of difficulty in breathing	Repeated hospitalizations Allergy shots Bronchodilators Mist inhalation Corticosteroids Antibiotics for infection Beta-agonists	Fear of dying by suffocation Fear of abandonment Maladaptive use of wheezing to express conflicts Physical and social restrictions Family disruption (sleep interruption, dietary and housekeeping problems) Growth retardation secondary to steroids
Diabetes: A metabolic disease in which there is a lack of insulin or impairment in the insulin mechanism	Insulin injections Diet restrictions Blood and urine testing Hospitalizations for acute episodes	Parent-child control struggle over insulin-food-exercise regimen Adolescent rebellion Pain of daily injections Fear of coma or insulin shock Anxiety over long term complications

(continued)

In some studies, severity of the disorder has been related to significant psychosocial adjustment problems (Cadman et al., 1987; Daniels et al., 1987; Wallander et al., 1988), but other investigations have not found severity of illness factors to be significantly associated with maladjustment (Breslau, 1985; Kashani et al., 1988; Tew & Laurence, 1985; Varni, Wilcox, & Hanson, 1988). Particularly, increased severity of physical

TABLE 12.1.   (Continued)

Illness	Stressful Medical Interventions	Possible Effects
Heart Defects: Congenital abnormalities of the heart structure	Catheterization for diagnosis and treatment Corrective surgery Palliative surgeries Antibiotics Digitalis for heart failure	Parental guilt and depression over defect Coping with a life-threatening illness Extensive painful procedures Prolonged separation during infancy Difficulty disciplining child (fear of precipitating symptoms) Child's fear of pain, mutilation, death Activity restrictions
Irritable Bowel Syndrome: A functional bowel disorder characterized by alternating diarrhea and constipation	Dietary restrictions Stool softeners Antispasmodic medication Exercise program Antidepressant medication Treatment of fecal impaction	Fear of loss of control Feelings of shame and inadequacy Emotional tension, anxiety, and depression Physical response to life stress Conflicts over holding back vs. letting go Difficulty dealing with anger and aggressive feelings
Juvenile Rheumatoid Arthritis: An inflammatory process affecting the joints	Aspirin Physical therapy Steroids Gold therapy injections Orthopedic intervention (splints and surgery)	Pain and feelings of maltreatment, punishment, and persecution Activity limitation Deformity and crippling Depression and mood alteration

(continued)

disability has *not* consistently related to poorer child adjustment. In fact, the contrary has sometimes been found—at times children experiencing a milder disability or better control of symptoms display greater maladjustment. This has been found in several studies of children with juvenile arthritis (McAnarney et al., 1974), adolescents who have generalized

TABLE 12.1.   (Continued)

Illness	Stressful Medical Interventions	Possible Effects
Muscular Dystrophy: A neuromuscular disorder in which striated muscle progressively deteriorates	Physical therapy Surgery for contractures Caloric-restricted diet Correction of spinal deformity Postural drainage exercises Orthopedic prosthesis and motorized equipment	Anguish and guilt over diagnosis Coping with knowledge of early crippling and death Chronic physical and mental exhaustion Progressive helplessness and dependency due to loss of strength Isolation and rejection by peers Great difficulty managing anger and aggressive feelings Sacrifices required by other family members Need for respite for parents and siblings

Acute CNS Infection (Bacterial Meningitis): An inflammation of the membranes surrounding the brain resulting from bacterial infection	Lumbar puncture
	Blood culture
	Spinal fluid culture
	Antibiotic therapy
	Respiratory isolation
	Treatment of increased intracranial pressure
		Fear of child's death
		Fear of residual brain damage
		Coping with possible residual deficits:
		    Mental retardation
		    Seizures
		    Hydrocephalus
		    Hemiparesis
		    Learning disability
		    Hearing impairment

tonic-clonic seizures (Hodgman et al., 1979), children with hemophilia (Bruhn, Hampton, & Chandler, 1971), and children with visual and hearing handicaps (Pless & Pinkerton, 1975). The reasons for such paradoxical findings are poorly understood but may involve denial of illness, failure to establish effective coping strategies, and difficulty competing with others when the disability is not sufficiently severe to result in special consideration and alternative school placements. Pless and Pinkerton (1975) speculate that "marginality and severity represent opposite poles of a disablement spectrum, each with its own special problems of management" (p. 171).

Significant age and sex effects among children with sickle cell disease have recently been reported by Hurtig, Koepke, and Park (1989). In their study, the limitations of the disease, affecting physical factors such as growth, delayed puberty, and physical activity, adversely affected the psychosocial development of adolescent boys but not girls in their sample.

Overall, the results of these studies suggest that adjustment cannot be predicted simply based on diagnostic category or severity indices, but rather is a complex process involving the interrelationships of disease, personal, familial, social, and medical variables. Mattsson (1972) has concluded that "the nature of the specific illness appears less influential for a child's successful adaptation than such factors as his developmental level and available coping techniques, the quality of the parent-child relationship, and the family's acceptance of the handicapped member" (p. 805).

These findings also illustrate that the stress may not be inherent in the illness, but rather may be a function of the child's perception of and response to the illness (Lazarus & Launier, 1978; Lipowski, 1970; Moos & Tsu, 1977). In this framework, an illness is considered a crisis, a challenge that creates a set of adaptational tasks. Lipowski (1970) provides an excellent outline of possible meanings an illness might have for a family, including their appraisal of the stress the illness presents to them. For example, he postulates that an illness may be perceived as: (1) a challenge, something to be mastered; (2) an enemy invading the body; (3) a punishment (just or unjust) for misconduct; (4) a sign of weakness or personal failing; (5) an opportunity to avoid the unpleasant demands of home or school; (6) a strategy for securing attention or affection; (7) an irreparable loss or change in function; or (8) an opportunity for moral growth and development.

Assessment of the different meanings an illness may have for the child and parent is critical in understanding the emotional and behavioral responses of the child and family to the adaptational tasks the illness presents. Such an assessment also can provide clues as to why the behavior of some children worsens and that of others with a similar disability improves. The determinants of individual outcome are extremely complex and difficult to predict without knowledge of multiple factors. Effective coping must be evaluated in multiple domains, including an assessment of the specific biological, psychological, and social stresses, and changes in these arenas over time and at different stages of the disease and the child's development (Lazarus & Folkman, 1984; O'Dougherty, 1983; Vitaliano et al., 1985).

In the rest of this chapter we address the fears and concerns typically experienced by children and their parents at each stage of development and highlight the specific factors that can influence the impact of an illness on a child's later adaptation. Each section focuses on the child's age and level of cognitive, emotional, and social development as critical factors in assessing the impact of illness and preventing stress. Table 12.2 summarizes the developmental changes that occur from infancy through adolescence, and Table 12.3 illustrates the types of fears and developmental crises that can occur in different age groups. These tables serve as an outline for the rest of the chapter.

INFANCY PERIOD: AGE 0 TO 1½ YEARS

During infancy the primary developmental goal is to establish trust in significant others. This trust involves the developing expectation that primary needs for comfort, food, and security will be met. When a baby experiences a serious illness, this sense of basic trust can be very difficult to establish. The baby is often separated from his or her parents and placed in a hospital setting, which can be frightening, unpredictable, chaotic, and unsatisfying. To understand the fears and developmental disruptions that can arise, it is important to take into account many intricate considerations, such as the special characteristics of the infant's medical problem, how severe the illness is, the occurrence of multiple complications, and the types of treatments provided. Equally important are the characteristics of the hospital caretaking staff, the parents, and the environment to which the infant returns after hospitalization.

It is important during the acute illness stage for the ill baby to have increased contact, comfort, and expression of affection from caretakers and nursing staff. This physical comforting can sometimes make the pain more bearable and it provides a degree of security to the infant. When such comfort cannot be given because the child's condition does not allow it (e.g., severe burns) or because the parents are absent or neglectful, the infant may develop symptoms of depression, including withdrawal, apathy, avoidance, or refusal to interact with his or her parents. Alternately, the baby can become clinging, demanding, and difficult to soothe (Ainsworth, 1973). Other behavioral indications that needs for stimulation and contact are not being met can include frequent crying, restlessness, difficulty sleeping, rocking, head banging, and disturbances in eating or gastrointestinal functions (Petrillo & Sanger, 1980).

Normal separation anxiety and fear of strangers are intensified because of the child's painful and frightening experiences (surgery, blood transfusions, isolation, injections, etc.). Continuity of care is extremely important at this time, and it is especially helpful to keep to a minimum the number of hospital staff interacting with the baby. Prolonged separation between parents and infant during this time can interfere with the parent's attachment to the baby and the development of competence in

TABLE 12.2. Developmental Changes—Infancy through Adolescence

Age	Psychosexual (Freud)	Cognitive (Piaget)	Personal-Social (Erikson)	Moral (Kohlberg)	Potential Adverse Impact
Infancy	Oral	Early Sensorimotor	Trust	No moral concepts	Insecure attachment Diminished responsiveness
Toddler	Anal	Late Sensorimotor	Autonomy	Fear of punishment	Excessive maternal control Power struggles Passivity
Preschooler	Phallic (Oedipal)	Preoperational Thought, Egocentrism	Initiative	Absolute good/bad	Extreme guilt Fear of mutilation Inhibition of initiative
Elementary School	Latent	Concrete Thinking and Problem Solving	Industry	General rules Obey authority	Sense of inferiority Feelings of inadequacy
Adolescent	Genital	Abstract, Logical, and Symbolic Problem Solving	Identity Intimacy	Abstract moral code	Authority conflict Low self-esteem

Source: O'Dougherty, M. M. (1983). *Counseling the chronically ill child: Psychological impact and intervention* (p. 10). New York: NY: Viking Penguin, Inc. Copyright © 1983 by Viking Penguin, Inc. Reprinted by permission.

TABLE 12.3. *Possible Stressors Affecting Children with Acute and Chronic Illness*

Stressor	Specific Age Risk Group	Possible Psychological Impact
Hospitalization and separation from parents	Infants and toddlers	Insecure attachment and difficulty establishing trust Separation anxiety Regression
	Young children	Feelings of rejection Behavioral disorders
	Adolescents	Difficulty establishing autonomy Conflict over heightened dependency on parents and staff
Surgical procedures causing pain or disfigurement	Infants and toddlers	Fear of strangers Fussiness, difficulty sleeping and eating, depression, apathy Defiance, negativism Parental overprotectiveness, permissiveness
	Young children	View pain as being punished for "bad behavior" or as mistreatment by parents Anxiety over rejection Fear of mutilation, castration
	Adolescents	Anxiety over impact of disfigurement on sexual attractiveness and body integrity Fear of death Fear of being different from peers
Restrictions on activity or diet	Younger children	Power struggles with parent Overdependency and passivity Loss of initiative and poor development of social skills with agemates
	Adolescents	Rebelliousness, acting out, noncompliance Apathy and withdrawal from social relationships with peers

(continued)

TABLE 12.3. (Continued)

Stressor	Specific Age Risk Group	Possible Psychological Impact
Heightened dependency on parents	Younger children	Loss of initiative, passivity
		Parental overprotection and permissiveness
	Aldolescents	Feelings of inadequacy, low self-esteem
		Authority conflict
		Difficulty establishing autonomy and separating successfully from parents
		Passive-aggressive, manipulative responses
Consumption of excess share of parental time and attention and other family resources	All age groups	Sibling jealousy and competition for parental affection
		Rejection, isolation, teasing of physically ill child
		Passive-aggressive expressions of anger
		Acting out by siblings to gain parental attention
Extent of financial and physical burden on family	All age groups	Heightened family stress
		Diminished parenting capacity due to extended work hours and prolonged care of ill child
		Financial strain and lack of adequate social and economic support contributing to family conflict and divorce
Lack of peer acceptance	Children and adolescents	Isolation, rejection, teasing, scapegoating
		Depression, withdrawal, loneliness
		Overdependency on parents
		Difficulty establishing a positive self-image and secure attachments to others

(continued)

334

TABLE 12.3.   (Continued)

Stressor	Specific Age Risk Group	Possible Psychological Impact
Frequent school absences	School-aged children	Failure to consolidate academic skills, resulting in frustration, school failure, and low self-esteem
Effect of disease on physical growth and development	Adolescent males	Small size, delayed puberty, limited physical activity can result in peer rejection, isolation, and lowered self-esteem for males
	Adolescent females	Impact on self-esteem and social adjustment affected more by disfigurement and infertility or problems with pregnancy

the necessary caretaking skills. Disruptions in the attachment process may result in an infant who fails to thrive and in disturbed parent-child interactions, including an increased likelihood of child abuse or neglect.

Parental attachment is facilitated by allowing the parents to "room in" when the infant is hospitalized and by permitting close contact and participation in the physical caretaking of the infant (Petrillo & Sanger, 1980). Some programs have been developed specifically to include parents in the provision of tactile and other sensory stimulation during hospitalization. These are aimed to promoting the child's motor, perceptual, and cognitive ability and social-interactive skills. Types of stimulation provided include non-nutritive sucking, rocking, stroking, massage, heartbeat recordings, visual decorating of the isolette, rocking waterbeds, cycled lighting patterns, recordings of the mother's voice, visual and auditory contacts with the mother, modeling of interactive strategies by nursing staff, or other parent education (Field et al., 1979; Holmes, Nagy, & Pasternak, 1984).

Such stimulation has been shown to affect the infants' functioning, at least for a short time. Some of the benefits documented are improvement in health status, weight gain, and responsiveness, and more optimal performance on newborn and early infant assessments. Although many of the programs focus on the infant, they actually have involved the parents directly and may have had their primary effect in enhancing the quality of the parent/infant attachment relationship. For example, parents participating in such programs increased the number and amount of visits to the intensive care nursery (Field et al., 1979). Some programs have focused more specifically on the parents, providing peer support, self-help groups, activities, and help in interacting with their infant. Such programs have also been successful in reducing negative behavioral sequelae, improving the quality and quantity of parent-child interactions and positively altering the parents' perceptions of their child and their expectations for his or her future well-being (Holmes et al., 1984).

TODDLER PERIOD: AGE 1 ½ TO 3 YEARS

The major developmental goal at this time is to establish autonomy or independence (Rothbaum & Weisz, 1989). In order for the normal process of separation-individuation to take place successfully, it is critical that the parent is present as a "secure base" from which the child can explore (Ainsworth, 1973). Attachment to the mother is very strong at this age and the child is often preoccupied with fears of abandonment when separated. Again, encouraging the parent to "room in" with the child can be particularly helpful in reducing separation anxiety. Petrillo and Sanger (1980) provide a variety of suggestions for reducing the stress that can accompany hospitalization, such as allowing the child to use transitional objects (stuffed animals, favorite blankets, etc.) for security, helping the parents establish a consistent pattern of visits, modeling effective ways to manage the child's fear and anxiety at separation, and providing an extensive play program in the hospital for cognitive, social, and motor stimulation.

Since separation anxiety is often most debilitating at this time, the toddler is likely to experience a great amount of regression. Signs of regression can include a return to more infantile behaviors such as soiling, wetting, thumb sucking, and bottle feeding. In part, this regression may stem from solicitous parental or nursing care which interferes with the child's responsibilities for self feeding, bathing, dressing, and toileting. The child can welcome this pampering or, conversely, perceive it as very threatening. Accepting such care, if needed, can allow the child to conserve energy and may facilitate recovery. However, if passivity and lack of autonomy persist for an unduly long time or become excessive, they can require intervention. The children particularly at risk here are those for whom achieving independence in these key areas has always been a struggle and who derive most of their satisfaction from passively receiving nurturance from others. They have not yet learned to assert their individuality. The opposite reaction, which can also occur during this period, is defiant negativism, saying NO to all requests and not allowing appropriate care to be given by others. Whenever possible, it is important to allow toddlers to continue familiar routines and to function independently in areas in which they have gained prior competence (Rothbaum & Weisz, 1989).

During this period, specific parental coping techniques can have the side effect of fostering either pathological dependency or defiance in the child. For example, an acute illness phase or initial diagnostic studies can be very frightening and traumatizing for the parents as well as the child. There is a natural tendency to be protective of or permissive with the child during these stressful times. If permissiveness extends for an unusually long period of time, the child may become overly dependent and demanding. When faced with the child's incessant demands, the parents may begin to feel resentful and angry. Periodically, this resentment may come out in inappropriately harsh expressions of anger or in rejection of the child. The guilt which often ensues then leads to more over-protectiveness and permissiveness, feeding a vicious cycle further (O'Dougherty, 1983).

During the toddler period, children are most often traumatized by the separation from their parents and the stress and pain of the medical procedures. Like preschool children, they often mistakenly believe that the illness is a punishment for misbehavior or a sign of rejection by their parents. At the toddler age, children display little cognitive understanding of what is wrong with them or what caused the disease. Doll play with appropriate hospital-like materials may facilitate expression of concerns and fears, but it is best to avoid giving most children at this age detailed information about the inside of their bodies since these concepts are not yet understood and may merely confuse them (Petrillo & Sanger, 1980).

PRESCHOOL PERIOD: AGE 3 TO 5 YEARS

During the preschool period, the primary developmental task is the development of conscience, a sense of right or wrong. When illness occurs during this period, the child often attributes the illness or the pain associated with its treatment to punishment for being bad or to mistreatment or rejection by the parents. Viewing illness as a punishment can inhibit initiative. Quotations throughout Petrillo and Sanger's (1980) book illustrate children's concepts of illness as punishment for misbehavior. For example, one little boy said, "Well, you know when you do something bad and your mother doesn't punish you? Then God has to do it" (p. 72). A 2-year-old child screamed, "I'm sorry; I said I'm sorry" (p. 69) over and over again when a nurse started an IV in preparation for chemotherapy. Clearly, both of these children viewed the infliction of pain as punishment.

If the child needs to be hospitalized, feelings of rejection can occur and cause great anxiety and distress. One 2-year-old child studied by Petrillo and Sanger (1980) was admitted to the hospital for repair of an umbilical hernia shortly after the birth of a new sibling. This child confided to her nurse that she was brought to the hospital "because her mother did not want her anymore" (p. 69). In other instances, a child may believe that his or her condition is the result of aggression or rejection by an older sibling.

The child's level of cognitive development is a particularly important factor contributing to fears and misconceptions at this age. Preschool children's thoughts are often superstitious and magical. For example, children at this age often believe that their thoughts and wishes are so powerful that they can cause direct harm to someone, such as the belief that hating someone can cause them to become sick or even die. They also may believe that good thoughts will protect them from harm. Misunderstandings of medical terminology or parent-doctor communications can result in substantial misconceptions: for example, "You get penisillin if you touch your penis" (Bergmann & Freud, 1965, p. 82) or the belief that a CT scan of the brain allows the doctor to read all of one's bad thoughts (Petrillo & Sanger, 1980). Children do interpret what is happening to them, and their interpretations, although amusing to adults, may be a source of great guilt and distress to them.

A normal developmental fear at this age is fear of mutilation. Surgical procedures and operations intensify this fear; castration anxieties and mutilation fantasies prior to surgery are particularly common to this age group. Some children think that surgical operations are similar to actions they have performed on their dolls: cutting heads off, ripping the arms and legs off, etc. It is extremely important to clarify the nature of any surgical procedure. When children are going to have an operation they need to know *what* is going to be removed (tonsils, appendix, etc.) and that that is *the only thing* that is going to be removed. It is particularly important to reassure the child that the illness or medical procedure is limited and specific, and to discuss repair and recovery of function when possible (O'Dougherty, 1983).

Preschool children begin to have a rudimentary understanding of internal body parts, illness, and health (Bibace & Walsh, 1980; Gellert, 1978). This understanding parallels the developmental progress observed in the cognitive area and is characterized by preoperational thought. Preschool children demonstrate a global awareness of the body and its activities, but are not able to differentiate structure and function. In Gellert's (1978) study of children's knowledge of body parts, she found that the mean number of body parts named increased steadily from 3.3 for preschoolers to 13 for older adolescents.

Some young children believe that *all* body parts are needed in order to live. Such a belief may well contribute to the anxiety a preschooler might experience if a part of the body is injured or must be removed through surgery. At this age, the skin is often thought to be vital in keeping the body together "so the blood won't fall out" (Gellert, 1978, p. 26). Given this view, it's not surprising that injections, cuts, incisions, and drawing blood samples are viewed with such concern and anxiety. The bandage is commonly thought to stop the blood from coming out of the hole made by the needle, and some children believe that without this bandage they could lose all of their blood (Petrillo & Sanger, 1980).

In this age period, children are prone to overgeneralize and often believe that all body parts are vulnerable. Phenomenism and contagion are characteristic of the explanations they generate to explain why an illness has occurred. Often the child centers on one aspect of the illness based on his or her unique experience (egocentrism) and cannot specify the causal mechanism involved other than to attribute it to simultaneous occurrence or spatial proximity (Bibace & Walsh, 1980, 1981).

During this period, play opportunities involving direct observation, action, and manipulation are important in fostering cognitive growth. When describing to children the type of illness they have, or in preparing a child for treatment, it is helpful to provide a body outline, visual aids, or a doll with visible internal parts to facilitate more accurate under-standing. After surgery or medical treatment, doll play utilizing toys or equipment similar to that used in surgery can increase the child's com-prehension, aid in the expression of fears, and promote a feeling of mending (Petrillo & Sanger, 1980).

All the examples given illustrate how important it is for the hospital staff and parents to understand that the children's level of cognitive development strongly influences their thinking about illness, even after receiving factual information. The child in this age period is particularly vulnerable to distortions and misconceptions about what is wrong, what is happening, and how it will turn out. Support, reassurance, specific examples, and illustrations can reduce the guilt and blame the child might mistakenly feel, as well as provide the milieu for expressing fears and concerns.

ELEMENTARY SCHOOL PERIOD: AGE 6 TO 12 YEARS

The primary developmental goal during elementary school involves achievement, industry, and work skills. It is during this age period that the internalization of conscience and the incorporation of parents' and society's values begins. Many of the fears and concerns that emerge during this stage overlap or are extensions of fears found in the pre-school period, particularly the belief that illness is a punishment for misbehavior. Breaking of rules and regulations is frequently thought to cause illness onset. For example, a child who received a skull fracture while riding his bike in the street concluded that the fracture was a punishment for disobeying his parents. This causal association may have been enhanced if the parent also remarked, "See, I told you you shouldn't have been riding your bike in the street." This type of reasoning is concurrent with Kohlberg's (1976) stage of moral development in which the school-age child makes evaluations which are strongly based on respect for authority and rules.

In comparison to the earlier periods, fears of castration or mutilation during surgery diminish and separation anxiety is significantly reduced. However, negative family interactions or conflict with siblings can mistakenly be thought to result in an illness or specific medical condition. In one instance, a 10-year-old boy thought that his undescended testicles were the result of being dropped by his older sister when he was two months old because she did not like him (Petrillo & Sanger, 1980).

Coping with pain caused by the illness or its treatment can be very difficult. Symbolically, pain is often associated with persecution and punishment. Children can perceive shots, surgeries, etc., as an attack on their body by a more powerful person. The natural reaction to being "attacked"—anger, rage, wish for revenge—must be blocked because the infliction of pain is a necessary, non-negotiable part of their treatment. Fear of being under someone's control can emerge. Children sometimes believe that the adults providing the treatment will hurt them more intensely if they do not behave or if the adult is upset with them or someone else. Petrillo and Sanger (1980) report an instance in which a 6-year-old girl was found playing doctor and saying to her doll, "If you don't hold still, I'm going to stick you ten times!"

The prolonged experience of pain can make it difficult to establish trust. This is particularly so when a child has been misled or lied to about an illness, hospitalization, or specific procedure. Some important principles of intervention to reduce feelings of mistreatment and mistrust include: (1) Allow the child to prepare for the procedure by giving information that will help him anticipate the experience (e.g., "First I'm going to wipe your finger with alcohol. It's going to feel very cold but it won't hurt you. Now I'm going to prick your finger. It will hurt for a little while.") (2) Let the child know what is and is not allowed (e.g., "It's okay to scream. It's okay to cry. It's not okay to move around, because moving around will make it hurt more and take longer.") (3) Prepare choices for the child and be aware of how the child can participate in the procedure and help you. (4) Let the child know how well things are going and provide reassurance, support, and praise. (5) Be aware of your own feelings and reactions to the role you have in caring for the child. (6) Encourage the child to vocalize fears, ask questions, and express feelings (Petrillo & Sanger, 1980).

The cognitive advances at this age allow for much greater understanding of the body, illness, and medical procedures. Most children in this age group have now attained concrete operational thought, in which they are able to use classification and causal reasoning concretely in relation to their own experiences. Children in this stage of cognitive development have a more scientific orientation, are less egocentric, and can conceptualize reversal of process. They are able to reason about real, concrete objects in systematic ways. They do, however, have difficulty in abstract thinking and an inability to consider hypothetical possibilities (Piaget, 1952/1963). In the concrete operational stage, children are able to differentiate the structure and function of various body parts and are able to name more internal organs. However, understanding or defining the processes involved in the various body systems (respiration, circulation, digestion, elimination) is very difficult for most children at this stage (Crider, 1981).

When Bibace and Walsh (1980, 1981) asked elementary school-aged children questions about specific illnesses, they found two primary types of explanations characteristic at this age: contamination and internalization. Explanations relying on contamination gave the cause of illness as an external person, object, or action that was harmful to or bad for the body. For example, bad behavior, smoking, dirt, or germs are all thought to cause illness. Children in this stage often believe that they can prevent illness by not allowing their bodies to touch the contaminated source. When internalization is given as the explanatory mechanism, the cause of the illness is either an external contaminant (dirt, germs, etc.) which was internalized through swallowing or inhaling, or an unhealthy internal state, such as old age, obesity, or high blood pressure.

At this age, body outlines illustrating anatomy and physiology are particularly useful. Before presenting the information, it is crucial to obtain an adequate picture of the child's knowledge and understanding so that information can be tailored to the child's level of understanding. Material that is too abstract or complex cannot be assimilated and is often misinterpreted. At this stage, children also enjoy opportunities to interact with same-sex peers and to meet in groups to work on projects or learn about their disease and its treatment. During hospitalization, opportunities for meaningful social interactions with peers and hospital staff can be very beneficial, if adequate preparation and support are provided (O'Dougherty, 1983).

It is important to provide alternative avenues to friendships and achievement when the child's illness and treatment necessitate prolonged absences from school. Medical restrictions or activity limitations at this time can interfere significantly with the child's sense of achievement, mastery, and skill development. If the child is bedridden or confined, play opportunities are diminished. Play restrictions can block one of the major channels available to the child for working out tension or resolving aggressive feelings. One serious consequence of chronic illness can be withdrawal from social relationships and retreat to a fantasy world of unhealthy proportions. The overly quiet, passive, compliant child, although certainly not a management problem, may be showing signs of poor coping and require intervention as intensive as for the child who is combative, resistive, and noncompliant. The more pro-longed the illness, the greater the likelihood of significant disruptions in the areas of home, school, and peer relations.

ADOLESCENCE: PUBERTY TO AGE 19 YEARS

The developmental tasks faced by adolescents are multifaceted and in-clude four separate but interrelated goals that must be completed in order for them to become functioning adults (Brown, 1978). First, the adolescents must separate effectively from their parents and establish a self-identity capable of independent action. Second, they need to de-velop a mature sense of sexuality, which infers the ability to become involved in a relationship on a caring, giving basis. Third, they must develop a realistic vocational goal. Finally, they need to develop a posi-tive self-image and a personal code of ethics and behavior. A severe or chronic illness during this period can interfere with development in any of these areas. Feelings of security and self-worth and a positive identity can be difficult to establish when an illness affects bodily functioning or physical appearance. Illness signifies weakness for many teenagers, and in fact, it is often accompanied by loss of strength, fatigue, and poor stamina. For boys, a chronic illness or physical disability may interfere with the development of their sense of masculinity and their ability to compete and interact successfully with male peers (Hurtig et al., 1989). For girls, an illness may lead to feelings of being different, defective, sexually unattractive, or without worth (O'Dougherty, 1983).

Issues that emerge during this stage of development differ in a variety of ways from issues that concerned younger children. Foremost among the concerns of adolescents are the needs for privacy, confidentiality, participation in decision making, consent for treatment, and deep con-cern over how illness or disability might affect relationships with the opposite sex, fertility, reproductive capacity, and vocational possibilities. These concerns directly relate to the developmental goals outlined above (Hofmann, 1983).

In order to understand the particular fears of adolescents, an under-standing of adolescent developmental processes is necessary. At no time outside of gestation and infancy do changes occur at a faster rate. During childhood, healthy individuals grow at the rate of 2 to 2 1/2 inches per year. This rate accelerates during adolescence, and during the year in which the adolescent growth spurt or peak height velocity occurs, the adolescent may grow 3 to 5 inches. At the same time this increase in size is occurring, the adolescent develops secondary sexual characteristics. Although almost all adolescents experience these changes between the ages of 8 and 17 years, age itself is a poor indicator of how far along an adolescent has developed physically. In order to better define adolescent physical maturation, the concept of grading development by use of the changes in configuration of secondary sex characteristics was developed by Dr. James Tanner of England (1962).

Important cognitive changes also occur at this time. Once the formal operational stage of cognitive development is attained, the adolescent is able to think and reason in abstract terms, to consider hypothetical possibilities and solutions, to approach a problem systematically and use combinatory logic, and to consider contrary-to-fact situations (Piaget, 1952/1963). These cognitive advances facilitate understanding of illness, the body, and body systems (Crider, 1981).

Formal operational explanations of illness are characterized by an ability to explain illness in terms of internal bodily dysfunction, to provide differentiated explanations of the etiology of various illnesses, and to speculate and hypothesize about cause-and-effect relationships. Bibace and Walsh (1980) report that adolescents who have attained formal operational thinking typically explain illness in terms of physiological and psychophysiological processes. (It is important to note that not all adolescents make this transition from concrete to formal operational thought.) When a physiological explanation is provided, illness is explained in terms of malfunctioning internal organs or processes. Multiple causes for a disease can be postulated. Psychophysiological explanations describe an illness in terms of internal physiological processes and also suggest that psychological processes such as thoughts and feelings can affect bodily functioning and be causally related to illness onset (Bibace & Walsh, 1980).

Substages of Adolescence

Because of the tremendous changes (biological, cognitive, psychosocial) that occur during adolescence, this stage is often subdivided into three phases: early (puberty to 14 years), middle (15 to 16 years), and late (17 to 19 years or older) (Brown, 1978). Particular issues are more salient in each period.

Early adolescence is a time of confusion—confusion about the body, confusion about sexuality, confusion about capacity to think and evaluate situations correctly—and vacillation between dependent and independent desires. Problems in following rules, regulations, and authority are typical, as are rebelliousness and defiance of parental values. Secretiveness, self-preoccupation, loneliness, and feelings of inadequacy are frequently encountered. The adolescent may use provocative, even hostile, ways of eliciting attention, may display hypochondriacal concerns, and might become quite egocentric and self-absorbed (Petrillo & Sanger, 1980).

Middle adolescence is a time of less rebelliousness and more reliance on peers for support, values, and recognition. There is a subtle and more intellectual testing of parents as well as a growing need for autonomy. Attempts to form relationships with the opposite sex, sexual experimentation, and reluctance to confide in parents are also common. The peer-group association can be a force for both good and bad. It can introduce the adolescent to harmful behaviors and substances, but it can also provide the adolescent a haven from the world of children and adults.

The *late adolescent* is much more future oriented and often is fairly emotionally independent from parents and peers. There is an effort to relate to parents as adults, and often values are established that are closer to those of the parents. This is often a period in which vocational goals are considered seriously and ideals, future aspirations, and personal relationships are evaluated. Late adolescents are concerned with the question, "As an adult, what will I do?" The refining of vocational goals and the development of intimate sexual relationships based on mutual concern for each other's welfare continues well into young adulthood. More success in these arenas is made possible because early physical and cognitive changes usually consolidate and feelings become more manageable and under control (Petrillo & Sanger, 1980).

Special Fears of Adolescents

Adolescents' perceptions of a physical problem or disability are dramatically influenced by their unique developmental status. One primary fear experienced by adolescents, particularly in the early and middle stages, is that of physical disruption. The *fear of loss of physical integrity* is considerable and sometimes overrides concerns about future prognosis and the implications of the illness for health status. For instance, an early or middle adolescent with cancer may be more concerned with the disfiguring effects of chemotherapy (hair loss, emaciation, etc.) than with the possibility of death.

The second fear that adolescents commonly experience when faced with a chronic illness or disability is the *fear that they will not be able to separate successfully from their parents.* A chronic illness can interfere significantly in the separation process by necessitating continued parental caregiving in various areas. For example, in the case of amputation resulting from malignancy or paraplegia resulting from spinal cord injury, adults may need to help with actual physical mobility, feeding, and dressing. A disease such as cystic fibrosis, which necessitates multiple treatments on a daily basis by a second person, usually the parent, will tend to prevent an adolescent from physically separating from the home. Unless the parents are quite attuned to the adolescent's need for independence, this task of adolescence is retarded. Coping mechanisms in such situations often are characterized by passive-aggressive or manipulative responses, which allow the adolescent to indirectly achieve control of the situation. Such responses are also used with health care providers, especially under periods of increased stress (hospitalization, exacerbations of the illness, outpatient clinic visits).

The *fear of loss of control* is closely tied to the fear of not being able to achieve independence. Adolescents are trying to become mature adults, able to achieve control over their own life. Feelings of helplessness and loss of control are particularly acute during hospitalization (Hofmann, 1983). These feelings are intensified when the setting demands complete compliance without allowing an opportunity for participation in decision making and discussion of alternatives. Adolescents may respond to this feeling of loss of control with several coping mechanisms: depression, acting out, regression, noncompliance. It is extremely important that persons working with adolescents involve them directly in their own care and management. Educational meetings, where information can be presented and questions encouraged, are essential. In addition, opportunities to talk privately (without parents present) with the physician and hospital staff can facilitate discussion of fears, concerns, and practices. Assurances of confidentiality are also appropriate, provided that the adolescent is informed about the limits of confidentiality (e.g., if the adolescent is suicidal, homicidal, or refusing needed treatments). If a confidence cannot be held, it is important to tell the adolescent and to discuss the reasons why confidentiality cannot be respected in that instance (Petrillo & Sanger, 1980).

The *fear of being different from peers* is also heightened by a chronic illness or disability. Any physical or physiological abnormality can heighten this sensitivity and interrupt the process of relating to peers, forming sexual attachments, and achieving a positive, realistic self-image. In order to protect themselves from these painful feelings of difference and inadequacy, some adolescents avoid peers while others deny the illness. These responses, carried to a pathological level, result in marked isolation with depressive thoughts and feelings or noncompliance with medical care (e.g., a diabetic adolescent denies the need to take daily insulin).

Another defense typically used by teenagers and adults is intellectualization, attempting to dissociate the technical aspects of the disease from the emotional impact. This strategy is adaptive if it prevents the adolescent from becoming overwhelmed by what is happening, but it can become a detriment if it blocks working through the grief over the diagnosis. Compensation is perhaps one of the most successful coping mechanisms, particularly if the adolescent can develop substitute activities or find alternative sources for peer support, such as therapeutic or social groups for adolescents with similar problems. Some ways in which the parents and medical staff facilitate compensation include helping the patient select clothing that will conceal any physical disfigurement, exploring new hair fashions, seeking consultation with a beautician, working on skill improvement in areas not dependent upon physical activity (reading, computers, chess), and encouraging expression of concerns, fears, and thoughts through poetry, music, and dance. Feelings of self-esteem and competence can also be enhanced by getting adolescents to teach others about their illness and its treatment.

The *fear of dying* is the ultimate fear that many ill adolescents face. This fear is particularly intense for adolescents who have a possibly fatal illness such as cancer, a degenerative illness such as muscular dystrophy, or an illness with potentially life-threatening episodes such as status asthmaticus or status epilepticus. The fear of dying can result in depression, acting out, isolation, suicide attempts, or intellectualization. Often the particular stage of adolescence will influence the type of coping mechanism employed. The early or middle adolescent is more likely to act out with a major change in physical behavior and is more likely to view isolation and suicide as a means to attaining a "safe haven." The older or middle adolescent tends to experience the affect more directly as depression and to have suicidal thoughts but better control over physical impulses. It is important to identify the adolescents' coping and defense strategies, differentiating those who have a realistic acceptance of their disease and prognosis from those who are inappropriately pessimistic, hopeless, and vulnerable to depression and suicide.

CONSULTATION AND INTERPROFESSIONAL COLLABORATION

When is it important to ask for consultation regarding a patient's response to his or her illness? Mental health consultation may be needed: (1) if depression or regression persists beyond the early stages of the disease or inhibits the return to normal developmental pursuits; (2) if suicidal ideation or marked isolation is observed; (3) whenever severe acting out or extreme denial of the illness interferes with medical management and compliance.

Because of the different skills needed in various situations, a multidisciplinary approach is necessary for children and adolescents with chronic health problems. No single profession can meet all the needs of chronically ill youth. Collaboration among physicians, nurses, social workers, psychologists, allied health professionals (physical, occupational, and speech therapists), nutritionists, educators, and religious personnel can be a key factor in forming a coordinated approach so as to allow the family to achieve mastery of the problem and allow the child to progress successfully into adulthood.

REFERENCES

Ainsworth, M. D. S. (1973). The development of mother-infant attachment. In B. Caldwell & H. N. Ricciuti (Eds.), *Review of child development research* (Vol. 3). Chicago: University of Chicago Press.

Bergmann, T., & Freud, A. (1965). *Children in the hospital.* New York: International Universities Press.

Bibace, R., & Walsh, M. E. (1980). Development of children's concepts of illness. *Pediatrics, 66,* 912–917.

Bibace, R., & Walsh, M. E. (Eds.). (1981). *New directions for child development: Children's conceptions of health, illness, and bodily functions* (Vol. 14). San Francisco: Jossey-Bass.

Breslau, N. (1985). Psychiatric disorder in children with physical disability. *Journal of American Academy of Child Psychiatry, 24,* 87–94.

Brown, R. T. (1978). Assessing adolescent development. *Pediatric Annals, 7,* 587–597.

Bruhn, J. G., Hampton, J. W., & Chandler, B. C. (1971). Clinical marginality and psychological adjustment in hemophilia. *Journal of Psychosomatic Research, 15,* 207–213.

Cadman, D., Boyle, M., Szatmari, P., & Offord, D. R. (1987). Chronic illness, disability, and mental health and social well-being findings of the Ontario Child Health Study. *Pediatrics, 79,* 805–813.

Crider, C. (1981). Children's conceptions of the body interior. In R. Bibace & M. E. Walsh (Eds.), *New directions for child development: Children's conceptions of health, illness, and bodily functions* (Vol. 14). San Francisco: Jossey-Bass.

Daniels, D., Miller, J. J., Billings, A. G., & Moos, R. H. (1987). Psychosocial functioning of siblings of children with rheumatic disease. *Journal of Pediatrics, 109,* 379–383.

Drotar, D., Doershuk, C. F., Stern, R. C., Boat, C. F., Boyer, W., & Matthews, L. (1981). Psychosocial functioning of children with cystic fibrosis. *Pediatrics, 67,* 338–343.

Field, T. M., Sostek, A. M., Goldberg, S., & Shuman, H. H. (Eds.). (1979). *Infants born at risk: Behavior and development.* New York: Spectrum Medical and Scientific Books.

Gellert, E. (1978). What do I have inside me? How children view their bodies. In E. Gellert (Ed.), *Psychosocial aspects of pediatric care.* New York: Grune & Stratton.

Hodgman, C. H., McAnarney, E. K., Myers, G. J., Iker, H., McKinney, R., Parmellee, D., Schuster, B., & Tutihasi, M. (1979). Emotional complications of adolescent grand mal epilepsy. *The Journal of Pediatrics, 95,* 309–312.

Hofmann, A. D. (1983). *Adolescent medicine.* Menlo Park, CA: Addison-Wesley.

Holmes, D. L., Nagy, J. N., & Pasternak, J. F. (1984). *The development of infants born at risk.* Hillsdale, NJ: Lawrence Erlbaum Associates.

Hurtig, A. L., Koepke, D., & Park, K. B. (1989). Relation between severity of chronic illness and adjustment in children and adolescents with sickle cell disease. *Journal of Pediatric Psychology, 14,* 117–132.

Kashani, J. H., Konig, P., Sheppard, J. A., Wilfley, D., & Morris, D. A. (1988). Psychopathology and self-concept in asthmatic children. *Journal of Pediatric Psychology, 13,* 509–520.

Kohlberg, L. (1976). Moral stages and moralization: The cognitive-developmental approach. In T. Lickona (Ed.), *Moral development and behavior.* New York: Holt, Rinehart, & Winston.

Lazarus, R. S., & Folkman, S. (1984). *Stress, appraisal, and coping.* New York: Springer.

Lazarus, R. S., & Launier, R. (1978). Stress-related transactions between person and environment. In L. H. Pervin & M. Lewis (Eds.), *Perspectives in international psychology.* New York: Plenum Press.

Lipowski, Z. J. (1970). Physical illness, the individual and the coping process. *Psychiatry in Medicine, 1,* 91–102.

Mattsson, A. (1972). Long-term physical illness in childhood: A challenge to psychosocial adaptation. *Pediatrics, 50,* 801–811.

McAnarney, E. R., Pless, I. B., Satterwhite, B., & Friedman, S. B. (1974). Psychological problems of children with chronic juvenile arthritis. *Pediatrics, 53,* 523–528.

Moos, R. H., & Tsu, V. D. (1977). The crisis of physical illness: An overview. In R. H. Moos (Ed.), *Coping with physical illness.* New York: Plenum Medical Book Company.

Mrazek, D., Anderson, I., & Strunk, R. (1985). Disturbed emotional development of severely asthmatic preschool children. In J. Stevenson (Ed.), *Recent research in developmental psychopathology. Journal of Child Psychology & Psychiatry.* (Book Suppl. No. 4, pp. 81–94). Oxford: Pergamon.

O'Dougherty, M. M. (1983). *Counseling the chronically ill child: Psychological impact and intervention.* New York: Viking Penguin.

Petrillo, M., & Sanger, S. (1980). *Emotional care of hospitalized children: An environmental approach* (2nd ed.). Philadelphia: J. B. Lippincott.

Piaget, J. (1963). *The origins of intelligence in children* (M. Cook, trans.). New York: W. W. Norton. (Originally published in 1952).

Pless, I. B., & Pinkerton, P. (1975). *Chronic childhood disorder: Promoting patterns of adjustment.* London: Henry Kimpton.

Pless, I. B., & Roghmann, K. J. (1971). Chronic illness and its consequences: Observations based on three epidemiological surveys. *Journal of Pediatrics, 79,* 351–359.

Pless, I. B., Roghmann, K. J., & Haggerty, R. J. (1972). Chronic illness, family functioning, and psychological adjustment: A model for the allocation of preventive mental health services. *International Journal of Epidemiology, 1,* 271–277.

Pless, I. B., & Satterwhite, B. B. (1975). Chronic illness. In R. J. Haggerty, K. J. Roghmann, & I. B. Pless (Eds.), *Child health and the community.* New York: John Wiley.

Rothbaum, F., & Weisz, J. R. (1989). Child psychopathology and the quest for control. In A. E. Kazdin (Ed.), *Developmental clinical psychology and psychiatry* (No. 17). Newbury Park, CA: Sage Publications.

Rutter, M., Tizard, J., & Whitmore, K. (Eds.). (1970). *Education, health, and behavior.* London: Longman.

Seidel, U. P., Chadwick, O. F. D., & Rutter, M. (1975). Psychological disorders in crippled children: A comparative study of children with and without brain damage. *Developmental Medicine and Child Neurology, 17,* 563–573.

Tanner, J. M. (1962). *Growth at adolescence* (2nd ed.). Oxford, England: Blackwell Scientific Publications.

Tavormina, J. B., Kastner, L. S., Slater, P. M., & Watt, S. (1976). Chronically ill children: A psychologically and emotionally deviant population. *Journal of Abnormal Child Psychology, 4,* 99–110.

Tew, B., & Laurence, K. M. (1985). Possible personality problems among 10 year old spina bifida children. *Child: Care, Health and Development, 11,* 375–390.

Varni, J. W., Wilcox, K. T., & Hanson, V. (1988). Mediating effects of family social support on child psychological adjustment in juvenile rheumatoid arthritis. *Health Psychology, 7,* 421–432.

Vitaliano, P. P., Russo, J., Carr, J. E., Maiuro, R. D., & Becker, J. (1985). The Ways of Coping Checklist: Revision and psychometric properties. *Multivariate Behavioral Research, 20,* 3–26.

Wallander, J. L., Varni, J. W., Babani, L., Banis, H. T., DeHaan, C. B., & Wilcox, K. T. (1989). Disability parameters, chronic strain, and adaptation of physically handicapped children and their mothers. *Journal of Pediatric Psychology, 14,* 23–42.

Wallander, J. L., Varni, J. W., Babani, L., Banis, H. T., & Wilcox, K. T. (1988). Children with chronic physical disorders: Maternal reports of their psychological adjustment. *Journal of Pediatric Psychology, 13,* 197–212.

CHAPTER THIRTEEN

Stress from Parental Depression: Child Risk, Self-Understanding, and a Preventive Intervention

William Beardslee

Portions of this chapter are reproduced with permission of the author from Beardslee, W. R. (1990). The development of a preventive intervention for families in which parents have serious affective disorder: Clinical issues. In G. I. Keitner (Ed.), *Depression and families: Recent advances*. Washington, DC: American Psychiatric Association Press.

Youngsters who grow up in families in which parents have serious mood disorder (affective illness, such as major depression) are more likely to develop psychopathology and social impairment over the course of adolescence than comparison groups (Beardslee, Keller, & Klerman, 1985; McKnew et al., 1979; Waters, 1987; Weissman et al., 1984; Welner et al., 1977; Welner & Garrison, 1985). Investigators have emphasized the need for preventive intervention programs for such youngsters (Grunebaum, 1984; Philips, 1983). Given the high rates of mood disorder in the population (Weissman & Myers, 1978) and the large number of clinicians of various disciplines who treat such disorders in adults, it is surprising that programs focused on preventive intervention for children and adolescents in these families have not yet appeared.

THE STRESS OF LIVING WITH DEPRESSED PARENTS

It has been clear to clinicians for a number of years that youngsters whose parents have serious mood disorder experience a wide range of stresses and are at special risk (see Table 13.1). Although the parental disorder is rarely labelled as an illness or given a diagnosis per se, the youngsters' lives are substantially disrupted by the presence of serious mood disorder in the parents. The disruptions most fundamentally involve parental caretaking functions. Youngsters experience their parents as limited in energy and attention that can be directed to their concerns. Other stresses often accompany a major mental illness, such as frequent moves, loss of income, loss of social supports, divorce, and marital dis-

TABLE 13.1. *Some Child and Adolescent Stressors Often Resulting From Parent Depression or Other Mood (Affective) Disorders*

Affective blunting or distance of parent
Confusion about parent's status (ill or not?)
Decreased parental caretaking energy
Economic hardship
Feeling of responsibility for ill parent
Identification with depressed parent
Increased risk of parental physical illness
Increased stress on healthy parent
Increased divorce risk
Marital tension and conflict
Frequent moves
Parental irritability
Psychological unavailability of parent

cord. Understandably, these are experienced as profound disruptions by children. Finally, the behavior of the parent with affective illness is very often incomprehensible to the child because it is placed on the continuum of normal behavior; affective illness is not often labelled as such in the family. Thus the symptoms of lack of interest, lack of energy, lack of attention, irritability, and sleeplessness that intermittently become severe are bewildering for the child. Sadly, children often blame themselves or, at least, try to cure or make their parents better without understanding what is going on. The following discussion describes a preventive intervention program that attempts to integrate empirical research observations with these clinical experiences of children.

PREVENTION METHODOLOGY

In the history of the mental hygiene movement, claims have often far outstripped what could be accomplished through prevention (Spaulding & Balch, 1983). Although an increasing sophistication has characterized both the dialogue and the research conducted in preventive intervention in recent years (Chassin, Presson, & Sherman, 1985; Earls, 1987; Eisenberg, 1981; Munoz, 1987; Rolf, 1985), there are substantial methodological problems in demonstrating preventive effects (Eisenberg, 1984; Rutter, 1982).

Nevertheless, advances in conceptualization and design have made possible some sound empirical studies of successful psychosocial preventive interventions, including early interventions with high-risk youngsters, such as Head Start (Berrueta-Clement et al., 1985; Lazar & Darlington, 1982; McKey et al., 1985; Zigler & Valentine, 1979), and a number of school-based interventions (Chandler et al., 1984; Kolvin et al., 1981).

Investigators have agreed that prevention programs must have specified interventions with clearly targeted goals and measurable outcomes in order to constitute reasonable empirical approaches to the problem. Two separate approaches have merit. One is based on disease prevention by the identification of a specific etiological agent and the removal of that agent, whether of genetic, infectious, metabolic, or psychosocial origin. The second is based on encouraging or developing the inherent adaptive capacities of individuals (e.g., Head Start). The review below of data on children of parents with mood disorder, specifically focused on what clinicians are likely to encounter in such families, suggests specific areas necessary for intervention. Similarly, a review of studies of resilient adults and youngsters suggests that self-understanding may be useful in preventive intervention.

EMPIRICAL FINDINGS IN CHILDREN OF PARENTS WITH MOOD DISORDER

Five separate empirical investigations—employing standard structured research interviews scored according to criterion-based diagnostic systems—concur in demonstrating higher lifetime rates of diagnosable general psychopathology and higher rates of major depression in the offspring (ages 6 to 19) of parents who presented for psychiatric treatment for mood (affective) disorder compared to children of control families (Beardslee et al., 1985; McKnew et al., 1979; Weissman et al., 1984; Welner et al., 1977; Welner & Garrison, 1985). Lower overall rates of adaptive functioning were also described in several of these studies. These findings are supported by a large number of other investigations employing various methodologies (e.g., Waters, 1987; Zuckerman & Beardslee, 1987). Adolescence is a time of heightened risk. The incidence of episodes of major depression in the children of parents with mood disorders increases significantly throughout adolescence. The occurrence of an episode of mood disorder by the end of adolescence in youngsters at risk ranges between 20% and 40% in the five studies.

The previously described studies all involved clinically referred populations. A more recent study (Beardslee et al., 1988) reported similar effects for parental mood disorder in a random sample of subjects recruited from a prepaid health plan. Such an investigation was necessary because the incidence of mood disorder in the general population, and presumably in parents, is greater than that which presents for clinical treatment. A selection skew could result in differences in the nature of mood disorder in clinical samples. In this study, 81 families with 153 children were recruited by random sampling from an HMO and assessed with standard diagnostic and psychosocial function measures. Most of the serious psychopathology and almost all of the cases of mood disorder in the children (27 of 28 cases) occurred in the offspring of parents with affective disorder. This effect was not due to age, sex, or IQ of the children, nor social class or marital status of the parents. A similar effect was found for overall adaptive functioning. The same rates of disorder were present as in samples recruited and identified clinically. This finding highlights the need for preventive intervention broadly involving those who deal with parents, such as internists and pediatricians, as well as psychiatrists.

Clinical Profile

Examination of nine cases of major depression from one of these risk studies (Beardslee et al., 1985b) has shown that these disorders cause major disruptions in the youngsters' lives. The subjects were studied because their parents had mood disorder. The following case report gives a sense of the complexity of the experience of family depression.

A single Caucasian girl was 18 at the time of interview. At age 15, when entering tenth grade, she experienced severe dysphoric affect, loss of concentration, loss of interest in her surroundings, anergy, and lack of participation in activities. She withdrew from social activities with friends. She gained weight and spent several hours in bed every morning, refusing to get up. She reported persistent feelings of worthlessness, guilt, and wanting to die. She planned suicide but did not attempt it. Although there was no history of drug use, her mother reported that she acted as if she might be using drugs because she behaved so differently from usual. A few weeks after the start of school, she dropped out and did not return.

She was symptomatic for eight months, during which there were two episodes when she met criteria for major depression. She saw a counselor for therapy briefly. After the second episode, her symptoms did not recur, but she did not return to school. Since then she had periods lasting one to two days each month when she has experienced dysphoric affect and tearfulness without precipitating events.

Everyone in her family had experienced at least one psychiatric disorder. Her father had chronic alcoholism; her mother had several episodes of major depression, recurrent episodes of alcoholism, and an intermittent depressive disorder with onset in early adulthood. The parents' marriage was characterized by frequent discord and quarreling. An older sister had several episodes of major depressive disorder. An older brother met criteria for drug and alcohol abuse and for antisocial behavior.

Both she and her mother reported that she was functioning well at the time of interview. She was involved with a boyfriend whom she saw daily, hoped to marry, and with whom she had a close confiding relationship. She had been working steadily for five months as a full-time clerk in a store where she liked the work, did well at the job, and took pride in it. She had passed her high school equivalency test and planned to attend college in the fall. Her activities outside of work were varied and extensive.

From the point of view of the stresses to which youngsters are subjected, it is important to note that the father's alcoholism, the mother's depression, and the older sister's several episodes of depression all involved major symptoms and long episodes of illness to which this girl was exposed. In addition, the discord and quarrelling created a family environment that made it very difficult for normal development to take place. It is likely that these stresses did contribute to this young woman's distress. At least her own depression was not fully responded to by the family (Beardslee et al., 1985a).

In seven of the nine cases, symptom severity and overall level of disturbance led to a judgment by the senior child psychiatrist that detailed evaluation and treatment would have been indicated. No children were treated with pharmacological methods, although three subjects received brief counseling. In five of the cases, the youngsters also met criteria for non-affective psychiatric disorder at some time in their lives in addition to the affective disorder.

Assessment of the phenomenology of the major depressive episodes themselves, the course of the disorder, neuropsychological test findings, school functioning, and associated psychopathology present evidence that these children and adolescents suffered serious disruptions in many areas. The chronic and recurrent nature of the mood disorders in a number of youngsters is highlighted. This emphasizes the need for a program that alerts families as to what youngsters are likely to experience and that assists them to get help as early as possible.

Retrospective assessments have demonstrated a variable pattern for the timing of adolescent disorder in relation to parental disorder: some youngsters become ill shortly after parental illness, others somewhat later, often at the onset of puberty or other related stressors. Some youngsters exhibit a diagnosable disorder while others only display limitations in their relationships or school performance (Beardslee, Schultz, & Selman, 1987). Thus, an intervention program must be flexible.

Studies of the parental predictors of child disorder have shown that lowered social status, poor marital functioning, and increased severity and chronicity of mood disorder are all correlated with poorer outcomes in the youngsters (Keller et al., 1986). The presence of several diagnoses in parents rather than just mood disorder often leads to poorer outcome in youngsters (Weissman et al., 1984). There has been increased awareness of the chronic nature of affective illness, particularly the combination of a chronic depression along with acute episodes (Keller et al., 1983; Keller et al., 1988; Kovacs et al., 1984). Only about a third of adults with depression receive adequate treatment (Keller et al., 1982). A number of authors have noted that both parents often are impaired in families with affective illness, either through assortative mating or other mechanisms (Merikangas, 1984). This has particularly severe consequences for youngsters (Beardslee et al., 1985; Weissman et al., 1984). Taken together, these data emphasize the need for ongoing treatment of mood disorder in adults for the sake of the children. Clinicians must also be alert to other factors, such as illness in the spouse and marital discord.

Mechanism for Child and Adolescent Depression: Genetics and Stress

A genetic component of affective illness for both bipolar (manic-depressive) and depressive disorder has been demonstrated by the evidence from studies of monozygotic twins reared apart (Nurnberger & Gershon, 1982) and by family studies demonstrating that relatives of those with affective disorder are at much higher risk for affective disorder themselves (Gershon, et al., 1982). The mode of genetic transmission is unclear and the relative weight of genetic factors as opposed to other risk factors remains to be elucidated.

Psychosocial stress factors in families with serious affective disorder contribute to disorders in youngsters (Beardslee, 1984; Waters, 1987). These include increased rates of divorce and marital difficulty, frequent moves, diminished economic resources, and, most importantly, the inability of the parents to attend to and focus on the needs of the child. These are not specific to affective illness and characterize families with a variety of parental mental disorders. Rutter's analyses of the differences between a London borough and the Isle of Wight, with respect to rates of childhood psychopathology, have highlighted the importance of such non-specific factors (Rutter et al., 1974).

There may well be specific psychosocial factors in the transmission of illness from parent to child. Anthony has argued that certain specific cognitive and affective dissonances, especially in the mother, may be assimilated during development (Anthony, 1977, 1983). The process of identification with the ill parent is also important (Anthony, 1975). Attempts by the child to get inside the world of the ill parent in order to communicate with him or her may lead the child to take on some of the characteristics of the ill parent and see the world through the parent's jaundiced eyes (Beardslee, 1984).

RESILIENCY AND SELF-UNDERSTANDING

In addition to defining risk and impairment as a function of risk, a striking finding in a wide variety of studies of youngsters at risk has been the considerable resiliency manifested by some children (Anthony & Cohler, 1987; Garmezy, 1984; Rutter, 1986). The study of resiliency offers important clues as to what protects individuals in the risk situation. This review focuses on a particular dimension, that of self-understanding. This has been important in the author's previous studies and has particular relevance to preventive intervention because it is potentially amenable to change through intervention.

In the general studies of resiliency, positive interpersonal relationships have been found protective for children (Eisenberg, 1979; Lieberman, 1982; Rutter, 1979, 1986) and they are characteristic of those who are resilient. Investigators have recognized the importance of other protective factors, such as certain temperamental characteristics (Porter & Collins, 1982) and ways of responding, thinking, and acting, such as coping styles, positive sense of self, and control over one's surroundings (Garmezy, 1983).

Within this broad domain of ways of responding, thinking, and acting falls the concept of self-understanding. Beardslee (1981, 1983, 1988, 1989) has described the nature and role of self-understanding in dealing with stress. It has been defined as an internal psychological process through which an individual makes causal connections between experiences in the world at large and inner feelings. The process of understanding leads to an explanatory and organizing framework for the individual. The organizing framework develops over time and eventually becomes a stable part of the individual's experience. Self-understanding requires not only the presence of thought and reflection about oneself and events, but also action congruent with the reflection. In mature self-understanding there is an emotional importance tied to the organizing framework that is involved. The individual believes that self-knowledge is valuable, takes the process of self-understanding seriously, and devotes time to it. In this sense, self-understanding is a higher level integrative ego function (Beardslee, 1989).

Interest in self-understanding arose from the conviction that the place to begin studying individuals who have come through difficult experiences well is in what they themselves say about their own lives, especially about what sustained them. Part of the reason for this is because standardized instruments for measuring resiliency do not exist and part of it is because the individuals studied—civil rights workers and children of parents with mood disorder—have lived and worked in life situations that were unusual and not well-characterized. To deal with this, an open-ended life history data-gathering method was developed and then applied first to civil rights workers and finally to resilient children of parents with mood disorder systematically selected from a larger study. The work represents an evolution in both conceptual and experimental terms from an initial study of a few remarkable men and women to a more quantitative approach for identification and description of adaptive behavior. It is based on an inductive process that builds from individual life experience towards a more general concept of self-understanding.

In the studies below, the method was an in-depth interview with two main components: an open-ended history, starting with the individual's current situation, and a focus on the individual's understanding of himself or herself. Questions were asked such as, "How do you understand yourself and your situation? What keeps you going?" "What are your sources of strength?" and "How would you advise others in this situation to best help themselves?"

Civil Rights Workers

From interviews of eleven prominent southern civil rights workers, these themes emerged: the total involvement initially in the movement; the importance of closeness to others; the necessity of living with grief, rage, and loss, and yet keeping on working; and the development over time of a sense of worth, belief, and acceptance. All workers reported a sense of joy and accomplishment in taking action and not being passive. Many saw their being active as the way to channel their anger. Taking action, being an organizer, was for them the visible expression of a new consciousness. Over time this came to be a stable part of their identities. All emphasized the importance of good, long-term, stable relationships with parents or parental figures in childhood. Their sense of acceptance of themselves, particularly of their limitations, grew out of that initial consciousness at work and a comfort with who they had become. Several said that through the movement they found expression for what they had been feeling all along. All emphasized that what sustained them most were their relationships to others, involving a deep, personal closeness to other civil rights workers and to the people in the community they were organizing.

The civil rights workers had an unusual capacity to perceive accurately the world in which they lived, to make careful judgments about the shifting social realities and political realities they faced, to make sense of their own lives, and so see their own actions as a continuity from earlier experience with important figures in their own lives. As John Lewis, head of SNCC, said:

> *Being involved tended to free you. You saw segregation, and you saw discrimination, and you had to solve the problem, but you also saw yourself as the free man, as the free agent, being able to act. . . . After what Martin Luther King, Jr. had to say, what he did . . . as an individual you couldn't feel alone again. It [being in the movement] gave a new sense of pride; it was a new sense of identity, really. You felt a sense of control over what was happening and what was going to happen.*

Both self-understanding and the deep immersion in relationships with others were perhaps ways of dealing with the uncertainty of their lives. They had to forge a new role for themselves, without models. Their lives were often in danger. They were constantly buffeted by forces they did not control. What they did have, what was stable and under their control, were their attempts to understand themselves on the one hand and, on the other, intense relationships. The importance of these two principles—relationships and self-understanding—seemed applicable to the study of children of parents with mood disorders.

Children of Parents with Mood Disorders

The same qualitative, in-depth examination of resilient youngsters was undertaken as with the civil rights workers (Beardslee & Poderefsky, 1988). However, these resilient youngsters were selected by quantitative means from a larger pool of subjects. We chose 20 individuals out of about 200 children of parents with mood disorders and assessed 18 of them in 14 families in depth, first in the regular cross-sectional assessment by quantitative means and then at follow-up with a briefer quantitative assessment of psychopathology and functioning and also with the open-ended life history technique.

The parents were quite impaired. They had very high rates of major depression, alcoholism, and intermittent depression. Of the 28 biological parents, 17 had experienced affective illness, only 4 had never been ill, and 7 had experienced nonaffective illness. Most of the illnesses were chronic. The mean duration of the child's exposure to parental mood disorder was $4^1/2$ years. In 10 of the 14 families, both parents were ill and in 9 (65%) there was separation or divorce. The mean age of the 18 youngsters at assessment was 19. Almost all displayed very high levels of function. Sixteen of the 18 described themselves as valuing close, confiding relationships; they emphasized that these relationships were a central part of their lives. Thirteen were attending school and most were extensively and deeply involved in academic pursuits. Several were in prestigious colleges. All, both in school and out, had extensive and varied work histories with a long history of good performance. In addition to work, all but 2 of the 18 reported extensive involvement in activities outside of work.

All of the young men and women were deeply affected by their parents' illness. They described their experiences in terms of changes in parental behavior or attitude. Many of them noted the isolation or loneliness of their parents' lives. They often described the disruption of their own lives. This disruption included economic hardship, change of household or apartment, lack of parental awareness and involvement, and divorce. The young people described their experiences as full of disillusionment, confusion, and feelings of helplessness. An important theme was the ill parent's unavailability to perform usual tasks. Relationships were crucial for many of these young people in allowing them to separate from their parents, whether this was during an acute illness episode or not. Surprisingly, eleven of the 18 young men and women assumed a caretaking role either within the family or outside of it. This included taking charge of all the family functionings, managing finances and living situations, caring for younger children, and calling attention to the parent's illness, which in some cases led to assistance and recovery. Two others, although not involved in the major caretaking role within their families, were pursuing careers in the helping professions. Three others were siblings of caretakers.

These young adults displayed an extraordinary understanding of their parents' illness. They were able to reflect on changes over time in themselves and in their parents' behavior. They were able to distinguish clearly between their own experiences and their parents' illness. They were able to talk about their parents' difficulties and be saddened by them and empathic yet not overwhelmed. For example, they did not expect that their own life experience in the future would be the same as those of their parents. They were clearly able to think and to act sepa-rately from the parents' illness system. Before the interview they had reflected on their relationships and made sense of them.

In all these cases, the young people who were functioning well had noticed that there was something wrong with their parents and had concluded that they were not the cause of the parents' illness. They claimed that the realization that they were not the cause was crucial to objective understanding and to their capacity to deal with the experience of having a sick parent.

Practical Conclusions

Based on studies such as those above, a number of dimensions that characterize a resilient individual's ability to understand himself/herself and function well have emerged (Beardslee, 1989).

Adequate Cognitive Appraisal. The life situations the individuals faced were complex and changed over time. The individuals were able to describe the major dimensions of the stresses and how they changed. The appraisal of the stresses allowed the individuals to focus their energies and take appropriate action. For example, the focus for the civil rights workers, early in the movement, was the need to draw local people into the struggle, to lead them in demonstrations, and to help them form organizations. The workers' accounts of their early involvement reflected this. In the late 1960s and into the 1970s those who stayed had to develop managerial and fund-raising skills and assume leadership positions. Some ran for public office. They had to appraise correctly the shifting political and social landscape in order to find opportunities for small projects. Appraisals of the changing circumstances, and of the need for concomitant change within themselves, were crucial components in their long-term commitment to being organizers.

For the children of parents with affective disorder, the course of the parental illness in their life situations changed. Some parents underwent hospitalization and recovered. Some parents experienced chronic, insid-ious disorder from which there was no recovery and which came to color and change their perception of the world. Some families underwent divorce, and relationships with their fathers were lost to the youths. In some families, extreme economic hardship was experienced and, indeed, the youngsters themselves became wage earners. In some instances, youngsters actually got their parents into treatment for their disorders. Each of the different aspects of parental disorder and the attendant life disruptions had to be identified and responded to separately. The set of issues to be dealt with changed over time; it was essential for the youngsters to recognize what they were dealing with at a given time and to change their strategies.

Realistic Appraisal of the Capacity for and Consequences of Action. This dimension has two main components: (1) the individual's assessment of personal capacity for action, and (2) the individual's assessment of the effects of personal actions. Perhaps most striking in this regard were the civil rights workers, who had dreams of transforming the society in which they lived. This vision was vital to their work. Nonetheless, those who stayed in the movement were also able to focus on limited, achievable goals, such as the election of a black county commissioner or the organization of a successful economic boycott. More and more they came to direct their energies to what they could do and learned not to blame themselves for dreams that were not realized. They shaped what they expected of themselves to their capacities and to their assessments of what could be done.

The children of parents with serious affective disorder who wished to cure their parents came to understand that this was not possible. At the same time they realized that their own lives would not be forfeit and that they could be of great help to their parents in limited ways. This, too, involved realistic appraisal. A sense of identity and of continuity is necessary for an individual to be able to exercise this capacity.

Action. In all studies, the individuals who proved to be resilient were those who engaged in actions in the world in addition to having an inner understanding. Children of parents with affective disorders saw themselves as active problem solvers and took a tremendous amount of pride in that. Civil rights workers defined themselves by the actions that they took.

Integration of the Risk and Self-Understanding Perspectives

Clearly a variety of approaches to preventive intervention are necessary in a problem such as depression. These include more empirical studies of the nature and quantification of risk and of the nature and description of the range of outcomes. More work is needed on the appropriate treatment for depression and other disorders in children in order to more fully be able to engage in secondary and tertiary as well as primary prevention. However, clinical work with the families and the work on self-understanding suggest that the development of understanding—which leads to psychological separateness and the capacity for action—may have an important primary role.

In many families where a parental depression or other affective illness occurs, the illness is not understood as an illness, like a heart attack or diabetes. It is either not talked about at all and misunderstood by the child, or it is perceived as the sick parent's sole responsibility. Second, when a disorder in a child in such a family develops, it is very often not responded to by the parents. Even serious disorders go untreated, sometimes for as long as several years. The parents simply have not been able to attend to their child's problem. Third, after clinical review, there is considerable misunderstanding on the children's part about what is occurring. Often these youngsters feel guilty and blame themselves for the parent's difficulty. Fourth, those youngsters in the high-risk situation who are doing well function independently, with varied activities and relationships outside of the home. They clearly are separate from and understand themselves as separate from their parent's illness system. Finally, and most importantly, the parents in such families are deeply concerned about the possible impacts on the children of their own serious illnesses. There is an intense motivation in these parents to care for and make provision for the youngsters. They often ask, "What can I do to protect my child?" This interest and motivation will provide the necessary foundation from which to undertake an intervention in families in which affective illness has occurred.

THE INTERVENTION—A COGNITIVE PSYCHOEDUCATIONAL APPROACH

The following intervention protocol was developed to translate the findings about risk and resiliency into a standard measurable intervention that could be empirically tested. It has been used in families in which parents have experienced a recent affective illness, often involving a hospitalization, and in which the youngsters are in early- to mid-adolescence and not yet ill. While the protocol is described for a two-parent family, it can be applied to a single-parent family. The number of sessions is variable, with no more than ten and no fewer than six sessions. Some sessions involve parents alone, some the child (or children) alone, and some the parents and child together. In its pilot form, the intervention was conducted by a clinician different from the one treating the parent's illness, but both functions could be carried out by the same individual.

Four main content areas are covered in the intervention: assessment, cognitive teaching, focus on the child's experience (both present and future), and family discussion of the parent's illness. Table 13.2 presents the aims of the intervention and specific objectives for each aim.

TABLE 13.2.   Aims and Specific Objectives of the Preventive Intervention

Aims	Objectives
I. Assessment	1. To obtain a history of the parent's illness and the various family members' response to it. 2. To assess the need for clinical referral for family members at the time of interview.
II. Teaching	To discuss specifically with parents cognitive information about depression, risks to youngsters in general and to their youngsters in particular, and findings about resiliency.
III. Focus on the Child's Experience	To direct parents' attention to their child's needs and to action plans to which they can commit themselves to foster the youngster's adaptation and resiliency.
IV. Family Communication	To allow an exploration by parents and children of the experience of parental illness in family sessions. Make it clear that the youngster is not to blame and should not feel guilty. Engage the family in a process of discussion and understanding that can continue after the intervention. Follow up in 6 months to ensure that this process continues.

I. Assessment

Initially, one or two parent history sessions are held, either with each parent alone or with both together. A history of the parents' recent understanding of the illness is taken. Effects of the illness, particularly on the child, are explored. A brief assessment of how the child is functioning from the parents' point of view is obtained, along with screening for the presence of serious illness. Finally, parents are asked what concerns and questions they would like help with.

In child sessions, the clinician explores the child's overall experience in school, with friends, in the family, and in outside activities. Major symptoms, if any, are explored. Concerns about the parental illness, a description of the child's experience of the parent's recent illness, and the child's questions are elicited.

II. Teaching

With the parents alone, the clinician reviews what is known about the etiology of depression, its psychosocial manifestations, and the risks to children in growing up in families with serious affective illness. The adaptive capacities of youngsters who function well in this and related risk situations are described.

III. Eliciting the Family Life History and Linking the Experience with the Cognitive Information

The experience of serious affective disorder has profound impact on the family. It changes the way people view themselves and view one another. Furthermore, an affective illness is not experienced as a diagnosis but as a series of concrete behaviors that change individuals from the way they usually function. Depression is a chronic, insidious disorder without an abrupt onset. There is often irritability, sometimes fearfulness about suicide, and very often listlessness and lack of energy. Children, spouses, and others around the family see and respond to these changes. A series of discrete life events, such as hospitalization, often characterize the illness.

The clinician elicits the family's actual experience, both individually and collectively. The family are encouraged to tell their own story and then change or modify that story in light of the information available about the biological causes of depression and about what is helpful to youngsters. This provides an opportunity for avoiding guilt and blaming, for understanding the illness properly, and for planning for the future.

IV. Integration of the Cognitive Teaching with the Life Experience of the Family

Once the link is made between the family's own experience and the cognitive information, then planning for the future takes place in light of an increased understanding.

Sessions with both parents specifically explore strategies that the family can employ in discussing the parent's illness and planning for the future. The major areas covered include:

1. Need for clarity on the child's part as to what has happened to the parent and to the family.
2. Provision to ensure that the child does not feel guilty or responsible.
3. Encouraging the child's understanding of the nature of the illness and realization that the parent's unavailability and incapacity need not limit the child.
4. Encouraging explorations of support networks for the child, particularly re-establishment of those that may have been disrupted by parental illness.
5. Discussion of difficulties the child may face.
6. Discussion of how to anticipate and seek prompt treatment for any development of illness within the child.
7. Discussion of how to continue the ongoing process of understanding in the family. At the end of these sessions, the parents define together what they hope to accomplish in the family sessions with the children.

Finally, the parents together are asked to accomplish a task: namely, to lead a family session with the clinician's help to discuss the matters with the children. The cognitive information is gone over, plans for the future are outlined, and each individual is given a full chance to speak about both strengths and difficulties within the family.

It is made clear to the child that he or she is not to blame. There is discussion about how the child can understand various things that have happened to the parent. The child is encouraged to ask questions. Plans for the future include continued exploration of the issue and also any specific concerns that have come up.

If a clear, diagnosable disorder requiring treatment is identified either in youngsters or in the other parent, referral for treatment is made. Help with any future needed referral is also offered by the clinician.

Follow-up

After this initial intervention, the clinician is available to the family by telephone as needed, and meets with the family at six and twelve months. These follow-up sessions review both the intervention and what has happened since in terms of understanding the parental illness and any difficulties the youngsters may have had to face.

This approach is being evaluated in an empirical study with blind assessment pre- and post-intervention. Clinical experience and research thus far have brought to light two issues related to understanding in a broader sense, which deserve mention in conclusion.

One of these issues in helping children understand is whether the parental behavior is continuous or discontinuous with normal behavior. There is a fair amount of evidence suggesting that the children of schizophrenic parents at some developmental stages do better than the children of depressed parents. Why? As Anthony (1975) has intimated, it may be because the children of schizophrenic parents can understand the illness of schizophrenia as discrete and apart from them. The manifestation is so bizarre, the psychosis so clearcut, that they can understand the parental behavior as discontinuous, as something strange and alien, not of their own causing. It is not on a continuum of the ongoing relationship between child and parent. Thus, children of schizophrenics are freer in a way than children of depressed parents. Depression usually is insidious and chronically continuous with normal behavior. A mother or father may become increasingly irritable or increasingly preoccupied without a clearcut precipitant. Individuals become impaired slowly and gradually. In the beginning a parent's withdrawal, sadness, crying, or irritability may be attributed by the child to the child's failure or acting up. Over time, that explanation may become part of the child's world view. It is essential to break through this, to provide a different explanation, and to emphasize that the behavior in depression is really discontinuous from normal behavior. It is not the way the parents want it to be, and there is an alternate framework of understanding rather than that the child is responsible.

The other issue is the role of the person doing the intervention. All kinds of fears, concerns, and unspoken guilts and shames are part of serious mental illness. We do not treat serious mental illness the way we treat physical illness. The parents themselves are quite prone to feel terribly guilty, to be ashamed, and to blame themselves. They are often very ashamed of talking about the depression or even mentioning that they have been treated or hospitalized. The children sense this. Someone doing an intervention must be honest, responsible, and above all open to talking about anything that concerns the parents or the child about the illness. We must be flexible in dealing with it and show that we are not thrown by it or overwhelmed by it. Thus, the example of how the professional deals with the material is a model for the family.

None of us would choose to have children grow up in families where depression has occurred, but with the widespread prevalence of depression, many children do. That is their life experience. The challenge is to help families understand this unavoidable life experience and provide an opportunity for adaptation and growth.

SUMMARY

Review of studies of children and adolescents whose parents have experienced mood disorder indicates that such youngsters experience serious difficulties during adolescence. These difficulties may well result from an interaction of genetic risk and the additional stresses of living with affectively ill parents. Study of a number of samples of individuals in high-stress situations who are functioning well, including children of parents with affective disorder, have emphasized the importance of the role of self-understanding. Implications of these two sets of studies are integrated into a family-based cognitive psychoeducational approach to preventive intervention.

REFERENCES

Anthony, E. J. (1975). The influence of a magic-depressive environment on the developing child. In E. J. Anthony & T. Benedek (Eds.), *Depression and human existence.* Boston: Little, Brown.

Anthony, E. J. (1977). Preventive measures for children and adolescents at high risk for psychosis. G. W. Albee & J. M. Joffee (Eds.), *Primary prevention of psychopathology. Vol. II: The issues.* Hanover, NH: University Press of New England.

Anthony, E. J. (1983). The preventive approach to children at high risk for psychopathology and psychosis. *Journal of Children in Contemporary Society, 15,* 67–72.

Anthony, E. J., & Cohler, B. J. (Eds.) (1987). *The invulnerable child,* New York: Clifford Publications.

Beardslee, W. R. (1981). Self-understanding and coping with cancer. In G. P. Koocher & J. E. O'Malley (Eds.), *The Damocles syndrome: Psychosocial consequences of surviving childhood cancer.* New York: McGraw-Hill.

Beardslee, W. R. (1983). *The way out must lead in: Life histories in the civil rights movement* (2nd ed.). Westport, CT: Lawrence Hill.

Beardslee, W. R. (1984). Familial influences in childhood depression. *Pediatric Annals, 13*(1), 32–36.

Beardslee, W. R. (1989). The role of self-understanding in resilient individuals: The development of a perspective. *American Journal of Orthopsychiatry, 59,* 266–278.

Beardslee, W. R. (1990). The development of a preventive intervention for families in which parents have serious affective disorder: Clinical issues. In G. I. Keitner (Ed.), *Depression and families: Recent advances.* Washington, DC: American Psychiatric Association Press.

Beardslee, W. R., Keller, M. B., & Klerman, G. L. (1985a). Children of parents with affective disorder. *International Journal of Family Psychiatry, 6,* 283–299.

Beardslee, W. R., Keller, M. B., Lavori, P. W., et al. (1988). Parental affective disorder and psychiatric disorder in adolescent offspring in a non-referred sample. *Journal of Affective Disorders, 15,* 331–322.

Beardslee, W. R., Klerman, G. L., Keller, M. B., et al. (1985b). But are they cases? Validity of DSM-III major depression in children identified in family study. *American Journal of Psychiatry, 142,* 687–691.

Beardslee, W. R., & Podorefsky, D. (1988). Resilient adolescents whose parents have serious affective and other psychiatric disorder: The importance of self-understanding and relationships. *American Journal of Psychiatry, 145,* 63–69.

Beardslee, W. R., Schultz, L. H., & Selman, R. L. (1987). Level of social-cognitive development, adaptive functioning, and DSM-III diagnoses in adolescent off-spring of parents with affective disorders: Implications of the development of the capacity for mutuality. *Developmental Psychology, 23*(6), 807–815.

Berrueta-Clement, J., Schweinhar, L., Barnett, W., et al. (1985). *Changed lives: The effects of the Perry Preschool Program on youths through age 19.* Ypsilanti, MI: High/Scope Press.

Chandler, C. L., Weissberg, R. P., Cowen, E. L., et al. (1984). Long-term effects of a school-based secondary prevention program for young maladapting children. *Journal of Consulting and Clinical Psychology, 52*(2), 165–170.

Chassin, L. A., Presson, C. C., & Sherman, S. J. (1985). Stepping backward in order to step forward: An acquisition oriented approach to primary prevention. *Journal of Clinical and Consulting Psychology, 53,* 612–622.

Earls, F. (1987). Toward the prevention of psychiatric disorders. In R. E. Hales & A. J. Frances (Eds.), *Annual Review* (Vol. 6). Washington, DC: American Psychiatric Press.

Eisenberg, L. (1979). A friend, not an apple, a day will help keep the doctor away. *American Journal of Medicine, 66,* 551–553.

Eisenberg, L. (1981). A research framework for evaluating the promotion of mental health and prevention of mental illness. *Prevention of Mental Illness, 96*(1), 3–19.

Eisenberg, L. (1984). Prevention: Rhetoric and reality. *Journal of the Royal Society of Medicine, 77,* 268–280.

Garmezy, N. (1983). Stressors of childhood. In N. Garmezy & M. Rutter (Eds.), *Stress, coping and development in children.* New York: McGraw-Hill.

Garmezy, N. (1984). Children vulnerable to major mental disorders: Risk and protective factors. In L. Grinspoon (Ed.), *Psychiatry update* (Vol. III). Washington, DC: American Psychiatric Press.

Gershon, E. S., Hamovit, J., Gunroff, J. J., et al. (1982). A family study of schizoaffective bipolar I, bipolar II, unipolar, and normal control probands. *Archives of General Psychiatry, 39,* 1157–1167.

Grunebaum, H. (1984). Parenting and children at risk. In L. Grinspoon (Ed.), *Psychiatry update* (Vol. III). Washington, DC: American Psychiatric Press.

Keller, M. B., Beardslee, W. R., Dorer, D. J., et al. (1986). Impact of severity and chronicity of parental affective illness on adaptive functioning and psychopathology in their children. *Archives of General Psychiatry, 43*(10), 930–937.

Keller, M. B., Beardslee, W. R., Lavori, P. W., Wunder, J., Dils, D. L., & Samueson, H. A. (1988). Course of major depression in non-referred adolescents: A retrospective study. *Journal of Affective Disorders, 15*, 235–244.

Keller, M. B., Klerman, G. K., Lavori, P. W., et al. (1982). Treatment received by depressed patients. *Journal of the American Medical Association, 16*, 229–240.

Keller, M. B., Lavori, P. W., Endicott, J., et al. (1983). Double depression: A two year follow-up. *American Journal of Psychiatry, 6*, 689–694.

Kolvin, I., Garside, R. F., Nicol, A. R., et al. (Eds.). (1981). *Help starts here: The maladjusted child in the ordinary school.* London: Tavistock Publications.

Kovacs, M., Feinberg, T. L., Crouse-Novak, M. A., Paulauskas, S. L., & Finkelstein, R. (1984). Depressive disorders in childhood: I. A longitudinal approach. *Archives of General Psychiatry, 41*, 229–287.

Lazar, I., & Darlington, B. (1982). Lasting effects of early education: A report from the consortium for longitudinal studies. *Monograph on Social Resiliency in Childhood Development, 47*(2–3, Serial No. 195).

Lieberman, M. A. (1982). The effects of social supports on response to stress. In I. Golberge & S. Breznit (Eds.), *Handbook of stress: Theoretical and clinical aspects.* New York: Free Press.

McKey, R. H., Condelli, L., Ganson, H., et al. (1985). *The impact of Head Start on children, family and communities: Final report of the Head Start Evaluation Synthesis and Utilization Project.* Washington, DC: U.S. Government Printing Office. U.S. Department of Health and Human Services Publication No. (OHDS) 85-31193.

McKnew, D. H., Cytryn, L., Effron, A. M., et al. (1979). Offspring of patients with affective disorder. *British Journal of Psychiatry, 134*, 148–152.

Merikangas, K. R. (1984). Divorce and assortative mating among depressed patients. *American Journal of Psychiatry, 141*, 75–76.

Munoz, R. F. (1987). Depression prevention research: Conceptual and practical considerations. In R. F. Munoz (Ed.), *Depression prevention.* New York: Hemisphere.

Nurnberger, J. I., & Gershon, E. S. (1982). Genetics of affective disorder. In E. S. Paykel (Ed.), *Handbook of affective disorders.* New York: Guilford Press.

Philips, I. (1983). Opportunities for prevention in the practice of psychiatry. *American Journal of Psychiatry, 140*, 389–395.

Porter, R., & Collins, G. M. (Eds.) (1982). Temperamental difference in infants and young children: Ciba Foundation Symposium 89. London: Pitman.

Rolf, J. E. (1985). Evolving adaptive theories and methods for prevention research with children. *Journal of Consulting and Clinical Psychology, 53*, 631–646.

Rutter, M. (1979). Protective factors in children's response to stress and disadvantage. In R. Rolf & M. D. Kent (Eds.), *Primary prevention of psychopathology: Vol. III. Social competence in children.* Hanover, NH: University Press of New England.

Rutter, M. (1982). Prevention of children's psychosocial disorders: Myth and substance. *Pediatrics, 70*(6), 883–894.

Rutter, M (1986). Meyerian psychobiology, personality development, and the role of life experiences. *American Journal of Psychiatry, 143*, 1077–1087.

Rutter, M., Yule, B., Quinton, D., et al. (1974). Attainment and adjustment in two geographical areas: III. Some factors accounting for area differences. *British Journal of Psychiatry, 125,* 520–533.

Spaulding, J., & Balch, P. (1983). A brief history of primary prevention in the twentieth century: 1908 to 1980. *American Journal of Community Psychology, 11*(1), 59–80.

Waters, B. G. (1987). Psychiatric disorders in the offspring of parents with affective disorder: A review. *Journal of Preventive Psychiatry, 3*(2), 191–206.

Weissman, M. M., & Myers, J. R. (1978). Affective disorders in a U.S. urban community. *Archives of General Psychiatry, 35,* 1304–1311.

Weissman, M. M., Prusoff, B. A., Gammon, G. D., et al. (1984). Psychopathology in the children (ages 6–18) of depressed and normal parents. *Journal of the American Academy of Child Psychiatry, 23*(1), 78–84.

Welner, A., Welner, A., McCrary, M. D., et al. (1977). Psychopathology in children of inpatients with depression: A controlled study. *Journal of Nervous Mental Disorders, 164,* 408–413.

Welner, Z., & Garrison, W. T. (1985). Blind high-risk study of depressives' offspring: Preliminary data. *International Journal of Family Psychiatry, 6,* 301–314.

Zigler, E. F., & Valentine, J. (1979). *Project Head Start: A legacy of the war on poverty.* New York: The Free Press.

Zuckerman, B. S., & Beardslee, W. R. (1987). Maternal depression: A concern for pediatricians. *Pediatrics, 79*(1), 110–117.

CHAPTER FOURTEEN

Child Divorce Stress

L. Eugene Arnold
John A. Carnahan

That divorce, its antecedents, and its aftermath are stressful to children cannot be doubted. Even crude measures reflect the distress and malfunction that result. For example, Kosky et al. (1985) found $2^{1}/_{2}$ times the rate of single-parent divorced families in a child psychiatric sample as prevailed in the general population from which it was drawn. More importantly, about one-quarter of the entire sample had suffered parental divorce in the preceding 12 months, suggesting a temporal link. Nevertheless, the chronic effects on children's mental, emotional, social, and functional/academic development are of even greater concern (Guidubaldi & Perry, 1985; Hetherington, Cox, & Cox, 1985; Kalter, 1987; Wallerstein, 1985, 1987; Wallerstein & Kelly, 1984; Zaslow, 1989).

Before discussing such effects, a qualification is in order. Most of the findings cited below, although statistically significant on group data, are often of rather modest magnitude in comparison to the wide range of individual variation within the population of children of divorce. Therefore, the main value is for public health considerations. These group statistical findings have limited applicability to individual cases. They should not be used to stereotype children of divorce. Nevertheless, they can be used as background knowledge to guide individual evaluation.

Table 14.1 lists some of the wide variety of child stressors that accompany divorce and its ramifications. Not all of these deserve equal attention. Inspection of the table suggests three main clusters: (1) loss of access to parents, (2) change in physical surroundings and living arrangements, and (3) hostilities between the parents and intrusion of the legal system into the family. These are discussed in the latter part of this chapter, with special attention to the third cluster.

AGE AND SEX RISKS AND CHRONICITY

The children's age at the time of parents' divorce influences the constellation of effects children have shown in various studies. There is often an interaction with sex. Table 14.2 summarizes the different immediate and long-term profiles resulting from divorce at different ages. It should be studied in conjunction with Table 14.1.

In the past, there was discussion of high-risk critical ages, such as the Oedipal stage. However, it now appears that children at any age are at risk for ill effects from parental divorce. Kalter and Rembar (1981) felt there may be a slightly greater risk for younger children (below $2^{1}/_{2}$ years), perhaps because of the cumulative effect over more years. Wallerstein (1987) corrected for the cumulative effect by following several age cohorts for ten years and found those who were age 6-13 at divorce were less well-adjusted ten years later than those who were age 5 or younger at divorce. In any event, Kalter and Rembar (1981) did not

TABLE 14.1. *Possible Stresses Impacting Children from Parental Separation/Divorce*

Stressor	Special Age/Sex Risk Groups	Likely Effects and Mechanisms
Preceding marital strife	Younger children at first; older children and adolescents for long term	Insecurity. Fearfulness. Distorted view of male-female relations. Long-term painful, vivid memories of marital violence (except if below age 5 at divorce).
Break-up of home; loss of familiar; loss of ideal family life	Younger children and adolescents; Boys; Families where divorce decision impulsive	Disorientation; anger at parents; loss of stability; confusion about concept of "family"; regression. Aggression and other antisocial behavior. Reconciliation fantasies. Self-blame.
Need to move	School-age and adolescents	Loss of friends, disruption of peer relations. Change of school, disruption of education.
Psychological demand of having two homes	School-age; Joint-custody children	Instability. Need to juggle two sets of friends or periodically leave them. Concerns about fairness.
Lowered standard of living (perhaps poverty)	School-age (younger children if severe poverty); girls slightly more	Varies from social embarrassment and peer-relation impairment to cultural deprivation, possible malnutrition. General adjustment and school affected. Lower SES, results in lower social and academic competence.
Loss of noncustodial parent in general	Younger children	Grieving, depression, denial, regression, fantasy of reunion, anger, separation anxiety. Fear of abandonment by both parents. Single-parent families linked with lower social and academic competence on school entry.

(continued)

TABLE 14.1. (Continued)

Stressor	Special Age/Sex Risk Groups	Likely Effects and Mechanisms
Loss of father in particular	Young boys (preschool and elementary) Adolescent girls Possibly toddler girls	Boys: poor grades and work habits: nonassertiveness; poor impulse control; cognitive stunting; gender identity problems. Girls (adolescent): aggression; seeking of male attention; sexual precocity; wide variance in heterosexual trust; lowered self-esteem; identification with mother who is perceived as rejected by father.
Change in frequency of grandparent contact (more or less)	Younger children	Possible loss of noncustodial grandparents takes away support at time most needed. If custodial parent moves in with own parents, constant contact with grandparent could sour relationship or make strong attachment. If latter, then loss when eventually move out.
Parent divorce stress (litigation, economic hardship, emotional loss, need to move)	Younger children	Attachment problems (insecure or anxious). Parent preoccupation. Child perception of neglect or rejection. Guilt from blaming self for parent distress.
Custody/visitation battles and other post-divorce hostilities: Witnessing parental fights	Early school age	Psychological, sometimes physical, danger in crossfire. Ambivalence. Duplicity. Affect constriction. Pseudomaturity. Anxiety, tension, depression, somatization. Identity problems if side with opposite-sex parent;

Pressure to take sides Loyalty conflict Court testimony Abuse allegation Child stealing	Late school (preadolescents) Early school age School-age and adolescent Younger children Younger children	heterosexual trust problems if side with same-sex parent. Self-blame. Distortion of reality; confusion; possible "brain washing." Witnessing parental fights leads to avoidance, attempts to control, submissive distress, some aggression. Abuse allegation leads to high risk whether true or false. Loss of contact with one parent.
Decreased parental availability (parents preoccupied with own problems, single parent spread thin)	Younger children; Resurgence of risk in adolescence	Feeling of rejection/neglect. Insecurity, fear of abandonment. Angry acting out of frustration/disappointment or attempt to seduce more attention by good behavior. Tension. Somatic complaints.
Chronic "after-shock" (knowledge that parents had divorced)	Age 8 and below	Sense of loss and vulnerability. Longing for ideal, intact family. At ten-year follow-up, divorce was central life experience for half of those 6–8 years at divorce.
Remarriage	Girls	Further changes in home. Both sexes at first externalizing problems, continuing beyond two years for girls. Interferes with reconciliation fantasies and with close mother-daughter bond. Further dilution of parental attention. Intrusion of stepparent, step-siblings, and half-siblings. In some cases positive, especially for boys (re-establish two-adult home; dampen parent hostility or grief).

Sources: Fergusson et al., 1986; Gamble & Zigler, 1986; Guidubaldi & Perry, 1984, 1985; Hetherington, 1972; Hetherington et al., 1985; Johnston et al., 1985; Kalter, 1985; Kalter et al., 1987; Kalter & Rembar, 1981; Radin, 1981; Soldano, 1990; Southworth & Schwartz, 1987; Wallerstein, 1985, 1987; Wallerstein & Kelly, 1984.

TABLE 14.2. Age and Time Considerations in Children's Responses to Stress of Parental Divorce: Typical Age Group Responses and Change in Stress Response Over Time

Age at Divorce	Early Response (First 2 Years)	Chronic or Delayed Response (4–10 Years After Divorce)
Preschool	Unable to understand finality; some deny divorce. Feeling of causing divorce, guilt feelings. Fear, bewilderment, repression. Preoccupation with replaceability. Separation anxiety, frustration, violent fantasies. Changes in aggression (increased or decreased). Loss of play and enjoyment. Fear of abandonment. Deterioration through first 18 months of divorce, especially boys. Impairment of social and academic competence on school entry.	Repression of divorce memories; lowered cognitive competence. Longing for ideal, intact family. Aggressive/antisocial and withdrawing behavior. Boys aggressive, antisocial. Girls anxious, depressed, lower social competence. One-third depressed at five-year follow-up. Better overall adjustment at 10-year follow-up than 10-year follow-up of children older at divorce. Reconciliation fantasies, continued awareness of father with renewed need in adolescence.	*If below 2¹/₂ years at divorce:* Girls: increased peer aggression Boys: academic problems and peer non-aggression in adolescence. Both sexes: non-aggression to parents in school age. *If age 3–5¹/₂ at divorce:* Boys: school behavior problems and subjective symptoms in school age. Girls: academic problems in adolescence. Both sexes: increased adolescent aggression (family and peers).

378

Elementary School Age	Girls communicate more with mothers, boys less. Worry about not being able to visit enough. Boys nonaggressive with peers but aggressive to objects. If *age 6–8*: Frightened, disorganized. Grieving. Reconciliation fantasies. Anger to mother; inhibited aggression to father. Loyalty conflicts. If *age 9–12*: Loyalty conflicts: likely to choose sides with ambivalence to other. Attempt to master through activity and play. Identity problems. Anger. Somatization. Half incur severe drop in schoolwork. Boys more troubled.	Worse adjustment than those younger at divorce. Dependency, irrelevance, withdrawal, blaming. School refusal, truancy. Inattentiveness, decrease in schoolwork, aggression, misbehavior, mainly in boys. Girls much better adjustment unless remarriage. If remarriage, both sexes initial externalizing problems, but boys adjust in two years. In adolescence, girls increase hostility, power struggles, antisocial rebellion, seeking male attention. Both sexes: adolescent regression to school-age dress, manner, and interests, or pseudo-maturity. If *age 6–8 at divorce:* At 10-year follow-up: Fear of disappointment in love. Low expectations for career and relationships. Sense of powerlessness. Muted anger. Anxiety about independence. Concerns about father loss, renewed adolescent need for father, and perceived rejection by father. Poor grades. Longing for ideal, intact family. Half experience vivid, painful memories of marital violence. Girls episodic recklessness, early sexual activity (one-fourth undergo abortions at age 13–16); depression, suicide. If *age 9–12 at divorce:* At 10-year follow-up: Memories of divorce worse than younger groups. Adolescent delinquency. Sadness, resentment, sense of deprivation. Conservative morality.

(continued)

TABLE 14.2. (Continued)

Age at Divorce	Early Response (First 2 Years)	Chronic or Delayed Response (4–10 Years After Divorce)
Adolescence	Concern about parents' motives. Withdrawal from parents. Mourning of parents' marriage and family stability. Concern about own ability for lasting marriage. Depression, angry outbursts. Vacillating loyalties. Regression or maturational spurt. Less sex differences than younger.	If early pubertal at divorce: midadolescent regression to school-age dress, interests, and interpersonal style, or pseudo-maturity. At 5-year follow-up: adjustment depended on quality of parenting, lowered divorce conflict and continuity of visits. Girls: low self-esteem and more variance in heterosexual relations at college age. In adulthood 10-year post-divorce: vivid, troubling memories of divorce; sadness, resentment, sense of deprivation; worry about repeating parents' unhappy marriage, especially in women. High unemployment. Low rate of college. Conservative morality.

Sources: Fergusson et al., 1986; Guidubaldi & Perry, 1984, 1985; Hetherington, 1972; Hetherington et al., 1985; Kalter 1985; Kalter et al., 1987; Kalter & Rembar, 1981; Soldano, 1990; Southworth & Schwartz, 1987; Wallerstein, 1985, 1987; Wallerstein & Kelly, 1984.

find significant overall quantitative differences in adjustment by age of divorce. Rather, they found considerably stronger qualitative effects on type of adjustment. For example, compared to children of intact families, children who experienced parental divorce by age 2$^1/_2$ later showed nonaggression with parents; those who experienced divorce at age 3–5$^1/_2$ later had academic problems; and those who experienced divorce at age 6 and over later showed school refusal and truancy. School-age boys with divorce at age 3–5$^1/_2$ showed school behavior problems, but those with divorce at age 6 or older were nonaggressive with peers. Girls with divorce by age 2$^1/_2$ were aggressive with peers in school age but showed few problems in adolescence. In contrast, girls with divorce at age 3–5$^1/_2$ had few school-age problems, but in adolescence were aggressive with parents and peers and had academic problems. Johnston, Campbell, and Mayes (1985) found that in families with continuing disputes about custody and care, 6- to 8-year-olds tended to have submissive distress and somatic symptoms, decreasing with age, while 9- to 12-year-olds were more likely to be co-opted into their parents' battle and take sides, increasing with age.

The recency hypothesis—that the severity of a child's symptoms correlates negatively with length of time since divorce—receives no more research support than does the critical stage hypothesis (e.g., Kalter & Rembar, 1981). In fact, some studies find a deterioration in the child's adjustment over the first year or two post-divorce. Wallerstein (1985, 1987) and Wallerstein and Kelly (1984) found on ten-year follow-up a sobering residue of emotional, mental, academic, social, and even socio-economic problems. These varied by age, but generally included as a core: feelings of sadness and deprivation; resentment; longing for an ideal, intact family; and underachievement. Vivid, troubling memories of interparental violence and hostility continued to haunt about half those children who were older at divorce, although children who were age 5 or younger at divorce seemed to have succeeded in repressing such memories. As young adults, the children of divorce worried about repeating their parents' mistakes and had career aspirations below their abilities and below their parents'. Thirty percent of those not in college were unemployed, even though a younger cohort showed at ten-year follow-up as 16- to 18-year-olds a remarkable degree of self-support and self-sufficiency, possibly pseudo-mature in view of their anxiety about independence. Southworth and Schwartz (1987) found in college daughters of divorce more variance in heterosexual trust (compared to daughters of intact families) and more plans to cohabit before making a marriage commitment.

Probably the variation in nature of stress response at different ages of divorce is based partly on the child's developmental stage of cognitive ability. McGurk and Glachan (1987) studied 4- to 14-year-old children's conceptions of the continuity of parenthood after divorce. Four-year-olds from intact families either had a naive belief in the unshakable continuity of parenthood and current home or considered parenthood contingent on residence or affection. Some children as old as 8 shared these views. However, most 8-year-olds either conditioned parenthood on subsequent marital status or on the sex of the parent, or distinguished the marital and parental relationships. All children over age 10 distinguished the marital and parental relationships. In the divorced families, children of all ages had given up the naive belief in unshakable continuity. The younger ones tended towards the affection contingency. Despite a general pressure towards more mature beliefs among children of divorce, 20% of 8-year-olds regressed relative to intact families, swelling the proportion who conditioned parenthood on residence or affection. Almost half of children age 6 and younger continued to view parenthood as contingent on living in the same home. This has startling implications for their view of the noncustodial parent's relationship.

Interactions of Sex, Age, and Time

Some interactions of sex, age, and time are noteworthy. In general, boys from divorced families have more adjustment problems at elementary school age, while girls often seem to function about as well as girls in intact families (unless the mother remarries). At adolescence, the girls' problems seem to blossom, and in young adulthood they show serious problems with self-esteem and heterosexual relations (Hetherington, 1972; Hetherington et al., 1985; Kalter et al., 1985; Southworth & Schwartz, 1987; Wallerstein, 1985). Although school-age boys fare worse than girls from the divorce status, girls have more problems with remarriage. Immediately after remarriage, children of both sexes show adjustment problems. In two years, boys usually make the adjustment and then seem to do better than in nonremarried families, almost as well as boys in intact families. However, girls' problems with remarriage seem to continue (Hetherington et al., 1985). Over time, externalizing symptoms are more stable for boys and internalizing ones for girls. One explanation offered for some of these interactions is that at younger ages, girls benefit from a closer relationship with their mother, while boys miss their father more; however, in adolescence and young adulthood, daughters suffer from identification with a mother they perceive as having been found unattractive by the father (Hetherington et al., 1985; Kalter, 1987; Kalter et al., 1985). Support for this hypothesis comes from the finding by Guidubaldi and Perry (1985) that after a divorce girls communicate more with their mother but boys less. Hetherington (1972) and Wallerstein (1987) report increased psychological need for the father in adolescence (both sexes), and that girls from divorced families seek male attention more and initiate sexual activity earlier than those from intact families. In Wallerstein's (1987) upper-middle-class sample, 25% of the girls had had abortions by age 16. Another protective factor for school-age girls may be that they are more likely than boys to witness reasoning by contesting parents, whereas both sexes are equally likely to witness violence (Johnston et al., 1985). It should be noted that Fergusson, Dimond, and Horwood (1986), in a large New Zealand longitudinal study of children up to age 6, did not find such sex differences. They proposed that perhaps only older children show sex differences in the effects of marital discord, divorce, and remarriage.

In a comprehensive review of sex differences in divorce effects, Zaslow (1989) concluded that across numerous studies:

1. The data are best explained by the hypothesis that boys fare worse both short-term and long-term in single-mother families, while girls fare worse in father custody or with a remarried mother and stepfather.

2. Since most divorced mothers tend to remarry with time, sex differences in severity of impact on the child tend to disappear over time, but not merely because of time elapsing since divorce; rather, sex differences attenuate because of changing family form.

3. In single-mother custody, boys tend to show more externalizing antisocial symptoms than girls, but about the same amount of internalizing symptoms. In stepfather families, girls show increased externalizing and internalizing symptoms.

4. Sex differences are not explained by sampling technique (clinical vs. nonclinical), variable selection, data sources (parent vs. teacher), or time since marital disruption.

Any consideration of age and time factors needs to take into account the inherent risk of mathematical skew related to age at parental divorce. Children whose parents divorce early are presumably exposed to a greater intensity and possibly different profile of associated risks than those whose parents stay together longer. Fergusson, Horwood, and Shannon (1984) found the risk of family breakdown in the first 6 years of life significantly associated with shorter length of marriage at birth, type of marriage (common-law = four times the risk), planning of pregnancy (unplanned = twice the risk), lower socioeconomic status, instability of maternal childhood, and each parent's age at birth (under age 20 = ten times the risk of 35-year-olds), education, ethnic status, and church attendance (nonattending = twice the risk), but not with family size. When classified on these risk factors, the "worst prognosis" families had a 99%

rate of breakdown in the child's first five years compared to 1% for the "best prognosis" families.

LOSS OF ACCESS TO PARENTS

The most important stress cluster in Table 14.1 concerns the loss of parent time and attention. This is most obvious for the noncustodial parent, but also involves the custodial parent, who is often spread thin by the demands of single parenthood. This often results in what amounts to a partial parent-child separation.

Normal Background of Separation Anxiety

As mammals with a long period of juvenile dependency, humans are endowed with a strong predisposition to separation anxiety. According to the age of the child, this is manifested variously as protesting, crying, searching, anger, calling for mommy, and autonomic arousal upon unexpected abrupt or prolonged separation from the parent figure. Such behaviors serve to maintain contact with the protective caretaker, which is necessary for survival of the young mammal. On this fact might be based an operational definition for psychological parent: the psychological parent is the person whose absence elicits the strongest evidence of separation anxiety. See Goldstein, Solnit, and Freud (1979) for an explanation of "psychological parent."

A normal developmental phase of separation anxiety occurs in late infancy and toddlerhood as the child begins experimenting with autonomy and independent exploration (Mahler's stages of practicing and rapprochement). Toddlers are interested in exploring their environment, but preferably within sight or sound of the parent. When they note that they are out of perceptual contact with the parent, they run back and reestablish the contact. The urge to maintain contact with the parents is accentuated in the presence of strangers. At a young enough age (especially 7–9 months), the child will even refuse to leave the parent's arms in the presence of a stranger ("stranger anxiety"). Through age 2 it is still normal for the child to refuse to be left by the parent with a stranger in strange surroundings. By age 4, children should be able to separate easily for short periods from their parents after the parent has introduced them to the stranger and shown at least nonverbally that the stranger and the situation can be trusted. The length of time for which a child can separate from the parent without distress gradually lengthens through the process of growing up. By school age, normal children can tolerate all-day separations and an occasional overnight separation. By adolescence, they can usually tolerate weeks of separation.

In the process of expanding the length of time during which they can tolerate separation from parents, many children make use of a transitional object. The object, whether it be security blanket, teddy bear, doll, pacifier, or anything else, represents the parent's presence. It gives the child a tangible substitute for the parent. Transitional objects are normal through the preschool years, and some children continue to need them into the early school years (for example, Linus of "Peanuts" fame). Any disruption of separation security (the normal process of gradual "weaning" from parental dependence) can induce regression to less mature function. See Chapter 19 for an example.

Divorce as Parent Loss

As might be expected, the stress most likely to induce regression to toddler-like separation anxiety is excessively prolonged separation from or loss of a parent. This can occur not only with death (see Chapter 15), but also with prolonged parental mental illness (Chapter 13), an unusually long parental business trip or childless vacation, or divorce. Other stresses that could induce regression include illness (see Chapter 12), fatigue, or severe disappointments. Of these, divorce may well be the most common chronic stressor of modern children. Of course, in some cases, the divorce is necessary to extricate the children from a damaging situation: for example, where there is violence (either toward the children or toward the mother or both), where there is incest or where the tension and anxiety caused by the hostility and anger between the parents clearly call for the departure of one parent from the daily scene. However, even in such situations the children usually miss the absent parent.

The "missing parent" is usually the father. The literature abounds with documentation of the impact of father loss on both sexes, but especially boys. For example, Guidubaldi and Perry (1985), in reporting boys' sadness, decreased schoolwork effort, and inappropriate behavior at 4 years post-divorce, noted that boys who had maintained frequent father contact fared better. A father figure's presence and influence is suspected to be necessary for optimum cognitive development, analytical thinking, and assertiveness in boys (Radin, 1981). Hetherington et al.'s (1985) finding that boys did better than girls in the long run if their mothers remarried tends to support the need for boys to have an easily accessible father figure, preferably in residence. A daughter's need for father, although not as immediately obvious and dramatic as a son's needs, surfaces in adolescence and is apparently not easily satisfied by a stepfather, with whom stepdaughters often have conflict, especially in adolescence. Both sexes experience a renewed need for father in adolescence, which provides a second chance for reworking unresolved parent-child problems from earlier years (Wallerstein, 1985). They often actively seek him out. Wallerstein (1987) found that over 40% of one cohort voluntarily moved to father's home during adolescence, most for a year or more. Over half expressed intense feelings of rejection by their father. Although more than half complained of painful, vivid memories of marital violence, their association to this was that divorce meant loss of father, not relief from conflict. Resentful feelings of rejection were often exacerbated by the father's failure to provide support. In sons, these feelings were associated with low self-esteem, poor academic performance, and weak aspirations (Wallerstein, 1987). As adolescents and young adults, daughters sought male attention, often dated older men, became sexually active younger, considered men weak and unfeeling, had a negative view of women, and had problems with heterosexual trust, believed to be related to absence of father during adolescence (Hetherington, 1972; Kalter et al., 1985; Wallerstein, 1985, 1987). Southworth and Schwartz (1987) reported negative correlations of such problems with amount of post-divorce father contact.

This discussion of father loss is not meant to downplay the equal or even greater importance of mothers. It simply reflects that fact that available divorce research has focused on father absence. The relevant issues for divorced mother availability that have been studied are single parenthood and parent stress. Guidubaldi and Perry (1984) found that even after correcting for socioeconomic status, the children of single-parent families had deficits in social and academic competence on school entry. Bronfenbrenner (1985) makes the point that children need daily interaction with more than one committed adult. Therefore, single parents, even if they had unlimited time and attention to devote (and never got sick or tired), would still be at a disadvantage in meeting the child's needs.

Realization of this fact is an added stress for single parents, who usually have less time and attention to spare for the child than they did before the divorce. In most cases, their time, energy, and attention are sapped by such demands as seeking a job or increased hours of work, litigation, the need to move, the burden of managing the household single-handedly, and financial worries (an unfortunately high proportion of divorced fathers fail to provide support, even when they can afford to). Such stresses are physically as well as psychologically taxing, and are reflected even in such crude measures as morbidity and mortality rates. Reviews by Kiecolt-Glaser and Glaser (1986, 1988) and Kennedy, Kiecolt-Glaser, and Glaser (1988) found that, compared to still-married spouses of the same age, separated/divorced individuals had 30% more acute illness and physician visits, six times more pneumonia deaths, higher rates of tuberculosis and heart disease, and a higher incidence of cancer. Much of this susceptibility is probably related to suppression of immune function on several measures. Recently separated/divorced women were shown to have impairments in blastogenic response to two mitogens, in percentages of T-helper lymphocytes and natural killer cells, and in cellular immunity to the Epstein-Barr virus (as reflected in higher plasma antibody titers). See Chapter 3 for more on stress and immune function.

Parent stress, of course, usually flows downhill to the child. Gamble and Zigler (1986) describe how parental stress can induce a maladaptive insecure attachment by the young child. They mentioned single parenthood as one causal stress. Guidubaldi and Perry (1985) felt that parents' adjustment predicted their children's adjustment four years after divorce.

Another potential loss of parent availability concerns grandparents. Often a grandparent has been the main caretaker, even the "psychological parent." If this grandparent happens to be the parent of the noncustodial parent, contact may be severely reduced or even severed. In other cases, the custodial parent moves in with her (or his) own parents, who become the main caretakers while the parent works, or at least they develop a close bond with the child. When the custodial parent eventually moves out (perhaps at remarriage), taking the child along, the child loses easy access to these beloved parent figures.

CHANGES IN PHYSICAL SURROUNDINGS AND LIVING ARRANGEMENTS

This cluster of stressors includes break-up of the family home, the need to move, a lowered living standard, the psychological demand of two homes, and remarriage, which has been discussed earlier in the section on sex, age, and time.

Physical surroundings and familiar routines are especially important to very young children, who often glean much security from them. Older children are more interested in friends and which school they attend. Thus, moves are stressful to all ages, but for different reasons. Unfortunately, the court often requires the family home to be sold as part of the divorce property settlement. Obviously, it would be much better to delay loss of the family home a few years until the children have adjusted to the marital split, because aggregated simultaneous stresses are less easily mastered than the same stresses spaced out over time. Moves are usually made to cheaper accommodations, and many children are as stressed by downgrading as adults are. The cost of keeping up two homes stretches the family's finances even when the father attempts to support generously, which in many cases he fails to do at all. Economic hardship often brings drift down the social ladder, and many studies have linked children's academic competence and other adjustment to socioeconomic status (e.g., Guidubaldi & Perry, 1984, 1985).

The psychological demands of two homes are a bit like old age: it's not so bad when you consider the alternative—in this case abandonment by the noncustodial parent. Nevertheless, it is a problem for some children, usually worse if the parents have greatly different social/moral values or both remarry. An attempt at finely apportioned joint custody may pose the worst risk. In one sample of children in joint custody, a third found the psychological demands of two homes overwhelming (Steinman, 1981).

Fergusson et al. (1986) imply that, at least for their preschool sample, maternal remarriage (or attempted reconciliation of the original spouses) had been one of the more destructive aspects of the child's divorce experience. Ratings by parents and teachers showed increased aggressive and antisocial behavior in children of divorce compared to intact families in the same longitudinal prospective birth cohort. This behavior was significantly worse in children whose parents reconciled or whose mother remarried than in children of single parents. The authors felt that the most likely explanation was increased home instability associated with reconciliations and remarriages.

DIVORCE WARS

Interparental hostilities are a major stressor for about half the children of divorce, resulting in painful memories of verbal and physical violence (Wallerstein, 1985, 1987). In fact, some experts suggest that it is the interparental hostility, rather than the divorce itself, that causes the deleterious effects summarized in this chapter. For the 25% of children whose parents carry their hostilities into custody and/or visitation battles, litigation may become a way of life. The legal system intrudes into the family through the gaping hole left by rupture of the marital bond, which should have protected the child from legal stress. Even if the parents, by heroic efforts, keep the child out of the dispute, the stress on the parents takes a toll on the child through decreased availability.

Custody and Its Legalities

The law in most jurisdictions is that mother and father "stand upon an equality" as to the care, custody, and control of their children (e.g., Ohio Revised Code 3109.03). It appears that in recent years this statutory language is being taken literally more frequently, with more father custody and joint custody. Nevertheless, the practical fact remains that the mother usually gets physical custody of the children, particularly very young children, either by agreement between the parties or by court decree. In a divorce, the court is required to decide "to whom the care, custody and control of the children shall be given." If it must make that decision in a case where custody is contested, it is guided by the comprehensive provisions of a specific statute (e.g., Sec. 3109.04 of the Ohio Revised Code). The court may grant the custody to either parent, but must take into account "that which would be in the best interests of the children."

Prior to trying the issue of custody, the court may request an investigation as to the character, family relations, past conduct, earning ability, and financial worth of the parties (the mother and father), and also may order the parties and the children to submit to medical, psychological, and psychiatric examinations. If the court finds that it would not be in the best interests of the child to grant custody to either parent, it may commit the child to a relative or simply certify its findings to the juvenile court for "further proceedings." At that point, the juvenile court is vested with exclusive jurisdiction, and can, among other things, place the child in the custody of the local child welfare board. But in order to justify this disposition, the domestic relations court must find that both parents are unfit. If one parent is "fit" then, under the law, custody goes to that parent.

The "Best Interests" Rule. In determining what serves the best interests of the child, the court must consider "all relevant factors," including the following:

(a) the wishes of the parents regarding the child's custody;
(b) the wishes of the children themselves if they are above a certain age (usually about puberty);
(c) the child's interaction and interrelationship with the parents;
(d) the child's adjustment to home, school, and community; and
(e) the "mental and physical health of all persons involved in the situation."

When it is essential to protect the interests of a child, the court may appoint a *guardian ad litem* and an attorney to represent the interests of that child. These may be the same person. That person, or those persons, conduct an independent investigation and make recommendations to the court accordingly [e.g., Ohio Rules of Civil Procedure #75(B)(2)].

The Child's Election. In determining the best interests of the child, the court must take into consideration, among other things, the wishes of the child if the child is of a statutory age (e.g., 11). If the child is a bit older (e.g., 12), the court may allow the child to choose the parent with whom he or she wishes to live, but the court can disregard such an election if it finds either that the parent so selected is unfit to take charge or that it would not be in the best interests of the child to have the choice. In practice, if an election is made by a child to live with one parent or the other, that election is usually honored by the court. The mechanics are simple, but sometimes the emotional interplay is extremely painful.

The child who is old enough may make the election in an original proceeding or in a proceeding where the noncustodial parent is seeking a change of custody. The election is made by signing a simple document. At times this process is handled crudely, if not cruelly. A child who loves both of his parents or, at the very least, wishes to antagonize neither, is asked to make a formal, written declaration that he or she chooses one over the other. It is a proceeding that should be avoided whenever possible. Even when the child seems eager, alternative mechanisms should be explored first.

Change of Custody. Even though most divorces involving children are initially "settled out of court" in pre-hearing agreements, about a third of these later return to court in a less amicable manner over custody/visitation issues. The philosophy of custodial law is that, once a custodian has been chosen, the child should remain with that custodian until adulthood. For example, one state law says that the court "shall" retain the custodian designated by the prior order *unless* one of the following situations apply:

(a) the custodian agrees to a change in custody;

(b) the child, with the consent of the custodian, "has been integrated into the family" of the person seeking the change of custody; or

(c) "the child's present environment endangers significantly his physical health or his mental, moral or emotional development and the harm likely to be caused by a change in environment is outweighed by the advantages of the change in environment to the child."

The mental health viewpoint might question under situation (b) whether the integration into the family of the person seeking the change of custody needs to be "with the consent of the custodian." Requiring the consent of the custodian seems to be based on a consideration of justice in regard to parents' rights. From the child's viewpoint, it does not matter whether integration into the family was with or without consent of the custodial parent; the psychological importance of staying in the family in which the child is currently integrated remains the same. However, that is not the way the law reads in most jurisdictions.

It appears that statutes make it difficult to obtain a change of custody. This is deliberate, and probably useful in preventing impulsive custody changes and frivolous litigation. However, remember that the child above a certain age may be allowed to make an election, and this applies both in original custodial proceedings and in proceedings for a change of custody. This offers an opportunity for parental manipulation. For example, suppose a father decides to seek a change of custody of a 14-year-old boy who has been in his mother's custody since age 3. (Sometimes, of course, a mother is eager to surrender custody of a 14-year-old boy; there are even occasional fights over who will be charged with the unpleasant task of *keeping* a child! But let's assume for the example that both want him.) Before the legal formalities, the father, who is usually more affluent than the mother, may "soften up" the boy by making it clear to him that various rewards would come his way: a new motor bike; the possibility of a car at age 16; a room of his own; a bigger, more luxurious house; access to the country club; glamorous trips; more chances to go hunting and fishing, and so on. Despite such inducements, though, the child often sees through the scheme and ultimately elects to remain with the original custodian. Of course, there can also be child election without parental manipulation. Wallerstein (1987) reported a high rate of young teens moving to their father's home even when they did not perceive enthusiasm for it on his part. Such moves were usually unofficial, without court involvement.

Outside of a child's election to change custodial parents, the ground most frequently cited in a change of custody proceeding is situation (c) above, danger in present environment: The words "mental, moral or emotional development" open wide the possibilities for arguments. A not-untypical example is the charge that a mother is an alcoholic or drug user who daily places the child in hazardous circumstances, uncared for and unsupervised. She may be accused of bringing into the home a variety of men, none of whom has a particular interest in the child. However, even when such allegations are true, it is not as easy as might be imagined to make a case that the child's moral well-being and emotional development are threatened. If the mother can convince the court that she has rehabilitated herself and, at the time of the hearing, has a reasonably stable home, it is by no means certain that the court will order a custody change. Maternal prostitution, particularly if it is performed outside the home, does not necessarily make one a "bad" mother, despite what some may think. Obviously, the court also must consider whether the alternative offered by the noncustodial parent is any better. The inducements for mutual parental mudslinging, both true and untrue, are obvious, with several kinds of stressful fallout for children.

Effects of Disputes on Children

Many children are immensely pained by witnessing parental hostility. Their pain may be aggravated by being more likely to see and hear the more violent parental interactions. Johnston et al. (1985) found in school-age children involved in custody and care disputes that over half of the parents' mutual physical aggression was witnessed by the children, while less than half of their attempts at reasoning were witnessed by the children. There was often a vicious cycle, with the child an unwilling pivot of the triangle: one parent would attack and blame the other for the child's crying and being upset, when the child was upset and crying because the parents were fighting. The school-age children responded to such stress by trying to avoid or control in four ways:

1. About one-fifth of the children attempted to maneuver between the two parents for what they needed and wanted, perhaps even manipulating. The younger ones (age 6–8) were not quite clever enough and sometimes blundered into trouble, but with age they were rather successful. Although this was the healthiest adaptation, it carried the danger of a "trickster" personality style.

2. Another fifth of the children tried to "equilibrate": stay calm and organized and be fair to both parents. In other words, they tried to do what the parents should have done. Naturally, they were doomed to repeated failure.

3. Two-fifths of Johnston's sample chose a less healthy adaptation: enmeshment and merging with the parental dispute as a way of life. They often chose sides and accepted parental distortions. The tendency to take sides and be co-opted into the battle increased with age, while the 6- to 8-year-olds tended to show more submissive distress with somatization, decreasing with age. Wallerstein (1985) confirms that the 9–12 year age group often handles its anger by siding with one parent and even enthusiastically joining in harassment of the other. Naturally, such behavior by the child should be firmly limited to prevent future repercussions on development and parent-child relationships.

4. The least healthy minority disorganize and diffuse under the stress, auguring serious disturbance (Johnston et al., 1985).

Hauser (1985) found the following characteristics in families contesting custody: disturbance of adjustment for both parents and children, little communication between parents, absence of parental accord, unstable parent-child relationships, unstable access of child to parent, and frequent relitigation despite joint custody.

Allegations of Abuse

One of the grounds sometimes used for claiming unfitness of one of the parents is an allegation of abuse, including sexual abuse. Sometimes, of course, the allegation is valid. However, with recent publicity about sexual abuse as well as other kinds of child abuse, there has been an increase in unfounded allegations. These are not necessarily trumped up deliberately by the accusing parent, but can result in a number of ways from the turmoil, conflict, and stress surrounding a divorce, and a child's reaction to these stresses. There was a time when a description of sexual abuse by a young child could be assumed valid merely because the child would have no other way of knowing such details. However, with cable television, home video recorders, more liberal rules about what is shown on commercial television, and increasing public attention focused on sexual abuse, it is very possible for a child to have access to explicit sexual details without actually having experienced sexual abuse. The possibilities for unfounded allegations form the following spectrum:

1. The accusing parent may deliberately brainwash or program the child to describe abuse by the accused parent. This may be done in order to obtain custody or terminate visitation, or merely for revenge.

2. A *folie à deux* (madness by two's) may develop in which one parent's paranoid hostility towards the other affects the child and leads to delusional statements by the child about abuse that did not occur. For example:

   > *A 3-year-old girl in joint custody was describing cunnilingus by her father. She would only tell her mother about this, and denied it to professionals until repeated visits and until her mother tape-recorded her statement about it. This abuse allegedly started at the time of the parents' separation a year before. When asked about her first clue that anything inappropriate was happening, the mother said that it was when the girl was an infant: "When she was about 9 months old, I was changing her diaper. I held her up to slide the diaper under her; I saw her little bottom and thought to myself: 'Is it possible that he could be stimulated even by the sight of a little baby's vagina?' After that I would not let him change her diaper." On further inquiry, she revealed that she had always disliked his voyeuristic preferences in their marital relations and had never actually seen him do anything inappropriate with the little girl. The mother's Minnesota Multiphasic Personality Inventory and projective testing confirmed a frank paranoid disturbance.*

3. The accusing parent, although not psychotic, may unwittingly brainwash or program the child to describe abuse by the accused parent because of overanxious concern (which may have been partly aroused by media attention focused on the problem). The parent begins making inquiries that suggest ideas to the child. In some cases, the accusing parent may be hoping for a description of abuse from the child and may unwittingly ask leading questions and reinforce the "right" answers.

4. The child may sense hostility between the parents and try to please the accusing parent by joining in the attack on the accused parent in a way that has been suggested by the media, by educational programs, or by chance remarks of some adult. Wallerstein (1985)

has described how children in other contexts may join with one divorced parent in harassing the other.

5. The child may be manipulating for attention or to negotiate between the two parents for "best deal." In a few cases, the child may dislike the accused parent and hence seizes on this manipulation as a way of getting out of contact with that parent or even taking revenge.

When we add to these possibilities that a child's detailed, naive description of abuse is probably valid (Everson & Boat, 1989), we can see that the court and its mental health consultants often face a difficult puzzle. Many authors have addressed the thorny issues involved and suggested resolutions (e.g., Benedek & Schetky, 1987; Bresas et al., 1986; de Young, 1986; Everson & Boat, 1989; Gardner, 1985, 1986; Green, 1986; Yates & Terr, 1988). The solution is extremely important and deserves adequate investment of professional time and energy. If the allegations are valid, the children need protection from the abusing parent. If they are not valid, it could be damaging to children to grow up with the assumption that they have been abused and with unnecessarily restricted contact with the accused parent. Bresas et al. (1986) make the cogent point that an allegation of abuse, whether true or not, is a sign that a child is at high risk. The stress of actual abuse is discussed by Johnson in Chapter 10.

Joint Custody

It was not always possible for parents to arrange for formal joint custody of a child. Now most jurisdictions in the United States provide for this. In some states it is even the presumed, automatic, or "default option," to take effect unless other arrangements are made. A distinction needs to be made between legal and physical joint custody (Isaacs, Leon, & Kline, 1987).

Joint custody arrangements sound good, and many work quite well, especially those that are only legally joint. This had led to an enthusiasm for joint custody without thorough study. Many authors are beginning to issue cautions and question this custodial Utopia (e.g., Hagen, 1987). Steinman, Zemmelman, and Knoblauch (1985), in a longitudinal study of 51 joint-custody families, found that 31% had already failed by the end of the first year. Only 27% were successful, with 42% classified as "stressed." Steinman (1981) felt that joint custody was more satisfying to parents than to children, although many children got some reassurance from it. Isaacs et al. (1987) found that it was the nature of relationships rather than type of custody that determined whether a child considered a parent peripheral. Of course, the type of custody was associated statistically with the child's perception: only 12% of joint-custody children (physical or legal) left one of the parents out of a family drawing, com-pared to 38% of sole-custody children. However, the statistical link with visiting frequency was more significant, and the child's perception of how the parents got along was as significant as the type of custody. Isaacs et al. felt that legal joint custody may help children perceive both parents as involved in their care and welfare, but the ability of the parents to cooperate, especially on visitation, was more important. Even without joint custody, agreements and decrees can be drawn to permit ample visitation and involvement of both parents.

Some parents attempt to fine-tune joint physical custody to a point that is not practical and may be harmful. For example, a child may spend Mondays and Tuesdays with mother, Wednesdays and Thursdays with father, Fridays with mother and alternate weekends with each, or spend alternate weeks with each parent. The child has no "home base." Never-theless, there may be an occasional case where the child enjoys and benefits from a finely sliced division of time.

One 8-year-old was brought for psychiatric evaluation because of disagreements among three pairs of parents: her natural father and stepmother, her natural mother and stepfather, and her adoptive father and adoptive stepmother. (A series of six divorces and remarriages had accomplished this.) She was spending approximately one-third of her time in each home, and each set of parents was concerned that she was suffering from inconsistencies in one or both of the other homes and wished to save her from that. They noted that she appeared unhappy. When seen privately, the child, a very intelligent, articulate girl, made it very clear that she wanted to retain the current visiting arrangement because she loved all six parents and enjoyed their company. The only thing that had made her obviously unhappy was the dissension among the three pairs of parents. With appropriate counseling, the three pairs of parents were able to begin cooperating with each other, and the child's apparent maladjust-ment evaporated without any change in visiting arrangements.

In another case, the parents bought homes in the same neighborhood so the children could alternate weeks while still riding the same school bus and enjoying the same friends, and the children liked this arrangement.

Such cases, however, may be exceptional. It should be noted that, from the children's viewpoint, the best joint physical custody arrangement is for the children to continue living in the family home and have each parent alternately live with them. This is not practical for most families economically, since it requires maintaining three homes, and it becomes virtually impossible when either parent remarries.

Visitation

The court may make any "just and reasonable order" permitting the noncustodial parent to visit at the times and under the conditions that the court directs (e.g., Ohio Revised Code 3109.05, 3109.11). Of course, all orders relating to minor children are subject to modification. Furthermore, the court has the discretion of granting to any other person "hav-ing an interest in the welfare of the child" reasonable companionship or visitation rights. Typically, this would be a favored grandparent or aunt.

Grandparent Visitation.   Recent expansion of possibilities for hostile litigation has arisen from laws passed in most states providing grandpar-ents a right to sue for visitation. The rationale for this is that grandchil-dren and grandparents should not be deprived of contact with each other merely because the parents cannot get along with each other or with their own parents (the grandparents). Especially in a hostile divorce situation, the grandparents might be able to provide a safe haven of neutral territory for the child. In some cases the grandparent is actually the psychological parent, who had been entrusted with the daily care of the child while both parents worked (or caroused). Certainly the grand-parent (usually grandmother) who is actually the psychological parent should not be discarded merely because she happens to be related to the noncustodial parent.

However, Derdeyn (1985) describes the pitfalls of attempting to legiti-mize grandparent visitation rights through legislation. If the custodial parent is not willing to let the child visit grandparents, the imposition of forced grandparent visitation may add more hostility and confusion to the child's world. A particular danger is that grandparent visitation may come to be viewed as a right of the grandparents rather than as a right of the child. Even in hostile divorces, most parents recognize their children's valid attachments to grandparents and continue to tolerate, if not promote, such visits, at least when the child indicates the desire to visit. If the grandparent is actually the psychological parent and the parents are not willing to allow continued contact, perhaps the grandpar-ent should have custody rather than visitation. Consider the following example:

A 9-year-old boy of normal intelligence was brought for psychiatric evaluation because he and his grandparents were resisting the reconciliation plan with his mother drawn up by Childrens' Services and approved by the court. He had lived with his grandparents for the previous four years, since being brought back from another state by Childrens' Services because of neglect by his divorced mother and her paramour. The mother had not bothered visiting him for several years. When the grandparents asked for permanent placement and a possible adoption, the mother began insisting upon visitation and demanded the reconcil-iation plan for him to eventually come and live with her again. The boy resisted in fright, fearing that she would take him again on an ill-advised vagabond pilgrimage. He refused even to visit her. Since the mother would not sign away her "rights," the placement remained in doubt, even though the boy's psychological parents were clearly his grand-mother and grandfather.

Split Custody and Sibling Separation

An especially close sibling bond may develop in divorced families when the children feel they can only depend on each other because neither parent is a permanent part of their life (Wallerstein, 1985). This can make sibling separations as painful as separation from the noncustodial parent.

Generally, courts are reluctant to separate siblings, although this may be occurring more frequently. In cases where a child is old enough to elect to go with the noncustodial parent, a sticky situation can be created when the electing child has younger brothers or sisters and one or more of them expresses the desire to follow the older child. In fact, having the older child elect to change custodians is a ploy sometimes used to obtain a change in custody of *all* the children. The argument is that detriment would result from the sibling breakup if the younger children's custody were not also changed.

A converse manipulation involves persuading the older child *not* to elect a change of custody in order to stay with siblings. Sometimes an older child will decide to stay with the younger ones to "protect" them. Nevertheless, in some cases, each sibling changes homes one by one as he or she reaches the age of election. Sometimes this splitting seems the lesser of two evils, a Solomonic prevention of parental hostilities, or perhaps a recognition that the custodial parent is wearing out. It also fits the developmental-stage renewed need of adolescents for their father that Wallerstein (1987) describes.

Even when all the children are below the age of election, there are exceptional cases where separating the siblings is the lesser of two evils. One example would be where one of the children has a special need that cannot be met by the parent to whom the other children are most attached. Another example is the following case:

> A 6-year-old girl and 4-year-old boy were evaluated for custody recommendations. The parents lived several states apart. The children had lived for awhile with the mother and then for awhile with the father, until the mother showed up with a court order to take the children back. The boy protested so much that the mother relented in regard to him, but took the girl with her. At the time of evaluation, the girl had been integrated into her mother's home, and the boy obviously was still integrated into his father's home. The siblings had been separated for almost a year. It seemed more important to leave each in the home into which they had been integrated than to rejoin them, even though they missed each other. The visitation recommendation in this case was crucial: to maximize children's time with each other, only one at a time should visit the respective noncustodial parent.

Child Stealing. Kidnapping or absconding with one's own children to keep them away from the other parent is the ultimate act of desperation in custody and visitation disputes. Parents who resort to this tactic are often unbalanced in their desperation, sometimes with a paranoid disturbance, and may even be dangerous to the child. At its best, such an experience means complete severance of contact with one parent and a semi-fugitive lifestyle. At its worst, it can be catastrophic (in rare cases, fatal) for the child. (See Chapter 2 for a discussion of post-traumatic stress disorders.)

The Child's Participation in Custody Disputes

In any custody dispute, the question arises as to whether to officially make the children themselves actors in the drama. They are certainly unofficially enmeshed in or reacting to the dispute (Johnston et al., 1985). Most experts like to avoid bringing children into court, but it is sometimes necessary, particularly when the child has the right to exercise a choice or preference as to custodian. A number of jurisdictions give the court the discretion to interview the child involved in the proceedings. This is often done.

If the court decides to interview the child, where should the interview take place and who should be present? Some jurisdictions require that a child be called to the witness stand to testify in open court. In others, the court must offer the electing child an "opportunity" to inform the court of his choice in chambers or in open court. If the child elects to inform the court of the choice in chambers, then often no person may be present in the chambers other than the child, the child's attorney, the judge, any necessary court personnel, and, at the judge's discretion, the attorney for each parent.

Many courts have held that it is error to refuse an attorney's request to call a child to the witness stand to testify, even though this is traumatic for the child. From the legal standpoint, an in-chambers interview raises constitutional questions about the parents' exclusion from the interview. The right of the parents to a due process hearing conflicts with the right of the child to be as free as possible from trauma and emotional distress. In this regard, most courts have decided in favor of the child (e.g., *Lincoln v. Lincoln*, 24 N.Y.2d 270, 272, 247 N.E.2d. 659, 660: 1969).

When a Judge Interviews the Child. Courts and authors speak of the need of the child to feel safe and comfortable in expressing a preference to the court, but no matter how it is done, the experience is traumatic for the child, and responsible attorneys try to avoid having the child exposed to the judicial process in custody proceedings to any extent greater than absolutely necessary. If the judge, after hearing the parties and other witnesses during the course of the custody proceeding, believes that there is already sufficient information upon which to base a decision, then the child ought to be left alone. But in some cases the independent evidence still leaves the court in doubt, and an interview with the child might be desirable. The objective, of course, is to gain information and insight toward the end of making a decision which serves the best interests and the welfare of the child.

Jones (1984) defined guidelines with which any judge interviewing a child should be familiar. One of the issues he considers is whether to ask the child directly for a custody preference. This gives the appearance of shifting the decision-making burden from the judge to the child. On the other hand, the child often has a clear preference and wants to state it. A compromise could be a two-step question: First, ask the children if they wish to state a preference, reminding them that they do not have to. If they reply affirmatively, then they can be asked the preference and reasons for it. If they reply negatively or not at all, they can be told empathically that this would be a hard choice for any kid, and that's why the judge decides.

AVOIDING DISPUTATION

A good many custody disputes are not "real." That is, one parent or the other uses custody as a pawn or a weapon: "If you don't let up on your demand for alimony, I'm going to ask for custody of Amy." Responsible attorneys will recognize that ploy for what it is and should not agree to raise custody as an issue when they know that the client has no genuine interest in obtaining custody of the child. Many custody disputes can be avoided with common sense and liberal thinking on the part of the attorneys, if not the parties. The trend toward mediation—now being mandated in some jurisdictions—should help.

One valuable insight is that a *business-like relationship* between the parents is a third alternative to friendship or hostility. The parents do not need to like each other to cooperate courteously in the common business of nurturing their children. All they need to do is love the children more than they dislike each other. Sometimes they need to be challenged with a direct question on this issue. They may need support in focusing on the children's needs rather than on how unfair the ex-spouse is. Sometimes it helps if they think of the other parent as the children's beloved, unpaid sitter. If the child cannot enjoy a loving, unified home and family, the deleterious effects of a divorce can be mitigated by enlightened attorneys who may need at times to call on other professionals, such as psychologists, psychiatrists, and social workers, for interprofessional advocacy for the child.

Role of Mental Health Professionals vis-à-vis Attorneys

Psychiatrists, psychologists, social workers, psychiatric nurses, and other mental health professionals are sometimes called on for evaluation and recommendations regarding custody and visitation, as well as for treatment of emotional disturbance in the children and/or parents. The function of these nonlegal professionals is quite different from that of the attorneys. It is important for the two types of professionals to work closely together within their respective roles. Each has certain strengths, both in training and in role, to bring to a peaceful resolution of the issues.

The attorneys are rightfully seen as advocates of the parties they represent. However, many enlightened attorneys also realize an obligation to work for what is good for the child. In some cases these two roles may be incompatible; it then becomes advisable to recommend a guardian ad litem to represent the child's interests and to work closely with the mental health consultants.

The mental health consultant should not assume the role of advocate for one of the parties as would the attorney. Rather, the mental health consultant attempts an objective evaluation from the viewpoint of what is best for the child. The mental health professional should insist on an opportunity to interview and examine not only the child, but each of the parents, their new mates, if any, and any other interested adults, and to observe the interaction between the children and each of these adults. Most responsible attorneys advise their clients to cooperate with such an evaluation. It is desirable if both sides can agree on one mental health consultant to evaluate and make recommendations rather than each side hiring its own.

It is sometimes useful for the mental health professional to meet with both of the attorneys after the evaluation to share the findings informally and see if some kind of agreement can be worked out without the necessity of a deposition or hearing. Attorneys sometimes are able to persuade their clients to compromise when the mental health professional could not. The parties know that their attorney is on their side, but are not always so confident about the mental health professional, who they realize must work with both sides.

While the mental health professional can better appreciate the psychological needs of the child and impact of the custody and visitation arrangements on the child's mental health, and be more impartial in evaluating advantages and disadvantages of the two homes, the attorneys are more likely to be heeded by the respective parties. Therefore, the attorneys are in a better position to implement recommendations in as amicable a way as possible. Thus, the roles of the attorneys and nonlegal professionals complement each other. By capitalizing on this complementarity, interprofessional cooperation can mitigate some of the stressful aspects of parental divorce for children.

REFERENCES

Benedek, E. P., & Schetky, D. H. (1987). Problems in validating allegations of sexual abuse. Part 2: Clinical evaluation. *Journal of the American Academy of Child and Adolescent Psychiatry, 26*(6), 916–921.

Bresas, P., Stearns, G. B., Bess, B. H., & Packer, L. S. (1986). Allegations of child sexual abuse in child custody disputes: A therapeutic assessment model. *American Journal of Orthopsychiatry, 56*(4), 560–569.

Bronfenbrenner, U. (1985). The parent-child relationship and our changing society. In L. E. Arnold (Ed.), *Parents, children, and change.* Lexington, MA: D.C. Heath.

Derdeyn, A. P. (1985). Grandparent visitation rights: Rendering family dissension more pronounced? *American Journal of Orthopsychiatry, 55*(2), 277–287.

de Young, M. (1986). A conceptual model for judging the truthfulness of a young child's allegation of sexual abuse. *American Journal of Orthopsychiatry, 56*(4), 550–559.

Everson, M. D., & Boat, B. W. (1989). False allegations of sexual abuse by children and adolescents. *Journal of the American Academy of Child and Adolescent Psychiatry, 28*(2), 230–235.

Fergusson, D. M., Dimond, M. E., & Horwood, L. J. (1986). Childhood family placement history and behavior problems in 6-year-old children. *Journal of Child Psychology and Psychiatry, 27*(2), 213–226.

Fergusson, D. M., Horwood, L. J., & Shannon, F. T. (1984, August). A proportional hazards model of family breakdown. *Journal of Marriage & Family,* 539–543.

Gamble, T. J., & Zigler, E. (1986). Effects of infant day care: Another look at the evidence. *American Journal of Orthopsychiatry, 56*(1), 26–42.

Gardner, R. A. (1986). *Child custody litigation: A guide for professionals.* Creskill, NY: Creative Therapeutics.

Goldstein, J., Freud, A., & Solnit, A. J. (1979). *Beyond the best interests of the child.* New York: Free Press.

Green, A. (1986). True and false allegations of sexual abuse in custody disputes. *Journal of the American Academy of Child and Adolescent Psychiatry, 25*(4), 449–456.

Guidubaldi, J., & Perry, J. D. (1984). Divorce, socioeconomic status, and children's cognitive-social competence at school entry. *American Journal of Orthopsychiatry, 54*(3), 459–468.

Guidubaldi, J., & Perry, J. D. (1985). Divorce and mental health sequelae for children: A two-year follow-up of a nationwide sample. *Journal of the American Academy of Child and Adolescent Psychiatry, 24*(5), 531–537.

Hagen, J. L. (1987, January-February). Proceed with caution: Advocating joint custody. *Social Work,* 26–30.

Hauser, B. B. (1985). Custody in dispute: Legal and psychological profiles of contesting families. *Journal of the American Academy of Child and Adolescent Psychiatry, 24*(5), 575–582.

Hetherington, E. M. (1972). Effects of father absence on personality development in adolescent daughters. *Developmental Psychology, 7,* 313–326.

Hetherington, E. M., Cox, M., & Cox, R. (1985). Long-term effects of divorce and remarriage on the adjustment of children. *Journal of the American Academy of Child and Adolescent Psychiatry, 24*(5), 518–530.

Isaacs, M. B., Leon, G. H., & Kline, M. (1987). When is a parent out of the picture? Different custody, different perceptions. *Family Practice, 26,* 101–110.

Johnston, J. R., Campbell, L. E. G., & Mayes, S. S. (1985). Latency children in post-separation and divorce disputes. *Journal of the American Academy of Child and Adolescent Psychiatry, 24*(5), 563–574.

Jones, C. J. (1984). Judicial questioning of children in custody and visitation proceedings. *Family Law Quarterly, 18,* 43.

Kalter, N. (1987). Long-term effects of divorce on children: A developmental vulnerability model. *American Journal of Orthopsychiatry, 57*(4), 587–599.

Kalter, N., Reimer, B., Brickman, A., et al. (1985). Implications of parental divorce for female development. *Journal of the American Academy of Child and Adolescent Psychiatry, 24*(5), 538–544.

Kalter, N., & Rembar, J. (1981). The significance of a child's age at the time of parental divorce. *American Journal of Orthopsychiatry, 51*(1), 85–100.

Kennedy, S., Kiecolt-Glaser, J. K., & Glaser, R. (1988). Immunological consequences of acute and chronic stressors: Mediating role of interpersonal relationships. *British Journal of Medical Psychology, 61,* 77–85.

Kiecolt-Glaser, J. K., & Glaser, R. (1986). Psychological influences on immunity. *Psychosomatics, 27*(9), 621–624.

Kiecolt-Glaser, J. K., & Glaser, R. (1988). Major life changes, chronic stress, and immunity. In T. P. Bridge, et al. (Eds.), *Psychological, neuropsychiatric, and substance abuse aspects of AIDS.* New York: Raven Press.

Kosky, R., McAlpine, I., Silburn, S., et al. (1985). A survey of child psychiatry outpatients. 1. Clinical and demographic characteristics. *Australian and New Zealand Journal of Psychiatry, 19,* 158–166.

McGurk, H., & Glachan, M. (1987). Children's conception of the continuity of parenthood following divorce. *Journal of Child Psychology and Psychiatry, 28*(3), 427–435.

Ohio Revised Code §3109.03 (parents stand upon an equality as to custody).

Ohio Revised Code §3109.04 ("the custody statute").

Ohio Revised Code §§3109.05, 3109.11 (visitation).

Ohio Rules of Civil Procedure # 75(B)(2) (appointment of guardian ad litem and attorney for child).

Radin, R. (1981). The role of the father in cognitive, academic, and intellectual development. In M. Lamb (Ed.), *The role of the father in child development.* New York: John Wiley.

Soldano, K. W. (1990). Divorce: Clinical implications for treatment of children. In B. D. Garfinkel, G. A. Carlson, & E. B. Weller (Eds.), *Psychiatric disorders in children and adolescents.* Philadelphia: W. B. Saunders.

Southworth, S., & Schwartz, J. C. (1987). Post-divorce contact, relationship with father, and heterosexual trust in female college students. *American Journal of Orthopsychiatry, 57*(3), 371–382.

Steinman, S. (1981). The experience of children in a joint-custody arrangement: A report of a study. *American Journal of Orthopsychiatry, 51*(3), 403–414.

Steinman, S. B., Zemmelman, S. E., & Knoblauch, T. M. (1985). A study of parents who sought joint custody following divorce: Who reaches agreement and sustains joint custody and who returns to court. *Journal of the American Academy of Child and Adolescent Psychiatry, 24*(5), 554–562.

Wallerstein, J. S. (1983). Children of divorce: The psychological tasks of the child. *American Journal of Orthopsychiatry, 53.*

Wallerstein, J. S. (1985). Children of divorce: Preliminary report of a ten-year follow-up of older children and adolescents. *Journal of the American Academy of Child and Adolescent Psychiatry, 24*(5), 545–553.

Wallerstein, J. S. (1987). Children of divorce: Report of a 10-year follow-up of early latency-age children. *American Journal of Orthopsychiatry, 57*(2), 199–211.

Wallerstein, J. S., & Kelly, J. (1984). Children of divorce: Preliminary report of 10-year followup of young children. *American Journal of Orthopsychiatry, 54,* 444–450.

Yates, A., & Terr, L. (1988). Anatomically correct dolls: Should they be used as the basis for expert testimony? *Journal of the American Academy of Child and Adolescent Psychiatry, 27*(2), 254–257.

Zaslow, M. J. (1989). Sex differences in children's response to parental divorce: 2. Samples, variables, ages, and sources. *American Journal of Orthopsychiatry, 59*(1), 118–141.

CHAPTER FIFTEEN

Parent Death in Childhood

Elliot M. Kranzler

Of all the life stresses a child might experience, the death of a parent seems most devastating, the loss least reparable, and the potential for harmful psychological consequences greatest. In fact, parental death during childhood has been implicated in the development of immediate, intermediate, and long-term psychiatric morbidity (Barry & Lindemann, 1960; Birtchnell, 1978; Dietrich, 1979; Felner, Stolberg, & Cowen, 1975; Lifshitz, 1976; Markusen & Fulton, 1971). However, results have been mixed in studies that retrospectively examine bereavement as a vulnerability factor by, for example, studying risk for depressive disorders in later life in those who have experienced childhood parental loss. Whereas many such studies have found increased risk (e.g., Beck, Sethi, & Tuthill, 1963; Birtchnell, 1972; Brown, Harris, & Copeland, 1977; Dennehy, 1966), others, frequently utilizing different methods, have not (e.g., Granville-Grossman, 1966; Gregory, 1966; Hopkinson & Reed, 1966; Roy, 1979).

Rutter (1986) makes the point that even if the risk for depression is increased, the majority of bereaved children do not go on to develop depressive disorders. The difference between those who do and those who do not probably is determined by a number of factors. Issues of biological predisposition, as well as preexisting and subsequent environmental circumstances, combine to impact on a child's response to loss. Harris, Brown, and Bifulco (1986) have argued that, in addition to the predisposing factors of parental loss, there must also be subsequent provoking agents—severe life events or major long-term difficulties—in order for the vulnerability to be expressed.

Garmezy (1986) states that, whereas in some children stress has a "sensitizing" effect, in others there appears to be a "steeling" effect if certain protective factors exist. That is, rather than a vulnerability, some children who have experienced such serious stressors as parental loss appear to develop a capacity to resist the negative effects of adversity. Garmezy argues that prospective studies are critical in order to investigate these questions, and complains that the prospective literature on bereavement, in particular, is extremely sparse.

Sample selection is critical in the assessment of studies of childhood bereavement. Samples are generally heterogeneous, small, and not representative. The presence and the nature of comparison samples will impact significantly on the conclusions drawn. There are a number of potentially important mediators that may complicate the study of bereavement. For one, the cause of death—suicide, murder, slow death due to cancer, or sudden, unexpected death due to heart attack—influences the reaction of both child and surviving parent and can result in very different grieving responses (Krupnick, 1984). The quality of the relationships that predated the loss will affect the degree and nature of the loss and its consequences (Elizur & Kaffman, 1983; Kranzler et al., in press). The sex of the child and deceased parent, as well as the age of the child, are likely to have particular relevance to the grieving process in childhood. The impact of multiple changes that often occur in the family in the aftermath of a parent's death also must be considered (Breier et al., 1988; Harris et al., 1986; Hetherington & Deur, 1971).

In this chapter we review some of the important descriptions of and controversies surrounding childhood bereavement, with a focus on the more recent and the prospective studies. We look at mediators that impact on a child's response to the death of a parent, attempting to delineate those factors that make some children more vulnerable and those that might help protect the child from negative long-term consequences. We point out some of the problems and complexities that have slowed the search for definitive answers to these questions. Finally, we review some important developmental and psychopathological issues and the implications for treatment and prevention.

OUTCOME OF CHILDHOOD BEREAVEMENT

Table 15.1 summarizes some of the effects of parent death reviewed below. Since Freud's paper, "Mourning and Melancholia," was published (1917/1957), some authors, particularly those reporting on children in treatment (Deutch, 1937; Nagera, 1970; Wolfenstein, 1969) have argued that children are unable to grieve "normally." Furman (1974) and Bowlby (1980) counter that while the process and clinical picture of grief in children is perhaps different from that of adults, it is certainly present and not necessarily abnormal. Furman argues that if a child has the capacity for object constancy and has the support of a consistent surviving parent who can both meet the child's real needs and provide the emotional environment needed for expression of grief, then a healthy adjustment is feasible, even after the death of a parent.

The conclusions drawn from case reports, while providing in-depth insights into the issues of some bereaved children, probably are not representative of the experience of the majority of bereaved children, who are untreated. There is a clear need for more studies of bereavement that utilize representative samples from which generalizable conclusions can be drawn.

Acute and Subacute Effects of Parent Death

Prospective studies of childhood bereavement often have been small in size, lacking in standardized assessment methods, or dependent on parent and teacher reports without directly interviewing the children. For example, Kaffman and Elizur (1979; 1983) and Van Eerdewegh et al.

TABLE 15.1.   Common Effects of Parental Death

Predominant Affect and Behaviors	Critical Stressors or Mediators
Anger	Anger, depression, and hopelessness of
Anxiety	surviving parent
Behavioral disturbance	Caretaking deficits
Denial of death	Concerns about surviving parent
Dependent, clingy behavior	Economic hardship
Disinterest	Loss of communication with surviving parent
Dysphoria, depression	Surviving parent's preoccupation with grief
Impaired school function	
Increased delinquency	
Irritability	
Night fears	
Regression	
Sadness, crying	
Separation difficulties	
Somatic symptoms	
Withdrawal	

(1982) provide information from surviving parents regarding their be-reaved children; in neither of these studies were the children inter-viewed.

Kaffman and Elizur (1983) studied 2- through 10-year-old children from Israeli kibbutzim whose fathers died in the war of October 1973. They found that in the first six months, almost half of the children showed significant behavioral disturbance, affecting their home and school functioning so severely as to require professional intervention. In the early months after the death, the predominant symptoms shown by these children were characteristic "mourning reactions" of sobbing, cry-ing, sadness and longing, searching for a substitute father, and recalling the deceased, yet in some ways denying the death. Children either avoided the subject of death or were preoccupied with the theme of death. These symptoms diminished during the second year after the loss.

Van Eerdewegh et al. (1982) interviewed widows and widowers about their children, one and thirteen months after the death of their spouses. In the initial assessment, at one month, most children were described as evidencing symptoms of "dysphoria," with sadness, crying, irritability, and fighting with siblings. Although most children did not meet criteria for a full-blown depression, there were significantly more bereaved chil-dren who did exhibit depressive syndromes than did controls. Although they concluded that there was a significant overall amelioration of the children's dysfunction at thirteen months, 43% of their sample contin-ued to show some depressive affect. Furthermore, the children showed more withdrawal, somatic symptoms, and disinterest in school.

With the bereaved showing significantly higher symptom rates than controls and with 70% of the bereaved at one month and 43% at thirteen months showing some evidence of depressive mood, it is perplexing how Van Eerdewegh and colleagues could conclude that their study confirms Wolfenstein's (1969) contention that children do not mourn. It is true as well for most adults that the overt manifestations of grief diminish over the course of the first year (Clayton & Darvish, 1979). This does not indicate an absence of mourning. It should also be noted that these so-called negative findings are the result of reports by parents, who have been shown to underreport the internalizing symptoms of their children.

Child Interview Findings.   In two recent studies, bereaved children of different ages were interviewed as a critical part of the assessment. Kranzler et al. (in press), studying 3- through 6-year-olds within six months of the death of their parent, found significantly higher rates of disturbance in bereaved children compared with controls, on both par-ent and teacher ratings. Over 40% of the bereaved sample showed symp-toms so severe as to reach clinical criterion on the Achenbach Child Behavior Checklist. Symptoms of depression and anxiety predominated. Bereaved preschoolers expressed more fearful and less happy affect than controls. Particularly when describing their feelings while remembering the deceased parent, the bereaved children expressed sad affects. Those who were capable of expressing feelings of sadness were less sympto-matic than those who expressed anger, fear, or happiness while remem-bering their deceased parent. We concluded that some preschoolers were able to actively, constructively grieve the death of a parent in the months after their loss.

Fristad et al. (1989), studying 6- through 12-year-olds at one month after the death of their parent, found sad affect (57%), irritability (57%), impaired concentration (46%), fatigue (43%), low self-esteem (41%), separation anxiety (41%), and loss of pleasure (40%). Most of these bereaved showed a decrease in symptoms at six months and even more so at thirteen months. However, one-third were most symptomatic six months after their parent's death. At six months, only two symptoms— sad affect and irritability—were reported by more than 40% of the sample. By thirteen months, none of the symptoms was reported by more than 40% of the sample. In a tandem study, Weller, Fristad, and Weller (1989) found that adolescents 13–18 years old reported sadness (75%), anger (54%), and anxiety (33%) at one month after the loss, and that overall they showed fewer depressive, anxiety, and somatic symptoms than children under age 13.

Summary and Conclusions about Early and Intermediate Bereavement Effects. Although there was a drop in "mourning symptoms" after the first year in Kaffman and Elizur's (1983) study, there was a persistently high rate of behavioral disturbance for as long as three-and-a-half years. They found that the second year, in fact, brought the most behavioral symptoms. The two common symptom clusters they described were those of the *overanxious dependent type* (fearful, separation-anxious, overdependent, and demanding) and the *unsocial-aggressive type* (aggressive, restless, prone to temper tantrums). Most children showed a combination of these symptoms. The fact that there were higher rates and greater persistence of symptoms in this study compared with those of Van Eerdewegh et al. (1982) and Fristad et al. (1989) might be explained in several ways. This study was homogeneous in its focus on *fathers,* all of whom had been *killed during a war;* perhaps both of these represent added risk. A sample that includes only surviving mothers may be more disturbed than a heterogeneous sample. Death during a war may pose greater stress on the family and the child. Both Van Eerdewegh et al. and Fristad et al. report on children at thirteen months. One does not know what the results of longer follow-up with these samples would show.

Taken together, these prospective studies of the early bereavement period for children suggest several important conclusions:

1. Like adults, children show evidence of disturbance in mood, particularly in the first months.

2. Symptoms of both depression and anxiety predominate, with the latter perhaps more prominent than in adults.

3. Although in all of these studies the bereaved children were significantly more symptomatic than were controls, the symptom severity for the majority of bereaved children often does not reach a clinical level, even at its most severe point.

4. It appears that for most bereaved children, there will be a natural decrement in overt symptoms, with many of them functioning better by the end of the first year.

5. There are some children at particular risk who might be identified for intervention.

The evidence shows that children react with expressions of sadness, anger, irritability, and pining similar to those seen in adults who are grieving. The process, timing, and pattern of response may differ as a result of developmental influences, and there may need to be reworking at different points later on, but clear evidence for a grief response in childhood exists.

Long-Term Outcome of Bereavement: Chronic Effects

Because long-term prospective studies are so sparse, they are supplemented with retrospective studies.

Prospective Studies. Gregory (1965), Markusen and Fulton (1971), and Bendiksen and Fulton (1976) all reported follow-ups at different times of a sample of ninth-graders. They were interested in predictors of school dropout and delinquency rates among three groups of ninth-graders: (1) children whose parent had died; (2) children of divorced parents, and (3) a control group. At three years, Gregory (1965) reported increased delinquency, as compared with controls, among children living with the opposite-sex parent as a result of death or separation. In their twenties, however, the bereaved and divorce groups did not show higher rates of marital disruption and violations of the law than controls (Markusen & Fulton, 1971). In their thirties, the bereaved group showed higher rates of serious medical problems and emotional distress (Bendiksen & Fulton, 1976).

The point at which children become symptomatic and the duration of disturbance can vary. Kaffman and Elizur reported that children with the most severe immediate reactions tended to be those with longer lasting disturbance. However, they also found that there were some who initially did not show evidence of disturbance, but became more symptomatic during the second and third year after their father's death. Rutter (1966) found that, particularly in children under five, the likelihood for referral for psychiatric care was greater five years or more following the death. This suggests that there might be delayed risk following parental loss, emphasizing the need for more long-term follow-up studies.

Retrospective Studies of Long-Term Outcome. Most of the studies on the impact of childhood bereavement have been retrospective. They have attempted to associate parental loss with psychiatric disorders, particularly depression (e.g., Beck et al., 1963; Birtchnell, 1972; Brown et al., 1977; Dennehy, 1966); personality disorder (Barry & Lindemann, 1960; Birtchnell, 1978; Dietrich, 1979; Felner et al., 1975); and cognitive and functional impairment (Lifshitz, 1976; Markusen & Fulton, 1971). The results of these studies are mixed. Some studies have failed to find greater risk among bereaved (e.g., Granville-Grossman, 1966; Gregory, 1966; Hopkinson & Reed, 1966; Roy, 1979). Lloyd (1980) reviewed the controlled retrospective literature, citing eight out of eleven that linked childhood parent loss with adult depression. Krupnick (1984) and Tenant, Bebbington, and Hurry (1980) point out that it is difficult to compare many of these contradictory studies, given the methodological and sample disparities, frequent absence of controls, and lack of consistent consideration of important mediators.

The recent studies by Breier et al. (1988) and Harris et al. (1986) point to the problems and clarify some of the confusion in this retrospective literature by carefully controlling for critical intervening mediators. Brown et al., in a 1977 epidemiologic study of female psychiatric inpatients, psychiatric outpatients, and nonpatient controls, found increased risk for depression, particularly psychotic depressions, but only in women who had lost their mothers before they were 11 years old. Father loss at any age and mother loss after age 11 was not found to increase risk for adult depression. However, in the next section we see how Harris et al., focusing on the intervening life circumstance, came to interpret the findings very differently.

MEDIATORS OF THE STRESS OF PARENT DEATH

Age

Many studies have found that parental death before a child reaches age 10, especially before age 7, causes the most negative impact on long-term follow-up (Barry & Lindemann, 1960; Brown et al., 1977; Greer, 1964; Haworth, 1964; Jacoson & Ryder, 1969; Lifshitz, 1976). Causal hypotheses include the younger child's greater cognitive and emotional immaturity, resulting difficulties in experiencing "normal grief," the child's ongoing need for basic caretaking and nurturance, and the possibility that the younger child is treated differently from older children in the same situation, e.g., in some way excluded from the family's grieving process.

Younger children show more regressive bereavement responses, including tantrums, night fears, separation difficulties, and dependent, clingy behavior (Kaffman & Elizur, 1983; Van Eerdewegh et al., 1982). Kranzler et al. (in press) found that although 3- through 6-year-olds were able to express grieving affects on interview, the younger (3- to 4-year-old) boys, who were the most symptomatic subgroup, were least expressive of grief affects, compared with girls of the same age and 5- and 6-year-olds of both sexes.

In Lifshitz's study (1976) of 9- to 14-year-olds, children who had lost their fathers before age 7 were especially likely to show cognitive deficiencies. The results from the Walthamstow study by Harris, Brown, and Bifulco (1986) may explain the heightened impact of parental loss in early childhood. Rather than separation from or death of the parent, it was subsequent inadequacy of care that determined increased risk or depression in later life. Those children who experience insufficient parenting or care are at greater risk for depressive disorders in adulthood, whereas those who are left in a situation that, despite the loss, provides a stable environment are not at greater risk than controls. Perhaps the association between parental death and later psychopathology is found particularly in young children because their needs for emotional parenting and practical sustenance are greatest and they might therefore be most sensitive to situations in which these needs are inadequately provided after their parent's death.

Concept of Death. Children between the ages of 2 and 7 undergo critical cognitive and affective development. Speece and Brent (1984) reviewed the literature on children's concepts of death. They concluded that during these ages, especially at the transition from preoperational to concrete operational thinking, an understanding of the irreversibility, nonfunctionality, and universality of death is acquired, at least partially. Does an incomplete understanding put younger bereaved children at greater risk for confusion and anxiety and result in creating unrealistic, perhaps guilt-engendering explanations? Or is it protective to believe that death is reversible and therefore that the deceased parent will eventually return?

Affective Development. From early through middle childhood and adolescence there is increasing developmental capacity to recognize one's own and other's emotions. As children grow older, they are, at least in some situations, less likely to express their affects overtly. Cummings, Zahn-Waxler, and Redke-Yarrow (1981), studying children's responses to anger, found that school-age children were better able than toddlers to control their own emotional responses and engage in purposive responses to their surviving parents' distress and conflict. Yet preschool children are in the process of developing real sympathetic behavior (Hoffman, 1975).

Sex

Kaffman and Elizur (1979) found more aggressivity and angry outbursts in boys than girls throughout their follow-up period. Kranzler et al. (in press) report that bereaved preschool boys were more vulnerable than were girls. Bereaved boys showed more externalizing and internalizing behavioral problems than control boys, whereas in the girls differences were significant only in the internalizing domain. The boys were also less expressive than girls regarding the sadness they felt about the death of their parent.

Both Rutter (1966) and Van Eerdewegh et al. (1982) reported that adolescent boys whose fathers died were at particular risk for depression. In Rutter's sample, the adolescent boys' depression was likely to start within six months of the parent's death, and they were likely to be treated in a psychiatric clinic sooner than other bereaved children.

Hetherington (1972) and Hetherington and Parke (1979) reported that adolescent girls whose fathers had died were anxious and shy around boys and eventually married successful but inhibited and controlled men. Archibald et al. (1962) found that boys who had experienced paternal loss in childhood had difficulties in masculine identification.

The impact of the sex of the deceased parent has been contested, with contradictory findings supporting the notion of either paternal (Glueck and Glueck, 1950) or maternal (Brown et al., 1977) loss as more critical. Recent evidence may help to clarify this complex question. Harris et al. (1986) and Breier et al. (1988) found that it was not the sex of the deceased parent per se that determined risk in children for later depression, but rather the extent to which the parenting function and the stability of the home life were disrupted. In some circumstances this may well be affected by the sex of the surviving parent.

Response of Surviving Parent

A potentially important influence on the risk to children after the death of a parent may be the particular difficulty experienced by young widows and widowers. Parkes (1970, 1972) and Madison and Walker (1967) have reported increased morbidity among younger widows. Van Eerdewegh, Clayton, and Van Eerdewegh (1985) has shown an association between the degree of parental psychopathology and children's symptoms. Kranzler et al. (in press) showed a strong relationship between parent's and child's adjustment. Parents of young children, left by the death of their spouse to raise the children alone, may be subject to greater feelings of anger, depression, and hopelessness. This directly impacts on how the children fare. Mothers with a history of affective disorders have been shown to be more disorganized, less active and effective, more overprotective, and more negative in affect toward their children (Davenport et al., 1984). It is possible that bereaved children are living in a parenting environment similar to that of children of depressed parents (see Chapter 13), at least temporarily. Their reaction to the loss of the deceased parent is colored by the additional stress of living with a grieving parent who may feel overwhelmed and unable to manage the task of parenting a bereaved child.

Raphael (1983) interviewed children from ten nonclinical families who had recently experienced the death of one of the parents. Particularly the younger children were focused on "oral concerns"—who was going to provide for them and feed them. Children were worried about the welfare of their surviving parents. Van Eerdewegh et al. (1982) found that 83% of the children who met criteria for depression had mothers who were themselves depressed prior to the death of the spouse. They concluded that the children of disturbed surviving parents were more vulnerable to the effects of bereavement than the children of "normal" surviving parents.

Kranzler et al. (in press) observed that bereaved preschoolers appeared to react to their surviving parents' grief and distress with anxiety and discomfort. Some were clearly aware of their parents' sadness and anger, but did not appear to have the capacity to effectively intervene and comfort them. Some parents reported a conscious effort to minimize their overt expression of grief in front of their children. They felt the children had given them the message that it was too painful for them to see their parents upset. Some children expressed hesitation about discussing their feelings and questions with their surviving parent, lest they upset them. This might at times be a mutually empathic protection by grieving parent and child, and therefore could be a useful coping strategy. It could also, however, lead to implied communication closure and denial, with resulting impairment of the grieving process.

Adequacy of Care

Harris et al. (1986) found that whether the loss was due to death, divorce, or separation was not crucial in determining outcome. Increased risk for depression in women who experienced childhood loss was seen in those who, in the aftermath of the death, experienced inadequate parenting and care. An index of high parental indifference and low control, which Harris and colleagues consider indications of material and emotional neglect by the surviving or substitute parents, was the measure most predictive of current depression in the grown women they studied. The low rates of inadequate care in the father-death group they studied explained the low rate of depression in that group. They hypothesized that surviving mothers in their sample were more likely than fathers to provide the necessary combination of breadwinning plus adequate emotional parenting. They concluded that lack of care rather than maternal loss was responsible for depression, because they found the same rates of depression in the adequate-care mother-loss groups as in the no-loss groups.

Similarly, Breier et al. (1988) found that adults with a history of psychopathology had a "poorer quality of childhood home life and personal adaptations" (p. 987) after the death of a parent than those without psychopathology. In particular, a nonsupportive relationship with the surviving parent, in which the child was burdened with the parent's emotional needs, was the most significant discriminator of later adult psychopathology. Family psychiatric history, age at the time of loss, and paternal versus maternal loss all failed to determine pathological outcome significantly. They concluded that the crucial mediator of adult outcome among those who had experienced early bereavement was the quality of the home life in the intervening years after the loss.

Prospective results reported by Kranzler et al. (in press) and Van Eerdewegh et al. (1985) lend support to the retrospective findings of Harris et al. (1986) and Breier et al. (1988). Kranzler et al. found that the most symptomatic bereaved preschoolers were (1) those whose surviving parents were most symptomatic in the aftermath of their spouse's death, (2) those whose surviving parents were comparatively uninvolved with them prior to the loss, and (3) those from families that experienced a drop in economic circumstances following the death. One might interpret these combined findings as reflections of ongoing loss, decrement in parental care, and inadequacy of environmental supports. It was not the death of a mother versus a father per se that determined outcome in this short-term assessment, but rather the preexisting relationship between each parent and the child and the capacity of the grieving parent to provide an adequate, safe atmosphere.

Pretraumatic Variables

Arthur and Kemme (1964), reporting a series of intensive case studies, argued that the most emotionally disturbed bereaved children were those who had significant pretraumatic personality deficiencies. They posited that the coping demands necessary to successfully withstand parental loss are so significant that children with prior ego fragility would suffer pervasive disruption. Elizur and Kaffman (1983) found that the children who had preexisting emotional disturbance as well as those from families where there were significant marital problems were at greater risk for pathological bereavement.

CONCLUSIONS AND APPLICATIONS

The evidence supports increased risk in some parentally bereaved children. In the year after the death of a parent, children exhibit many of the behaviors and emotions seen in grieving adults, with dysthymia and anxiety predominating. This, however, does not indicate pathological bereavement. Vargas, Loya, and Hodde-Vargas (1989), in a study of adult grief reactions, concluded that aspects of the grief response that previously have been considered pathological may in fact be seen in most bereaved individuals. They suggest that pathology is determined by the frequency and intensity of these symptoms rather than by their mere presence.

Some children survive the stress of parent loss without developing major psychiatric dysfunction, either short- or long-term. The specific protective constitutional or environmental mediators that improve the child's chances of coping and adjusting well over the long run must be identified and fostered when possible. Recent research implicates some critical mediators that impact outcome. These findings will help to identify those children in need of treatment.

A critical question is whether those who are most symptomatic initially are the same ones who remain at risk in the long term. To answer this question, long-term prospective studies are needed. Clayton (1974) and Clayton and Darvish (1979) found that a significant percentage of young widows went on to develop full-blown depressive episodes within one year after the death of their husbands, complicating the course of their adjustment to the loss. Given the purported association between childhood parent loss and later adult depression, it is important to investigate the degree to which there is continuity between the bereaved child's acute condition and subsequent long-term outcome. Identifying children who are functioning poorly in the short term may have important preventive implications.

An important aspect of the bereavement experience has not been addressed in the research literature so far. Outcome measures used in studies of childhood bereavement, for both short- and long-term adjustment, are relatively gross indices of disturbance. It is more difficult to assess the more subtle aspects of emotional pain experienced by even those children who on the surface may be coping successfully. Their capacity for intimacy and trust and many subsequent career, friendship, and marital choices could be affected. These effects may have a large impact on their lives, even though they do not develop the degree of dysfunction or the major psychiatric disturbances that generally have been measured in the literature.

Treatment and Prevention

Little is known about when treatment should be instituted and which interventions are most effective. Clinicians have argued in favor of differing modalities, including individual, family, and group interventions. Nevertheless, the research to date suggests several guidelines.

Consistent findings regarding the impact of the surviving parent's clinical state on the bereaved child indicate that the parent be assessed as part of the child's evaluation. Whenever the parent shows need for intervention, this should be included as an integral part of the treatment plan. If the parent's needs are great and potentially overwhelming to the child, this will be best accomplished by arranging for separate treatment of the parent. In other situations it can be important to foster the shared grieving process by seeing parent and child together in family sessions.

Goals of clinical intervention include: (1) to support the child's experience of parental loss; (2) to help in the identification and expression of grieving affects; (3) to clarify misconceptions and distortions about the death of the parent; (4) to assist children with the resultant loss of well-being and economic or family structure changes; (5) to help the child understand and deal with the surviving parent's grief; and (6) to help the parent understand and deal with the child's grief.

Interventions should enhance the capacity of family members to express their feelings to one another appropriately, especially when the nature or timing of their reactions differs. Active strategies should be developed for mutual support within the family. Younger children in particular may need help in recognizing or verbalizing their feelings and relating them to their loss. Families may need strengthening so that the children are assured of the stability and security that can be threatened after the loss. This strategy includes assuring that consistent caretakers supplement surviving parents where needed and that the support of friends and extended family be engaged.

Like adults, some children find mutual support groups particularly useful. Bereaved children describe a feeling of being forever different from their peers. They will no longer be able to have both parents attend their school plays or Little League games as their peers will. This can become a salient aspect of their loss experience. They can find comfort in meeting with other bereaved children, with the guidance of trained therapists, to share the common aspects of their experience.

REFERENCES

Archibald, H., Bell, D., Miller, C., & Tuddenham, P. (1962). Bereavement in childhood and adult psychiatric disturbance. *Psychosomatic Medicine, 4*, 343–351.

Arthur, B., & Kemme, M. L. (1964). Bereavement in childhood. *Journal of Child Psychology and Psychiatry, 5*, 37–49.

Barry, H., & Lindemann, E. (1960). Critical ages for maternal bereavement in psychoneurosis. *Psychosomatic Medicine, 22*, 366–381.

Beck, A. T., Sethi, B. B., & Tuthill, R. H. (1963). Childhood bereavement and adult depression. *Archives of General Psychiatry, 9*, 295–302.

Bendiksen, R., & Fulton, R. (1976). Death and the child: An anterospective test of the childhood bereavement and later behavior disorder hypothesis. In R. Fulton (Ed.), *Death and identity* (pp. 274–287). Bowie, MD: Charles Press.

Birtchnell, J. (1972). Early parent death and psychiatric diagnosis. *Social Psychiatry, 7*, 202–210.

Birtchnell, J. (1978). Early parent death and the clinical scales of the MMPI. *British Journal of Psychiatry, 132*, 574–579.

Bowlby, J. (1980). *Attachment and loss: III. Loss, sadness and depression.* New York: Basic Books.

Breier, A., Kelsoe, J. R., Kirwin, P., Beller, S., Wolkowitz, W., & Pickar, D. (1988). Early parental loss and development of adult psychopathology. *Archives of General Psychiatry, 45,* 987–993.

Brown, G., Harris, T., & Copeland, J. (1977). Depression and loss. *British Journal of Psychiatry, 30,* 1–18.

Clayton, P. J. (1974). Mortality and morbidity in the first year of widowhood. *Archives of General Psychiatry, 30,* 747–750.

Clayton, P., & Darvish, H. (1979). Course of depressive symptoms following the stress of bereavement. In J. E. Barrett et al. (Eds.), *Stress and mental disorder* (pp. 121–126). New York: Raven Press.

Cummings, E. M., Zahn-Waxler, C., & Redke-Yarrow, M. (1981). Young children's responses to expressions of anger and affection by others in the family. *Child Development, 52,* 1274–1282.

Davenport, Y. V., Zahn-Waxler, C., Adland, M. L., & Mayfield, A. (1984). Early child rearing practices in families with a manic-depressive parent. *American Journal of Psychiatry, 141,* 230–235.

Dennehy, C. M. (1966). Childhood bereavement and psychiatric illness. *British Journal of Psychiatry, 112,* 1049–1069.

Deutch, H. (1937). The absence of grief. *Psychoanalysis Quarterly, 6,* 12–22.

Dietrich, D. R. (1979). Psychopathology and death fear. *Dissertation abstracts international.* Ann Arbor, MI: University of Michigan [Films # 7918593].

Elizur, E., & Kaffman, M. (1983). Factors influencing the severity of childhood bereavement reactions. *American Journal of Orthopsychiatry, 53,* 668–676.

Felner, R., Stolberg, A., & Cowen, E. (1975). Crisis events and school mental health referral patterns of young children. *Journal of Consulting Clinical Psychology, 43,* 305–310.

Freud, S. (1957). Mourning and melancholia. In J. Strachey (Ed.), *The standard edition of the complete psychological works of Sigmund Freud* (Vol. 14, pp. 227–260). London: Hogarth Press and Institute for Psychoanalysis. (Originally published in 1917).

Fristad, M., Weller, E., Weller, R., & Grosshans, B. (1989). Children's bereavement during the first year post-parental death. In *Scientific Proceedings of the Annual Meeting of the American Academy of Child and Adolescent Psychiatry,* (Vol. 5, pp. 62–63).

Furman, E. (1974). *A child's parent dies.* New Haven: Yale University Press.

Garmezy, N. (1986). Developmental aspects of children's responses to the stress of separation and loss. In M. Rutter, C. E. Izzard, & P. B. Reed (Eds.), *Depression in young people.* New York: Guilford Press.

Glueck, S., & Glueck, E. (1950). *Unraveling juvenile delinquency.* Cambridge, MA: Harvard University Press.

Granville-Grossman, K. (1966). Early bereavement and schizophrenia. *British Journal of Psychiatry, 112,* 1027–1034.

Greer, S. (1964). The relationship between parental loss and attempted suicide: A control study. *British Journal of Psychiatry, 110,* 698–705.

Gregory, I. (1965). Anterospective data following childhood loss of a parent. *Archives of General Psychiatry, 13,* 99–109.

Gregory, I. (1966). Retrospective data concerning childhood loss of a parent. *Archives of General Psychiatry, 15,* 362–367.

Harris, T., Brown, G. W., & Bifulco, A. (1986). Loss of parent in childhood and adult psychiatric disorder: The role of lack of adequate parental care. *Psychological Medicine, 16,* 641–659.

Haworth, M. (1964). Parental loss in children as reflected in projected responses. *Journal of Projective Techniques, 28,* 31–45.

Hetherington, E. M. (1972). Effects of father absence on personality development in adolescent daughters. *Developmental Psychology, 7,* 313–326.

Hetherington, E., & Deur, J. (1971). Effects of father absence on child development. *Young Children, 26,* 233–248.

Hetherington, E. M., & Parke, R. (1979). *Child psychology: A contemporary viewpoint* (2nd ed.). New York: McGraw-Hill.

Hoffman, M. (1975). Developmental synthesis of affect and cognition and its implications for altruistic maturation. *Developmental Psychology, 11,* 607–622.

Hopkinson, G., & Reed, G. F. (1966). Bereavement in childhood and depressive psychosis. *British Journal of Psychiatry, 112,* 743–751.

Jacobson, G., & Ryder, R. (1969). Parental loss and some characteristics of the early marriage relationship. *American Journal of Orthopsychiatry, 39,* 779–787.

Kaffman, M., & Elizur, E. (1979). Children's bereavement reactions following death of father: The early months of bereavement. *International Journal of Therapy, 1,* 203–229.

Kaffman, M., & Elizur, E. (1983). Bereavement responses of kibbutz and non-kibbutz children following the death of a father. *Journal of Child Psychology and Psychiatry, 24,* 435–442.

Kranzler, E. M., Shaffer, D., Wasserman, G., & Davies, M. (in press). Early childhood bereavement. *Journal of the American Academy of Child and Adolescent Psychiatry.*

Krupnick, J. (1984). Bereavement during childhood and adolescence. In M. Osterweis, F. Solomon, & M. Green (Eds.), *Bereavement: Reactions, consequences and care.* Washington, DC: National Academy Press.

Lifshitz, M. (1976). Long range effects of father's loss: The cognitive complexity of bereaved children and their school adjustment. *British Journal of Medical Psychology, 49,* 189–197.

Lloyd, C. (1980). Life events and depressive disorders reviewed: Events of predisposing factors. *Archives of General Psychiatry, 37,* 529–535.

Madison, D. C., & Walker, W. L. (1967). Factors affecting the outcome of conjugal bereavement. *British Journal of Psychiatry, 113,* 1057–1067.

Markusen, E., & Fulton, R. (1971). Childhood bereavement and behavior disorders: A critical review. *Omega, 2,* 107–117.

Nagera, G. (1970). Children's reactions to the death of important objects. *The Psychoanalytic Study of the Child, 25,* 360–400.

Parkes, C. M. (1970). The first year of bereavement: A longitudinal study of the reaction of London widows to the death of their husbands. *Psychiatry, 33,* 444–467.

Parkes, C. M., & Brown, R. J. (1972). Health after bereavement: A controlled study of young Boston widows and widowers. *Psychosomatic Medicine, 34,* 449–469.

Raphael, B. (1983). *The anatomy of bereavement.* New York: Basic Books.

Roy, A. (1979). Correction to vulnerability factors and depression in women. *British Journal of Psychiatry, 134,* 552.

Rutter, M. (1966). Bereaved children. In *Children of sick parents, Maudsley Monograph XVI* (pp. 66–75). New York: Oxford University Press.

Rutter, M. (1986). The developmental psychopathology of depression: Issues and perspectives. In M. Rutter, C. E. Izzard, & P. B. Reed (Eds.), *Depression in young people.* New York: Guilford Press.

Speece, M. W., & Brent, S. S. (1984). Children's understanding of death: A review of three components of a death concept. *Child Development, 55,* 1671–1686.

Tenant, C., Bebbington, P., & Hurry, J. (1980). Parental death in childhood and risk for adult depressive disorders: A review. *Psychological Medicine, 10,* 289–299.

Van Eerdewegh, M., Bieri, M., Parilla, R., & Clayton, P. (1982). The bereaved child. *British Journal of Psychiatry, 140,* 23–29.

Van Eerdewegh, M. M., Clayton, P. J., & Van Eerdewegh, P. (1985). The bereaved child: Variables influencing early psychopathology. *British Journal of Psychiatry, 147,* 188–194.

Vargas, L. A., Loya, F., & Hodde-Vargas, J. (1989). Exploring the multidimensional aspects of grief reactions. *American Journal of Psychiatry, 146,* 1484–1488.

Weller, E., Fristad, M., & Weller, R. (1989). Adolescent bereavement post parental death. *Scientific proceedings of the annual meeting of the American Academy of Child and Adolescent Psychiatry* (Vol. 5, p. 63).

Wolfenstein, M. (1969). Loss, rage, and repetition. *Psychoanalytic Study of the Child, 24,* 432–460.

CHAPTER SIXTEEN

Social Stressors in Childhood: Poverty, Discrimination, and Catastrophic Events

Beverly G. Toomey
Daniel J. Christie

The recent public recognition that 500,000 children are homeless in America (*New York Times,* 1988) has increased interest in the stress caused by social forces on the lives of children. The image of the homeless child graphically illustrates the stresses that occur when basic needs for food, shelter, and safety are unmet. Berry and Chiappelli (1985) remark, "whenever there is social disorganization, school-age children, especially the young, must carry a large part of the burden" (p. 303).

Existing child development literature has focused largely on the stress in children's lives related to micro-social variables, such as parental and sibling relationships and supports. This is true for two reasons: parents are most significant in the child's life, and parents are the mediators of community stressors for their children. Both theory and conventional wisdom recognize the significant role of parents in protecting their children from trauma imposed by the forbidding outside world. Further, child development theorists contend that the coping strength the child will have to deal with the stress is, to a large degree, a function of the relationships within the home (Coles & Piers, 1969). Nevertheless, they also suggest that children are stressed by events in the world outside of the family; they may have an experience of stress from poverty, discrimination, or catastrophe, independent of the parental response. Researchers have identified a void in the literature discussing how children experience the impact of these sociostructural variables. Brim (1975), in an address to the American Orthopsychiatric Association, called for a survey of children so they could "speak for themselves." Benedek (1985) and Beardslee and Mack (1982), discussing research on disaster, note there is little data on how children experience these events.

DEFINITIONS OF STRESS AND CHAPTER FRAMEWORK

In the literature, the concept of stress has been defined in a number of different ways. It is defined both as the stimulus causing disequilibrium (often labelled the stressor) and as the non-specific response of disequilibrium (labelled the stress reaction). Behavioral scientists often use the word "stress" interchangeably for these two different ideas. Therefore the comparison of research findings is conceptually cloudy. Further, there is confusion in the overlap of the terms *fears, anxieties,* and *stresses.* The word "fear" is used to describe a normal emotion in response to something the child can identify as a threat, something of which he or she is afraid. The terms "stress" and "anxiety" refer to a factor that causes the child pain or discomfort over time. It may or may not be something the child is able to identify specifically. Often the identification of a fear names the factors that are assumed to cause the stress reaction.

Macro-sociocultural factors that cause stress reactions in children have not been examined carefully. The literature is particularly deficient in the identification of children's perception of these types of stressors and their respective fears. In this chapter we review three major social forces: poverty/unemployment, discrimination, and natural and social disasters.

The study of poverty covers the impact of being poor, children's awareness of parental unemployment and financial setbacks, and the effects of loss of income, such as eviction, excessive mobility, school displacement, and homelessness. While Coles (1967), Gottlieb and Ramsey (1967), Harrington (1962), and others have noted the devastating effects of poverty on children, there is less research on how children experience poverty, what they think about it, and what stress reactions they have because of it.

Discrimination is an acknowledged force in many cultures. The discrimination may be based on gender, race, ethnicity, age, religion, or beliefs. Although there is some study of the impact of differential treatment on children's success in education and occupational choice, there is limited knowledge of the stress children experience because of prejudice and discrimination.

The effect of experiencing natural disasters or traumatic social events such as war, nuclear accidents, or crime is a potential threat to a child's sense of safety and security. However, most of the literature focuses on community response and adult reactions. Children have been considered extensions of their parents. Only recently has there been recognition that parental stability during such turmoil cannot completely mitigate the impact of such events (Benedek, 1985).

The Maslow model of a hierarchy of needs provides a framework for looking at the elements in the social environment causing stress and fear in children. Maslow's model suggests that the most basic needs of human beings are those meeting physical sustenance requirements for food and shelter. Once those needs are met, the individual needs to feel safe and secure. On the third level, the human animal has needs for belonging and love, which are foundations for the fourth level, the need for self-esteem and identity. Finally, Maslow posits that when all of these needs are met, the individual can reach for self-actualization. The threats to basic sustenance, safety and security, belonging and self-esteem are evident in the macro-social variables explored in this review.

POVERTY AND UNEMPLOYMENT

It is well accepted that economic depression and unemployment are related to many social problems impacting on children: infant mortality, child abuse (see Chapter 10), child deaths from abuse, children in out-of-home placements, school truancy and displacement, and homelessness (Brown, 1983; Edelman, 1983; Justice & Justice, 1976). If the strength of the family is the buffer for children, then the loss of family strength through economic hardship reduces the protection for the child. In addition to loss of support, the child may also be the target for family frustration. The incidence of problems increases with loss of income, whether the poverty is the chronic, long-term type experienced by the poor, or the crisis type experienced by the middle-class family that suddenly loses income, but the type or severity of outcomes may be different. For example, Brown (1983) found that one in eight workers laid off from an aircraft plant said their marital stability broke down and problems with their children increased.

Berry and Chiappelli (1985) have summarized the literature on the impact of unemployment on school-age children. It reduces family resources, the adequacy of family diet, and the amount of medical care, recreation, and clothing the family has. They suggest that of particular importance to children is the loss of things that facilitate peer acceptance, such as special types of clothing, games, and fad items. Using a data base of middle-class families who suddenly became poor in the Great Depression, Elder (1974) found that income loss also created uncertainty and ambiguity as to family status and social standing.

The recent attention to the growing number of homeless families has increased public awareness of some of the most serious effects of poverty on children. Interviews with 83 families residing in shelters and hotels in New York City documented that two-thirds of the children were not attending school, that half of the families reported negative behaviors and depression in the children, and that children were exposed to dangerous physical and emotional environments (Citizens Committee for Children, 1984). The 1987 Congressional Report on the effects of homelessness on children and families presents testimony from the homeless and their advocates that "homelessness is threatening the physical health and safety of thousands of children; placing them at risk of serious developmental delays and academic failure; and it is stretching the fabric of family life to its limits" (Select Committee on Children, Youth & Families, 1987, p. 2). Bassuk and Rubin (1987), studying homeless families living in shelters, identified developmental delays and increased depression and anxiety in the children. Jonathan Kozol (1988) adds journalistic anecdotal information, but the serious impact of homelessness on physical and psychological development is still largely unstudied. Advocates identify the loss of privacy and the limited opportunity for parent-child intimacy as contributing to the arrested development of homeless children.

The impact of poverty on children can be studied as a direct effect or as an indirect effect. One can document how being poor or worrying about security directly affects children by measuring traditional indicators of social status, school performance, misbehavior, or sense of well-being. In addition, one can study the indirect effect of poverty as it diminishes the ability of parents to provide emotional sustenance or increases parental rejection, thereby affecting the child's feelings of security and love and interfering with normal development.

Direct Effect of Poverty

Direct effects of poverty were supported by Elmer (1978) in a study originally designed to identify the long-term effects of abuse. She matched low-income infants (under 24 months) who were abused with a group of low-income, non-abused children who had been injured in an accident, and followed them for eight years. She found that both groups were seriously damaged, exhibiting poor language development, low achievement, and a pervading sense of sadness, anxiety, and fear. Elmer concluded, "We must inquire whether membership in the lower classes is in itself dwarfing the potential of young children" (p. 18).

In a study of how elementary school children are affected by unemployment of their parents, Mirage (1982) reports that children of unemployed families display increased maladaptive behavior—daydreaming, asocial behavior, and academic loss. The analysis of the Oakland Growth Study found that adolescent girls from economically stressed families were perceived to be less well-groomed by peers, rated themselves as more socially unhappy, and felt more excluded (Elder, 1974, Chap. 61).

There are few studies that directly ask children if they are concerned about unemployment, poverty, or financial losses in their families. Pryor-Brown et al. (1986) included unemployment of parent in a study of stressful life events. Subjects were 503 fourth- through sixth-graders in urban and suburban schools. They report that urban, lower socioeconomic level children experience more stressful events than suburban, higher socioeconomic level children. Of 22 events rated, parental unemployment was eleventh in frequency; it occurred more often for urban youngsters and was rated more upsetting by urban children. In a study of more than a thousand Canadian boys and girls from an economically depressed area, Paulter and Lewko (1983, cited in Rayman, 1988) found that children from unemployed families reported more worries on a 75-item worry inventory. Age level was an important variable. Children from grades 6, 9, and 12 were surveyed, and sixth-graders were found to have the greatest effect.

Indirect Effect of Poverty

A number of studies have documented that poverty, unemployment, and economic loss cause depression in parents, decreasing their emotional availability and responsiveness (Leana & Ivancevich, 1987). The resultant emotional deprivation causes children to be insecure and dependent, resulting in inept social behavior and peer rejection (Friedemann, 1986).

Kasl and Cobb (1967) studied children reared in economic hardship. They reported that parents had poor self-images and were insecure, less affectionate, and less responsive to their children. They contend that this situation resulted in the children feeling rejected.

Depression due to economic setbacks appears to occur more often in fathers than mothers. Mothers, however, are likely to become depressed if the economic losses affect their neighborhood status or their marital relationship (Elder, 1974; Friedemann, 1986). The effect of mothers' depression and subsequent emotional unavailability or rejection impacts on children's emotional development (Cohler & Musick, 1982; Crook, Raskin, & Eliot, 1981; Grunebaum et al., 1974; see also Chapter 13 by Beardslee) and may increase a child's suicidal tendencies (Pfeiffer, 1981).

Friedemann (1986) studied 52 families with a kindergarten child and found lower peer acceptance for children from families with greater income setbacks. She documented an unusual effect of father depression on girls in this study, with two distinct response patterns emerging. One group of girls was quiet, rather withdrawn, inattentive, and uninvolved, and the other was the opposite: very active, fast moving, assertive, noisy, and somewhat scattered. The depression of the mother did not seem to affect the girls in this study. The link between economic loss and father rejection on adolescent girls was explored by Elder, Nguyen, and Caspi (1985). They report that girls were more likely to be affected by the rejection of their fathers. Girls of rejecting fathers had lower aspirations, held a lower opinion of themselves, and saw their mothers as more moody and irritable. Further, less attractive girls were more likely to be rejected.

Implications of Poverty for Interprofessional Practice

It has been well documented that level of socioeconomic status is a significant stress variable in describing the lives of children, and experts analyzing differences in school performance, family conflict, community activities, and delinquent behavior attribute the cause to poverty. Nevertheless, there is still only minimal work directly measuring what children observe and think about living in poverty or their response to short-term economic deprivation during childhood and adolescence. The poignancy of fictional characters like the Little Match Girl or Tiny Tim is evidence of society's recognition of the impact of poverty on children. When parents either cannot or will not provide the consistent basic level of care needed for growth, children are damaged. Their physical health and well-being may be harmed, their mental acuity may be reduced, and their sense of trust and security is threatened. Children suffer the embarrassment of being poor among their peers and grow up with a diminished self-image. Poor children live at the mercy of public programs and private charities.

Persons in the helping professions struggle in separate service systems to ameliorate the numerous symptoms of poverty. Interprofessional cooperation to identify and provide services in a coordinated manner has been described as an ideal model in some human service settings; however, only limited implementation has occurred. Income maintenance programs offer social services through Title XX, health care is offered through Medicaid, and case work attempts to link to other needed community resources. Public health professionals collaborate with social workers, nutritionists, teachers, and clergy in offering care from a holistic paradigm. However, the model frequently breaks down as agency policies become barriers to coordinated services. Interprofessional collaboration on the development of policy to ameliorate the impact of poverty on children is essential. For example, some of the issues that need to be addressed are creative investment strategies to finance low-income housing, jobs, and a wage structure that fosters the independence of the low-income family.

The public schools are a potential locus for service. Since children attend (or should attend) school daily, school-based multiservice centers are suggested for the delivery of interprofessional services. The school is already recognized as an important socializing agent of society. It is also a nutrition and health center, with food programs, health education, and even medical clinics. The counseling and guidance provided now are only a beginning for what could become family support centers. The school is an ideal setting because teachers are in a unique position to recognize the multiple problems of poverty in children. However, schools do not have the resources to provide all these services. Although schools have been consistently recognized as ideal settings for tackling new problems, their budgets rarely are expanded to allow this role. A solution might be to bring other agency services into the school with financial support from outside the education budget, perhaps with private initiative.

Social workers, psychologists, physicians, and other professionals bring creative strength and professional expertise, but joint efforts of professionals, business and labor leaders, and politicians are essential to formulate and support public policy for the development of programs, housing, and jobs. Social policy to provide for the economic welfare of children is necessary if future productivity is to be ensured.

DISCRIMINATION

This section focuses on racial and ethnic discrimination as a particular type of social stressor. First, the intended usages of key terms are clarified—*prejudice, racism, discrimination,* and *stereotypes*—then a model that integrates research on children who are the brunt of racial and ethnic discrimination is offered. In its most simple form, the model posits a relationship between discrimination as a stressor and various stress reactions. The model takes on greater complexity when variables that mediate the relationship between discrimination and stress reactions are examined.

Definitions and Clarifications

Traditionally, social scientists have conceptualized *prejudice* as an attitude with three-components: affective, cognitive, and behavioral (Jaspars, 1978; Milner, 1981).

The *affective* component engenders feelings of dislike, antipathy, perhaps even hatred for the target of prejudice. The *cognitive* component of an attitude refers to mental processes that result in a particular mental representation of the target, one that may bear little resemblance to reality. Selective attention, perception, categorization, beliefs, expectations, and other aspects of information processes are included in the cognitive component. These aspects of information processing are used by everyone and serve the function of simplifying social information that otherwise would overload and overwhelm the individual with complexity. Social *stereotypes,* which amount to generalizations or oversimplified mental images of some category of person (Tajfel, 1981), represent a particular kind of cognitive simplification.

The third component of an attitude includes *behavioral* tendencies. The behavioral component of prejudice may range from social rejection to outright aggression. While not everyone who is prejudiced actually engages in behaviors aimed at the target, the predisposition or readiness to behave in a negative way is assumed to be present. Certain situational conditions will be necessary for the behavior to occur. *Discrimination* may be regarded as a manifestation of the behavioral component of an attitude. The target of discrimination is treated unfairly or unequally because of membership in a particular social category or group.

Prejudice may be directed at any individual who has an identifiable feature that can be used for the purpose of categorization. *Racism* is more limited in scope—the target is those who are identified as belonging to a particular racial category. In the United States, old-fashioned racism typically involved the triple creed of white supremacy, black inferiority, and racial segregation (Sniderman & Tetlock, 1986). Katz and Taylor (1988a) note that "racism" entered the lexicon in the 1949 edition of *Webster's Intercollegiate Dictionary,* perhaps because of the racist philosophy officially sanctioned in Nazi Germany. In subsequent editions, the term retained its emphasis on the belief component and concomitant behavioral tendencies. The belief component engenders notions of inherent superiority and inferiority due to presumed biologically based differences, while the behavioral component is akin to discrimination, the unequal treatment of individuals because of their membership in a particular group.

Survey research suggests that the main behavioral dimension of racism in the United States—white discrimination toward blacks—has declined in the past 20 or so years. White public opinion has moved toward acceptance of black and white students attending the same schools, acceptance of blacks as neighbors, and acceptance of equal treatment for blacks with regard to the use of transportation and access to jobs (Smith & Sheatsley, 1984; Taylor, Sheatsley, & Greeley, 1978). Firebaugh and Davis (1988) have analyzed trends in racism, using data from the General Social Survey (Davis & Smith, 1984). The results suggest two conclusions that are relevant to our consideration of racism as a particular kind of stressor: first, the decline in racism has continued, at least until 1984; second, the decline has been due mainly to cohort replacement (i.e., replacement of old, more prejudiced cohorts with younger, less prejudiced ones) and, to a lesser extent, to people changing their existing attitude.

While the general trend in racism is one of decline, opinions about interracial marriage have changed little since 1972 (Schuman, Steeh, & Bobo, 1985, p. 82). There remains substantial support for laws that prohibit black-white marriages, with a third of the public in 1982 either favoring or undecided about antimiscegenation laws (Kluegel & Smith, 1986). If a substantial percentage of respondents favor laws against black-white marriages, it seems likely that a large percentage of the white population would oppose having a family member date or marry a black person.

While most forms of blatant, old-fashioned racism have declined in recent years, some social scientists have suggested that a more subtle and pervasive form of racism continues to exist. It has been suggested that symbolic racism (Sears & Kinder, 1971) underlies whites' continued resistance to efforts designed to bring about racial equality, such as busing and affirmative action. There are problems with the clarity of "symbolic racism" as a hypothetical construct (cf. Sniderman & Tetlock, 1986). The construct has been measured in various ways and has had myriad meanings, such as "the blending of racist sentiment and such treasured values as individualism and self-reliance" (Sears & Kinder, 1971); "a blend of antiblack affect and the kind of traditional values embodied in the Protestant Ethic" (Kinder & Sears, 1981, p. 416); "a 'witches brew,' in which traditional values merely camouflage racism" (Sneiderman & Hagen, 1985, p. 10). Part of the problem is the difficulty of inferring what motives underlie opposition to things like busing and having black candidates running for office, two typical items that are used to measure symbolic racism. Presumably, if the motives underlying opposition are a

mix of anti-black affect combined with traditional values of individualism and self-reliance, then symbolic racism is the appropriate label. On
the other hand, if anti-black affect is the main cause of the opposition,
then old-fashioned racism is implicated. (For completeness we need to
add the possibility of nonracial motivation, either classist or pragmatic.)
In any case, to the extent that whites hold stereotypes of blacks that
violate cherished values, such as those embodied by the Protestant Ethic
(Weber, 1958)—hard working, individualistic, repressing sexuality, and
delaying gratification—there is likely to be opposition to actions that
promote equality.

Racism may be viewed as a stressor to the target of racist actions or
racial discrimination. This chapter focuses on racial discrimination at
the individual level, using the American experience as an example. This
is not meant to devalue the impact of institutional racism. When opportunities for primary wealth, such as land acquisition, proliferated some
250 years ago, blacks were systematically excluded by racist institutions.
Prior to legislation in the mid-1960s, major institutions in the United
States remained closed to black people (Jones, 1988). While this chapter
is concerned with micro-forces, undoubtedly the macro-forces of institutional racism have had a major, if immeasurable, impact on black people.

Although social scientists generally are in agreement about the perni-
cious nature of prejudice, discrimination, and racism, there is less agreement as to the depth and breadth of the problem and its likely effects,
causes, and remedies. In the discussion that follows, a model is presented
that attempts to clarify relationships between discrimination, a particular kind of stressor (or cause of disequilibrium), and the stress reaction
(i.e., non-specific response to disequilibrium).

A Model of the Discrimination Stressor/Stress Reaction

Much of the research literature on racial and ethnic discrimination can
be integrated by the model shown in Figure 16.1, which is organized by
three sets of variables: antecedent variables, intervening variables, and
consequent variables. Antecedent and consequent variables are observable and can be subjected to qualitative and quantitative analyses. Intervening variables are hypothetical constructs that are inferred on the basis
of observations of antecedents and consequent variables. Moreover, intervening variables are presumed to mediate the relationship between antecedents and consequences. Hence, a particular antecedent or stressor
(e.g., verbal abuse) may lead to a consequence or stress reaction such as
aggression. However, the relationship between the stressor and stress
reaction will vary, depending upon characteristics of the individual
along with other intervening variables.

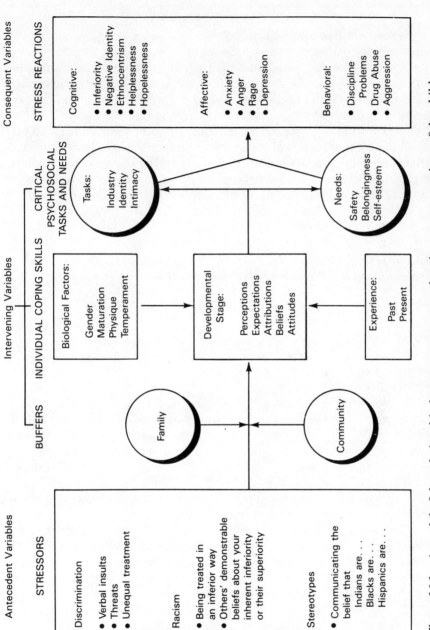

Figure 16.1. A model of the relationship between stressors and various stress reactions of the child.

Stressors.   Surprisingly little research has been designed to identify the kind of discrimination to which members of an ethnic or racial group are subjected. Instead, one must turn to anecdotal evidence and case studies. These can be a rich source of information, but offer little hard data as to the incidence and prevalence of prejudice, discrimination, and racism.

Lyles et al. (1985) presented a case study of an 11-year-old biracial girl who was subjected to verbal insults (e.g., "zebra," "bitch") and who had difficulties achieving an identity in the Eriksonian sense. Other forms of discrimination and racism have been reported in retrospective accounts of black children. What follows are examples cited by Howard (1980):

Child 1

I can remember when I was real small how children would be drawn away from me by their mothers and told that I was a black African cannibal, and that black was evil (p. 371).

Child 2

A small child came over and called me a nigger. Having lived in an all-Negro town all my life, I had never been called a nigger like that before. I thought something terrible had happened to me. Of course, I knew that I was another color but I was proud of our people until that time (p. 372).

Incidents that serve to deprecate or devalue others may take subtle forms, not always racially motivated but imbedded in the culture and language. Consider, for example, the first-grade teacher who equates the color black with sadness or evil (Taylor, 1980). Similarly, using phrases like "blackball" and "black sheep," and describing sin as "a 'black mark' on an otherwise white soul," all represent widespread instances in which black is associated with bad and white with good.

Phyllis Katz (Katz & Taylor, 1988) has reported some preliminary data on the subtle ways in which parents transmit racism. When either black or white parents are asked to go through a picture book with their children in any way they would like, parents tend to direct their children's attention to those pictures that depict characters of the same race. The transmission process appears early, for the children in the study are only 12 to 36 months of age, and the process is subtle. Katz suggests that such an emphasis may accentuate the child's perceptions of group differences, and may even diminish their empathy for others who are unlike themselves.

Modern forms of racism may be difficult to eradicate because of their subtlety and indirectness. For example, when compared to white applicants, black applicants who are interviewed by white interviewers receive less eye contact, less foward body lean, shorter interviews, greater inter-personal distance, and other nonverbal and verbal behaviors indicative of negative interaction or rejection (Pettigrew & Martin, 1987).

Prejudice toward other minorities in the United States has been exam-ined. While not identifying specific stressors or instances of discrimina-tion toward Hispanics, Ramirez (1988) has argued that negative interethnic relations may be due to "a monolithic system in which the dominant cultural group has the power, resources, and authority to define itself in positive, normative ways and to define the out-group in negative, dysfunctional ways" (p. 138). Accordingly, low self-esteem, a low level of aspiration, and negative attitudes toward education may be viewed as consequences of discrimination.

The stereotypical ways in which American Indians have been por-trayed, particularly in the media, have done little to foster appreciation for cultural diversity and promote positive intergroup relations (Trim-ble, 1988). Moreover, it has been suggested that racism and discrimina-tion are contributing factors in mental health problems, the conse-quences of which may be seen in the inordinately high rates of suicide and alcoholism among American Indian youth (Kelso & Attneave, 1981; Mail & McDonald, 1980; Trimble, 1988).

The stressor/stress-reaction model proposed here posits a relationship between various manifestations of racial and ethnic prejudice (e.g., dis-crimination, racism, and stereotypes) and stress reactions. The relation-ship is complex. Stressors do not lead directly to a particular stress reaction; instead, a number of intervening variables mediate the relation-ship between stressors and stress reactions. One set of intervening vari-ables that may alter the effect of a stressor consists of buffers, a variable which will now be addressed.

Buffers: The Family and Community

The family and community can support a child's acquisition of skills that will help the child meet needs and successfully deal with psychosocial tasks. Consider, for example, two different social environments in which the child may develop (Brill, 1984). In the first case, the child's primary caregiver may feel powerless to change the situation, have no interest in seeing the child receive a good education, have no expectations for the child, provide no guidance, neglect the child's needs, and offer a negative role model for the child to observe. The parent, perhaps having been raised in a similar environment, might provide inconsistent discipline and offer little support and encouragement as the child faces such psy-chosocial tasks as the development of trust and initiative. It is difficult to imagine a child acquiring effective coping skills in a neighborhood in which distrust and hostility pervade, with inadequate housing, adult models lacking skills and dependent on welfare, and in a culture inhabited by prostitutes, drug addicts, drug pushers, juvenile delinquents, criminals, deinstitutionalized psychotics, and pimps, with hostility toward the police, a sense of alienation from society, and a feeling of victimization.

In contrast, a child would be more likely to cope effectively with stressors when raised in a social environment in which the mother wanted the child and had good prenatal nutrition and care, and in which both parents were present, exuded a sense of efficacy, provided guidance and consistent discipline, inculcated the value of education, provided high expectations and support, and encouraged in the child a future orientation.

Attempts have been made to identify the ways in which family support can serve as a buffer for stress reactions (Eckenrode & Gore, 1981; Lindblad-Goldberg, Dukes, & Lasley, 1988; Pearlin & Schooler, 1978). Families can eliminate or help modify the conditions that lead to problems; they can influence the way in which the child perceives an event; they can help the child moderate emotional reactions, thereby keeping the reactions manageable (cf. Pearlin & Schooler, 1978).

Some stress in daily life is inevitable. Social support may act as a buffer so that events like discrimination are interpreted or appraised in ways that minimize stress reactions. Family members may appraise an event as potentially harmful or helpful. Indeed, healthy families have been distinguished from unhealthy ones not by the number and kinds of stressors experienced, but by the tendency to emphasize positive events more than negative events (Lindblad-Goldberg et al., 1988).

At the community level, a racial or ethnic group may serve as a buffer against discrimination in the larger society. Black children, for example, may turn to persons in their immediate environment—family, friends, teachers, most of whom will be of the same racial/ethnic group—and so those persons who matter most may be the ones who tend to regard the child positively (Milner, 1981; Simmons, 1978). Put a slightly different way, the black (or other) community, through solidarity, a shared sense of norms, and self-determination, can serve as a filter that attenuates the harmful effects of a society that discriminates against minorities (Barnes, 1980).

Individual Coping Skills

It is suggested that the child's developmental stage sets the limits on the kind of coping skills that can be brought to bear on stressors. Presumably, biological factors (e.g., temperament, gender) also make a difference in the child's coping skills, yet little research bears directly on the nature of relationships between biological factors and coping skills.

There is evidence, for example, that the child's temperament may affect the quality of the attachment between the child and the primary caregiver (Goldsmith, Bradshaw, & Riesser-Danner, 1986), and it seems reasonable to expect that the quality of the attachment would impact on the child's repertoire of coping skills, such as the frequency with which the child would use the caregiver for support or as a consultant when discrimination occurs.

Developmental psychologists suggest that the developmental stage of the child is determined by the interaction of maturation and experience. The emergence of a particular coping skill requires a certain degree of readiness, maturationally given, combined with appropriate experiences. For instance, one would not expect preschool children to be able to take the perspective of another person very easily. Instead, they are egocentric or embedded in their own viewpoint. Gradually, with age, the child becomes maturationally ready to take another's viewpoint when the opportunity (experience) arises.

As cognitive development proceeds, the child eventually will be able to think about the nature of discrimination in complex ways, with greater flexibility and more differentiated categories of experience. The ability to take another person's perspective—or social perspective taking—is an integral part of many educational programs that are designed to reduce prejudice. This is not to suggest that the child who is a victim of discrimination should take the racist's perspective and excuse instances of racism. Rather, the child would be able to understand some of the situational factors that lead to racism or, more broadly, would realize that prejudice is learned, that instances of prejudice do not reflect on the worth of the victim. Refusal to internalize instances of discrimination was referred to by Andy Young, Mayor of Atlanta, when he gave an invited address to the American Psychological Association in 1988. He explained that from the time he was a young child, a key family member encouraged him to realize that instances of prejudice were not a reflection of his worth; rather, ownership of the problem rested with the person who insulted fellow human beings.

Similarly, a certain level of cognitive complexity is required to break down oversimplified images of others. The victim of discrimination may tend to lump together all members of another race or dominant ethnic group and believe that they are all alike. However, with age, greater cognitive flexibility, and the ability to make finer differentiations, it should become possible for the child to perceive heterogeneity in the other group (e.g., "not all whites are racists"), given appropriate opportunities.

Metacognitive analysis—being able to think about one's thinking—usually develops in late childhood or adolescence. At this time, the child may develop an awareness of biases in the kind of thinking and the kind of coping patterns that he or she typically uses. For example, a black child may realize that blaming "whitey" for one's shortcomings has become a convenient attribution that effectively blames external causes and relieves the individual from taking personal responsibility for his or her behavior (Auletta, 1982).

Psychosocial Tasks and Needs Impacted by Discrimination

Some key psychosocial tasks of childhood and adolescence include: (a) industry versus inferiority (school age); (b) identity versus role confusion (adolescence); and (c) intimacy versus isolation (late adolescence and young adulthood). The first issue, industry versus inferiority, is conceptually similar to the problem of self-esteem, a need that will be addressed shortly, after the issues of identity formation and intimacy are discussed.

With the development of abstract thinking, the child is able to grapple with *identity* questions: Who am I? Where am I going in life? What is my purpose? Erikson (1968) has made the point that deprecatory messages and other instances of racism and discrimination can place children at risk for developing "negative identities" in that the children may develop a negative sense of self and identify with negative elements in society.

The problem of identity formation is part of the larger problem of relations between different cultural groups in a pluralistic society. A policy of *assimilation,* for example, would encourage members of the minority group to adopt the culture of the mainstream. An *integration* policy would encourage the minority to retain its customs and coordinate the goals of the groups (Triandis, 1988). Some research indicates that a policy of integration (e.g., Canada) is preferred over assimilation (i.e., melting pot) in terms of mental health outcomes such as number of psychiatric hospitalizations among minority group members (Berry, Kalin, & Taylor, 1976; Murphy, 1965).

Berry (1984) has conceptualized *integration* as a condition in which (a) customs are retained and (b) positive relations with the larger society are sought. In contrast, the former is not present in *assimilation,* while the latter is not present in *segregation.* Finally, neither condition is present in the case of a society that has a policy of *deculturation.*

Thus, the crux of the identity issue for minority children can be conceptualized in terms of two questions: (1) Should I retain the values, attitudes, and behavior patterns of the minority group? (2) Should I seek positive relations with the majority group? Table 16.1 presents the child's "identity state" as a function of the way in which these questions are resolved.

In industrially and technologically developed societies, identity issues loom large as the child prepares for the future. While most children in such societies will face the issue of identity, in a sense minority children have a wider array of identity states to consider, along with the added

TABLE 16.1. *The Minority Child's "Identity State" in a Pluralistic Society*

Question 1: Should I retain the values, attitudes, and behavior patterns of the minority group?		Question 2: Should I seek positive relations with the majority group?
Yes	No	
Bi-cultural identity state	Assimilated identity state	Yes
Segregated identity state	Unresolved identity state	No

stress of intermittent assaults on their sense of worth, assaults that may occur in a highly unpredictable way.

Intimacy also takes on added complexity for the child who is a member of a minority group. While there have been consistent increases in the percentage of whites favoring equal treatment of blacks across a variety of issues, by 1983 the approval of interracial marriages had reached only about the same percentage as the approval of integrated transportation had reached some 45 years before (Schuman et al., 1985). Thus, a black youth may experience difficulties related to friendships, and later, inter-racial dating.

A related issue is Maslow's need to have a feeling of *belonging*. It is difficult to imagine how the victim of discrimination can satisfy the need to belong under conditions in which identity issues are in flux, for the problem of belonging is, in part, the problem of arriving at some sense of group membership and mutual acceptance.

Much of the research on minority children's *self-esteem* can be traced back to the doll studies of Clark and Clark (1947). These investigators presented a pair of black and white dolls to black children and asked them the question: "Which of these two dolls looks most like you?" The startling finding was that about a third of the black children indicated that the *white* doll looked more like them. Misidentifications by black children were not because they misperceived; instead, researchers argued that black children chose the white doll because of the derogatory connotations that society attached to black people. It was never clear whether or not the racial dimension of the self was important in the individual's overall sense of self-esteem. Nonetheless, the doll studies suggested that blacks valued being white more highly than being black. The first indication of a favorable change in blacks' self-esteem appeared in studies conducted in the 1960s and early 1970s (Hraba & Grant, 1970; Zirkel & Moses, 1971). It is not clear why the shift in self-esteem took place. Explanations range from criticisms of methodological shortcomings of the early studies to suggestions that the shift reflected real and significant sociological changes.

Stress Reactions to Discrimination

Although it is possible to find professionals who maintain that stress is a contributing factor in almost all disorders, there is uncertainty from a scientific viewpoint as to whether or not specific stressors such as discrimination actually cause the reactions that are observed in disproportionate numbers among minority group members. Practitioners, on the other hand, typically operate under the assumption that stress causes stress reactions and may predispose the individual to adopt inefficient and self-destructive behavior patterns.

Alton Kirk (1976), a psychologist and suicidologist, is representative of the practitioner's viewpoint. He found a disproportionately high rate of suicide among young black males when compared to the general population. In addition, Kirk (1986) suggests that depression among minority group members also may be a result of discrimination and related insults. Both *endogenous depression,* which arises without a clearcut precipitating event, and *reactive depression,* which is triggered by a specific life event, may be common among blacks because of their second-class position in U.S. society. Moreover, *internal rage* may be expressed by overreaction to minor annoyances or inappropriate reactions to provocations. The problem is that depression is not just a psychological state; it also creates an intrapsychic state that may set the context for self-destructive behavior. While the causes of suicide are many and varied, the mental state accompanying a suicide attempt is often one of depression, helplessness, and hopelessness. Under conditions in which hopelessness and helplessness pervade, escape and relief by way of drugs and other ineffective coping strategies would also seem more likely.

Some Implications of Discrimination for Professionals

Helping professionals can play an important role in reducing the stress of discrimination and related problems. Psychiatrists, for example, traditionally have focused on the individual as the locus of pathology as well as the unit of change. Comer and Hill (1985) have suggested that psychiatric training programs ought to offer trainees activities beyond the clinical setting, such as field experiences in the social policy-making process and exposure to extant social policies as they impact on child and family functioning. It does seem plausible that societal conditions are producing mental health casualties at a rate that is far greater than could ever be treated by focusing exclusively on the individual unit of analysis.

Psychiatrists are in a good position to assess and inform a variety of policies, including those related to income, education, and housing as they affect the well-being of children and families. In addition to influencing policies at the community level, psychiatrists can provide well-informed testimony to legislators who are responsible for the formation of policy and funding priorities.

The legal profession could play a more active role in the enforcement of civil rights as a remedy for discrimination and racism. Padgett (1984) has reviewed the legal cases and statutes related to racially motivated violence and intimidation. He makes the point that the basic rights of minorities depend on more rigorous enforcement of federal civil rights acts. Compensatory damages have been awarded under conditions in which the victim of racism has suffered severe emotional distress (e.g., shame, humiliation) because of the willful and outrageous conduct of the perpetrator of racism. Professionals in the helping professions can play an important role in determining whether or not the victim of racism has suffered "severe emotional distress."

Ever since *Brown vs. Board of Education* in 1954, increasing attention has focused on the schools as a remedy to the problem of discrimination. The interethnic curricula now available (Stephan & Stephan, 1984) typically present the history of a particular ethnic group and highlight the achievements of members of that group. School integration has been the major legal remedy for the problem of discrimination and prejudice. Part of the problem with this approach is that it attempts to produce instant harmony by merely putting people together in a room. Unfortunately, the contact seldom occurs under conditions that promote harmony. In particular, at least four conditions should be met to reduce prejudice: interdependence (i.e., both groups dependent upon one another), superordinate goals or goals that both groups strive to attain, support from authorities who can construct norms for intergroup behavior, and sanctions provided by authorities. Indeed, contact under conditions in which the specified conditions are not met can lead to increased prejudice (Amir, 1976). *Eliminating Racism* (Katz & Taylor, 1988b) provides a detailed and comprehensive analysis of the means of reducing racism and prejudice.

DISASTERS (CATASTROPHES)

Defining Disaster

The term *disaster* is used frequently in social science parlance; however, just as with the term *stress,* the word is used interchangeably to identify both the stimulus (event) and its impact. Dimensions descriptive of disaster include suddenness of the occurrence, the physical harm caused to people and the environment, and the need for a social response to ameliorate the effects. The designation of an event as a disaster is a social process (Quarantelli & Dynes, 1977), taking into account individual and communal reactions to the event and an assessment of the usual resources available for coping. A disaster is "declared" upon recognition that extraordinary efforts are needed to restore social order.

Kreps (1984) suggests that the term *disaster* is perhaps a global sensitizing concept rather than a singular and specific one. Building on the work of Fritz, Kreps offers the following operational definition: "Disasters are events, observable in time and space, in which societies or their larger subunits (e.g., communities, regions) incur physical damages and losses and/or disruption of their routine functioning. Both the causes and consequences of these events are related to the social structures and processes of societies or their subunits" (p. 312). Disaster designations have been applied both to natural occurrences and to human-induced events.

A major limitation of the research on the impact of natural and social disasters is that it is always conducted after the event. This means that there are usually no baseline data on individuals for comparison. Another limitation for this review is that children are less often the unit of analysis than are adults and communities (Anthony, 1986). Further, when children are studied they are usually in clinical treatment. Benedek (1985) laments the lack of a common framework or research protocol for studying the effect of disaster on children. The time lapse after a disaster is another limitation. It is difficult for social scientists to respond immediately after a disaster; obtaining funding takes time. This means the immediate crisis may not be well documented. Studies are also deficient in generalizability. There are few studies of a representative population of children describing their fears or their experience. Instead, most studies either cite increased rates of deviant behavior collected from community records or discuss clinical symptoms of children in treatment. Beardslee and Mack (1982) contend that "research concerning what children think has been neglected."

The literature reviewed below includes studies of natural occurrences like fires, floods, tornadoes, earthquakes, and volcanic eruptions, and socially defined disasters such as war, accidents, group hostage situations and crime experienced in school or other group situations.

Responding to Disaster

Studies of disasters disprove common myths about panic and immediate incapacitating stress reactions in major catastrophes (Tierney & Baisden, 1979). Instead, some social scientists have identified a therapeutic communal response evident in disaster situations and describe the use of formal and informal resources to cope (Rossi et al., 1982). Others reject the panic myth for different reasons. Focusing on the individual rather than communal response, they identify a "disaster syndrome" which is characterized by a numbing or lack of response in most people in the aftermath of the event (Erikson, 1976). This concept is similar to that of "psychic closing off" described by Lifton (1982) in his studies of survivors of Hiroshima. He posits that the immediate feelings in a disaster are rage and insecurity. The total repression in psychic closing off functions to avoid these feelings. He even suggests that the lack of research on these topics is an indicator of a societal repression of the fear of catastrophe (cited in Beardslee & Mack, 1982).

With the passage of time, disaster victims experience many types of stress as they cope with living in the disorder that follows. McGee (1973) reports 20% of flood victims expressed "emotional problems." Hall and Landreth (1975) report that a community experienced more family problems after a flood, as evidenced by an increase in divorce and annulments and in applications for Aid to Dependent Children. In a review of ten major disaster studies, Tierney and Baisden (1979) conclude that victims experience "considerable stress and strain and varying degrees of concern, worry, and depression and anxiety, together with numerous problems of living and adjustment postdisaster" (p. 36). However, they suggest that only a few researchers would claim that disasters cause severe or chronic mental disorder to any large degree.

Symptoms of Catastrophic Distress in Children

Studies of the impact of catastrophic events on children report effects over two time periods: short-term crisis symptoms and long-term symptoms, including post-traumatic stress disorder (PTSD). (See Chapter 2 for more about these.)

In the short term, numbing or denial are common in adults. However, Beardslee and Mack (1982), reporting on adolescent fears of nuclear war, concluded that children differ from adults in that they do not rely mainly on "denial or psychic shutdown" as a defense (p. 73). Terr (1979) agrees. She said the children did not seem to display psychic numbing in the crisis immediately after the Chowchilla bus kidnapping. However, Freud and Burlingham (1942) did identify the numbing phenomenon in their studies of World War II children. Newman (1976) reports that children and adolescents may not appear to experience the psychic numbing characteristic of adults in disaster; however they respond by "withdrawing into uncustomary behavior patterns" (p. 81). Working with children in Buffalo Creek, Newman identified an avoidance response where children initially resisted drawing anything related to the flood. She contends that the impact of the stress may actually be overlooked because the child appears not to respond. It is evident that there is a need for much more study of the immediate response of children to traumatic situations.

Frederick (1985) summarizes the most common symptoms children display in the short term across a range of disastrous events. He compared children who experienced natural disasters with those who were victims of sexual and physical abuse. The symptoms include "sleep disorders (bad dreams), persistent thoughts of the trauma, belief that another traumatic event will occur, conduct disturbances, hyperalertness, avoidance of any stimulus or situation symbolic of the event, psychophysiological disturbances, and in younger children, regression to enuresis, thumb sucking and more dependent behavior" (p. 76). He found that these children had significantly more disturbed behaviors than expected in the population they represented. He found more disturbance in children who experienced sexual abuse than in those who experienced physical abuse or disasters. Other short-term effects identified in research include time distortion, including a foreshortened view of the future; distortion and symbolization of the disaster; obsessiveness about the event; feeling vulnerable; and excessive attachment behaviors.

As stated earlier, studies of natural disasters focus primarily on adults. However, some have identified children as a special needs group. These studies reported community statistics of increases in school truancy and delinquency and lessening of parental authority as indicators of effects on children (Newman, 1976). Adams and Adams (1984) reported that children and adults were equally likely to suffer from increased domestic violence and stress-related physical and mental illness following the Mount St. Helen eruption. They also reported an increase in juvenile crime, vandalism, and disorderly conduct.

Those who have studied PTSD in children often fail to define the length of time considered "post" or "long-term," but they confirm its existence. Howard and Gordon (1972), providing mental health services to children who experienced an earthquake, documented that these children suffered more symptoms than a control group one year after the event. Sleep disorders and fearfulness were the most common symptoms. Eth and Pynoos (1985) think post-traumatic, long-term effects are different in children than they are in adults. They distinguish child PTSD from adult by the following: not necessarily having any preexisting psychiatric symptoms, being related to the developmental stage of the child, and having different types of impairment. Terr concurs that PTSD is different for children. She suggests that children are more vulnerable and that the trauma is more likely to have serious impact on the child's personality. Frederick (1985), comparing children and adults who have suffered from human-induced catastrophes, reports that 77% of children suffer from PTSD as compared with 57% of the adults. Erikson (1976) and Stern (1976) both identified stress in children through years of legal battles in Buffalo Creek, and there is evidence that children who were transferred out of their home schools after the Xenia, Ohio, tornado felt like outsiders and experienced long-term difficulty in coping with the arrangements necessitated by the disaster.

Factors Mediating the Impact of Disasters on Children

Newman (1976) proposes three factors that mediate the impact of disasters on children and adolescents: (1) the child's developmental level, (2) the child's perceptions of family reactions, and (3) the child's direct exposure to the traumatic event. These factors are described below as discrete categories, but they overlap and interact in the child's life. For example, the child's exposure may be controlled by the parents, the parents' reaction may affect how the child experiences the trauma, and the parents' reaction may be influenced by the child's developmental stage.

Another factor that appears to influence the impact of a disastrous event is the situation and people in the experience. Terr (1979), who studied 27 children kidnapped on the Chowchilla school bus, attributes some of her findings to the fact that the children shared a group experience during the trauma and following it. She identified symptom contagion and group fragmentation. Children's symptoms included fantasy of the kidnapping, perception of ghosts, misperception of time passage, and post-traumatic play, which spread among the child victims and also to non-victimized siblings and friends. Contrary to the expectation that the event would be a bond for the group, Terr reported that children seemed to break friendships after the event. Only one pair of friends maintained their friendship five years after the kidnapping.

Developmental Level

Escalona (1965) noted the interaction of developmental level and the impact of the fear of a disaster on the child. Studying children's fear of war, she concluded that the process of identity development would be hampered depending on the stage when the fear is salient. Children in elementary school are at the developmental level where accomplishment and achievement are critical to identity. The instrumental self grows as the child risks and succeeds at new tasks. Facing the threat of disaster and the feelings of powerlessness inherent in these situations can impede the sense of effective self. The problem is further complicated by the fact that children see their adult role models unable to reduce fear or ensure security. Observing the powerlessness of adults can weaken a child's identification. Escalona concludes that this may reduce or block the child's normal motivation to enter the adult world. Beardslee and Mack (1982) support this idea. They suggest that adolescents' ego ideal is impacted negatively when they see the future as uncertain because of adult incompetence, greed, lust for power, or ineffectiveness.

Other scholars (Law, 1973; Schwebel, 1965) contend that adolescents cope with the fear of war in one of two ways: either they accept it as inevitable (feeling powerless) and live in fear, or they develop a denial system. Neither outcome is desirable. Law points out that living in societies that are at war or are accepting of war teaches youth that organized killing is natural. This, too, causes real or imaginary stressors in the lives of children and adolescents.

Studies of the actual impact of war on children are few, are fraught with methodological limitations, and provide variable findings. Nevertheless, they expand our understanding of the differential stresses children experience by developmental stage. Arroyo and Eth (1985) reviewed the major studies of the impact of war on children and concluded the following: "First, war and extreme civil strife can adversely affect the local children and adolescents psychologically, and disrupt their normal development. And secondly, the more intimately (or personally) and catastrophically the youth are victimized, the greater is the risk of developing seriously disabling psychiatric symptoms" (p. 107). In psychiatric evaluations of 30 children who had experienced war in Central America before emigrating, Arroyo and Eth found serious mental illness, behavioral disorders, and somatic complaints, differing by developmental level. Young children were severely withdrawn and showed symptoms of regression. School-age children had more learning and behavioral problems in school than immigrants who had not experienced war. They seemed bothered by frightening flashbacks, fears of parental separation, and somatic complaints. Adolescents, as might be expected, demonstrated their problems by acting out sexually, using drugs, and aggressing against themselves and others. All ages suffered from severe deprivation of minimal resources during the war, which adversely affected their physical, mental, and psychosocial development. Many children feared abandonment; they had often been separated from parents in the war.

Newman's (1976) observations of children under 12 who experienced the Buffalo Creek flood are consistent with the responses of children in war. Feelings of depression, powerlessness, and vulnerability were common in latency-age children. Preschoolers were more likely to regress to earlier behaviors. They had difficulty distinguishing fantasy and dreams from reality, and they reported fears of separation and chronic anxiety. Erikson (1976) found adolescents in Buffalo Creek less responsive to community codes. They slipped from the control of their parents into socially unacceptable behaviors.

Studying 5- to 12-year-olds after a school accident, Bloom (1986) identified gender and developmental differences. More than 100 school children witnessed the fall of an overpass skywalk with children on it. Six weeks following the event, Bloom found that 19% of the families responding to a questionnaire reported distress. He also reports that boys took longer to recover and had more sleep disturbances, fighting, and fear responses. Girls had more startle reactions and asked more questions about the accident. The younger children (5 to 8 years old) showed more phobic and somatic responses than the 9- to 12-year-olds. The older children were more likely to express their distress in sleep disturbances, in worrying about friends, and in thinking about the accident.

Child's Perception of Family Reactions

Numerous child theorists contend that the response of the parents to the disaster is the most significant factor determining how the child will be affected. Reviewing the major studies of World War II, Janis (1958) noted that they largely attributed children's anxiety to the responses of parents or other adults around the children. He accepts the plausibility of this logic with very young children who are not able to fully understand the potential danger. However, Janis challenges the validity of the conclusion with school-age children; they are able to appreciate that there is danger in many situations without adult interpretation. Nevertheless, the literature looks not at "if," but rather at "how," the parental response mediates the impact of the disaster experience for the children.

Newman (1976) noted that one preschooler reported distress that his father was unable to save some neighborhood children from the flood. This example is an illustration of the truism that children expect their parents to take care of all threats from the outside world. Most children continue to benefit from the security of this belief unchallenged until later childhood or adolescence. Some even continue to hold it in the face of ordinary contradiction. Numerous responses from children in Buffalo Creek reveal the fearfulness children felt upon realizing that their parents were powerless in the face of the rushing water. Erikson (1976) suggests that this loss of belief in the adults results in the breakdown of adult authority, manifest in juvenile misconduct.

Children of war suffer a great deal from the awareness that their parents are unable to protect them. In fact, they may feel abandoned when parents are separated from them or killed. They are also affected by viewing adults who are aggressive and brutal and who sanction mutilating and terrorizing behavior. Arroyo and Eth (1985) contend this interferes with a child's development of impulse control and contributes to antisocial behavior on the part of adolescents. Jackson (1982) defined a phase of "moral nihilism" in children who actually participated in combat. He contends they are affected by the immorality of the adults in their environment and are unable to integrate the experience into the superego.

Evidence of the positive impact of familial support in a period of stress is found in a study of families surviving a house fire and the follow-up of children in a Boston flood. Cohen and Ahearn (1980) found evidence of stress reduction measured by children's blood pressures when their family's post-flood stress was reduced. In a qualitative study of 12 families after home fires, Rosenfeld and Krim (1983) found the mutuality of the relationship between parent and child was related to successful adjustment. In families where parents communicated their distress and exchanged support with the children, there was less stress. These parents were sensitive to their children's needs and found that the children were responsive in return. The families with negative adjustment had limited communication. Parents were authoritarian, making unmanageable demands on the children. They had two major response patterns: ignoring the children or punishing them.

Degrees of Exposure to the Disaster

Many of the studies of disaster do not make a distinction about proximity to the trauma because all the children in the study have been seriously affected. Newman (1976) has suggested that the intensity of the impact of a disaster on the child is increased if the child has greater direct contact with the event. Her hypothesis is based on her observations after the Buffalo Creek flood. The children who witnessed the flood waters sweeping away the people and possessions in their lives were more intensely disturbed than those who did not directly view the rushing flood and only observed the damage in the aftermath. Consistent with this is the finding that children in war who are involved in the violence are more damaged than those who are not pressed into the fight (Arroyo & Eth, 1985).

The Challenger 10 explosion is an example that offers a contrast. This event was a more distant experience. Millions of children watched the actual lift-off or saw replays on television. Few had a direct relationship with the shuttle crew, but most felt some attachment because of the educational element of the mission. Responses of these individuals to the disaster were less intense and disabling than those of children who actually experience a disastrous event firsthand. Nevertheless, a significant grief reaction occurred. Children varied in response according to age, with minimal understanding in the preschool child, questions about death from the elementary-age child, and more intellectualizing and denial in high school children (Blume et al., 1986).

The amount of contact the child has with a disastrous event is some-times controlled by adults in the child's life. Parents and teachers try to shield children from the experience where possible, but sometimes children are either witnesses or victims of events in which adults cannot intervene. In some instances, the response of the children may be quite independent of that of the parents because the parents did not share the experience. The skywalk accident, the Chowchilla bus kidnapping, and the recent shootings in school settings are all examples of situations in which the child's intense experience of the event is greater than the parents' because the parents were not present. Terr, Eth, Pynoos, Good-win, and Nir all have conducted research involving children who experi-enced the disastrous event directly and without their parents. These authors report PTSD in children occurring quite independently of the parental reactions (Benedek, 1985).

Implications for Interprofessional Practice

It is clear that interprofessional collaboration for amelioration of the stress after natural and social disasters is desirable. There is usually a generous response from the community of professionals. Studies of the efforts to restore order clearly demonstrate the cooperative model. Pre-vention of disaster is still an underdeveloped possibility. While the pre-vention of natural disasters may be impossible, there is much that can be done to reduce psychological damage in the wake of these events. In the case of human-induced disasters, prevention is quite possible, but some-times not politically feasible. The power of professional opinion could be significant in preventing future tragedy. For example, gun control and peace curricula are public policy strategies which have the potential to prevent violence, yet there is little organized support by professional groups either separately or interprofessionally. These are areas where interprofessional cooperation could create a meaningful change in the social structure, with benefits for the security of children.

SOCIAL STRESS INTERACTIONS
AND PREVENTION STRATEGY

The impact of poverty, discrimination, and disaster on children is sub-stantial and significant. While they are discussed in separate sections of this chapter, they are related: poverty is a correlate of discrimination and disaster. Poverty strikes children at their core; poor nutrition, health care, and housing limit the potential for child growth and development. Children who are poor or who are threatened by crime, discrimination, disruption, or violence cannot develop a sense of trust, safety, and security. The literature supports the notion that parents who are under a great deal of stress (as from poverty, discrimination, or disaster) may be unable to provide enough love and affection for their children. The indirect effect of these structural variables is felt in less effective parenting. Prejudice and discrimination, as well as poverty, play a central role in hindering the child's development of sense of self or of belonging in the society. Clinical literature has long recognized these problems. It has offered individual restorative treatment, but has done little to prevent the stresses, perhaps because prevention requires structural rather than individual solutions.

It is certainly necessary that professionals continue to treat the stress reactions of children who experience poverty, discrimination, and disaster. The current social institutions may need restructuring to facilitate new interprofessional treatment. For example, the school has become more than an educational setting. It could be expanded even more to a community center for serving families. The separation of service domains creates barriers in integrated service for children. Planning must look beyond placing a greater burden on the current educational system; it must integrate other service systems with the school.

Unfortunately, professionals in general have focused little attention on macro-solutions. With some significant exceptions, such as Physicians for Social Responsibility, which won the Nobel Peace Prize, the efforts of professionals as policy advocates have been minimal. Professional lobbying groups advocate largely on behalf of the profession rather than on behalf of the clients of the profession or the general well-being of the community.

Because the problems are structural, full solutions demand an overwhelming amount of change. These models for massive change are difficult to devise, let alone accomplish. Perhaps this is why social scientists and helping professionals expend so little effort in this frustrating direction. Weick (1984) offers a method for attacking these massive social issues by redefining the scale of the problem to a more manageable size. He notes that the large problem taxes our rational powers, overwhelms our abilities, and stimulates dysfunctional levels of arousal. Large-scale problems also tend to generate large-scale resistance to change in the target system. Conversely, restructuring the problem so that tasks are manageable provides a more hopeful attitude, reduces the dysfunctional arousal, and incites less systemic resistance. Each of these factors is conducive to a successful change, which may be small but is more certain. Interprofessional collaboration on public policy might well adopt this approach by pursuing small rather than major structural changes.

REFERENCES

Adams, P. R., & Adams, G. R. (1984). Mount St. Helen's ashfall: Evidence for a disaster stress reaction. *American Psychologist, 39,* 252–260.

Amir, Y. (1976). The role of intergroup contact in change of prejudice and ethnic relations. In P. A. Katz (Ed.), *Toward the elimination of racism.* New York: Pergamon Press.

Anthony, E. J. (1986). The response to overwhelming stress: Some introductory comments. *Journal of the American Academy of Child Psychiatry, 25,* 299–305.

Arroyo, W., & Eth, S. (1985). Children traumatized by Central American warfare. In S. Eth & R. S. Pynoos (Eds.), *Post-Traumatic Stress Disorder in children* (pp. 101–120). Washington, DC: American Psychiatric Press.

Auletta, K. (1982). *The underclass.* New York: Random House.

Barnes, E. J. (1980). The Black community as the source of positive self concept for Black children. In R. L. Jones (Ed.), *Black psychology* (pp. 106–130). New York: Harper & Row.

Bassuk, E., & Rubin, L. (1987). Homeless children: A neglected population. *American Journal of Orthopsychiatry, 57,* 279–287.

Beardslee, W., & Mack, J. (1982). The impact on children and adolescents of nuclear developments. In *Psychosocial aspects of nuclear developments* (pp. 64–93). Washington, DC: American Psychiatric Association.

Benedek, E. P. (1985). Children and psychic trauma: A brief review of contemporary thinking. In S. Eth & R. S. Pynoos (Eds.), *Post-Traumatic Stress Disorder in children* (pp. 1–16). Washington, DC: American Psychiatric Press.

Berry, G. L., & Chiappelli, F. (1985). The state of the economy and the psychosocial development of the school-age child. *Elementary School Guidance and Counseling, 19,* 300–306.

Berry, J. W. (1984). Cultural relations in plural societies: Alternatives to segregation and their sociopsychological implications. In N. Miller & M. B. Brewer (Eds.), *Groups in contact* (pp. 11–26). New York: Academic Press.

Berry, J. W., Kalin, R., & Taylor, D. M. (1976). *Multiculturism and ethnic attitudes in Canada.* Ottawa: Ministry of Supply and Services.

Bloom, G. E. (1986). A school disaster—Intervention and research aspects. *Journal of the American Academy of Child Psychiatry, 25,* 336–345.

Blume, D., Whitley, E., Stevenson, R. G., Van Buskirk, A., et al. (1986). Challenger 10 and our schoolchildren: Reflections on the catastrophe. *Death Studies, 10,* 95–118.

Brill, N. Q. (1984). The hard core. *The Psychiatric Journal of the University of Ottawa, 9,* 1–7.

Brim, O. G., Jr. (1975). Macro-structural influences on child development and the need for childhood social indicators. *American Journal of Orthopsychiatry, 45,* 516–524.

Brown, B. (1983). Impact of political and economic changes upon mental health. *American Journal of Orthopsychiatry, 53,* 583–592.

Brown v. Board of Education of Topeka. (1954). *347*, U.S. 483.

Citizens' Committee for Children of New York, Inc. (1984). *7000 homeless children: The crisis continues.* New York: Author.

Clark, K. B., & Clark, M. (1947). Racial identification and preferences in Negro children. In T. M. Newcomb & Hartley (Eds.), *Readings in social psychology.* New York: Holt.

Cohen, R. E, & Ahearn, F. L. (1980). *Handbook for mental health care victims.* Baltimore, MD: Johns Hopkins University Press.

Cohler, B. J., & Musick, J. (1982, March). *Psychopathology of parenthood: Implications for mental health of children.* Paper presented at the 6th annual meeting of the Michigan Association for Infant Mental Health, Ann Arbor.

Coles, R. (1967). *Children of crisis: A study of courage and fear.* Boston: Little Brown.

Coles, R., & Piers, M. (1969). *Wages of neglect.* Chicago: Quadrangle Books.

Comer, J. P., & Hill, H. (1985). Social policy and the mental health of Black children. *Journal of the American Academy of Child Psychiatry, 24,* 175–181.

Crook, T., Raskin, A., & Eliot, J. (1981). Parent-child relationship and adult depression. *Child Development, 52,* 950–957.

Davis, J. A., & Smith, T. W. (1984). *General social surveys, 1972–1984.* Distributed by Roper Public Opinion Research Center, New Haven, CT.

Eckenrode, J., & Gore, S. (1981). Stressful events and social supports: The significance of context. In B. Gottlieb (Ed.), *Social networks and social support.* Beverly Hills, CA: Sage.

Edelman, M. W. (1983). Death by poverty, arms, or moral numbness. *American Journal of Orthopsychiatry, 53,* 593–601.

Elder, G. H., Jr. (1974). *Children of the Great Depression.* Chicago: University of Chicago Press.

Elder, G. H., Jr., Nguyen, T. V., & Caspi, A. (1985). Linking family hardship to children's lives. *Child Development, 56,* 361–375.

Elmer, E. (1978). Effects of early neglect and abuse on latency age children. *Journal of Pediatric Psychology, 3,* 14–19.

Erikson, E. H. (1968). *Identity: Youth and crisis.* New York: Norton.

Erikson, K. T. (1976). *Everything in its path.* New York: Simon and Schuster.

Escalona, S. (1965). Children and the threat of nuclear war. In M. Schwebel (Ed.), *Behavioral science and human survival.* Palo Alto, CA: Science and Behavior Books.

Eth, S., & Pynoos, R. S. (1985). Intervention of trauma and grief in childhood. In S. Eth & R. S. Pynoos (Eds.), *Post-Traumatic Stress Disorder in children* (pp. 169–186). Washington, DC: American Psychiatric Press.

Firebaugh, G., & Davis, K. E. (1988). Trends in antiblack prejudice, 1972–1984: Region and cohort effects. *American Journal of Sociology, 94,* 251–272.

Frederick, C. J. (1985). Children traumatized by catastrophic situations. In S. Eth & R. S. Pynoos (Eds.), *Post-Traumatic Stress Disorder in children* (pp. 71–100). Washington, DC: American Psychiatric Press.

Freud, A., & Burlingham, D. (1942). *The writings of Anna Freud* (Report 12, p. 3). New York: International Universities Press.

Friedemann, M. (1986). Family economic stress and unemployment: Child's peer behavior and parents' depression. *Child Study Journal, 16,* 125–143.

Goldsmith, H. H., Bradshaw, D. L., & Riesser-Danner, L. A. (1986). Temperament as a potential developmental influence on attachment. *New Directions for Child Development, 31,* 5–34.

Gottlieb, D., & Ramsey, C. E. (1967). *Understanding children of poverty.* Chicago: Science Research Associates.

Grunebaum, H., Weiss, J., Gallant, D., & Cohler, B. (1974). Attention in young children of psychotic mothers. *American Journal of Psychiatry, 131,* 887–891.

Hall, P. S., & Landreth, P. W. (1975). Assessing some long-term consequences of a natural disaster. *Mass Emergencies, 1,* 55–61.

Harrington, M. (1962). *The other America: Poverty in the United States.* New York: Macmillan.

Howard, J. H. (1980). Toward a social psychology of colonialism. In R. L. Jones (Ed.), *Black psychology* (pp. 367–375). New York: Harper & Row.

Howard, S. I., & Gordon, N. S. (1972). *Final progress report: Mental health investigation in a major disaster* (NIMH Small Resource grant MH 21649-01). Van Nuys, CA: San Fernando Valley Child Guidance Clinic.

Hraba, J., & Grant, G. (1970). Black is beautiful: a re-examination of racial preference and identification. *Journal of Personality and Social Psychology, 16,* 398–402.

Jackson, H. C. (1982). Moral nihilism: Developmental arrest as a sequel to combat stress. In S. L. Feinstein et al. (Eds.), *Adolescent psychiatry, 10.* Chicago, IL: University of Chicago Press.

Janis, I. (1958). *Psychological Stress.* New York: John Wiley.

Jaspars, J. M. (1978). The nature and measurement of attitudes. In H. Tajfel & C. Fraser (Eds.), *Introduction to social psychology.* Harmondsworth, Middlesex: Penguin.

Jones, J. M. (1988). Racism in Black and White: A bicultural model of reaction and evolution. In P. A. Katz & D. A. Taylor (Eds.), *Eliminating racism* (pp. 117–136). New York: Plenum Press.

Justice, B., & Justice, R. (1976). *The abusing family.* New York: Human Services Press.

Kasl, S., & Cobb, S. (1967). Effects of parental status incongruence and discrepancy on physical and mental health of adult offspring. *Journal of Personality and Social Psychology Monograph, 7,* 2.

Katz, P. A. (1988). *Children and Social Issues, 44*(1), 193–201.

Katz, P. A., & Taylor, D. A. (1988a). Introduction. In P. A. Katz & D. A. Taylor (Eds.), *Eliminating racism* (pp. 7–18). New York: Plenum Press.

Katz, P. A., & Taylor, D. A. (Eds.). (1988b). *Eliminating racism.* New York: Plenum Press.

Kelso, D. R., & Attneave, C. L. (Eds.). (1981). *Bibliography of North American Indian mental health.* Westport, CT: Greenwood.

Kinder, D. R., & Sers, D. O. (1981). Prejudice and politics: Symbolic racism versus racial threats to the good life. *Journal of Personality and Social Psychology, 40,* 414–431.

Kirk, A. R. (1976). *Socio-psychological factors in attempted suicide among urban Black males.* Unpublished doctoral dissertation, Michigan State University.

Kirk, A. R. (1986). Destructive behaviors among members of the Black community with a special focus on males: Causes and methods of intervention. *Journal of Multicultural Counseling and Development, 14,* 3–9.

Kluegel, J. R., & Smith, E. R. (1986). *Beliefs about inequality.* New York: Aldine.

Kozol, J. (1988). *Rachel and her children: Homeless families in America.* New York: Crown.

Kreps, G. A. (1984). Sociological inquiry and disaster research. *Annual Review of Sociology, 10,* 309–330.

Law, N. (1973, February). *Children and war.* Association for Childhood Education International.

Leana, C. R., & Ivancevich, J. M. (1987). Involuntary job loss: Institutional interventions and a research agenda. *Academy of Management Review, 12,* 301–312.

Lifton, R. J. (1982). *Death in life: Survivors of Hiroshima.* New York: Basic Books.

Lindblad-Goldberg, M., Dukes, J. L., & Lasley, J. H. (1988). Stress in Black, low-income, single-parent families: Normative and dysfunctional patterns. *American Journal of Orthopsychiatry, 58,* 104–120.

Lyles, M. R., Yancey, A., Grace, C., & Cater, J. H. (1985). Racial identity and self-esteem: Problems peculiar to biracial children. *Journal of the American Academy of Child Psychiatry, 24,* 150–153.

Mail, P. D., & McDonald, D. R. (Eds.). (1980). *Tulapai to Tokay.* New Haven, CT: HRAF Press.

McGee, R. K. (1973). *The role of crisis intervention services in disaster recovery.* Paper presented at National Institute of Mental Health meeting.

Milner, D. (1981). Racial prejudice. In H. Giles & J. C. Turner (Eds.), *Intergroup behavior* (pp. 102–143). Oxford: Basil Blackwell.

Mirage, T. (1982, December). Unemployment's youngest victims. *Education Week,* 1–15.

Murphy, H. M. (1965). Migration and the major mental disorders: A reappraisal. In M. B. Kantor (Ed.), *Mobility and mental health.* Springfield, IL: Charles C. Thomas.

Newman, C. (1976). Children of disaster: Clinical observations at Buffalo Creek. *American Journal of Psychiatry, 133,* 306–312.

New York Times, December 20, 1988.

Padgett, G. L. (1984). Racially-motivated violence and intimidation: Inadequate state enforcement and federal civil rights remedies. *The Journal of Criminal Law & Criminology, 75,* 103–138.

Pearlin, L., & Schooler, C. (1978). The structure of coping. *Journal of Health and Social Behavior, 19,* 2–21.

Pettigrew, T. F., & Martin, J. (1987). Shaping the organizational context for Black American inclusion. *Journal of Social Issues, 43*, 41–78.

Pfeiffer, C. R. (1981). The family system of suicidal children. *American Journal of Psychotherapy, 35*, 330–341.

Pryor-Brown, L., Cowen, E. L., Hightower, A. D., & Lofyczewski, B. S. (1986). Demographic differences among children in judging and experiencing specific stressful life events. *The Journal of Special Education, 20*, 339–345.

Quarantelli, E. L., & Dynes, R. R. (1977). Response to social crisis and disaster. *Annual Review of Sociology, 3*, 23–49.

Ramirez, A. (1988). Racism toward Hispanics: The culturally monolithic society. In P. A. Katz & D. A. Taylor (Eds.), *Eliminating racism*. New York: Plenum Press.

Rayman, P. (1988). Unemployment and family life: The meaning for children. In P. Voydanoff & L. C. Majka (Eds.), *Families and economic distress* (pp. 119–134). Newbury Park, CA: Sage.

Rosenfeld, J. M., & Krim, A. (1983, November). Adversity as opportunity: Urban families who did well after a fire. *Social Casework, 64*, 561–565.

Rossi, P. H., Wright, J. D., Weber-Burdin, E., & Pereira, J. (1982). *Acts of God, acts of man: Victimization by natural hazards in the United States*. Amherst, MA: Social and Demographic Research Institute, University of Massachusetts.

Schuman, H., Steeh, C., & Bobo, L. (1985). *Racial attitudes in America: Trends and interpretations*. Cambridge, MA: Harvard University Press.

Schwebel, M. (1965). Nuclear cold war: Student opinions and professional responsibility. In M. Schwebel (Ed.), *Behavioral science and human survival*. Palo Alto, CA: Science and Behavior Books.

Sears, D. O., & Kinder, D. R. (1971). Racial tensions and voting in Los Angeles. In W. Z. Hirsch (Ed.), *Los Angeles: Viability and prospects for metropolitan leadership*. New York: Praeger.

Select Committee on Children, Youth, and Families. (1987). *The crisis in homelessness: Effect on children and families*. Washington, DC: U.S. Government Printing Office.

Simmons, R. (1978). Blacks and high self-esteem: A puzzle. *Social Psychology, 41*, 54–57.

Smith, T. W., & Sheatsley, P. B. (1984, October/November). American attitudes toward race relations. *Public Opinion*, 14–15, 50–53.

Sniderman, P. M., & Hagen, M. G. (1985). *Race and inequality: A study in American values*. Chatham, NJ: Chatham House.

Sniderman, P. M., & Tetlock, P. E. (1986). Symbolic racism: Problems of motive attribution in political analysis. *Journal of Social Issues, 42*, 129–150.

Stephan, W. G., & Stephan, C. W. (1984). The role of ignorance in inter-group relations. In N. Miller & M. B. Brewer (Eds.), *Groups in contact: The psychology of desegregation* (pp. 229–255). New York: Academic Press.

Stern, G. M. (1976). *The Buffalo Creek disaster: The story of the survivors' unprecedented lawsuit*. New York: Random House.

Tajfel, H. (1981). Social stereotypes and social groups. In H. Giles & J. C. Turner (Eds.), *Intergroup behavior* (pp. 144–167). Oxford: Basil Blackwell.

Taylor, J. (1980). Dimensionalizations of racialism and the Black experience: The Pittsburgh project. In R. L. Jones (Ed.), *Black psychology* (pp. 384–400). New York: Harper & Row.

Taylor, D. G., Sheatsley, P. B., & Greeley, A. M. (1978). Attitudes toward racial integration. *Scientific American, 238,* 42–51.

Terr, L. C. (1979). Children of Chowchilla: A study of psychic trauma. *Psychoanalytic Study of Children, 34,* 547–623.

Tierney, K. J., & Baisden, B. (1979). *Crisis intervention programs for disaster victims: A sourcebook and manual of mental health.* Rockville, MD: National Institute of Mental Health.

Triandis, H. C. (1988). The future of pluralism revisited. In P. A. Katz & D. A. Taylor (Eds.), *Eliminating racism* (pp. 31–52). New York: Plenum Press.

Trimble, J. E. (1988). Stereotypical images, American Indians, and prejudice. In P. A. Katz & D. A. Taylor (Eds.), *Eliminating racism* (pp. 181–202). New York: Plenum Press.

Weber, M. (1958). *The Protestant ethic and the spirit of capitalism.* New York: Scribners.

Weick, K. E. (1984). Small wins? Redefining the scale of social problems. *American Psychologist, 39,* 40–49.

Young, A. (1988, August). Keynote address to opening session of the American Psychological Association Annual Convention, Atlanta, GA.

Zirkel, P. A., & Moses, E. G. (1971). Self-concept and ethnic group membership among public school students. *American Educational Research Journal, 8,* 253–265.

Part IV

Assessing, Preventing, and Treating Childhood Stress

CHAPTER SEVENTEEN

The Adaptation of Children to a Stressful World: Mastery of Fear

Norman Garmezy
Ann Masten

Acknowledgments: This chapter was supported by grants from the William T. Grant Foundation, the National Institute of Mental Health, and a Research Career Award (NIMH-USPHS) to the senior author.

Fear and stress are often commingled in both children and adults. This linkage of children's fears with stress has both a normative and a non-normative aspect.

NORMAL STRESSES AND FEARS OF INFANTS AND CHILDREN

In the course of development, one witnesses with a high degree of regularity the emergence of specific, normal fears that are reflected in the behavior of infants and children. For example, there are points of agreement on the age sequence for the fearful response of infants to the presence of strangers. Fear of loss and separation from loved ones exists not only in infancy, but in childhood, adolescence, and into adulthood as well. If there is any single stressor with near universal impact, it is the threat of such loss. It is that universality that validates its normative properties. Evidence for this with respect to the developmental aspects of children's responses to the stress of separation and loss has been provided by Garmezy (1985).

Again on the normative side, there have been repeated efforts to catalogue the specific developmental fears of childhood, such as the early volume of Jersild and Holmes (1935) on *Children's Fears;* and the more recent studies by Barnett (1969), Miller and his colleagues (1971a,b; 1974) and Scherer and Nakamura (1968), which have emphasized the modal fears of children between the ages of 7 and 12.

It is important to discriminate normal fears, which reflect developmental growth, from those that reflect a disordered state. An example of the former is the appearance of "stranger anxiety" in the 8-month-old. At that age, if mother leaves the infant and a stranger appears, the infant will become apprehensive, cry, and begin to search for mother. At 5 months of age, this is a far less common behavioral pattern. The newly formed response constellation is a *normal* fear response to mother's disappearance, which serves as a stressor, triggering the consequent response of anxiety in the infant.

Fear of the stranger occurs in the third quarter of the first year, with the modal date of onset the eighth month of life. The infant becomes wary of strangers; being picked up by a stranger is no longer a positive occurrence: the infant turns its gaze toward mother and seeks to return to the safer, nurturant individual who is now fixed in the infant's memory. However, individual differences exist in both the age of the onset of the fear as well as in the intensity of its expression. Although the precise interaction between genes, maturation, and experiences is not known, each undoubtedly plays a role in the manifestation of fearful behavior at this point in development. Furthermore, stability of fearfulness varies over both the short and long term, with fluctuations of function evident in response to many state and situational variables.

Although a high degree of group consistency is evident, individual and situational variables result in a high degree of inter-individual variation. Recent excellent research has produced a more precise description of fears in the first year of life than was present before developmental psychologists began to study the phenomenon. The understanding of this behavioral phenomenon is now made comprehensible by knowledge of the development of cognition and emotion in the very young infant, together with knowledge of the quality of the infant's prior history of caretaking. The latter element can be a protective factor (Waters, Wittman, & Sroufe, 1979) or a risk factor (Egeland & Sroufe, 1981), depending upon the early pattern of mother-infant interaction. In most cases, fear of strangers toward the latter portion of the first year of life does not evoke clinical concern unless the infant engages in specific behaviors that have been demonstrated to be associated with patterns of undesirable caregiving by mother or a mother surrogate (Bowlby, 1969; Egeland & Sroufe, 1981; Sameroff & Chandler, 1975).

RISK AND PROTECTIVE FACTORS IN CHILDREN UNDER ABNORMAL STRESS

This chapter is not focused on such normal fear-evoking situations, but rather on more powerful traumatizing events that do not occur with developmental regularity, but do occur sufficiently often to warrant attention to their serious consequences for adaptation in the lives of children. (For a discussion of various traumata, see Garmezy and Rutter, 1985, and the preceding section of this book.)

Three markedly different stressful contexts will be discussed: (1) premature birth, a profound stressor for both infant and parent; (2) delinquency as a potential response to severe ecological and familial disadvantage; and (3) the adaptational patterns of children of the Holocaust. Whereas the first two examples emphasize the nature of stressors as "risk" factors, the third emphasizes the concept of "protective" factors.

In this discussion we are taking advantage of a *Zeitgeist* (spirit of the times), in which a set of concepts has become as much a part of the lay language as it is the language of science. A poet once termed ours "the age of anxiety"; a more commercial rendition depicts our times as "the era of the stress tab." However described, one indicator of this element of contemporary life is the readiness with which terms such as "stress," "risk," "vulnerability," and "coping" have become a part of everyday conversation.

For the scientist, adoption of these terms has the virtue of their being readily understood by ordinary citizens, yet such universal acceptance invariably invites ambiguity and stereotype. Any concept that is so much a part of our daily language tends to become overinclusive and to bear markedly different meanings. This imposes an imprecision that is a deterrent to the research enterprise. Researchers have a need to define concepts, to make them operational, and in doing so to allow research studies and their outcomes to be appraised, compared, and then integrated.

How does one contain a topic marked by the multiplicity and diversity of stressors to which children are subjected? There are stressors imposed by developmental transitions: the fearfulness of a child going off to school for the first time, the advance of a child from elementary to junior high school, the onset of puberty, the adolescent experience with its threats of insecurities and the exploration of the forbidden, the shame evoked by apparent differences between the adolescent and the all-powerful peer in-group, the stress of graduation and entry into the work force. There are the chronic stressors: poverty, physical handicap, and prejudice in its various guises experienced by children who are not part of the advantaged majority. There are acute stressors: the loss of a parent in childhood by the uncommon mishap of a parent's death or by the common mishap of divorce; there are accidents and illnesses. There is academic failure or rejection by a school of one's choice. There are man-made and natural disasters: war, famine, floods, and earthquakes.

Many of these stressors are almost daily occurrences for some children on this globe, and we witness images of children's pain, suffering, loss, and trauma in our press and on daily telecasts. Our newspapers and magazines reiterate the frequency of post-traumatic stress consequences in adult and child victims of war and violence.

However, there is another, more positive development which does not elicit as much attention: a relatively new literature that focuses on mastery, competence, coping, and pro-social behaviors in children under stress. This emergent literature remains small, but it is compensatory to the emphasis on threat, disruption, and despair in the lives of children exposed to disadvantage. Until now, the traumatic event and its severe negative consequences have commanded our attention to an extent that normal development and efficacy under disadvantage have not. In turning to this more recent literature, it becomes necessary to clarify some of the definitional uncertainties that surround several of the constructs related to stress, its elicitation, and its consequences.

Definitions and Delineations

Defining *stress* typically implicates four factors: (1) the presence of a manifest stimulus event; (2) the event is one capable of modifying the organism's physiological and psychological equilibrium; (3) the disequilibrium is reflected in a state of arousal marked by neurophysiological, cognitive, and emotional consequences for the individual; (4) these changes, in turn, disrupt the adaptation of the person.

The response to stress is an effort at resolution that is termed *coping*. A determiner of the adequacy of the coping response to stress is an act of *appraisal* by the individual (Lazarus & Folkman, 1984). Such an appraisal presumably involves matching the demands imposed by the stressful event with an evaluation of one's abilities to meet them. If demand is perceived to exceed ability, the event will have disruptive consequences; if ability matches or exceeds demand, the event may serve as a "growth experience." However, even this generalization has its limits. There are exceptional situations, such as mandatory retirement or a fruitless job search by an able handicapped or minority person, wherein the denial of employment can be the result of factors unrelated to ability. In such cases, when the victim is prevented from using a manifest ability to cope, the event may prove to be extremely stressful and frustrating.

Risk

Another concept requiring brief discussion is that of risk. In Chapter 13, Beardslee applies this specific concept to his research with the offspring of affectively disordered parents. In a non-specific sense, risk implies the identification of variables or factors in biology, person, family, and/or environment that heighten the probability of a negative outcome (e.g., mental or physical disorder) for the individual. Certain types of powerful stressors can impose long-term risk consequences. Thus, the famine in Ethiopia may well leave its mark on children who have been its victims. In this nation, Elder (1974) has written extensively on the later effects of the Great Depression on the children of the 1930s, who as adults have now reached senior citizen status. Prolonged hunger and deprivation can have long-term consequences for those who have had to endure such disadvantage. Thus, the event and the trauma it induces become risk factors both at the time the event occurs and potentially at a later period, especially if the victim is exposed to situations similar to the original trauma.

Risk factors include personal, familial, and environmental factors, and each of these can have biological, psychological, or social components. Personal factors such as socioeconomic status, sex, age, and other demographic variables can enhance risk for numerous outcomes. In the world of a child, being male carries distinctly greater risk for conduct disorder than being female. In the case of eating disorders in late adolescence, females are at far greater risk than are males. On the other hand, poverty can constitute a risk factor across the life span for both sexes. A frequent correlate of maternal poverty—that of poor prenatal care during pregnancy—constitutes a risk factor for the subsequent development of the fetus and infant. Prolonged and early disadvantaged status can compromise subsequent cognitive, educational, and social performance.

Familial history constitutes a risk factor for genetically linked disorders. If a child has a first-degree relative who has suffered a schizophrenic or bipolar (manic-depressive) disorder, the risk for these disorders in the child is multiplied several fold. Similarly, there appears to be a genetic as well as environmental risk in families marked by alcoholism, criminality, and violence. Other biological and physical defects also serve as risk factors, particularly if they impose behavioral constraints. Specific events that are markedly stressful, such as the death of a parent early in a child's life, can impose additional risk for children. Certain environments accentuate risk: slum areas carry greater risk potential than do middle-class neighborhoods. However, this risk is not overriding, for there is evidence of diverse outcomes in individuals reared in disadvantaged neighborhoods (Long & Vaillant, 1984). Excessive mobility patterns, familial and cultural characteristics, the non-availability of social support networks when one faces adversity, all can add to risk.

Although the multiplicity of potential risk elements is obvious, merely listing them does not adequately delineate risk. One must ask a number of questions: Can we identify and measure the presumed risk factors? Do such measures have stability over time? Are the factors modifiable, and if so, can the modifiers be specified? Is the risk factor relevant only to some specific disorder, or does it apply to a variety of disorders? What underlying processes are activated by the risk variable? Is it a "sensitive" or a "specific" factor?

By *sensitivity*, the epidemiologist means the proportion of individuals who will actually develop the disorder who are identified as being at risk by the presence of the risk factor. By contrast, *specificity* refers to the proportion of all individuals who do not develop the disorder subsequently who are identified as lacking the risk factor.

Protective Factors

In contrast to risk, there are also protective factors. Although important, far less is known about them (See Chapter 18). Protective factors presumably inhibit the expression of disorder. Thus, studies of such factors direct the researcher away from an emphasis on negative adaptation and toward the search for (often unanticipated) positive outcomes in individuals exposed to the relevant risk elements.

This new theme has a universal quality. Everyone knows of individuals who, despite their exposure to grim trauma, appear to have emerged healthy. In such cases, we assume that there are protective factors operating. The search to identify these factors and their correlates has become one of the exciting new areas in stress research. The manifest evidence that such factors exist makes their past neglect seem rather incomprehensible. However, there are many instances in scientific research in which the obvious has escaped attention. Fortunately, researchers have begun to attend to the evident majority of persons who do adapt to stressful circumstances.

Where to begin that scientific quest? First, one must discard disciplinary prejudices, for there is little gain in being either exclusively psychosocial/environmental or exclusively biological/genetic in one's orientation. The potential contributions of biology, psychology, and sociology must be examined in the search for adaptive factors, just as in the study of psychopathological processes. Temperament, with its biogenetic origins, is a case in point. From the moment of birth, infants differ in their temperaments. Babies vary in arousal level and in the degree of manifest anxiety they exhibit in new situations, and they habituate at different rates to disequilibrating events in their environments. But they are also cared for by temperamentally different parents or parental surrogates. Environmental factors such as parent-child relations modify temperament as an adaptive or maladaptive influence. Environments, too, can be cruel or supportive; variations in temperament can also be modified by the nature of experiences in such environments. This provides but one example of what is meant by gene-environment interaction.

The concept of "goodness of fit" suggested by Henderson (1913) and Kagan (1971) and elaborated by Thomas and Chess (1977) emphasizes the interaction of environmental demands and the organism's capacities, characteristics, and behavioral style in the process of adaptation (see also Chess & Thomas, 1984).

THREE EXAMPLES OF RISK AND PROTECTIVE FACTORS IN STRESS

Prematurity as Stressor

The presence of risk and protective factors acting in concert is exemplified by the developmental risks that accompany premature birth. Premature birth to socioeconomically disadvantaged mothers heightens the overall risk to infants (Field, 1980; Kopp, 1983; Sigman & Parmalee, 1979). Maternal undernourishment, drinking, smoking, and drug taking, inadequate prenatal care, toxicity, and delivery complications are all risk factors that can have profound developmental consequences for the newborn. Continuation of the disadvantaged economic status of the mother can create other postnatal risk elements such as malnutrition and inadequate pediatric care. Not only biological, but also behavioral risk factors can burden such infants: the quality of caregiving is correlated to some extent with maternal socioeconomic status; low socioeconomic status creates stressed mothers which, in turn, modifies their effectiveness as caregivers.

Nevertheless, variation in infant outcome is evident even in the more disadvantaged segments of the population. This suggests the necessity for studying the environmental elements that provide both positive (protective) and negative (risk) modifiers of biological risk (Kopp & Krakow, 1983). The context of this type of research for the study of resilience in children has been described recently by Masten & Garmezy (1985).

The Familial Environment as Stressor

Moving up the age scale, there comes into focus a behavioral disorder that evokes clinical and community concern. It is denoted as *conduct disorder* in younger children, as *delinquency* in adolescence, and as *antisocial personality* in adulthood. What is intriguing about the behavioral pattern of conduct disorder is its cross-national similarity. If one compares the epidemiological data on delinquency in Great Britain (West & Farrington, 1973), or on the European continent (Friday, 1980; Lie, 1981; Olweus, 1978), with similar data derived in the United States (Patterson, 1982; Robins, 1966, 1978), there is powerful evidence of parallel risk factors that run through this particular classification of deviant behavior. One can inquire into these risk factors, but to do so, other questions must be asked.

First, we must define conduct disorder and delinquent behaviors. There is difficulty in tagging the delinquent because of variations in the *frequency* and in the *severity* of delinquent behavior and in the selection of delinquent samples. There are variations in the way cohorts of such children are organized and data about them are gathered. Information about antisocial acts can be provided by children's self-reports; by children's presence in clinics because of acts against persons and property that have come to community, school, or parental attention; or by the in-court appearances of children for more severe disturbances. The latter, however, can become a net for capturing heterogeneous subgroups of children—socialized delinquents who travel in gangs and have a loyalty to their group, and unsocialized delinquents who are loners without attachments to others. To complicate the problem of identification, social class factors can facilitate or inhibit the identification of delinquents. If one is poor, the probability is heightened for an appearance in court with an attendant juvenile police record; by contrast, the middle-class child can often enjoy the intercession of a lawyer before a court appearance is arranged.

Despite these variations, there exists strong evidence of continuities of conduct-disordered behavior over time (Robins, 1978): (1) for a substantial proportion of cases, antisocial behavior in children seems to be predictive of antisocial behavior in adulthood; (2) from a retrospective perspective, serious adult antisocial disorder almost invariably is preceded by childhood conduct disorder and adolescent delinquent behavior; (3) antisocial behavior in childhood is also associated with other types of maladaptive outcomes other than criminal activity in adulthood, including asociality and even severe mental disorders such as schizophrenia.

However, from a prospective standpoint *a substantial majority of antisocial children do not become manifestly antisocial adults.* These findings pose an interesting problem as to identification of the starting point for preventive efforts to thwart the severe consequences seemingly predicted by early childhood signs of antisocial externalizing behaviors.

Whereas severe antisocial disorder in adulthood reveals a consistent history of childhood antisocial behaviors (approximately 90%), less than 50% of children who manifest antisocial disorder go on to highly antisocial adult careers (Robins, 1978). What happens to the majority of conduct-disordered children who do not become antisocial in adulthood? Are these outcomes suggestive of the operation of protective factors? If so, can we develop predictors of such non-disordered outcomes? It is critically important for the nation to know as much about the half who escape adult criminal lives as it is to know about the other half, who constitute a major concern for residents in our large urban centers. Before we can develop rational means of prevention, we must know the nature of risk and protective factors. This task of scientific uncovering must begin with apparent risk factors for antisocial behavior in childhood and adolescence.

West and Farrington (1973) at the Institute of Criminology at Cambridge University have produced a large body of research in an effort to capture the risk factors implicated in early antisocial behavior. They began their research with groups of children at the age of 8, typically a predelinquent period, in their effort to learn which children would then go on to delinquent careers. Research has shown that at least by the age of 8, and probably even before they go to school, some boys (this is a disorder far more typical of boys than of girls) can be identified as potential delinquents. They note:

> *Typically, they are socially and intellectually backward, the product of poor homes with too many children, and reared by parents whose standards of care, supervision and training are woefully inadequate. Perceived by teachers as difficult, resistive children, they fit uncomfortably into the scholastic system. Their parents have little or no contact with the schools, and display minimal concern about their children's scholastic progress or leisure pursuits. Aggressive and impulsive in temperament, these boys resist the constraints of school, learn poorly, attend badly, and leave early. Unattracted by organized activities or by*

training schemes, they spend their time on the streets and gravitate to unskilled, dead-end jobs for the sake of the higher wages offered. (p. 202)

A fascinating issue is posed by two groups characterized by atypical outcomes: (1) children marked by such risk factors who do not become delinquent; and (2) delinquents with identifiable life histories not revealing of any of these risk factors.

Studies cited by Rutter and Giller (1983) based on the research of West and Farrington (1973) and West (1982) focus on a so-called "paradoxical" group—boys from a high-risk background who do *not* become delinquent. Follow-up studies of these children are not encouraging, for while they do not exhibit antisocial behavior, they are not, in most instances, exemplars of competence. They tend to be somewhat asocial, have little contact with their families, are of lower intelligence, and have poor work histories. They have been described as "socially handicapped, nervous, withdrawn, and unhappy individuals" (Rutter & Giller, 1983, p. 224).

Another group is composed of several boys who became delinquent without any predisposing risk factors in their records. Rutter and Giller (1983) view this small subgroup as an "enigma" whose existence makes evident the current lack of an "adequate understanding" of the developmental nature of delinquent behavior.

Thus, most research on delinquency, while providing reliable and valid evidence of recurrent risk factors in antisocial behavior, as yet fails to provide insights into protective factors for those children who show positive adaptations despite their exposure to cumulative numbers of risk factors. A recent general review suggests that three types of protective factors may be important: dispositional personality variables, the presence of a positive family atmosphere, and the availability and utilization of social supports when needed (Garmezy, 1985). However, the extent to which these apply to the "atypicals" from a predisposing delinquent subculture needs to be ascertained.

Children of the Holocaust: Resilience Under Supreme Stress

In a recent publication, Garmezy & Rutter (1985) described studies of children's behavior when exposed to different types of severe stressors: war, disasters, concentration camp experiences, kidnapping, severe burns, etc. The concentration camp experience especially commands our attention, for here were children reared under the most dire and dangerous circumstances.

Among the millions who died in the camps were one million child victims (under age 16). When Auschwitz was liberated by Russian soldiers in January 1945, only 300 surviving children were found, and their physical condition was desperate. They were rachitic, emaciated, starving, and tubercular. The stresses to which they were subjected had been both chronic and cumulative. Moskovitz (1983) has described the observations recorded by an adult prisoner who watched the arrival of more than 1,000 children at the Theresienstadt camp:

> *They were frightened and speechless, many barefoot, all in a sorry state and half-starved. . . . They were taken immediately in groups to a disinfection bath where they made terrible scenes. These children knew of gas chambers and would not set foot in the bath area. They screamed desperately "No, no, not gas." They would not obey the SS men. Consequently, they were pushed in by force. They cried and clung to each other . . . [Later] fathers, mothers, and older brothers and sisters were then shot before their eyes. (p. 12)*

Camp conditions for the children precluded play for the very young children and schooling for the older ones. Hunger, cold, hard labor, and maltreatment by guards were daily occurrences. The children lived under an omnipresent fear of death, with self-preservation serving as their guide to action. Reports indicate that many of the children turned to lying and stealing, formed gangs, and engaged in antisocial acts. However, mental disorders and overt neurotic symptoms were absent from their behavior, while aggression, expressions of vengeance, and overt, crippling anxiety were contained (cited in Garmezy & Rutter, 1985, as derived from Langmeier & Matejcek, 1975).

When liberated, many of the children were returned to their own countries while others were sent to England, Israel, and the United States. Short-term observations of the children's adaptation at that point were rather consistent: one reads of developmental lags in physical hygiene, social play, and interaction with others; of behavior marked by destructive aggression, irritability, temper outbursts, and aimlessness. Adults became targets for mistrust and fear of separation; older children were suspicious of adults, and their interpersonal relationships were disturbed; the children sought to avoid discussing the trauma they had witnessed, while many expressed a preference to remain with their companions in displacement camps, fearing the move to a new family setting. While still in the camps, there were initial moves to steal and hoard food, but this passed quickly as did the delinquent acts.

Most of the children made a surprisingly rapid adjustment to new surroundings. Moral and social behavior improved rapidly and most children did not show signs of serious mental disorder. Minor stresses, however, revealed the potential for breakdown in some children. In Israel, children who were assigned to the kibbutzim did best, while those placed in private homes showed the greatest difficulty. Adolescent boys often showed anger and destructiveness; girls, heightened passivity. In comparison to evacuated children, the camp victims showed reduced adaption, but the behaviors of both groups revealed individual variation. Camp victims who had been reared in stable families (a potential protective factor) survived the trauma with a surprising degree of strength, tolerance, and competence. Overt disorders were rare in this group. On the other hand, some children from previously unstable families developed more severe disturbances, but even in this risk group, good care produced a more favorable prognosis.

Obviously, a critical question remained: What happened subsequently to these wounded children? In the volume *Love Despite Hate,* Moskovitz (1983) has provided detailed data based on interviews with 24 child survivors of the Holocaust. Her search carried her to seven different countries on three continents. Her recorded interviews with these children, now grown to adulthood, provides a descriptive account of adaptation despite severe early trauma.

Six children in particular have held great interest for investigators of stress responsivity in children. These were the children cared for by Anna Freud and her colleagues in Great Britain following their release from the camps. What happened to these very young children, reared from infancy in the camps, had at first remained in the closed files of Freud's clinic in London. Freud and Dann (1951) initially wrote a monograph on the adaptation of the six children when they were first brought into their care. Upon arrival in the children's home, their behavior had a most interesting quality. The children acted almost as a collective, shown by reciprocal concern for each other's welfare. Initially they were markedly hostile to the staff, but gradually shifted to more cooperative and engaged behavior.

Moskovitz (1983) reveals the continuity to their development in adulthood. She writes of their striking positive qualities, their strong reaffirmation of life, their stubborn durability, their desire to rear their children in a manner that would ensure their wholeness. She concludes that "contrary to previously accepted notions, we learn powerfully from these lives that lifelong emotional disability does not automatically follow early trauma, even such devastating, pervasive trauma as experienced here. Apparently what happens later matters enormously."

What did happen "later"? Moskovitz, in a concluding chapter, touches upon some of the events and experiences that were unveiled in the course of her interviews with the child survivors now grown to adulthood. Their reflections reveal the importance of the reconstructive efforts that took place in England following the children's liberation. She writes of the strong and loving caregiver who individualized her concern for each child and who is still remembered by them for her "pride and passion" in caring for them. Decades later, this sense of love and purpose is still evident in the recital of their childhood and adult accomplishments.

Moskovitz cites the power of religious belief, of "ethical and spiritual involvement" that mobilizes the activism of these survivors. The power of their own families and their children has added to a personal sense of strength through bonds that have tied their children and their parenting responsibilities and community together. Other themes include the evolution of a Jewish identity and a sense of historical continuity with Judaism and the Jewish people; humane consideration evoked by belief and affiliation; imagery of the dead parents and their hopes and aspirations for their children, attitudes of compassion toward others, including the "awesome responsibility" that fell on some to care for even younger children left behind; a sense of social responsibility derived from service to country and to community.

What one sees in a tabulation is only a portion of listings that appear in other studies of resilience under adversity. Thus, resilience seems to result from admixtures of environmental context, significant figures in those environments, and personal attributes (traits, temperaments) that undoubtedly generate an interplay of biological, psychological, and psychosocial factors reflected in variations in resilience under adversity. We cannot speak of "invulnerability," for the enormity of loss and suffering undoubtedly left its mark on victims of the Holocaust. But despite the suffering, Moskovitz' clinical research points to the retention of competence and adaptation in children who have undergone dire experiences; they still have emerged as competent, functional, responsible adults.

The fact that this occurs does not mean that responsible agencies should play a do-nothing role simply because nature appears to have endowed many of our young with strong adaptive potentialities. What it does mean is that psychopathology tends to be an outcome of stressful experiences for only a *minority* of children. For many others, a quality of resilience would appear to be more characteristic of children in adversity.

The scientific agenda seems evident. The search will have to be an interdisciplinary one, for there is no single discipline capable of elaborating the basic biogenetic, psychosocial, and developmental factors implicated in this striving for adaptation. An even more difficult scientific task is the discovery of the more basic processes and mechanisms that underlie the interaction among these many variables.

If the goal is achieved of discovering those risk and protective factors that play a role in the lives of children who grow up under the multiple stressors of living in a complex, technological society, then the way will have been cleared for a program of preventive intervention with children who are at risk for later disorder, but who need not be the future adult victims of their early exposure to disadvantage.

REFERENCES

Barnett, J. T. (1969). *Development of children's fears: The relationship between three systems of fear measurement.* Unpublished master's thesis, University of Wisconsin-Madison.

Bowlby, J. (1969). *Attachment and loss. Vol. 1: Attachment.* New York: Basic Books.

Chess, S., & Thomas, A. (1984). *Origins and evolution of behavior disorders.* New York: Brunner/Mazel.

Egeland, B., & Sroufe, L. A. (1981). Developmental sequelae of maltreatment in infancy. In R. Rizley & D. Cichetti (Eds.), *New directions for child development: Developmental perspectives in child treatment.* San Francisco: Jossey Bass.

Elder, G. H., Jr. (1974). *Children of the Great Depression.* Chicago: University of Chicago Press.

Field, T. M. (Ed.). (1980). *High-risk infants and children: Adult and peer interactions.* New York: Academic Press.

Freud, A., & Dann, S. (1951). An experiment in group upbringing. In *The psychoanalytic study of the child* (Vol. 6). New York: International Universities Press.

Friday, P. (1980). International review of youth crime and delinquency. In G. Newman (Ed.), *Deviance and crime: International perspectives.* London: Sage Publications.

Garmezy, N. (1985). Stress-resistant children: The search for protective factors. In J. E. Stevenson (Ed.), *Recent research in developmental psychopathology. Journal of Child Psychology and Psychiatry Book Supplement No. 4* (pp. 213–233). Oxford: Pergamon Press.

Garmezy, N., & Rutter, M. (1985). Acute reactions to stress. In M. Rutter & L. Hersov (Eds.), *Child psychiatry: Modern approaches* (2nd ed., pp. 152–176). Oxford: Blackwell Scientific.

Henderson, L. J. (1913). *The fitness of the environment.* New York: Macmillan.

Jersild, A. T., & Holmes, F. G. (1935). *Children's fears.* New York: Teachers College Press.

Kagan, J. (1971). *Change and continuity in infancy.* New York: Wiley.

Kopp, C. B. (1983). Risk factors in development. In P. H. Mussen (Ed.), *Handbook of child psychology* (4th ed.). *Vol. 2: Infancy and developmental psychology* (pp. 1081–1188). New York: Wiley.

Kopp, C. B., & Krakow, J. B. (1983). The developmentalist and the study of biological risk: A view of the past with an eye toward the future. *Child Development, 54,* 1086–1108.

Langmeier, J., & Matejcek, Z. (1975). *Psychological deprivation in childhood.* New York: Halstead Press.

Lazarus, R. S., & Folkman, S. (1984). *Stress, appraisal, and coping.* New York: Springer.

Lie, N. (1981). Young law breakers: A prospective longitudinal study. *Acta Paediatrica Scandinavica,* Suppl. 288.

Long, J. V. F., & Vaillant, G. E. (1984). Natural history of male psychological health. XI: escape from the underclass. *American Journal of Psychiatry, 141,* 341–346.

Masten, A. S., & Garmezy, N. (1985). Risk, vulnerability, and protective factors in developmental psychopathology. In B. B. Lahey & A. E. Kazdin (Eds.), *Advances in clinical child psychology* (Vol. 8, pp. 1–52). New York: Plenum Press.

Miller, L. C., Barrett, C., & Hampe, E. (1974). Phobias of childhood in a prescientific era. In A. Davis (Ed.) *Child personality and psychopathology: Current topics* (pp. 89–134). New York: Wiley.

Miller, L. C., Barrett, C., Hampe, E., & Noble, H. (1971a). Revised anxiety scales for the Louisville Behavior Checklist. *Psychological Reports, 29,* 503–511.

Miller, L. C., Hampe, E., Barrett, C., & Noble, H. (1971b). Children's deviant behavior within the general population. *Journal of Consulting and Clinical Psychology, 34,* 16–22.

Moskovitz, S. (1983). *Love despite hate: Child survivors of the Holocaust and their adult lives.* New York: Schocken Books.

Olweus, D. (1978). *Aggression in the schools: Bullies and whipping boys.* Washington, DC: Hemisphere.

Patterson, G. R. (1982). *Coercive family process.* Eugene, OR: Castalia.

Robins, L. N. (1966). *Deviant children grown up.* Baltimore: Williams & Wilkins.

Robins, L. N. (1978). Sturdy childhood predictors of adult antisocial behavior: Replications from longitudinal studies. *Psychological Medicine, 8,* 611–622.

Rutter, M., & Giller, H. (1983). *Juvenile delinquency: Trends and perspectives.* Harmondsworth, Middlesex, England: Penguin Books.

Sameroff, A. J., & Chandler, M. J. (1975). Reproductive risk and the continuum of caretaking casualty. In F. D. Horowitz, M. Hetherington, S. Scarr-Salapatek, & G. Siegel (Eds.), *Review of child development research* (Vol. 4, pp. 187–243). Chicago: University of Chicago Press.

Scherer, M. W., & Nakamura, C. Y. (1968). A fear survey schedule for children (FSS-FC): A factor analytic comparison with manifest anxiety (CMAS). *Behavior Research and Therapy, 6,* 173–182.

Sigman, M., & Parmalee, A. M., Jr. (1979). Longitudinal evaluation of the preterm infant. In T. M. Field, A. M. Sostek, S. Goldberg, & H. H. Shuman (Eds.), *Infants born at risk: Behavior and development.* New York: Spectrum

Thomas, A., & Chess, S. (1977). *Temperament and development.* New York: Brunner/Mazel.

Waters, E., Wittman, J., & Sroufe, L. A. (1979). Attachment, positive affect, and competence in the peer group: Two studies in construct validation. *Child Development, 50,* 821–829.

West, D. J. (1982). *Delinquency: Its roots, careers, and prospects.* Cambridge, MA: Harvard University Press.

West, D. J., & Farrington, D. P. (1973). *Who becomes delinquent?* London: Heinemann.

CHAPTER EIGHTEEN

Childhood Protective Factors and Stress Risk

Judith Kimchi
Barbara Schaffner

What is a stressor for one person is an episode of zestful living for
another. Could this be also true in children? Protective factors help a
child deal with a stress as an exciting, growth-stimulating event rather
than as a stressor. They have already been mentioned in special contexts
in earlier chapters (e.g., 1, 7, and 17). This chapter attempts a more
comprehensive overview.

RISK VS. PROTECTIVE FACTORS

Historically, attempts to study children of parents with various psycho-
pathologies led to studies of risk factors and vulnerability. When these
studies revealed that children facing adversity do not necessarily develop
emotional problems, factors such as competence began to be studied.
Then came the study of invulnerability and resiliency, and now of protective factors. Each of these concepts has a slightly different meaning, but
they overlap considerably.

Risk factors are those factors that, if present, increase the likelihood of
a child developing an emotional or behavioral disorder in comparison
with a randomly selected child from the general population (Garmezy,
1983). For example, parental psychiatric illness has been documented as
a risk factor (Anthony, 1987a).

Protective factors are those attributes of persons, environments, situations, and events that appear to temper predictions of psychopathology
based upon an individual's at-risk status. They provide resistance to risk.
They foster outcomes marked by patterns of adaptation and competence
(Rutter, 1979). Protective factors include both individual characteristics,
such as IQ and gender, and environmental characteristics, such as socioeconomic status and religious affiliation. Examples of protective factors
can be found in Table 18.1. These factors ameliorate or buffer a person's
response to constitutional risk factors or stressful life events (Masten &
Garmezy, 1985).

Some protective factors can be conceptualized as the reverse of respective risk factors. For example, if poverty is a risk factor, then financial
security is a protective factor. However, not all protective factors are so
neatly categorized. Risk factors that lead to pathology are often culturally
bound; in contrast, many protective factors may have a more cross-
cultural universality (Werner, 1988). Seifer and Sameroff (1987) identified problems with the existing definitions of risk, pointing to the lack of
criteria for determination of what variable should be considered a risk
factor. This void makes the identification of protective factors, or what
differentiates the vulnerable from the resilient children, more difficult.

Resiliency (or resilience) is an individual characteristic, whereas protective factors include both individual and environmental characteristics

TABLE 18.1. *Protective Factors*

Individual Factors	Social Factors (family and others)
Ability to elicit caregiver's attention	*Family Factors*
Achievement orientation	
Adequate sensorimotor and language development	Adequate rule setting and structure during adolescence
Adequate verbal comprehension and reading/writing skills	Alternative caretakers
Challenge	Ample attention by primary caretaker during first year of life
Competence	Age of opposite-sex parent (for girls, fathers over 30; for boys, mothers below 30)
Commitment	
Efforts toward self-improvement	
Flexibility	Birth order (first)
Freedom from serious illnesses and accidents	Family cohesion
	Family size of four or less children
Gender (female for most stresses, male for some)	High socioeconomic status
	Little parental conflict the first two years
Good communication skills	
Good coping mechanisms	Maternal perception of the infant as highly active and socially responsive
Good problem-solving skills	
Hardiness	Open communication
High endorphines (decreased discomfort?)	Parenting gradualism (gradual exposure to stress better prepares to deal with real life?)
High scores on measures of responsibility, socialization, femininity/masculinity	
	Parental anticipatory guidance
	Positive, self-confident mother
Humor	Stable behavior of the parents during chaotic times (war, disasters)
Independence, advanced self-help skills as a toddler	
	Supportive family milieu
Internal locus of control	Sibling relations good
Internal psychic strength	Warmth toward child
Internalized values	
Physical activity	*External Social Support Factors*
Positive personality disposition	
Positive sense of self	A close adult with whom to share experiences
Self-confidence	
Sociability, social perceptiveness	A support figure who can serve as identification model for the child
Temperament (cheerful, responsive)	Dedication to a cause
Thrill seeking	Ethnicity
Touch seeking	Friendship
	Good day care/school teacher
	Informal sources of support through peers, kin, neighbors, ministers, and teachers
	Peers
	Positive recognition for activities
	Religious affiliation

(Masten & Garmezy, 1985). Resiliency is a summary concept implying a track record of successful adaptation following exposure to biological and psychosocial risk factors and/or stressful life events, and implying an expectation of continued lower susceptibility to future stressors (Werner, 1981). However, children that may be identified as vulnerable (low resiliency) in infancy or early childhood are not necessarily doomed for life..A portion of these have been identified by Anthony (1987b) and Werner (1989) as resilient: those that bounce back. Murphy and Moriarty (1976) describe Helen, an odd-looking, sickly infant who was rated as of low functional ability and one of the most vulnerable children in their project. Her mother referred to her as a "very dumb" baby, and her caretakers rapidly became impatient and disenchanted with her. Contrary to the predicted outcome, Helen, a "late bloomer," grew up to become a lovely and healthy young adult. She was strongly religious, active at church, and successful in her academic endeavors. The source of individuals' resiliency are both environmental and constitutional, and the degree of resistance to stress varies over time and is partly dependent on life's circumstances (Rutter, 1985). The term *ego-resilient* does not differ essentially from *resilient*.

Invulnerability has been defined as the display of competent behavior in spite of deleterious circumstances. Any child who displays competent behavior at any developmental stage could be viewed as competent while at risk (Fisher et al., 1987). *Stress resistance* typically is used to refer to a greater likelihood of successful adaptation despite exposure to stressful life events (Masten & Garmezy, 1985).

Competence can be defined as the ability to cope with events, relationships, and task demands in ways appropriate to one's developmental stage.

Thus, protective factors are constitutional and environmental factors that make a child resilient or invulnerable. "Invulnerable" emphasizes the consistency of behavior while "resilient" acknowledges the possibility of change with recovery. Although resilient children can be described as good copers, and although they manifest high degree of competence, their ways of coping and their type of competence may vary considerably (Anthony, 1987a).

Factors vs. Mechanisms or Processes

Rutter (1987) points out that protection or risk is not a quality of the factor itself, but rather of the way in which the factor or variable interacts with other factors (variables). In fact, in the absence of stress factors, "protective factors" or "risk factors" as such have no impact. Furthermore, whether a factor functions as a direct stressor or as a vulnerability factor cannot be determined from the factor itself, only from the circumstances in which it is studied. For example, loss of a parent is obviously a direct stress and also can be documented as a vulnerability factor, leading to susceptibility to other stresses. Also, one cannot tell from the general ambience (positive or negative) of a factor whether it is protective or risk-enhancing. Unpleasant or stressful factors, like immunization, may be protective in the long run.

Therefore, Rutter (1987) proposes the terms *protective mechanisms* and *risk mechanisms* or *protective process* and *risk process* rather than "factors," to emphasize their interactive and contextual nature. While this proposal has much merit, we retain the more traditional and popularly recognized term "protective factors" in this chapter. Nevertheless, the reader is cautioned to remember that the term actually refers to an interactive process frequently associated with the factor in question, not to the factor itself.

The Dynamic Balance

As long as the balance between stressful events and protective factors is manageable for an individual, he or she can cope. But when stressful events outweigh the protective factors, even the most resilient child can develop problems (Werner, 1988). Werner and Smith (1982, 1989) suggest that the interaction of risk and protective factors is a balance between the power of the person and the power of the social and physical environment. This balance is necessary throughout life, although different factors assume different degrees of importance at different developmental stages. Constitutional factors are most important during infancy and childhood, and interpersonal factors such as locus of control, sense of control over the future, and a plan to obtain realistic goals, appear more important in adolescence.

CLASSIFICATION OF PROTECTIVE FACTORS

Protective factors fall into three broadly defined categories (Garmezy, 1984): (1) positive personality disposition of the child; (2) a supportive family milieu; and (3) an external support system that encourages and reinforces the child's coping efforts and strengthens them by inculcating positive values. Table 18.1 classifies some of the better known protective factors into these categories.

Three models for the operation of protective factors are suggested by Garmezy, Masten, & Tellegen (1984). Each model can be used to analyze the relations between major situational stressors and individual protective factors. In the *compensatory model*, stress factors and individual attributes are seen as combining additively in the prediction of outcome. In this model, the impact of severe stress can be counteracted by personal qualities of strength. For example, a brilliant youngster may be able to overcome the stress and disadvantage of poverty, discrimination, and poor schooling. In the *challenge model,* moderate stress is treated as a potential enhancer of competence, and the relation between stress and competence may be curvilinear. For example, a resilient child may be spurred to a greater growth and maturity by the loss or depression of one parent, while the loss of both parents may be overwhelming to the same child. In the *immunity-versus-vulnerability model,* protective factors modulate (dampen or amplify) the impact of stress as a variable. When protective factors are present, adaptation to a stressful situation will be easier than when these factors are lacking. This suggests that protective factors impart a kind of "immunity" against stress. For example, a strong support network or religious affiliation may allow a child to weather a crippling injury that would depress the average child. The three models are not mutually exclusive.

SPECIFIC PROTECTIVE FACTORS

The following discussion of specific factors is based on the literature review summarized in Table 18.2.

Temperament and Constitution

Resilient infants appear to elicit positive attention. They tend to be active, alert, responsive, and sociable babies who have experienced nurturance and learned to trust in its availability. Several classical longitudinal studies in the last three decades shed light on the constitution of the resilient child.

One of the best known is the Kauai study by Emmy Werner and her associates (Werner, Bierman, & French, 1971; Werner & Smith, 1977, 1982, 1989). In this study, 698 Asian and Polynesian children born in 1955 on a rural Hawaiian island were monitored for the impact of a variety of biological and psychosocial factors, stressful life events, and protective factors. Data on the children were collected at various intervals ranging from birth to age 30. Other studies support and supplement Werner's findings. From these studies, one can compile a profile of the resilient temperament at different developmental stages. Resilient infants were characterized by their caregivers as active, affectionate, goodnatured, alert, responsive, sociable, and easy to deal with. Few had distressing feeding or sleeping habits. All tended to elicit a great deal of attention and warmth from their caregivers (Werner et al., 1971; Werner,

TABLE 18.2. *Research Relevant to Protective Factors and Resiliency*

Investigator/s	Project Name Location/Design	Sample Characteristics N / Age / Sex / SES / Race	Findings
Anthony, E. J. (1987b)	*The St. Louis Risk Project Prospective, longitudinal Started 1966	238 6–12 year children of mentally ill parents 130 control children of healthy parents, intact families 218 caucasians 150 blacks	• 10% "resilient" (R): sound normal defenses, wide range of coping skills, constructive and creative capacities. Pursued hobbies with schoolmates. Curiosity about parent's diagnosis; compassion, but detached approach to ill parent. • Adult support and encouragement important.
Beardslee, W., & Podorefsky, D. (1988)	Prospective, longitudinal (2½ years) Massachusetts General Hospital	275 adolescents of parents with affective disorders Only 18 subjects interviewed by 2½ years	• R. adolescents: evident self-understanding and understanding of parent's illness; did not blame self for parent's problem.
Bleuler, M. 1984	*Prospective, longitudinal Zurich Started 1941	184 newborns of schizophrenic parents	• 90% became normal adolescents, sometimes with outstanding intelligence & stability. • Steeling effect: pain & suffering render children capable of mastering life despite inherent disadvantages.

(continued)

481

TABLE 18.2. (Continued)

Investigator/s	Project Name Location/Design	Sample Characteristics N / Age / Sex / SES / Race	Findings
Block, J. H. (1981) Block, J. H., & Block, J. (1984)	*Berkeley Study Prospective, longitudinal Data collected at 3, 4, 5, 7, 11 & 14 years. Started 1969	130 3-year-olds 60% caucasians 25% blacks 5% others	• High scorers on experimentally derived ego resiliency index described by teachers as competent, novelty seekers, self-reliant.
Earls, F., Beardslee, W., & Garrison, W. (1987)	Epidemiological survey Northeastern United States Data collected at 3 & 12 years	100 3-year-olds in rural community	• 20 children ego-resilient by play observation. All had "easy" temperament, self-initiative, adaptibility, positive response to environmental stress, high involvement in play.
Farber, E. A., & Egeland, B. (1987)	*Minnesota Mother-Child Interaction Project Prospective, longitudinal Tested with barrier	86 infants at risk for abuse Low SES	• Resilient (R) infants: alert, easy to sooth, socially responsive; secure attachment to a supportive family member. • R. preschooler: securely attached at 24 months = less vulnerable to abuse at 48 months. Competent problem-solving in frustrating situations.

Fisher, L., Kokes, R. F., Cole, R. E., Perkins, P. M., & Wynne, L. C. (1987)	University of Rochester Child & Family Study	77 7–10-year old children of a mentally ill parent	• Positive, supportive figures can compensate for negative influences of parental illness • R. child: ability to objectify the disturbed parent.
Garmezy, N., Masten, A. S., & Tellegen, A. (1984)	*The Project Competence Studies of Stress Resistance in Children Cross sectional, community cohort	200 healthy 3rd–6th graders 32 with congenital heart defects 29 mainstreamed severely physically handicapped All from urban community schools	• 3 operative models for protective factors: compensatory, challenge, immunity. Protective factors differentiate children in high stress levels. High SES—protective, makes up for stressful life events.
Halverson, C. F., & Waldrop, M. P. (1974)	Prospective, longitudinal Data collected pre-school age & 7 1/2 years Tested with barrier	74 preschoolers, 30–34 months White, upper-middle-class, intact families	• Preschoolers who coped successfully with the barrier: fear less, socially at ease; initiative; played vigorously. • Correlated positively with age: coping, imagination, and verbal development.
Hetherington, E. M., Cox, R., & Cox, R. (1982)	Prospective, longitudinal (2 years) Virginia	36 preschoolers of divorcing parents 36 control families	• R. boys: needed structured school environment. • R. girls: needed nurturing school environment; chance to assume responsibility.

(continued)

483

TABLE 18.2. (Continued)

Investigator/s	Project Name Location/Design	Sample Characteristics N / Age / Sex / SES / Race	Findings
Jenkins, J. M., & Smith, M. A. (1990)	London Cross-sectional comparison of effects of 7 putative protective factors on child symptom ratings	57 disharmonious families 62 matched controls with harmonious marriage Children age 9–12	• Quality of marriage interacted with: good sibling relations, positive recognition for activity, and relationship with adult outside family. (All inversely significant with symptoms.) • Parent-child relationships significant in both harmonious and disharmonious. • Friendships significant.
Kauffman, C., Grunebaum, H., Cohler, B., & Gamer, E. (1979)	Children at risk for psychosis (follow up) Boston and vicinity Started 1977	52 children of 30 mentally ill mothers & 22 healthy control mothers	• 6 children highly competent (but not gifted): extensive positive contact with extrafamilial adult; warm relationship with the mother; at least one lose friend; mother Parent Death in Childhood functioned at an adequate level of social interaction.
Lewis, J. M., & Looney, J. D. (1983)	The Healthy Family Project, Texas	18 black adolescents from intact working-class families	• R. adolescents: well-functioning, active, energetic, and future-oriented. Knew they had to struggle for a good future; family ties & religion important in the struggle.
Masten, A. S. (1986)	Humor and Competence in School-aged children	93 10–14-year-olds from urban community schools	• Humor and competence positively related. Children with humor abilities more attentive, cooperative, responsive, and productive in classroom. Viewed by peers as popular, happy leaders.

Reference	Sample	Findings
Murphy, L. B., & Moriarty, A. E. (1976)	*The Coping Project of the Menninger Foundation, Topeka, Kansas Prospective, longitudinal Started 1953	32 infants, 4–32 months middle-class caucasians	• Infants: good copers had intense drive and vigor, responsiveness to people and objects, and good energy resources. • Preschoolers: good copers played vigorously, sought out novel experiences. Self-reliant, but able to seek an adult's or peer's help. Humorous, prepared to take realistic risks; able to tolerate frustration and handle anxiety.
Music, J. S., Cohler, B. J., & Dincin, J. (1982)	*Risk & Recovery in the Children of Mentally Ill Mothers, Illinois	25 5-year and older children of mentally ill mothers Heterogeneous sample	• R. child-mother relationships: maternal responsiveness, availability and warmth regardless of psychiatric disorder; mother enabled child to use growth-enhancing alternative caretaking environment.
Rae-Grant, N., Thomas, B. H., Offord, D. R., & Boyle, M. H. (1989)	*Ontario Child Health Study Started 1983	3294 4–16-year-old residents of Ontario Large, small urban areas, & rural	• Protective factors for 4–11-year-olds: getting along with others, good students; participation in one or more activities. Competence more protective in high SES. • Protective factors for 12–16-year-olds: being a good student, presence of a confidante. Good friendship greater protective effect in adolescent girls.
Rolf, J. E., Crowther, J., Teri, L., & Bond, L. (1984)	*Vermont Vulnerable Child Development Project Prospective, longitudinal Started 1972	52 2–6-year-olds of hospitalized (N = 24) & nonhospitalized (N = 28) mentally ill parents Well matched groups	• Higher social status a protective influence. • Children more adversely affected by a hospitalized father. • Children of depressed parent more affected than children of schizophrenic parent.

(continued)

TABLE 18.2. (Continued)

Investigator/s	Project Name Location/Design	Sample Characteristics N / Age / Sex / SES / Race	Findings
Rubenstein, J. L., Heeren, T., Housman, D., Rubin, C., & Stechler, G. (1989)	Suicide behavior in "normal" adolescents Northeastern United States Correlational	300 9–12 graders: 204 females, 96 males Middle class 45 adolescents in private psychiatric hospital: 30 females, 15 males	• Family cohesion direct protective effect. • Friendship indirect protection by preventing depression.
Rutter, M. (1979)	*Isle of Wight & inner London borough Prospective, longitudinal (7 years)	103 10-year-old children from severely quarrelsome, discordant, unhappy homes	• R. child: Positive temperament; parental warmth, affection, & support; positive school environment.
Seifer, R., & Sameroff, A. J. (1987)	*Rochester Longitudinal Study (RLS) Prospective, longitudinal Data collected at 4, 12, 30, & 48 months Started 1970	215 newborn–4 years 65% caucasians, 35% blacks SES: heterogeneous	• Social status directly related to child performance.
Wallerstein, J. S., & Kelly, J. B. (1980)	*The California Children of Divorce Project Prospective,	131 preschool and school age children of divorcing parents White middle-class	• 34% R. at 5-year follow-up: high self-esteem, coping competently in school, playground, and home. • R. preschoolers: related well to peers and teachers; socially mature. Distance from parental conflict by

Study	Design	Sample	Findings
Wallerstein, J. S., & Blakeslee (1989)	longitudinal (5 years)		adherence to own daily routine. • R. schoolagers: good students; enjoyed classmates and teachers, pursued hobbies.
Werner, E. (1986)	Resilient Offspring of Alcoholics Kauai Island Data collected at birth, 1, 2, 10, 18 years Started 1955	49 Asian & Polynesian children of alcoholic parents 38 alcoholic father 6 alcoholic mother 5 both parents	• R. child: positive temperament; elicited attention from caretaker; at least average intelligence; adequate communication skills; achievement-oriented, responsible, caring; positive self-concept, internal LOC, belief in self-help. • Environment of R. Child: plenty of attention from primary caretaker first year of life; absence of prolonged separation first year of life. In first 2 years of life: no additional siblings, no parental conflict.
Werner, E. E., Bierman, J. S., French, F. E., (1971) Werner, E. E., & Smith, R. S. (1977, 1982, 1989) Werner, E. E., (1989)	*Kauai Longitudinal Study Prospective, longitudinal Data collected at birth and at 1, 2, 10, 18, & 30 years Started 1955	698 newborns; Asians & Polynesians Half in chronic poverty, half in relative affluence Most exposed to multiple risk factors	• 72 children identified as resilient (R). • R. infants: positive temperamental characteristics and ability to elicit caregivers' attention. Close bond with at least 1 caretaker. • R. preschoolers: cheerful, responsive, self-confident, independent. Advanced in communication, locomotion, self-help skills, social play. • R. schoolagers: good problem-solving and communication skills; sociable, independent. • R. adolescents: internal locus of control; high self-concept; achievement-oriented; social maturity; internalized values; nurturant, socially perceptive.

Several projects started as risk studies but found protective factors. R = Resilient. * = Major study.

487

1985). As they progressed to the preschool year, they acquired a pronounced sense of autonomy and social orientation. These children were especially skilled at recruiting substitute parents. During middle childhood, girls tended to be autonomous and independent and boys tended to be emotionally expressive. Both sexes displayed flexible coping strategies that allow them to master adversity.

Researchers have found that children who demonstrate resiliency seem to have an outgoing social personality at all ages. Resilient infants were characterized as very responsive to people and objects (Murphy, 1987; Murphy & Moriarty, 1976), and as affectionate and cuddly (Werner, 1985). Werner and Smith (1982) found high-risk resilient toddlers to be more communicative and more actively involved in social play. Preschoolers classified as ego-resilient were also found to have a high involvement in play (Earls, Beardslee, & Garrison, 1987; Murphy & Moriarty, 1976). Wallerstein and Kelly (1980) found that preschoolers who successfully dealt with the stress of divorce appeared more socially mature than their counterparts who had more difficulty.

In the New York longitudinal temperament study (Thomas & Chess, 1982), 131 children were followed from age 1–5 years to age 18–22. Interview and a temperament questionnaire were used. "Difficult" versus "easy" temperament at 3 and 5 years of age was significantly associated with early adult "difficult" or "easy" temperament, adjustment, and presence or absence of a clinical psychiatric diagnosis.

Genetic Effects

It appears that one of the ways in which genetic factors operate is through an influence on responsiveness to environmental stresses. This effect was suggested in Rutter's (1979) study, where the children most likely to be damaged by the effects of severe family discord were those whose parents had a lifelong personality disorder. Children of depressed parents were more affected than children of schizophrenic parents (Anthony, 1987b).

It is hypothesized that people may be more or less susceptible to stressors because of individual differences in endogenous factors. One of these factors is genotype. It is believed that just as embryonic and fetal development is determined, in part, by the actions of genes (Schaie, et al., 1975), so also is postnatal development. Furthermore, it is speculated that a complex interaction exists between heredity, environment, and the organism's developmental stage (Farber, 1982). It is believed that some individuals are more or less susceptible because of a genetic loading. This formulation is often described as the diathesis-stressor model: the greater the innate susceptibility, the lower the degree of external stressors needed to bring the individual over the threshold for symptom expression (Farber, 1982). Conversely, genetic "good protoplasm" is protective.

Birth Order and Spacing

For boys, being a first-born was found to be a protective factor in several studies (Werner, 1985; Williams et al., 1987). In the Kauai study, most of the resilient boys were first-born and most of the children did not have to share their parents' attention for the first 20 months of their life. This fact might have some implications for family planning. White (1975) suggests that the ideal interval between first and second child is about three years, with emotional benefits for both the older and younger child. When the difference between the children is between two and three years, the smaller sibling is often subjected to aggressive behavior by the older child, who is driven by jealousy.

Gender

Gender appears to have some bearing on a child's resistance to stress. However, which gender is protective depends on the age of the child and other circumstances. In the Kauai study, Werner (1981) concluded that girls on the whole were more resilient in the first decade of life and boys were more resilient toward the end of the second decade. Boys generally reported or perceived more stressful life events in childhood than did girls, whereas girls reported more stress in adolescence. At birth, more boys than girls in the study had been exposed to moderate to marked perinatal stress, but fewer of the boy babies survived. Boys at risk because of perinatal stress, congenital defects, or parental defects, especially maternal mental illness, appeared to be more vulnerable than did girls with the same predisposing conditions.

Resilient girls tend to come from households that combine an absence of overprotection, an emphasis on risk-taking and independence, and reliable emotional support from the primary caregiver. Resilient boys tend to come from families where there is greater structure, rules, parental supervision, emotional expressiveness, and a male who serves as a model of identification. Thus, family socialization that emphasizes independence and an absence of overprotection appears to favor the resilience of girls more than of boys (Block & Gjerde, 1986).

Werner (1981) observed that "if there are sex differences in susceptibility to biological and psychological stress, then the characteristics of resiliency in the face of both internal and external stress may also differ with the sexes, the stage of the life cycle, and the cognitive and social demands made on males and females in childhood, adolescence, and adulthood." For example, in the California Children of Divorce Project (Wallerstein

& Blakeslee, 1989; Wallerstein & Kelly, 1980), boys recovered slower from the initial parental separation than did girls.

Age of the opposite-sex parents is also a protective factor: for girls, fathers over 30; for boys, mothers below 30 (Werner, 1981). In families with an alcoholic parent, the gender of the child and the gender of the parent make a significant difference in the outcome: girls and the offspring of alcoholic fathers had a better outcome than boys and the offspring of alcoholic mothers (Werner, 1986).

Intelligence

In a study of 168 middle-class school children, those with higher scholastic achievement improved with moderate to high family stress levels; less scholastically competent children deteriorated with the same level of family stress (Barton, 1985). Lewis and Looney (1983) found that adolescents with higher IQ scores tended to describe themselves as more poised and self-confident, as having a greater sense of self-worth, as being better socialized, and as being more flexible. School achievement and social competence have been reliable predictors of stress resistance in children (Rutter, 1987).

Caretakers and Family

Regardless of their actual parental situation—single parent, absent father, divorced parents, marital discord, parental alcoholism, or parental mental illness—all the resilient children studied had the opportunity to establish a secure attachment with at least one stable adult caregiver in infancy. An intact family is not a consistent, identifiable correlate. The mother's parenting and coping style seemed to have been the deciding factor. The caregivers tended to reward these children for their risk-taking and independence, encourage the assumption of responsibility, and model examples of helpfulness and caring. They also fostered the belief that adversities can be overcome by personal effort and with the emotional support of kith and kin (Werner, 1988). Favorable family factors include parents that were competent, loving, and patient; family closeness; and adequate rule setting. In families with a schizophrenic mother, children whose mothers were nevertheless responsive, warm, and communicative on an adequate level survived psychologically. Jenkins and Smith (1990) found that good sibling relations were related significantly to lower psychiatric symptom scores.

Friends

Resilient children tend to be well liked by their peers. They are able to develop close relationships and maintain those friendships over time

(Garmezy, 1981; Kauffman et al., 1979; Werner & Smith, 1982, 1989). In examining children from unstable homes, Anthony (1987a) and Werner and Smith (1982, 1989) found friends from stable families to be particularly helpful to the resilient children. Friends from stable families helped resilient children gain a perspective on family life and maintain a constructive distance from the turmoil in their own families. Interaction with friends provided enrichment and expanded the quality of life for children who are effectively dealing with parental divorce (Wallerstein & Kelly, 1980). Kennedy, Kiecolt-Glaser, and Glaser (1988) contend that interpersonal resources such as supportive interpersonal relationships may attenuate distress-related decline in immune function, and thus may favorably affect health.

Societal Protective Factors

Support from societal sources has been found to serve as a buffer from the physiological and psychological consequences of exposure to stressful situations. Social support has been identified by Antonovsky (1979) as one of several "resistance resources" that strengthen an individual in the presence of stress. Societal factors that have been identified as protective factors in resilient children include friends, teachers, and school and religious affiliations. From whatever source the child receives support, an essential protective factor for resilient children appears to be a significant adult who can provide a support system important to the child's well-being (Spielberger, Sarason, & Milgram, 1982; Werner, 1988). Empirical studies confirm that exposure to high stress by individuals receiving adequate support does not increase the risk of mental and physical illness (Caplan, 1981). The relationship between perceived stress and symptom patterns as mediated by social support was investigated in 136 seventh- and eighth-grade students. When early adolescents perceived life events (developmental and nondevelopmental) as stressful but also perceived high social support, the stress-buffering effect of social support on symptom patterns was evident (Yarcheski & Mahon, 1986).

Resilient children tend to rely on friendly teachers and other school and religious affiliations in times of stress and crisis and continue to do so in adulthood (Werner, 1989; Werner & Smith, 1982). Resilient children are skillful at garnering social support. Their ability to elicit a supportive social network may be key to their resiliency. In the Kauai Longitudinal Study (Werner & Smith, 1982, 1989), school-age "vulnerable but invincible" children were reported by their teachers as being highly sociable. Sociability was a personality characteristic of resilient school age children found in studies by Wallerstein and Kelly (1980), Anthony (1987a, 1987b), Cohler (1987), and Kauffman et al. (1979). Resilient adolescents were rated as having a higher level of social maturity and scored higher on the California Psychological Inventory (CPI) scale on sociability (Lewis & Looney, 1983; Masen, 1967; Werner & Smith, 1982).

School

Resilient children seem to enjoy school at all ages (Kellam, Ensminger, & Turner, 1977). A positive school environment with a responsive, nurturant atmosphere has been associated with mitigating the effects of stress.

Zuckerman-Barlee (1982), studying children in Israel who are frequently exposed to border incidents, found that school and education enhance flexibility in problem solving. An increased ability in effective problem solving was related to stress resistance. Rutter (1979) studied students who attended school in a poor section of London and found that a positive school environment can mitigate the effects of home stress. Characteristics of the schools that had the most beneficial effects included high academic standards, feedback, praise, incentives, rewards, and opportunities for students to obtain positions of responsibility. Hetherington, Cox, and Cox (1982) found similar school characteristics, including an organized and predictable environment, to be helpful to children successfully adapting to parental divorce. Structure within the school setting was also found to be important to high academic achievers in divorce-prone homes (Wallerstein & Kelly, 1980), and for talented, high-achieving Hispanic females (Gandara, 1982).

Different characteristics of the schools were found to be more important to boys than to girls (Hetherington et al., 1982). More important to boys was an environment with structure and control, whereas resiliency in girls was fostered by a nurturing environment that allowed for the assumption of responsibility. These are the same characteristics that are associated with the differing home environments that foster resiliency differently in each sex.

Teachers

Resilient children who were able to overcome economic and social disadvantages had at least one adult who had a significant influence on their lives. For many of these children, the significant adult was a teacher. In the Kauai study (Werner & Smith, 1982), the most frequently identified positive role model and confidante identified by the children was a teacher. Pederson, Faucher, and Eaton (1978) interviewed 60 adults who had grown up in an economically disadvantaged neighborhood and had a first-grade teacher rated as highly effective. All the subjects stated that their first-grade teacher had a profound effect on their lives, especially their valuing of the importance of education. Twenty four survivors of the Holocaust were interviewed as adults by Moskovitz (1983). All these subjects identified the nursery school teacher who interacted with them immediately after leaving the concentration camp as among the most potent influences on their lives.

Religious Affiliations

Affiliation with a religious denomination has been found to provide stability and meaning in the lives of resilient children. The effect of religious associations crossed socioeconomic classes and ethnic backgrounds. In the studies on religion and resilient children, multiple denominations were examined, including Buddhism, Mormonism, Catholicism, Judaism, and fundamental to liberal Protestantism (Anthony, 1987a, 1987b; Blum, 1972; Lewis & Looney, 1983; Moskovitz, 1983; Murphy & Moriarty, 1976; Werner & Smith, 1982).

Religious beliefs appear to enhance resistance to stress. Such beliefs can provide a sense of coherence and rootedness (Antonovsky, 1979); give life meaning and provide an optimistic outlook (Segal, 1986); provide love for a child despite living in a hateful world, and instruct a child on how to behave compassionately (Moskovitz, 1983). In the St. Louis Risk Project, several children who seemed at risk within a disadvantageous milieu climbed to success and health through affiliation with religious groups (Anthony, 1984). A significant adult, whether in the family or external, played a role in religious affiliations as a protective factor. Introduction of the child to the religious denomination is essential in providing religious exposure.

Exercise

Studies with adults show that vigorous exercise is associated with reductions in anxiety, tension, and moderate depression (Morgan & O'Connor, 1988). Several studies suggest that exercise can augment mental coping skills for managing stress (Kobasa, Maddi, & Puccetti, 1982; Morgan & O'Connor, 1988). The development of such skills in childhood needs to be studied (Dishman & Dunn, 1988). Convincing exercise studies in normal children and adolescents have not been conducted, but among obese and physically impaired children, fitness training increased self-esteem and perceived physical competence (Gruber, 1986; Sonstroem, 1984). Such findings may have important implications for behavioral health, because self-esteem and perceived competence are viewed as mediators for coping with mental stress.

Hardiness

The concept of hardiness is related to the concept of resiliency. It was introduced by Kobasa (1979) as a possible personality disposition mediating the stressful life events/illness relationship. Hardiness developed from the theoretical framework of existential personality theory (Kobasa & Maddi, 1977) and flows consistently from the authentic personality described by that theory. The personality disposition of hardiness combines three tendencies: commitment, control, and challenge. Commitment is expressed as a tendency to involve oneself in one's life. Control is expressed by a feeling that one can influence the events taking place in one's life. Challenge is expressed by a belief that change is normal in life and that the anticipation of change leads to growth (Kobasa, 1979).

In the studies of hardiness, subjects high on the hardiness scale, even though high on the stressful life events scale, were found to have less illness than subjects low on the hardiness scale (Kobasa, 1979; Kobasa, Maddi, & Courington, 1981; Kobasa & Puccetti, 1983; Kobasa, Maddi, & Puccetti, 1982). The personality disposition of hardiness does seem to be an effective mediator against stressful events for the samples tested.

One weakness in the research on hardiness is the homogeneity of the samples studied. Most of the work has been conducted on white, middle- to upper-class adults. There are no studies with children. Further research on the relationship between hardiness, stress, and illness is needed with samples of children.

Currently, research is being conducted to determine if the characteristics of hardiness (commitment, control, and challenge) can be taught. If this is found to be possible, the indications for examining hardiness in children multiply. If a personality disposition that allows persons to decrease the incidence of illness in the face of stress can be learned, what better time to begin such instruction than in childhood, when the benefits of such instruction can be felt throughout life?

DEVELOPMENTAL PROFILE OF RESILIENT CHILDREN

Resilient infants are alert, responsive to people and objects, and cheerful. They readily gain caretakers' attention and are easily soothed. They are good copers, with intense drive and vigor. At this age, a close bond with one primary individual for the first year has a protective effect.

Resilient preschoolers maintain these positive temperamental characteristics. They are self-confident, independent, highly involved in play, and advanced in communication, locomotion, and self-help skills. They play vigorously and seek novel experiences. They are able to tolerate frustrations and handle anxiety. They are ready to take realistic risks, but seek assistance when necessary. They manifest adaptability and self-initiative. They relate well to peers and teachers and are socially mature.

Resilient school-age children are good students, enjoy classmates and teachers, and pursue hobbies. They have a wide range of coping skills, with constructive and creative capacities. They enjoy humor. They get along well with others and develop good friendships.

Resilient adolescents are well-functioning, active, energetic, future-oriented, achievement-oriented, responsible, and caring. They have positive self-concept, internal locus of control, and belief in self-help. They have high internalized values and are nurturant, socially perceptive, and socially mature.

The *resilient child's family* tends to be middle-class and cohesive, with very few conflicts. The parents are competent, loving, compatible, and patient. The primary caretaker gives plenty of attention in the first year of life. There are no additional closely spaced siblings.

In summary, the resilient child is a very "easy" and cheerful infant, born without any complications into a stable, loving family, a hard-playing preschooler, and a good student with fairly high IQ, high-achieving and future oriented. This child is well liked by peers and teachers, develops friendships, and has a strong self-concept.

Over a decade ago, Rutter (1979) stated that the exploration of protective factors in children's responses to stress and disadvantage had only just begun. In evaluating this field of inquiry, it seems that we are still not at the stage when satisfying overall practical conclusions can be drawn. Although a vast amount of information is available on constitutional factors, these are the factors that clinicians can modify the least. Individual differences caused by constitutional and experiential factors, the development of self-esteem, the availability of personal bonds and intimate relationships, and the acquisition of coping skills are much clearer now than in 1979. The compensating experiences outside the home, the scope and range of available opportunities outside the home, and appropriate degree of environmental structure and control—these are less well understood. One partial conclusion about avenues of intervention is to target the development of self-esteem and improvement of coping skills by utilizing day care, school teachers, and elder mentors. Compensating experiences outside the home, available opportunities, and appropriate environmental structure and control need further study, preferably longitudinal-developmental studies of various risk groups.

REFERENCES

Anthony, E. J. (1984). The St. Louis Risk Project. In N. F. Watt, E.J. Anthony, L.C. Wynne, & J. Roth (Eds.), *Children at risk of schizophrenia: A longitudinal perspective.* Cambridge, England: Cambridge University Press.

Anthony, E. J. (1987a). Risk, vulnerability, and resilience: An overview. In E. J. Anthony & B. J. Cohler (Eds.), *The invulnerable child.* New York: The Guilford Press.

Anthony, E. J. (1987b). Children at high risk for psychosis growing up successfully. In E. J. Anthony & B. J. Cohler (Eds.), *The invulnerable child.* New York: The Guilford Press.

Antonovsky, A. (1979). *Health, stress, and coping: New perspectives on mental and physical well-being.* San Francisco: Jossey-Bass.

Barton, M. (1985). *Behavioral stability in elementary school years and the effects of environmental stress.* Paper presented at the American Psychological Association meeting, Los Angeles, California.

Beardslee, W. R., & Podorefsky, D. (1988). Resilient adolescents whose parents have serious affective and other psychiatric disorders: Importance of self-understanding and relationships. *American Journal of Psychiatry, 145,* 63–69.

Bleuler, M. (1984). Different forms of childhood stress and patterns of adult psychiatric outcome. In N. F. Watt, E. J. Anthony, L. C. Wynne, & J. E. Rolf (Eds.), *Children at risk for schizophrenia: A longitudinal perspective.* London: Cambridge University Press.

Block, J. H. (1981). Growing up vulnerable and growing up resistant: Preschool personality, pre-adolescent personality and intervening family stresses. In D. Moore (Ed.), *Adolescence and stress.* Washington, DC: U. S. Government Printing Office.

Block, J. H., & Block, J. (1984). A longitudinal study of personality and cognitive development. In S. A. Mednick, M. Harway, & K. M. Finello (Eds.), *Handbook of longitudinal research.* New York: Praeger.

Block, J., & Gjerde, P. F. (1986). *Early antecedents of ego resiliency in late adolescence.* Paper presented at the American Psychological Association meeting, Washington, DC.

Blum, R. (1972). *Horatio Alger's children: The role of the family in the origin and prevention of drug risk.* San Francisco: Jossey-Bass.

Caplan, G. (1981). Mastery of stress: Psychological aspects. *American Journal of Psychiatry, 138*(4), 413–420.

Cohler, B. J. (1987). Adversity, resilience and the study of lives. In E. J. Anthony & B. J. Cohler (Eds.), *The invulnerable child.* New York: The Guilford Press.

Dishman, R. K., & Dunn, A. L. (1988). Exercise adherence in children and youth: Implications for Adulthood. In R. K. Dishman, (Ed.), *Exercise adherence: Its impact on public health.* Champaign, IL: Human Kinetics Books.

Earls, F., Beardslee, W., & Garrison, W. (1987). Correlates and predictors of competence in young children. In E. J. Anthony & B. J. Cohler (Eds.), *The invulnerable child.* New York: The Guilford Press.

Farber, E. A., & Egeland, B. (1987). Invulnerability among abused and neglected children. In E. J. Anthony & B. J. Cohler (Eds.), *The invulnerable child.* New York: The Guilford Press.

Farber, S. L. (1982). Genetic diversity and differing reactions to stress. In L. Goldberger & S. Breznitz (Eds.), *Handbook of stress: Theoretical and clinical aspects.* New York: The Free Press.

Fisher, L., Kokes, R. F., Cole, R. E., Perkins, P. M., & Wynne, C. (1987). Competent children at risk: A study of well-functioning offsprings of disturbed parents. In E. J. Anthony & B. J. Cohler (Eds.), *The invulnerable child.* New York: The Guilford Press.

Gandara, P. (1982). Passing through the eye of the needle: High achieving Chicanas. *Hispanic Journal of Behavioral Sciences, 4,* 167–180.

Garmezy, N. (1981). Children under stress: Perspectives on antecedents and correlates of vulnerability and resistance to psychopathology. In A.I. Fabin, J. Aronoff, A.N. Barclay, & R.A. Zucker (Eds.), *Further explorations in personality* (pp. 196–269). New York: Wiley.

Garmezy, N. (1983). Stressors of childhood. In N. Garmezy & M. Rutter (Eds.), *Stress, coping and development in children.* New York: McGraw Hill.

Garmezy, N. (1984). Stress-resistant children: The search for protective factors. In J. E. Stevenson (Ed.), *Recent research in developmental psychopathology,* Book Supplement No. 4, *Journal of Child Psychology and Psychiatry.* Oxford: Pergamon Press.

Garmezy, N., Masten, A. S., & Tellegen, A. (1984). The study of stress and competence in children: A building block for developmental psychopathology. *Child Development, 55,* 97–111.

Gruber, J. J. (1986). Physical activity and self-esteem development in children: A meta-analysis. In G. A. Stull & H. M. Eckert (Eds.), *Effects of physical activity on children: American Academy of Physical Education papers, 19,* 30–48. Champaign, IL: Human Kinetics.

Halverson, C. F., & Waldrop, M. F. (1974). Relations between preschool barrier behaviors and early school-age measures of coping, imagination, and verbal development. *Developmental Psychology, 10*(5), 716–720.

Hetherington, E. M., Cox, M., & Cox, R. (1982). Effects of divorce on parents and children. In M. E. Lamb (Ed.), *Nontraditional families: Parenting and child development.* Hillsdale, NJ: Lawrence Erlbaum.

Jenkins, J. M., & Smith, M. A. (1990). Factors protecting children living in disharmonious homes: Maternal reports. *Journal of American Academy of Child and Adolescent Psychiatry, 29*(1), 60–69.

Kauffman, C., Grunebaum, H., Cohler, B., & Gamer, E. (1979). Superkids: Competent children of psychotic mothers. *American Journal of Psychiatry, 136*(11) 1398–1402.

Kellam, S. G., Ensminger, M. T., & Turner, R. J. (1977). Family structure and the mental health of children. *Archives of General Psychiatry, 34,* 1012–1022.

Kennedy, S., Kiecolt-Glaser, J. K., & Glaser, R. (1988). Immunological consequences of acute and chronic stressors: Mediating role of interpersonal relationships. *British Journal of Medical Psychology, 61,* 77–85.

Kobasa, S. C. (1979). Stressful life events, personality and health: An inquiry into hardiness. *Journal of Personality and Social Psychology, 37,* 1–11.

Kobasa, S. C., & Maddi, S. R. (1977). Existential personality theory. In R. J. Corsini (Ed.), *Current personality theories.* Itaca, IL: F. E. Peacock.

Kobasa, S. C., Maddi, S. R., & Courington, S. (1981). Personality and constitution as mediators in the stress-illness relationship. *Journal of Health and Social Behavior, 22,* 368–378.

Kobasa, S. C., Maddi, S. R., & Puccetti, M. C. (1982). Personality and exercise as buffers in the stress-illness relationship. *Journal of Behavioral Medicine, 5,* 391.

Kobasa, S. C., & Puccetti, M. C. (1983). Personality and social resources in stress resistance. *Journal of Personality and Social Psychology, 45*(4), 839–850.

Lewis, J. M., & Looney, J. G. (1983). *The long struggle: Well-functioning working-class black families.* New York: Brunner/Mazel.

Masen, E. P. (1967). Comparison of personality characteristics of junior high school students from American Indian, Mexican and Caucasian ethnic backgrounds. *Journal of Social Psychology, 73,* 115–128.

Masten, A. S. (1986). Humor and competence in school-aged children. *Child Development, 57,* 461–473.

Masten, A. S., & Garmezy, N. (1985). Risk, vulnerability, and protective factors in developmental psychopathology. In B. B. Lahey & A. E. Kazdin (Eds.), *Advances in clinical child psychology* (Vol. 8). New York: Plenum Press.

Morgan, W. P., & O'Connor, P. J. (1988). Exercise and mental health. In R. K. Dishman (Ed.), *Exercise adherence: Its impact on public health.* Champaign, IL: Human Kinetics Books.

Moskovitz, S. (1983). *Love despite hate: Child survivors of the Holocaust and their adult lives.* New York: Schocken.

Murphy, L. B. (1987). Further reflections on resilience. In E. J. Anthony & B. J. Cohler (Eds.), *The invulnerable child.* New York: The Guilford Press.

Murphy, L. B., & Moriarty, A. E. (1976). *Vulnerability, coping and growth: From infancy to adolescence.* New Haven: Yale University Press.

Music, J. S., Cohler, B. J. & Dinein, J. (1982). Risk and recovery in the children of mentally ill mothers. (Grant No. 8252–01). Chicago: Department of Mental Health and Developmental Disabilities.

Pederson, E., Faucher, T. A., & Eaton, W. W. (1978). A new perspective on the effects of first-grade teachers on children's subsequent adult status. *Harvard Educational Review, 48*(1), 1–31.

Rae-Grant, N., Thomas, B. H., Offord, D. R., & Boyle, M. H. (1989). Risk, protective factors, and the prevalence of behavioral and emotional disorders in children and adolescents. *Journal of American Academy of Child Adolescent Psychiatry, 28*(2), 262–268.

Rolf, F. E., Crowther, L., Teri, L., & Bond, L. (1984). Contrasting developmental risks in preschool children of psychiatrically hospitalized parents. In N. F. Watt, E. J. Anthony, L. C. Wynne & J. E. Rolf (Eds.), *Children at risk for schizophrenia: A longitudinal perspective.* London: Cambridge University Press.

Rubenstein, J. L., Heeren, T., Housman, D., Rubin, C. R., & Stechler, G. (1989). Suicidal behavior in normal adolescents: Risk and protective factors. *American Journal of Orthopsychiatry, 59,* 59–71.

Rutter, M. (1979). Protective factors in children's responses to stress and disadvantage. In: M. W. Kent & J. E. Rolf (Eds.), *Primary prevention of psychopathology.* Hanover, NH: University Press of New England.

Rutter, M. (1985). Resilience in the face of adversity: Protective factors and resistance to psychiatric disorder. *British Journal of Psychiatry, 147,* 598–611.

Rutter, M. (1987). Psychosocial resilience and protective mechanisms. *American Journal of Orthopsychiatry, 57,* 316–331.

Schaie, K. W., Anderson, V. E., McClearn, G. E., & Money, J. (Eds.). (1975). *Developmental Human Behavior Genetics.* Lexington, MA: DC Heath.

Seifer, R., & Sameroff, A. J. (1987). Multiple determinants of risk and invulnerability. In E. J. Anthony & B. J. Cohler (Eds.), *The invulnerable child.* New York: The Guilford Press.

Segal, J. (1986). *Winining life's toughest battles: Roots of human resilience.* New York: McGraw Hill.

Sonstroem, R. J. (1984). Exercise and self-esteem. *Exercise and Sport Sciences Reviews, 12,* 100–130.

Spielberger, C. D., Sarason, I. G., & Milgram, N.A. (Eds.). (1982). *Stress and anxiety* (Vol. 8). Washington, DC: Hemisphere.

Thomas, A., & Chess, S. (1982). Temperament and follow-up to adulthood. In *Temperamental differences in infants and young children.* Ciba Foundation symposium. London: Pitman.

Wallerstein, J. S., & Blakeslee, S. (1989). *Second chances: Men, women, and children a decade after divorce.* New York: Ticknor and Fields.

Wallerstein, J. S., & Kelly, J. B. (1980). *Surviving the breakup: How children and parents cope with divorce.* New York: Basic Books.

Werner, E. E. (1981). *Adolescent and stress. Report of an NIMH conference* (DHHS Publication No. ADM 81-1098). Rockville, MD: National Institute of Mental Health, U.S. Department of Health and Human Services Alcohol, Drug Abuse, and Mental Health Administration.

Werner, E. E. (1985). Stress and protective factors in children's lives. In A. R. Nicol (Ed.), *Longitudinal studies in child psychology and psychiatry.* Chichester, England: Wiley.

Werner, E. E. (1986). Resilient offspring of alcoholics: A longitudinal study from birth to age 18. *Journal of Studies on Alcohol, 4,* 34–40.

Werner, E. E. (1988). Individual differences, universal needs: A 30-year study of resilient high risk infants. In *Zero to three: Bulletin of the National Center for Clinical Infant Programs* (Vol. III, No. 4). Washington, DC: National Center for Clinical Infant Programs.

Werner, E. E. (1989). High risk children in young adulthood: A longitudinal study from birth to age 32. *American Journal of Orthopsychiatry, 59*(1), 72–78.

Werner, E. E., Bierman, J. S., & French, F. E. (1971). *The children of Kauai: A longitudinal study from the prenatal period to age ten.* Honolulu: University of Hawaii Press.

Werner, E. E., & Smith, R. S. (1977). *Kauai's children come of age.* Honolulu: University of Hawaii Press.

Werner, E. E., & Smith, R. S. (1982). *Vulnerable but invincible: A longitudinal study of resilient children and youth.* New York: McGraw Hill.

Werner, E. E., & Smith, R. S. (1989). *Vulnerable but invincible: A longitudinal study of resilient children and youth* (paperback edition). New York: Adams, Bannister, Cox.

White, B. (1975). *The first three years.* Tel Aviv: Zmora, Bitan, Modan Publishers.

Williams, P. D., William, A. R., Landa, A., & Decena, A. (1987). *Risk and resilience: Another look at the excluded child.* Paper presented at the 5th International Conference on Early Identification of Children at Risk, Durango, CO.

Yarcheski, A., & Mahon, N. E. (1986). Perceived stress and symptom patterns in early adolescents: The role of mediating variables. *Research in Nursing and Health, 9,* 289–297.

Zukerman-Barlee, C. (1982). The effect of border tension on the adjustment of kibbutzim and moshavim on the northern border of Israel. In C.D. Spielberger, I. G. Sarason, & N. A. Milgram (Eds.), *Stress and anxiety* (Vol. 8). Washington, DC: Hemisphere.

CHAPTER NINETEEN

Case Illustration of Stress Assessment and Interprofessional Prevention Opportunities

L. Eugene Arnold

The following case was chosen to illustrate the clinical assessment of stress in a common childhood stress situation: parental divorce. With almost half of children expected to experience parental divorce, it may be the most ubiquitous and serious child stressor with which helping professionals need to deal from day to day. Certainly it is more frequent than death of a parent or death of a sibling, the only two stressors that surpass it in the empirically derived weightings of seriousness on the Coddington Life Event Scales for Children and Adolescents (Coddington, 1981). It also involves secondary stressors, such as household moves and caretaker changes, as this case illustrates. Furthermore, such stresses impact the children even when the divorced parents are devoted to them, sincerely attempt to cooperate for their welfare, and have adequate financial resources for two homes. Since stresses are cumulative and synergistic, any softening of the stress or additional support at any point in the children's time-life-space should help. This points the way to interprofessional prevention opportunities. In the first part of this chapter an illustrative case from the author's clinical practice is presented, and in the rest of the chapter the issues as illuminated by the case material are discussed.

KURT AND MARGE

Kurt and Marge Brown, ages 7 and 5, were referred by their mother's attorney in March 1990 for mental health evaluation regarding an impending custody hearing. They were brought to the first appointment by their mother and stepfather, Mr. and Mrs. Plumber, and to the second appointment by their father, Nate Brown. They had been in their father's custody the previous two years, and Mrs. Plumber was suing to recover custody.

Background

Mrs. Plumber said she had been their main caretaker until February 1, 1988. In July 1987 she had initiated a divorce suit against their father. She moved out, taking the children with her. During the period of separation from September 1987 to February 1988, the children were living with her. She refused to sign a joint custody agreement for the children to spend half the time with each parent because she felt that the father would not be able to devote half his time to the children because of business demands on his time. When she refused, he went to court with affidavits that he had been the main caretaker. Her attorney was unprepared for this and did not raise objections. In February 1988 the children were required to move from the mother's home to the father's home, which had been the original family home. The mother then experienced feelings of sadness, loss, and depression, which persisted to the time of referral. Shortly after the divorce she met Bud Plumber, and married him after a year.

Mr. Brown was liberal with visiting time until Mrs. Plumber filed for change of custody in October 1989. At that point he began restricting visiting to the decreed times, even when he had to be away and had to hire a housekeeper to stay with the children despite their mother being willing to keep them. Although he didn't like keeping the children away from their mother, he did this on advice of his attorney, who felt that the more time Mrs. Plumber had the children, the stronger her case would be in the custody litigation. He went through a series of five housekeepers, to each of whom the children had become attached. The current one was planning to leave before the custody hearing.

Developmental and School Histories

Kurt was born prematurely, weighing 2400 grams. He walked at 18 months. His development was otherwise unremarkable, with three-word sentences by 2 years, and he did well in kindergarten and first grade, although his grades dropped a bit in the second grade. Nevertheless, his teacher told his mother that he was progressing well. By telephone, his teacher confirmed that he was doing well academically in school but that in the past few months he had become irritable. Also, he had begun having headaches every Thursday morning, for which he went to the school nurse's office for an aspirin and then felt O.K. The teacher had thought of having the counselor talk with Kurt, but the problem did not seem serious enough in view of his continuing good academic work. Nevertheless, she was planning to mention it to his parents at their next regular parent-teacher conference. Both parents always attended these, and the teacher had not realized that they were engaged in custody litigation.

Marge was born one week early after third-month hemorrhage. Although she weighed 3400 grams at birth, she showed many developmental lags. For example, she did not walk until 22 months of age and was late talking, eventually requiring speech therapy. She had an IQ of 98 at age 3, but on retesting at age 5 dropped to 83 full scale (101 verbal, 75 performance). Mr. Brown enrolled her in a preschool at age $4^{1}/_{2}$ because of his concerns about her lags. Her teacher there described her as a bit clingy, especially right after being dropped off by either parent. However, she seemed likeable, made friends, and was progressing in academic readiness skills. She occasionally complained of a tummy ache, which usually left as the teacher read her a story. She seemed fearful of the more aggressive children. Although both parents were of normal height, Marge was below the tenth percentile and had once been worked up for failure to thrive with no definite findings.

Interview and Mental Status

Both children enthusiastically greeted the interviewer, who first saw them briefly with their mother and stepfather to establish the reason for the appointment. When it was explained that both parents wanted the children to live with them, that the judge would have to decide, and that the interviewer was to advise the judge, Kurt interrupted to say that the kids should decide. When it was explained to him that he could decide at age 12, but that meanwhile he would have to live where the judge decided, he seemed a bit upset and became insistent that the kids should decide. His mother later told the examiner that she thought his father had been telling him that it's up to the kids to decide where they will live.

When the Plumbers left to go to the waiting room (five or ten minutes after the start of the interview), Marge objected, began crying, and clung to her mother. It was possible to distract her with toy animals while mother slipped out of the room, but then she gave a brief burst of crying and wanted to go out the door after mother. She was quickly consoled (in less than 30 seconds) by the examiner, whom she hugged. Then she cooperated enthusiastically with the toy animal play and with drawings for another half hour to 45 minutes. Kurt did not show any obvious concern about her behavior, apparently accepting it as the usual course. On a second visit, with her father, Marge showed similar separation symptoms when he left the room. The two children were a bit competitive at times, but were able to share a box of toy animals. The competition for attention sometimes led to Kurt's regressing to Marge's level of function.

The examiner lined up two toy horses on one side of the table, one on the other, and 2 colts in the middle, and explained that there was a daddy horse who wanted the two baby horses to live with him and a mommy and stepfather horse who wanted them to live with them. The children were asked which one they would want the two baby horses to live with. In his eagerness to have the examiner's attention (or to maintain control), Kurt quickly volunteered to decide, but when he grasped the two baby colts, he hesitated. Then he started moving them towards the mother and stepfather horse, then brought them back to the middle, hesitated again, and with a grin of relief said, "Oh, I know," and put one colt on each side. However, when he was asked which colt was the little girl horse and which was the little boy horse, his grin of relief turned to a look of consternation. He pulled the two baby horses back into the middle, and then finally put them on the father's side, saying twice that they can visit the mother and stepfather anytime they want to. When Marge was asked what she wanted to do, she immediately pushed both horses towards the mother and stepfather's side and said, "with the mommy horse and Bud horse," indicating by her slip of the tongue that she fully understood the transparent ruse. Both children then volunteered confirmation of their play decision: Kurt indicated he would want to live with father "but visit mom and Bud anytime I wanted to." Marge wished to live with her mother and stepfather even if Kurt did not.

When asked what animal they would want to be if they had to be one, Kurt said that he would want to be a strong animal, and picked the bear. He explained that he could beat up on anybody who tried to hurt him. Marge picked a bunny rabbit because if she were a rabbit she could hop away from a skunk, and could hop to mommy's house.

The children described their housekeepers in detail, most of whom they liked and missed when they left. They volunteered that they did not see much of father even when living with him because he was so busy. They did not indicate resentment or blame of him for this, but merely a sadness that he seemed to have more important things to do. While drawing, Kurt accused Marge of copying from him. He complained several times that she was copying from him, until the examiner held Marge's security blanket up between the two of them so that Marge could not see his drawing. Then Kurt pulled the blanket aside and reinstituted the bickering.

Marge presented as a guileless, friendly, appealing, diminutive girl with a waif-like appearance. She clutched a blanket, which she often held to her cheek. Many times during the interview she sucked her fingers, especially after Kurt left the room and she was alone with the examiner, but also whenever the subject turned to family or living arrangements. She was able to draw a cross and square. She was able to spell her own name. When asked about her security blanket, she readily agreed that she liked it. She said that her daddy did not let her keep a security blanket, but takes it away from her and throws it away. She indicated a sadness and disappointment about this. On inquiry, she stated that she keeps the blanket with her mother, and gets to have it when she visits her mother, but has to leave it behind when she goes back to father's so he will not throw it away.

Kurt was a likeable, attractive boy of superior intelligence. Although he established immediate rapport with the examiner, he showed flashes of negativism and opposition. He appeared tense. Toward the end of the session, he seemed to tire, and appeared less mature. He even began aping Marge and clinging to mother. His three wishes were to have a computer, to have his mother and father get back together again, and that it be summer all the time. (In the summer he spent half his time at mother's, more than during the school year.)

When the comment was made that he must want mother and Bud to divorce if he wants father and mother back together again, he said that he did not want them to divorce; he wanted them to stay together, but he just wanted mother and father to get together. When the incompatibility of these two desires was pointed out, he modified his wish: that mother and Bud stay together and never get a divorce, but if mother does ever divorce Bud, that she and father get back together again. When it was pointed out that if they wanted to be together, they would have been together already—that the reason they are divorced is because they did not want to be together—he reluctantly agreed to this logic, but his nonverbal demeanor indicated that he really had not given up the hope. He refused to tell about any dreams, but did say that they were all scary. At a second interview, when brought by father, Kurt admitted that he was stating a preference for living with his father as a way of pleasing him. He wanted more time and attention from his father, and was fearful of displeasing him and losing his approval.

Psychological Testing

On the Draw-a-Person test, Kurt scored a Goodenough mental age of almost 9, and Marge scored a mental age over 5. Both childrens' initial person drawings were of the opposite sex. (Only 13% of boys and 22% of girls in one clinic sample drew the opposite sex first; a higher percentage of depressed (27%) and developmentally disordered (28%) children drew the opposite sex first.) Kurt's first drawing was of his mother, and Marge's was of Bud. When Marge was asked to draw a female, she drew her mother. When Kurt was asked to draw a male, he drew "Webster," a comic strip arch-villain. On kinetic family drawing, although the instruction was repeated twice to include themselves, neither child included either child in the drawing. Kurt drew his mother and father together. Marge drew Bud and her mother together. Overall, the drawings revealed a preoccupation with parent figures, a feeling of not belonging, an intensification of sibling rivalry by felt parental deprivation, and a wish to reunite the parents. Marge's drawings suggested an acceptance of Bud as her primary father figure.

As rated by Mrs. Plumber, Marge's Conners hyperkinetic index was 18 (significant), but her Davids hyperkinetic scale was only 10 (normal). Kurt's score on the Conners hyperkinetic index was 20 and on the Davids hyperkinetic scale was 32, both significant. Kurt's Bender-Gestalt was hastily done in about 4 minutes, and he complained that he couldn't do it right. He had 8 Koppitz errors (excessive for his age), and came close to additional errors. He expanded to a second sheet of paper. He became visibly more impatient and impulsive as he worked on it. His subtle signs neurological exam suggested unevenness of development.

Attachment to Parents

Both children showed a warm attachment to each parent. Kurt's was about equal with the two natural parents, slightly favoring his father. Although not as attached to his stepfather, this was also a good relation-ship. Marge showed a clinging attachment to all three parents, but seemed more attached to her mother and stepfather than to her father.

Parents

The father, Nate Brown, was a successful 30-year-old engineer who needed to spend a lot of time on business, including trips. He was not remarried, but had a girlfriend with whom he sometimes left Marge when he took Kurt to his Little League games. He had resisted the divorce. Mrs. Plumber described him as not showing much overt affec-tion to the children, and his own parents as not showing much affection either to him or their grandchildren. On interview he showed excellent intellectual function. He seemed conscientious about the children's wel-fare and cooperative with professional advice. He nondefensively admit-ted persuading Marge to give up her security blanket after her dentist told him her thumbsucking was creating an orthodontic problem and that it would probably continue as long as she kept the security blanket. He was surprised to learn that Marge perceived the persuasion as his taking the blanket away with no choice by her. He agreed to let her have it. Follow-up inquiry confirmed that he did. His MMPI (Minnesota Multi-phasic Personality Inventory) was normal.

The mother, Mrs. Plumber, was a 29-year-old programmer who readily admitted feelings of depression and anxiety which dated from the loss of the children and for which she had sought treatment. She had intact intellectual functions. She was reported by her psychologist to have an essentially normal MMPI, but with subclinical depression, hysterical fea-tures, and guardedness. She described the divorce as bitter, but reported that the two parents were treating each other civilly at this point. She believed, however, that Mr. Brown had been "brainwashing" the children since she filed for custody. She related that Kurt recently called her up and told her he wanted to get everything over with; he would just live with dad, and to please stop trying to change custody.

The stepfather, Bud Plumber, was a pleasant, warm, 39-year-old associ-ate professor of English who made a good impression, seemed to relate well to the children, and described himself as biased when asked his assessment of the situation. He had intact intellectual functions and normal MMPI.

Information from Other Professionals

The children's pediatrician stated by telephone that both parents ordinarily came for the children's health care appointments, and they seemed to cooperate in this regard. The children were currently in good health and had been growing at a normal rate, except that Marge had since age 6 months been consistently below the 10th percentile for length/height.

The children's dentist confirmed that she had advised both parents to do something about the thumbsucking and had suggested that they might try to get the security blanket away as a means of stopping the thumbsucking. However, she had cautioned the parents that this was not her field of expertise and that they should check with a psychologist or psychiatrist about it. She had not expected that they would proceed solely on this comment when they were so conscientious and careful about the children's care in other regards.

The children's pastor, whom the father wanted contacted as a character reference for himself, confirmed that the father was a good citizen of the congregation and community and a good parent, but also volunteered that the mother had been the same prior to her moving out of the congregation at the time of the divorce.

DISCUSSION AND ASSESSMENT

By displaying separation anxiety symptoms inappropriate for her age, Marge illustrates explicitly what many children of divorce feel in a more subtle manner, usually discovered only by careful interview and observation. Kurt's symptoms were more typical: he continued to function in a satisfactory way academically, and made a good impression on first contact. But on closer inquiry and observation, he admitted scary dreams and fear of displeasing his father if he were to say where he really wanted to live. Most children, even in intact families, have an occasional worry about abandonment or not belonging (for example, unrealistic adoption fantasies), but in most cases these worries are tolerable and fleeting. Children of divorce, however, are faced with constant reminders of the possibility of abandonment. They already have partially lost one parent and may fear total loss of that parent, as well as loss of the other parent. The stability and security that allows a child to separate for ever longer periods of time from the parent in the growing-up process is threatened. Under such stress, it should not be surprising to find regression to earlier levels of functioning and lower levels of tolerance for short periods of separation.

It is important to note that Marge and Kurt's sad plight occurred with parents that most professionals would agree are "good parents." They both were sincerely interested in the children's welfare, did not appear to be using the children as pawns (at least not deliberately), cooperated with each other in the children's health care and educational supervision, and were seen as good parents by the professionals with whom they came in contact. Neither spent a great deal of time criticizing the other parent to the evaluator, and each took the opportunity to request professional advice as to the best way to handle various problems the children had. To top it off, there was even a good stepfather involved as an additional support for the children, and there did not seem to be any conflict between the father and the stepfather about the stepfather's role. (Although the divorce literature reports that remarriage of one of the parents frequently is stressful to the children, especially in the first year or two [see Chapter 14], this does not appear to be the case here.) One of the biggest problems the children had, in fact, was that they were highly valued by both parents, each of whom wanted full custody. In summary, this case illustrates about as well as any the adage that divorce is hard on children even under the best circumstances.

The issue of housekeepers deserves further comment. In the absence of more frequent and pervasive contact with their mother, the children had become attached to their father's housekeeper as a surrogate mother. Even in intact families with continual presence of mother, children tend to develop such attachments to a live-in sitter, housekeeper, or nanny. It was not clear that Mr. Brown was aware of the importance of this attachment. Although he did not appear to be deliberately sabotaging it, as a few jealous parents have been known to do, he was not able to arrange a consistent, enduring housekeeper, which, with his considerable financial resources, he might have been able to arrange if he had fully realized the importance.

The children's developmental vulnerability may have been a red herring in this case. Although both children had birth histories suggesting neurological vulnerability, had at least one delayed developmental milestone, and showed some subtle neurological signs excessive for their age (including Kurt's visual-motor dysfunction), Kurt at least was functioning as well as anyone could expect in light of the stress that he was under. The fact that the children were functioning as well as they were under the circumstances speaks for both parents having provided good nurturing earlier in the children's lives. Another protective factor was undoubtedly an inherently very high intelligence, which allowed Kurt to compensate for his visual-motor dysfunction and other neurological impairments and allowed Marge to function at a normal level despite her severe performance impairment. No doubt at least some of her drop in IQ score can be attributed to anxiety, and some could be ascribed to retest measurement error, but we also need to wonder about effects of mild maternal deprivation she was experiencing. A further protective factor was a good social support system, with friends, a supportive school, and high socioeconomic status. The children show several paradoxes in the nature-versus-nurture dialogue. Their situation and performance cannot be used as more of an argument on one side or on the other. There is no doubt that they both would have been better off without their neurological and developmental handicaps and would also have been better off without the divorce stress. Marge's more severe developmental problems and her younger age both tended to make her more vulnerable to the separation stress.

The children's attitude toward their father as elucidated in the interview deserves some comment. If an evaluator entered this case as an advocate for the mother's position, it would not have been too difficult to extract from the children's projective data a rejection of their father. Marge, in her Oedipal first human figure drawing, drew Bud rather than her father. Kurt, who indicated that he was drawing parent figures by first drawing his mother, then drew a monster for his second drawing, which we might assume represented his father. Finally, Marge in her animal fantasy wanted to hop away from the skunk and hop to her mommy's house. This seemed to indicate denigration of her father. However, the total context suggested that the children were angry with their father for depriving them of the more frequent visits with their mother that they had enjoyed in the past. This was illustrated rather explicitly by Kurt's deciding to place the baby horses with the father horse yet repeating several times, "but they can visit the mother and stepfather horse anytime they want to." It was obvious that the big issue was being allowed access to the mother. Marge had an additional complaint and reason for calling her father a skunk in that he had, in her perception, taken away her security blanket, which symbolically represented her mother. The solution here was to get the father to understand the children's needs, not to decide that they did not want him. In fact, observation of the children together with their father indicated a very loving, normal relationship. This shows but one of the reasons why a mental health professional doing a custody or visitation evaluation needs to suspend judgment until all parties are interviewed and observed in various combinations.

Quantitative Assessment: Measuring Stress

The two best-known means of quantifying childhood stressors are Axis IV of the five-axis diagnostic system in DSM-III-R (American Psychiatric Association, 1987) and the Coddington Life Event Scales for Children and Adolescents (Coddington, 1981, 1983). Each approaches the quantification somewhat differently, and each has certain advantages. Both will be applied to Kurt and Marge. The Feel Bad Scale (Lewis, Siegel, & Lewis, 1984) assesses stress from the child's perspective and is described in Chapter 4. More specialized scales to measure specific stresses, such as the Test Anxiety Scale for Children (TASC), are also available (Speilberger et al., 1978).

Axis IV. Axis IV of DSM-III-R is a six-point scale of estimated severity using a table of examples to which the case is compared (Table 19.1). The examples in the table are not exhaustive; of particular relevance for children is the fact that developmental phases such as puberty are legitimate stressors for consideration (DSM-III-R, p. 20). Whether in the table or not, the estimation of severity is based on how stressful an average person of the same age and sex would find the stressor, regardless of individual vulnerabilities or strengths. The rating generally is determined by the child's single most severe stressor, but up to four relevant stressors are listed in order of importance as specifications to the rating.

TABLE 19.1. DSM-III-R Axis IV

Severity of Psychosocial Stressors Scale: Children and Adolescents

| Code | Term | Examples of Stressors | |
		Acute Events	Enduring Circumstances
1	None	No acute events that may be relevant to the disorder	No enduring circumstances that may be relevant to the disorder
2	Mild	Broke up with boyfriend or girlfriend; change of school	Overcrowded living quarters; family arguments
3	Moderate	Expelled from school; birth of sibling	Chronic disabling illness in parent; chronic parental discord
4	Severe	Divorce of parents; unwanted pregnancy; arrest	Harsh or rejecting parents; chronic life-threatening illness in parent; multiple foster home placements
5	Extreme	Sexual or physical abuse; death of a parent	Recurrent sexual or physical abuse
6	Catastrophic	Death of both parents	Chronic life-threatening illness
0	Inadequate information, or no change in condition		

Source: American Psychiatric Association. (1987). *Diagnostic and statistical manual of mental disorders* (3rd ed., rev.) (DSM-III-R). Washington, DC: Author. Reprinted by permission.

In cases of multiple stressors, the severity rating may be subjectively raised above the single most severe one, in a kind of cumulative "fudging." Stressors are supposed to be classified as predominantly acute (6 months or less) or predominantly enduring circumstances (greater than 6 months). Only stressors present in the past 12 months are supposed to be counted (except for post-traumatic stress disorder, which has no time limit for the stressor). However, in practice many clinicians liberalize the time frame, especially for serious stressors directly related to symptoms.

In the case of Kurt and Marge, the divorce as an acute event occurred over two years before, technically disqualifying it from Axis IV consideration. However, the continuing parental conflict extended as an enduring stressful circumstance to the time of assessment. This warrants an Axis IV rating of "3—Moderate." Additional stressors may upgrade this rating. The recent restriction on mother's visitation was like another divorce in loss of access to mother. Whether this in itself warrants the "4—Severe" rating assigned to divorce is debatable. Both children had suffered recent losses of beloved live-in sitters who had been mother surrogates. While this is not listed in the table of severity examples, it would seem to qualify for at least a "moderate" rating in itself. In some ways it was like another divorce, in that the children again lost access to their mother figure, the only adult female in their home. From this perspective, one might argue for a rating of "4—Severe." Further, Marge was deprived of her transitional object. Coming at a time when she was having access to her natural mother unreasonably limited and was losing her mother surrogate (the live-in sitter), its loss undoubtedly appeared "extreme" or "catastrophic" to her, especially with her natural immaturity. However, since we are not allowed to consider the child's special vulnerabilities, we must rate this as loss of a transitional object would affect a normal 5-year-old girl, yielding a "mild" to "moderate" rating. Kurt felt a pressure to side with his father, whom he feared displeasing; this in itself would warrant a "mild" to "moderate" rating for him. Consideration of all this leads to the following Axis IV diagnoses:

For Kurt:

Axis IV: Psychosocial Stressors: Restriction of maternal visits, loss of live-in sitter, parental conflict with pressure to take sides, and fear of displeasing father.
Severity: 4. Severe (predominantly enduring circumstances)

For Marge:

Axis IV: Psychosocial Stressors: Restriction of maternal visits, loss of live-in sitter, loss of transitional object, and continuing parental conflict.
Severity: 4. Severe (predominantly acute events)

Note that although several stressors were common to both children, the order of importance to each was slightly different. Note also that both children received the same rating ("severe"), even though Marge seemed more stressed than Kurt. Each severity rating encompasses a range. It did not seem that Marge's cumulative stress quite justified raising her to the next rating ("extreme"), which typically is used for abuse or parental death.

Life Events Scales. The Coddington Life Events Scales for Children and Adolescents (Coddington, 1981) focus on acute events and therefore do not account well for enduring stressful circumstances. This disadvantage is balanced by several advantages in quantification. The various events are assigned relative weights derived empirically from relative severity estimates by professionals, which have a kind of "consensus" validity. This allows multiple stressors to be added up in a more precise manner. The time elapsed since the event is also accounted for by a formula multiplying the weight by a fraction proportional to recency of event. For an event in the most recent 3 months, the multiplier is 1.0; for an event in the next most recent 3-month period, the multiplier is 0.75; for the third most recent 3-month period, the multiplier is 0.5; and for events up to 1 year old, the multiplier is 0.25. (Like Axis IV, the Coddington Scales disregard stressors over 1 year old.) Age cut-off norms are provided, below which 75% score and above which behavioral symptoms reportedly double or triple. Interestingly, the cut-off norms increase gradually with age, almost doubling from age 8 to age 19. This suggests that as children age, they typically suffer more stress each year than the year before. Another advantage of the Coddington Scales is the inclusion of positive events as possible stressors. This is compatible with opinions of authors such as Sears and Milburn (Chapter 8), who point out that success can be stressful.

There are two Coddington Scales, one for children age 6–11 years and one for ages 12 and over ("Adolescent Scale"). The 6–11 year scale is shown in Table 19.2 with Kurt and Marge's scores marked in. The Adolescent Scale is similar except for the addition of items such as "getting pregnant or fathering a pregnancy" (weighted 88 for girls, 66 for boys) and "getting your first driver's license" (weight 32).

Technically, Marge, at age 5, is too young to be rated on the Coddington Scale, but we will proceed for sake of illustration. Since not all of Kurt and Marge's stress events are listed on the scale (Table 19.2), we have written in the additional events in the space provided, with estimated weighting compared to those listed. The loss of live-in sitter was weighted at 60 because in this case it seemed more important than losing a grandparent and close to the kind of loss involved in marital separation. Marge's loss of her transitional object (security blanket) was

TABLE 19.2. Coddington Life Event Scale—Children (Age 6 through 11)*

K = Kurt; M = Marge

NAME: _____ DATE: _____ SEX: _____ RACE: _____

INSTRUCTIONS:
1. If any of the events listed below occurred in the PAST 12 MONTHS, write the weight in the correct column on the right.

	WEIGHT	SUMMER June July Aug.	FALL Sept. Oct. Nov.	WINTER Dec. Jan. Feb.	SPRING Mar. April May
The death of a parent	109				
The death of a brother or sister	86				
Divorce of your parents	73				
Marital separation of your parents	66				
The death of a grandparent	56				
Hospitalization of a parent	52				
Remarriage of a parent to a step parent	53				
Birth of a brother or sister	50				
Hospitalization of a brother or sister	47				
Loss of a job by your father or mother	37				
Major increase in your parents' income	28				
Major decrease in your parents' income	29				
Start of a new problem between your parents	44		K44 M44		
End of a problem between your parents	27				
Change in father's job so he has less time home	39				
A new adult moving into your home	41	K41 M41			
Mother beginning to work outside the home	40				

Life event	Value			
Beginning the first grade	20			
Move to a new school district	35			
Failing a grade in school	45			
Suspension from school	30			
Start of a new problem between you and your parents	43			
End of a problem between you and your parents	34			
Recognition for excelling in a sport or other activity	21			
Appearance in juvenile court	33			
Failing to achieve something you really wanted	28			
Becoming an adult member of a church	21			
Being invited to join a social organization	15			
Death of a pet	40			
Being hospitalized for illness or injury	53			
Death of close friend	52			
Becoming involved with drugs	38			
Stopping the use of drugs	23			
Finding an adult who really respects you	20			
Outstanding personal achievement (special prize)	34			

2. List below any events that occurred in the PAST 12 MONTHS but were not included in our list and place a check mark in the correct column.

Loss of live-in sitter	60	K60 M60		
Loss of transitional object (security blanket)	40		M40	
Restriction of maternal visits	55		K55 M55	

K20

K60 M60

weighted at 40 because it seemed roughly as severe as mother beginning to work outside the home. The restriction of maternal visits was weighted 55 because it seemed similar in severity to hospitalization of a parent or death of a grandparent and worse than birth of a sibling. The "new problem between parents" was the renewed custody suit the previous September. The "new adult" moving into the home was the previous sitter change. Note that the Coddington Scale may unearth some stressors (e.g., Kurt's beginning first grade) that did not come to mind in using Axis IV.

Since the assessment occurred in the spring, that is the most recent quarter. Therefore the formula is: Spring sum + 0.75 (Winter sum) + 0.50 (Fall sum) + 0.25 (Summer sum) = 1-year life event stress sum.

For Kurt:

$$60 + 0.5(44 + 20 + 55) =$$
$$60 + 59.5 + 25.2 =$$
$$144.7 = \text{year's sum}$$

For Marge:

$$60 + 0.75(40) + 0.5(44 + 55) + 0.25(41 + 60) =$$
$$60 + 30 + 49.5 + 25.2 =$$
$$164.7 = \text{year's sum}$$

The scores of both children are above the cut-off norms for their age at both three months (50) and one year (110).

Time Limit On Counting Stress.   One frustrating aspect of both Axis IV and the Coddington scales is the disregard of events occurring more than a year before assessment. It seems common-sense obvious that events like parental death or divorce continue to affect children beyond 1 year. However, closer scrutiny usually discloses the more recent secondary stressors through which such major events exert their continuing effect. These can then be rated to approximate the appropriate quantification. This principle is illustrated in Kurt and Marge's case by such secondary stressors as renewed litigation, restriction of maternal visits, and changes of live-in sitters who would not have been necessary or so important without the divorce. One value of such quantification attempts is in being forced to think specifically and critically about the child's environment and time-space.

INTERPROFESSIONAL PREVENTION

All helping professionals have at times experienced parents ignoring their advice to the detriment of the children. Mr. Brown illustrates the opposite problem: a parent *heeding* professional advice to the detriment of a child. By taking Marge's security blanket away on the dentist's advice and by restricting her mother's visits on his attorney's advice, he twice threatened Marge's security inadvertently and with good intentions. The lesson here is not for professionals to stop offering advice, but to think through the consequences thoroughly and to communicate with other professionals, making referrals as appropriate. The ability to harm is a proof of potency; and the potency of professional intervention can, with reasonable effort, be channeled to the children's benefit.

At the time of the two premature deliveries, the obstetrician, nurse, pediatrician, or other member of the health care team may have had an opportunity for some preventive counseling about special needs of the children. Developmental or child psychologists and educators could help advise about the children's special needs. Either they or the pediatrician or nurse practitioner who saw the children for their routine child health care could have educated both parents about the need for transitional objects and the regressive effects of prolonged separation from either parent.

We do not know how much mental health consultation was involved in Marge's failure-to-thrive work-up, but we might hope that a psychiatrist, psychologist, or social worker could have assisted the physician and nurses in picking up the marital strain that must have preceded the separation and divorce. Appropriate marriage counseling or couple therapy at that time might have prevented the divorce and all of its consequent stresses for the children.

At the time of the divorce, the possibility of joint custody might have been salvaged if the attorneys had made the case with the parents that joint custody did not have to include equal time with each parent, but could be a symbolic indication that the children belonged to both parents. Mr. Brown's attorney could have called on psychiatric, psychological or social work consultation to help persuade his client that the children were better left with an available parent than with sitters or housekeepers. For some attorneys this might involve a rethinking of priorities. Traditionally, most attorneys saw their ethical task as obtaining the most that they could for the party that had engaged their services. More recently, many enlightened attorneys are considering it their ethical obligation to consider what is best for the child as well as for their client in a divorce proceeding.

It is not clear why Mrs. Plumber's attorney did not raise objections at the hearing about the affidavit saying that Mr. Brown was the primary caretaker. Perhaps her attorney had been so confident that she was obviously the caretaker that there did not seem to be a need to prepare for such a move, and therefore no need to go to additional expense. The question arises as to whether Mr. Brown's attorney should have apprised the mother's attorney that he was planning to introduce affidavits showing that Mr. Brown was the primary caretaker. From the point of view of gaining the most for his client, it would be foolish to tip off the other attorney. However, from the point of view of giving the children the best chance to be with their primary caretaker, it would seem desirable to let both parents be prepared to present evidence that they were primary caretaker and then let the court decide, rather than using a strategy of surprise to win the point.

From the children's viewpoint, some problems could have been prevented by better communication among the professionals. For example, the dentist could have actually referred the parents to a psychiatrist or psychologist about Marge's thumbsucking and security blanket. Even communication with the pediatrician might have prevented depriving Marge of her transitional object at the time when she needed it the most. If Mr. Brown's attorney had checked with a psychologist or psychiatrist or with the children's pediatrician before recommending that Mr. Brown restrict visiting to the decreed times, even more trauma for the children could have been prevented. Any of these professionals could have taken responsibility for recommending to the parents that they apprise the children's teacher of the custody situation so that the teacher could understand and be more supportive. Also, some direct communication with the teacher (with the parents' permission) might have been helpful in developing interprofessional teamwork. Kurt's teacher, for her part, could have paid more attention to the behavioral signs of trouble. Bright children are often deprived of the emotional and other supports they need because they continue to achieve at a satisfactory level; it is not obvious that "one cylinder is missing" because they had so much horsepower to begin with.

Divorce has become so frequent and common that it is easy for parents and professionals to forget how hard it is on children. The fears and anxieties that divorce begets require extra understanding and support from the adults in their lives. The most devastating of the fears is that of being separated from both parents, a fear that is given some reality credence by the fact that the child does undergo at least partial separation from one of the parents, no matter how reasonably the parents try to handle the divorce and the issues of custody and visitation. When there is disagreement between the parents about custody and visitation, the child's fears and anxieties are aggravated. Most parents, even though they may have difficulty cooperating with their ex-spouse, will accept some guidance from a professional who identifies with the child's viewpoint. Since many children do not have the opportunity to have their psychological security advocated for by a mental health professional, it behooves all of the helping professions to keep these facts in mind when dealing with divorced parents or their children.

REFERENCES

American Psychiatric Association. (1987). *Diagnostic and statistical manual of mental disorders* (DSM-III-R) (3rd ed., rev.). Washington, DC: Author.

Coddington, R. D. (1981). *Life event scales for children and adolescents.* (Available from R. Dean Coddington, M.D., 100 W. Main Street, St. Clairsville, OH 43950.)

Coddington, R. D. (1983). Measuring the stressfulness of a child's environment. In J. H. Humphrey (Ed.), *Stress in childhood.* New York: AMS Press.

Lewis, L. E., Siegel, J. M., & Lewis, M. A. (1984). Feeling bad: Exploring sources of distress among pre-adolescent children. *American Journal of Public Health,* 74(2), 117–122.

Speilberger, C. D., Gonzalez, H. P., Taylor, C. J., Algaze, B., & Anton, W. D. (1978). Examination stress and test anxiety. In C. D. Speilberger & I. G. Sarason (Eds.), *Stress and anxiety.* Washington, DC: Hemisphere.

Prevention and Treatment of Stress in Preschool Children: Psychotherapeutic Interventions

Paul V. Trad
Edward Greenblatt

Stress may be described as the lack of balance between environmental demands and a child's coping resources, which results in physiological, behavioral, or affective feelings of disregulation (Masten, 1985). Stressors are the events or stimuli impinging upon normal functioning, while coping resources refer to the child's ability to adapt to these stressors, either by instrumentally changing the stressful conditions or regulating the emotions.

Five categories of stressors have been outlined in Chapter 1: loss; chronically disturbed relationships; events that change the family structure, such as the birth of a sibling; events that require social adaptation; and acute events, such as physical trauma. Each of these areas of stress may cause a series of responses based on children's perception of the event and their ability to cope with the impinging phenomenon. Anxiety is the usual feeling that occurs in response to stress. The various stressors in the child's life may not only affect current behavior, but may also trigger physical and emotional symptoms which can affect future development and coping mechanisms. Therefore, treatment of acute or immediate symptoms constitutes secondary prevention of these "snowball" stress sequelae. Furthermore, many treatment techniques also are used in primary prevention of anticipated stress reactions.

TREATMENT AND PREVENTION OPTIONS

Several treatment options are available for a child who is exposed to stress. Many of these can also be used preventively in anticipation of known stressful experiences. Among the most frequently used modalities are: cognitive-behavioral modification, parental guidance, hypnosis and related relaxation techniques, play therapy, pharmacotherapy, and psychotherapy, which may integrate one or several of these modalities. This chapter focuses on psychotherapy, especially psychodynamic therapy, while the following chapter more broadly covers other therapeutic and preventive modalities.

Cognitive-behavioral modification allows the therapist to initiate changes in the child's perceptions of events by focusing the treatment on techniques that are appropriate to the child's developmental status. These techniques, described by Noshpitz in Chapter 21, acknowledge that the child may have difficulty comprehending notions of intentionality and causality in the same way as adults. They allow for the natural egocentrism of the preoperational child, who may resist the therapist's interpretations because the child lacks the developmental capacity to adopt the psychological perspective of the other. As described by Harter (1983), therapists can use play sequences to enable the child to act out emotionally disturbing events while making interpretations that are appropriate for the child's cognitive level.

Parental guidance instructs parents in techniques that they can administer directly to their children. This form of treatment generally relies on candid discussion and open communication between parent and child. It lends itself to both treatment and primary prevention. Kaplan (1987) recommends this modality for children whose parents are about to divorce. It is also used in preparation for surgery, hospitalization, change of school, sibling birth, and moves. It is often used in conjunction with direct therapy of the child and is described more fully below.

Hypnosis or *hypnotherapy* has been found effective for ameliorating stress among families with chronically ill children, according to Negley-Parker and Araoz (1986). This form of hypnosis minimizes induction rituals and instead relies heavily on the patient's capacity to visualize images and describe feelings while being guided by the therapist. Related to hypnotherapy are *relaxation techniques* that focus on deep breathing and sense centering, slow movement, and imagery. According to Campbell (1986), such techniques are effective in alleviating stress among children about to undergo cardiac catherization.

Play therapy has been found to be of benefit among children who have experienced stressful events. Terr (1981b) suggests that this form of play in front of the therapist can aid the child in symbolically confronting the trauma of the event without having to experience fear in a direct fashion. Play, in other words, permits the child to control the stress to a certain degree.

Pharmacotherapy is not common for treating stress among preschoolers and young children, yet some reports have suggested that GABAergic drugs such as benzodiazepines and L-glutamine may be useful for treating anxiety among these young populations (Cocchi, 1980). Since pharmacotherapy is more likely to be used with older children (Campbell & Spencer, 1988), further discussion of this modality is deferred to the next chapter.

Psychodynamic Treatment Strategies

A number of psychodynamic treatment strategies, ranging from insight-oriented therapy to supportive psychotherapy, have been demonstrated to have ameliorating effects in young children. Insight-oriented therapy seeks to balance children's self-regulatory capacities by helping them develop awareness of their internal sense of self. Treatment focuses on the way in which the inner conflicts and transference reactions are experienced internally. Supportive psychotherapy, by contrast, is more goal-oriented, seeking to resolve symptoms of stress by promoting coping and mastery behaviors in the external world. Table 20.1 summarizes some treatment strategies.

As Mishne (1983) noted, psychotherapy is indicated for children with mild neurotic conflicts, separation-individuation difficulties, or structural ego defects. Analysis is indicated for children presenting with conflicts that have been pervasively internalized. Freedheim and Russ (1983), who advocate an analytic approach, focus on the development of the child's inner structure, resulting ultimately in better self/other definitions and object relationships. Mishne notes, however, that analysis is contraindicated for children who do not have adequate ego development, for those who have cognitive deficits, rigid defense systems, an inability to learn from their behavior, or a history of psychotic behavior, or when there is a lack of both a supportive home and community environment for successful treatment.

TABLE 20.1. Principles of Treatment. All verbal communications must be couched in wording at the child's level of understanding.

Intervention Strategy/Tactic	Explanation/Example/Goal
1. Setting Statements	Discuss and clarify with the child why he or she is in therapy, to create a therapeutic setting.
2. Attention Statements	Comment to the child upon behaviors that are either present or absent during play situations.
3. Reductive Statements	Define origins of child's behaviors.
4. Situational Statements	Objectify for the child the origins of his feelings by drawing attention to the specific situations that trigger the same feelings.
5. Transference Interpretation Statements	Address the child's projection onto the therapist of internal thoughts and emotions regarding objects and roles.
6. Etiological Statements	Recall and reconstruct past events in the child's life to provide a link for understanding present behaviors.
7. Family Involvement	Promote parental participation in parent training specific to areas of adaptive difficulty.
8. Social Support	Persuade family to make contact with social networks.

Unfortunately, there are no significant statistical data that compare the relative effectiveness of different psychodynamic treatment strategies with preschool children. The therapist must, therefore, select a strategy by clinical common sense or intuition. This can be facilitated by assessing the child comprehensively, considering biographical information, the nature and intensity of the disturbance, intrafamilial relations, the parent-child relationship, and the nature and prognosis of the specific disorder (Trad, 1989).

Freedheim and Russ (1983) have grouped child psychotherapeutic approaches into three broad categories: insight-oriented, supportive, and development of the child's inner structure. (The latter is a form of cognitive-behavioral therapy.) Insight-oriented therapy concentrates on conflict resolution and the mastery of developmental crises. This form of therapy should be used only with children who are motivated, have adequate ego development for conflict resolution, and have supportive homes. Supportive psychotherapy strives to help the child devise coping strategies and develop problem-resolving techniques. In contrast to analysis, this form of therapy is indicated for children with a less developed ego, those who would have difficulty with anxiety-producing phenomena, or those who have developmental deficits. Dewald (1983) has suggested that supportive psychotherapy is appropriate for children who are denying physiological illness, for those pressured by family and/or community to get treatment, for the withdrawn or suspicious child, and for the child who has difficulties establishing object relationships. The goal is helping the child develop an internal structure, a better definition of self/other boundaries, and object relationships. This form of therapy assumes that the therapist is familiar with the cognitive stages of development. It is readily applicable to children with narcissistic disorders.

PSYCHOTHERAPEUTIC INTERVENTION TECHNIQUES

Lewis (1974) views psychotherapeutic intervention as a means of enhancing communication by creating an environment in which the transference and countertransference reaction in child and therapist may emerge and be understood. Fraiberg (1962) contends that intervention techniques should focus on the emotional and/or cognitive difficulties that have been detected in the child's functioning. Anna Freud (1966) posits that the child's ego should be the focus of attention during therapy, since the ego is the structure that defends the child from subconscious impulses. The therapist works to facilitate the emergence of subconscious residues into consciousness. This task can be accomplished by interpreting the child's defensive operations, affective responses and resistances. A correlate to such an approach is the increased interaction between therapist and child. Amster (1964) warns, however, that some children are not able to tolerate the emergence of subconscious impulses, and cautions therapists to be careful when relaying interpretations of such unconscious material to the child. Interpretations lacking an empathic understanding of the child's emotional make-up run the risk of forcing the child to isolate and withdraw from the therapeutic process in order to defend against the anxiety provoked by the interpretation.

Play therapy, a technique that may be readily integrated into the child's psychotherapeutic sessions, operates by allowing child and therapist to interact (Ekstein, 1983; Esman, 1983). During play therapy, the therapist's primary function is to interpret the child's overall behavior. For example, once the child creates a pretend episode the therapist should follow the child's lead and may begin a dialogue in order to clarify and learn as much as possible about the child's emotional condition. A child who is given the necessary encouragement during episodes of play will be more likely to continue initiating play activities and engaging in fantasy behaviors in the therapist's presence.

When testing hypotheses that derive from clinical observations regarding the origins of the child's behavior, the therapist should weigh both confirmations and disconfirmations equally (Harter, 1983). This is because therapeutic interventions can be orchestrated to test the validity of these hypotheses. Therapists must also be able to communicate their interpretations to the child on a level that is both commensurate and appropriate to the child's cognitive skills (Harter, 1983). Therapists should chart the child's reactions to a particular interpretation by noting whether the child accepts, rejects, denies, or shows no reaction to the therapist's interpretation. When the child displays no reaction to the proposed interpretation, the therapist should consider a new hypothesis.

Types of Psychotherapeutic Intervention

Lewis (1974) observed that there are six types of intervention statements that a therapist may use when interacting with a child. Each has a specific purpose designed to enhance the therapeutic process. Setting statements explore and clarify why the child is in treatment. For example, the therapist may ask the child, "Do you know why your mother brought you here today?" Attention statements, the second type of intervention, draw attention to particular behaviors of the child, providing either factual information about play behaviors or commenting upon the lack of specific behaviors. The third type of intervention, reductive statements, has the goal of reducing the child's disparate behaviors into forms that define their origins. Situational statements, the fourth type of intervention, aim to draw attention to behavior that provokes feeling (e.g., anger), in an attempt to show children both the origins of their feelings and the repetition of their feelings both within and outside the treatment setting. Transference interpretation statements, the fifth type of intervention, refer to the child's projection of emotions and intentions felt toward objects, roles, behaviors, and dreams onto the therapist. Transference is seen most commonly when children attribute to the therapist thoughts and feelings regarding their parents. However, any kind of transference lends itself to the therapist's interpretations. Etiological statements, the sixth form of intervention, derive from past events in the child's life which are recalled and reconstructed in order to link them to the child's present behavior.

Formulating an interpretation and presenting it to the child is an important step which must be approached skillfully. The therapist should keep in mind the child's fundamental needs and developmental status, taking care not to press the child into an interaction that is beyond his or her comprehension. Fraiberg (1962) noted that interpretation of symbolic play should not be grounded in the general models of definition, but should instead call upon the child's personal experiences. Lowenstein (1951) suggests five steps involved in making an interpretation: (1) make the child aware that events have certain elements in common, (2) point out the child's similar behaviors in these particular situations, (3) demonstrate the motivating circumstances to the child, (4) point out the unconsciously motivated behavior that may be replaced by more adaptive behavior, and (5) show the correlations of these behaviors to critical events in the child's life.

The therapist then may use play techniques to both assess and modify the child's psychopathology, interweaving interpretation and play to help the child overcome difficulties. Interpreting play behaviors is one mode through which the therapist may work through conflicts until the nature of the conflict can be broken down into its constituent elements. In this fashion, the child is able to perceive and articulate the origins of the conflict.

Imagery in Psychotherapy

Imagery is another important tool in the diagnosis and treatment of preschoolers with psychiatric disorders. Conceptual thinking is viewed as a residual skill that derives from the process of assimilation, which is itself a function of imagery (Piaget & Inhelder, 1971). Assimilation refers to the ability to inculcate experiences from the environment. Imagery is therefore a useful treatment for children with poor verbal abilities because it facilitates learning visual material and transfers learning to a domain in which the child is more adept.

Self-report, behavioral, physiological, and projective measures can all be used to assess a child's imagery abilities (Tower & Singer, 1981) and to help distinguish the dimensions of the imagery. The choice of intervention depends on these dimensions. Wilkins (1974) has suggested that a desensitization effect occurs when children are helped to develop such imagery skills.

Psychodrama and guided imagery are two therapeutic techniques that directly use imagery. Psychodrama functions by allowing group members to play roles designed to encourage both the expression of feelings and conflict resolution. This technique is used primarily to enhance a child's decision-making skills (Elliott & Ozolins, 1983). In guided imagery, the child is given suggestions designed to elicit information about a specific imaginary situation. This technique is used as a tool for teaching imagery skills.

Hypnotherapy in the Psychotherapeutic Setting

Recent studies have suggested that hypnosis can be a valuable adjunct to interpersonal psychotherapy that relies on the discussion of emotionally charged issues. As described by Negley-Parker and Araoz (1986), hypnosis may be especially useful for treating young children exposed to stress, because the techniques currently used rely on induction techniques—deep breathing and imaging—that are particularly in accord with the child's level of cognitive processing.

Negley-Parker and Araoz used this form of hypnosis with children with chronic illnesses, such as diabetes and cancer, and their families. Family members at the beginning of the induction were first asked to find a symbol or image that was characteristic of the sick child. They were then asked to visualize the symbol and describe it. As a variant on this exercise, family members were asked to breathe deeply and to focus on the forces of health rather than illness. In each family that underwent such sessions, there was improvement in the child's symptoms and in the behaviors of the family members toward the child.

These researchers (1985) also found deep breathing and imaging exercises of value in helping stressed children relax. One reason why these techniques may be so efficacious is that they provide the child with a sense of control and mastery over the situation. The child may be frightened and yet can learn to control breathing, heart rate, and state of mind. This sense of control often allows the child to surmount the stress.

Videotape within the Psychotherapeutic Setting

Videotape is another important tool in treating the TV generation, because it helps to focus attention and ascertain nonobvious clues during important events in the treatment session. Replaying the visual recording of the session makes it difficult for the child to repress underlying conflicts. It might be considered a kind of forced imagery. Videotape replay also fosters both self-reflection and the formation of cause-effect hypotheses in the child. The therapist watching the videotape with the child can either offer immediate interpretations or can guide the child toward spontaneous insight. Voice-overs can be used to incorporate the therapist's interpretations and to promote the child's self-reflective skills. The taped image can also be replayed silently, so that the therapist and child can focus attention on a particular characteristic without added distraction. Freeze-frames may be used to discuss unconscious conflicts, since a freeze-frame can highlight subtle nonverbal behavior (Heilveil, 1983).

Videotape is used most often with preschool children who have low self-esteem, poor body image, social withdrawal, passivity, and behavioral difficulties. On the other hand, this technique is contraindicated for children who are extremely depressed, psychotic, or paranoid (Heilveil, 1983), because these psychopathologic conditions do not manifest in vivid behaviors that are capable of being captured on videotape.

Parents may be given a videotape of a model therapy session prior to the initiation of formal therapy, so that the child may become sensitized to the treatment setting in advance. Heilveil (1983) explains that a videotape depicting a "model" patient in a "model" session may be shown to a prospective patient before treatment begins. Thus, the patient is provided with observable behaviors that may be emulated and is familiarized with what therapy will be like. Anxiety about treatment may be alleviated. Children particularly may benefit from observing such a videotape since they are by nature eager to imitate. Tapes may also be used to transfer information from one setting, such as a group therapy session, to another, such as an individual session. In cases where family roles are contributing to a child's problems, a tape of family interactions may help identify patterns of interaction and encourage family members to contribute to the treatment. Children may also be given tapes of treatment sessions to bring home in order to view them away from the inhibiting presence of the therapist.

PARENT GUIDANCE

The therapist must also be aware that there are other factors outside of the therapeutic setting, such as parental psychopathology, which may affect the child's life and thus the response to treatment. Conflicts specifically reinforced by the child's parents are especially difficult for the child to work through (Lewis, 1974). It is therefore both therapeutic and prophylactic to see parents regularly in order to increase their understanding of the child's behavior and psychopathology. Goals for intervention with parents include increasing parental empathy, obtaining information regarding the child, clarifying the child's developmental

needs, and resolving possible fantasies about the treatment or the therapist that might impinge upon therapy (Liebowitz & Kernberg, 1988).

Numerous studies have found that the presence of supportive parents
who are willing to talk about the stressful event with the child is often the
most significant factor in ameliorating psychological trauma. This finding was confirmed by Masten (1985), who reported that in the hospital
atmosphere, known to be a particularly stressful environment for young
children because of potential separation from parents, the reassurance
or even the mere availability of the parent served to reduce stress and
promote cooperation.

But just as parents can serve as models for alleviating stress, so too in
certain situations may the parents themselves exacerbate the stress and
emotional trauma that the child is experiencing. Elkind (1986), for example, has reported that parents can sometimes inappropriately pressure
their children by imposing unrealistic demands for academic or athletic
achievement. In these cases, parents are often projecting their own needs
onto the child and experiencing achievement vicariously through the
child. For such parents, pressure-reducing strategies should be introduced. These include teaching the parent to ease up on expectations and
to confront issues of separation that may have resulted in placing undue
pressure on the child initially. Parents who place undue pressure on the
child to achieve from an early age should also be informed of the work of
Eskilson et al. (1986). These researchers found that if a pattern of pressure is placed on the child from early school age, by high school such
children tend to possess lower self-esteem and resort to more deviant
activities than their peers.

It is also important for parents to recognize that they represent the
most significant role models in their child's life. Gallagher, Beckman,
and Cross (1983) reported on stress in the families of handicapped children. These researchers discovered that while parents were often the
cause of provoking stress in their children, parents were also the family
members most flexible with respect to modifying debilitating patterns.
No matter what the specific technique used for treating the young child
who is under stress, therefore, it is likely that the treatment will be
facilitated if parental guidance and support are interwoven into the
regimen.

Tripartite therapeutic design (Elkish, 1953; Mahler, 1968) is the simultaneous treatment of mother and child. This form of intervention is indicated in cases of separation anxiety, especially when the mother finds it
more difficult to separate than the child. The focus of treatment in this
form of therapy is the mother-child dyad, with the therapist functioning
in this instance as both a model to the mother and as an auxiliary ego
conveying mastery skills to the child. Therapists should also compare and
contrast the child's behaviors in and outside of therapy, guiding the child

towards an awareness of the differences between these behaviors and the implications of these differences. Armed with the awareness of their behaviors and with new adaptive strategies to replace old ones, children will break the cycle of behavior that has prevented them from developing adaptively.

PLAY THERAPY FOR TREATING POST-TRAUMATIC STRESS

Play is the mechanism by which children are able to cope with and master the various stressors that impinge on their development. While play allows children to re-experience previously mastered experiences as well as to anticipate future experiences (S. Freud, 1909), it also provides an experimental outlet for the child to handle such anxieties as separation anxiety or the Oedipal conflict. In this type of ordinary play, children can identify with such well-meaning aggressors as parents or teachers, and by scolding or punishing a doll, for example, can diminish their own anxieties. However, play therapy may also be a valuable technique in instances where the child has been subjected to unusual forms of stress. Sigmund Freud (1920) defined psychic trauma as the injury to the personality which happens as a result of anxiety so sudden, intense, and unexpected that it overwhelms ordinary coping and defensive mechanisms.

Terr (1979, 1981a, 1981b), studying child-kidnap victims in Chowchilla, California, discovered that 14 of the 23 children involved manifested certain symptomatology which she termed "post-traumatic play." Terr found that the children who engaged in post-traumatic play were attempting to use ordinary play mechanisms in an attempt to dissipate the overwhelming anxiety of the traumatic event. Terr noted that since these children are not fully able to identify with either the aggressors or the helpers in the event, and since they already know that a happy ending (one in which they were able to cope) to the event is not possible, they cannot gain enough emotional distance from the event to dispel anxious feelings. The more the play aggravates rather than soothes the children's anxieties, the more they will repeat this play in an attempt to overcome the stress aroused by the trauma. This repeated post-traumatic play creates additional anxiety in the child because it literally recreates the original traumatic event.

Terr (1981b) listed 11 characteristics of post-traumatic play that distinguish it from ordinary play, including: compulsive repetition of the entire play sequence; modes of repetitious play such as drawing, talking, or listening to tapes; an unconscious link between the trauma and the play; the play's failure to relieve the child's anxieties; a wide age range in the children engaging in this form of play; a time lag between the original traumatic event and the development of post-traumatic play; an atmosphere of danger; the ability of these children to communicate and enact post-traumatic play episodes with other, non-traumatized children, such as younger children who have not experienced the trauma; and the possibility for a therapist to trace this form of play back to a previous traumatic event.

Post-traumatic play may remain excluded from the therapeutic context because of its secrecy and ritualization (Terr, 1981a, 1981b). Therefore, a therapist who learns from parents, a teacher, or other children about a child's repeated, monotonous "strange" play should consider the possibility of the child's previous exposure to a traumatic event. Terr has outlined four techniques for therapeutic reconstruction and interpretation of this form of play. These techniques include: (1) therapeutic reconstruction in which previous knowledge from parents or others regarding the child's post-traumatic play is utilized; (2) therapeutic interpretation based on direct observation within an outpatient setting; (3) interpretation based on observed play behaviors within a residential setting; and (4) intervention based on observation of post-traumatic stories, art, or recordings. After post-traumatic play has been reconstructed within the therapy setting, there are several play therapy techniques which may be utilized to help the child overcome the trauma that motivated this form of play.

As one method for treating a child who is exhibiting post-traumatic play, Levy (1938, 1939, 1945) suggests *release therapy*, in which the therapist allows the child to re-enact stressful feelings through play. In this abreactive form of treatment, the therapist's interpretative function is minimal or even absent. *Spontaneous play*, another therapeutic technique, allows the child to engage in anxiety-related play activities. The therapist then may interpret these behaviors and prescribe a course of action for the parents without providing a direct interpretation to the child (Erikson, 1950). In *pre-set* or *pre-arranged play*, the therapist may set up a play situation designed to be directly applicable to the child's traumatic experience. The child then will spontaneously play with the materials the therapist has pre-set. Although such play may appear to resemble post-traumatic play, the context has been set by the therapist, not the child.

Corrective denouement play, as noted by Terr (1981a, 1981b), refers to play during which the therapist helps the child to retrospectively find a solution which might have avoided or ended the trauma. In this type of intervention, the solution provided is not magical but real. This solution not only allows the children to realize that they previously lacked the proper skills to avoid the traumatic event, but also that they have now developed the skills necessary to cope with any similar future event. Terr observes that this type of therapeutic intervention is contraindicated for children who have undergone massive natural disasters, other events that were random and unprovoked, or catastrophic illness.

THE TRANSFERENCE RELATIONSHIP

Transference, first alluded to by Sigmund Freud (1905), occurs when the child unconsciously projects onto the therapist thoughts and feelings about his or her caregivers, displacing to the therapist the attitudes aroused in the child by the parents (Fraiberg, 1962; Freud, 1905; Markowitz, 1959). It is especially important when caretakers have been a source of stress, as in abusive, rejecting, or ill parents. The therapist's presence during treatment gives the child opportunities to forge this transference relationship, making understanding, interpretation, and reconstruction possible.

"Transference neurosis" as defined and identified by Anna Freud (1928), refers to the child replacing previous neurotic functioning with caregivers or important others by neurotic reactions in relation to the therapist. When a child in treatment expresses behaviors, attitudes, or feelings to the therapist that formerly have been expressed toward important others, while decreasing those behaviors elsewhere, then a transference neurosis is said to be occurring (Tyson & Tyson, 1986).

Children in a transference relationship with the therapist must be helped to overcome the ego split that enables them to maintain their defensive, conflicting beliefs. Transference relationships are, however, related to the developmental status of the child (Neubauer, 1980). Object constancy, which develops at about 3 1/2 years of age (Mahler, Pine, & Bergman, 1975), must first be developed before the child can have a transference reaction (Kohrman et al., 1971; Neubauer, 1980). In young children who have attained this developmental level, however, transference allows the child to re-experience past events (Neubauer, 1980).

Since it revives feelings associated with old memories and imbues them with immediacy, transference is more than just a mere reenactment of the past (Ritvo, 1978). It is a process that allows direct exploration of the foundations of conflict. The major therapeutic tool of change in the therapeutic setting is the therapist's interpretation of the conflicts aroused by the transference relationship (A. Freud, 1928). The therapist must, however, discriminate carefully between the transference and the nontransference elements being projected by the child, noting which responses are projected onto the situation itself and which are projected onto the therapist as authority figure.

One major complication in managing the transference relationship is young children's inability to process abstract thoughts, which limits their understanding of the therapist's interpretations. Full understanding of the therapist's interpretations is key in helping the child to distinguish between the influences of the past, present, and fantasy. Telling a story about an animal or a child is one method of overcoming this problem. This technique, though, is limited by the fact that these symbolic stories may not engage the focus of intervention—the child's ego.

The Countertransference Relationship and Other Therapist Feelings

Sigmund Freud (1933) was the first to describe the countertransference phenomenon as the numerous emotions triggered in the therapist as a consequence of the patient's influence on the therapist's unconscious. Technically, countertransference denotes only feelings from the therapist's own past relationships that are transferred to the patient. In practice, however, the term is often broadened to include any feelings that the patient provokes in the therapist. In therapy with children, countertransference may be used for understanding and interpreting the child's internal perceptions. Berlin (1987) noted, however, that the therapist must consider the child's detrimental past relationships in order to avoid repeating any of the same interactions. Therapists, then, must understand the subjective elements of their experience with the child, and use them to formulate treatment strategies (Stein, 1985a, 1985b, 1985c). The more therapists can perceive and analyze their own countertransference feelings, the more adept they will become at deciphering the child's internal reality.

The child in the therapeutic setting, unaware of the countertransference reactions that can be provoked in the therapist, may actively seek to elicit action-oriented responses. The therapist must then proceed carefully and objectively in order to respond optimally to the child's needs (Winnicott, 1949). Acting out—a spontaneous discharge of impulse, emotion, fantasy, or memory by the child—frequently evokes countertransference feelings in the therapist. In such instances, the child may be unconsciously testing the therapist.

Children who have been exposed to a traumatic incident may have a tremendous reservoir of anxiety fueling their play activities. Terr (1981a, 1981b) has mentioned that one of the characteristics of post-traumatic play is the ability to draw non-traumatized children into this form of play. The therapist therefore should consider the potency of such anxiety and how it may effect the transference-countertransference relationship. Overidentification may be a possible result for the therapist who, in an attempt to protect and shield the child, may lose objectivity, thereby thwarting the therapeutic process.

An objective, sufficiently neutral perspective is key in order not to overidentify with, misinterpret, or become seduced by the child (Esman,

1983). Warning signs for the therapist include an overreluctance to see parents, a view of being a better parent to the child, anxiety, and/or guilt aroused by the child. Possible emotional responses of child therapists include identification or overidentification, counteridentification, experiencing the child as an extension of the self, and responding to the child as a non-patient real person (Esman, 1983). Identification and counteridentification occur when therapists begin to perceive the child as their own and begin to view themselves as the child's parent. Like identification and counteridentification, viewing the child as a narcissistic extension of the self will hamper therapy if not rectified. Viewing the child as a non-patient real person occurs as a response to sudden provocative behaviors such as pushing away by the child. Because these behaviors may occur so suddenly, the therapist can be caught off guard and respond in a non-objective manner.

Therapists who remain unaware of these countertransference reactions may nurture the child in a manner that undermines the therapy (Bick, 1962). Self-analysis is of continual importance to the therapist, who must recognize any negative feelings toward the child and prevent them from entering the therapeutic relationship (Bick, 1962).

Therapists who can handle their countertransference feelings objectively can also diagnose the child's progress objectively. To maintain objectivity and enhance the potential usefulness of countertransference feelings, therapists may use free-floating attention and response techniques, allowing their daydreams, random thoughts, and associations to emerge freely while observing and listening to the child.

Resistance in the Therapeutic Setting

The child may employ resistance consciously or unconsciously in order to evade the therapist's efforts to establish an alliance. Abused children, for example, may resist therapy because they fear that the therapist, like their parents, will punish them randomly or arbitrarily for their behaviors. The scrutiny of a stranger (the therapist) and the distress of expressing ostensibly dangerous, forbidden, or unpleasant emotions also may tend to make a child resistant. In addition, by thwarting the therapist's attempts to establish an alliance, resistance provides a child with the secondary gain of controlling an adult. Resistance in a child exposed to a traumatic situation may be much greater than the resistance displayed by a non-traumatized child because of the amount of anxiety involved.

Resolution of the child's initial resistance is imperative. The therapist must intervene actively from the outset to direct the child's behaviors and/or thoughts in order to alleviate the child's anxieties and to induce feelings of trust. The child then will begin to perceive the therapist as a person whose intent is not to punish maladaptive behavior, but to relieve the dysphoric feelings that such behavior triggers. Introducing therapy through the child's parents (if they are not the source of the stress) is one way of alleviating the child's initial fears (Gardner, 1979). Exploring the child's feelings about being in therapy and explaining the therapeutic process are other means of alleviating some of the child's initial fears. In cases of abused children, dispelling resistance may be in itself the main therapeutic goal.

Three forms of resistance can emerge in the therapeutic setting: repression, transference, and secondary gain resistance. Both transference and secondary gain resistance refer to acted-out behaviors designed to avoid interpretation and/or their modification. Transference resistance evolves when the child repeats with the therapist past modes of reacting. Secondary gain resistance is born from the need to maintain a symptom because of the gains derived from doing so. Over time, as the child's fear and apprehension of the therapeutic situation diminish, so too do these phenomena, and thus an adaptive alliance is finally established between therapist and child. Repression resistance is not, however, a defense activated by an external event such as the therapy itself, but is instead a defensive mechanism that has evolved in response to the internal conflict. The resolution of this type of resistance happens when the child experiences the therapist as empathic, interested, and understanding. The therapist, translating observations into language that is readily understandable to the child, helps the child draw conclusions and grow in the direction of self-assessment (Frankl & Hellman, 1964; Gardner, 1979).

Young children often expose their unconscious wishes and impulses for interpretation. Frankl and Hellman (1964) warn, however, that the therapist must be wary of bypassing ego defenses in order to make interpretations. If such defenses are bypassed, resistance may be evoked. Direct confrontation of the child's unconscious makes the therapist appear like a person who can read the child's secret, inner thoughts and may induce anxiety in the child, thereby undermining the benefits of the therapeutic situation. The therapist who first establishes an alliance with the child based on trust and then communicates interpretations through the child's ego will prevent anxiety from overwhelming the child while accessing derivatives of the child's unconscious.

Termination

The ultimate goals of therapy, as outlined by Liebowitz and Kernberg (1988), are opportunities for further normal growth and development, positive identifications with the therapist, and corrective emotional experiences. Changes in the child that have occurred through therapy are assessed in order to know when the specific therapeutic goals have been attained and normal development has resumed.

According to Smirnoff (1971), criteria for termination of therapy include: symptomatic improvement, the development of a fantasy life, and structural criteria. Symptomatic improvement includes abatement or disappearance of such symptoms as poor schoolwork, aggressive behavior, and poor family relations. The development of a fantasy life corresponds with increased freedom of play and expression, as well as a gradual lessening of inhibitions. Structural criteria for termination include the manifestation of flexible defenses, ego mastery, and improved adaptation.

It is important for the therapist to know when therapy may be diminished or terminated successfully, so that the child and parents can continue unaided. As Carek (1979) has noted, psychotherapy does not have as a goal the reconstruction of children so that they become invulnerable to any stress and symptom-free for the rest of their life. Rather, liberating them from their oppressive symptoms and maladaptive developmental course, in order that they may continue to develop to their fullest potential, is the ultimate therapeutic goal.

BEFORE THE NEED FOR THERAPY: PREVENTION

In many instances, episodes of childhood stress can be anticipated and even averted if parents are alert to the kinds of events that may trigger a sensitive response in the child (Trad, 1990). For example, Graudins and Harris (1985) examined how children responded when their mothers went to the hospital to have a new baby. Although this event is readily understood by adults, children may be traumatized by the possibility that their mother may be sick, has abandoned them, and may not return from the hospital. To prepare for this type of event, the researchers recommend that a substitute primary caregiver be designated for the child during the period of the mother's absence and that the mother explain the reason for her departure and reassure the child of her return. Many events likely to cause stress in the young child can be handled in an analogous fashion. For example, when a preschooler first attends school, the caregiver should reassure the child that she will return to pick the child up at the end of the day. Research by other investigators, such as Eskilson et al. (1986) indicates that as the child grows older, parents should continue their supportive stance and should refrain from placing unwarranted expectations upon the child. Such expectations can lead to stress and deviant behavior patterns.

Given the fact that some methods of deflecting or managing stress are more desireable than others, is it possible to encourage good coping skills while downplaying maladaptive ones? From the data presented in Chapter 1, it seems that the ideal prescription for "stress-proofing" children is to ensure that they come from a home that is warm, loving, and supportive and is not socially or economically disadvantaged; that their nature be adaptive, curious, and optimistic; and that they have a strong network of support contacts. We cannot guarantee these things for all children—would that we could! But perhaps certain kinds of coping mechanisms can be encouraged in a child who appears to be at risk for stress-related disorders.

Lazarus and his colleagues (Lazarus & Launier, 1978; Roskies & Lazarus, 1980) suggest that coping mechanisms can be divided into those actions designed to mitigate the stress itself and those designed to change reactions to the stressor. The modes of coping within those categories include direct action, information seeking, inhibition of action, and a number of intrapsychic modes. These researchers suggest that these coping mechanisms may be activated in advance of the stress event or in response to it (Lazarus, 1975). Some of these mechanisms may be highly effective where others will be ineffective. The most important "trick" to coping appears to be the ability to discern correctly which environmental forces can be mitigated and which must be accepted and adapted to. Table 20.2 summarizes some preventive strategies. For more about preschool stress prevention, see Chapters 7, 10, 12, 14, 16, 17, and 19.

CASE EXAMPLE

A 3 1/2-year-old boy was referred for treatment following complaints by his preschool teacher of disruptive outbursts during which he reportedly threatened to "kill" his father. The child's mother reported several incidents of destructive behavior dating back to the father's abrupt abandonment of the household. She also reported sleeping disturbances, a tendency to engage in sudden, inexplicable silences, and a particular fascination for playing with fire.

The child was living with his mother. The parents had been through multiple separations during the two years prior to therapy. The parents were unmarried at the time of conception, the pregnancy was unplanned, and the mother reported she had considered abortion throughout the gestation period. As a result of family pressure, she finally married the father in her seventh month of pregnancy. She had abused alcohol and amphetamines sporadically during the pregnancy, and had felt deeply depressed from the fifth month of pregnancy until at least the second month after the boy's birth. She also discussed her disappointment in having a son instead of a daughter.

According to the mother, the father lived with the family sporadically

TABLE 20.2. *Preventive Strategies.* Preventive strategies and tactics include data gathering and interventions. Sometimes the data gathering is an intervention in itself, by calling attention to some issue.

1. Identify the qualities of the child's relationship to his caregivers that may hinder adaptation (e.g., insecurity in the attachment relationship) or the qualities that enhance adaptation (e.g., security of the attachment relationship).
2. Identify the temperamental dimensions that may hinder adaptation (e.g., negative mood) and those that enhance adaptation (e.g., persistence).
3. Utilize and optimize the child's relationship to pediatrician and nursery personnel, all of whom mobilize the effectiveness of the child's most powerful preventive asset—a competent caregiver.
4. Identify buffers (e.g., extended family) against stressful events.
5. Obtain information from multiple sources about the child's coping repertoire shown during past stressful events.
6. Identify and reinforce coping successes: goals that have been reached.
7. Reinforce adaptive expectations about future events (e.g., if mommy dies, Aunt Jane will care for child; or if abused again, child will know how to escape and call for help).
8. Delineate behavioral diffusion that emerged from negative expectations.
9. Identify the parental characteristics (e.g., affectively disordered parents) that influence the child's ability to cope with stressors.
10. Define the current sources of social support (including networks of social and professional assistance) available to the family.
11. Review the reactions of the child and the child's family to physical illness and other stressors.
12. Control for timing and awareness of stressor threats; titrate child's exposure to necessary stressors when possible (e.g., with preliminary desensitization exposures).

during the first three years of the child's life. The parent's marital relationship was stormy, punctuated with frequent and often violent fights. The child witnessed several fights during which his father would both physically and verbally abuse his mother. On one occasion, during a period of separation, the child and his mother returned home to discover that the father had burned the family photo album and other family mementos.

The child became fascinated with fire around the time his father first left the home. On one occasion, his mother discovered him trying to set his mattress afire; on another, she found him throwing balls of burning paper out of the window. Several weeks later, she found him attempting to burn a toy soldier. When the child exhibited behavioral outbursts or played with fire, his mother devised a method of "calming him down." Bringing the child into the bedroom, she would lie with him on the bed, holding him, singing songs, and stroking his back and hair. This technique appeared to soothe him so that he often fell asleep in her arms. The mother also exercised with the child in her bedroom, after which she would shower while he would lie in bed and "wait" for her.

During the initial interview, the child was reticent about communicating with the therapist, although he would intermittently smile directly and seductively bat his eyelashes at the male therapist. He was cooperative about drawing pictures, which were comprised of animals and humans such as a wrestler with exaggerated teeth and large, clenched fists. During the first few months of treatment, he revealed his preoccupation with fire by relating several dreams involving burning houses and "children laughing." He hit the therapist when not allowed to do something.

As treatment progressed, the therapist worked to establish a therapeutic alliance. One day in the third month of therapy, the child entered the office without greeting and moved immediately to the toy cabinet. Slowly and systematically, he removed several toys and showed them one by one to the therapist. After the therapist commented upon each toy, the child replaced it in the cabinet and removed another. The therapist began to verbalize the child's behavior, suggesting that the child's motions seemed to be an exercise in concealing and revealing.

This behavior was key in establishing the transference bond. The child felt able to trust the therapist, as evidenced by the fact that during the session immediately following the toy-revealing session, the child displayed the first of his three forms of suicide-like behavior. At the beginning of the session, he entered the office appearing agitated and disoriented. For the first few minutes he pounded the blackboard eraser against the blackboard, ignoring the therapist and chanting "it won't erase, it won't erase," while clouds of chalk enveloped him. As the chalk dust became more dense, the child blurted out, "I burned my finger on Daddy's cigarette." The therapist asked to see the injury and the child approached cautiously, showing a fresh scar on his index finger. The child then jerked his finger away and began to talk of "fire engines" he had heard the previous night and of a dream featuring, cops, robbers, firemen, and magic snakes. Then he rose abruptly and without warning ran to the window, hurled himself against the sill, and yelled, "I'm going to jump" several times in rapid succession. When the therapist approached him and inquired about the incident, he appeared oblivious to the inquiry. Eventually, he left the window, returned to the play area and began to play calmly with a toy truck.

The window-running scenario continued intermittently for the next several months and then gradually abated, eventually replaced by the child walking slowly to the window and quietly gazing out. When asked about what he was doing, he would reply that he was "looking for Daddy." During the child's second year of treatment, a repetitive fantasy about knives surfaced. The child commented on how he had cut himself in the abdomen while raising his shirt and tracing an imaginary scar. When questioned about the incident, he replied that the injury was accidental, because the knife just "popped up" in his hands. This fantasy diminished by the end of the second year of treatment, when the patient reported that his father had taught him "karate" to "block the knife" and keep it from "hurting people."

During the third and final year of treatment, the child engaged in his own version of the Goldilocks fairy tale. He would recount the story to the therapist, emphasizing the details involving Goldilock's ability to find a place that was "just right" for her within the Bear's household. At the tale's conclusion, the child would approach the therapist enthusiastically and urge him to repeat in unison the phrase "just right." By this juncture, both parental and teacher reports indicated that the child's disruptive outbursts and profanity had ceased, and the "window crashing" behavior and fire and knife fantasies had abated. Shortly thereafter, psychotherapy was terminated, although monthly reassessments were maintained.

Discussion of the Stressors and Psychodynamic Intervention in the Case

This child had experienced several stressors: gestational drugs, paternal abandonment, parental marital strife, paternal abuse, maternal rejection, seductive enmeshment, and physical trauma. Child therapy is particularly prone to evoking countertransference (Kohrman et al., 1971). As Kohrman and co-workers note, children's instinctual drives are frequently conveyed actively, which in turn evokes a potent response in the therapist. Initially, the child in the above case history conversed little with the therapist, yet intermittently approached the therapist seductively, thereby revealing his tendency to engage in manipulative behavior in order to achieve drive gratification. In the first few months of therapy, these behaviors, as well as physically hitting the therapist, were observed in the child whenever he was not allowed to do something or told his behavior was unacceptable.

The child's extreme expression of his drives evoked an intense countertransference response in the therapist. Overidentification, in which the therapist identifies so strongly with the child's plight and vulnerabilities that a protective relationship develops which threatens the therapeutic relationship, was a strong factor in the case. Here, the therapist, discovering his overidentification with the child's problems within the first few months of treatment, was forced to resurrect his own childhood memories and analyze his feelings in an attempt to understand why this overidentification had arisen at that particular juncture in the treatment. Overidentification occurred here because the therapist, like the patient, was also a younger son. Because of the intensity of this countertransference reaction, constant analysis and interpretation of such feelings by the therapist was key in maintaining the therapeutic relationship.

Events in the child's life and family situation may have influenced his maladaptive development. Such stressors as the parents' separation, the accompanying loss of his father, and the highly enmeshed, subtly seductive relationship with his mother, were factors in the development of his symptoms. His mother's depression during pregnancy and her disappointment with his sex may have fostered an ambivalence toward him which undermined attachment, thus hindering both his ability to separate and individuate from her and the development of adequate coping mechanisms to deal with the various stressors in his life. For this child, completed suicide would seem to offer a means to separate from his mother, a means which would parallel his father's abrupt departure from the family.

The child's suicidal tendencies can also be examined in light of the Oedipal conflict (S. Freud, 1912, 1913, 1923, 1930). The child may have feared that the father, upon discovering the extreme enmeshment he shared with his mother, would retaliate violently, destroying any chance for identification between the child and mother. Self-destructive behaviors would provide him with an opportunity to free himself from his overattachment to his mother, thereby allowing him to both relieve sexual desires for her and reunite with his father.

Feelings of lack of control, described in Seligman's (1975) model of learned helplessness, were an additional factor in the child's psychopathology. The child, repeatedly subjected to uncontrollable stressors, internalized feelings of incapacity and lack of control over his environment. This lack of control made him subject to periodic overwhelming feelings of depression and helplessness, and, in turn, these feelings of helplessness manifested as confusion, disorientation, and lack of interest in academic pursuits. The child began engaging in self-destructive behaviors in an attempt to experience a sense of internal control.

The therapist focused on treatment strategies that allowed the child to comprehend the consequences of his self-destructive behavior and helped him learn alternative methods for managing the negative feelings that propelled him toward such suicide-like behavior.

A preschooler's concept of death, as documented by Piaget (1976) and Speece and Brent (1984), does not include an understanding of the irreversibility and finality of death. The therapist therefore needed to expand the child's cognitive capabilities, so that the child would be able to comprehend the unchangeable consequences of his self-destructive fantasies.

To aid this comprehension, the therapist primarily engaged in verbal exchange. When the child expressed a desire to jump from the window, the therapist would respond with questions about such an act's outcome, reasoning with the child and sharing perceptions about such results. This gentle motivation, stimulating better coordination of the child's cognitive abilities, enabled him to progress from a conception of reparable damage to one in which the damage could be permanent and irreparable.

Play videotapes were used to circumvent the child's limited understanding of death. When the child announced a desire to jump from the window, the therapist would give the child a doll, occasionally allowing him to throw it from the window. Using videotapes to record these events, the therapist and child would leave the room to retrieve the doll. The therapist would then initiate a discussion of the doll's damage, comparing the doll to the child under the same circumstances. The videotape would then be reviewed and discussed later, with the therapist keying in specifically on the child's feelings prior to the urge to jump, his feelings regarding the empty office, and finally, his feelings about the reconstruction of the broken doll. These dialogues helped the child identify the feelings that precipitated his self-destructive impulses. In addition, the therapist encouraged the supportive efforts of the caregiver by alerting her to episodes that would trigger stress in her son.

The continued reality-testing by the child during the therapeutic sessions combined with his increased cognitive capabilities to enable him to identify the emotions which triggered his self-destructive impulses. By replacing these impulses with less damaging alternatives, the child was able to construct new strategies that ultimately enabled him to respond adaptively to his frustrations and limitations.

CONCLUSION

Psychotherapy offers young children the opportunity to communicate their inner thoughts and feelings in a predictable and empathic environment. Within the psychotherapeutic setting, the child is given free reign to practice and master such skills as separating fantasy from reality, regulating affect, and controlling impulse processes. In turn, the exercise of these skills fosters individuation. By helping the child to regulate emotional states, therapy serves to promote adaptive development of the social, emotional, and cognitive spheres. Play therapy, an important psychotherapeutic strategy for preschoolers, simultaneously offers children a fertile means to represent their innermost feelings and fantasies while also providing the therapist with insight into the child's inner reality.

The therapist, by both supporting and interpreting behaviors during treatment, facilitates the child's disclosure of subconscious feelings and thoughts. The discussion of such phenomena by the therapist allows the child to reason about them and to develop insights into their cause and effect. The gradual enhancement of adaptive, cognitive, and affective skills that emerges through psychotherapeutic treatment helps the child to cope progressively within the developmental challenges that surface as the child progresses to adolescence.

A major technique used within the therapeutic setting to promote change is the interpretation of transference and countertransference phenomena. In this respect, individual psychotherapy with children is not radically different from such therapy conducted with adults. Transference reactions—the unconscious projection of the child's thoughts and feelings onto the therapist—enable the therapist to gain access to the core of psychological conflict, thus providing a basis for interpretation. Positive transference reactions also serve to forge a therapeutic alliance between therapist and child—a process indispensable for reducing the child's resistance to intervention.

REFERENCES

Amster, F. (1964). Differential uses of play in treatment of young children. In M. R. Haworth (Ed.), *Child psychotherapy: Practice and theory*. New York: Basic Books.

Berlin, I. N. (1987). Some transference and countertransference issues in the playroom. *Journal of the American Academy of Child and Adolescent Psychiatry, 26,* 101–107.

Bick, E. (1962). Symposium on child analysis: I. Child analysis today. *International Journal of Psychoanalysis, 43,* 328–332.

Campbell, S. B. (1986). Parent-initiated problem preschoolers: Mother-child interaction during play at intake and 1-year follow-up. *Journal of Abnormal Child Psychology, 14,* 425–440.

Campbell, M., & Spencer, E. K. (1988). Psychopharmacology in child and adolescent psychiatry: A review of the past five years. *Psychopharmacology in Child Psychiatry, 27,* 269–279.

Carek, D. J. (1979). Individual psychodynamically oriented therapy. In S. I. Harrison (Ed.), *Basic handbook of child psychiatry* (Vol. 3, pp. 35–57). New York: Basic Books.

Cocchi, R. (1980). Psychopharmacotherapy of anxiety in the first years of life. *Third Symposium de psychopharmacologie Smolennice,* 20–22 October.

Dewald, P. A. (1983). Elements of change and cure in psychoanalysis. *Archives of General Psychology, 40,* 89–95.

Ekstein, R. (1983). Play therapy for borderline children. In C. E. Schaefer & K. J. O'Connor (Eds.), *Handbook of play therapy* (pp. 412–418). New York: Wiley.

Elkind, D. (1986). David Elkind discusses parental pressures. *Pediatric Nursing, 12,* 417–418.

Elkish, P. (1953). Simultaneous treatment of a child and his mother. *American Journal of Psychotherapy, 7,* 105–130.

Elliott, C., & Ozolins, M. (1983). Use of imagery and imagination in treatment of children. In C. E. Waler & M. C. Roberts (Eds.), *Handbook of clinical psychology* (pp. 1026–1049). New York: Wiley.

Erikson, E. (1950). *Childhood and society.* New York: Norton.

Eskilson, A., Wiley, M. G., Muehlbauer, G., & Dodder, L. (1986). Parental pressure, self-esteem and adolescent reported deviance: bending the twig too far. *Adolescence, 83,* 501–515.

Esman, A. (1983). Psychoanalytic play therapy. In C. Schaefer & K. O'Connor (Eds.), *Handbook of play therapy* (pp. 11–20). New York: Wiley.

Fraiberg, S. (1962). Technical aspects of the analysis of a child with a severe behavior disorder. *Journal of the American Psychoanalytic Association, 10,* 338–367.

Frankl, L., & Hellman, I. (1964). The ego's participation in the therapeutic alliance. In M. R. Haworth (Ed.), *Child psychotherapy: Practice and theory* (pp. 229–235). New York: Basic Books.

Freedheim, D. K., & Russ, S. R. (1983). Psychotherapy with children. In C. E. Walker & M. C. Roberts (Eds.), *Handbook of clinical child psychology* (pp. 978–994). New York: Wiley.

Freud, A. (1928). Introduction to the technique of child analysis. *Nervous and Mental Disease Monograph Series, 48,* 30–41.

Freud, A. (1966). *The ego and the mechanisms of defense.* New York: International Universities Press.

Freud, S. (1905). Three essays on the theory of sexuality. *Standard Edition, 7.*

Freud, S. (1909). Creative writers and day-dreaming. *Standard Edition, 9,* 141–153.

Freud, S. (1912). On the universal tendency to the debasement in the sphere of love. *Standard Edition, 11,* 178–190.

Freud, S. (1913). Totem and taboo. *Standard Edition, 13,* 140–161.

Freud, S. (1920). Beyond the pleasure principle. *Standard Edition, 18,* 7–64.

Freud, S. (1923). The ego and the id. *Standard Edition, 19,* 57–59.

Freud, S. (1930). Civilization and its discontents. *Standard Edition, 21,* 64–132.

Freud, S. (1933). New introductory lectures on psycho-analysis. *Standard Edition, 22,* 81–111.

Gallagher, J. J., Beckman, P., & Cross, A. H. (1983). Families of handicapped children: Sources of stress and its amelioration. *Exceptional Children, 50,* 10–19.

Gardner, R. A. (1979). Helping children cooperate in therapy. In J. D. Noshpitz & S. I. Harrison (Eds.), *Basic handbook of child psychiatry* (Vol. 3, pp. 414–432). New York: Basic Books.

Graudins, A., & Harris, M. J. (1985). The care of older children when a sibling is born. *Australian and New Zealand Journal of Obstetrics and Gynaecology, 25*(1), 74–76.

Harter, S. (1983). Cognitive-developmental perspectives on self-esteem. In E. M. Hetherington (Ed.), *Socialization, personality, and social development. Vol. 4. Handbook of child psychiatry* (pp. 275–385). New York: Wiley.

Heilveil, I. (1983). *Video in mental health practice.* New York: Springer-Verlag.

Kaplan, C. J. (1987). Children's responses to the loss of a parent: The interaction between the family and the intrapsychic mourning process. *Dissertation Abstracts International, 47*(9-B), 3959.

Kohrman, R., Fineberg, H., Gerlman, R. L., & Weiss, S. (1971). Technique of child analysis: Problems of countertransference. *International Journal of Psycho-Analysis, 52,* 487–497.

Lazarus, R. B. (1975). A cognitively oriented psychologist looks at biofeedback. *American Psychologist, 30,* 553–561.

Lazarus, R. S., & Launier, R. (1978). Stress-related transactions between person and environment. In L. A. Pervin & M. Lewis (Eds.), *Perspectives in interactional psychology* (pp. 287–327). New York: Plenum.

Lewis, M. (1974). Interpretation in child analysis. *Journal of Child Psychiatry, 13,* 32–53.

Levy, D. (1938). Release therapy in young children. *Psychiatry, 1,* 387–390.

Levy, D. (1939). Release therapy. *American Journal of Orthopsychiatry, 9,* 713–736.

Levy, D. (1945). Psychic trauma of operations in children and a note on combat neurosis. *American Journal of Diseases of Children, 69,* 7–25.

Liebowitz, J. H., & Kernberg, P. F. (1988). Psychodynamic psychotherapies. In C. J. Kestenbaum & D. T. Williams (Eds.), *Handbook of clinical assessment of children and adolescents* (pp. 1045–1065). New York: New York University Press.

Lowenstein, R. M. (1951). The problem of interpretation. *Psychoanalytic Quarterly, 20,* 1–14.

Mahler, M. S. (1968). *On human symbiosis and the vicissitudes of individuation.* New York: International Universities Press.

Mahler, M. S., Pine, F., & Bergman, A. (1975). *The psychological birth of the human infant.* New York: Basic Books.

Markowitz, J. (1959). The nature of the child's initial resistances to psychotherapy. *Social Work, 4,* 40–52.

Masten, A. S. (1985). Stress, coping and children's health. *Pediatric Annals, 14*(8), 543–547.

Mishne, J. M. (1983). *Clinical work with children.* New York: Free Press.

Negley-Parker, E., & Araoz, D. L. (1986). Hypnotherapy with families of chronically ill children. *International Journal of Psychosomatics, 33*(2), 9–11.

Neubauer, P. (1980). The life cycle as indicated by the nature of the transference in the psychoanalysis of children. *International Journal of Psycho-Analysis, 61,* 137–144.

Piaget, J. (1976). *The psychology of intelligence.* Totowa, NJ: Littlefield, Adams.

Piaget, J., & Inhelder, B. (1971). *Mental imagery in the child.* New York: Basic Books.

Ritvo, S. (1978). The psychoanalytic process in childhood. *Psychoanalytic Study of the Child, 33,* 295–305.

Roskies, E., & Lazarus, R. (1980). Coping theory and the teaching of coping skills. In P. Davidson & S. M. Davidson (Eds.), *Banff International Conference on Behavior*

Modification: Behavioral medicine: Changing health lifestyles (pp. 38–69). New York: Brunner/Mazel.

Seligman, M. E. P. (1975). *Helplessness: On depression, development and death.* San Francisco: Freeman.

Smirnoff, V. (1971). *The scope of child analysis.* New York: International Universities Press.

Speece, M. W., & Brent, S. B. (1984). Children's understanding of death: A review of three components of a death concept. *Child Development, 55,* 1671–1686.

Stein, H. F. (1985a). The ebb and flow of the clinical relationship. In H. F. Stein & M. Apprey (Eds.), *Series in ethnicity, medicine, and psychoanalysis: Vol. I. Context and dynamics in clinical knowledge* (pp. 211–220). Charlottesville: University Press of Virginia.

Stein, H. F. (1985b). Physician self-insight as a tool of patient care: A case study of behavioral science supervision in family medicine. In H. F. Stein & M. Apprey (Eds.), *Series in ethnicity, medicine, and psychoanalysis: Vol. I. Context and dynamics in clinical knowledge* (pp. 56–77). Charlottesville: University Press of Virginia.

Stein, H. F. (1985c). Whatever happened to countertransference? The subjective in medicine. In H. F. Stein & M. Apprey (Eds.), *Series in ethnicity, medicine, and psychoanalysis: Vol. I. Context and dynamics in clinical knowledge* (pp. 1–55). Charlottesville: University Press of Virginia.

Terr, L. (1979). Children of Chowchilla: A study of psychic trauma. *Psychoanalytic Study of the Child, 34,* 547–623.

Terr, L. (1981a). Psychic trauma in children: Observations following the Chowchilla schoolbus kidnapping. *American Journal of Psychiatry, 138,* 14–19.

Terr, L. (1981b). Forbidden games: post-traumatic child's play. *Journal of the American Academy of Child Psychiatry, 20,* 741–760.

Tower, R. B., & Singer, J. L. (1981). The measurement of imagery: How can it be clinically useful? In P. C. Kendall & S. Hollon (Eds.), *Assessment methods for cognitive-behavioral interventions* (pp. 265–281). New York: Academic.

Trad, P. V. (1989). *The preschool child.* New York: Wiley.

Trad, P. V. (1990). *Infant previewing: Predicting and sharing interpersonal outcome.* New York: Springer-Verlag.

Tyson, R. L., & Tyson, P. (1986). The concept of transference in child psychoanalysis. *Journal of the American Academy of Child Psychiatry, 25*(1), 30–39.

Wilkins, W. (1974). Parameters of therapeutic imagery: Directions from case studies. *Psychotherapy: Theory, Research, and Practice, 11*(2), 163–171.

Winnicott, D. W. (1949). Hate in the counter-transference. *International Journal of Psycho-Analysis, 30,* 69–74.

CHAPTER TWENTY-ONE

Prevention and Treatment of School-Age and Adolescent Stress Disorders

Joseph D. Noshpitz

The nature of stress is complex. Only by understanding some of the complexity can one hope eventually to reach the simplifying generalizations that must underlie any rational attempt at intervention, whether preventive or therapeutic.

BACKGROUND COMPLEXITIES OF STRESS

The essence of stress is *perceptual-experiential.* The stress value of an event must be measured in terms of its meaning to a given individual or group. What is catastrophic to one boy or girl may be a source of pleasurable excitement to another. Thus, stress is in the mind's eye of the experiencer. What determines the meaning of an event derives from the interplay of the child's unique heritage and the context within which that child has developed. On one level, the genetic distribution of the great variety of human traits (or dispositions) will determine some portion of the child's vulnerability. On another, the vagaries of circumstance and environment will make for given states of greater or lesser capacity to cope.

Wholesome experience does not imply an absence of stress. Indeed, an optimum level of stress is biologically and psychologically necessary. This is visible on the simple level of large muscle tone: without the right amount of challenge, muscles grow flabby and soon atrophy. Albeit less easy to document, a similar relationship seems to hold true for cognitive functions, talents, and the human spirit in general—a certain level of stress is necessary for growth. To grow well, it is important for children to learn, and learning may be demanding; it may involve discipline, anxiety, tension, application, occasional failure, and various degrees of social challenge.

Moreover, not only is stress necessary, but also some forms of it can be desired and sought out. Certain types of stress are associated with pleasure, e.g., many forms of athletics or exhilarating (terrifying?) amusement park rides or seeing a horror movie. All of these may indeed be stressful, but may be exciting and sensuously rewarding to the point that one is willing to pay for the experience. Hence, in arriving at a definition of stress, we must be careful to define the range of stressors.

Clinical Stress Definition

Our concern here is with stress that has clinical implications: stress that affects physical and mental health, produces unwanted and unwholesome suffering, and thwarts optimal growth. Putting the many qualifiers and exceptions aside for the moment, we come to the following definition: clinical stress is a deforming force in a child's life that begets undue pain and/or produces growth-impeding deformity in the child's development. In general, all subsequent reference to stress in the following material should be understood to mean clinical stress.

Attributes and Variables of Clinical Stress

Quality and Quantity. Stress may be of either macro or micro proportions. On the macro level, there is encounter with fire, flood, tornado, hurricane, earthquake, volcanic eruption, or other natural disasters; perhaps even more mordantly, there is the experience of human assault, as in wartime, child battering, sexual abuse, rape, kidnapping, or other forms of violent victimization.

On the micro level, in an average home, let us consider a case where the 7-year-old gets excited in some game he is playing at home. He knocks over mother's favorite vase, which shatters on the floor. The resultant maternal reaction and the ensuing interplay between mother and son will never be recorded in the newspapers or perhaps even recalled later as an item to report to the mental health professional. Nonetheless, the traumatic impact on the child might be considerable.

Timing. Stress may be acute, usually deriving from a single major event, such as one of the natural disasters or human assaults listed above; or it may be chronic, which usually implies a recurrent sequence of microevents, e.g., a pattern of malicious teasing, repeated critical outbursts by an irritable parent, or longstanding victimization by a bullying family member or peer. However, under conditions of severe socioeconomic deprivation, the recurrent events that comprise the chronic stress may again and again be of major character, e.g., in a single week, a 12-year-old girl may learn of an eviction notice served on her family, be suspended from school for fighting, have the police come to her house because of a violent family quarrel, and be attacked sexually by a drunken member of her household. Several serious mental health syndromes have been linked to such chronic stress, including multiple personality (Putnam, 19) and conduct disorder (Patterson, 1983). Acute stresses, of course, are causally linked to adjustment disorder and to post-traumatic stress disorder; depression is known to follow both acute and chronic stress experiences.

Analogy to Physical Stress. Stress has a physical meaning which captures something of the kernel of its general realm of psychological applicability. In physics, stress implies a deforming force visited on a resistant object. If the force is sufficiently powerful, the object will lose its original form and take on a new configuration in response to the pressures impinging upon it. Most objects, however, have a certain quality of "give" or elasticity, which allows them to resist the effects of the stress and spring back toward the original shape.

This brings us to our next definition, *resiliency*. This term describes the ability to regain original form after the stressor is removed. In effect, it depicts a child's elasticity, his or her capacity for spontaneous recovery.

This brings us to another important term, *vulnerability*, which has two dimensions. One is the degree of deformity an object may undergo in the face of a given stress; objects composed of differing materials or structured in different fashions will deform uniquely in keeping with their inherent nature. Indeed, some objects may shatter rather than merely deform, whereas others subjected to the same degree of deforming stress may seem unaffected. The other dimension of vulnerability is the degree of residual deformation that persists after the stress is removed. Thus, a glass that falls to the floor may show no evident change, yet a fault line may have been set up in its crystalline structure which will subsequently cause it to shatter in the face of a second stress, even a minor one.

Risk. This is another term with two dimensions. One is the likelihood of encountering a given stress (e.g., the risk of encountering a life-threatening flood within the confines of New York City is exceedingly small); the other is the likelihood of undergoing permanent deformity in the face of that stress (e.g., a young child who is kidnapped is likely to be permanently affected by that experience).

Interaction of Variables. It might be illuminating to look at how Patterson (1983) traces the etiology of conduct disorder to the experience of chronic stress. He recognizes that for conduct disorder to appear, the child must possess an inherent array of particular traits. However, the actual manifestation of the condition depends on an ongoing interactive process between the child and the primary caretaker. By disposition, the child may tend to initiate aggressive reactions from the family, but it is only when the family responds in aggressive and retaliatory ways—provoking more of the same reaction from the child and more of the same response from the family in an ascending spiral—that the full feedback cycle gets established and the conduct disorder takes form. Indeed, Patterson (1981, 1982, 1983) has been able to demonstrate that ". . . the greater the likelihood the parent will react irritably, the greater the likelihood the child will display high rates of social aggression" (1983, p. 236).

PREVENTION

How is society to prevent children from experiencing undue and deforming stresses? What shall we seek to prevent, for whom, and how shall we go about it?

There are two systems within the larger social framework where professionals interact routinely with school-age children: the school system and the national network of pediatric care. Each of these is an obvious site for potential encounter and evaluation. The implication of this is that increased training in stress assessment can be added to the preparation of both teachers and pediatricians. This currently is coming about piecemeal. Teachers, for example, are being given some background in evidences of child abuse, both violent and sexual. They are learning what evidence to mark as significant if it thrusts itself on their attention, and they are learning to what channels to turn when such indications appear. Pediatricians are diagnosing Attention-deficit Hyperactivity Disorder with some regularity and are beginning to notice depression. Clearly a major focus of training in both disciplines should be how to discern the expressions of stress in childhood, and when and how to refer children for further evaluation when such evidence appears.

In many instances, the key observation is a change in the child's demeanor from a reasonably comfortable status to one that suggests disturbance. This can be physical, as in marked weight loss or weight gain; it can be physiological, as in unwonted sleepiness or hyperactivity. It can be cognitive: a falling off in schoolwork or unusual concern and worry about schoolwork; or attentional: inability to concentrate or obsessive preoccupation with tasks that previously could be handled easily. It can be affective, as when the formerly comfortable child displays evident sadness and tearfulness, avoidance and fearfulness, irritability punctuated by unexpected outbursts of rage, or an unprovoked and unusual level of excitement. Or it can be behavioral, as when a conduct disorder appears, with provocativeness and serious aggression. Sometimes strikingly symptomatic behavior becomes manifest: the child starts to masturbate in class, to engage in bizarre antics, to talk continuously despite reproof, or to be unable to stay seated. Such symptomatic behaviors are commonly observed in classrooms and are responded to in highly diverse ways. They should be referred to a mental health professional.

Levels of Prevention and Criteria

Prevention is usually thought of as occurring on three levels. Primary prevention is the anticipatory activity that precedes the potential appearance of the trauma; it is truly preventive in that it avoids the occurrence of the disturbing event. Its effectiveness is measured by the degree to which target behaviors (e.g., drunk driving) do *not* appear. Secondary prevention implies catching some condition early and intervening so that it does not continue or get worse. Tertiary prevention is the management of a full-blown condition so that it does not develop complications or deteriorate further.

In the realm of mental health practice, primary prevention has two distinct sublevels. The first sublevel involves the *larger social dimension,* such as the availability and quality of housing, employment, nutrition, health care, retirement benefits, unemployment insurance, and the like. These are of the essence; it is fruitless to identify or try to treat a child's mental health problem when the patient's family is homeless, starving, or in a state of chronic alarm because of realistic threats to its existence. Of course, these factors do not, by and large, fall within the province of mental health practice. For example, special services such as health clinics for pregnant adolescent girls or special classes for mentally retarded children are matters of social policy and are not implemented by mental health professionals. Surely any given practitioner may be an advocate for appropriate social policies; it is not likely, however, that mental health practitioners would have been trained in their design or implementation.

A second sublevel of primary prevention involves *special projects.* It is here that the efforts of mental health practitioners can find more ready expression. Realistically, however, the skills involved may be at the farthest reaches of these practitioners' original training. In the typical training environment, the learning experiences most intimately involved with preventive efforts would have been present in some programs but not in others (e.g., the trainee conducting a junior high school class in how to handle one's feelings); when present, they are likely to have been taught only as electives; and by and large, they would have been regarded as peripheral to one's core skills.

Any such prevention project must start with a target symptom and a theory of causality as to what brings that symptom about—what makes a child become learning disabled, or delinquent, or addicted, or pregnant, or a victim of abuse? It must then include a series of communicable techniques to deal with the target behavior. These techiques will have to have certain essential characteristics, among which are that they be reasonably cost efficient, teachable to mental health aides, and acceptable to the community. Many other elements will have to be present as well—cost control, ethical issues, clinical backup, etc.; among them a *sine qua non* is that there must be some way to establish whether or not the desired result has been attained. To date, merely stating what these many elements are and how they may be brought to bear in a given program has by no means been easy to accomplish. In fact, rarely has the formulation, much less the actual implementation, of such a mental health prevention program been accomplished. Many projects have been undertaken, but few would pass critical scrutiny.

Primary Prevention

Many nagging questions remain: which problems to address, whom to work with, how to work with them, what goals to strive for, and how to know if what one has done has any merit. All this was considered recently by a task force appointed by the American Psychological Association (Price et al., 1989). Designated as the APA Task Force on Promotion, Prevention, and Intervention Alternatives, it set itself the goal of review-ing all preventive programs it could learn about. The APA Task Force included in its evaluation each program's theory of causality, population addressed, mode of intervention assayed, the way the staff was recruited, the goals of the project, the evaluative design, the associated clinical issues, the community-relations dimension, the degree to which the tech-niques involved could be transferred to other settings, and the availabil-ity of both the professionals and non-professionals necessary to carry it out. Out of 900 projects surveyed, 52 emerged as meeting the criteria of the Task Force, and of those, 14 model programs were selected for the report. On the basis of this overview, the Task Force members concluded that careful evaluation of outcome was scarce—indeed, only about one-third of the initial 900 projects had even tried to accomplish such an evaluation. Even of the 52 programs selected for final screening, nearly a quarter lacked adequate follow-up.

The Task Force also commented on the fact that it is difficult to estimate cost/benefit ratios. After all, if taxpayers are asked to put out money today for a preschool program, how does one determine who ultimately gains and loses and how much? And how does one calculate the worth of the suffering or humiliation that the program might have prevented? But the bottom line of the study was that prevention works. It is definable, it is measurable, and it can be demonstrably effective. Such a conclusion is a major advance, and one worth celebrating.

Two of the 14 programs selected for review involved latency-age chil-dren; four others primarily involved adolescents. It is not surprising that both of the latency programs were school based. One was aimed at kindergarten children and first-graders, the other at 9- and 10-year-olds in the fourth and fifth grades. Each program involved a 12-week course; each sought to teach positive social skills and problem-solving behavior. For two hours each week, the fourth- and fifth-graders were given group-based social-skills and assertiveness training, reinforced by role-play techniques and discussions. The younger group of kindergartners and first-graders were in formal training programs threaded through the school day; they were taught how to deal with interpersonal problems and how to consider the consequences of their acts. In both projects, the follow-up demonstrated that there were solid benefits in academic achievement as well as in scores on personal/social adjustment.

As the associated technology matures, we should see a wealth of such endeavors appearing. Indeed, with a proper advance in public understanding over the ensuing decades, it is not too much to hope for that training in interpersonal skills and impulse regulation may in time become part of the normal school curriculum.

Practical Prevention: Injury as an Example

If we consider the crises that tend to occur during children's latency years, there are a number of sites where efforts at prevention are at least coherent and reasonable if not of demonstrated worth. The stresses of school, of home, and of neighborhood are all implicit in such a review. The multiple vicissitudes of family life, of peer interaction, of adaptation to authority, and of coping with cognitive requirements all merit address. To focus the discussion, let us arbitrarily select a fairly simple example as a model of the kind of thinking each aspect of childhood stress merits: the phenomenon of physical injury and its many consequences.

Historically, illness has been an obvious source of much distress, unhappiness, and, all too often, residual dysfunction in the lives of many children. During the twentieth century, antibiotics, clean milk and water, vaccination, better understanding of nutrition, and robust public health programs have banished such diseases as smallpox and polio. Hence, in recent years, injuries have emerged as the major threat to the integrity of child development (Institute of Medicine, 1985). Between the ages of 1 and 14 years, more than half (55%) of all deaths are due to injury (Margolis & Runyan, 1983). Even more important for our purposes are the permanent disabilities and the various degrees and kinds of emotional trauma that attend the more transient disabilities. In Chapter 12, O'Dougherty and Brown describe the stress consequences of illness and injury. Here we will discuss the prevention of the stressor.

Sources of Injury. Children sustain injuries from many sources, but perhaps the most destructive are those visited on the child by a caretaker. In planning prevention, one must draw a distinction between intended and inadvertent injuries. But even that distinction is too simple. One may bring about childhood injuries passively, by neglect, as well as actively, by assault. Parents who are neglectful or who are unconsciously resentful of the child will characteristically expose the youngster to the kinds of situations that make for "accidents." Thus, the distinction between the intentional and the happenstance tends to blur.

Garbarino (1988) divides childhood injuries into four types: those that occur randomly, those that are preventable, those due to negligence, and those occasioned by assault. Random accidents are those visited on a child by genuine happenstance (e.g., the child is in the back seat of a properly driven car that is struck by another car whose driver has had a stroke). In contrast to random accidents, preventable accidents attain that status by social definition. Events such as a child running out into the street after a ball and into the path of an oncoming vehicle were once considered inevitable products of chance; now, however, they often are regarded as the product of poor child training or neighborhood planning. Children can be taught to behave safely in relation to streets, and limited speed zones can be instituted where high concentrations of children exist. This moves us toward the third category, childhood injury due to negligence. An adult who does not insist that the child put on a seat belt might well be regarded as negligent. The latch-key child is vulnerable to the consequences of unsupervised behavior at home with access to knives, gas, or electricity. Or a child might be provided with an all-terrain vehicle by indulgent parents despite a known record of dangerous accidents associated with that vehicle. The parental motivation, of course, might be quite complex. The fourth category of childhood injury, child abuse, both violent and sexual, is discussed in detail in Chapter 10.

The sources of risk are many. Some arise from the environment (e.g., inadequately patroled high-speed highways near residential neighborhoods), and some from dangerous child behavior (e.g., adolescents crowded into a car with spirits high and beer flowing freely). Other sources are mismanagement and assaults, including neglectful and abusive behavior by both the immediate family and others (pedophiles, vengeful gang members, etc.). Overall, something like 10% to 14% of children are assaulted each year in potentially serious ways. Of the many children who suffer fatal accidents each year, in-depth investigations show that elements of neglect and assault frequently are present.

Interventions. How can a community respond to such a set of circumstances? It is possible to do so on three levels. The focus of efforts can be directed toward the community itself, toward the caregiver, or toward the child.

Community endeavors may take the form of legislation, such as laws banning corporal punishment in the public schools, regulations requiring the reporting of child abuse, or stipulations about how old one must be before being permitted to drive. A second means of community address is through the mass media: TV spots illustrating how children should behave when approached by strangers, the importance of having and using seat belts, etc. Programs of public information can be launched targeting specific behaviors (e.g., how to prevent drunk driving, or how to avoid contracting AIDS) and supported by the distribution of comic books, videocassettes, posters, and similar visual communications. Yet another approach involves group instruction, such as free workshops, classes, and discussion groups offered to families and children. Finally, the slowest but possibly most effective means of conveying the safety message is on a case-by-case basis: giving each individual youngster both training and instruction in significant areas of safety. Thus, children can be taught individually how to deal with the telephone, both in terms of coping with dubious callers and in terms of contacting emergency services.

Some care needs to be taken in selecting the *targets for preventive efforts*. A great hullabaloo is made about children being kidnapped by strangers, yet that is rather a rare occurrence—Garbarino (1988) cites less than 80 cases a year—whereas thousands of children are kidnapped annually by estranged parents. Familiar but unrelated males, such as boyfriends of unmarried mothers, male baby sitters, and stepfathers, account for a heavily disproportionate number of child assaults and acts of negligence, yet there is almost no concentration on that population as a target for preventive efforts (Daly & Wilson, 1985).

If one turns to *behavior that the children themselves initiate,* a major source of injuries in childhood is vehicle use. In the 5- to 14-year age range, a principal danger is bicycles. Children can learn to balance themselves and stay aboard a bicycle a good deal earlier than they can navigate safely through traffic or handle themselves well in emergencies. Bicycles are sometimes deceptively easy to manage; the illusion of control is often greater than the actual mastery achieved. For the older teenager, the car is the principal source of injury and death. A quantitative estimate of the degree of such vulnerability is found in the additional premium added to a family auto insurance policy when a teenager is added to the list of drivers. This is not an argument for doing away with bicycles or cars, though it might well be a rationale for developing mass educational programs about bicycle safety or for raising the driving age.

Summary of Stress Prevention Principles

Having studied this one example, let us summarize the import of the preventive message. To prevent childhood trauma, one must consider both general measures and specific modalities of action. General measures involve better demographic surveys, better case finding, and better training of those community service deliverers who contact children and families (e.g., teachers, pediatricians, welfare workers, certain volunteers, etc.). The specific modalities, on the other hand, take form as projects designed to address predetermined issues. Such a project would focus on one of the many specific sources of distress; isolate a target problem; identify a vulnerable target population; analyze the factors contributing to that specific kind of stress; design a program that rationally could be expected to help youngsters avoid that kind of experience (e.g., driving when drunk, becoming pregnant out of wedlock, setting fires, etc.); work with the community so that the project will have understanding, acceptance, and support; institute measures to determine the effectiveness of the approach employed (matched controls, follow-up of both groups for a number of years, means for ascertaining whether or not the target behavior was indeed avoided, such as questionnaires, periodic structured interviews, or checking court records); maintain the records that would allow for adequate determination of cost/benefit ratios; and make the findings—positive or negative—available to the larger professional community. It is the accumulated wisdom and efforts of many interveners that ultimately will give rise to the necessary strategies to avoid much preventable childhood stress.

Stress Prevention in Adolescence

Although we will examine society's role in engendering stress in adolescence, it should be kept in mind that the developmental epoch itself is inherently a time of change and often of turmoil. The achievement of fertility and of full physical prowess, the arrival at the capacity to think abstractly, the flowering of talents, the natural tendency to reexplore the superego and its precepts, the need to achieve autonomy while still being socially and economically dependent, all these and more make for a state of uncertainty and multipotentiality. With these dilemmas come attempts at solution: inevitable cross-purposes between teenagers and caretakers, a measure of family conflict, and stress. In the majority of homes, these conflicts are not extreme, and many young people go through a happy and successful adolescence (Offer & Offer, 1975). But a significant percentage do not, and at best there are likely to be some significant stress points in the course of the average sequence of growing up.

Cultural Stresses. Adolescents are peculiarly culture conscious. They are at a point in development that allows them for the first time to understand conceptually the nature of their society and to grasp the character of the ethical and political forces at work in their milieu. They are also developmentally disposed to question and challenge the world in which they find themselves growing up. As a result, the mode of their induction into adult society is of vital character in determining how they are likely to adjust and to orient themselves in the new setting of which they gradually become aware.

It is characteristic of Western society that we have no defined pathway to adulthood. About the closest we come is the issuance of a driver's license or the granting of a high school diploma. A marriage ceremony could dub a youngster as an adult, but many young people reach their majority well before they marry. For some teenagers, college entrance is the symbolic pathway to certain adult patterns of behavior; it acts as a sort of releasing mechanism for a host of activities that formerly were eschewed. For other youngsters, having a first job conveys the significant message that one has come of age. In short, there is no common cere- mony, no pubertal ordeal, no rite of passage to mark the trail into the further reaches of development, and this lack in itself can create enor- mous amounts of stress (Bloch & Niederhoffer, 1958). The lack of a cultural definition of adulthood throws the matter into a limbo from which each family must find its own way out. Within a given home, the freedom to decide one's own hours, one's own course curriculum at school, one's own pattern of employment, one's own disposition of the money one earns (or has been given), even one's own choice of friends, clothes, and hairdo can all be contested issues evoking enormous bouts of emotion from teenager and parents.

Clearly some sort of ceremony, some way to mark the transition and to define when one has passed over into adulthood would have a profound effect on this cluster of problems. For example, some sort of National Youth Service period would probably serve such a function and say, in effect: Up to this point you were a child; beyond this you are a young man or woman. Obviously there would be many knotty cultural tangles to pick apart before such a program could be developed. Whatever its problems, such as institution would probably lower the level of adolescent stress by a sizable percentage.

The many ways that laws and social practice can influence the experi- ence of teenagers are too involved to be detailed exhaustively here. The age for being allowed to drive, to enter a bar or to buy liquor, to drop out of school, to sign a check or a contract, to obtain a business license, to have an abortion without parental consent, and so on—all of these im- pact directly on adolescent experience and the experience of adolescent stress. Our cultural uncertainty about what our young should or should not be allowed to do is clearly a major source of adolescent stress. Nor should we forget that, for the most part, the mental health specialist does not have answers for these vexing questions. One might be able to say with some certainty what is best for a given young person one has studied in depth, but that is a far cry from being able to state what is demograph- ically valid.

On the other hand, there are at least some issues about which the evidence is reasonably conclusive. For example, the transitions into ju- nior high (Botvin et al., 1984) and high school (Feiner, Ginter, & Prima- vera, 1982) have been demonstrated repeatedly to expose many young people to considerable challenge. The disruptive effects on the lives of adolescents of early patterns of alcohol use and drug abuse are also too well documented to need additional verification. The cluster of events around juvenile delinquency, police action, court involvement, and institutional placement is self-evident in its capacity for engendering multiple sources of stress. Adolescent suicidal behavior speaks for the life-threatening power of adolescent stress and provokes enormous consequences for both youth and family. Finally, it is clear that teenage pregnancy, however well it may have worked out in some individual instances, is a source of chronic stress in the lives of young people in general and of black, low-income youngsters in particular (Lindblad-Goldberg, Dukes, & Lasley, 1988). Effective prevention in any of these realms would be of enormous benefit to both the cohort of youth and society at large.

Teenage Prevention: Pregnancy as an Example.   To illustrate the issues involved, let us take one of these stressors—the matter of teenage pregnancy—and survey some of its attendant problems. This is by no means a random selection; students of the field consider this a major problem. When the National Mental Health Association established a Commission on the Prevention of Mental-Emotional Disabilities, the Commission set itself only three goals, one of which was the prevention of adolescent pregnancy (Long, 1986).

Curiously enough, the American Psychological Association Task Force on Promotion, Prevention, and Intervention Alternatives referred to earlier (Price et al., 1989), in the course of summarizing their findings, did not list a single successful program for preventing teenage pregnancy. They did mention a visiting nurse program that was successful in lowering the rate of subsequent child abuse among poor, unmarried teenagers (Olds, Henderson, & Tatelbaum, 1986), but apparently no true preventive strategy has been demonstrated for the pregnancy itself. And this despite considerable social effort to find a way to cope with the issue.

The chances are that we cannot prevent it because we do not understand it. No consistent picture emerges from the literature. For example, in her review, Franklin (1987) presented five explanatory theories of adolescent pregnancy. These involved: access to contraceptive knowledge, adolescent cognitive development, social influence, psychological factors, and decision making. On the basis of this survey, Franklin concluded that most adolescent decision making was based on erroneous information. The indicated intervention, therefore, was better communication through a variety of public and familial networks. On the other hand, Hanson, Myers, and Ginsberg (1987) studied the report of a survey conducted by the National Center for Education Statistics of 10,000 never-married female high school sophomores. The investigators sought to determine the impact of two factors: knowledge and attitudes. Knowledge was estimated in terms of whether or not the youngsters had taken sex-education courses and whether they reported familiarity with or ignorance of birth control measures. Values included such elements as being reared in an atmosphere that stressed responsibility. In the face of such an analysis, it turned out that knowledge had no effect on the chances that a girl (black or white) would get pregnant during her teens. Those whose values emphasized responsibility, however, showed a significantly reduced probability of becoming pregnant. Thus, the one report stresses a cognitive deficit to be remedied by appropriate cognitive interventions, and the other refutes this in favor of value training.

Perhaps the best marker for future work is that suggested by Zabin et al. (1986), who launched a program for pregnancy prevention, but who in addition built in a mechanism for evaluative research. They gave questionnaires to 1,709 black students attending junior and senior high school, gave a second round of questionnaires a year later, and a third round a year after that. In the interim, the students had access to a clinic staffed by a nurse and a social worker, and contraceptives were made available on request. The investigators were able to demonstrate a 13% increase in knowledge (of contraception and pregnancy) and decrease in pregnancy risk by round two, with little further change by the following year. These are somewhat meager results, but at least one knows where one's efforts have led.

Thus, we have much work to do to understand the etiology of some forms of adolescent behavior, and even more to accomplish if we are to intervene meaningfully in a preventative fashion. Considering what is at stake, however, adolescent prevention research is probably one of the best investments our society could make in terms of both the targeting of professional effort and the expenditure of public money.

TREATMENT OF STRESS DISORDERS

Clinical stress involves a challenge of such intensity and/or duration as to overwhelm the established patterns of coping and to pose a threat to the young person's sense of inner integrity. In the face of such stress, a variety of tactics are resorted to, some naturally and intuitively, and others as special forms of adaptation to these unusual circumstances. The goal of treatment is to facilitate the most adaptive coping. In a sense, treatment is prevention of permanent clinical stress consequences. "Treatments" range from naturalistic ones to sophisticated, professional ones.

Family and Friends: A Natural Treatment

For most youngsters, the first line of defense in the face of clinical stress is the intensification of bonds with the family. There are many unfortunate situations where children and teenagers have no family or cannot take recourse to the people at home. For example, a sexually abused girl may have run away from her rural home, found her way to the city, and finally come to rest as a street prostitute who is managed by a pimp. At some point, however, the pimp accuses her of withholding money, beats her up to the point of inducing fractures and internal injuries, and throws her out. She is taken from the street to a hospital, physically wounded, destitute, and alone. The stress is catastrophic. She dares not seek out the abusing family, and she is engulfed by feelings of loneliness, powerlessness, helplessness, hopelessness, frustrated rage, and self-hatred.

One may compare her situation to that of a youngster who lives in an average home with both parents and who sustains a serious accident. After the acute medical management, there is continuing active interaction with both parents who sustain, comfort, and reassure the child as best they can; the extended family often rallies round with phone calls, cards, visits, and gifts; the family doctor is an active presence, visiting following, and caring for the child; and the religious affiliation (where it is present—and it commonly is) leads to visits by the clergyman and, often enough, by other members of the congregation. The youngster is exposed to the supportive rituals of prayer, the chance to join with a group in the religious practice, and the comfort of the religious ideas as such (Whitehead & Stout, 1989). Beyond all these, the school and neighborhood may contribute to the total pattern of supports in a variety of ways. The affected child will have his or her own set of meanings to contend with ("It's all my fault," or "I'm the victim of someone else's error," or "God is punishing me," etc.), but the massive infusion of interest, attention, and reassurance that such an environmental network offers can go far to beat back the tides of guilt, rage, despair, and hopelessness which might otherwise engulf the boy or girl.

Hence, a first line of treatment is the cloak of immediate environmental caring that can be drawn around the afflicted individual. It may not be enough by itself to prevent stress-related symptoms, but it may be a powerful moderating force, and it is often a *sine qua non* to permit any other treatment to work.

Self-Help Groups

A second line of defense against clinical stress is the resort to self-help groups (Borman, 1989). This term encompasses mutual-help (e.g, Alcoholics Anonymous) and peer-help groups (e.g., suicide hotlines). It covers a wide range of activities in which people meet together to consider means of handling a variety of stresses. Many such groups are formed around specific health conditions (e.g., spina bifida or mental retardation), and many others around special circumstances (recent widows and widowers, or Parents Without Partners). For the stressed individual, the central reality of most such encounters is the opportunity for shared experiences with people in similar situations. The chance to join forces with others who bear burdens similar to one's own is a powerful renewing force. It diminishes feelings of isolation, overcomes the sense of social rejection, and opens up channels for communication with people who necessarily understand. Ultimately it is a chance for constructive identification with many who have mastered the stress successfully. Beyond this, it allows the sufferer to participate in helping other victims: instead of being merely a passive victim, one can thus become an active intervener. It gives access to a group feeling, even a group ideology, which makes the work toward recovery a powerful mission. It leads to the formation of friendships and warm relationships with other group members. If the group becomes interested in learning more about the associated issues, it exposes the individual to the latest scientific knowledge about the stress. The group activity also can allow for participation in projects, fund raising, classes, and lobbying activities associated with the traumatic core of the problem, all of which inspire and give hope to the stressed individual.

Many such self-help entities are designed specifically for adolescents (Shore & Mannino, 1989). Al-Ateen is surely the best known, and has been a positive force in the lives of many children of alcoholic parents. The shame, guilt, rage, ambivalence, and despondency that such a home life generates is often materially benefited by the encounter with other young people who are in the same straits. Self-help arrangements have been created for youngsters on drugs, for suicide attempters, and for others. It is difficult to estimate just how efficacious such groups are, but there is much to suggest that a directed peer group is probably even more effective in adolescence than it is in adulthood.

Professional Interventions

After the recourse to family, family doctor, friends, religion, and self-help groups, there remain the possibilities for more formal therapeutic efforts. These include crisis intervention, behavioral therapy, brief therapy, dynamic psychotherapy, psychopharmacotherapy, group therapy, and family therapy. Besides these more commonly practiced methods, supplementary techniques include hypnotherapy, Amytal interviews, and transcendental meditation.

There are certain principles (Swanson & Carbon, 1989) that pervade almost all of these methods: They should be invoked as soon as possible after the onset of the symptoms, be organized directly around the traumatic event, be designed to bring relief as quickly as possible, and be discontinued once the relief is attained. Wherever possible, they should be administered by trained, skilled, and experienced professionals.

Psychopharmacology. Psychopharmacology (Kelly & Frosch, 1989), albeit not a definitive form of treatment, can offer symptom relief in acute overwhelming stress and enable the patient to be receptive to other forms of treatment. The two most pressing symptom syndromes stressed individuals experience are anxiety and depression; fortunately, both are responsive to several of the medications currently available. However, such medications carry the risk of side effects and the possibility of misuse (e.g., for suicide attempts, as street drugs, etc.). Hence, one should prescribe as little as possible, with due regard for the circumstances of administration.

Alprazolam (Xanax®) is probably the optimal benzodiazepine for treatment of anxiety. It needs the usual precautions for use of any benzodiazepine: it should not be used during pregnancy, it should not be mixed with alcohol, it can be habit forming, it must not be terminated abruptly, and during early stages of use the patient should not ride a bike or drive a car. It is, on the other hand, an effective agent and, when properly administered, has brought relief to many patients tormented by high anxiety levels. Alprazolam is usually prescribed within a dosage range of 1 to 4 milligrams per day in divided doses.

Fluoxetine (Prozac®) is among the desirable antidepressants. It belongs to the class of agents that inhibit the re-uptake of serotonin. Although not a more effective antidepressant, it has the advantage over the tricyclic antidepressants of relatively fewer side effects. An additional benefit is that most patients respond to a single dose of 20 milligrams daily. On the other hand, it shares the property common to the antidepressants of attaining its full effects only after two or more weeks of treatment. Its principal side effects are nervousness, irritability, and insomnia.

Occasionally major stress reactions involve a transient psychotic episode. This can occur even where no previous indication of psychotic potential has been noted. Antipsychotic medication such as a phenothiazine [e.g., thioridazine (Mellaril®)] or a butyrophenone [haloperidol (Haldol®)] is then indicated until symptoms clear. The antipsychotic may then be tapered off.

In general, the use of any of these agents is at best only part of the therapeutic address such patients require. The meaning of the stress remains a critical entity that needs appropriate management. The chief use of the psychopharmacologic agent is to bring symptomatic relief on the one hand, and to make the patient more available for psychotherapeutic work on the other.

Group Therapy. Among the several forms of psychotherapy available, young people often relate themselves particulary readily to group therapy (Weiner, 1989). This has the advantages noted above in regard to the self-help groups, but also offers the powerful additional element of a group therapist competent to introduce interpretative and supportive comments. The therapist must set the tone: optimism, hope, a sense of working toward change, and a quality of learning about the condition and about how to master it. The term "reframing" has come to be employed; it refers to a technique for redefining catastrophic experiences so that they lose some of their awesome character and become instead practical problems that need solution.

From the outset, the realities of the situation are set forth and addressed. Everyone in the group has faced the disaster, whether it be a flood, the loss of a limb, or a death in the family. The sharing of pain, the cathartic expression of feelings, and the extending of support from one to another are cardinal aspects of the group experience. The group members grow accustomed both to hearing and pronouncing the unsayable, and thus become gradually inured to the painful themes that haunt their lives. They share in each other's mourning and are in this way buffered against the enormous sense of isolation, exclusion, and condemnation ("why me?") that characteristically dogs the victims of trauma. The chance to set the experience against the backdrop of group perception and validation offers a major buffer for some of the more corrosive aspects of stress reactions.

Family Therapy. Beal (1989) describes family therapy for treatment of stress. Most family therapists regard the family as the primary unit of treatment. The individual family members have inherent and stable patterns of relationship with one another, so that an enduring context is formed that maintains a relatively fixed configuration over time. Implicitly, if one would seek to affect the behavior and/or the emotional status of a given individual, one must do so by dealing with family dynamics. According to the family theorists, it is these dynamics that determine the responses of the family members. In particular, when a family addresses a problem, it may seek to resolve this by attacking, extruding, or redefining the status of a given family member. The assignment of the "sick" role is a favorite device that families unconsciously employ; in the face of stress, one individual becomes the scapegoat, the injured or defective one. The family can evade its own internal conflicts by concentrating on the difficulties of the problematic one. Many a child thus has been cast in a symptomatic role to divert attention from the threat of a split between mother and father. In a dysfunctional family encountering stress, the various members may turn on one another, or away from one another; or a given child or adolescent may develop serious symptoms, bring everyone together around his or her problem, and thus buffer the otherwise destructive impact of the stress. The family dysfunction usually takes the form of excessive enmeshment of the family members in each other's lives. Where boundaries are inadequate and personalities fuse, the ability to cope with life's stresses is diminished accordingly.

Therefore, treatment primarily addresses family dynamics and the way roles are assigned within that context. The major therapeutic effort is directed to turning the focus of concern away from the individual child and redirecting it to the interplay among family members. To the extent that boundaries can be strengthened, intergenerational identities redefined, and a measure of honesty restored in the exchange among the several participants, the child's symptomatic picture will be proportionately relieved and stress more adequately coped with.

Behavioral Therapy

There are two general styles of psychotherapy currently practiced. One is based on behavioral techniques. It was developed within the framework of experimental psychology, particularly from the work of Pavlov and Skinner, and is called behavior therapy or cognitive-behavioral therapy. The other derives from medical psychology and psychoanalysis, and owes its origins to Freud, Adler, Rank, and other psychiatrists from the late nineteenth and early twentieth centuries. It is called psychodynamic (including psychoanalytic) psychotherapy and it is described extensively in Chapter 20.

The behavioral methods are research-based and tend to be directed at specific symptoms (Suinn, 1989). Numerous highly varied tactics have been described in the literature. Only a few of the better known methods are described here. It is important to note that one thing they have in common is the idea of an initial analysis of the patient's inner life, what troubles the patient, and what rewards him or her. This kind of study is key to formulating any behavioral treatment.

Relaxation Training. Of particular importance to stress consequences are the relaxation techniques. Clearly, for individuals who have been subjected to excessive stress, one highly disturbing symptom is likely to be chronic tension. Accordingly, the ability to relax is of critical importance. This is facilitated by having a systematic way of relaxing. Patients are taught to concentrate on and relax one muscle group at a time, e.g., the right foot and leg, then the left foot and leg, then the knees, then the thighs, and so on upward for the whole body, area by area. Eventually there is a limp, easy feeling all over, and this is maintained for a specified number of minutes. This can be enhanced by saying such phrases as, "Easy," "Calm down," "Easy does it," etc. As the process continues, it can be further assisted by careful control of one's breathing.

A refinement is to encourage the patient to recall the traumatic event and then to interrupt the memory, again and again, with the relaxation sequence. Thus, with increasing practice, the memory of the trauma no longer produces feelings of panic but tends instead to be neutralized by an evoked feeling of relaxation.

Biofeedback.   A different way of relieving tension is biofeedback. This is a form of relaxation directed toward the autonomic system. The patient is hooked up to instruments that read out pulse rate, blood pressure, muscle tension, or other such objective findings in numerical detail. The patient then concentrates on lowering these numbers to a safe range. By dint of practice, many people can gain a good deal of control over their autonomic processes. Tension headaches, palpitations, and other expressions of stress thus can be addressed. In effect, it is a method that allows the child or adolescent to view a record of his or her own physiologic responses. By a relaxed kind of "passive volition" (Smith & Womack, 1987), the child learns to alter these physiologic values and, presumably, to regulate them toward an optimum level. The attention of very young children can be maintained by such gimmicks as rigging an electric train to the biofeedback machine in such a way that maintaining physiologic parameters in a safe range makes the train run.

Desensitization.   Many techniques involve controlling the content of thought. In one variety, under the guidance of the therapist, the patient allows himself or herself to encounter the disturbing and distressing memories; in effect, the patient permits his or her mind to be flooded by the traumatic recall under safe and well-controlled conditions. This allows for eventual desensitization to those disturbing thoughts so that they lose their power to alarm.

Alternative methods require the patient to recall positive experiences whenever the stressful thought comes to mind. For example, if the patient faces a scary interview, he or she is asked to recall a successful interview and to couple that memory with each flare of fear about the forthcoming experience. Again, the patient can be asked to consider a story of someone who succeeded at the dreaded task (perhaps facing surgery), to watch a movie of someone who mastered it, or to observe a live model.

Cognitive Therapy.   There is a theory that many disturbing symptoms are due to false beliefs—low self-esteem is attributed to distorted conceptions of the self, certain kinds of anxiety involve a baseless sense of threat from the environment, etc. The therapeutic tactic, then, is to explore the patient's ideas and to challenge irrational belief as it appears. Such cognitive restructuring must go on gradually over time; it involves the patient in much rehearsal and practice.

Brief Therapy and Crisis Intervention

There is a group of methods which is sometimes called crisis intervention and sometimes brief therapy. Such methods are built on a conception of disturbed equilibrium that must be brought back to a state of homeostatic balance (Swanson & Carbon, 1989). The stressor, acute or chronic, has initiated a condition of failed coping capacity. Symptoms ensue, and the therapeutic effort seeks to undo the symptomatic state. The tactics employed share several elements in common. By and large, these are designed as brief, time-limited, goal-directed, intensive programs (Horowitz, 1989). From the outset, a specific number of hours is planned for, and the patient knows that the work has to be accomplished within that time frame. A set of specific goals is articulated, and the focus of the work is on reaching those goals (the relief of identified symptoms) within the designated time. Much attention is given to the patient's strengths and the patient's ability to build on those in order to overcome the current difficulties. Among those assets is the patient's network of supports. Although many therapists prefer to confine their efforts to work with the patient, other therapists make active attempts to reinforce or, where necessary, create such a support system.

When therapist and patient first meet, an initial review is made that covers the story of what happened, the patient's understanding of the problem, and the efforts put forth thus far to seek relief. Special attention is given to the element of danger, either the danger of self-injury or of attack on others. Where a significant threat of this kind exists, hospitalization is indicated. Once it is clarified that no significant danger exists, it is appropriate to go forward with outpatient treatment. The patient and therapist must agree together on what goals should be set for the work. This depends on the current symptoms, the sense of where the patient would like to be, and the therapist's judgment on where the patient reasonably can hope to be. With the goals agreed on, the length of therapy is then specified. By and large, brief therapy does not last more than 12 weeks. The element of brevity is of considerable importance, and a termination date is set at the outset.

With these preparatory steps accomplished, the definitive effort is set in motion. Depending on one's theoretical stance, this may involve special psychotherapeutic initiatives; it may include parallel work with the family; or it may require getting the patient connected with one or more self-help groups (e.g., where excessive alcohol use is present, one of the goals may be to have the patient join AA). The particular style of treatment that has been selected is then pursued through the agreed time frame. The final stage involves a closing out of the exchanges and a formal termination. If the patient should desire continued therapeutic help, a referral for long-term therapy may be made.

The psychotherapeutic tactics likely to be employed usually fall under some form of cognitive therapy or a version of brief dynamic psychotherapy. For the cognitive therapist, much energy is directed toward correcting the many misconceptions to which patients are prone, e.g., theories about the cause of the difficulties, inflated expectations about what treatment can do, and inappropriate efforts to remedy the situation by drinking or self-injury. By calling the patient's attention again and again to these misrepresentations of reality and by working with the patient to correct these false beliefs, a more rational and realistic outlook presently can be achieved.

Brief Dynamic Psychotherapy. For the dynamic therapist (Carek, 1989), the patient is assumed to be pressed by painful memories and disturbing emotions that are being warded off by resort to the symptoms. The major elements in building this pathological shield against pain are the unconscious mechanisms of defense. These include repression, displacement, isolation, reaction-formation, projection, splitting, and other such powerful and active mental organizations. (For a more complete list and explanation, see Table 9.3 in Chapter 9.) By means of defense interpretations, the therapist seeks to reduce these means for warding off feelings and to bring the stressful affects into fuller awareness. The therapist then seeks to help the patient encounter the feelings, cope with them, and master them. The patient may be asked to keep a diary or a log of each occurrence or recurrence of trauma-related experience. As the work proceeds, the patient is likely to bring in references to earlier events in life where similar emotional challenges arose. These are of special importance; both the links and the differences between past and present need exploration. Where relationship issues arise, even in brief therapy the therapist must be both vigilant and vigorous in addressing any expressions of negative transference. It is not unusual for the patient to seek unconsciously to recreate the traumatic event within the therapist-patient interaction. In effect, the patient seeks to engender in the therapist some of the same affects that were evoked within the patient by the recent stressor. This requires recognition, clarification, and confrontation by the therapist.

As the midpoint of the preset therapy interval approaches, the therapist must mention the termination date. Sometimes patients will have forgotten that such a date was set; sometimes they are surprised that the time frame continues to be adhered to. In any case, themes of termination are likely to come up thereafter. The expression of affects related to prior separations and losses should be encouraged, and the work of termination should be pressed insistently.

The brief therapies work especially well with adolescents, but many younger children need more conventional psychotherapeutic work in which the process is open ended, with no predetermined time frame. The modalities of therapy have been well described elsewhere (e.g., Axline, 1947; Carek, 1989; Chapter 20 of this book). The basic techniques include support of injured narcissism, play techniques, interpretation of the experiences of the play figures (especially of defenses and transference feelings), clarification of confused emotional states, and empathic mirroring. All in all, as the therapy proceeds, the patient should feel an ever-increasing freedom to encounter and to express the trauma-engendered affects. To the extent that this is achieved, symptomatic relief will follow.

Other Therapies. Besides the more standard treatment techniques designed for stress relief, there exists a number of other methods. For most of these the literature is scanty and confirmatory studies in children still await the doing.

Meditation has been "demystified" by Benson (Benson, 1975; Smith & Womack, 1987) and converted into a relatively simple procedure; it involves conscious breathing and concentrating on a single word for 20 minutes. Certain adolescents can carry this out with apparent success.

Hypnosis has gained a certain credibility in recent years, and there is even a hypnotic clinical scale for children (Morgan & Higard, 1979). The emphasis in the literature appears to be on teaching children self-hypnotic techniques (Kohen et al., 1984).

In some ways, all such methods overlap. They involve a redirection of interest and attention inwardly, an altered state of consciousness, a considerable degree of relaxation, and a special kind of concentration. For some children and teenagers, such approaches may offer considerable relief from the vicissitudes of excessive stress. Whether this is true for most youngsters, whether there is a specific, identifiable subset who would be likely to benefit from a given technique, whether there are any troublesome side effects not yet recognized, and how these approaches compare in efficacy with the more standard methods are among the many questions that remain to be addressed.

REFERENCES

Axline, V. M. (1947). *Play therapy.* Boston: Houghton Mifflin.

Beal, E. M. (1989). Family therapy. In American Psychiatric Association, *Treatment of psychiatric disorders: A Task Force report of the American Psychiatric Association* (Vol. 3, pp. 2566–2577). Washington, DC: Author.

Benson, H. (1975). *The relaxation response.* New York: William Morrow.

Bloch, H. A., & Niederhoffer, A. (1958). *The gang: A study in adolescent behavior.* New York: Philosophical Library.

Borman, L. D. (1989). Self-help and mutual aid groups for adults. In American Psychiatric Association, *Treatment of psychiatric disorders: A Task Force report of the American Psychiatric Association* (Vol. 3, pp. 2596–2606). Washington, DC: Author.

Botvin, G. J., Baker, E., Renick, N. L., Filazzola, A. D., & Botvin, E. M. (1984). A cognitive behavioral approach to substance abuse prevention. *Addictive Behaviors, 9,* 137–174.

Carek, D. J. (1989). Individual child psychotherapy. In American Psychiatric Association, *Treatment of psychiatric disorders: A Task Force report of the American Psychiatric Association* (Vol. 3, pp. 2557–2565). Washington, DC: Author.

Daly, M., & Wilson, M. (1985). Child abuse and other risks of not living with both parents. *Ethology and Sociobiology, 6,* 197–210.

Felner, R. D., Ginter, M., & Primavera, J. (1982). Primary prevention during school transitions. *American Journal of Community Psychology, 10,* 277–290.

Franklin, D. L. (1987). Black adolescent pregnancy: A literature review. Special Issue: The black adolescent parent. *Child and Youth Services, 9*(1), 15–39.

Garbarino, J. (1988). Preventing childhood injury: Developmental and mental health issues. *American Journal of Orthopsychiatry, 58*(1), 25–45.

Hanson, S. L., Myers, D. E., & Ginsberg, A. L. (1987). The role of responsibility and knowledge in reducing teenage out-of-wedlock childbearing. *Journal of Marriage and the Family, 49*(2), 241–256.

Horowitz, M. J. (1989). Brief dynamic psychotherapy. In American Psychiatric Association, *Treatment of psychiatric disorders: A Task Force report of the American Psychiatric Association* (Vol. 3, pp. 2548–2556). Washington, DC: Author.

Institute of Medicine. (1985). *Injury in America.* Washington, DC: National Academy Press.

Kelly, K. V., & Frosch, W. A. (1989). Pharmacotherapy. In American Psychiatric Association, *Treatment of psychiatric disorders: A Task Force report of the American Psychiatric Association* (Vol. 3, pp. 2585–2589). Washington, DC: Author.

Kohen, D. P., Olness, K. N., Colwell, S. O., & Heimel, A. (1984). The use of relaxation-mental imagery (self-hypnosis) in the management of 505 pediatric behavior encounters. *Developmental Behavioral Pediatrics, 5,* 21–25.

Lindblad-Goldberg, M., Dukes, J. L., & Lasley, J. H. (1988). Stress in low-income, single-parent families: Normative and dysfunctional patterns. *American Journal of Orthopsychiatry, 58*(1), 104–120.

Long, B. B. (1986). The prevention of mental-emotional disabilities: A report from a National Mental Health Association Commission. *American Psychologist, 41*(7), 825–829.

Margolis, L., & Runyan, C. (1983). Accidental policy: An analysis of the problem of unintended injuries in childhood. *American Journal of Orthopsychiatry, 53,* 629–644.

Morgan, A. H., & Higard, J. R. (1979). The Stanford Hypnotic Clinical Scale for Children. *American Journal of Clinical Hypnosis, 21,* 148–169.

Offer, D., & Offer, J. B. (1975). *From teenage to young manhood: A psychological study.* New York: Basic Books.

Olds, D. L., Henderson, C. R., & Tatelbaum, R. (1986). Preventing child abuse and neglect: A randomized trial of nurse home visitation. *Pediatrics, 78,* 65–78.

Patterson, G. R. (1981). *A bilateral definition for the social aggression trait.* Presented at Conference of Relations between Developmental and Social Psychology, Vanderbilt University.

Patterson, G. R. (1982). *A social learning approach: Volume 3: Coercive family process.* Eugene, OR: Castalia.

Patterson, G. R. (1983). Stress: A change agent for family process. In N. Garmezy & M. Rutter (Eds.), *Stress, coping and development in children* (pp. 235–264). New York: McGraw-Hill.

Price, R. H., Cowan, E. L., Lorion, R. P., & Ramos-McKay, J. (1989). The search for effective preventive programs: What we learned along the way. *American Journal of Orthopsychiatry, 59*(1), 49–58.

Putnam, F. (1989). *Diagnosis and treatment of multiple personality disorder.* New York: Guilford.

Shore, M. F., & Mannino, F. V. (1989). Self-help, mutual-help, and peer-helping services for youth. In American Psychiatric Association, *Treatment of psychiatric disorders: A Task Force report of the American Psychiatric Association* (Vol. 3, pp. 2607–2616). Washington, DC: Author.

Smith, M. S., & Womack, W. M. (1987). Stress management techniques in childhood and adolescence. *Clinical Pediatrics, 26*(11), 581–585.

Suinn, R. M. (1989). Stress management by behavioral methods. In American Psychiatric Association, *Treatment of psychiatric disorders: A Task Force report of the American Psychiatric Association* (Vol. 3, pp. 2532–2547). Washington, DC: Author.

Swanson, W. C., & Carbon, J. B. (1989). Crisis intervention: Theory and technique. In American Psychiatric Association, *Treatment of psychiatric disorders: A Task Force report of the American Psychiatric Association* (Vol. 3, pp. 2520–2531). Washington, DC: Author.

Weiner, M. F. (1989). Group therapy. In American Psychiatric Association, *Treatment of psychiatric disorders: A Task Force report of the American Psychiatric Association* (Vol. 3, pp. 2578–2584). Washington, DC: Author.

Whitehead, P. L., & Stout, R. J. (1989). Religion as ego support. In American Psychiatric Association, *Treatment of psychiatric disorders: A Task Force report of the American Psychiatric Association* (Vol. 3, pp. 2590–2595). Washington, DC: Author.

Zabin, L. S., Hirsch, M. B., Smith, E. A., Streett, R., & Hardy, J. B. (1986). Adolescent pregnancy-prevention program: A model for research and evaluation. *Journal of Adolescent Health Care, 7*(2), 77–87.

Author Index

Subject Index